Epitaph for a Soldier

"Among the celebrities at Sherman's funeral, as every astute reporter observed, was Confederate General Joseph E. Johnston. Twice during the Civil War the mourned and this mourner from the South had been antagonists—at the first Bull Run, when Sherman had been one of the greenest commanders on the field; and again during the campaign for Atlanta, when Sherman, a seasoned practitioner in the art of killing his fellow man, had forged one of the greatest strategic victories in military history. So even in death, Sherman remained unpredictable, astonishing, a man to stir the heart and the imagination:

". . . a friend said to Joe Johnston: 'General, please put on your hat; you might get sick.' The proud Confederate, then eighty-two years of age, shook his head. 'If I were in his place and he were standing here in mine, he would not put on his hat.'

"And so, ten days later, bells tolled also for Sherman's old foe. Johnston had died of pneumonia."

—from the Foreword by EARL SCHENCK MIERS

THE COLLIER BOOKS CIVIL WAR CLASSICS

EARL SCHENCK MIERS, *General Editor*

Jefferson Davis
The Rise and Fall of the Confederate Government
Foreword by Earl Schenck Miers

Ulysses Grant
Grant's Civil War
Edited, with a Foreword by Earl Schenck Miers

The Official Story of the Decisive Battles of the Civil War
Edited, with a Foreword by Earl Schenck Miers

Noah Brooks
Washington, D.C., in Lincoln's Time
Edited, with an Introduction by Herbert Mitgang

Thomas C. DeLeon
Four Years in Rebel Capitals
Introduction by E. B. Long

Thomas Wentworth Higginson
Army Life in a Black Regiment
Introduction by Howard N. Meyer

Sam R. Watkins
Company "Aytch," A Side Show of the Big Show
Introduction by Roy Basler

Those Who Knew Lincoln
Edited by Lloyd Dunlap

Other Collier Books by Earl Schenck Miers
 The Great Rebellion: The Emergence of the American Conscience from Sumter to Appomattox

 Gettysburg, with Richard A. Brown

SHERMAN'S

CIVIL WAR

Selected and Edited from His Personal

Memoirs, with a Foreword by

EARL SCHENCK MIERS

 COLLIER BOOKS
NEW YORK, N.Y.

A Collier Books Original

First Edition 1962

Collier Books is a division of The Crowell-Collier Publishing Company

Library of Congress Catalog Card Number: 62-17495

Foreword

FEBRUARY, 1891, was a fatal month for old heroes. On the tenth, front-page headlines told of the death of James Redpath, struck down by one of those clanging streetcars that now made New York City a cobblestoned jungle mocking human values, and devoted readers of Redpath's *Life of John Brown* and *Echoes of Harper's Ferry* must have believed that fate had dealt a wry end to this famous journalist and political agitator who had been risking his neck since his days as a follower of John Brown in Bloody Kansas. Also in that month, Admiral David Dixon Porter was languishing near death in Washington, D.C. He was the foster brother of the immortal Farragut and celebrated in his own right in naval history for the part he played in the capture of New Orleans in '62, and the surrender of Vicksburg the following July; poor Porter, suffering "from fatty degeneration of the heart," was slipping fast, according to the bulletins, and on the thirteenth, he too, passed away.

At the moment, however, a saddened nation was absorbed in another impending calamity. The front pages on Feburary 11 had carried the first news of the serious illness of William Tecumseh Sherman. The facts were sparse and even difficult to credit: only a week earlier, seeming to be in full vigor as he approached his seventieth birthday, the General had tramped off to a theater party at the Casino in the company of several old cronies from the Army and Navy. No event could have been more in character for a Sherman once more adored by a nation because he said and did as he pleased, and it was a pleasant joke among friends that the General kept a valise packed and waiting by the door in order to dash off at an instant's notice to any social, military, or civic gathering to which he was invited. Now, unexpectedly, the nation learned that its greatest hero was lying unconscious in his home at Seventy-five West Seventy-first Street with "but little hope for his recovery" and unable to take any nourishment, or so the New York *Evening Post* reported, except whisky and milk. A cold, a product of the night's hilarity at the Casino, had been followed by an attack of erysipelas. Now, the members of his immediate family, with the exception of the son who was a student in the Jesuit Theological Seminary in the Isle of Jersey, were gathered gloomily at his bedside, and on February 12 the headline in the *Evening Post* recorded sorrowfully: HIS DEATH ONLY A QUESTION OF HOURS.

That night Sherman slept comfortably and the nation rejoiced in his TURN FOR THE BETTER. As though mitigating the General's illness, a telegram from his brother, Senator John Sherman, told Secretary of War Redfield Proctor: "Asthma, his old disease, his chief trouble." But the optimism was short-lived; at ten minutes to two the following afternoon William Tecumseh Sherman breathed his last. Next day, a Sunday, afforded editorial writers and eulogy makers a respite in which to sharpen their sentiments, and they responded in bright spirit. Declared the New York *Evening Post*:

> Sherman's personal character gave the man a hold upon the popular heart such as his achievements had won him in the popular imagination. He came home to the people in a way that neither Grant nor Sheridan ever did. Utterly unlike Lincoln, there was yet about him that refreshing individuality which distinguished the war President and which won for both the affection of the people to a degree that not either [Secretary of State] Seward or [Secretary of War] Stanton, on the one hand, nor either Grant or Sheridan on the other, ever approached.[1]

That "refreshing individuality," which so impressed the editors of the *Evening Post,* also delighted the Reverend Dr.

[1] The New York *Evening Post,* February 16, 1891.

Talmadge who, addressing a memorial service in Brooklyn's Academy of Music, recalled Sherman as "simple as a child, brave as a lion, sympathetic as a woman, firm as a rock, wrathful as a tempest when aroused against wrong, lovely as a June morning among his friends." Upstate, the Poughkeepsie *Twice Weekly Eagle*, which boasted in its motto that it was "Neutral in Nothing," recalled Sherman somewhat less metaphorically: "He was no austere and unapproachable divinity, wrapped in the dignities of the past, but one of the people, alive to the thought and feeling of the day, and keenly interested in the questions and the progress of his times"; while across the river in New Jersey the *Daily Times* of New Brunswick called Sherman "the noble old citizen whom all the world honored."[2]

Among the celebrities at Sherman's funeral, as every astute reporter observed, was Confederate General Joseph E. Johnston. Twice during the Civil War the mourned and this mourner from the South had been antagonists—at First Bull Run, when Sherman had been one of the greenest commanders on the field, and again during the campaign for Atlanta, when Sherman, a seasoned practitioner in the art of killing his fellow man, had forged one of the greatest strategic victories in military history. So, even in death, Sherman remained unpredictable, astonishing, a man to stir the heart and the imagination.

II

No trait in Sherman ever had been more fascinating than the way in which he won friends, lost them, and won them back. His march to the sea had made him by 1865 one of the men most hated in the South, but within a decade many Southerners were beginning to look upon Sherman as a warmly understanding friend. Who more vigorously than he had scorned the carpetbaggers, the policies of Andrew Johnson (whom he characterized as "Lear roaring at the wild storm, bareheaded and helpless"), or the Fifteenth Amendment? Who had spoken out more bluntly against Republican "stupidity" in those first post-bellum years?

Then in 1875 Sherman published his *Memoirs*. With sullen

[2] The Poughkeepsie (N.Y.) *Twice Weekly Eagle*, February 18, 1891; The New Brunswick (N.J.) *Daily Times*, February 14, 1891.

scowls Southerners read these two highly individualistic volumes and began to hate Sherman anew. Sherman's obvious contempt for the quality of the bulk of Confederate generalship stripped the South of its pride, the only compensation remaining to it after four tragic years of bloodshed and tears. Who cared if Sherman spoke no more highly of Northern generalship? Grasping the pen in place of the sword, Sherman was still seeking to crush the South by destroying its sentimentality toward the war; he was, indeed, the same blackhearted rascal who had ravished Georgia, burned Columbia to the ground, and threatened to bring every Southern woman to the washtub!

In these years *The Galaxy,* an influential journal in America, called itself "A Magazine of Entertaining Reading," but it is doubtful if Sherman enjoyed altogether the bitter attack of its reviewer upon his *Memoirs.* Two long articles were devoted to picking at the work, chapter by chapter. *The Galaxy's* critic concluded, in part:

> The [Sherman's *Memoirs*] are written in a remarkably terse, clear, energetic, and flowing style, and are plentifully interspersed with anecdotes of the camp and field, which give life and interest to the story, although in many instances they are inexcusably profane, sometimes indelicate, and occasionally inapplicable or badly told. . . . The gravest fault of the work . . . is the frequent recurrence of unjust censure and criticism of men who, to say the least, were serving their country as patriotically as the author himself. . . . We are forced to express the opinion that these memoirs have been hastily written, perhaps to while away the hours which hung heavily upon him in "the piping times of peace," and that they will neither reward him for the trouble they will bring, nor increase his reputation for fairness and prudence, while it is equally sure that they will cause him to be assigned a lower place than might otherwise have fallen to his lot among the great captains of history.[3]

How widely *The Galaxy's* critic had missed his mark was evident on that February day, fifteen years later, when the country rang with eulogies to the departed Sherman. Gen-

[3] *The Galaxy,* Vol. XX, 464.

eral Jacob D. Cox, who wrote the review in *The Nation*, proved a much more perceptive judge of the importance of Sherman's *Memoirs*, and he understood how Grant's somewhat grudging decision not to stand for a third term as President had influenced the critics:

It is a pity that a book of this kind should be received with an outburst of partisan attack and partisan laudation, and yet, such is the public temper just now [1875], that anything like a calm judgment seems next to impossible. The personal recollections of a great soldier ought not to excite political feeling, and, nevertheless, the criticisms on Sherman's "Memoirs" are very generally colored by the politics of the writers of them. To us it seems that it would be difficult for an important public figure to show that he had "turned his back on politics" by any better proof than the publication of such a book. If there is anywhere in it a purpose to court political favor, we are quite unequal to the subtlety required to discover it. To our way of thinking, the man would be crazy indeed who should expect it to help him into the Presidency; and no less a quarry is supposed to be worthy the aim of the writer. It looks to us like a more intelligible and explicit renunciation of worldly ambition than the President's [Grant's] late letter to the Pennsylvania Republicans; and we cannot, by any effort of the imagination, make a hope for a political nomination consist with the printing of so much matter that will touch powerful enemies on the raw.

Cox, of course, was right—Sherman wanted no part of the Presidency. And Cox understood also why it was within Sherman's character to publish his *Memoirs* while he was still alive so that no one could say he was too timid "to face the storm of his own brewing." Knowing his subject, Cox added: "We suspect that for lack of other fighting he more than half enjoys the rattling skirmish just now going on in his literary front." Yet Cox, while appreciating Sherman's "quick eye for the humorous" and knowing how any false accusation would "exasperate a man like Sherman," could still comment reproachfully: "There are personal quarrels and even personal wrongs which the successful man can afford to forget, and which it is not generous to perpetuate." Again, Cox could put his finger squarely on the weakest point in Sherman's literary armor: "In narrating his own experience, the writer grows more general as his career widens. As a captain, he speaks of his regimental mess and his company officers. As a brigadier, he tells us of his colonels and their regiments; but when he becomes the commander of a great army, he rarely has occasion to extend his notice beyond the commandants of the wings of his army."[4]

The author of the commentary on Sherman's *Memoirs* in *The North American Review* was Francis Winthrop Palfrey, one time colonel of the 20th Massachusetts and a brigadier general by brevet. Sherman's work, following closely the publication of Joseph E. Johnston's *Narrative of Military Operations,* should be applauded first of all, in Palfrey's opinion, for reviving an interest in the Civil War that had become "perceptibly deadened" by the times and "the many cares of our intense and nervous American life." To Palfrey, Sherman wrote with "the cheerfulness of success," whereas Johnston reflected "the depression of disappointment and failure," and *The North American Review*'s critic had no unkind word for Sherman; he was "always clear, rapid and interesting," a man "in advance of his time" who "always has his wits about him and his eyes open"; and who, in conclusion, could best be described as "the kindly man in the relentless soldier."[5]

III

Given time, Sherman succeeded in baffling both friend and foe, for he was, as a newspaperman once remarked, a person of "crotchets and prejudices." As a youngster he had detested his red hair but could do nothing about it, although he experimented with various dyes. The name of Tecumseh, affixed on him by a Dartmouth-educated father who adored the Shawnee leader, he had lived with comfortably by shortening to "Cump." When at the age of nine his father died from typhoid, young Sherman was adopted by a neighbor, old Tom Ewing, a Whig power in Ohio politics. The Ewings, devout Catholics and incapable of asking any priest to administer the rites of the church to a lad named after a heathen redskin, had prefixed the William to the Tecumseh. Tom Ewing's Whig connections managed an appointment to West Point for

4 *The Nation,* Vol. XX, 397–98, 411–12.
5 *The North American Review,* Vol. CXXI, 337–40, 365.

the lad; he was then sixteen—by his own description, "an un-tamed animal just caught in the Far West"—but he did well at the Academy, standing highest in engineering, geology, rhetoric, mental philosophy, and demerits.

Sherman's military experiences afterward hardly prepared him for the renown that would one day come to him; sent to chase Indians in Florida, his only conquests were waltzing with the belles of St. Augustine. Four years at Fort Moultrie found Sherman dabbling in painting and wishing he could be an artist, and when the Mexican War came along, providing a proving ground for such future generals as Grant and Lee, Sherman was tramping through the misty mountains of Cali-fornia in quest of Mexicans who kept well out of reach. His business ventures in subsequent years likewise added little luster to his record. Beginning with a failure in San Francisco, where he became a self-styled "Jonah of banking," he moved to Leavenworth, Kansas, where he became a self-styled "dead cock in a pit." Ostensibly Sherman had moved to Kansas to manage the Ewing properties there, but he decided to have a fling at the law and hardly survived his first and only case—fresh evidence that a fiery temper nestled under his red thatch. Old army friends—notably Braxton Bragg and Pierre G. T. Beauregard—came to Sherman's rescue, securing his appointment as superintendent of a new state military college in Louisiana. For really the the first time since leaving the army, Sherman was thoroughly happy, but the War Between the States quickly ended this love affair between schoolmaster and students. He might have known it couldn't last, Sherman sighed, explaining why to his daughter Lizzie: "Men are blind and crazy."

At this point in his career, *Sherman's Civil War* begins. Edited for the modern reader, it serves as a companion volume to *Grant's Civil War*, another Collier Book. These two men, Grant and Sherman—devoted friends and comrades-in-arms —became the architects of Unon victory on the battlefield, and if ever history could be influenced by an attraction of opposites, here was the classic example! Slouching Sam Grant, placid, unafraid, tried sorely the "nervous-sanguine tempera-ment" of "Uncle Billy" Sherman; and W. F. G. Shanks, a shrewd reporter for *Harper's New Monthly Magazine,* watch-ing the two smoking, caught the difference at once: Grant used "his tobacco as the Chinese do opium," whereas Sher-man smoked "as if it were a duty to be finished in the shortest imaginable time." Sherman was well aware of his assets and his shortcomings, compared to Grant, and one day, when "Uncle Billy" was in a confidential mood, General James Harrison Wilson heard him explode:

> Wilson, I am a damned sight smarter man than Grant. I know a great deal more about war, military history, strategy, and grand tactics than he does. I know more about organization, supply, and administration, and about everything else than he does, but I'll tell you where he beats me and where he beats the world. He don't care a damn for what the enemy does out of his sight, but it scares me like hell! I am more nervous than he is. I am more likely to change my orders or to counter-march my command than he is. He uses such information as he has according to his best judgment; he issues his orders and does his level best to carry them out without much reference to what is going on about him and, so far, experience seems to have fully justified him.[6]

Sooner or later, whatever was on Sherman's mind came out—the good with the bad. His friends understood and forgave (or even defended) him, whereas his enemies, trying to make capital out of this weakness, were perplexed by their failure. H. V. Boynton, who had served in the Army of the Cumberland under Don Carlos Buell and George H. Thomas, was the Washington correspondent for the Cincinnati *Gazette* when Sherman's *Memoirs* appeared. Boynton rushed to Grant with wild stories of how Sherman had discredited him, and Grant's temper flared, but after Grant read the volumes he thought that Sherman had treated him kindly, and only wished he had done as well with Frank P. Blair and John A. Logan. Sherman bided his time for dealing with Boynton, finally telling the Cleveland *Leader* that the reporter would "slander his own mother for a thousand dollars." Boynton, threatening a libel suit, asked if the statement were true, and, calmly, Sherman replied: "This is a hard thing to say of any man, but I believe it of you."

Sherman—"the concentrated quintessence of Yankeedom," a friend once said—simply had to be himself. Critics spoke

---

[6] James Harrison Wilson, *Under the Old Flag* (New York: 1912), Vol. II, page 17.

of his "eccentricity of mind" without denying its brilliance. He was, in an age that liked to drape lace curtains over the ugliness of life, an unremitting realist. He proved to be even better than he believed, and, not surprisingly, he was named Lieutenant General on July 25, 1866, and General on March 4, 1869. Four days later he succeeded Grant as Commander in Chief of the army, a post that he filled for fourteen years.

At Sherman's funeral a friend said to Joe Johnston: "General, please put on your hat; you might get sick."

The proud Confederate, then eighty-two years of age, shook his head. "If I were in his place and he were standing here in mine, he would not put on his hat."

And so, ten days later, bells tolled also for Sherman's old foe. Johnston had died of pneumonia.

EARL SCHENCK MIERS

Edison, New Jersey
January 2, 1962

Contents

Sherman's Civil War

Chapter 1

St. Louis:
"This Distracted and Anarchical People"
April–May, 1861

WHEN SECESSION overtook Louisiana, I was in constant correspondence with my brother, [Senator] John Sherman, at Washington. I had managed to maintain my family comfortably at Lancaster, Ohio, but was extremely anxious about the future. It looked like the end of my career, for I did not suppose that "civil war" could give me an employment that would provide for the family. I thought, and may have said, that the national crisis had been brought about by the politicians, and, as it was upon us, they "might fight it out." Therefore, when I turned North from New Orleans, I felt more disposed to look to St. Louis for a home, and to Major [H. S.] Turner[1] to find me employment, than to the public service.

I left New Orleans about the 1st of March, 1861, by rail to Jackson and Clinton, Mississippi, Jackson, Tennessee, and Columbus, Kentucky, where we took a boat to Cairo, and thence, by rail, to Cincinnati and Lancaster. All the way, I heard, in the cars and boats, warm discussions about politics; to the effect that, if Mr. Lincoln should attempt coercion of the seceded States, the other slave or border States would make common cause, when, it was believed, it would be madness to attempt to reduce them to subjection. In the South, the people were earnest, fierce and angry, and were evidently organizing

---

[1] A warm friend and former business associate.

for action; whereas, in Illinois, Indiana, and Ohio, I saw not the least sign of preparation. It certainly looked to me as though the people of the North would tamely submit to a disruption of the Union, and the orators of the South used, openly and constantly, the expressions that there would be no war, and that a lady's thimble would hold all the blood to be shed. On reaching Lancaster, I found letters from my brother John, inviting me to come to Washington, as he wanted to see me; and from Major Turner, at St. Louis, that he was trying to secure for me the office of president of the Fifth Street Railroad, with a salary of twenty-five hundred dollars; that Mr. [J. H.] Lucas and D. A. January held a controlling interest of stock, would vote for me, and the election would occur in March. This suited me exactly, and I answered Turner that I would accept, with thanks. But I also thought it right and proper that I should first go to Washington, to talk with my brother, Senator Sherman.

Mr. Lincoln had just been installed, and the newspapers were filled with rumors of every kind indicative of war; the chief act of interest was that Major Robert Anderson had taken by night into Fort Sumter all the troops garrisoning Charleston Harbor, and that he was determined to defend it against the demands of the State of South Carolina and of the Confederate States. I must have reached Washington about the 10th of March. I found my brother there, just appointed Senator, in place of Mr. [Salmon P.] Chase, who was in the cabinet, and I have no doubt my opinions, thoughts, and feelings, wrought up by the events in Louisiana, seemed to him gloomy and extravagant. About Washington I saw but few signs of preparation, though the Southern Senators and Representatives were daily sounding their threats on the floors of Congress, and were publicly withdrawing to join the Confederate Congress at Montgomery. Even in the War Department and about the public offices there was open, unconcealed talk, amounting to high-treason.

One day, John Sherman took me with him to see Mr. Lincoln. He walked into the room where the secretary to the President now sits, we found the room full of people, and Mr. Lincoln sat at the end of the table, talking with three or four gentleman, who soon left. John walked up, shook hands, and took a chair near him, holding in his hand some papers referring to minor appointments in the State of Ohio, which formed the subject of conversation. Mr. Lincoln took the papers, said he would refer them to the proper heads of departments, and would be glad to make the appointments asked for, if not already promised. John then turned to me, and said, "Mr. President, this is my brother, Colonel Sherman, who is just up from Louisiana, he may give you some information you want." "Ah!" said Mr. Lincoln, "how are they getting along down there?" I said, "They think they are getting along swimmingly—they are preparing for war." "Oh, well!" said he, "I guess we'll manage to keep house." I was silenced, said no more to him, and we soon left. I was sadly disappointed, and remember that I broke out on John, d—ning the politicians generally, saying, "You have got things in a hell of a fix, and you may get them out as you best can," adding that the country was sleeping on a volcano that might burst forth at any minute, but that I was going to St. Louis to take care of my family, and would have no more to do with it. John begged me to be more patient, but I said I would not; that I had no time to wait, that I was off for St. Louis; and off I went. At Lancaster I found letters from Major Turner, inviting me to St. Louis, as the place in the Fifth Street Railroad was a sure thing, and that Mr. Lucas would rent me a good house on Locust Street, suitable for my family, for six hundred dollars a year.

Mrs. Sherman and I gathered our family and effects together, started for St. Louis March 27th, where we rented of Mr. Lucas the house on Locust Street, between Tenth and Eleventh, and occupied it on the 1st of April. Charles Ewing and John Hunter had formed a law-partnership in St. Louis, and agreed to board with us, taking rooms on the third floor. In the latter part of March, I was duly elected president of the Fifth Street Railroad, and entered on the discharge of my duties April 1, 1861. We had a central office on the corner of Fifth and Locust, and also another up at the stables in Bremen. The road was well stocked and in full operation, and all I had to do was to watch the economical administration of existing affairs, which I endeavored to do with fidelity and zeal. But the whole air was full of wars and rumors of wars. The struggle was going on politically for the border States. Even in Missouri, which was a slave State, it was manifest that the Governor of the State, Claiborne Jackson, and all the leading politicians, were for the South in case of a war. The house on the northwest corner of Fifth and Pine was the rebel headquarters, where the rebel flag was hung publicly, and the crowds about the Planters' House were all more or less rebel. There was also a camp in Lindell's Grove, at the end of Olive Street, under command of General D[aniel] M. Frost, a Northern man, a graduate of West Point, in open sympathy with the Southern leaders. This camp was nominally a State camp of instruction, but, beyond doubt, was in the interest of the Southern cause, designed to be used against the national authority in the event of the General Government's attempting to coerce the Southern Confederacy. General William S. Harney was in command of the Department of Missouri, and resided in his own house, on Fourth Street, below Market; and there were five or six companies of United States troops in the arsenal, commanded by Captain N[athaniel] Lyon; throughout the city, there had been organized, almost exclusively out of the German part of the population, four or five regiments of "Home Guards," with which movement Frank Blair, B. Gratz Brown, John M. Schofield, Clinton B. Fisk, and others, were most active on the part of the national authorities. Frank Blair's brother Montgomery was in the cabinet of Mr. Lincoln at Washington, and to him seemed committed the general management of affairs in Missouri.

The newspapers fanned the public excitement to the highest pitch, and threats of attacking the arsenal on the one hand, and the mob of d———d rebels in Camp Jackson on the other, were bandied about. I tried my best to keep out of the current, and only talked freely with a few men; among them Colonel John O'Fallon, a wealthy gentleman who resided above St. Louis. He daily came down to my office in Bremen, and we walked up and down the pavement by the hour, deploring the sad condition of our country, and the seeming drift toward dissolution and anarchy. I used also to go down to the arsenal occasionally to see Lyon, Totten, and other of my army acquaintance, and was glad to see them making preparations to defend their post, if not to assume the offensive.

The bombardment of Fort Sumter, which was announced by telegraph, began April 12th, and ended on the 14th. We then knew that the war was actually begun, and though the South was openly, manifestly the aggressor, yet her friends and apologists insisted that she was simply acting on a justifiable defensive, and that in the forcible seizure of the public fort within her limits the people were acting with reasonable prudence and foresight. Yet neither party seemed willing to invade, or cross the border. [Jefferson] Davis, who ordered the bombardment of Sumter, knew the temper of his people well, and foresaw that it would precipitate the action of the border States; for almost immediately Virginia, North Carolina, Arkansas, and Tennessee, followed the lead of the cotton States, and conventions were deliberating in Kentucky and Missouri.

On the night of Saturday, April 6th, I received the following dispatch:

WASHINGTON, *April* 6, 1861.

Major W. T. SHERMAN:

Will you accept the chief clerkship of the War Department? We will make you assistant Secretary of War when Congress meets.

M. BLAIR, *Postmaster-General.*

To which I replied by telegraph, Monday morning, "I cannot accept"; and by mail as follows:

OFFICE ST. LOUIS RAILROAD COMPANY, }
Monday, April 8, 1861.   }

Hon. M. BLAIR, *Washington, D. C.:*

I received, about nine o'clock Saturday night, your telegraph dispatch, which I have this moment answered, "I cannot accept."

I have quite a large family, and when I resigned my place in Louisiana, on account of secession, I had no time to lose; and, therefore, after my hasty visit to Washington, where I saw no chance of employment, I came to St. Louis, have accepted a place in this company, have rented a house, and incurred other obligations, so that I am not at liberty to change.

I thank you for the compliment contained in your offer, and assure you that I wish the Administration all success in its almost impossible task of governing this distracted and anarchical people.

Yours truly,   W. T. SHERMAN.

I was afterward told that this letter gave offense, and that some of Mr. Lincoln's cabinet concluded that I too would prove false to the country.

Later in that month, after the capture of Fort Sumter by

the Confederate authorities, a Dr. Cornyn came to our house on Locust Street, one night after I had gone to bed, and told me he had been sent by Frank Blair, who. was not well, and wanted to see me that night at his house. I dressed and walked over to his house on Washington Avenue, near Fourteenth, and found there, in the front-room, several gentlemen, among whom I recall Henry T. Blow. Blair was in the back-room, closeted with some gentleman, who soon left, and I was called in. He there told me that the Government was mistrustful of General Harney, that a change in the command of the department was to be made; that he held it in his power to appoint a brigadier-general, and put him in command of the department, and he offered me the place. I told him I had once offered my services, and they were declined; that I had made business engagements in St. Louis, which I could not throw off at pleasure; that I had long deliberated on my course of action, and must decline his offer, however tempting and complimentary. He reasoned with me, but I persisted. He told me, in that event, he should appoint Lyon, and he did so.

Finding that even my best friends were uneasy as to my political status, on the 8th of May I addressed the following official letter to the Secretary of War:

OFFICE OF ST. LOUIS RAILROAD COMPANY,
May 8, 1861.

Hon. S. CAMERON, *Secretary of War, Washington, D. C.*

DEAR SIR: I hold myself now, as always, prepared to serve my country in the capacity for which I was trained. I did not and will not volunteer for *three months,* because I cannot throw my family on the cold charity of the world. But for the *three-years* call, made by the President, an officer can prepare his command and do good service.

I will not volunteer as a soldier, because rightfully or wrongfully I feel unwilling to take a mere private's place, and, having for many years lived in California and Louisiana, the men are not well enough acquainted with me to elect me to my appropriate place.

Should my services be needed, the records of the War Department will enable you to designate the station in which I can render most service.

Yours truly,   W. T. SHERMAN.

To this I do not think I received a direct answer; but, on the 14th of the same month, I was appointed colonel of the Thirteenth Regular Infantry.

I remember going to the arsenal on the 9th of May, taking my children with me in the street-cars. Within the arsenal wall were drawn up in parallel lines four regiments of the "Home Guards," and I saw men distributing cartridges to the boxes. I also saw General Lyon running about with his hair in the wind, his pockets full of papers, wild and irregular, but I knew him to be a man of vehement purpose and of determined action. I saw of course that it meant business, but whether for defense or offense I did not know. The next morning I went up to the railroad-office in Bremen, as usual, and heard at every corner of the streets that the "Dutch" were moving on Camp Jackson. People were barricading their houses, and men were running in that direction. I hurried through my business as quickly as I could, and got back to my house on Locust Street by twelve o'clock. Charles Ewing and Hunter were there, and insisted on going out to the camp to see "the fun." I tried to dissuade them, saying that in case of conflict the by-standers were more likely to be killed than the men engaged, but they would go. I felt as much interest as anybody else, but staid at home, took my little son Willie, who was about seven years old, and walked up and down the pavement in front of our house, listening for the sound of musketry or cannon in the direction of Camp Jackson. While so engaged Miss Eliza Deans, who lived opposite us, called me across the street, told me that her brother-in-law, Dr. Scott, was a surgeon in Frost's camp, and she was dreadfully afraid he would be killed. I reasoned with her that General Lyon was a regular officer; that if he had gone out, as reported, to Camp Jackson, he would take with him such a force as would make resistance impossible; but she would not be comforted, saying that the camp was made up of the young men from the first and best families of St. Louis, and that they were proud, and would fight. I explained that young men of the best families did not like to be killed better than ordinary people. Edging gradually up the street, I was in Olive Street just about Twelfth, when I saw a man running from the direction of Camp Jackson at full speed, calling, as he went, "They've surrendered, they've surrendered!" So I turned back and rang the bell at Mrs. Deans's. Eliza came to the door, and

I explained what I had heard; but she angrily slammed the door in my face! Evidently she was disappointed to find she was mistaken in her estimate of the rash courage of the best families.

I again turned in the direction of Camp Jackson, my boy Willie with me still. At the head of Olive Street, abreast of Lindell's Grove, I found Frank Blair's regiment in the street, with ranks opened, and the Camp Jackson prisoners inside. A crowd of people was gathered around, calling to the prisoners by name, some hurrahing for Jeff Davis, and others encouraging the troops. Men, women, and children, were in the crowd. I passed along till I found myself inside the grove, where I met Charles Ewing and John Hunter, and we stood looking at the troops on the road, heading toward the city. A band of music was playing at the head, and the column made one or two ineffectual starts, but for some reason was halted. The battalion of regulars was abreast of me, of which Major Rufus Saxton was in command, and I gave him an evening paper, which I had bought of the newsboy on my way out. He was reading from it some piece of news, sitting on his horse, when the column again began to move forward, and he resumed his place at the head of his command. At that part of the road, or steet, was an embankment about eight feet high, and a drunken fellow tried to pass over it to the people opposite. One of the regular sergeant file-closers ordered him back, but he attempted to pass through the ranks, when the sergeant barred his progress with his musket "a-port." The drunken man seized his musket, when the sergeant threw him off with violence, and he rolled over and over down the bank. By the time this man had picked himself up and got his hat, which had fallen off, and had again mounted the embankment, the regulars had passed, and the head of [Peter J.] Osterhaus's regiment of Home Guards had come up. The man had in his hand a small pistol, which he fired off, and I heard that the ball had struck the leg of one of Osterhaus's staff; the regiment stopped; there was a moment of confusion, when the soldiers of that regiment began to fire over our heads in the grove. I heard the balls cutting the leaves above our heads, and saw several men and women running in all directions, some of whom were wounded. Of course there was a general stampede. Charles Ewing threw Willie on the ground and covered him with his body. Hunter ran behind the hill, and I also threw myself on the ground. The fire ran back from the head of the regiment toward its rear, and as I saw the men re-loading their pieces, I jerked Willie up, ran back with him into a gulley which covered us, lay there until I saw that the fire had ceased, and that the column was again moving on, when I took up Willie and started back for home round by way of Market Street. A woman and child were killed outright; two or three men were also killed, and several others were wounded. The great mass of the people on that occasion were simply curious spectators, though men were sprinkled through the crowd calling out, "Hurrah for Jeff Davis!" and others were particularly abusive of the "damned Dutch." Lyon posted a guard in charge of the vacant camp, and marched his prisoners down to the arsenal; some were paroled, and others held, till afterward they were regularly exchanged.

A very few days after this event, May 14th, I received a dispatch from my brother Charles in Washington, telling me to come on at once; that I had been appointed a colonel of the Thirteenth Regular Infantry, and that I was wanted at Washington immediately.

Of course I could no longer defer action. I saw Mr. Lucas, Major Turner, and other friends and parties connected with the road, who agreed that I should go on. I left my family, because I was under the impression that I would be allowed to enlist my own regiment, which would take some time, and I expected to raise the regiment and organize it at Jefferson Barracks. I repaired to Washington, and there found that the Government was trying to rise to a level with the occasion. Mr. Lincoln had, without the sanction of law, authorized the raising of ten new regiments of regulars, each infantry regiment to be composed of three battalions of eight companies each; and had called for seventy-five thousand State volunteers. Even this call seemed to me utterly inadequate; still it was none of my business. I took the oath of office, and was furnished with a list of officers, appointed to my regiment, which was still incomplete. I reported in person to General [Winfield] Scott, at his office on Seventeenth Street, opposite the War Department, and applied for authority to return West, and raise my regiment at Jefferson Barracks, but the general said my lieutenant-colonel, [Sidney] Burbank, was fully qualified to superintend the enlistment, and that he wanted me there; and he at once dictated an order for me to report to him in person for inspection duty.

Satisfied that I would not be permitted to return to St.

Louis, I instructed Mrs. Sherman to pack up, return to Lancaster, and trust to the fate of war.

I also resigned my place as president of the Fifth Street Railroad, to take effect at the end of May, so that in fact I received pay from that road for only two months' service, and then began my new army career

Chapter 2

Bull Run to Paducah:
"I Saw Cannonballs Strike Men"
June, 1861—February, 1862

AND NOW THAT, in these notes, I have fairly reached the period of the civil war, which ravaged our country from 1861 to 1865—an event involving a conflict of passion, of prejudice, and of arms, that has developed results which, for better or worse, have left their mark on the world's history—I feel that I tread on delicate ground.

I have again and again been invited to write a history of the war, or to record for publication my personal recollections of it, with large offers of money therefor; all of which I have heretofore declined, because the truth is not always palatable, and should not always be told. Many of the actors in the grand drama still live, and they and their friends are quick to controversy, which should be avoided. The great end of peace has been attained, with little or no change in our form of government, and the duty of all good men is to allow the passions of that period to subside, that we may direct our physical and mental labor to repair the waste of war, and to engage in the greater task of continung our hitherto wonderful national development.

What I now propose to do is merely to group some of my personal recollections about the historic persons and events of the day, prepared not with any view to their publication, but rather for preservation till I am gone; and then to be allowed to follow into oblivion the cords of similar papers, or to be used by some historian who may need them by way of illustration.

I have heretofore recorded how I again came into the military service of the United States as a colonel of the Thirteenth Regular Infantry, a regiment that had no existence at the time, and that, instead of being allowed to enlist the men and instruct them, as expected, I was assigned in Washington City, by an order of Lieutenant-General Winfield Scott, to inspection duty near him on the 20th of June, 1861.

At that time Lieutenant-General Scott commanded the army in chief, with Colonel E[dward] D. Townsend as his adjutant-general, Major G[eorge] W. Cullum, United States Engineers, and Major Schuyler Hamilton, as aides-de-camp. The general had an office upstairs on Seventeenth Street, opposite the War Department, and resided in a house close by, on Pennsylvania Avenue. All fears for the immediate safety of the capital had ceased, and quite a large force of regulars and volunteers had been collected in and about Washington. Brigadier-General J[oseph] K. Mansfield commanded in the city, and Brigadier-General Irvin McDowell on the other side of the Potomac, with his headquarters at Arlington House. His troops extended in a semicircle from Alexandria to above Georgetown. Several forts and redoubts were either built or in progress, and the people were already clamorous for a general forward movement. Another considerable army had also been collected in Pennsylvania under General [Robert] Patterson, and, at the time I speak of, had moved forward to Hagerstown and Williamsport, on the Potomac River. My brother, John Sherman, was a volunteer aide-de-camp to General Patterson, and, toward the end of June, I went up to Hagerstown to see him. I found that army in the very act of moving, and we rode down to Williamsport in a buggy, and were present when the leading division crossed the Potomac River by fording it waist-deep. My friend and classmate, George H. Thomas, was there, in command of a brigade in the leading division. I talked with him a good deal, also with General [George] Cadwalader, and with the staff-officers of General Patterson, viz., Fitz-John Porter, Belger, [Edward G.] Beckwith, and others, all of whom seemed encouraged to think that the war was to be short and decisive, and that, as soon as it was demonstrated that the General Government meant in earnest to defend its rights and property, some general compromise would result.

Patterson's army crossed the Potomac River on the 1st or 2d of July, and, as John Sherman was to take his seat as a Senator in the called session of Congress, to meet July 4th, he resigned his place as aide-de-camp, presented me his two horses and equipment, and we returned to Washington together.

The Congress assembled punctually on the 4th of July, and the message of Mr. Lincoln was strong and good: it recognized the fact that civil war was upon us, that compromise of any kind was at an end; and he asked for four hundred thousand men, and four hundred million dollars, wherewith to vindicate the national authority, and to regain possession of the captured forts and other property of the United States.

It was also immediately demonstrated that the tone and temper of Congress had changed since the Southern Senators and members had withdrawn, and that we, the military, could now go to work with some definite plans and ideas.

The appearance of the troops about Washington was good, but it was manifest they were far from being soldiers. Their uniforms were as various as the States and cities from which they came; their arms were also of every pattern and calibre; and they were so loaded down with overcoats, haversacks, knapsacks, tents, and baggage, that it took from twenty-five to fifty wagons to move the camp of a regiment from one place to another, and some of the camps had bakeries and cooking establishments that would have done credit to Delmonico.

While I was on duty with General Scott, viz., from June 20th to about June 30th, the general frequently communicated to those about him his opinions and proposed plans. He seemed vexed with the clamors of the press for immediate action, and the continued interference in details by the President, Secretary of War, and Congress. He spoke of organizing a grand army of invasion, of which the regulars were to constitute the "iron column," and seemed to intimate that he himself would take the field in person, though he was at the time very old, very heavy, and very unwieldy. His age must have been about seventy-five years.

At that date, July 4, 1861, the rebels had two armies in front of Washington; the one at Manassas Junction, commanded by General [Pierre G. T.] Beauregard, with his advance guard at Fairfax Court House, and indeed almost in sight of Washington. The other, commanded by General Joe Johnston, was at Winchester, with its advance at Martinsburg and Harper's Ferry; but the advance had fallen back before Patterson, who then occupied Martinsburg and the line of the Baltimore & Ohio Railroad.

The temper of Congress and the people would not permit the slow and methodical preparation desired by General Scott; and the cry of "On to Richmond!" which was shared by the volunteers, most of whom had only engaged for ninety days, forced General Scott to hasten his preparations, and to order a general advance about the middle of July. McDowell was to move from the defenses of Washington, and Patterson from Martinsburg. In the organization of McDowell's army into divisions and brigades, Colonel David Hunter was assigned to command the Second Division, and I was ordered to take command of his former brigade, which was composed of five regiments in position in and about Fort Corcoran, and on the ground opposite Georgetown. I assumed command on the 30th of June, and proceeded at once to prepare it for the general advance. My command constituted the Third Bridgade of the First Division, which division was commanded by Brigadier-General Daniel Tyler, a graduate of West Point, but who had seen little or no actual service. I applied to General [Irvin] McDowell for some staff-officers, and he gave me, as adjutant-general, Lieutenant [George C.] Piper, of the Third Artillery, and, as aide-de-camp, Lieutenant [John C.] McQuiston, a fine young cavalry-officer, fresh from West Point.

I selected for the field the Thirteenth New York, Colonel [Isaac F.] Quimby; the Sixty-ninth New York, Colonel [Michael] Corcoran; the Seventy-ninth New York, Colonel [James] Cameron; and the Second Wisconsin, Lieutenant-Colonel [Henry W.] Peck. These were all good, strong, volunteer regiments, pretty well commanded; and I had reason to believe that I had one of the best brigades in the whole army. Captain [Romeyn B.] Ayres's battery of the Fifth Regular Artillery was also attached to my brigade. The other regiment, the Twenty-ninth New York, Colonel Bennett, was destined to be left behind in charge of the forts and camps during our absence, which was expected to be short. Soon after I had assumed the command, a difficulty arose in the Sixty-ninth, an Irish regiment. This regiment had volunteered in New York, early in April, for ninety days; but, by reason of the difficulty of passing through Baltimore, they had come *via* Annapolis, had been held for duty on the railroad as a guard for nearly a month before they actually reached Washington, and were then mustered in about a month after enrollment. Some of the men claimed that they were entitled to their discharge in ninety days from the time of enrollment, whereas the muster-roll read ninety days from the date of muster-in. One day, Colonel Corcoran explained this matter to me. I advised him to reduce the facts to writing, and that I would submit it to the War Department for an authoritative decision. He did so, and the War Department decided that the muster-roll was the only contract of service, that it would be construed literally; and that the regiment would be held till the expiration of three months from the date of muster-in, viz., to about August 1, 1861. General Scott at the same time wrote one of his characteristic letters to Corcoran, telling him that we were about to engage in battle, and he knew his Irish friends would not leave him in such a crisis. Corcoran and the officers generally wanted to go to the expected battle, but a good many of the men were not so anxious. In the Second Wisconsin, also, was developed a personal difficulty. The actual colonel was Dr. Coon, a good-hearted gentleman, who knew no more of the military art than a child; whereas his lieutenant-colonel, Peck, had been to West Point, and knew the drill. Preferring that the latter should remain in command of the regiment, I put Colonel Coon on my personal staff, which reconciled the difficulty.

In due season, about July 15th, our division moved forward, leaving our camps standing; [Erasmus D.] Keyes's brigade in the lead, then [Robert C.] Schenck's, then mine, and [Israel B.] Richardson's last. We marched *via* Vienna, Germantown, and Centreville, where all the army, composed of five divisions, seemed to converge. The march demonstrated little save the general laxity of discipline; for with all my personal efforts I could not prevent the men from straggling for water, blackberries, or any thing on the way they fancied.

At Centreville, on the 18th, Richardson's brigade was sent by General [Daniel] Tyler to reconnoitre Blackburn's Ford across Bull Run, and he found it strongly guarded. From our camp, at Centreville, we heard the cannonading, and then a sharp musketry-fire. I received orders from General Tyler to send forward Ayres's battery, and very soon after another order came for me to advance with my whole brigade. We marched the three miles at the double-quick, arrived in time to relieve Richardson's brigade, which was just drawing back from the ford, worsted, and stood for half an hour or so under a fire of artillery, which killed four or five of my men. General Tyler was there in person, giving directions, and soon after he ordered us all back to our camp in Centreville. This reconnoissance had developed a strong force, and had been made without the orders of General McDowell; however, it satisfied us that the enemy was in force on the other side of Bull Run, and had no intention to leave without a serious battle. We lay in camp at Centreville all of the 19th and 20th, and during that night began the movement which resulted in the battle of Bull Run, on July 21st. Of this so much has been written that more would be superfluous; and the reports of the opposing commanders, McDowell and Johnston, are fair and correct. It is now generally admitted that it was one of the best-planned battles of the war, but one of the worst-fought. Our men had been told so often at home that all they had to do was to make a bold appearance, and the rebels would run; and nearly all of us for the first time then heard the sound of cannon and muskets in anger, and saw the bloody scenes common to all battles, with which we were soon to be familiar. We had good organization, good men, but no cohesion, no real discipline, no respect for authority, no real knowledge of war. Both armies were fairly defeated, and, whichever had stood fast, the other would have run. Though the North was overwhelmed with mortification and shame, the South really had not much to boast of, for in the three or four hours of fighting their organization was so broken up that they did not and could not follow our army, when it was known to be in a state of disgraceful and causeless flight. It is easy to criticise a battle after it is over, but all now admit that none others, equally raw in war, could have done better than we did at Bull Run; and the lesson of that battle should not be lost on a people like ours.

I insert my official report, as a condensed statement of my share in the battle:

HEADQUARTERS THIRD BRIGADE, FIRST DIVISION, }
FORT CORCORAN, *July* 25, 1861. }

To Captain A. BAIRD, *Assistant Adjutant-General, First Division (General Tyler's).*

SIR: I have the honor to submit this my report of the operations of my brigade during the action of the 21st instant. The brigade is composed of the Thirteenth New York Volunteers, Colonel Quimby; Sixty-ninth New York, Colonel Corcoran; Seventy-ninth New York, Colonel Cameron; Second Wisconsin, Lieutenant-Colonel Peck; and Company E, Third Artillery, under command of Captain R. B. Ayres, Fifth Artillery. We left our camp near Centreville, pursuant to orders, at half-past 2 A. M., taking place in your column, next to the brigade of General Schenck, and proceeded as far as the halt, before the enemy's position, near the stone bridge across Bull Run. Here the brigade was deployed in line along the skirt of timber to the right of the Warrenton road, and remained quietly in position till after 10 A. M. The enemy remained very quiet, but about that time we saw a rebel regiment leave its cover in our front, and proceed in double-quick time on the road toward Sudley Springs, by which we knew the columns of Colonels [David] Hunter and [Samuel P.] Heintzelman were approaching. About the same time we observed in motion a large mass of the enemy, below and on the other side of the stone bridge. I directed Captain Ayres to take position with his battery near our right, and to open fire on this mass; but you had previously detached the two rifle-guns belonging to this battery, and finding that the smooth-bore guns did not reach the enemy's position, we ceased firing, and I sent a request that you would send to me the thirty-pounder rifle-gun attached to Captain [John H.] Carlisle's battery. At the same time I shifted the New York Sixty-ninth to the extreme right of the brigade. Thus we remained till we heard the musketry-fire across Bull Run, showing that the head of Colonel Hunter's column was engaged. This firing was brisk, and showed that Hunter was driving before him the enemy, till about noon, when it became certain the enemy had come to a stand, and that our forces on the other side of Bull Run were all engaged, artillery and infantry.

Here you sent me the order to cross over with the whole brigade, to the assistance of Colonel Hunter. Early in the day, when reconnoitring the ground, I had seen a horseman descend from a bluff in our front, cross the stream, and show himself in the open field on this side; and, inferring that we could cross over at the same point, I sent forward a company as skirmishers, and followed with the whole brigade, the New York Sixty-ninth leading.

We found no difficulty in crossing over, and met with no opposition in ascending the steep bluff opposite with our infantry, but it was impassable to the artillery, and I sent word back to Captain Ayres to follow if possible, otherwise to use his discretion. Captain Ayres did not cross Bull Run, but remained on that side, with the rest of your division. His report herewith describes his operations during the remainder of the day. Advancing slowly and cautiously with the head of the column, to give time for the regiments in succession to close up their ranks, we first encountered a party of the enemy retreating along a cluster of pines; Lieutenant-Colonel Haggerty, of the Sixty-ninth, without orders, rode out alone, and endeavored to intercept their retreat. One of the enemy, in full view, at short range, shot Haggerty, and he fell dead from his horse. The Sixty-ninth opened fire on this party, which was returned; but, determined to effect our junction with Hunter's division, I ordered this fire to cease, and we proceeded with caution toward the field where we then plainly saw our forces engaged. Displaying our colors conspicuously at the head of our column, we succeeded in attracting the attention of our friends, and soon formed the brigade in rear of Colonel Porter's. Here I learned that Colonel Hunter was disabled by a severe wound, and that General McDowell was on the field. I sought him out, and received his orders to join in pursuit of the enemy, who was falling back to the left of the road by which the army had approached from Sudley Springs. Placing Colonel Quimby's regiment of rifles in front, in column, by division, I directed the other regiments to follow in line of battle, in the order of the Wisconsin Second, New York Seventy-ninth, and New York Sixty-ninth. Quimby's regiment advanced steadily down the hill and up the ridge, from which he opened fire upon the enemy, who had made another stand on ground very favorable to him, and the regiment continued advancing as the enemy gave way, till the head of the column reached the point near which [James B.] Rickett's battery was so severely cut up. The other regiments descended the hill in line of battle, under a severe cannonade; and, the ground affording comparative shelter from the enemy's artillery, they changed direction, by the right flank, and followed the road before mentioned. At the point where this road crosses the ridge to our left front, the ground was swept by a most severe fire of artillery, rifles, and musketry, and we saw, in succession, several regiments driven from it; among them the Zouaves and battalion of marines. Before reaching the crest of this hill, the roadway was worn deep enough to afford shelter, and I kept the several regiments in it as long as possible; but when the Wisconsin Second was abreast of the enemy, by order of Major Wadsworth, of General McDowell's staff, I ordered it to leave the roadway, by the left flank, and to attack the enemy.

This regiment ascended to the brow of the hill steadily, received the severe fire of the enemy, returned it with spirit, and advanced, delivering its fire. This regiment is uniformed in gray cloth, almost identical with that of the great bulk of the secession army; and, when the regiment fell into confusion and retreated toward the road, there was a universal cry that they were being fired on by our own men. The regiment rallied again, passed the brow of the hill a second time, but was again repulsed in disorder. By this time the New York Seventy-ninth had closed up, and in like manner it was ordered to cross the brow of the hill, and drive the enemy from cover. It was impossible to get a good view of this ground. In it there was one battery of artillery, which poured an incessant fire upon our advancing column, and the ground was very irregular with small clusters of pines, affording shelter, of which the enemy took good advantage. The fire of rifles and musketry was very severe. The Seventy-ninth, headed by its colonel, Cameron, charged across the hill, and for a short time the contest was severe; they rallied several times under fire, but finally broke, and gained the cover of the hill.

This left the field open to the New York Sixty-ninth, Colonel Corcoran, who, in his turn, led his regiment over the crest, and had in full, open view the ground so severely contested; the fire was very severe, and the roar of cannon, musketry, and rifles, incessant; it was manifest the enemy was here in great force, far superior to us at that point. The Sixty-ninth held the ground for some time, but finally fell back in disorder.

All this time Quimby's regiment occupied another ridge,

to our left, overlooking the same field of action, and similarly engaged. Here, about half-past 3 P. M., began the scene of confusion and disorder that characterized the remainder of the day. Up to that time, all had kept their places, and seemed perfectly cool, and used to the shell and shot that fell, comparatively harmless, all around us; but the short exposure to an intense fire of small-arms, at close range, had killed many, wounded more, and had produced disorder in all of the battalions that had attempted to encounter it. Men fell away from their ranks, talking, and in great confusion. Colonel Cameron had been mortally wounded, was carried to an ambulance, and reported dying. Many other officers were reported dead or missing, and many of the wounded were making their way, with more or less assistance, to the buildings used as hospitals, on the ridge to the west. We succeeded in partially reforming the regiments, but it was manifest that they would not stand, and I directed Colonel Corcoran to move along the ridge to the rear, near the position where we had first formed the brigade. General McDowell was there in person, and used all possible efforts to reassure the men. By the active exertions of Colonel Corcoran, we formed an irregular square against the cavalry which were then seen to issue from the position from which we had been driven, and we began our retreat toward the same ford of Bull Run by which we had approached the field of battle. There was no positive order to retreat, although for an hour it had been going on by the operation of the men themselves. The ranks were thin and irregular, and we found a stream of people strung from the hospital across Bull Run, and far toward Centreville. After putting in motion the irregular square in person, I pushed forward to find Captain Ayres's battery at the crossing of Bull Run. I sought it at its last position, before the brigade had crossed over, but it was not there; then passing through the woods, where, in the morning, we had first formed line, we approached the blacksmith's shop, but there found a detachment of the secession cavalry and thence made a circuit, avoiding Cub Run Bridge, into Centreville, where I found General McDowell, and from him understood that it was his purpose to rally the forces, and make a stand at Centreville.

But, about nine o'clock at night, I received from General Tyler, in person, the order to continue the retreat to the Potomac. This retreat was by night, and disorderly in the extreme. The men of different regiments mingled together, and some reached the river at Arlington, some at Long Bridge, and the greater part returned to their former camp, at or near Fort Corcoran. I reached this point at noon the next day, and found a miscellaneous crowd crossing over the aqueduct and ferries. Conceiving this to be demoralizing, I at once commanded the guard to be increased, and all persons attempting to pass over to be stopped. This soon produced its effect; men sought their proper companies and regiments. Comparative order was restored, and all were posted to the best advantage.

W. T. SHERMAN, *Colonel commanding Brigade.*

This report, which I had not read probably since its date till now, recalls to me vividly the whole scene of the affair at Blackburn's Ford, when for the first time in my life I saw cannonballs strike men and crash through the trees and saplings above and around us, and realized the always sickening confusion as one approaches a fight from the rear; then the night-march from Centreville, on the Warrenton road, standing for hours wondering what was meant; the deployment along the edge of the field that sloped down to Bull Run, and waiting for Hunter's approach on the other side from the direction of Sudley Springs away off to our right; the terrible scare of a poor Negro who was caught between our lines; the crossing of Bull Run, and the fear lest we should be fired on by our own men; the killing of Lieutenant-Colonel [Peter] Haggerty, which occurred in plain sight; and the first scenes of a field strewed with dead men and horses. Yet, at that period of the battle, we were the victors and felt jubilant. At that moment, also, my brigade passed Hunter's division; but Heintzelman's was still ahead of us, and we followed its lead along the road toward Manassas Junction, crossing a small stream and ascending a long hill, at the summit of which the battle was going on. Here my regiments came into action well, but successively, and were driven back, each in its turn. For two hours we continued to dash at the woods on our left front, which were full of rebels; but I was convinced their organization was broken, and that they had simply halted there and taken advantage of these woods as a cover, to reach which we had to pass over the intervening fields about the Henry House, which were clear, open, and gave them a decided advantage. After I had put in each of my regiments, and had them driven back to the cover of the road, I had no idea that we were beaten, but reformed the regiments in line in their proper order, and only wanted a little rest, when I found that my brigade was almost alone, except [George] Syke's regulars, who had formed square against cavalry and were coming back. I then realized that the whole army was "in retreat," and that my own men were individually making back for the stone bridge. Corcoran and I formed the brigade into an irregular square, but it fell to pieces; and, along with a crowd, disorganized but not much scared, the brigade got back to Centreville to our former camps. Corcoran was captured, and held a prisoner for some time; but I got safe to Centreville. I saw General McDowell in Centreville, and understood that several of his divisions had not been engaged at all, that he would reorganize them at Centreville, and there await the enemy. I got my four regiments in parallel lines in a field, the same in which we had camped before the battle, and had lain down to sleep under a tree, when I heard someone asking for me. I called out where I was, when General Tyler in person gave me orders to march back to our camps at Fort Corcoran. I aroused my aides, gave them orders to call up the sleeping men, have each regiment to leave the field by a flank and to take the same road back by which we had come. It was near midnight, and the road was full of troops, wagons, and batteries. We tried to keep our regiments separate, but all became inextricably mixed. Toward morning we reached Vienna, where I slept some hours, and the next day, about noon, we reached Fort Corcoran.

A slow, mizzling rain had set in, and probably a more gloomy day never presented itself. All organization seemed to be at an end; but I and my staff labored hard to collect our men into their proper companies and into their former camps, and, on the 23d of July, I moved the Second Wisconsin and Seventy-ninth New York closer in to Fort Corcoran, and got things in better order than I had expected. Of course, we took it for granted that the rebels would be on our heels, and we accordingly prepared to defend our posts. By the 25th I had collected all the materials, made my report, and had my brigade about as well governed as any in that army; although most of the ninety-day men, especially the Sixty-ninth, had become extremely tired of the war, and wanted to go home. Some of them were so mutinous, at one time, that

I had Ayres's battery to unlimber, threatening, if they dared to leave camp without orders, I would open fire on them. Drills and the daily exercises were resumed, and I ordered that at the three principal roll-calls the men should form ranks with belts and muskets, and that they should keep their ranks until I in person had received the reports and had dismissed them. The Sixty-ninth still occupied Fort Corcoran, and one morning, after reveille, when I had just received the report, had dismissed the regiment, and was leaving, I found myself in a crowd of men crossing the drawbridge on their way to a barn close by, where they had their sinks; among them was an officer, who said: "Colonel, I am going to New York today. What can I do for you?" I answered: "How can you go to New York? I do not remember to have signed a leave for you." He said, "No; he did not want a leave. He had engaged to serve three months, and had already served more than that time. If the Government did not intend to pay him, he could afford to lose the money; that he was a lawyer, and had neglected his business long enough, and was then going home." I noticed that a good many of the soldiers had paused about us to listen, and knew that, if this officer could defy me, they also would. So I turned on him sharp, and said: "Captain, this question of your term of service has been submitted to the rightful authority, and the decision has been published in orders. You are a soldier, and must submit to orders till you are properly discharged. If you attempt to leave without orders, it will be mutiny, and I will shoot you like a dog! Go back into the fort *now*, instantly, and don't dare to leave without my consent." I had on an overcoat, and may have had my hand about the breast, for he looked at me hard, paused a moment, and then turned back into the fort. The men scattered, and I returned to the house where I was quartered, close by.

That same day, which must have been about July 26th, I was near the river-bank, looking at a block-house which had been built for the defense of the aqueduct, when I saw a carriage coming by the road that crossed the Potomac River at Georgetown by a ferry. I thought I recognized in the carriage the person of President Lincoln. I hurried across a bend, so as to stand by the road-side as the carriage passed. I was in uniform, with a sword on, and was recognized by Mr. Lincoln and Mr. Seward, who rode side by side in an open hack. I inquired if they were going to my camps, and

Mr. Lincoln said: "Yes; we heard that you had got over the big scare, and we thought we would come over and see the 'boys.'" The roads had been much changed and were rough. I asked if I might give directions to his coachman, he promptly invited me to jump in and to tell the coachman which way to drive. Intending to begin on the right and follow round to the left, I turned the driver into a side-road which led up a very steep hill, and, seeing a soldier, called to him and sent him up hurriedly to announce to the colonel (Bennett, I think) that the President was coming. As we slowly ascended the hill, I discovered that Mr. Lincoln was full of feeling, and wanted to encourage our men. I asked if he intended to speak to them, and he said he would like to. I asked him then to please discourage all cheering, noise, or any sort of confusion; that we had had enough of it before Bull Run to ruin any set of men, and that what we needed were cool, thoughtful, hard-fighting soldiers—no more hurrahing, no more humbug. He took my remarks in the most perfect good-nature. Before we had reached the first camp, I heard the drum beating the "assembly," saw the men running for their tents, and in a few minutes the regiment was in line, arms presented, and then brought to an order and "parade rest!"

Mr. Lincoln stood up in the carriage, and made one of the neatest, best, and most feeling addresses I ever listened to, referring to our late disaster at Bull Run, the high duties that still devolved on us, and the brighter days yet to come. At one or two points the soldiers began to cheer, but he promptly checked them, saying: "Don't cheer, boys. I confess I rather like it myself, but Colonel Sherman here says it is not military; and I guess we had better defer to his opinion." In winding up, he explained that, as President, he was commander-in-chief; that he was resolved that the soldiers should have every thing that the law allowed; and he called on one and all to appeal to him personally in case they were wronged. The effect of this speech was excellent.

We passed along in the same manner to all the camps of my brigade; and Mr. Lincoln complimented me highly for the order, cleanliness, and discipline, that he observed. Indeed, he and Mr. Seward both assured me that it was the first bright moment they had experienced since the battle.

At last we reached Fort Corcoran. The carriage could not enter, so I ordered the regiment, without arms, to come outside, and gather about Mr. Lincoln, who would speak to them. He made to them the same feeling address, with more personal allusions, because of their special gallantry in the battle under Corcoran, who was still a prisoner in the hands of the enemy; and he concluded with the same general offer of redress in case of grievance. In the crowd I saw the officer with whom I had had the passage at reveille that morning. His face was pale, and lips compressed. I foresaw a scene, but sat on the front seat of the carriage as quiet as a lamb. This officer forced his way through the crowd to the carriage, and said: "Mr. President, I have a cause of grievance. This morning I went to speak to Colonel Sherman, and he threatened to shoot me." Mr. Lincoln, who was still standing, said, "Threatened to shoot you?" "Yes, sir, he threatened to shoot me." Mr. Lincoln looked to him, then at me, and stooping his tall, spare form toward the officer, said to him in a loud stage-whisper, easily heard from some yards around: "Well, if I were you, and he threatened to shoot, I would not trust him, for I believe he would do it." The officer turned about and disappeared, and the men laughed at him. Soon the carriage drove on, and, as we descended the hill, I explained the facts to the President, who answered, "Of course I didn't know any thing about it, but I thought you knew your own business best." I thanked him for his confidence, and assured him that what he had done would go far to enable me to maintain good discipline, and it did.

By this time the day was well spent. I asked to take my leave, and the President and Mr. Seward drove back to Washington. This spirit of mutiny was common to the whole army, and was not subdued till several regiments or parts of regiments had been ordered to Fort Jefferson, Florida, as punishment.

General McDowell had resumed his headquarters at the Arlington House, and was busily engaged in restoring order to his army, sending off the ninety-days men, and replacing them by regiments which had come under the three-years call. We were all trembling lest we should be held personally accountable for the disastrous result of the battle. General [George B.] McClellan had been summoned from the West to Washington, and changes in the subordinate commands were announced almost daily. I remember, as a group of officers were talking in the large room of the Arlington House, used as the adjutant-general's office, one evening, some young officer came in with a list of the new brigadiers just announced at the War Department, which embraced the names of Heintzelman, Keyes, Franklin, Andrew Porter, W. T. Sherman, and others, who had been colonels in the battle, and all of whom had shared the common stampede. Of course, we discredited the truth of the list; and Heintzelman broke out in his nasal voice, "By—— ——, it's all a lie! Every mother's son of you will be cashiered." We all felt he was right, but, nevertheless, it was true; and we were all announced in general orders as brigadier-generals of volunteers.

General McClellan arrived, and, on assuming command, confirmed McDowell's organization. Instead of coming over the river, as we expected, he took a house in Washington, and only came over from time to time to have a review or inspection. I had received several new regiments, and had begun two new forts on the hill or plateau, above and farther out than Fort Corcoran; and I organized a system of drills, embracing the evolutions of the line, all of which was new to me, and I had to learn the tactics from books; but I was convinced that we had a long, hard war before us, and made up my mind to begin at the very beginning to prepare for it.

August was passing, and troops were pouring in from all quarters; General McClellan told me he intended to organize an army of a hundred thousand men, with one hundred field-batteries, and I still hoped he would come on our side of the Potomac, pitch his tent, and prepare for real hard work, but his headquarters still remained in a house in Washington City. I then thought, and still think, that was a fatal mistake. His choice as general-in-chief at the time was fully justified by his high reputation in the army and country, and, if he then had any political views or ambition, I surely did not suspect it.

About the middle of August I got a note from Brigadier-General Robert Anderson, asking me to come and see him at his room at Willard's Hotel. I rode over and found him in conversation with several gentlemen, and he explained to me that events in Kentucky were approaching a crisis; that the Legislature was in session, and ready, as soon as properly backed by the General Government, to take open sides for the Union cause; that he was offered the command of the Department of the Cumberland, to embrace Kentucky, Tennessee, etc., and that he wanted help, and that the President had offered to allow him to select out of the new brigadiers four of his own choice. I had been a lieutenant in Captain

Anderson's company, at Fort Moultrie, from 1843 to 1846, and he explained that he wanted me as his right hand. He also indicated George H. Thomas, D[on] C[arlos] Buell, and [Ambrose B.] Burnside, as the other three. Of course, I always wanted to go West, and was perfectly willing to go with Anderson, especially in a subordinate capacity. We agreed to call on the President on a subsequent day, to talk with him about it, and we did. It hardly seems probable that Mr. Lincoln should have come to Willard's Hotel to meet us, by my impression is that he did, and that General Anderson had some difficulty in prevailing on him to appoint George H. Thomas, a native of Virginia, to be brigadier-general, because so many Southern officers had already played false; but I was still more emphatic in my indorsement of him by reason of my talk with him at the time he crossed the Potomac with Patterson's army, when Mr. Lincoln promised to appoint him and to assign him to duty with General Anderson. In this interview with Mr. Lincoln, I also explained to him my extreme desire to serve in a subordinate capacity, and in no event to be left in a superior command. He promised me this with promptness, making the jocular remark that his chief trouble was to find places for the too many generals who wanted to be at the head of affairs, to command armies, etc.

After some days, I was relieved in command of my brigade and post by Brigadier General Fitz-John Porter, and at once took my departure for Cincinnati, Ohio, *via* Cresson, Pennsylvania, where General Anderson was with his family; and he, Thomas, and I, met by appointment at the house of his brother, Larz Anderson, Esq., in Cincinnati. We were there on the 1st and 2d of September, when several prominent gentlemen of Kentucky met us to discuss the situation, among whom were O. L. Jackson, [James] Harlan, [James] Speed, and others. At that time, William Nelson, an officer of the navy, had been commissioned a brigadier-general of volunteers, and had his camp at Dick Robinson, a few miles beyond the Kentucky River, south of Nicholasville; and Brigadier-General L[ovell] H. Rousseau had another camp at Jeffersonville, opposite Louisville. The State Legislature was in session at Frankfort, and was ready to take definite action as soon as General Anderson was prepared, for the State was threatened with invasion from Tennessee, by two forces: one from the direction of Nashville, commanded by Generals Albert Sidney Johnston and [Simon B.] Buckner; and the other from the direction of Cumberland Gap, commanded by Generals [George B.] Crittenden and [Felix K.] Zollicoffer. General Anderson saw that he had not force enough to resist these two columns, and concluded to send me in person for help in Indianapolis and Springfield, to confer with Governors of Indiana, and Illinois, and to General [John C.] Fremont, who commanded in St. Louis.

McClellan and Fremont were the two men toward whom the country looked as the great Union leaders, and toward them were streaming the newly-raised regiments of infantry and cavalry, and batteries of artillery; nobody seeming to think of the intervening link covered by Kentucky. While I was to make this tour, Generals Anderson and Thomas were to go to Louisville and initiate the department. None of us had a staff, or any of the machinery for organizing an army, and, indeed, we had no army to organize. Anderson was empowered to raise regiments in Kentucky, and to commission a few brigadier-generals.

At Indianapolis I found Governor [Oliver P.] Morton and all the State officials busy in equipping and providing for the new regiments, and my object was to divert some of them toward Kentucky; but they were called for as fast as they were mustered in, either for the army of McClellan or Fremont. At Springfield also I found the same general activity and zeal, Governor [Richard] Yates busy in providing for his men; but these men also had been promised to Fremont. I then went on to St. Louis, where all was seeming activity, bustle, and preparation. Meeting R. M. Renick at the Planters' House (where I stopped), I inquired where I could find General Fremont. Renick said, "What do you want with General Fremont?" I said I had come to see him on business; and he added, "You don't suppose that he will see such as you?" and went on to retail all the scandal of the day: that Fremont was a great potentate, surrounded by sentries and guards; that he had a more showy court than any real king; that he kept senators, governors, and the first citizens, dancing attendance for days and weeks before granting an audience, etc.; that if I expected to see him on business, I would have to make my application in writing, and submit to a close scrutiny by his chief of staff and by his civil surroundings. Of course I laughed at all this, and renewed my simple inquiry as to where was his office, and was informed that he resided and had his office at Major Brant's new house on Chouteau Avenue. It was then late in the afternoon, and I concluded to wait till the next morning; but that night I received a dispatch from General Anderson in Louisville to hurry back, as events were pressing, and he needed me.

Accordingly, I rose early next morning before daybreak, got breakfast with the early railroad-passengers, and about sunrise was at the gate of General Fremont's headquarters. A sentinel with drawn sabre paraded up and down in front of the house. I had on my undress uniform indicating my rank, and inquired of the sentinel, "Is General Fremont up?" He answered, "I don't know." Seeing that he was a soldier by his bearing, I spoke in a sharp, emphatic voice, "Then find out." He called for the corporal of the guard, and soon a fine-looking German sergeant came, to whom I addressed the same inquiry. He in turn did not know, and I bade him find out, as I had immediate and important business with the general. The sergeant entered the house by the front-basement door, and after ten or fifteen minutes the main front-door above was slowly opened from the inside, and who should appear but my old San Francisco acquaintance Isaiah C. Woods, whom I had not seen or heard of since his flight to Australia, at the time of the failure of Adams & Co. in 1855! He ushered me in hastily, closed the door, and conducted me into the office on the right of the hall. We were glad to meet, after so long and eventful an interval, and mutually inquired after our respective families and special acquaintances. I found that he was a commissioned officer, a major on duty with Fremont, and Major [Joseph H.] Eaton, now of the Paymaster's Department, was in same office with him. I explained to them that I had come from General Anderson, and wanted to confer with General Fremont in person. Woods left me, but soon returned, said the general would see me in a very few minutes, and within ten minutes I was shown across the hall into the large parlor, where General Fremont received me very politely. We had met before, as early as 1847, in California, and I had also seen him several times when he was senator. I then in a rapid manner ran over all the points of interest in General Anderson's new sphere of action, hoped he would spare us from the new levies what troops he could, and generally act in concert with us. He told me that his first business would be to drive the rebel General [Sterling] Price and his army out of Missouri, when he would turn his attention down the Mississippi. He asked my opinion about the various kinds of field-artillery which manufacturers were thrusting on him, especially the then newly-invented James gun, and afterward our conversation took a wide turn about the character of the principal citizens of St. Louis, with whom I was well acquainted.

Telling General Fremont that I had been summoned to Louisville, and that I should leave in the first train, viz., at 3 P. M., I took my leave of him. Returning to Wood's office, I found there two more Californians, viz., Messrs. Palmer and Haskell, so I felt that, while Fremont might be suspicious of others, he allowed free ingress to his old California acquaintances.

Returning to the Planters' House, I heard of Beard, another Californian, a Mormon, who had the contract for the line of redoubts which Fremont had ordered to be constructed around the city, before he would take his departure for the interior of the State; and while I stood near the office-counter, I saw old Baron Steinberger, a prince among our early California adventurers, come in and look over the register. I avoided him on purpose, but his presence in St. Louis recalled the maxim, "Where the vultures are, there is a carcass close by;" and I suspected that the profitable contracts of the quartermaster, [Justus] McKinstry, had drawn to St. Louis some of the most enterprising men of California. I suspect they can account for the fact that, in a very short time, Fremont fell from his high estate in Missouri, by reason of frauds, or supposed frauds, in the administration of the affairs of his command.

I left St. Louis that afternoon and reached Louisville the next morning. I found General Anderson quartered at the Louisville Hotel, and he had taken a dwelling house on——— Street as an office. Captain O[liver] D. Greene was his adjutant-general, Lieutenant [Charles B.] Throckmorton his aide, and Captain [Frederick E.] Prime, of the Engineer Corps, was on duty with him. General George H. Thomas had been dispatched to camp Dick Robinson, to relieve Nelson.

The city was full of all sorts of rumors. The Legislature, moved by considerations purely of a political nature, had taken the step, whatever it was, that amounted to an adherence to the Union, instead of joining the already-seceded States. This was universally known to be the signal for action. For it we were utterly unprepared, whereas the rebels were fully prepared. General Sidney Johnston immediately crossed into Kentucky, and advanced as far as Bowling Green, which he began to fortify, and thence dispatched General Buckner with a division forward toward Louisville; General Zollicoffer, in like manner, entered the State and advanced as far as Somerset. On the day I reached Louisville the excitement ran high. It was known that Columbus, Kentucky, had been occupied, September 7th, by a strong rebel force, under Generals [Gideon J.] Pillow and [Leonidos K.] Polk, and that General Grant had moved from Cairo and occupied Paducah in force on the 6th. Many of the rebel families expected Buckner to reach Louisville at any moment. That night, General Anderson sent for me, and I found with him Mr. Guthrie, president of the Louisville & Nashville Railroad, who had in his hands a dispatch to the effect that the bridge across the Rolling Fork of Salt Creek, less than thirty miles out, had been burned, and that Buckner's force, *en route* for Louisville, had been detained beyond Green River by a train thrown from the track. We learned afterward that a man named Bird had displaced a rail on purpose to throw the train off the track, and thereby give us time.

Mr. Guthrie explained that in the ravine just beyond Salt Creek were several high and important trestles which, if destroyed, would take months to replace, and General Anderson thought it well worth the effort to save them. Also, on Muldraugh's Hill beyond, was a strong position, which had in former years been used as the site for the State "Camp of Instruction," and we all supposed that General Buckner, who was familiar with the ground, was aiming for a position there, from which to operate on Louisville.

All the troops we had to counteract Buckner were Rousseau's Legion, and a few Home Guards in Louisville. The former were still encamped across the river at Jeffersonville; so General Anderson ordered me to go over, and with them, and such Home Guards as we could collect, make the effort to secure possession of Muldraugh's Hill before Buckner could reach it. I took Captain Prime with me, and crossed over to Rousseau's camp. The long-roll was beaten, and within an hour the men, to the number of about one thousand, were marching for the ferry-boat and for the Nashville depot. Meantime General Anderson had sent to collect some Home Guards, and Mr. Guthrie to get the trains ready. It was after midnight before we began to move. The trains proceeded slowly, and it was daybreak when we reached Lebanon

Junction, twenty-six miles out, where we disembarked, and marched to the bridge over Salt River, which we found had been burnt; whether to prevent Buckner coming into Louisville, or us from going out, was not clear. Rousseau's Legion forded the stream and marched up to the State Camp of Instruction, finding the high trestles all secure. The railroad-hands went to work at once to rebuild the bridge. I remained a couple of days at Lebanon Junction, during which General Anderson forwarded two regiments of volunteers that had come to him. Before the bridge was done we advanced the whole camp to the summit of Muldraugh's Hill, just back of Elizabethtown. There I learned definitely that General Buckner had not crossed Green River at all, that General Sidney Johnston was fortifying Bowling Green, and preparing for a systematic advance into Kentucky, of which he was a native, and with whose people and geography he must have been familiar.

As fast as fresh troops reached Louisville, they were sent out to me at Muldraugh's Hill, where I was endeavoring to put them into shape for service, and by the 1st of October I had the equivalent of a division of two brigades preparing to move forward toward Green River. The daily correspondence between General Anderson and myself satisfied me that the worry and harassment at Louisville were exhausting his strength and health, and that he would soon leave. On a telegraphic summons from him, about the 5th of October, I went down to Louisville, when General Anderson said he could not stand the mental torture of his command any longer, and that he must go away, or it would kill him. On the 8th of October he actually published an order relinquishing the command, and, by reason of my seniority, I had no alternative but to assume command, though much against the grain, and in direct violation of Mr. Lincoln's promise to me. I am certain that, in my earliest communication to the War Department, I renewed the expression of my wish to remain in a subordinate position, and that I received the assurance that Brigadier-General Buell would soon arrive from California, and would be sent to relieve me.

By that time I had become pretty familiar with the geography and the general resources of Kentucky. We had parties all over the State raising regiments and companies; but it was manifest that the young men were generally inclined to the cause of the South, while the older men of property wanted to be let alone—i.e., to remain neutral. As to a forward movement that fall, it was simply impracticable; for we were forced to use divergent lines, leading our columns farther and farther apart; and all I could attempt was to go and collect force and material at the two points already chosen, viz., Dick Robinson and Elizabethtown. General George H. Thomas still continued to command the former, and on the 12th of October I dispatched Brigadier-General A[lexander] McD. McCook to command the latter, which had been moved forward to Nolin Creek, fifty-two miles out of Louisville, toward Bowling Green. Staff-officers began to arrive to relieve us of the constant drudgery which, up to that time, had been forced on General Anderson and myself; and these were all good men. Colonel Thomas Swords, quartermaster, arrived on the 13th; Paymaster Larned on the 14th; and Lieutenant Smyzer, Fifth Artillery, acting ordnance-officer, on the 20th; Captain Symonds was already on duty as the commissary of subsistence; Captain O. D. Greene was the adjutant-general, and completed a good working staff.

The everlasting worry of citizens complaining of every petty delinquency of a soldier, and forcing themselves forward to discuss politics, made the position of a commanding general no sinecure. I continued to strengthen the two corps forward and their routes of supply; all the time expecting that Sidney Johnston, who was a real general, and who had as correct information of our situation as I had, would unite his force with Zollicoffer, and fall on Thomas at Dick Robinson, or McCook at Nolin. Had he done so in October, 1861, he could have walked into Louisville, and the vital part of the population would have hailed him as a deliverer. Why he did not, was to me a mystery then and is now; for I know that he saw the move, and had his wagons loaded up at one time for a start toward Frankfort, passing between our two camps. Conscious of our weakness, I was unnecessarily unhappy, and doubtless exhibited it too much to those near me; but it did seem to me that the Government at Washington, intent on the larger preparations of Fremont in Missouri and McClellan in Washington, actually ignored us in Kentucky.

About this time, say the middle of October, I received notice, by telegraph, that the Secretary of War, Mr. [Simon] Cameron (then in St. Louis), would visit me at Louisville, on his way back to Washington. I was delighted to have an opportunity to properly represent the actual state of affairs, and got Mr. Guthrie to go with me across to Jeffersonville, to meet the Secretary of War and escort him to Louisville. The train was behind time, but Mr. Guthrie and I waited till it actually arrived. Mr. Cameron was attended by Adjutant-General Lorenzo Thomas, and six or seven gentlemen who turned out to be newspaper reporters. Mr. Cameron's first inquiry was, when he could start for Cincinnati, saying that, as he had been detained at St. Louis so long, it was important he should hurry on to Washington. I explained the regular mail-boat would leave very soon—viz., at 12 M.—but I begged him to come to Louisville; that I wanted to see him on business as important as any in Washington, and hoped he would come and spend at least a day with us. He asked if everything was not well with us, and I told him far from it; that things were actually bad, as bad as bad could be. This seemed to surprise him, and Mr. Guthrie added his persuasion to mine; when Mr. Cameron, learning that he could leave Louisville by rail *via* Frankfort next morning early, and make the same connections at Cincinnati, consented to go with us to Louisville, with the distinct understanding that he must leave early the next morning for Washington.

We accordingly all took hacks, crossed the river by the ferry, and drove to the Galt House, where I was then staying. Brigadier-General T[homas] J. Wood had come down from Indianapolis by the same train, and was one of the party. We all proceeded to my room on the first floor of the Galt House, where our excellent landlord, Silas Miller, Esq., sent us a good lunch and something to drink. Mr. Cameron was not well, and lay on my bed, but joined in the general conversation. He and his party seemed to be full of the particulars of the developments in St. Louis of some of Fremont's extravagant contracts and expenses, which were the occasion of Cameron's trip to St. Louis, and which finally resulted in Fremont's being relieved, first by General Hunter, and after by General H[enry] W. Halleck.

After some general conversation, Mr. Cameron called to me, "Now General Sherman, tell us of your troubles." I said I preferred not to discuss business with so many strangers present. He said, "They are all friends, all members of my family, and you may speak your mind freely and without restraint." I am sure I stepped to the door, locked it to prevent intrusion, and then fully and fairly represented the state of affairs in Kentucky, especially the situation and numbers of my troops. I complained that the new levies of Ohio and Indiana were diverted East and West, and we got scarcely anything; that our forces at Nolin and Dick Robinson were powerless for invasion, and only tempting to a general such as we believed Sidney Johnston to be; that, if Johnston chose, he could march to Louisville any day. Cameron exclaimed: "You astonish me! Our informants, the Kentucky Senators and members of Congress, claim that they have in Kentucky plenty of men, and all they want are arms and money." I then said it was not true; for the young men were arming and going out openly in broad daylight to the rebel camps, provided with good horses and guns by their fathers, who were at best "neutral;" and as to arms, he had, in Washington, promised General Anderson forty thousand of the best Springfield muskets, instead of which we had received only about twelve thousand Belgian muskets, which the Governor of Pennsylvania had refused, as had also the Governor of Ohio, but which had been adjudged good enough for Kentucky. I asserted that volunteer colonels raising regiments in various parts of the State had come to Louisville for arms, and when they saw what I had to offer had scorned to receive them—to confirm the truth of which I appealed to Mr. Guthrie, who said that every word I had spoken was true, and he repeated what I had often heard him say, that no man who owned a slave or a mule in Kentucky could be trusted.

Mr. Cameron appeared alarmed at what was said, and turned to Adjutant-General L. Thomas, to inquire if he knew of any troops available, that had not been already assigned. He mentioned [James S.] Negley's Pennsylvania Brigade, at Pittsburg, and a couple of other regiments that were then *en route* for St. Louis. Mr. Cameron ordered him to divert these to Louisville, and Thomas made the telegraphic orders on the spot. He further promised, on reaching Washington, to give us more of his time and assistance.

In the general conversation which followed, I remember taking a large map of the United States, and assuming the people of the whole South to be in rebellion, that our task was to subdue them, showed that McClellan was on the left, having a frontage of less than a hundred miles, and Fremont the right, about the same; whereas I, the centre, had from the Big Sandy to Paducah, over three hundred miles of frontier; that McClellan had a hundred thousand men, Fremont sixty thousand, whereas to me had only been allotted about eighteen thousand. I argued that, for the purpose of defense, we should have sixty thousand men at once, and for offense, would need two hundred thousand, before we were done. Mr. Cameron, who still lay on the bed, threw up hands and exclaimed, "Great God! where are they to come from?" I asserted that there were plenty of men at the North, ready and willing to come, if he would only accept their services; for it was notorious that regiments had been formed in all the Northwestern States, whose services had been refused by the War Department, on the ground that they would not be needed. We discussed all these matters fully, in the most friendly spirt, and I thought I had aroused Mr. Cameron to a realization of the great war that was before us, and was in fact upon us. I heard him tell General Thomas to make a note of our conversation, that he might attend to my requests on reaching Washington. We all spent the evening together agreeably in conversation, many Union citizens calling to pay their respects, and the next morning early we took the train for Frankfort; Mr. Cameron and party going on to Cincinnati and Washington, and I to Camp Dick Robinson to see General Thomas and the troops there.

I found General Thomas in a tavern, with most of his regiments camped about him. He had sent a small force some miles in advance toward Cumberland Gap, under Brigadier-General [Albin F.] Schoepf. Remaining there a couple of days, I returned to Louisville; on the 22d of October, General Negley's brigade arrived in boats from Pittsburg, was sent out to Camp Nolin; and the Thirty-seventh Indiana, Colonel Hazzard, and Second Minnesota, Colonel Van Cleve, also reached Louisville by rail, and were posted at Elizabethtown and Lebanon Junction. These were the same troops which had been ordered by Mr. Cameron when at Louisville, and they were all that I received thereafter, prior to my leaving Kentucky. On reaching Washington, Mr. Cameron called on General Thomas, as he himself afterward told me, to submit his memorandum of events during his absence, and in that memorandum was mentioned my *insane* request for two hundred thousand men. By some newspaper man this was seen and published, and, before I had the least conception of it, I was universally published throughout the country as "insane, crazy," etc. Without any knowledge, however, of this fact, I had previously addressed to the Adjutant-General of the army at Washington this letter:

HEADQUARTERS DEPARTMENT OF THE CUMBERLAND, }
    LOUISVILLE, KENTUCKY, *October* 22, 1861. }

To General L. THOMAS, *Adjutant-General, Washington, D. C.*

SIR: On my arrival at Camp Dick Robinson, I found General Thomas had stationed a Kentucky regiment at Rock Castle Hill, beyond a river of the same name, and had sent an Ohio and an Indiana regiment forward in support. He was embarrassed for transportation, and I authorized him to hire teams, and to move his whole force nearer to his advance-guard, so as to support it, as he had information of the approach of Zollicoffer toward London. I have just heard from him, that he had sent forward General Schoepf with Colonel Wolford's cavalry, Colonel Steadman's Ohio regiment, and a battery of artillery, followed on a succeeding day by a Tennessee brigade. He had still two Kentucky regiments, the Thirty-eighth Ohio and another battery of artillery, with which he was to follow yesterday. This force, if concentrated should be strong enough for the purpose; at all events, it is all he had or I could give him.

I explained to you fully, when here, the supposed position of our adversaries, among which was a force in the valley of Big Sandy, supposed to be advancing on Paris, Kentucky. General [William] Nelson at Maysville was instructed to collect all the men he could, and Colonel Gill's regiment of Ohio Volunteers. Colonel [L. A.] Harris was already in position at Olympian Springs, and a regiment lay at Lexington, which I ordered to his support. This leaves the line of Thomas's operations exposed, but I cannot help it. I explained so fully to yourself and the Secretary of War the condition of things, that I can add nothing new until further developements. You know my views that this great centre of our field is too weak, far too weak, and I have begged and implored till I dare not say more.

Buckner still is beyond Green River. He sent a detachment of his men, variously estimated at from two to four thousand toward Greenburg. General [William T.] Ward, with about one thousand men, retreated to Campbellsburg, where he called to his assitance some partially-formed regiments to the number of about two thousand. The enemy did not advance, and General Ward was at last dates at Campbellsburg. The officers charged with raising regiments must of necessity be near their homes to collect men, and for this reason are out of position; but at or near Greensburg and Lebanon, I desire to assemble as large a force of the Kentucky Volunteers as possible. This organization is necessarily irregular, but the necessity is so great that I must have them, and therefore have issued to them arms and clothing during the process of formation. This has facilitated their enlistment; but inasmuch as the Legislature has provided money for organizing the Kentucky Volunteers, and intrusted its disbursement to a board of loyal gentlemen, I have endeavored to coöperate with them to hasten the formation of these corps.

The great difficulty is, and has been, that as volunteers offer, we have not arms and clothing to give them. The arms sent us are, as you already know, European muskets of uncouth pattern, which the volunteers will not touch.

General McCook has now three brigades—[Robert] Johnson's, Wood's, and Rousseau's. Negley's brigade arrived today, and will be sent out at once. The Minnesota regiment has also arrived, and will be sent forward. Hazzard's regiment of Indiana troops I have ordered to the mouth of Salt Creek, an important point on the turnpike-road leading to Elizabethtown.

I again repeat that our force here is out of all proportion to the importance of the position. Our defeat would be disastrous to the nation; and to expect of new men, who never bore arms, to do miracles, is not right.

I am, with much respect, yours truly,

W. T. SHERMAN, *Brigadier-General commanding.*

About this time my attention was drawn to the publication in all the Eastern papers, which of course was copied at the West of the report that I was "crazy, insane, and mad," that "I had demanded two hundred thousand men for the defense of Kentucky;" and the authority given for this report was stated to be the Secretary of War himself, Mr. Cameron, who never, to my knowledge, tooks pains to affirm or deny it. My position was therefore simply unbearable, and it is probable I resented the cruel insult with language of intense feeling. Still I received no orders, no reënforcements, not a word of encouragement or relief. About November 1st General McClellan was appointed commander-in-chief of all the armies in the field, and by telegraph called for a report from me. It is herewith given:

HEADQUARTERS DEPARTMENT OF THE CUMBERLAND, }
    LOUISVILLE, KENTUCKY, *November* 4, 1861. }

General L. THOMAS, *Adjutant-General, Washington, D. C.*

SIR: In compliance with the telegraphic orders of General McClellan, received late last night, I submit this report of the forces in Kentucky, and of their condition.

The tabular statement shows the position of the several regiments. The camp at Nolin is at the present extremity of the Nashville Railroad. This force was thrown forward to meet the advance of Buckner's army, which then fell back to Green River, twenty-three miles beyond. These regiments were substantially without means of transportation, other than the railroad, which is guarded at all dangerous points, yet is liable to interruption at any moment, by the tearing up of a rail by the disaffected inhabitants or a hired enemy. These regiments are composed of good materials, but devoid of company officers of experience, and have been put under thorough drill since being in camp. They are generally well clad, and provided for. Beyond Green River, the enemy has masked his forces, and it is very difficult to ascertain even the approximate numbers. No pains have been spared to ascertain them, but without success, and it is well known that they far outnumber us. Depending, however, on the railroads to their rear for transportation, they have not thus far advanced this side of Green River, except in marauding parties. This is the proper line of advance, but will require a very large force, certainly fifty thousand men, as their railroad facilites south enable them to concentrate at Munfordsville the entire strength of the South. General McCook's command is divided into four brigades, under Generals Wood, R. W. Johnson, Rousseau, and Negley.

General Thomas's line of operations is from Lexington, toward Cumberland Gap and Ford, which are occupied by a force of rebel Tennesseeans, under the command of Zollicoffer. Thomas occupies the position at London, in front of two roads which lead to the fertile part of Kentucky, the one by Richmond, and the other by Crab Orchard, with his reserve at Camp Dick Robinson, eight miles south of the Kentucky River. His provisions and stores go by railroad from Cincinnati to Nicholasville, and thence in wagons to his several regiments. He is forced to hire transportation.

Brigadier-General Nelson is operating by the line from Olympian Springs, east of Paris, on the Covington & Lexington Railroad, toward Prestonburg, in the valley of the Big Sandy where is assembled a force of from twenty-five to thirty-five hundred rebel Kentuckians waiting reënforcements from Virginia. My last report from him was on October 28th, at which time he had Colonel Harris's Ohio Second, nine hundred strong; Colonel Norton's Twenty-first Ohio, one thousand; and Colonel [Joshua W.] Sill's Thirty-third Ohio, seven hundred and fifty strong; with two irregular Kentucky regiments, Colonels Marshall and Metcalf. These troops were on the road near Hazel Green and West Liberty, advancing toward Prestonburg.

Upon an inspection of the map, you will observe these are all divergent lines, but rendered necessary, from the fact that our enemies choose them as places of refuge from pursuit, where they can receive assistance from neighboring States. Our lines are all too weak, probably with the exception of that to Prestonburg. To strengthen these, I am thrown on the raw levies of Ohio and Indiana, who arrive in detachments, perfectly fresh from the country, and loaded down with baggage, also upon the Kentuckians, who are slowly forming regiments all over the State, at points remote from danger, and whom it will be almost impossible to assemble together. The organization of this latter force is, by the laws of Kentucky, under the control of a military board of citizens, at the capital, Frankfort, and they think they will be enabled to have fifteen regiments toward the middle of this month, but I doubt it, and deem it unsafe to rely on them. There are four regiments forming in the neighborhood of Owensboro', near the mouth of Green River, who are doing good service, also in the neighborhood of Campbellsville, but it is unsafe to rely on troops so suddenly armed and equipped. They are not yet clothed or uniformed. I know well you will think our force too widely distributed, but we are forced to it by the attitude of our enemies, whose force and numbers the country never has and probably never will comprehend.

I am told that my estimate of troops needed for this line, viz., two hundred thousand, has been construed to my prejudice, and therefore leave it for the future. This is the great centre on which our enemies can concentrate whatever force is not employed elsewhere.

With great respect, your obedient servant,

W. T. SHERMAN, *Brigadier-General commanding.*

And, in order to conclude this subject, I also add copies of two telegraphic dispatches, sent for General McClellan's use about the same time, which are all the official letters received at his headquarters, as certified by the Adjutant-General, L. Thomas, in a letter of February 1, 1862, in answer to an application of my brother, Senator John Sherman, and on which I was adjudged insane:

LOUISVILLE, *November* 3, 10 P. M.

To General McCLELLAN, *Washington, D. C.:*

Dispatch just received. We are forced to operate on three lines, all dependent on railroads of doubtful safety, requiring strong guards. From Paris to Prestonburg, three Ohio regiments and some militia—enemy variously reported from thirty-five hundred to seven thousand. From Lexington toward Cumberland Gap, Brigadier-General Thomas, one Indiana and five Ohio regiments, two Kentucky and two Tennessee; hired wagons and badly clad. Zollicoffer, at Cumberland Ford, about seven thousand. Lee reported on the way with Virginia reënforcements. In front of Louisville, fifty-two miles, Mc-Cook, with four brigades of about thirteen thousand, with four regiments to guard the railroad, at all times in danger. Enemy along the railroad from Green River to Bowling Green, Nashville, and Clarksville. Buckner, [William J.] Hardee, Sidney Johnston, Polk, and Pillow, the two former in immediate command, the force as large as they want or can subsist, from twenty-five to thirty thousand. Bowling Green strongly fortified. Our forces too small to do good, and too large to sacrifice.

W. T. SHERMAN, *Brigadier-General.*

HEADQUARTERS DEPARTMENT OF THE CUMBERLAND, ⎱
LOUISVILLE, KENTUCKY, *November* 6, 1861. ⎰

General L. THOMAS, *Adjutant-General.*

SIR: General McClellan telegraphs me to report to him daily the situation of affairs here. The country is so large that it is impossible to give clear and definite views. Our enemies have a terrible advantage in the fact that in our midst, in our camps, and along our avenues of travel, they have active partisans, farmers and business-men, who seemingly pursue their usual calling, but are in fact spies. They report all our movements and strength, while we can procure information only by circuitous and unreliable means. I inclose you the copy of an intercepted letter, which is but the type of others. Many men from every part of the State are now enrolled under Buckner—have gone to him—while ours have to be raised in neighborhoods, and cannot be called together except at long notice. These volunteers are being organized under the laws of the State, and the 10th of November is fixed for the time of consolidating them into companies and regiments. Many of them are armed by the United States as home guards, and many by General Anderson and myself, because of the necessity of being armed to guard their camps against internal enemies. Should we be overwhelmed, they would scatter, and their arms and clothing will go to the enemy, furnishing the very material they so much need. We should have here a very large force, sufficient to give confidence to the Union men of the ability to do what should be done—possess ourselves of all the State. But all see and feel we are brought to a stand-still, and this produces doubt and alarm. With our present force it would be simple madness to cross Green River, and yet hesitation may be as fatal. In like manner the other columns are in peril, not so much in front as rear, the railroads over which our stores must pass being much exposed. I have the Nashville Railroad guarded by three regiments, yet it is far from being safe; and, the moment actual hostilities commence, these roads will be interrupted, and we will be in a dilemma. To meet this in part I have put a cargo of provisions at the mouth of Salt River, guarded by two regiments. All these detachments weaken the main force, and endanger the whole. Do not conclude, as before, that I exaggerate the facts. They are as stated, and the future looks as dark as possible. It would be better if some man of sanguine mind were here, for I am forced to order according to my convictions. Yours truly,

W. T. SHERMAN, *Brigadier-General commanding.*

After the war was over, General Thomas J. Wood, then in command of the district of Vicksburg, prepared a statement addressed to the public, describing the interview with the Secretary of War, which he calls a "Council of War." I did not then deem it necessary to renew a matter which had been swept into oblivion by the war itself; but, as it is evidence by an eyewitness, it is worthy of insertion here.

STATEMENT.

On the 11th of October, 1861 the writer, who had been personally on mustering duty in Indiana, was appointed a brigardier-general of volunteers, and ordered to report to General Sherman, then in command of the Department of the Cumberland, with his headquarters at Louisville, having succeeded General Robert Anderson. When the writer was about leaving Indianapolis to proceed to Louisville, Mr. Cameron, returning from his famous visit of inspection to General Fremont's department, at St. Louis, Missouri, arrived at Indianapolis, and announced his intention to visit General Sherman.

The writer was invited to accompany the party to Louisville. Taking the early morning train from Indianapolis to Louisville on the 16th of October, 1861, the party arrived in Jeffersonville shortly after mid-day. General Sherman met the party in Jeffersonville, and accompanied it to the Galt House, in Louisville, the hotel at which he was stopping.

During the afternoon General Sherman informed the writer that a council of war was to be held immediately in his private room in the hotel, and desired him to be present at the council. General Sherman and the writer proceeded directly to the room. The writer entered the room first, and observed in it Mr. Cameron, Adjutant-General L. Thomas, and some other persons, all of whose names he did not know, but whom he recognized as being of Mr. Cameron's party. The name of one of the party the writer had learned, which he remembers as Wilkinson, or Wilkerson, and who he understood was a writer for the *New York Tribune* newspaper. The Hon. James Guthrie was also in the room, having been invited, on account of his eminent position as a citizen of Kentucky, his high civic reputation, and his well-known devotion to the Union, to meet the Secretary of War in the council. When General Sherman entered the room he closed the door, and turned the key in the lock.

Before entering on the business of the meeting, General

Sherman remarked substantially: "Mr. Cameron, we have met here to discuss matters and interchange views which should be known only by persons high in the confidence of the Government. There are persons present whom I do not know, and I desire to know, before opening the business of the council, whether they are persons who may be properly allowed to hear the views which I have to submit to you." Mr. Cameron replied, with some little testiness of manner, that the persons referred to belonged to his party, and there was no objection to their knowing whatever might be communicated to him.

Certainly the legitimate and natural conclusion from this remark of Mr. Cameron's was that whatever views might be submitted by General Sherman would be considered under the protection of the seal of secrecy, and would not be divulged to the public till all apprehension of injurious consequences from such disclosure had passed. And it may be remarked, further, that justice to General Sherman required that if, at any future time, his conclusions as to the amount of force necessary to conduct the operations committed to his charge should be made public, the grounds on which his conclusions were based should be made public at the same time.

Mr. Cameron then asked General Sherman what his plans were. To this General Sherman replied that he had no plans; that no sufficient force had been placed at his disposition with which to devise any plan of operations; that, before a commanding general could project a plan of campaign, he must know what amount of force he would have to operate with.

The general added that he had views which he would be happy to submit for the consideration of the Secretary. Mr. Cameron desired to hear General Sherman's views.

General Sherman began by giving his opinion of the people of Kentucky, and the then condition of the State. He remarked that he believed a very large majority of the people of Kentucky were thoroughly devoted to the Union, and loyal to the Government, and that the Unionists embraced almost all the older and more substantial men in the State; but, unfortunately, there was no organization nor arms among the Union men; that the rebel minority, armed (this having been done in advance by their leaders), and, beyond the reach of the Federal forces, overawed and prevented the Union men from organizing; that, in his opinion, if Federal protection were extended throughout the State to the Union men, a large force could be raised for the service of the Government.

General Sherman next presented a *résumé* of the information in his possession as to the number of the rebel troops in Kentucky. Commencing with the force at Columbus, Kentucky, the reports varied, giving the strength from ten to twenty thousand. It was commanded by Lieutenant-General Polk. General Sherman fixed it at the lowest estimate; say, ten thousand. The force at Bowling Green, commanded by General A. S. Johnston, supported by Hardee, Buckner, and others, was variously estimated at from eighteen to thirty thousand. General Sherman estimated this force at the lowest figures given to it by his information— eighteen thousand.

He explained that, for purposes of defense, these two forces ought, owing to the facility with which troops might be transported from one to the other, by the net-work of railroads in Middle and West Tennessee, to be considered almost as one. General Sherman remarked, also, on the facility with which reënforcements could be transported by railroad to Bowling Green, from the other rebellious States.

The third organized body of rebel troops was in Eastern Kentucky, under General Zollicoffer, estimated, according to the most reliable information, at six thousand men. This force threatened a descent, if unrestrained, on the bluegrass region of Kentucky, including the cities of Lexington, and Frankfort, the capital of the State; and if successful in its primary movements, as it would gather head as it advanced, might endanger the safety of Cincinnati.

General Sherman said that the information in his possession indicated an intention, on the part of the rebels, of a general and grand advance toward the Ohio River. He further expressed the opinion that, if such advance should be made, and not checked, the rebel force would be swollen by at least twenty thousand recruits from the disloyalists in Kentucky. His low computation of the organized rebel soldiers then in Kentucky fixed the strength at about thirty-five thousand. Add twenty thousand for reënforcements gained in Kentucky, to say nothing of troops drawn from other rebel States, and the effective rebel force in the State, at a low estimate, would be fifty-five thousand men.

General Sherman explained forcibly how largely the difficulties of suppressing the rebellion would be enhanced, if the rebels should be allowed to plant themselves firmly, with strong fortifications, at commanding points on the Ohio River. It would be facile for them to carry the war thence into the loyal States north of the river.

To resist an advance of the rebels, General Sherman stated that he did not have at that time in Kentucky more than some twelve to fourteen thousand effective men. The bulk of this force was posted at camp Nolin, on the Louisville & Nashville Railway, fifty miles south of Louisville. A part of it was in Eastern Kentucky, under General George H. Thomas, and a very small force was in the lower valley of Green River.

This disposition of the force had been made for the double purpose of watching and checking the rebels, and protecting the raising and organization of troops among the Union men of Kentucky.

Having explained the situation from the defensive point of view, General Sherman proceeded to consider it from the offensive stand-point. The Government had undertaken to suppress the rebellion; the *onus faciendi*, therefore, rested on the Government. The rebellion could never be put down, the authority of the paramount Government asserted, and the union of the States declared perpetual, by force of arms, by maintaining the defensive; to accomplish these grand desiderata, it was absolutely necessary the Government should adopt, and maintain until the rebellion was crushed, the *offensive*.

For the purpose of expelling the rebels from Kentucky, General Sherman said that at least sixty thousand soldiers were necessary. Considering that the means of accomplishment must always be proportioned to the end to be achieved, and bearing in mind the array of rebel force then in Kentucky, every sensible man must admit that the estimate of the force given by General Sherman, for driving the rebels out of the State, and reëstablishing and maintaining the authority of the Government, was a very low one. The truth is that, before the rebels were driven from Kentucky, many more than sixty thousand soldiers were sent into the State.

Ascending from the consideration of the narrow question of the political and military situation in Kentucky, and the extent of force necessary to redeem the State from rebel thraldom, forecasting in his sagacious intellect the grand and daring operations which, three years afterward, he realized in a campaign, taken in its entirety, without a parallel in modern times, General Sherman expressed the opinion that, to carry the war to the Gulf of Mexico, and destroy all armed opposition to the Government, in the entire Mississippi Valley, at least two hundred thousand troops were absolutely requisite.

So soon as General Sherman had concluded the expression of his views, Mr. Cameron asked, with much warmth and apparent irritation, "Where do you suppose, General Sherman, all this force is to come from?" General Sherman replied that he did not know; that it was not his duty to raise, organize, and put the necessary military force into the field; that duty pertained to the War Department. His duty was to organize compaigns and command the troops after they had been put into the field.

At this point of the proceedings, General Sherman suggested that it might be agreeable to the Secretary to hear the views of Mr. Guthrie. Thus appealed to, Mr. Guthrie said he did not consider himself, being a civilian, competent to give an opinion as to the extent of force necessary to carry the war to the Gulf of Mexico; but, being well informed of the condition of things in Kentucky, he indorsed fully General Sherman's opinion of the force required to drive the rebels out of the State.

The foregoing is a circumstantial account of the deliberations of the council that were of any importance.

A good deal of desultory conversation followed, on immaterial matters; and some orders were issued by telegraph, by the Secretary of War, for some small reënforcements to be sent to Kentucky immediately, from Pennsylvania and Indiana.

A short time after the council was held—the exact time is not now remembered by the writer—an imperfect narrative of it appeared in the *New York Tribune*. This account announced to the public the conclusions uttered by

General Sherman in the council, without giving the reasons
on which his conclusions were based. The unfairness of
this course to General Sherman needs no comment. All
military men were shocked by the gross breach of faith
which had been committed.

TH. J. WOOD, *Major-General Volunteers.*
VICKSBURG, MISSISSIPPI, *August* 24, 1866.

Brigadier-General Don Carlos Buell arrived at Louisville
about the middle of November, with orders to relieve me, and
I was transferred for duty to the Department of the Missouri,
and ordered to report in person to Major-General H. W. Halleck at St. Louis. I accompanied General Buell to the camp
at Nolin, where he reviewed and inspected the camp and
troops under the command of General A. McD. McCook,
and on our way back General Buell inspected the regiment of
Hazzard at Elizabethtown. I then turned over my command
to him, and took my departure for St. Louis.

At the time I was so relieved I thought, of course, it was
done in fulfillment of Mr. Lincoln's promise to me, and as a
necessary result of my repeated demand for the fulfillment of
that promise; but I saw and felt, and was of course deeply
moved to observe, the manifest belief that there was more or
less of truth in the rumor that the cares, perplexities, and
anxiety of the situation had unbalanced my judgment and
mind. Still, on a review of the only official documents before
the War Department at the time, it was cruel for a Secretary
of War to give a tacit credence to a rumor which probably
started without his wish or intention, yet through his instru-
mentality. Of course I could not deny the fact, and had to
submit to all its painful consequences for months; and, moreover, I could not hide from myself that many of the officers
and soldiers subsequently placed under my command looked
at me askance and with suspicion. Indeed, it was not until
the following April that the battle of Shiloh gave me personally the chance to redeem my good name.

On reaching St. Louis and reporting to General Halleck, I
was received kindly, and was shortly afterward (viz., November 23d) sent up to Sedalia to inspect the camp there, and the
troops located along the road back to Jefferson City, and I
was ordered to assume command in a certain contingency. I
found General Steele at Sedalia with his regiments scattered

about loosely; and General Pope at Otterville, twenty miles back, with no concert between them. The rebel general, Sterling Price, had his forces down about Osceola and Warsaw. I advised General Halleck to collect the whole of his men into one camp on the La Mine River, near Georgetown, to put them into brigades and divisions, so as to be ready to be handled, and I gave some preliminary orders looking to that end. But the newspapers kept harping on my insanity and paralyzed my efforts. In spite of myself, they tortured from me some words and acts of imprudence. General Halleck telegraphed me on November 26th: "Unless telegraph-lines are interrupted, make no movement of troops without orders"; and on November 29th: "No forward movement of troops on Osceola will be made; only strong reconnoitring-parties will be sent out in the supposed direction of the enemy; the bulk of the troops being held in position till more reliable information is obtained."

About the same time I received the following dispatch:

HEADQUARTERS, ST. LOUIS, MISSOURI, }
November 28, 1861. }

Brigadier-General SHERMAN, *Sedalia:*

Mrs. Sherman is here. General Halleck is satisfied, from reports of scouts received here, that no attack on Sedalia is intended. You will therefore return to this city, and report your observations on the condition of the troops you have examined. Please telegraph when you will leave.

SCHUYLER HAMILTON, *Brigadier-General and Aide-de-Camp.*

I accordingly returned to St. Louis, where I found Mrs. Sherman, naturally and properly distressed at the continued and reiterated reports of the newspapers of my insanity, and she had come from Lancaster to see me. This recall from Sedalia simply swelled the cry. It was alleged that I was recalled by reason of something foolish I had done at Sedalia, though in fact I had done absolutely nothing, except to recommend what was done immediately thereafter on the advice of Colonel [John B.] McPherson, on a subsequent inspection. Seeing and realizing that my efforts were useless, I concluded to ask for a twenty days' leave of absence, to accompany Mrs. Sherman to our home in Lancaster, and to allow the storm to blow over somewhat. It also happened to be mid-winter, when nothing was doing; so Mrs. Sherman and I returned to Lancaster, where I was born, and where I supposed I was better known and appreciated.

The newspapers kept up their game as though instigated by malice, and chief among them was the *Cincinnati Commercial,* whose editor, [Murat] Halsted, was generally believed to be an honorable man. P. B. Ewing, Esq., being in Cincinnati, saw him and asked him why he, who certainly knew better, would reiterate such a damaging slander. He answered, quite cavalierly, that it was one of the news-items of the day, and he had to keep up with the time; but he would be most happy to publish any correction I might make, as though I could deny such a malicious piece of scandal affecting myself. On the 12th of November I had occasion to write to General Halleck, and I have a copy of his letter in answer:

St. Louis, *December* 18, 1961.

Brigadier-General W. T. Sherman, *Lancaster, Ohio.*

My dear General: Yours of the 12th was received a day or two ago, but was mislaid for the moment among private papers, or I should have answered it sooner. The newspaper attacks are certainly shameless and scandalous, but I cannot agree with you, that they have us in their power "to destroy us as they please."I certainly get my share of abuse, but it will not disturb me.

Your movement of the troops was not countermanded by me because I thought it an unwise one in itself, but because I was not then ready for it. I had better information of Price's movements than you had, and I had no apprehension of an attack. I intended to concentrate the forces on that line, but I wished the movement delayed until I could determine on a better position.

After receiving Lieutenant-Colonel McPherson's report, I made precisely the location you had ordered. I was desirous at the time not to prevent the advance of Price by any movement on our part, hoping that he would move on Lexington; but finding that he had determined to remain at Osceola for some time at least, I made the movement you proposed. As you could not know my plans, you and others may have misconstrued the reason of my countermanding your orders. . . .

I hope to see you well enough for duty soon. Our organization goes on slowly, but we will effect it in time.

Yours truly,

H. W. HALLECK.

And subsequently, in a letter to Hon. Thomas Ewing, in answer to some inquiries involving the same general subject, General Halleck wrote as follows:

St. Louis, *February* 15, 1862.

Hon. THOMAS EWING, *Lancaster, Ohio.*

DEAR SIR: Your note of the 13th, and one of this date, from Mr. Sherman, in relation to Brigadier-General Sherman's having being relieved from command in Sedalia, in November last, are just received. General Sherman was not put in command at Sedalia; he was authorized to assume it, and did so for a day or two. He did not know my plans, and his movement of troops did not accord with them. I therefore directed him to leave them as they were, and report here the result of his *inspection,* for which purpose he had been ordered there.

No telegram or dispatch of any kind was sent by me, or by any one with my knowledge or authority, in relation to it. After his return here, I gave him a leave of absence of twenty days, for the benefit of his health. As I was then pressing General McClellan for more officers, I deemed it necessary to explain why I did so. I used these words: "I am satisfied that General Sherman's physical and mental system is so completely broken by labor and care as to render him, for the present, unfit for duty; perhaps a few weeks' rest may restore him." This was the only communication I made on the subject. On no occasion have I ever expressed an opinion that his mind was affected otherwise than by over-exertion; to have said so would have done him the greatest injustice.

After General Sherman returned from his short leave, I found that his health was nearly restored, and I placed him temporarily in command of the camp of instruction, numbering over fifteen thousand men. I then wrote to General McClellan that he would soon be able to again take the field. I gave General Sherman a copy of my letter. This is the total of my correspondence on the subject. As evidence that

I have every confidence in General Sherman, I have placed him in command of Western Kentucky—a command only second in importance in this department. As soon as divisions and columns can be organized, I propose to send him into the field where he can render most efficient service. I have seen newspaper squibs charging him with being "crazy," etc. This is the grossest injustice; I do not, however, consider such attacks worthy of notice. The best answer is General Sherman's present position, and the valuable services he is rendering to the country. I have the fullest confidence in him.

Very respectfully, your obedient servant,
H. W. HALLECK, *Major-General.*

On returning to St. Louis, on the expiration of my leave of absence, I found that General Halleck was beginning to move his troops: one part, under General U. S. Grant, up the Tennessee River; and another part, under General S[amuel] R. Curtis, in the direction of Springfield, Missouri. General Grant was then at Paducah, and General Curtis was under orders for Rolla. I was ordered to take Curtis's place in command of the camp of instruction, at Benton Barracks, on the ground back of North St. Louis, now used as the Fair Grounds, by the following order:

[Special Order No. 87].
HEADQUARTERS DEPARTMENT OF THE MISSOURI,
ST. LOUIS, *December* 23, 1861.

[EXTRACT.]

Brigadier-General W. T. Sherman, United States Volunteers, is hereby assigned to the command of the camp of instruction and post of Benton Barracks. He will have every armed regiment and company in his command ready for service at a moment's warning, and will notify all concerned that, when marching orders are received, it is expected that they will be instantly obeyed; no excuses for delay will be admitted. General Sherman will immediately report to these headquarters what regiments and companies, at Benton Barracks, are ready for the field.

By order of Major-General Halleck,
J. C. KELTEN, *Assistant Adjutant-General.*

I immediately assumed command, and found, in the building constructed for the commanding officer, Brigadier-General Strong, and the family of a captain of Iowa cavalry, with whom we boarded. Major Curtis, son of General Curtis, was the adjutant-general, but was soon relieved by Captain J. H. Hammond, who was appointed assistant adjutant-general, and assigned to duty with me.

Brigadier-General [Stephen A.] Hurlbut was also there, and about a dozen regiments of infantry and cavalry. I at once gave all matters pertaining to the post my personal attention, got the regiments in as good order as possible, kept up communication with General Halleck's headquarters by telegraph, and, when orders came for the movement of any regiment or detachment, it moved instantly. The winter was very wet, and the ground badly drained. The quarters had been erected by General Fremont, under contract; they were mere shells, but well arranged for a camp, embracing the Fair Grounds, and some forty acres of flat ground west of it. I instituted drills, and was specially ordered by General Halleck to watch Generals Hurlbut and [William K.] Strong, and report as to their fitness for their commissions as brigadier-generals. I had known Hurlbut as a young lawyer, in Charleston, South Carolina, before the Mexican War, at which time he took a special interest in military matters, and I found him far above the average in the knowledge of regimental and brigade drill, and so reported. General Strong had been a merchant, and he told me that he never professed to be a soldier, but had been urged on the Secretary of War for the commission of a brigadier-general, with the expectation of becoming quartermaster or commissary-general. He was a good, kind-hearted gentleman, boiling over with patriotism and zeal. I advised him what to read and study, was considerably amused at his receiving instruction from a young lieutenant who knew the company and battalion drill, and could hear him practise in his room the words of command, and tone of voice, "Break from the right, to march to the left!" "Battalion, halt!" "Forward into line!" etc. Of course I made a favorable report in his case. Among the infantry and cavalry colonels were some who afterward rose to distinction—David Stuart, Gordon Granger, [Cyrus] Bussey, etc., etc.

Though it was mid-winter, General Halleck was pushing his preparations most vigorously, and surely he brought order out of chaos in St. Louis with commendable energy. I remember, one night, sitting in his room, on the second floor of the Planters' House, with him and General Cullum, his chief of staff, talking of things generally, and the subject then was of the much-talked-of "advance," as soon as the season would permit. Most people urged the movement down the Mississippi River; but Generals Polk and Pillow had a large rebel force, with heavy guns in a very strong position, at Columbus, Kentucky, about eighteen miles below Cairo. Commodore [Andrew] Foote had his gunboat fleet at Cairo; and General U. S. Grant, who commanded the district, was collecting a large force at Paducah, Cairo, and Bird's Point. General Halleck had a map on his table, with a large pencil in his hand, and asked, "Where is the rebel line?" Cullum drew the pencil through Bowling Green, Forts Donelson and Henry, and Columbus, Kentucky. "That is their line," said Halleck. "Now, where is the proper place to break it?" And either Cullum or I said, *Naturally* the centre." Halleck drew a line perpendicular to the other, near its middle, and it coincided nearly with the general course of the Tennessee River; and he said, "That's the true line of operations." This occurred more than a month before General Grant began the movement, and, as he was subject to General Halleck's orders, I have always given Halleck the full credit for that movement, which was skillful, successful, and extremely rich in military results; indeed, it was the first real success on our side in the civil war. The movement up the Tennessee began about the 1st of February, and Fort Henry was captured by the joint action of the navy under Commodore Foote, and the land-forces under General Grant, on the 6th of February, 1862. About the same time, General S. R. Curtis had moved forward from Rolla, and, on the 8th of March, defeated the rebels under [Ben] McCulloch, [Earl] Van Dorn, and Price, at Pea Ridge.

As soon as Fort Henry fell, General Grant marched straight across to Fort Donelson, on the Cumberland River, invested the place, and, as soon as the gunboats had come round from the Tennessee, and had bombarded the water-front, he assaulted; whereupon Buckner surrendered the garrison of twelve thousand men; Pillow and ex-Secretary of War General Floyd having personally escaped across the river at night, occasioning a good deal of fun and criticism at their expense.

Before the fall of Donelson, but after that of Henry, I received, at Benton Barracks, the following orders:

HEADQUARTERS DEPARTMENT OF THE MISSOURI,
ST. LOUIS, *February* 13, 1862.

Brigadier-General SHERMAN, *Benton Barracks:*

You will immediately repair to Paducah, Kentucky, and assume command of that post. Brigadier-General Hurlbut will accompany you. The command of Benton Barracks will be turned over to General Strong.

H. W. HALLECK, *Major-General.*

I started for Paducah the same day, and think that General Cullum went with me to Cairo; General Halleck's purpose being to push forward the operations up the Tennessee River with unusual vigor. On reaching Paducah, I found this dispatch:

HEADQUARTERS DEPARTMENT OF THE MISSOURI,
ST. LOUIS, *February* 15, 1862.

Brigadier-General SHERMAN, *Paducah, Kentucky:*

Send General Grant every thing you can spare from Paducah and Smith land; also General Hurlbut.

Bowling Green has been evacuated entirely.

H. W. HALLECK, *Major-General.*

The next day brought us news of the surrender of Buckner, and probably at no time during the war did we all feel so heavy a weight raised from our breasts, or so thankful for a most fruitful series of victories. They at once gave Generals Halleck, Grant, and C. F. Smith, great fame. Of course, the rebels let go their whole line, and fell back on Nashville and Island No. Ten, and to the Memphis & Charleston Railroad. Everybody was anxious to help. Boats passed up and down constantly, and very soon arrived the rebel prisoners from Donelson. I saw General Buckner on the boat, he seemed self-sufficient, and thought their loss was not really so serious to their cause as we did.

From the time I had left Kentucky, General Buell had really made no substantial progress, though strongly reënforced beyond even what I had asked for. General Albert Sidney Johnston had remaind at Bowling Green until his line was broken at Henry and Donelson, when he let go Bowling Green and fell back hastily to Nashville; and, on Buell's approach, he did not even tarry there, but continued his retreat southward.

Chapter 3

Shiloh:
"Our Men Were in Good Spirits"
March—April, 1862

IN THE MIDDLE of February, 1862, Major-General Halleck commanded all the armies in the valley of the Mississippi, from his headquarters in St. Louis. These were, the Army of the Ohio, Major-General Buell, in Kentucky; the Army of the Tennessee, Major-General Grant, at Forts Henry and Donelson; and General S. R. Curtis, in Southern Missouri. He posted his chief of staff, General Cullum, at Cairo, and me at Paducah, chiefly to expedite and facilitate the important operations then in progress up the Tennessee and Cumberland Rivers.

Fort Donelson surrendered to General Grant on the 16th of February, and there must have been a good deal of confusion resulting from the necessary care of the wounded, and disposition of prisoners, common to all such occasions, and there was a real difficulty in communicating between St. Louis and Fort Donelson.

General Buell had also followed up the rebel army, which had retreated hastily from Bowling Green to and through Nashville, a city of so much importance to the South, that it was at one time proposed as its capital. Both Generals Grant and Buell looked to its capture as an event of great importance. On the 21st General Grant sent General Smith with his division to Clarksville, fifty miles above Donelson, toward Nashville, and on the 27th went himself to Nashville to meet and confer with General Buell, but returned to Donelson the next day.

Meantime, General Halleck at St. Louis must have felt that his armies were getting away from him, and began to send dispatches to me at Paducah, to be forwarded by boat, or by a rickety telegraph-line up to Fort Henry, which lay entirely in a hostile country, and was consequently always out of repair. On the 1st of March I received the following dispatch, and forwarded it to General Grant, both by telegraph and boat:

St. Louis, *March* 1, 1862.

To General GRANT, *Fort Henry:*

Transports will be sent you as soon as possible, to move your column up the Tennessee River. The main object of this expedition will be to destroy the railroad-bridge over Bear Creek, near Eastpoint, Mississippi; and also the railroad connections at Corinth, Jackson, and Humboldt. It is thought best that these objectives be attempted in the order named. Strong detachments of cavalry and light artillery, supported by infantry, may by rapid movements reach these points from the river, without any serious opposition.

Avoid any general engagements with strong forces. It will be better to retreat than to risk a general battle. This should be strongly impressed on the officers sent with expeditions from the river. General C. F. Smith or some very discreet officer shoud be selected for such commands. Having accomplished these objects, or such of them as may be practicable, you will return to Danville, and move on Paris.

Perhaps the troops sent to Jackson and Humboldt can reach Paris by land as easily as to return to the transports. This must depend on the character of the roads and the position of the enemy. All telegraphic lines which can be reached must be cut. The gunboats will accompany the transports for their protection. Any loyal Tennesseeans who desire it, may be enlisted and supplied with arms. Competent officers should be left to command Forts Henry and Donelson in your absence. I have indicated in general terms the object of this.

H. W. HALLECK, *Major-General.*

Again on the 2d:

CAIRO, *March* 2, 1862

To General GRANT:

General Halleck, February 25th, telegraphs me: "General Grant will send no more forces to Clarksville. General Smith's division will come to Fort Henry, or a point higher up on the Tennessee River; transports will also be collected at Paducah. Two gunboats in Tennessee River with Grant. General Grant will immediately have small garrisons detailed for Forts Henry and Donelson, and all other forces made ready for the field."

From your letter of the 28th, I learn you were at Fort Donelson, and General Smith at Nashville, from which I infer you could not have received orders. Halleck's telegram of last night says: "Who sent Smith's division to Nashville? I ordered it across to the Tennessee, where they are wanted immediately. Order them back. Send all spare transports up Tennessee to General Grant." Evidently the general supposes you to be on the Tennessee. I am sending all the transports I can find for you, reporting to General Sherman for orders to go up the Cumberland for you, or, if you march across to Fort Henry, then to send them up the Tennessee.

G. W. CULLUM, *Brigadier-General.*

On the 4th came this dispatch:

ST. LOUIS, *March* 4, 1862.

To Major-General U. S. GRANT:

You will place Major-General C. F. Smith in command of expedition, and remain yourself at Fort Henry. Why do you not obey my orders to report strength and positions of your command?

H. W. HALLECK, *Major-General.*

Halleck was evidently working himself into a passion, but he was too far from the seat of war to make due allowance for the actual state of facts. General Grant had done so much, that General Halleck should have been patient. Meantime, at Paducah, I was busy sending boats in every direction—some under the orders of General Halleck, others of General Cullum; others for General Grant, and still others for General Buell at Nashville; and at the same time I was organizing out of the new troops that were arriving at Paducah a division for myself when allowed to take the field, which I had been promised by General Halleck. His purpose was evidently to operate up the Tennessee River, to break up Bear Creek Bridge and the railroad communications between the Mississippi and Tennessee Rivers, and no doubt he was provoked that Generals Grants and Smith had turned aside to Nashville. In the mean time several of the gunboats, under Captain [S. L.] Phelps, United States Navy, had gone up the Tennessee as far as Florence, and on their return had reported a strong Union feeling among the people along the river. On the 10th of March, having received the necessary orders from General Halleck, I embarked my division at Paducah. It was composed of four brigades.

We steamed up to Fort Henry, the river being high and in splendid order. There I reported in person to General C. F. Smith, and by him was ordered a few miles above, to the remains of the burned railroad bridge, to await the rendezvous of the rest of his army. I had my headquarters on the Continental.

Among my colonels I had a strange character—Thomas Worthington, colonel of the Forty-sixth Ohio. He was a graduate of West Point, of the class of 1827; was, therefore, older than General Halleck, General Grant, or myself, and claimed to know more of war than all of us put together. In ascending the river he did not keep his place in the column, but pushed on and reached Savannah a day before the rest of my division. When I reached that place, I found that Worthington had landed his regiment, and was flying about giving orders, as though he were commander-in-chief. I made him get back to his boat, and gave him to understand that he must thereafter keep his place. General C. F. Smith arrived about the 13th of March, with a large fleet of boats, containing Hurlbut's division, Lew. Wallace's division, and that of himself, then commanded by Brigadier-General W[illiam] H. L. Wallace.

General Smith sent for me to meet him on his boat, and ordered me to push on under escort of the two gunboats, Lexington and Tyler, commanded by Captains [William]

Gwin and [James W.] Shirk, United States Navy. I was to land at some point below Eastport, and make a break of the Memphis & Charleston Railroad, between Tuscumbia and Corinth. General Smith was quite unwell, and was suffering from his leg, which was swollen and very sore, from a mere abrasion in stepping into a small-boat. This actually mortified, and resulted in death about a month after, viz., April 25, 1862. He was adjutant of the Military Academy during the early part of my career there, and afterward commandant of cadets. He was a very handsome and soldierly man, of great experience, and at Donelson had acted with so much personal bravery that to him many attributed the success of the assault. I immediately steamed up the Tennessee River, following the two gunboats, and, in passing Pittburg Landing, was told by Captain Gwin that, on his former trip up the river, he had found a rebel regiment of cavalry posted there, and that it was the usual landing-place for the people about Corinth, distant thirty miles. I sent word back to General Smith that, if we were detained up the river, he ought to post some troops at Pittsburg Landing. We went on up the river cautiously, till we saw Eastport and Chickasaw, both of which were occupied by rebel batteries and a small rebel force of infantry.

We then dropped back quietly to the mouth of Yellow River, a few miles below, whence led a road to Burnsville, a place on the Memphis & Charleston road, where were the company's repair-shops. We at once commenced disembarking the command: first the cavalry, which started at once for Burnsville, with orders to tear up the railroad-track, and burn the depots, shops, etc.; and I followed with the infantry and artillery as fast as they were disembarked. It was raining very hard at the time. Daylight found us about six miles out, where we met the cavalry returning. They had made numerous attempts to cross the streams, which had become so swollen that mere brooks covered the whole bottom; and my aide-de-camp, [Dan] Sanger, whom I had dispatched with the cavalry, reported the loss, by drowning, of several of the men. The rain was pouring in torrents, and reports from the rear came that the river was rising very fast, and that, unless we got back to our boats soon, the bottom would be simply impassable. There was no alternative but to regain our boats; and even this was so difficult, that we had to unharness the artillery-horses, and drag the guns under water through the bayous, to reach the bank of the river. Once more embarked, I concluded to drop down to Pittsburg Landing, and to make the attempt from there. During the night of the 14th, we dropped down to Pittsburg Landing, where I found Hurlbut's division in boats. Leaving my command there, I steamed down to Savannah, and reported to General Smith in person, who saw in the flooded Tennessee the full truth of my report; and he then instructed me to disembark my own division, and that of General Hurlbut, at Pittsburg Landing; to take positions well back, and to leave room for his whole army; telling me that he would soon come up in person, and move out in force to make the lodgment on the railroad, contemplated by General Halleck's orders.

Lieutenant-Colonel McPherson, of General C. F. Smith's, or rather General Halleck's, staff, returned with me, and on the 16th of March we disembarked and marched out about ten miles toward Corinth, to a place called Monterey or Pea Ridge, where the rebels had a cavalry regiment, which of course de-camped on our approach, but from the people we learned that trains were bringing large masses of men from every direction into Corinth. McPherson and I reconnoitred the ground well, and then returned to our boats. On the 18th, Hurlbut disembarked his division and took post about a mile and a half out, near where the roads branched, one leading to Corinth and the other toward Hamburg. On the 19th I disembarked my division, and took post about three miles back, three of the brigades covering the roads to Purdy and Corinth, and the other brigade (Stuart's) temporarily at a place on the Hamburg Road, near Lick Creek Ford, where the Bark Road came into the Hamburg Road. Within a few days, [Benjamin M.] Prentiss's division arrived and camped on my left, and afterward [John A.] McClernand's and W. H. L. Wallace's divisions, which formed a line to our rear. Lew Wallace's division remained on the north side of Snake Creek, on a road leading from Savannah or Crump's Landing to Purdy.

General C. F. Smith remained back at Savannah, in chief command, and I was only responsible for my own division. I kept pickets well out on the roads, and made myself familiar with all the ground inside and outside my lines. My personal staff was composed of Captain J. H. Hammond, assistant adjutant-general; Surgeons Hartshorn and L'Hommedieu; Lieutenant Colonels [Milo S.] Hascall and Sanger, inspector-generals; Lieutenants McCoy and John Taylor, aides-de-camp. We were all conscious that the enemy was collecting at Corinth, but in what force we could not know, nor did we know what was going on behind us. On the 17th of March, General U. S. Grant was restored to the command of all the troops up the Tennessee River, by reason of General Smith's extreme illness, and because he had explained to General Halleck satisfactorily his conduct after Donelson; and he too made his headquarters at Savannah, but frequently visited our camps. I always acted on the supposition that we were an invading army; that our purpose was to move forward in force, make a lodgment on the Memphis & Charleston road, and thus repeat the grand tactics of Fort Donelson, by separating the rebels in the interior from those at Memphis and on the Mississippi River. We did not fortify our camps against an attack, because we had no orders to do so, and because such a course would have made our raw men timid. The position was naturally strong, with Snake Creek on our right, a deep, bold stream, with a confluent (Owl Creek) to our right front; and Lick Creek, with a similar confluent, on our left, thus narrowing the space over which we could be attacked to about a mile and a half or two miles.

At a later period of the war, we could have rendered this position impregnable in one night, but at this time we did not do it, and it may be it is well we did not. From about the 1st of April we were conscious that the rebel cavalry in our front was getting bolder and more saucy; and on Friday, the 4th of April, it dashed down and carried off one of our picket-guards, composed of an officer and seven men, posted a couple of miles out on the Corinth road. Colonel [Ralph P.] Buckland sent a company to its relief, then followed himself with a regiment, and, fearing lest he might be worsted, I called out his whole brigade and followed some four or five miles, when the cavalry in advance encountered artillery. I then, after dark, drew back to our lines, and reported the fact by letter to General Grant, at Savannah; but thus far we had not positively detected the presence of infantry, for cavalry regiments generally had a couple of guns along, and I supposed the guns that opened on us on the evening of Friday, April 4th, belonged to the cavalry that was hovering along our whole front.

Saturday passed in our camps without any unusual event, the weather being wet and mild, and the roads back to the steamboat-landing being heavy withm ud; but on Sunday morning, the 6th, early, there was a good deal of picket-firing, and I got breakfast, rode out along my lines, and, about four hundred yards to the front of [Jesse J.] Appler's regiment, received from some bushes in a ravine to the left front a volley which killed my orderly, Holliday. About the same time I saw the rebel lines of battle in front coming down on us as far as the eye could reach. All my troops were in line of battle, ready, and the ground was favorable to us. I gave the necessary orders to the battery ([Allen C.] Waterhouse's) attached to [Jesse] Hildebrand's brigade, and cautioned the men to reserve their fire till the rebels had crossed the ravine of Owl Creek, and had begun the ascent; also, sent staff-officers to notify Generals McClernand and Prentiss of the coming blow. Indeed, McClernand had already sent three regiments to the support of my left flank, and they were in position when the onset came.

In a few minutes the battle of "Shiloh" began with extreme fury, and lasted two days. Its history has been well given, and it has been made the subject of a great deal of controversy. Hildebrand's brigade was soon knocked to pieces, but Buckland's and McDowell's kept their organization throughout. Stuart's was driven back to the river, and did not join me in person till the second day of the battle. I think my several reports of that battle are condensed and good, made on the spot, when all the names and facts were fresh in my memory, and are herewith given entire:

HEADQUARTERS FIRST DIVISION, ⎫
PITTSBURG LANDING, *March* 17, 1862. ⎰

Captain WM. MCMICHAEL, *Assistant Adjutant-General to General* C. F. SMITH, *Savannah, Tennessee.*

SIR: Last night I dispatched a party of cavalry, at 6 P. M., under the command of Lieutenant-Colonel [Thomas T.] Heath, Fifth Ohio Cavalry, for a strong reconnoissance, if possible, to be converted into an attack upon the Memphis road. The command got off punctually, followed at twelve o'clock at night by the First Brigade of my division, commanded by Colonel McDowell, the other brigades to follow in order.

About one at night the cavalry returned, reporting the road occupied in force by the enemy, with whose advance-guard they skirmished, driving them back about a mile, taking two prisoners, and having their chief guide, Thomas Maxwell, Esq., and three men of the Fourth Illinois wounded.

As soon as the cavalry returned, I saw that an attempt on the road was frustrated, and accordingly have placed McDowell's brigade to our right front, guarding the pass of Snake Creek; Stuart's brigade to the left front, to watch the pass of Lick Creek; and I shall this morning move directly out on the Corinth road, about eight miles to or toward Pea Ridge, which is a key-point to the southwest.

General Hurlbut's division will be landed to-day, and the artillery and infantry disposed so as to defend Pittsburg, leaving my division entire for any movement by land or water.

As near as I can learn, there are five regiments of rebel infantry at Purdy; at Corinth, and distributed along the railroad to Iuca, are probably thirty thousand men; but my information from prisoners is very indistinct. Every road and path is occupied by the enemy's cavalry, whose orders seem to be, to fire a volley, retire, again fire and retire. The force on the Purdy road attacked and driven by Major [Samuel M.] Bowman yesterday, was about sixty strong. That encountered last night on the Corinth road was about five companies of Tennessee cavalry, sent from Purdy about 2 P. M. yesterday.

I hear there is a force of two regiments on Pea Ridge, at the point where the Purdy and Corinth roads come together.

I am satisfied we cannot reach the Memphis & Charleston road without a considerable engagement, which is prohibited by General Halleck's instructions, so that I will be governed by your orders of yesterday, to occupy Pittsburg strongly, extend the pickets so as to include a semi-circle of three miles, and push a strong reconnoissance as far out as Lick Creek and Pea Ridge.

I will send down a good many boats to-day, to be employed as you may direct; and would be obliged if you would send a couple of thousand sacks of corn, as much hay as you can possibly spare, and, if possible, a barge of coal.

I will send a steamboat under care of the gunboat, to collect corn from cribs on the river-bank.

I have the honor to be your obedient servant,

W. T. SHERMAN,
Brigadier-General commanding First Division.

HEADQUARTERS, STEAMBOAT CONTINENTAL, }
PITTSBURG, *March* 18, 1862. }

Captain RAWLINS, *Assistant Adjutant-General to General* GRANT.

SIR: The division surgeon having placed some one hundred or more sick on board the Fanny Bullitt, I have permitted her to take them to Savannah. There is neither house nor building of any kind that can be used for a hosiptal here.

I hope to receive an order to establish floating hospitals, but in the mean time, by the advice of the surgeon, allow these sick men to leave. Let me hope that it will meet your approbation.

The order for debarkation came while General Sherman was absent with three brigades, and no men are left to move the effects of these brigades.

The landing, too, is small, with scarcely any chance to increase it; therefore there is a great accumulation of boats. Colonel [John] McArthur has arrived, and is now cutting a landing for himself.

General Sherman will return this evening. I am obliged to transgress, and write myself in the mean time,

Respectfully your obedient servant,
J. H. HAMMOND, *Assistant Adjutant-General.*

P.S.—4 P. M.—Just back; have been half-way to Corinth and to Purdy. All right. Have just read this letter, and approve all but floating hospitals; regimental surgeons can take care of all sick, except chronic cases, which can always be sent down to Paducah.

Magnificent plain for camping and drilling, and a military point of great strength. The enemy has felt us twice, at great loss and demoralization; will report at length this evening; am now much worn out.

W. T. SHERMAN, *Brigadier-General.*

HEADQUARTERS FIRST DIVISION, }
PITTSBURG LANDING, *March* 19, 1862. }

Captain RAWLINS, *Assistant Adjutant-General to General* GRANT, *Savannah, Tennessee.*

SIR: I have just returned from an extensive reconnoissance

toward Corinth and Purdy, and am strongly impressed with the importance of this position, both for its land advantages and its strategic position. The ground itself admits of easy defense by a small command, and yet affords admirable camping-ground for a hundred thousand men. I will as soon as possible make or cause to be made a topographical sketch of the position. The only drawback is that, at this stage of water, the space for landing is contracted too much for the immense fleet now here discharging.

I will push the loading and unloading of boats, but suggest that you send at once (Captain Dodd, if possible) the best quartermaster you can, that he may control and organize this whole matter. I have a good commissary, and will keep as few provision afloat as possible.   Yours, etc.,

W. T. SHERMAN, *Brigadier-General commanding.*

HEADQUARTERS SHERMAN'S DIVISION,
CAMP SHILOH, NEAR PITTSBURG LANDING, TENNESSEE,
April 2, 1862.

Captain J. A. RAWLINS, *Assistant Adjutant-General to General* GRANT.

SIR: In obedience to General Grant's instructions of March 31st, with one section of Captain Muench's Minnesota Battery, two twelve-pound howitzers, a detachment of Fifth Ohio Cavalry of one hundred and fifty men, under Major Ricker, and two battalions of infantry from the Fifty-seventh and Seventy-seventh Ohio, under the command of Colonels Hildebrand and Mungen, I marched to the river, and embarked on the steamers Empress and Tecumseh. The gunboat Cairo did not arrive at Pittsburg, until after midnight, and at 6 A. M. Captain Bryant, commanding the gunboat, notified me that he was ready to proceed up the river. I followed, keeping the transports within about three hundred yards of the gunboat. About 1 P. M., the Cairo commenced shelling the battery above the mouth of Indian Creek, but elicited no reply. She proceeded up the river steadily and cautiously, followed close by the Tyler and Lexington, all throwing shells at the points where, on former visits of the gunboats, enemy's batteries were found. In this order all followed, till it was demonstrated that all the enemy's batteries, including that at Chickasaw, were abandoned.

I ordered the battalion of infantry under Colonel Hildebrand to disembark at Eastport, and with the other battalion proceeded to Chickasaw and landed. The battery at this point had evidently been abandoned some time, and consisted of the remains of an old Indian mound, partly washed away by the river, which had been fashioned into a two-gun battery, with a small magazine. The ground to its rear had evidently been overflowed during the late freshet, and led to the removal of the guns to Eastport, where the batteries were on high, elevated ground, accessible at all seasons from the country to the rear.

Upon personal inspection, I attach little importance to Chickasaw as a military position. The people, who had fled during the approach of the gunboats, returned to the village, and said the place had been occupied by one Tennessee regiment and a battery of artillery from Pensacola. After remaining at Chickasaw some hours, all the boats dropped back to Eastport, not more than a mile below, and landed there. Eastport Landing during the late freshet must have been about twelve feet under water, but at the present stage the landing is the best I have seen on the Tennessee River.

The levee is clear of trees or snags, and a hundred boats could land there without confusion.

The soil is of sand and gravel, and very firm. The road back is hard, and at a distance of about four hundred yards from the water begin the gravel hills of the country. The infantry scouts sent out by Colonel Hildebrand found the enemy's cavalry mounted, and watching the Iuca road, about two miles back of Eastport. The distance to Iuca is only eight miles, and Iuca is the nearest point and has the best road by which the Charleston & Memphis Railroad can be reached. I could obtain no certain information as to the strength of the enemy there, but am satisfied that it would have been folly to have attempted it with my command. Our object being to dislodge the enemy from the batteries recently erected near Eastport, and this being attained, I have returned, and report the river to be clear to and beyond Chickasaw.

I have the honor to be, your obedient servant,

W. T. SHERMAN,
Brigadier-General commanding Division.

HEADQUARTERS FIFTH DIVISION, }
CAMP SHILOH, *April* 5, 1862. }

Captain J. A. RAWLINS, *Assistant Adjutant-General, District of Western Tennessee.*

SIR: I have the honor to report that yesterday, about 3 P. M., the lieutenant commanding and seven men of the advance pickets imprudently advanced from their posts and were captured. I ordered Major Ricker, of the Fifth Ohio Cavalry, to proceed rapidly to the picket-station, ascertain the truth, and act according to circumstances. He reached the station, found the pickets had been captured as reported, and that a company of infantry sent by the brigade commander had gone forward in pursuit of some cavalry. He rapidly advanced some two miles, and found them engaged, charged the enemy, and drove them along the Ridge road, till he met and received three discharges of artillery, when he very properly wheeled under cover, and returned till he met me.

As soon as I heard artillery, I advanced with two regiments of infantry, and took position, and remained until the scattered companies of infantry and cavalry had returned. This was after night.

I infer that the enemy is in some considerable force at Pea Ridge, that yesterday morning they crossed a brigade of two regiments of infantry, one regiment of cavalry, and one battery of field-artillery, to the ridge on which the Corinth road lies. They halted the infantry and artillery at a point about five miles in my front, sent a detachment to the lane of General Meaks [?], on the north of Owl Creek, and the cavalry down toward our camp. This cavalry captured a part of our advance pickets, and afterward engaged the two companies of Colonel Buckland's regiment. Our cavalry drove them back upon their artillery and Infantry, killing many, and bringing off ten prisoners, all of the First Alabama Cavalry, whom I send to you.

We lost of the pickets one first-lieutenant and seven men of the Ohio Seventieth Infantry (list inclosed); one major, one lieutenant, and one private of the Seventy-second Ohio, taken prisoners; eight privates wounded.

We took ten prisoners, and left two rebels wounded and many killed on the field.

I have the honor to be, your obedient servant,

W. T. SHERMAN,
Brigadier-General, commanding Division.

HEADQUARTERS FIFTH DIVISION, }
CAMP SHILOH, *April* 10, 1862. }

Captain J. A. RAWLINS, *Assistant Adjutant-General to General*
GRANT.

SIR: I had the honor to report that, on Friday the 4th inst., the enemy's cavalry drove in our pickets, posted about a mile and a half in advance of my centre, on the main Corinth road, capturing one first-lieutenant and seven men; that I caused a pursuit by the cavalry of my division, driving them back about five miles, and killing many. On Saturday the enemy's cavalry was again very bold, coming well down to our front; yet I did not believe they designed any thing but a strong demonstration. On Sunday morning early, the 6th inst., the enemy drove our advance-guard back on the main body, when I ordered under arms all my division, and sent word to General McClernand, asking him to support my left; to General Prentiss, giving him notice that the enemy was in our front in force, and to General Hurlbut, asking him to support General Prentiss. At that time—7 A. M.—my division was arranged as follows:

First Brigade, composed of the Sixth Iowa, Colonel J. A. McDowell; Fortieth Illinois, Colonel Hicks; Forty-sixth Ohio, Colonel Worthington; and the Morton battery, Captain Behr, on the extreme right, guarding the bridge on the Purdy road over Owl Creek.

Second Brigade, composed of the Fifty-fifth Illinois, Colonel D. Stuart; the Fifty-fourth Ohio, Colonel T. Kilby Smith; and the Seventy-first Ohio, Colonel Mason, on the extreme left, guarding the ford over Lick Creek.

Third Brigade, composed of the Seventy-seventh Ohio, Colonel Hildebrand; the Fifty-third Ohio, Colonel Appler; and the Fifty-seventh Ohio, Colonel Mungen, on the left of the Corinth road, its right resting on Shiloh meeting-house.

Fourth Brigade, composed of the Seventy-second Ohio, Colonel Buckland; the Forty-eighth Ohio, Colonel Sullivan; and the Seventieth Ohio, Colonel Cockerill, on the right of the Corinth road, its left resting on Shiloh meeting-house.

Two batteries of artillery—Taylor's and Waterhouse's—were posted, the former at Shiloh, and the latter on a ridge to the left, with a front-fire over open ground between Mungen's and Appler's regiments. The cavalry, eight companies of the Fourth Illinois, under Colonel Dickey, were posted in a large open field to the left and rear of Shiloh meeting-house, which I regarded as the centre of my position.

Shortly after 7 A. M., with my entire staff, I rode along a

portion of our front, and when in the open field before Appler's regiment, the enemy's pickets opened a brisk fire upon my party, killing my orderly, Thomas D. Holliday, of Company H, Second Illinois Cavalry. The fire came from the bushes which line a small stream that rises in the field in front of Appler's camp, and flows to the north along my whole front.

This valley afforded the enemy partial cover; but our men were so posted as to have a good fire at them as they crossed the valley and ascended the rising ground on our side.

About 8 A. M. I saw the glistening bayonets of heavy masses of infantry to our left front in the woods beyond the small stream alluded to, and became satisfied for the first time that the enemy designed a determined attack on our whole camp.

All the regiments of my division were then in line of battle at their proper posts. I rode to Colonel Appler, and ordered him to hold his ground at all hazards, as he held the left flank of our first line of battle, and I informed him that he had a good battery on his right, and strong support to his rear. General McClernand had promptly and energetically responded to my request, and had sent me three regiments which were posted to protect Waterhouse's battery and the left flank of my line.

The battle opened by the enemy's battery, in the woods to our front, throwing shells into our camp. Taylor's and Waterhouse's batteries promptly responded, and I then observed heavy battalions of infantry passing obliquely to the left, across the open field in Appler's front; also, other columns advancing directly upon my division. Our infantry and artillery opened along the whole line, and the battle became general. Other heavy masses of the enemy's forces kept passing across the field to our left, and directing their course on General Prentiss. I saw at once that the enemy designed to pass my left flank, and fall upon Generals McClernand and Prentiss, whose line of camps was almost parallel with the Tennessee River, and about two miles back from it. Very soon the sound of artillery and musketry announced that General Prentiss was engaged; and about 9 A. M. I judged that he was falling back. About this time Appler's regiment broke in disorder, followed by Mungen's regiment, and the enemy pressed forward on Waterhouse's battery thereby exposed.

The three Illinois regiments in immediate support of this battery stood for some time; but the enemy's advance was so vigorous, and the fire so severe, that when Colonel Raith, of the Forty-third Illinois, received a severe wound and fell from his horse, his regiment and the others manifested disorder, and the enemy got possession of three guns of this (Waterhouse's) battery. Although our left was thus turned, and the enemy was pressing our whole line, I deemed Shiloh so important, that I remained by it and renewed my orders to Colonels McDowell and Buckland to hold their ground; and we did hold these position until about 10 A. M., when the enemy had got his artillery to the rear of our left flank and some change became absolutely necessary. Two regiments of Hildebrand's brigade—Appler's and Mungen's—had already disappeared to the rear, and Hildebrand's own regiment was in disorder. I therefore gave orders for Taylor's battery—still at Shiloh—to fall back as far as the Purdy and Hamburg road, and for McDowell and Buckland to adopt that road as their new line. I rode across the angle and met [Frederick] Behr's battery at the cross-roads, and ordered it immediately to come into battery, action right. Captain Behr gave the order, but he was almost immediately shot from his horse, when drivers and gunners fled in disorder, carrying off the caissons, and abandoning five out of six guns, without firing a shot. The enemy pressed on, gaining this battery, and we were again forced to choose a new line of defense. Hildebrand's brigade had substantially disappeared from the field, though he himself bravely remained. McDowell's and Buckland's brigades maintained their organizations, and were conducted by my aides, so as to join on General McClernand's right, thus abandoning my original camps and line. This was about 10½ A. M., at which time the enemy had made a furious attack on General McClernand's whole front. He struggled most determinedly, but, finding him pressed, I moved McDowell's brigade directly against the left flank of the enemy, forced him back some distance, and then directed the men to avail themselves of every cover—trees, fallen timber, and a wooded valley to our right. We held this position for four long hours, sometimes gaining and at others losing ground; General McClernand and myself acting in perfect concert, and struggling to maintain this line. While we were so hard pressed, two Iowa regiments approached from the rear, but could not be brought up to the severe fire that was raging in our front, and General Grant, who visited us on that ground, will remember our situation about 3 P. M.; but about 4 P. M. it was evident that Hurlbut's line had been driven back to the river; and knowing that General Lew Wallace was coming with reënforcements from Crump's Landing, General McClernand and I, on consultation, selected a new line of defense, with its right covering a bridge by which General Wallace had to approach. We fell back as well as we could, gathering in addition to our own such scattered forces as we could find, and formed the new line.

During this change the enemy's cavalry charged us, but were handsomely repulsed by the Twenty-ninth Illinois Regiment. The Fifth Ohio Battery, which had come up, rendered good service in holding the enemy in check for some time, and Major Taylor also came up with another battery and got into position, just in time to get a good flank-fire upon the enemy's column, as he pressed on General McClernand's right, checking his advance; when General McClernand's division made a fine charge on the enemy and drove him back into the ravines to our front and right. I had a clear field, about two hundred yards wide, in my immediate front, and contented myself with keeping the enemy's infantry at that distance during the rest of the day. In this position we rested for the night. My command had become decidedly of a mixed character. Buckland's brigade was the only one that retained its organization. Colonel Hildebrand was personally there, but his brigade was not. Colonel McDowell had been severely injured by a fall off his horse, and had gone to the river, and the three regiments of his brigade were not in line. The Thirteenth Missouri, Colonel Crafts J. Wright, had reported to me on the field, and fought well, retaining its regimental organization; and it formed a part of my line during Sunday night and all Monday. Other fragments of regiments and companies had also fallen into my division, and acted with it during the remainder of the battle. Generals Grant and Buell visited me in our bivouac that evening, and from them I learned the situation of affairs on other parts of the field. General Wallace arrived from Crump's Landing shortly after dark, and formed his line to my right rear. It rained hard during the night, but our men were in good spirits, lay on their arms, being satisfied with such bread and meat as could be gathered at the neighboring camps, and determined to redeem on Monday the losses of Sunday.

At daylight of Monday I received General Grant's orders to advance and recapture our original camps. I dispatched several members of my staff to bring up all the men they could find, especially the brigade of Colonel Stuart, which had been separated from the division all the day before; and at the appointed time the division, or rather what remained of it, with the Thirteenth Missouri and other fragments, moved forward and reoccupied the ground on the extreme right of General McClernand's camp, where we attracted the fire of a battery located near Colonel McDowell's former headquarters. Here I remained, patiently waiting for the sound of General Buell's advance upon the main Corinth road. About 10 A. M. the heavy firing in that direction, and its steady approach, satisfied me; and General Wallace being on our right flank with his well-conducted division, I led the head of my column to General McClernand's right, formed line of battle, facing south, with Buckland's brigade directly across the ridge, and Stuart's brigade on its right in the woods; and thus advanced, steadily and slowly, under a heavy fire of musketry and artillery. Taylor had just got to me from the rear, where he had gone for ammunition, and brought up three guns, which I ordered into position, to advance by hand firing. These guns belonged to Company A, Chicago Light Artillery, commanded by Lieutenant P. P. Wood, and did most excellent service. Under cover of their fire, we advanced till we reached the point where the Corinth road crosses the line of McClernand's camp, and here I saw for the first time the well-ordered and compact columns of General Buell's Kentucky forces, whose soldierly movements at once gave confidence to our newer and less disciplined men. Here I saw [August] Willich's regiment advance upon a point of water-oaks and thicket, behind which I knew the enemy was in great strength, and enter it in beautiful style. Then arose the severest musketry-fire I ever heard, and lasted some twenty minutes, when this splendid regiment had to fall back. This green point of timber is about five hundred yards east of Shiloh meeting-house, and it was evident here was to be the struggle. The enemy could also be seen forming his lines to the south. General McClernand sending to me for artillery, I detached to him the three guns of Wood's battery, with which he speedily drove them back, and, seeing some others to the rear, I sent one of my staff to bring them forward, when, by almost providential decree, they proved to be two twenty-four-pound howitzers belonging to McAlister's battery, and served as well as guns ever could be.

This was about 2 P. M. The enemy had one battery close by

Shiloh, and another near the Hamburg road, both pouring grape and canister upon any column of troops that advanced upon the green point of water-oaks. Willich's regiment had been repulsed, but a whole brigade of McCook's division advanced beautifully, deployed, and entered this dreaded wood. I ordered my second brigade (then commanded by Colonel T. Kilby Smith, Colonel Stuart being wounded) to form on its right, and my fourth brigade, Colonel Buckland, on its right; all to advance abreast with this Kentucky brigade before mentioned, which I afterward found to be Rousseau's brigade of McCook's division. I gave personal direction to the twenty-four-pounder guns, whose well-directed fire first silenced the enemy's guns to the left, and afterward at the Shiloh meeting-house.

Rousseau's brigade moved in splendid order steadily to the front, sweeping every thing before it, and at 4 P. M. we stood upon the ground of our original front line; and the enemy was in full retreat. I directed my several brigades to resume at once their original camps.

Several times during the battle, cartridges gave out; but General Grant had thoughtfully kept a supply coming from the rear. When I appealed to regiments to stand fast, although out of cartridges, I did so because, to retire a regiment for any cause, has a bad effect on others. I commend the Fortieth Illinois and Thirteenth Missouri for thus holding their ground under heavy fire, although their cartridge-boxes were empty. . . .

I am, with much respect, your obedient servant,

W. T. SHERMAN,
Brigadier-General commanding Fifth Division.

HEADQUARTERS FIFTH DIVISION, }
Tuesday, April 8, 1862. }

SIR: With the cavalry placed at my command and two brigades of my fatigued troops, I went this morning out on the Corinth road. One after another of the abandoned camps of the enemy lined the roads, with hospital-flags for their protection; at all we found more or less wounded and dead men. At the forks of the road I found the head of General T. J. Wood's division of Buell's Army. I ordered cavalry to examine both roads leading toward Corinth, and found the enemy on both. Colonel [T. Lyle] Dickey, of the Fourth Illinois Cavalry, asking for reënforcements, I ordered General Wood to advance the head of his column cautiously on the left-hand road, while I conducted the head of the third brigade of my division up the right-hand road. About half a mile from the forks was a clear field, through which the road passed, and, immediately beyond, a space of some two hundred yards of fallen timber, and beyond that an extensive rebel camp. The enemy's cavalry could be seen in this camp; after reconnoissance, I ordered the two advance companies of the Ohio Seventy-seventh, Colonel Hildebrand, to deploy forward as skirmishers, and the regiment itself forward into line, with an interval of one hundred yards. In this order we advanced cautiously until the skirmishers were engaged. Taking it for granted this disposition would clear the camp, I held Colonel Dickey's Fourth Illinois Cavalry ready for the charge. The enemy's cavalry came down boldly at a charge, led by General [Nathan B.] Forrest in person, breaking through our line of skirmishers; when the regiment of infantry, without cause, broke, threw away their muskets, and fled. The ground was admirably adapted for a defense of infantry against cavalry, being miry and covered with fallen timber.

As the regiment of infantry broke, Dickey's Cavalry began to discharge their carbines, and fell into disorder. I instantly sent orders to the rear for the brigade to form line of battle, which was promptly executed. The broken infantry and cavalry rallied on this line, and, as the enemy's cavalry came to it, our cavalry in turn charged and drove them from the field. I advanced the entire brigade over the same ground and sent Colonel Dickey's cavalry a mile farther on the road. On examining the ground which had been occupied by the Seventy-seventh Ohio, we found fifteen of our men dead and about twenty-five wounded. I sent for wagons and had all the wounded carried back to camp, and caused the dead to be buried, also the whole rebel camp to be destroyed.

Here we found much ammunition for field-pieces, which was destroyed; also two caissons, and a general hospital, with about two hundred and eighty Confederate wounded, and about fifty of our own wounded men. Not having the means of bringing them off, Colonel Dickey, by my orders, took a surrender, signed by the medical director (Lyle) and by all the attending surgeons, and a pledge to report themselves to you as prisoners of war; also a pledge that our wounded should be carefully attended to, and surrendered to us to-morrow as soon as ambulances could go out. I inclose this written document, and request that you cause wagons or ambulances for our wounded to be sent to-morrow, and that wagons be sent to bring in the many tents belonging to us which are pitched along the road for four miles out. I did not destroy them, because I knew the enemy could not move them. The roads are very bad, and are strewed with abandoned wagons, ambulances, and limber-boxes. The enemy has succeeded in carrying off the guns, but has crippled his batteries by abandoning the hind limber-boxes of at least twenty caissons. I am satisfied the enemy's infantry and artillery passed Lick Creek this morning, travelling all of last night, and that he left to his rear all his cavalry, which has protected his retreat; but signs of confusion and disorder mark the whole road. The check sustained by us at the fallen timber delayed our advance, so that night came upon us before the wounded were provided for and the dead buried, and our troops being fagged out by three days' hard fighting, exposure, and privation, I ordered them back to their camps, where they now are.

I have the honor to be, your obedient servant,

W. T. SHERMAN,
Brigadier-General commanding Division.

General Grant did not make an official report of the battle of Shiloh, but all its incidents and events were covered by the reports of division commanders and subordinates. Probably no single battle of the war gave rise to such wild and damaging reports. It was publicly asserted at the North that our army was taken completely by surprise; that the rebels caught us in our tents; bayoneted the men in their beds; that General Grant was drunk; that Buell's opportune arrival saved the Army of the Tennessee from utter annihilation, etc. These reports were in a measure sustained by the published opinions of Generals Buell, Nelson, and others, who had reached the steamboat-landing from the east, just before nightfall of the 6th, when there was a large crowd of frightened, stampeded men, who clamored and declared that our army was all destroyed and beaten. Personally I saw General Grant, who with his staff visited me about 10 A. M. of the 6th, when we were desperately engaged. But we had checked the headlong assault of our enemy, and then held our ground. This gave him great satisfaction, and he told me that things did not look as well over on the left. He also told me that on his way up from Savannah that morning he had stopped at Crump's Landing, and had ordered Lew Wallace's division to cross over Lick Creek, so as to come up on my right, telling me to look out for him. He again came to me just before dark, and described the last assault made by the rebels at the ravine, near the steamboat-landing, which he had repelled by a heavy battery collected under Colonel J[oseph] D. Webster and other officers, and he was convinced that the battle was over for that day. He ordered me to be ready to assume the offensive in the morning, saying that, as he had observed at Fort Donelson at the crisis of the battle, both sides seemed defeated, and whoever assumed the offensive was sure to win. General Grant also explained to me that General Buell had reached the bank of the Tennessee River opposite Pittsburg Landing, and was in the act of ferrying his troops across at the time he was speaking to me.

About half an hour afterward General Buell himself rode up to where I was, accompanied by Colonels [James B.] Fry, Michler, and others of his staff. I was dismounted at the time, and General Buell made of me a good many significant inquiries about matters and things generally. By the aid of a manuscript map made by myself, I pointed out to him our positions as they had been in the morning, and our then positions; I also explained to him that my right then covered the bridge over Lick Creek by which we had all day been expecting Lew Wallace; that McClernand was on my left, Hurlbut on his left, and so on. But Buell said he had come up from the landing, and had not seen our men, of whose existence in fact he seemed to doubt. I insisted that I had five thousand good men still left in line, and thought that McClernand had as many more, and that with what was left of Hurlbut's, W. H. L. Wallace's, and Prentiss's divisions, we ought to have eighteen thousand men fit for battle. I reckoned that ten thousand of our men were dead, wounded, or prisoners, and that the enemy's loss could not be much less. Buell said that Nelson's, McCook's, and Crittenden's divisions of his army, containing eighteen thousand men, had arrived and could cross over in the night, and be ready for the next day's battle. I argued that with these reënforcements we could sweep the field. Buell seemed to mistrust us, and repeatedly said that he did not like the looks of things, especially about the boat-landing, and I really feared he would not cross over his army that night, lest he should become involved in our general disaster. He did not, of course, understand the shape of the ground, and asked me for the use of my map, which I lent him on the promise that he would return it. He handed it to Major Michler to have it copied, and the original returned to me, which Michler did two or three days after the battle. Buell did cross over that night, and the next day we assumed the offensive and swept the field, thus gaining the battle decisively. Nevertheless, the controversy was started and kept up, mostly to the personal prejudice of General Grant, who as usual maintained an imperturbable silence.

After the battle, a constant stream of civilian surgeons, and sanitary commission agents, men and women, came up the Tennessee to bring relief to the thousands of maimed and wounded soldiers for whom we had imperfect means of shelter and care. These people caught up the camp-stories, which on their return home they retailed through their local papers, usually elevating their own neighbors into heroes, but decrying all others. Among them was Lieutenant-Governor Stanton, of Ohio, who published in Belfontaine, Ohio, a most abusive article about General Grant and his subordinate generals. As General Grant did not and would not take up the cudgels, I did so. My letter in reply to Stanton, dated June 10, 1862, was published in the *Cincinnati Commercial* soon after its date. To this Lieutenant-Governor Stanton replied, and I further rejoined in a letter dated July 12, 1862. These letters are too personal to be revived. By this time the good people of the North had begun to have their eyes opened, and to give us in the field more faith and support. Stanton was never again elected to any public office, and was commonly spoken of as "the late Mr. Stanton." He is now dead, and I doubt not in life he often regretted his mistake in attempting to gain popular fame by abusing the army-leaders, then as now an easy and favorite mode of gaining notoriety, if not popularity. Of course, subsequent events gave General Grant and most of the other actors in that battle their appropriate place in history, but the danger of sudden popular clamors is well illustrated by this case.

The battle of Shiloh, or Pittsburg Landing, was one of the

most fiercely contested of the war. On the morning of April 6, 1862, the five divisions of McClernand, Prentiss, Hurlbut, W. H. L. Wallace, and Sherman, aggregated about thirty-two thousand men. We had no intrenchments of any sort, on the theory that as soon as Buell arrived we would march to Corinth to attack the enemy. The rebel army, commanded by General Albert Sidney Johnston, was, according to their own reports and admissions, forty-five thousand strong, had the momentum of attack, and beyond all question fought skillfully from early morning till about 2 P. M., when their commander-in-chief was killed by a Minié-ball in the calf of his leg, which penetrated the boot and severed the main artery. There was then a perceptible lull for a couple of hours, when the attack was renewed, but with much less vehemence, and continued up to dark. Early at night the division of Lew Wallace arrived from the other side of Snake Creek, not having fired a shot. A very small part of General Buell's army was on our side of the Tennessee River that evening, and their loss was trivial.

During that night, the three divisions of McCook, Nelson, and Crittenden, were ferried across the Tennessee, and fought with us the next day (7th). During that night, also, the two wooden gunboats, Tyler, commanded by Lieutenant Gwin, and Lexington, Lieutenant Shirk, both of the regular navy, caused shells to be thrown toward that part of the field of battle known to be occupied by the enemy. Beauregard afterward reported his entire loss as ten thousand six hundred and ninety-nine. Our aggregate loss, made up from official statements, shows seventeen hundred killed, seven thousand four hundred and ninety-five wounded, and three thousand and twenty-two prisoners; aggregate, twelve thousand two hundred and seventeen, of which twenty-one hundred and sixty-seven were in Buell's army, leaving for that of Grant ten thousand and fifty. This result is a fair measure of the amount of fighting done by each army.

Chapter 4

Memphis:
"Now I Was in High Feather"
April—July, 1862

WHILE THE "Army of the Tennessee," under Generals Grant and C. F. Smith, was operating up the Tennessee River, another force, styled the "Army of the Mississippi," commanded by Major-General John Pope, was moving directly down the Mississippi River, against that portion of the rebel line which, under Generals Polk and Pillow, had fallen back from Columbus, Kentucky, to Island Number Ten and New Madrid. This army had the full coöperation of the gunboat fleet, commanded by Admiral Foote, and was assisted by the high flood of that season, which enabled General Pope, by great skill and industry, to open a canal from a point above Island Number Ten to New Madrid below, by which he interposed between the rebel army and its available line of supply and retreat. At the very time that we were fighting the bloody battle on the Tennessee River, General Pope and Admiral Foote were bombarding the batteries on Island Number Ten, and the Kentucky shore abreast of it; and General Pope having crossed over by steamers a part of his army to the east bank, captured a large part of this rebel army, at and near Tiptonville.

General Halleck still remained at St. Louis, whence he gave general directions to the armies of General Curtis, General

Grant, and General Pope; and instead of following up his most important and brilliant successes directly down the Mississippi, he concluded to bring General Pope's army around to the Tennessee, and to come in person to command there. The gunboat fleet pushed on down the Mississippi, but was brought up again all standing by the heavy batteries at Fort Pillow, about fifty miles above Memphis. About this time Admiral [David] Farragut, with another large sea-going fleet, and with the coöperating army of General [Benjamin F.] Butler, was entering the Mississippi River by the Passes, and preparing to reduce Forts Jackson and St. Philip in order to reach New Orleans; so that all minds were turned to the conquest of the Mississippi River, and surely adequate means were provided for the undertaking.

The battle of Shiloh had been fought, as described, on the 6th and 7th of April; and when the movement of the 8th had revealed that our enemy was gone, in full retreat, leaving killed, wounded, and much property by the way, we all experienced a feeling of relief. The struggle had been so long, so desperate and bloody, that the survivors seemed exhausted and nerveless; we appreciated the value of the victory, but realized also its great cost of life. The close of the battle had left the Army of the Tennessee on the right, and the Army of the Ohio on the left; but I believe neither General Grant nor Buell exercised command, the one over the other; each of them having his hands full in repairing damages. All the division, brigade, and regimental commanders were busy in collecting stragglers, regaining lost property, in burying dead men and horses, and in providing for their wounded. Some few new regiments came forward, and some changes of organization became necessary. Then, or very soon after, I consolidated my four brigades into three, which were commanded: First, Brigadier-General Morgan L. Smith; Second, Colonel John A. McDowell; Third, Brigadier-General J. W. Denver. About the same time I was promoted to major-general of volunteers.

The Seventy-first Ohio was detached to Clarksville, Tennessee, and the Sixth and Eighth Missouri were transferred to my division.

In a few days after the battle, General Halleck arrived by steamboat from St. Louis, pitched his camp near the steamboat-landing, and assumed personal command of all the armies. He was attended by his staff, composed of General

G. W. Cullum, U. S. Engineers, as his chief of staff; Colonel George Thom, U. S. Engineers; and Colonels Kelton and Kemper, adjutants-general. It soon became manifest that his mind had been prejudiced by the rumors which had gone forth to the detriment of General Grant; for in a few days he issued an order, reorganizing and rearranging the whole army. General Buell's Army of the Ohio constituted the centre; General Pope's army, then arriving at Hamburg Landing, was the left; the right was made up of mine and Hurlbut's divisions, belonging to the old Army of the Tennessee, and two new ones, made up from the fragments of the divisions of Prentiss and C. F. Smith, and of troops transferred thereto, commanded by Generals T. W. Sherman and [Thomas A.] Davies. General George H. Thomas was taken from Buell, to command the right. McClernand's and Lew Wallace's divisions were styled the reserve, to be commanded by McClernand. General Grant was substantially left out, and was named "second in command," according to some French notion, with no clear, well-defined command or authority. He still retained his old staff, composed of [John] Rawlins, adjutant-general; [John] Riggin, [Clarn B.] Lagow, and [William S.] Hilyer, aides; and he had a small company of the Fourth Illinois Cavalry as an escort. For more than a month he thus remained, without any apparent authority, frequently visiting me and others, and rarely complaining; but I could see that he felt deeply the indignity, if not insult, heaped upon him.

General Thomas at once assumed command of the right wing, and, until we reached Corinth, I served immediately under his command. We were classmates, intimately acquainted, had served together before in the old army, and in Kentucky, and it made to us little difference who commanded the other, provided the good cause prevailed.

Corinth was about thirty miles distant, and we all knew that we should find there the same army with which we had so fiercely grappled at Shiloh, reorganized, reënforced, and commanded in chief by General Beauregard in place of Johnston, who had fallen at Shiloh. But we were also reënforced by Buell's and Pope's armies; so that before the end of April our army extended from Snake River on the right to the Tennessee River, at Hamburg, on the left, and must have numbered nearly one hundred thousand men.

Ample supplies of all kinds reached us by the Tennessee

River, which had a good stage of water; but our wagon transportation was limited, and much confusion occurred in hauling supplies to the several camps. By the end of April, the several armies seemed to be ready, and the general forward movement on Corinth began. My division was on the extreme right of the right wing, and marched out by the "White House," leaving Monterey or Pea Ridge to the south. Crossing Lick Creek, we came into the main road about a mile south of Monterey, where we turned square to the right, and came into the Purdy road, near "Elams." Thence we followed the Purdy road to Corinth, my skirmishers reaching at all times the Mobile & Ohio Railroad. Of course our marches were governed by the main centre, which followed the direct road from Pittsburg Landing to Corinth; and this movement was provokingly slow. We fortified almost every camp at night, though we had encountered no serious opposition, except from cavalry, which gave ground easily as we advanced. The opposition increased as we neared Corinth, and at a place called Russell's we had a sharp affair of one brigade, under the immediate direction of Brigadier-General Morgan L. Smith, assisted by the brigade of General Denver. This affair occurred on the 19th of May, and our line was then within about two miles of the northern intrenchments of Corinth.

On the 27th I received orders from General Halleck "to send a force the next day to drive the rebels from the house in our front, on the Corinth road, to drive in their pickets as far as possible, and to make a strong demonstration on Corinth itself"; authorizing me to call on any adjacent division for assistance.

I reconnoitred the ground carefully, and found that the main road led forward along the fence of a large cotton-field to our right front, and ascended a wooded hill, occupied in some force by the enemy, on which was the farm-house referred to in General Halleck's orders. At the farther end of the field was a double log-house, whose chinking had been removed; so that it formed a good block-house from which the enemy could fire on any person approaching from our quarter.

General Hurlbut's division was on my immediate left, and General McClernand's reserve on our right rear. I asked of each the assistance of a brigade. The former sent General [James C.] Veatch's, and the latter General John A. Logan's brigade. I asked the former to support our left flank, and the latter our right flank. The next morning early, Morgan L. Smith's brigade was deployed under cover on the left, and Denver's on the right, ready to move forward rapidly at a signal. I had a battery of four twenty-pound Parrott guns, commanded by Captain [Axel] Silversparre. Colonel Ezra Taylor, chief of artillery, had two of these guns moved up silently by hand behind a small knoll, from the crest of which the enemy's block-house and position could be distinctly seen; when all were ready, these guns were moved to the crest, and several quick rounds were fired at the house, followed after an interval by a single gun. This was the signal agreed on, and the troops responded beautifully, crossed the field in line of battle, preceded by their skirmishers who carried the position in good style, and pursued the enemy for half a mile beyond.

The main line halted on the crest of the ridge, from which we could look over the parapets of the rebel works at Corinth, and hear their drum and bugle calls. The rebel brigade had evidently been taken by surprise in our attack; it soon rallied and came back on us with the usual yell, driving in our skirmishers, but was quickly checked when it came within range of our guns and line of battle. Generals Grant and Thomas happened to be with me during this affair, and were well pleased at the handsome manner in which the troops behaved. That night we began the usual entrenchments, and the next day brought forward the artillery and the rest of the division, which then extended from the Mobile & Ohio Railroad, at Bowie Hill Cut, to the Corinth & Purdy road, there connecting with Hurlbut's division. That night, viz., May 29th, we heard unusual sounds in Corinth, the constant whistling of locomotives, and soon after daylight occurred a series of explosions followed by a dense smoke rising high over the town. There was a telegraph line connecting my headquarters with those of General Halleck, about four miles off, on the Hamburg road. I inquired if he knew the cause of the explosions and of the smoke, and he answered to "advance with my division and feel the enemy if still in my front." I immediately dispatched two regiments from each of my three brigades to feel the immediate front, and in a very short time advanced with the whole division. Each brigade found the rebel parapets abandoned, and pushed straight for the town, which lies in the northeast angle of intersection of the Mobile & Ohio and

Memphis & Charleston Railroads. Many buildings had been burned by the enemy on evacuation, which had begun the night before at 6 P.M., and continued through the night, the rear-guard burning their magazine at the time of withdrawing, about daybreak. Morgan L. Smith's brigade followed the retreating rear-guard some four miles to the Tuscumbia Bridge, which was found burned. I halted the other brigades at the college, about a mile to the southwest of the town, where I was overtaken by General Thomas in person.

The heads of all the columns had entered the rebel lines about the same time, and there was some rather foolish clamor for the first honors, but in fact there was no honor in the event. Beauregard had made a clean retreat to the south, and was only seriously pursued by cavalry from General Pope's flank. But he reached Tupelo, where he halted for reorganization; and there is no doubt that at the moment there was much disorganization in his ranks, for the woods were full of deserters whom we did not even take prisoners, but advised them to make their way home and stay there. We spent the day at and near the college, when General Thomas, who applied for orders at Halleck's headquarters, directed me to conduct my division back to the camp of the night before, where we had left our trains. The advance on Corinth had occupied all of the month of May, the most beautiful and valuable month of the year for campaigning in this latitude. There had been little fighting, save on General Pope's left flank about Farmington; and on our right I esteemed it a magnificent drill, as it served for the instruction of our men in guard and picket duty, and in habituating them to out-door life; and by the time we had reached Corinth I believe that army was the best then on this continent, and could have gone where it pleased. The four subdivisions were well commanded, as were the divisions and brigades of the whole army. General Halleck was a man of great capacity, of large acquirements, and at the time possessed the confidence of the country, and of most of the army. I held him in high estimation, and gave him credit for the combinations which had resulted in placing this magnificent army of a hundred thousand men, well equipped and provided, with a good base, at Corinth, from which he could move in any direction.

Had he held his force as a unit, he could have gone to Mobile, or Vicksburg, or anywhere in that region, which

would by one move have solved the whole Mississippi problem; and, from what he then told me, I believe he intended
such a campaign, but was overruled from Washington. Be
that as it may, the army had no sooner settled down at
Corinth before it was scattered: General Pope was called to
the East, and his army distributed among the others; General
Thomas was relieved from the command of the right wing,
and reassigned to his division in the Army of the Ohio; and
that whole army under General Buell was turned east along
the Memphis & Charleston road, to march for Chattanooga.
McClernand's "reserve" was turned west to Bolivar and
Memphis. General Halleck took post himself at Corinth, assigned Lieutenant-Colonel McPherson to take charge of the
railroads, with instructions to repair them as far as Columbus,
Kentucky, and to collect cars and locomotives to operate them
to Corinth and Grand Junction. I was soon dispatched with
my own and Hurlbut's divisions northwest fourteen miles to
Chewalla, to save what could be of any value out of six trains
of cars belonging to the rebels which had been wrecked and
partially burned at the time of the evacuation of Corinth.

A short time before leaving Corinth I rode from my camp
to General Halleck's headquarters, then in tents just outside of
the town, where we sat and gossiped for some time, when he
mentioned to me casually that General Grant was going away
the next morning. I inquired the cause, and he said that he
did not know, but that Grant had applied for a thirty days'
leave, which had been given him. Of course we all knew that
he was chafing under the slights of his anomalous position,
and I determined to see him on my way back. His camp was
a short distance off the Monterey road, in the woods, and consisted of four or five tents, with a sapling railing around the
front. As I rode up, Majors Rawlins, Lagow, and Hilyer,
were in front of the camp, and piled up near them were the
usual office and camp chests, all ready for a start in the morning. I inquired for the general, and was shown to his tent,
where I found him seated on a camp-stool, with papers on a
rude camp-table; he seemed to be employed in assorting
letters, and tying them up with red tape into convenient
bundles. After passing the usual compliments, I inquired if
it were true that he was going away. He said, "Yes." I then
inquired the reason, and he said: "Sherman, you know. You
know that I am in the way here. I have stood it as long as I

can, and can endure it no longer." I inquired where he was going to, and he said, "St. Louis." I then asked if he had any business there, and he said, "Not a bit." I then begged him to stay, illustrating his case by my own.

Before the battle of Shiloh, I had been cast down by a mere newspaper assertion of "crazy"; but that single battle had given me new life, and now I was in high feather; and I argued with him that, if he went away, events would go right along, and he would be left out; whereas, if he remained, some happy accident might restore him to favor and his true place. He certainly appreciated my friendly advice, and promised to wait awhile; at all events, not to go without seeing me again, or communicating with me. Very soon after this, I was ordered to Chewalla, where, on the 6th of June, I received a note from him, saying that he had reconsidered his intention, and would remain. I cannot find the note, but my answer I have kept.

CHEWALLA, *June* 6, 1862.

Major-General GRANT.

MY DEAR SIR: I have just received your note, and am rejoiced at your conclusion to remain; for you could not be quiet at home for a week when armies were moving, and rest could not relieve your mind of the gnawing sensation that injustice had been done you.

My orders at Chewalla were to rescue the wrecked trains there, to reconnoitre westward and estimate the amount of damage to the railroad as far as Grand Junction, about fifty miles. We camped our troops on high, healthy ground to the south of Chewalla, and after I had personally reconnoitred the country, details of men were made and volunteer locomotive-engineers obtained to superintend the repairs. I found six locomotives and about sixty cars, thrown from the track, parts of the machinery detached and hidden in the sourrounding swamp, and all damaged as much by fire as possible. It seems that these trains were inside of Corinth during the night of evacuation, loading up with all sorts of commissary stores, etc., and about daylight were started west; but the cavalry-picket stationed at the Tuscumbia bridge had, by mistake or panic, burned the bridge before the trains got to them. The trains, therefore, were caught, and the engineers and guards hastily scattered the stores into the swamp, and disabled the trains as far as they could, before our cavalry had discovered their critical situation. The weather was hot, and the swamp fairly stunk with the putrid flour and fermenting sugar and molasses; I was so much exposed there in the hot sun, pushing forward the work, that I got a touch of malarial fever, which hung on me for a month, and forced me to ride two days in an ambulance, the only time I ever did such a thing during the whole war. By the 7th I reported to General Halleck that the amount of work necessary to reëstablish the railroad between Corinth and Grand Junction was so great, that he concluded not to attempt its repair, but to rely on the road back to Jackson (Tennessee), and forward to Grand Junction; and I was ordered to move to Grand Junction, to take up the repairs from there toward Memphis.

The evacuation of Corinth by Beauregard, and the movements of General McClernand's force toward Memphis, had necessitated the evacuation of Fort Pillow, which occurred about June 1st; soon followed by the further withdrawal of the Confederate army from Memphis, by reason of the destruction of the rebel gunboats in the bold and dashing attack by our gunboats under command of Admiral [Charles H.] Davis, who had succeeded Foote. This occurred June 7th. Admiral Farragut had also captured New Orleans after the terrible passage of Forts Jackson and St. Philip on May 24th, and had ascended the river as high as Vicksburg; so that it seemed as though, before the end of June, we should surely have full possession of the whole river. But it is now known that the progress of our Western armies had aroused the rebel government to the exercise of the most stupendous energy. Every man capable of bearing arms at the South was declared to be a soldier, and forced to act as such. All their armies were greatly reënforced, and the most despotic power was granted to enforce discipline and supplies. Beauregard was replaced by Bragg, a man of more ability—of greater powers of organization, of action, and discipline—but naturally exacting and severe, and not possessing the qualities to attract the love of his officers and men. He had a hard task to bring into order and discipline that mass of men to whose command he succeeded at Tupelo, with which he afterward fairly outmanœuvred General Buell, and forced him back from Chattanooga to Louisville. It was a fatal mistake, however, that halted General Halleck at Corinth, and led him to disperse and scatter the best materials for a fighting army that, up to that date, had been assembled in the West.

During the latter part of June and first half of July, I had my own and Hurlbut's divisions about Grand Junction, Lagrange, Moscow, and Lafayette, building railroad-trestles and bridges, fighting off cavalry detachments coming from the south, and waging an everlasting quarrel with planters about their negroes and fences—they trying, in the midst of moving armies, to raise a crop of corn. On the 17th of June I sent a detachment of two brigades, under General M. L. Smith, to Holly Springs, in the belief that I could better protect the railroad from some point in front than by scattering our men along it; and, on the 23d, I was at Lafayette Station, when General Grant, with his staff and a very insignificant escort, arrived from Corinth *en route* for Memphis, to take command of that place and of the District of West Tennessee. He came very near falling into the hands of the enemy, who infested the whole country with small but bold detachments of cavalry. Up to that time I had received my orders direct from General Halleck at Corinth, but soon after I fell under the immediate command of General Grant, and so continued to the end of the war; but, on the 29th, General Halleck notified me that "a division of troops under General C[harles] S. Hamilton of 'Rosecrans's army corps,' had passed the Hatchie from Corinth," and was destined for Holly Springs, ordering me to "coöperate as far as advisable," but "not to neglect the protection of the road." I ordered General Hurlbut to leave detachments at Grand Junction and Lagrange, and to march for Holly Springs. I left detachments at Moscow and Lafayette, and, with about four thousand men, marched for the same point. Hurlbut and I met at Hudsonville, and thence marched to the Coldwater, within four miles of Holly Springs. We encountered only small detachments of rebel cavalry under Colonels [William H.] Jackson and Pierson, and drove them into and through Holly Springs; but they hung about, and I kept an infantry brigade in Holly Springs to keep them out. I heard nothing from General Hamilton till the 5th of July, when I received a letter from him dated Rienzi, saying that he had been within nineteen miles of Holly Springs and had turned back for Corinth; and on the next day, July 6th, I got a telegraph order from General Halleck, of July 2d, sent me by courier from Moscow, "not to attempt to hold Holly Springs, but to fall back and protect the railroad." We accordingly marched back twenty-five miles—Hurlbut to Lagrange, and I to Moscow. The enemy had no infantry nearer than the Tallahatchee bridge, but their cavalry was saucy and active, superior to ours, and I despaired of ever protecting a railroad, presenting a broad front of one hundred miles, from their dashes.

About this time, we were taunted by the Confederate soldiers and citizens with the assertion that Lee had defeated McClellan at Richmond; that he would soon be in Washington; and that our turn would come next. The extreme caution of General Halleck also indicated that something had gone wrong, and, on the 16th of July, at Moscow, I received a dispatch from him, announcing that he had been summoned to Washington, which he seemed to regret, and which at that moment I most deeply deplored. He announced that his command would devolve on General Grant, who had been summoned around from Memphis to Corinth by way of Columbus, Kentucky, and that I was to go into Memphis to take command of the District of West Tennessee, vacated by General Grant. By this time, also, I was made aware that the great army that had assembled at Corinth at the end of May had been scattered and dissipated, and that terrible disasters had befallen our other armies in Virginia and the East.

I soon received orders to move to Memphis, taking Hurlbut's division along. We reached Memphis on the 21st, and on the 22d I posted my three brigades mostly in and near Fort Pickering, and Hurlbut's division next below on the river-bank by reason of the scarcity of water, except in the Mississippi River itself. The weather was intensely hot. The same order that took us to Memphis required me to send the division of General Lew Wallace (then commanded by Brigadier-General A[lvin] P. Hovey) to Helena, Arkansas, to report to General Curtis, which was easily accomplished by steamboat. I made my own camp in a vacant lot, near Mr. Moon's house, and gave my chief attention to the construction of Fort Pickering, then in charge of Major Prime, United States Engineers; to perfecting the drill and discipline of the two divisions under my command; and to the administration of civil affairs.

At the time when General Halleck was summoned from Corinth to Washington, to succeed McClellan as commander-in-chief, I surely expected of him immediate and important results. The Army of the Ohio was at the time marching toward Chattanooga, and was strung from Eastport by Huntsville to Bridgeport, under the command of General Buell. In like manner, the Army of the Tennessee was strung along the same general line, from Memphis to Tuscumbia, and was commanded by General Grant, with no common commander for both these forces: so that the great army which General Halleck had so well assembled at Corinth, was put on the defensive, with a frontage of three hundred miles. Soon thereafter the rebels displayed peculiar energy and military skill. General Bragg had reorganized the army of Beauregard at Tupelo, carried it rapidly and skillfully toward Chattanooga, whence he boldly assumed the offensive, moving straight for Nashville and Louisville, and compelling General Buell to fall back to the Ohio River at Louisville.

The army of Van Dorn and Price had been brought from the trans-Mississippi Department to the east of the river, and was collected at and about Holly Springs, where, reënforced by [Frank C.] Armstrong's and Forrest's cavalry, it amounted to about forty thousand brave and hardy soldiers. These were General Grant's immediate antagonists, and so many and large detachments had been drawn from him, that for a time he was put on the defensive. In person he had his headquarters at Corinth, with the three divisions of Hamilton, Davies, and [Thomas J.] McKean, under the immediate orders of General [William S.] Rosecrans. General [Edward O. C.] Ord had succeeded to the division of McClernand (who had also gone to Washington), and held Bolivar and Grand Junction. I had in Memphis my own and Hurlbut's divisions, and other smaller detachments were strung along the Memphis & Charleston road. But the enemy's detachments could strike this road at so many points, that no use could be made of it, and General Grant had to employ the railroads, from Columbus, Kentucky, to Corinth and Grand Junction, by way of Jackson, Tennessee, a point common to both roads, and held in some force.

In the early part of September the enemy in our front manifested great activity, feeling with cavalry at all points, and on the 13th General Van Dorn threatened Corinth, while General Price seized the town of Iuka, which was promptly abandoned by a small garrison under Colonel [Robert] Murphy. Price's force was about eight thousand men, and the general impression was that he was *en route* for Eastport, with the purpose to cross the Tennessee River in the direction of Nashville, in aid of General Bragg, then in full career for Kentucky. General Grant determined to attack him in force, prepared to regain Corinth before Van Dorn could reach it. He had drawn Ord to Corinth, and moved him, by Burnsville, on Iuka, by the main road, twenty-six miles. General Grant accompanied this column as far as Burnsville. At the same time he had dispatched Rosecrans by roads to the south, *via* Jacinto, with orders to approach Iuka by the two main roads, coming into Iuka from the south, viz., the Jacinto and Fulton roads.

On the 18th General Ord encountered the enemy about four miles out of Iuka. His orders contemplated that he should not make a serious attack, until Rosecrans had gained his position on the south; but, as usual, Rosecrans had encountered difficulties in the confusion of roads, his head of column did not reach the vicinity of Iuka till 4 P.M. of the 19th, and then his troops were long drawn out on the single Jacinto road, leaving the Fulton road clear for Price's use. Price perceived his advantage, and attacked with vehemence the head of Rosecrans's column, Hamilton's division, beating it back, capturing a battery, and killing and disabling seven hundred and thirty-six men, so that when night closed in Rosecrans was driven to the defensive, and Price, perceiving his danger, deliberately withdrew by the Fulton road, and the next morning was gone. Although General Ord must have been within four or six miles of this battle, he did not hear a sound; and he or General Grant did not know of it till advised the next morning by a courier who had made a wide circuit to reach them. General Grant was much offended with General Rosecrans because of this affair, but in my experience these concerted movements generally fail, unless with the very best kind of troops, and then in a country on whose roads some reliance can be placed, which is not the case in Northern Mississippi. If Price was aiming for Tennessee, he failed, and was therefore beaten. He made a wide circuit by the south, and again joined Van Dorn.

On the 6th of September, at Memphis, I received an order from General Grant dated the 2d, to send Hurlbut's division to Brownsville, in the direction of Bolivar, thence to report by letter to him at Jackson. The division started the same day, and, as our men and officers had been together side by side from the first landing at Shiloh, we felt the parting like the breaking up of a family. But General Grant was forced to use every man, for he knew well that Van Dorn could attack him at pleasure, at any point of his long line. To be the better prepared, on the 23d of September he took post himself at Jackson, Tennessee, with a small reserve force, and gave Rosecrans command of Corinth, with his three divisions and some detachments, aggregating about twenty thousand men. He posted General Ord with his own and Hurlbut's divisions at Bolivar, with outposts toward Grand Junction and Lagrange. These amounted to nine or ten thousand men, and I held Memphis with my own division, amounting to about six thousand men. The whole of General Grant's men at that time may have aggregated fifty thousand, but he had to defend a frontage of a hundred and fifty miles, guard some two hundred miles of railway, and as much river. Van Dorn had forty thousand men, united, at perfect liberty to move in any direction, and to choose his own point of attack, under cover of woods, and a superior body of cavalry, familiar with every foot of the ground. Therefore General Grant had good reason for telegraphing to General Halleck, on the 1st of October, that his position was precarious, "but I hope to get out of it all right." In Memphis my business was to hold fast that important flank, and by that date Fort Pickering had been made very strong, and capable of perfect defense by a single brigade. I therefore endeavored by excursions to threaten Van Dorn's detachments to the southeast and east. I repeatedly sent out strong detachments toward Holly Springs, which was his main depot of supply; and General [Benjamin] Grierson, with his Sixth Illinois, the only cavalry I had, made some bold and successful dashes at the Coldwater, compelling Van Dorn to cover it by Armstrong's whole division of cavalry. Still, by the 1st of October, General Grant was satisfied that the enemy was meditating an attack in force on Bolivar or Corinth; and on the 2d Van Dorn made his appearance near Corinth, with his entire army. On the 3d he moved down on that place from the north and northwest. General Rosecrans went out some four miles to meet him, but was worsted and compelled to fall back within the line of his forts. These had been begun under General Halleck, but were much strengthened by General Grant, and consisted of several detached redoubts, bearing on each other, and inclosing the town and the depots of stores at the intersection of the two railroads. Van Dorn closed down on the forts by the evening of the 3d, and on the morning of the 4th assaulted with great vehemence. Our men, covered by good parapets, fought gallantly, and defended their posts well, inflicting terrible losses on the enemy, so that by noon the rebels were repulsed at all points, and drew off, leaving their dead and wounded in our hands. Their losses, were variously estimated, but the whole truth will probably never be known, for in that army reports and returns were not the fashion. General Rosecrans admitted his own loss to be three hundred and fifteen killed, eighteen hundred and twelve wounded, and two hundred and thirty-two missing or prisoners, and claimed on the part of the rebels fourteen hundred and twenty-three dead, two thousand and twenty-five prisoners and wounded. Of course, most of the wounded must have gone off or been carried off, so that, beyond doubt, the rebel army lost at Corinth fully six thousand men.

Meantime, General Grant, at Jackson, had dispatched Brigadier-General McPherson, with a brigade, directly for Corinth, which reached General Rosecrans after the battle; and, in anticipation of his victory, had ordered him to pursue instantly, notifying him that he had ordered Ord's and Hurlbut's divisions rapidly across to Pocahontas, so as to strike the rebels in flank. On the morning of the 5th, General Ord reached the Hatchie River, at Davis's bridge, with four thousand men; crossed over and encountered the retreating army, captured a battery and several hundred prisoners, dispersing the rebel advance, and forcing the main column to make a wide circuit by the south in order to cross the Hatchie River. Had General Rosecrans pursued promptly, and been on the heels of this mass of confused and routed men, Van Dorn's army would surely have been utterly ruined; as it was, Van Dorn regained Holly Springs somewhat demoralized.

General Rosecrans did not begin his pursuit till the next morning, the 5th, and it was then too late. General Grant was again displeased with him, and never became fully reconciled. General Rosecrans was soon after relieved, and transferred to the Army of the Cumberland, in Tennessee, of which he afterward obtained the command, in place of General Buell, who was removed.

The effect of the battle of Corinth was very great. It was, indeed, a decisive blow to the Confederate cause in our quarter, and changed the whole aspect of affairs in West Tennessee. From the timid defensive we were at once enabled to assume the bold offensive. In Memphis I could see its effects upon the citizens, and they openly admitted that their cause had sustained a death-blow. But the rebel government was then at its maximum strength; Van Dorn was reënforced, and very soon Lieutenant-General J[ohn] C. Pemberton arrived and assumed the command, adopting for his line the Tallahatchie River, with an advance-guard along the Coldwater, and smaller detachments forward at Grand Junction and Hernando. General Grant, in like manner, was reënforced by new regiments.

Out of those which were assigned to Memphis I organized two new brigades, and placed them under officers who had gained skill and experience during the previous campaign.

Chapter 5

Vicksburg and Arkansas Post:
"More Patience Than I Usually Possess"
July, 1862—January, 1863

WHEN WE FIRST entered Memphis, July 21, 1862, I found the place dead; no business doing, the stores closed, churches, schools, and every thing shut up. The people were all more or less in sympathy with our enemies, and there was a strong prospect that the whole civil population would become a dead weight on our hands. Inasmuch as the Mississippi River was then in our possession northward, and steamboats were freely plying with passengers and freight, I caused all the stores to be opened, churches, schools, theatres, and places of amusement to be reëstablished, and very soon Memphis resumed its appearance of an active, busy, prosperous place. I also restored the mayor (whose name was Parks) and the city government to the performance of their public functions, and required them to maintain a good civil police.

Up to that date neither Congress nor the President had made any clear, well-defined rules touching the Negro slaves, and the different generals had issued orders according to their own political sentiments. Both Generals Halleck and Grant regarded the slave as still a slave, only that the labor of the slave belonged to his owner, if faithful to the Union, or to the United States, if the master had taken up arms against the Government, or adhered to the fortunes of the rebellion. Therefore, in Memphis, we received all fugitives, put them to work on the fortifications, supplied them with food and clothing, and reserved the question of payment of wages for future decision. No force was allowed to be used to restore a fugitive slave to his master in any event; but if the master proved his loyalty, he was usually permitted to see his slave, and, if he could persuade him to return home, it was permitted. Cotton, also, was a fruitful subject of controversy. The Secretary of the Treasury, Mr. Chase, was extremely anxious at that particular time to promote the purchase of cotton, because each bale was worth, in gold, about three hundred dollars, and answered the purpose of coin in our foreign exchanges. He therefore encouraged the trade, so that hundreds of greedy speculators flocked down the Mississippi, and resorted to all sorts of measures to obtain cotton from the interior, often purchasing it from Negroes who did not own it, but who knew where it was concealed. This whole business was taken from the jurisdiction of the military, and committed to Treasury agents appointed by Mr. Chase.

Other questions absorbed the attention of military commanders; and by way of illustration I here insert a few letters from my "letter-book," which contains hundreds on similar subjects:

HEADQUARTERS FIFTH DIVISION,
MEMPHIS, TENNESSEE, *August* 11, 1862.

Hon. S. P. CHASE, *Secretary of the Treasury*.

SIR: Your letter of August 2d, just received, invites my discussion of the cotton question.

I will write plainly and slowly, because I know you have no time to listen to trifles. This is no trifle; when one nation is at war with another, all the people of the one are enemies of the other: then the rules are plain and easy of understanding. Most unfortunately, the war in which we are now engaged has been complicated with the belief on the one hand that all on the other are *not* enemies. It would have been better if, at the outset, this mistake had not been made, and it is wrong longer to be misled by it. The Government of the United

States may now safely proceed on the proper rule that all in the South *are* enemies of all in the North; and not only are they unfriendly, but all who can procure arms now bear them as organized regiments, or as guerrillas. There is not a garrison in Tennessee where a man can go beyond the sight of the flag-staff without being shot or captured. It so happened that these people had cotton, and, whenever they apprehended our large armies would move, they destroyed the cotton in the belief that, of course, we would seize it, and convert it to our use. They did not and could not dream that we would pay money for it. It had been condemned to destruction by their own acknowledged government, and was therefore lost to their people; and could have been, without injustice, taken by us, and sent away, either as absolute prize of war, or for future compensation. But the commercial enterprise of the Jews[1] soon discovered that ten cents would buy a pound of cotton behind our army; that four cents would take it to Boston, where they could receive thirty cents in gold. The bait was too tempting, and it spread like fire, when here they discovered that salt, bacon, powder, fire-arms, percussion-caps, etc., etc., were worth as much as gold; and, strange to say, this traffic was not only permitted, but encouraged. Before we in the interior could know it, hundreds, yea thousands of barrels of salt and millions of dollars had been disbursed; and I have no doubt that Bragg's army at Tupelo, and Van Dorn's at Vicksburg, received enough salt to make bacon, without which they could not have moved their armies in mass; and that from ten to twenty thousand fresh arms, and a due supply of cartridges, have also been got, I am equally satisfied. As soon as I got to Memphis, having seen the effect in the interior, I

---

[1] At this period, when caricature was much in vogue, the word "Jews" was used to denote a type of merchant rather than a race or religion. Grant's famous order, barring Jews from the Department of Tennessee, had brought a tactful letter from Halleck: "The President, has no objection to your expelling traitors and Jew peddlars, which I suppose was the object of your order; but, as its terms proscribe an entire religious class, some of whom are fighting in our ranks, the President deemed it necessary to revoke it." Occasionally Sherman used the word "nigger," and it has been allowed to stand; again, its use reflects a spirit of an age that had not outgrown thinking loosely in terms of caricature.

ordered (only as to my own command) that gold, silver, and Treasury notes, were contraband of war, and should not go into the interior, where all were hostile. It is idle to talk about Union men here; many want peace, and fear war and its results; but all prefer a Southern, independent government, and are fighting or working for it. Every gold dollar that was spent for cotton, was sent to the seaboard, to be exchanged for bank-notes and Confederate scrip, which will buy goods here, and are taken in ordinary transactions. I therefore required cotton to be paid for in such notes, by an obligation to pay at the end of the war, or by a deposit of the price in the hands of a trustee, viz., the United States Quartermaster. Under these rules cotton is being obtained about as fast as by any other process, and yet the enemy receives no "aid or comfort." Under the "gold" rule, the country people who had concealed their cotton from the burners, and who openly scorned our greenbacks, were willing enough to take Tennessee money, which will buy their groceries; but now that the trade is to be encouraged, and gold paid out, I admit that cotton will be sent in by our open enemies, who can make better use of gold than they can of their hidden bales of cotton.

I may not appreciate the foreign aspect of the question, but my views on this may be ventured. If England ever threatens war because we don't furnish her cotton, tell her plainly if she can't employ and feed her own people, to send them here, where they cannot only earn an honest living, but soon secure independence by moderate labor. We are not bound to furnish her cotton. She has more reason to fight the South for burning that cotton, than us for not shipping it. To aid the South on this ground would be hypocrisy which the world would detect at once. Let her make her ultimatum, and there are enough generous minds in Europe that will counteract her in the balance. Of course her motive is to cripple a power that rivals her in commerce and manufactures, that threatens even to usurp her history. In twenty more years of prosperity, it will require a close calculation to determine whether England, her laws and history, claim for a home the Continent of America or the Isle of Britain. Therefore, finding us in a death-struggle for existence, she seems to seek a quarrel to destroy both parts in detail.

Southern people know this full well, and will only accept

the alliance of England in order to get arms and manufactures in exchange for their cotton. The Southern Confederacy will accept no other mediation, because she knows full well that in *Old* England her slaves and slavery will receive no more encouragement than in *New* England.

France certainly does not need our cotton enough to disturb her equilibrium, and her mediation would be entitled to a more respectful consideration than on the part of her present ally. But I feel assured the French will not encourage rebellion and secession anywhere as a political doctrine. Certainly all the German states must be our ardent friends; and, in case of European intervention, they could not be kept down.

With great respect, your obedient servant,
W. T. SHERMAN, *Major-General.*

HEADQUARTERS FIFTH DIVISION,
MEMPHIS, TENNESSEE, *August* 26, 1862.

Major-General GRANT, *Corinth, Mississippi.*

SIR: In pursuance of your request that I should keep you advised of matters of interest here, in addition to the purely official matters, I now write.

I dispatched promptly the thirteen companies of cavalry, nine of Fourth Illinois, and four of Eleventh Illinois, to their respective destinations, punctually on the 23d instant, although the order was only received on the 22d. I received at the same time, from Colonel Dickey, the notice that the bridge over Hatchie was burned, and therefore I prescribed their order of march *via* Bolivar. They started at 12 M. of the 23d, and I have no news of them since. None of the cavalry ordered to me is yet heard from.

The guerrillas have destroyed several bridges over Wolf Creek; one at Raleigh, on the road by which I had prescribed trade and travel to and from the city. I have a strong guard at the lower bridge over Wolf River, by which we can reach the country to the north of that stream; but, as the Confederates have burned their own bridges, I will hold them to my order, and allow no trade over any other road than the one prescribed, using the lower or Randolph road for our own convenience. I am still satisfied there is no large force of rebels anywhere in the neighborhood. All the navy gunboats are below except the St. Louis, which lies off the city. When Commodore Davis passes down from Cairo, I will try to see him, and get him to exchange the St. Louis for a fleeter boat not iron-clad; one that can move up and down the river, to break up ferry-boats and canoes, and to prevent all passing across the river. Of course, in spite of all our efforts, smuggling is carried on. We occasionally make hauls of clothing, gold-lace, buttons, etc., but I am satisfied that salt and arms are got to the interior somehow. I have addressed the Board of Trade a letter on this point, which will enable us to control it better.

You may have been troubled at hearing reports of drunkenness here. There was some after pay-day, but generally all is as quiet and orderly as possible. I traverse the city every day and night, and assert that Memphis is and has been as orderly a city as St. Louis, Cincinnati, or New York.

Before the city authorities undertook to license saloons, there was as much whiskey here as now, and it would take all my command as customhouse inspectors, to break open all the parcels and packages containing liquor. I can destroy all groggeries and shops where soldiers get liquor just as we would in St. Louis.

The newspapers are accusing me of cruelty to the sick; as base a charge as was ever made. I would not let the Sanitary Committee carry off a boat-load of sick, because I have no right to. We have good hospitals here, and plenty of them. Our regimental hospitals are in the camps of the men, and the sick do much better there than in the general hospitals; so say my division surgeon and the regimental surgeons. The civilian doctors would, if permitted, take away our entire command. General Curtis sends his sick up here, but usually no nurses; and it is not right that nurses should be taken from my command for his sick. I think that, when we are endeavoring to raise soldiers and to instruct them, it is bad policy to keep them at hospitals as attendants and nurses.

I send you Dr. Derby's acknowledgment that he gave the leave of absence of which he was charged. I have placed him in arrest, in obedience to General Halleck's orders, but he remains in charge of the Overton Hospital, which is not full of patients.

The State Hospital also is not full, and I cannot imagine what Dr. Derby wants with the Female Academy on Vance Street. I will see him again, and now that he is the chief at Overton Hospital, I think he will not want the academy. Still, if he does, under your orders I will cause it to be vacated by the children and Sisters of Mercy. They have just advertised for more scholars, and will be sadly disappointed. If, however, this building or any other be needed for a hospital, it must be taken; but really, in my heart, I do not see what possible chance there is, under present circumstances, of filling with patients the two large hospitals now in use, besides the one asked for. I may, however, be mistaken in the particular building asked for by Dr. Derby, and will go myself to see.

The fort is progressing well, Captain Jenney having arrived. Sixteen heavy guns are received, with a large amount of shot and shell, but the platforms are not yet ready; still, if occasion should arise for dispatch, I can put a larger force to work. Captain Prime, when here, advised that the work should proceed regularly under the proper engineer officers and laborers.

> I am, etc.,
> W. T. SHERMAN, *Major-General commanding.*

Satisfied that, in the progress of the war, Memphis would become an important depot, I pushed forward the construction of Fort Pickering, kept most of the troops in camps back of the city, and my own headquarters remained in tents on the edge of the city, near Mr. Moon's house, until, on the approach of winter, Mrs. Sherman came down with the children to visit me, when I took a house nearer the fort.

About the 17th of November I received an order from General Grant, dated—

LAGRANGE, *November* 15, 1862.

Meet me at Columbus, Kentucky, on Thursday next. If you have a good map of the country south of you, take it up with you.

> U. S. GRANT, *Major-General.*

I started forthwith by boat, and met General Grant, who had reached Columbus by the railroad from Jackson, Tennessee. He explained to me that he proposed to move against Pemberton, then intrenched on a line behind the Tallahatchie River below Holly Springs; that he would move on Holly Springs and Abberville, from Grand Junction; that McPherson, with the troops at Corinth, would aim to make junction with him at Holly Springs; and that he wanted me to leave in Memphis a proper garrison, and to aim for the Tallahatchie, so as to come up on his right by a certain date. He further said that his ultimate object was to capture Vicksburg, to open the navigation of the Mississippi River, and that General Halleck had authorized him to call on the troops in the Department of Arkansas, then commanded by General S. R. Curtis, for coöperation. I suggested to him that if he would request General Curtis to send an expedition from some point on the Mississippi near Helena, then held in force, toward Grenada, to the rear of Pemberton, it would alarm him for the safety of his communications, and would assist us materially in the proposed attack on his front. He authorized me to send to the commanding officer at Helena a request to that effect, and, as soon as I reached Memphis, I dispatched my aide, Major McCoy, to Helena, who returned, bringing me a letter from General Frederick Steele, who had just reached Helena with Osterhaus's division, and who was temporarily in command, General Curtis having gone to St. Louis. This letter contained the assurance that he "would send from Friar's Point a large force under Brigadier-General A. P. Hovey in the direction of Grenada, aiming to reach the Tallahatchie at Charleston, on the next Monday, Tuesday, or Wednesday (December 1st) at furthest." My command was appointed to start on Wednesday, November 24th, and meantime Major-General S. A. Hurlbut, having reported for duty, was assigned to the command of Memphis, with four regiments of infantry, one battery of artillery, two companies of Thielman's cavalry and the certain prospect of soon receiving a number of new regiments, known to be *en route*.

I marched out of Memphis punctually with three small divisions, taking different roads till we approached the Tallahatchie, when we converged on Wyatt to cross the river, there a bold, deep stream, with a newly-constructed fort behind. I had Grierson's Sixth Illinois Cavalry with me, and with it opened communication with General Grant when we were abreast of Holly Springs. We reached Wyatt on the 2d day of

December without the least opposition, and there learned that Pemberton's whole army had fallen back to the Yalabusha, near Grenada, in a great measure by reason of the exaggerated reports concerning the Helena force, which had reached Charleston; and some of General Hovey's cavalry, under General [Cadwallader C.] Washburn, having struck the railroad in the neighborhood of Coffeeville, naturally alarmed General Pemberton for the safety of his communications, and made him let go his Tallahatchie line with all the forts which he had built at great cost in labor. We had to build a bridge at Wyatt, which consumed a couple of days, and on the the 5th of December my whole command was at College Hill, ten miles from Oxford, whence I reported to General Grant in Oxford.

On the 8th I received the following letter:

OXFORD, MISSISSIPPI, *December* 8, 1862.—*Morning.*

General SHERMAN, *College Hill.*

DEAR GENERAL: The following is a copy of dispatch just received from Washington:

WASHINGTON, *December* 7, 1862.—12 M.

General GRANT:

The capture of Grenada may change our plans in regard to Vicksburg. You will move your troops as you may deem best to accomplish the great object in view. You will retain, till further orders, all troops of General Curtis now in your department. Telegraph to General [Robert] Allen in St. Louis for all steamboats you may require. Ask Porter to coöperate. Telegraph what are your present plans.

H. W. HALLECK, *General-in-Chief.*

I wish you would come over this evening and stay tonight, or come in the morning. I would like to talk with you about this matter. My notion is to send two divisions back to Memphis, and fix upon a day when they should effect a landing, and press from here with this command at the proper time to coöperate. If I do not do this I will move our present force to Grenada, including Steele's, repairing road as we proceed, and establish a depot of provisions there. When a good ready is had, to move immediately on

Jackson, Mississippi, cutting loose from the road. Of the two plans I look most favorably on the former.

Come over and we will talk this matter over.

Yours truly,

U. S. GRANT, *Major-General.*

I repaired at once to Oxford, and found General Grant in a large house with all his staff, and we discussed every possible chance. He explained to me that large reënforcements had been promised, which would reach Memphis very soon, if not already there; that the entire gunboat fleet, then under the command of Admiral D[avid] D. Porter, would coöperate; that we could count on a full division from the troops at Helena; and he believed that, by a prompt movement, I could make a lodgment up the Yazoo and capture Vicksburg from the rear; that its garrison was small, and he, at Oxford, would so handle his troops as to hold Pemberton away from Vicksburg. I also understood that, if Pemberton should retreat south, he would follow him up, and would expect to find me at the Yazoo River, if not inside Vicksburg. I confess, at that moment I did not dream that General McClernand, or anybody else, was scheming for the mere honor of capturing Vicksburg. We knew at the time that General Butler had been reënforced by General Banks at New Orleans, and the latter was supposed to be working his way up-stream from New Orleans, while we were working down. That day General Grant dispatched to General Halleck, in Washington, as follows:

OXFORD, *December* 8, 1862.

Major-General H. W. HALLECK, *Washington, D. C.:*

General Sherman will command the expedition down the Mississippi. He will have a force of about forty thousand men; will land above Vicksburg (up the Yazoo, if practicable), and cut the Mississippi Central road and the road running east from Vicksburg, where they cross Black River. I will coöperate from here, my movements depending on those of the enemy. With the large cavalry force now at my command, I will be able to have them show themselves at different points on the Tallahatchie and Yalabusha; and, when an opportunity occurs, make a real attack. After cutting the two roads, General Sherman's movements to secure the end desired will necessarily be left to his judgment.

I will occupy this road to Coffeeville.

U. S. GRANT, *Major-General.*

I was shown this dispatch before it was sent, and afterward the general drew up for me the following letter of instructions in his own handwriting, which I now possess:

HEADQUARTERS THIRTEENTH ARMY CORPS,
DEPARTMENT OF THE TENNESSEE, OXFORD, MISSISSIPPI,
December 8, 1862.

Major-General W. T. SHERMAN, *commanding Right Wing Army in the Field, present.*

GENERAL: You will proceed with as little delay as practicable to Memphis, Tennessee, taking with you one division of your present command. On your arrival at Memphis you will assume command of all the troops there, and that portion of General Curtis's forces at present east of the Mississippi River, and organize them into brigades and divisions in your own way.

As soon as possible move with them down the river to the vicinity of Vicksburg, and, with the coöperation of the gunboat fleet under command of Flag-Officer Porter, proceed to the reduction of that place in such manner as circumstances and your own judgment may dictate.

The amount of rations, forage, land transportation, etc., necessary to take, will be left entirely to yourself.

The quartermaster in St. Louis will be instructed to send you transportation for thirty thousand men. Should you still find yourself deficient, your quartermaster will be authorized to make up the deficiency from such transports as may come into the port of Memphis.

On arriving in Memphis put yourself in communication with Admiral Porter, and arrange with him for his coöperation.

Inform me at the earliest practicable day of the time when you will embark, and such plans as may then be matured. I will hold the forces here in readiness to coöperate with you in such manner as the movements of the enemy may make necessary.

Leave the District of Memphis in the command of an efficient officer and with a garrison of four regiments of infantry, the siege-guns, and what ever cavalry force may be there.

One regiment of infantry and at least a section of artillery will also be left at Friar's Point or Delta, to protect the stores of the cavalry post that will be left there.

Yours truly,

U. S. GRANT, *Major-General.*

I also insert here another letter, dated the 14th instant, sent afterward to me at Memphis, which completes all instructions received by me governing the first movement against Vicksburg:

HEADQUARTERS DEPARTMENT OF THE TENNESSEE, OXFORD, MISSISSIPPI, *December* 14, 1862.

Major-General SHERMAN, *commanding, etc., Memphis, Tennessee:*

I have not had one word from Grierson since he left, and am getting uneasy about him. I hope General [Willis A.] Gorman will give you no difficulty about retaining the troops on this side the river, and Steele to command them. The twenty-one thousand men you have, with the twelve thousand from Helena, will make a good force. The enemy are as yet on the Yalabusha. I am pushing down on them slowly, but so as to keep up the impression of a continuous move. I feel particularly anxious to have the Helena cavalry on this side of the river; if not now, at least after you start. If Gorman will send them, instruct them where to go and how to communicate with me. My headquarters will probably be in Coffeeville one week hence. In the mean time I will order transportation, etc. . . . It would be well if you could have two or three small boats suitable for navigating the Yazoo. It may become necessary for me to look to that base for supplies before we get through. . . .

U. S. GRANT, *Major-General.*

When we rode to Oxford from College Hill, there happened a little circumstance which seems worthy of record. While General Van Dorn had his headquarters in Holly Springs, viz., in October, 1862, he was very short of the comforts and luxuries of life, and resorted to every possible device to draw from the abundant supplies in Memphis. He had no difficulty whatever in getting spies into the town for information, but he had trouble in getting bulky supplies out through our guards, though sometimes I connived at his supplies of cigars, liquors, boots, gloves, etc., for his individual use; but medicines and large supplies of all kinds were confiscated, if attempted to be passed out. As we rode that morning toward Oxford, I observed in a farmer's barn-yard a wagon that looked like a city furniture-wagon with springs. We were always short of wagons, so I called the attention of the quartermaster, Colonel J. Condit Smith, saying, "There is a good wagon; go for it." He dropped out of the retinue with an orderly, and after we had ridden a mile or so he overtook us, and I asked him, "What luck?" He answered, "All right; I have secured that wagon, and I also got another," and explained that he had gone to the farmer's house to inquire about the furniture-wagon, when the farmer said it did not belong to him, but to some party in Memphis, adding that in his barn was another belonging to the same party. They went to the barn, and there found a handsome city hearse, with pall and plumes. The farmer said they had had a big funeral out of Memphis, but when it reached his house, the coffin was found to contain a fine assortment of medicines for the use of Van Dorn's army. Thus under the pretense of a first-class funeral, they had carried through our guards the very things we had tried to prevent. It was a good trick, but diminished our respect for such pageants afterward.

As soon as I was in possession of General Grant's instructions of December 8th, with a further request that I should dispatch Colonel Grierson, with his cavalry, across by land to Helena, to notify General Steele of the general plan, I returned to College Hill, selected the division of Brigadier-General Morgan L. Smith to return with me to Memphis; started Grierson on his errand to Helena, and ordered Generals [James W.] Denver and [Jacob G.] Lauman to report to General Grant for further orders. We started back by the most direct route, reached Memphis by noon of December 12th, and began immediately the preparations for the Vicksburg movement. There I found two irregular divisions which had arrived at Memphis in my absence, commanded respectively by Brigadier-General A. J. Smith and Brigadier-General George W. Morgan. These were designated the First and Third Divisions, leaving the Second Division of Morgan L. Smith to retain its original name and number.

I also sent orders, in the name of General Grant, to General Gorman, who meantime had replaced General Steele in command of Helena, in lieu of the troops which had been east of the Mississippi and had returned, to make up a strong division to report to me on my way down. This division was accordingly organized, and was commanded by Brigadier-General Frederick Steele, constituting my Fourth Division.

Meantime a large fleet of steamboats was assembling from St. Louis and Cairo, and Admiral Porter dropped down to Memphis with his whole gunboat fleet, ready to coöperate in the movement. The preparations were necessarily hasty in the extreme, but this was the essence of the whole plan, viz., to reach Vicksburg as it were by surprise, while General Grant held in check Pemberton's army about Grenada, leaving me to contend only with the smaller garrison of Vicksburg and its well-known strong batteries and defenses. On the 19th the Memphis troops were embarked, and steamed down to Helena, where on the 21st General Steele's division was also embarked.

At the same time were communicated the following instructions:

HEADQUARTERS RIGHT WING, THIRTEENTH ARMY CORPS, }
    FOREST QUEEN, *December* 23, 1862. }

To Commanders of Divisions, Generals F. STEELE, GEORGE W. MORGAN, A. J. SMITH, *and* M. L. SMITH:

With this I hand to each of you a copy of a map, compiled from the best sources, and which in the main is correct. It is the same used by Admiral Porter and myself. Complete military success can only be accomplished by united action on some *general plan*, embracing usually a large district of country. In the present instance, our object is to secure the navigation of the Mississippi River and its main branches, and to hold them as military channels of communication and for commercial purposes. The river, above Vicksburk, has been gained by conquering the country to its rear, rendering its possession by our enemy useless and unsafe to him, and of great value to us. But the enemy still holds the river from Vicksburg to Baton Rouge, navigating it with his boats, and the possession of it enables him to connect his communications and routes of supply, east and west. To deprive him of this will be a severe blow, and, if done effectually, will be of great advantage to us, and probably the most decisive act of the war. To accomplish this important result we are to act our part—an important one of the great *whole*. General Banks, with a large force, has reënforced General Butler in Louisiana, and from that quarter an expedition, by water and land, is coming northward. General Grant, with the Thirteenth Army Corps, of which we compose the right wing, is moving southward. The naval squadron (Admiral Porter) is operating with his gunboat fleet by water, each in perfect harmony with the other.

General Grant's left and centre were at last accounts approaching the Yalabusha, near Grenada, and the railroad to his rear, by which he drew his supplies, was reported to be seriously damaged. This may disconcert him somewhat, but only makes more important our line of operations. At the Yalabusha General Grant may encounter the army of General Pemberton, the same which refused him *battle* on the line of the Tallahatchie, which was strongly fortified; but, as he will not have time to fortify it, he will hardly stand there; and, in that event, General Grant will immediately advance down the high ridge between the Big Black and Yazoo, and will expect to meet us on the Yazoo and receive from us the supplies which he needs, and which he knows we carry along. Parts of this general plan are to coöperate with the naval squadron in the reduction of Vicksburg; to secure possession of the land lying between the Yazoo and Big Black; and to act in concert with General Grant against Pemberton's forces, supposed to have Jackson, Mississippi, as a point of concentration. Vicksburg is doubtless very strongly fortified, both against the river and land approaches. Already the gunboats have secured the Yazoo up for twenty-three miles, to a fort on the Yazoo at Haines's Bluff, giving us a choice for a landing-place at some point up the Yazoo below this fort, or on the island which lies between Vicksburg and the present mouth of the Yazoo.

But, before any actual collision with the enemy, I purpose, after our whole *land-force* is rendezvoused at Gaines's Landing, Arkansas, to proceed in order to Milliken's Bend, and there dispatch a brigade, without wagons or any incumbrances whatever, to the Vicksburg & Shreveport Railroad, to destroy that effectually, and to cut off that fruitful avenue of supply; then to proceed to the mouth of the Yazoo, and, after possessing ourselves of the latest and most authentic information from naval officers now there, to land our whole force on the Mississippi side, and then to reach the point where the Vicksburg & Jackson Railroad crosses the Big Black; after which to attack Vicksburg *by land,* while the gunboats assail it by water. It may be necessary (looking to Grant's approach), before attacking Vicksburg, to reduce the battery at *Haines's Bluff* first, so as to enable some of the lighter gunboats and transports to ascend the Yazoo and communicate with General Grant. The detailed manner of accomplishing all these results will be communicated in due season, and these general points are only made known at this time, that commanders may study the maps, and also that in the event of non-receipt of orders all may act in perfect concert by following the general movement, unless specially detached.

You all now have the same map, so that no mistakes or confusion need result from different names of localities. All possible preparations as to wagons, provisions, axes, and intrenching-tools, should be made in advance, so that when we do land there will be no want of them. When we begin to act on shore, we must do the work quickly and effectually. The gunboats under Admiral Porter will do their full share, and I feel every assurance that the army will not fall short in its work.

Division commanders may read this to regimental commanders, and furnish brigade commanders a copy. They should also cause as many copies of the map to be made on the same scale as possible, being very careful in copying the names.

The points marked (Allan's and Mount Albans) are evidently strategical points that will figure in our future operations, and these positions should be well studied.

I am, with great respect, your obedient servant,

W. T. SHERMAN, *Major-General*

The Mississippi boats were admirably calculated for handling troops, horses, guns, stores, etc., easy of embarkation and disembarkation, and supplies of all kinds were abundant, except fuel. For this we had to rely on wood, but most of the woodyards, so common on the river before the war, had been exhausted, so that we had to use fence-rails, old dead timber, the logs of houses, etc. Having abundance of men and plenty of axes, each boat could daily procure a supply.

In proceeding down the river, one or more of Admiral Porter's gunboats took the lead; others were distributed throughout the column, and some brought up the rear. We manœuvred by divisions and brigades when in motion, and it was a magnificent sight as we thus steamed down the river. What few inhabitants remained at the plantations on the river-bank were unfriendly, except the slaves; some few guerrilla-parties infested the banks, but did not dare to molest so strong a force as I then commanded.

We reached Milliken's Bend on Christmas-day, when I detached one brigade ([Stephen G.] Burbridge's), of A. J. Smith's division, to the southwest, to break up the railroad leading from Vicksburg toward Shreveport, Louisiana. Leaving A. J. Smith's division there to await the return of Burbridge, the remaining three divisions proceeded, on the 26th, to the mouth of the Yazoo, and up that river to Johnson's plantation, thirteen miles, and there disembarked—Steele's division above the mouth of Chickasaw Bayou, Morgan's division near the house of Johnson (which had been burned by the gunboats on a former occasion), and M. L. Smith's just below. A. J. Smith's division arrived the next night, and disembarked below that of M. L. Smith. The place of our disembarkation was in fact an island, separated from the high bluff known as Walnut Hills, on which the town of Vicksburg stands, by a broad and shallow bayou—evidently an old channel of the Yazoo. On our right was another wide bayou, known as Old River; and on the left still another, much narrower, but too deep to be forded, known as Chickasaw

Bayou. All the island was densely wooded, except Johnson's plantation, immediately on the bank of the Yazoo, and a series of old cotton-fields along Chickasaw Bayou. There was a road from Johnson's plantation directly to Vicksburg, but it crossed numerous bayous and deep swamps by bridges, which had been destroyed; and this road debouched on level ground at the foot of the Vicksburg bluff, opposite strong forts, well prepared and defended by heavy artillery. On this road I directed General A. J. Smith's division, not so much by way of a direct attack as a diversion and threat.

Morgan was to move to his left, to reach Chickasaw Bayou, and to follow it toward the bluff, about four miles above A. J. Smith. Steele was on Morgan's left, across Chickasaw Bayou, and M. L. Smith on Morgan's right. We met light resistance at all points, but skirmished, on the 27th, up to the main bayou, that separated our position from the bluffs of Vicksburg, which were found to be strong by nature and by art, and seemingly well defended. On reconnoitring the front in person, during the 27th and 28th, I became satisfied that General A. J. Smith could not cross the intervening obstacles under the heavy fire of the forts immediately in his front, and that the main bayou was impassable, except at two points— one near the head of Chickasaw Bayou, in front of Morgan, and the other about a mile lower down, in front of M. L. Smith's division.

During the general reconnoissance of the 28th General Morgan L. Smith received a severe and dangerous wound in his hip, which completely disabled him and compelled him to go to his steamboat, leaving the command of his division to Brigadier-General D. Stuart; but I drew a part of General A. J. Smith's division, and that general himself, to the point selected for passing the bayou, and committed that special task to his management.

General Steele reported that it was physically impossible to reach the bluffs from his position, so I ordered him to leave but a show of force there, and to return to the west side of Chickasaw Bayou in support of General Morgan's left. He had to countermarch and use the steamboats in the Yazoo to get on the firm ground on our side of the Chickasaw.

On the morning of December 29th all the troops were ready and in position. The first step was to make a lodgment on the foot-hills and bluffs abreast of our position, while diversions were made by the navy toward Haines's Bluff, and by the first division directly toward Vicksburg. I estimated the enemy's forces, then strung from Vicksburg to Haines's Bluff, at fifteen thousand men, commanded by the rebel Generals Martin Luther Smith and Stephen D. Lee. Aiming to reach firm ground beyond this bayou, and to leave as little time for our enemy to reënforce as possible, I determined to make a show of attack along the whole front, but to break across the bayou at the two points named, and gave general orders accordingly. I pointed out to General Morgan the place where he could pass the bayou, and he answered, "General, in ten minutes after you give the signal I'll be on those hills." He was to lead his division in person, and was to be supported by Steele's division. The front was very narrow, and immediately opposite, at the base of the hills about three hundred yards from the bayou, was a rebel battery, supported by an infantry force posted on the spurs of the hill behind. To draw attention from this, the real point of attack, I gave instructions to commence the attack at the flanks.

I went in person about a mile to the right rear of Morgan's position, at a place convenient to receive reports from all other parts of the line; and about noon of December 29th gave the orders and signal for the main attack. A heavy artillery-fire opened along our whole line, and was replied to by the rebel batteries, and soon the infantry-fire opened heavily, especially on A. J. Smith's front, and in front of General George W. Morgan. One brigade (De Courcey's[?]) of Morgan's troops crossed the bayou safely, but took to cover behind the bank, and could not be moved forward. Frank Blair's brigade, of Steele's division, in support, also crossed the bayou, passed over the space of level ground to the foot of the hills; but, being unsupported by Morgan, and meeting a very severe cross-fire of artillery, was staggered and gradually fell back, leaving about five hundred men behind, wounded and prisoners; among them Colonel Thomas Fletcher, afterward Governor of Missouri. [John M.] Thayer's brigade, of Steele's division, took a wrong direction, and did not cross the bayou at all; nor did General Morgan cross in person. This attack failed; and I have always felt that it was due to the failure of General G. W. Morgan to obey his orders, or to fulfill his promise made in person. Had he used with skill and boldness one of his brigades, in addition to that of Blair's, he could have made a lodgment on the bluff, which would have opened the door for our whole force to follow. Meantime the Sixth Missouri Infantry, at heavy loss, had also crossed the bayou at the narrow passage lower down, but could not ascend the steep bank; right over their heads was a rebel battery, whose fire was in a measure kept down by our sharp-shooters (Thirteenth United States Infantry) posted behind logs, stumps, and trees, on our side of the bayou.

The men of the Sixth Missouri actually scooped out with their hands caves in the bank, which sheltered them against the fire of the enemy, who, right over their heads, held their muskets outside the parapet vertically, and fired down. So critical was the position, that we could not recall the men till after dark, and then one at a time. Our loss had been pretty heavy, and we had accomplished nothing, and had inflicted little loss on our enemy. At first I intended to renew the assault, but soon became satisfied that, the enemy's attention having been drawn to the only two practicable points, it would prove too costly, and accordingly resolved to look elsewhere for a point below Haines's Bluff, or Blake's plantation. That night I conferred with Admiral Porter, who undertook to cover the landing; and the next day (December 30th) the boats were all selected, but so alarmed were the captains and pilots, that we had to place sentinels with loaded muskets to insure their remaining at their posts. Under cover of night, Steele's division, and one brigade of Stuart's, were drawn out of line, and quietly embarked on steamboats in the Yazoo River. The night of December 30th was appointed for this force, under the command of General Fred Steele, to proceed up the Yazoo just below Haines's Bluff, there to disembark about daylight, and make a dash for the hills. Meantime we had strengthened our positions near Chickasaw Bayou, had all our guns in good position with parapets, and had every thing ready to renew our attack as soon as we heard the sound of battle above.

At midnight I left Admiral Porter on his gunboat; he had his fleet ready and the night was propitious. I rode back to camp and gave orders for all to be ready by daybreak; but when daylight came I received a note from General Steele reporting that, before his boats had got up steam, the fog had settled down on the river so thick and impenetrable, that it was simply impossible to move; so the attempt had to be abandoned. The rain, too, began to fall, and the trees bore water-marks ten feet above our heads, so that I became convinced that the part of wisdom was to withdraw. I ordered the stores which had been landed to be reëmbarked on the boats, and preparations made for all the troops to regain their proper boats during the night of the 1st of January, 1863. From our camps at Chickasaw we could hear the whistles of the trains arriving in Vicksburg, could see batallions of men marching up toward Haines's Bluff, and taking post at all points in our front. I was more than convinced that heavy reënforcements were coming to Vicksburg; whether from Pemberton at Grenada, Bragg in Tennessee, or from other sources, I could not tell; but at no point did the enemy assume the offensive; and when we drew off our rear-guard, on the morning of the 2d, they simply followed up the movement, timidly. Up to that moment I had not heard a word from General Grant since leaving Memphis; and most assuredly I had listened for days for the sound of his guns in the direction of Yazoo City. On the morning of January 2d, all my command were again afloat in their proper steamboats, when Admiral Porter told me that General McClernand had arrived at the mouth of the Yazoo in the steamboat Tigress, and that it was rumored he had come down to supersede me. Leaving my whole force where it was, I ran down to the mouth of the Yazoo in a small tug-boat, and there found General McClernand, with orders from the War Department to command the expeditionary force on the Mississippi River. I explained what had been done, and what was the actual state of facts; that the heavy reënforcements pouring into Vicksburg must be Pemberton's army, and that General Grant must be near at hand. He informed me that General Grant was not coming at all; that his depot at Holly Springs had been captured by Van Dorn, and that he had drawn back from Coffeeville and Oxford to Holly Springs and Lagrange; and, further, that Quimby's division of Grant's army was actually at Memphis for stores when he passed down. This, then, fully explained how Vicksburg was being reënforced. I saw that any attempt on the place from the Yazoo was hopeless; and, with General

McClernand's full approval, we all came out of the Yazoo, and on the 3rd of January rendezvoused at Milliken's Bend, about ten miles above. On the 4th General McClernand issued his General Order No. 1, assuming command of the Army of the Mississippi, divided into two corps; the first to be commanded by General Morgan, composed of his own and A. J. Smith's divisions; and the second, composed of Steele's and Stuart's divisions, to be commanded by me. Up to that time the army had been styled the right wing of (General Grant's) Thirteenth Corps, and numbered about thirty thousand men. The aggregate loss during the time of my command, mostly on the 29th of December, was one hundred and seventy-five killed, nine hundred and thirty wounded, and seven hundred and forty-three prisoners. According to [Adam] Badeau, the rebels lost sixty-three killed, one hundred and thirty-four wounded, and ten prisoners.

It afterward transpired that Van Dorn had captured Holly Springs on the 20th of December, and that General Grant fell back very soon after. General Pemberton, who had telegraphic and railroad communciation with Vicksburg, was therefore at perfect liberty to reënforce the place with a garrison equal, if not superior, to my command. The rebels held high, commanding ground, and could see every movement of our men and boats, so that the only possible hope of success consisted in celerity and surprise, and in General Grant's holding all of Pemberton's army hard pressed meantime. General Grant was perfectly aware of this, and had sent me word of the change, but it did not reach me in time; indeed, I was not aware of it until after my assault of December 29th, and until the news was brought me by General McClernand as related. General McClernand was appointed to this command by President Lincoln in person, who had no knowledge of what was then going on down the river. Still, my relief, on the heels of a failure, raised the usual cry, at the North, of "repulse, failure, and bungling." There was no bungling on my part, for I never worked harder or with more intensity of purpose in my life; and General Grant, long after, in his report of the operations of the siege of Vicksburg, gave us all full credit for the skill of the movement, and described the almost impregnable nature of the ground; and, although in all official reports I assumed the whole responsibility, I have ever felt that had General Morgan promptly and skillfully sustained the lead of Frank Blair's brigade on that day, we should have broken the rebel line, and effected a lodgment on the hills behind Vicksburg. General Frank Blair was outspoken and indignant against Generals Morgan and De Courcey at the time, and always abused me for assuming the whole blame. But, had we succeeded, we might have found ourselves in a worse trap, when General Pemberton was at full liberty to turn his whole force against us.

While I was engaged at Chickasaw Bayou, Admiral Porter was equally busy in the Yazoo River, threatening the enemy's batteries at Haines's and Snyder's Bluffs above. In a sharp engagement he lost one of his best officers, in the person of Captain Gwin, United States Navy, who, though on board an iron-clad, insisted on keeping his post on deck, where he was struck in the breast by a round shot, which carried away the muscle, and contused the lung within, from which he died a few days after. We of the army deplored his loss quite as much as his fellows of the navy, for he had been intimately associated with us in our previous operations on the Tennessee River, at Shiloh and above, and we had come to regard him as one of us.

On the 4th of January, 1863, our fleet of transports was collected at Milliken's Bend, about ten miles above the mouth of the Yazoo, Admiral Porter remaining with his gunboats at the Yazoo. General John A. McClernand was in chief command, General George W. Morgan commanded the First Corps and I the Second Corps of the Army of the Mississippi.

I had learned that a small steamboat, the Blue Wing, with a mail, towing coal-barges and loaded with ammunition, had left Memphis for the Yazoo, about the 20th of December, had been captured by a rebel boat which had come out of the Arkansas River, and had been carried up that river to Fort Hindman. We had reports from this fort, usually called the "Post of Arkansas," about forty miles above the mouth, that it was held by about five thousand rebels, was an inclosed work, commanding the passage of the river, but supposed to be easy of capture from the rear. At that time I don't think General McClernand had any definite views or plans of action. If so, he did not impart them to me. He spoke in general terms of opening the navigation of the Mississippi, "cutting his way to the sea," etc., etc., but the *modus operandi* was not so clear. Knowing full well that we could not carry on operations against Vicksburg as long as the rebels held the Post of Arkansas, whence to attack our boats coming and going without convoy, I visited him on his boat, the Tigress, took with me a boy who had been on the Blue Wing, and had escaped, and asked leave to go up the Arkansas, to clear out the Post. He made various objections, but consented to go with me to see Admiral Porter about it. We got up steam in the Forest Queen, during the night of January 4th, stopped at the Tigress, took General McClernand on board, and proceeded down the river by night to the admiral's boat, the Black Hawk, lying in the mouth of the Yazoo. It must have been near midnight, and Admiral Porter was in *déshabille*. We were seated in his cabin and I explained my views about Arkansas Post, and asked his coöperation. He said that he was short of coal, and could not use wood in his iron-clad boats. Of these I asked for two, to be commanded by Captain Shirk or Phelps, or some officer of my acquaintance. At that moment, poor Gwin lay on his bed, in a state-room close by, dying from the effect of the cannon shot received at Haines's Bluff, as before described. Porter's manner to McClernand was so curt that I invited him out into a forward-cabin where he had his charts, and asked him what he meant by it. He said that "he did not like him"; that in Washington, before coming West, he had been introduced to him by President Lincoln, and he had taken a strong prejudice against him. I begged him, for the sake of harmony, to waive that, which he promised to do. Returning to the cabin, the conversation was resumed, and, on our offering to tow his gunboats up the river to save coal, and on renewing the request for Shirk to command the detachment, Porter said, "Suppose I go along myself?" I answered, if he would do so, it would insure the success of the enterprise. At that time I supposed General McClernand would send me on this business, but he concluded to go himself, and to take his whole force. Orders were at once issued for the troops not to disembark at Milliken's Bend, but to remain as they were on board the transports. My two divisions were commanded—the First, by Brigadier-General Frederick Steele, with three brigades, commanded by Brigadier-Generals F. P. Blair, A. E. Hovey, and J. M.

Thayer; the Second, by Brigadier-General D. Stuart, with two brigades, commanded by Colonels G. A. Smith and T. Kilby Smith.

The whole army, embarked on steamboats convoyed by the gunboats, of which three were iron-clads, proceeded up the Mississippi River to the mouth of White River, which we reached January 8th. On the next day we continued up White River to the "Cut-off"; through this to the Arkansas, and up the Arkansas to Notrib's farm, just below Fort Hindman. Early the next morning we disembarked. Stuart's division, moving up the river along the bank, soon encountered a force of the enemy intrenched behind a line of earthworks, extending from the river across to the swamp. I took Steele's division, marching by the flank by a road through the swamp to the firm ground behind, and was moving up to get to the rear of Fort Hindman, when General McClernand overtook me, with the report that the rebels had abandoned their first position, and had fallen back into the fort. By his orders, we countermarched, recrossed the swamp, and hurried forward to overtake Stuart, marching for Fort Hindman. The first line of the rebels was about four miles below Fort Hindman, and the intervening space was densely wooded and obscure, with the exception of some old fields back of and close to the fort. During the night, which was a bright moonlight one, we reconnoitred close up, and found a large number of huts which had been abandoned, and the whole rebel force had fallen back into and about the fort. Personally I crept up to a stump so close that I could hear the enemy hard at work, pulling down houses, cutting with axes, and building intrenchments. I could almost hear their words, and I was thus listening when, about 4 A. M. the bugler in the rebel camp sounded as pretty a reveille as I ever listened to.

When daylight broke it revealed to us a new line of parapet straight across the peninsula, connecting Fort Hindman, on the Arkansas River bank, with the impassable swamp about a mile to its left or rear. This peninsula was divided into two nearly equal parts by a road. My command had the ground to the right of the road, and Morgan's corps that to the left. McClernand had his quarters still on the Tigress, back at Notrib's farm, but moved forward that morning (January 11th) to a place in the woods to our rear, where he had a man up a tree to observe and report the movements.

There was a general understanding with Admiral Porter that he was to attack the fort with his three iron-clad gunboats directly by its water-front, while we assaulted by land in the rear. About 10 A. M. I got a message from General McClernand, telling me where he could be found, and asking me what we were waiting for. I answered that we were then in close contact with the enemy, viz., about five or six hundred yards off; that the next movement must be a direct assault; that this should be simultaneous along the whole line; and that I was waiting to hear from the gunboats; asking him to notify Admiral Porter that we were all ready. In about half an hour I heard the clear ring of the navy-guns; the fire gradually increasing in rapidity and advancing toward the fort. I had distributed our field-guns, and, when I judged the time had come, I gave the orders to begin. The intervening ground between us and the enemy was a dead level, with the exception of on or two small gullies, and our men had no cover but the few standing trees and some logs on the ground. The troops advanced well under a heavy fire, once or twice falling to the ground for a sort of rest or pause. Every tree had its group of men, and behind each log was a crowd of sharp-shooters, who kept up so hot a fire that the rebel troops fired wild. The fire of the fort proper was kept busy by the gunboats and Morgan's corps, so that all my corps had to encounter was the direct fire from the newly-built parapet across the peninsula. This line had three sections of field-guns, that kept things pretty lively, and several round-shot came so near me that I realized that they were aimed at my staff; so I dismounted, and made them scatter.

As the gunboats got closer up I saw their flags actually over the parapet of Fort Hindman, and the rebel gunners scamper out of the embrasures and run down into the ditch behind. About the same time a man jumped up on the rebel parapet just where the road entered, waving a large white flag, and numerous smaller white rags appeared above the parapet along the whole line. I immediately ordered, "Cease firing!" and sent the same word down the line to General Steele, who had made similar progress on the right, following the border of the swamp. I ordered my aide, Colonel Dayton, to jump on his horse and ride straight up to the large white flag, and when his horse was on the parapet I followed with the rest of my staff. All firing had ceased, except an occasional shot away to the right, and one of the captains (Smith) of the Thirteenth Regulars was wounded after the display of the white flag. On entering the line, I saw that our muskets and guns had done good execution; for there was a horse-battery, and every horse lay dead in the traces. The fresh-made parapet had been knocked down in many places, and dead men lay around very thick. I inquired who commanded at that point, and a Colonel [James A.] Garland stepped up and said that he commanded that brigade. I ordered him to form his brigade, stack arms, hang the belts on the muskets, and stand waiting for orders. Stuart's division had been halted outside the parapet. I then sent Major Hammond down the rebel line to the right, with orders to stop Steele's division outside, and to have the other rebel brigade stack its arms in like manner, and to await further orders. I inquired of Colonel Garland who commanded in chief, and he said that General [Thomas J.] Churchill did, and that he was inside the fort. I then rode into the fort, which was well built, with good parapets, drawbridge, and ditch, and was an inclosed work of four bastions. I found it full of soldiers and sailors, its parapets toward the river well battered in, and Porter's gunboats in the river, close against the fort, with their bows on shore. I soon found General Churchill, in conversation with Admiral Porter and General A. J. Smith, and about this time my adjutant-general, Major J. H. Hammond, came and reported that General [James] Deshler, who commanded the rebel brigade facing and opposed to Steele, had refused to stack arms and surrender, on the ground that he had received no orders from his commanding general; that nothing separated this brigade from Steele's men except the light parapet, and that there might be trouble there at any moment. I advised General Churchill to send orders at once, because a single shot might bring the whole of Steele's division on Deshler's brigade, and I would not be responsible for the consequences; soon afterward, we both concluded to go in person. General Churchill had the horses of himself and staff in the ditch; they were brought in, and we rode together to where Garland was standing, and Churchill spoke to him in an angry tone, "Why did you display the white flag!" Garland replied, "I received orders to do so from one of your staff." Churchill denied giving such an order, and angry words passed between them. I stopped them, saying that it made little difference then, as they were in our power. We continued to ride down the line to its extreme point, where we found Deshler in person, and his troops were still standing to the parapet with their muskets in hand. Steele's men were on the outside. I asked Deshler: "What does this mean? You are a regular officer, and ought to know better." He answered, snappishly, that "he had received no orders to surrender"; when General Churchill said: "You see, sir, that we are in their power, and you may surrender." Deshler turned to his staff-officers and ordered them to repeat the command to "stack arms," etc., to the colonels of his brigade. I was on my horse, and he was on foot. Wishing to soften the blow of defeat, I spoke to him kindly, saying that I knew a family of Deshlers in Columbus, Ohio, and inquired if they were relations of his. He disclaimed any relation with people living north of the Ohio, in an offensive tone, and I think I gave him a piece of my mind that he did not relish. He was a West Point graduate, small but very handsome, and was afterward killed in battle. I never met him again.

Returning to the position where I had first entered the rebel line, I received orders from General McClernand, by one of his staff, to leave General A. J. Smith in charge of the fort and prisoners, and with my troops to remain outside. The officer explained that the general was then on the Tigress, which had moved up from below, to a point in the river just above the fort; and not understanding his orders, I concluded to go and see him in person. My troops were then in possession of two of the three brigades which composed the army opposed to us; and my troops were also in possession of all the ground of the peninsula outside the "fort proper" (Hindman). I found General McClernand on the Tigress, in high spirits. He said repeatedly: "Glorious! glorious! my star is ever in the ascendant!" He spoke complimentarily of the troops, but was extremely jealous of the navy. He said: "I'll make a splendid report"; "I had a man up a tree"; etc. I was very hungry and tired, and fear I did not appreciate the honors in reserve for us, and asked for something to eat and drink. He very kindly ordered something to be brought, and explained to me that by his "orders" he did not wish to interfere with the actual state of facts; that General A. J. Smith would occupy "Fort Hindman," which his troops had first entered, and I could hold the lines outside, and go on securing the prisoners and stores as I had begun. I returned to the position of Garland's brigade and gave the necessary orders for marching all the prisoners, disarmed, to a pocket formed by the river and two deep gullies just above the fort, by which time it had become quite dark. After dark another rebel regiment arrived from Pine Bluff, marched right in, and was also made prisoners. There seemed to be a good deal of feeling among the rebel officers against Garland, who asked leave to stay with me that night, to which I of course consented. Just outside the rebel parapet was a house which had been used for a hospital. I had a room cleaned out, and occupied it that night. A cavalry-soldier lent me his battered coffee-pot with some coffee and scraps of hard bread out of his nose-bag; Garland and I made some coffee, ate our bread together, and talked politics by the fire till quite late at night, when we lay down on straw that was saturated with the blood of dead or wounded men. The next day the prisoners were all collected on their boats, lists were made out, and orders given for their transportation to St. Louis, in charge of my aide, Major Sanger. We then proceeded to dismantle and level the forts, destroy or remove the stores, and we found in the magazine the very ammunition which had been sent for us in the Blue Wing, which was secured and afterward used in our twenty-pound Parrott guns.

On the 13th we reëmbarked; the whole expedition returned out of the river by the direct route down the Arkansas during a heavy snow-storm, and rendezvoused in the Mississippi, at Napoleon, at the mouth of the Arkansas. Here General Mc-Clernand told me he had received a letter from General Grant at Memphis, who disapproved of our movement up the Arkansas; but that communication was made before he had learned of our complete success. When informed of this, and of the promptness with which it had been executed, he could not but approve. We were then ordered back to Milliken's Bend, to await General Grant's arrival in person. We reached Milliken's Bend January 21st.

McClernand's report of the capture of Fort Hindman almost ignored the action of Porter's fleet altogether. This was unfair, for I know that the admiral led his fleet in person in the river-attack, and that his guns silenced those of Fort Hindman, and drove the gunners into the ditch.

The aggregate loss in my corps at Arkansas Post was five hundred and nineteen, viz., four officers and seventy-five men killed, thirty-four officers and four hundred and six men wounded. I never knew the losses in the gunboat fleet, or in Morgan's corps; but they must have been less than in mine, which was more exposed. The number of rebel dead must have been nearly one hundred and fifty; of prisoners, by actual count, we secured four thousand seven hundred and ninety-one, and sent them north to St. Louis.

Chapter 6

Vicksburg:
"Our Enemy Was Shut Up in a Large Fort"
January—July, 1863

THE CAMPAIGN OF 1863, resulting in the capture of Vicksburg, was so important, that its history has been well studied and well described in all the books treating of the civil war, more especially by Dr. Draper, in his "History of the Civil War in America," and in Badeau's "Military History of General Grant." In the latter it is more fully and accurately given than in any other, and is well illustrated by maps and original documents. I now need only attempt to further illustrate Badeau's account by some additional details. When our expedition came out of the Arkansas River, January 18, 1863, and rendezvoused at the river-bank, in front of the town of Napoleon, Arkansas, we were visited by General Grant in person, who had come down from Memphis in a steamboat. Although at this time Major-General J. A. McClernand was in command of the Army of the Mississippi, by virtue of a confidential order of the War Department, dated October 21, 1862, which order bore the indorsement of President Lincoln, General Grant still exercised a command over him, by reason of his general command of the Department of the Tennessee. By an order (No. 210) of December 18, 1862, from the War Department, received at Arkansas Post, the Western armies had been grouped into five *corps d'armée,* viz.: the Thirteenth, Major-General McClernand; the Fourteenth, Major-General

George H. Thomas, in Middle Tennessee; the Fifteenth, Major-General W. T. Sherman; the Sixteenth, Major-General Hurlbut, then at or near Memphis; and the Seventeenth, Major-General McPherson, also at and back of Memphis. General Grant when at Napoleon, on the 18th of January, ordered McClernand with his own and my corps to return to Vicksburg, to disembark on the west bank, and to resume work on a canal across the peninsula, which had been begun by General Thomas Williams the summer before, the object being to turn the Mississippi River at that point, or at least to make a passage for our fleet of gunboats and transports across the peninsula, opposite Vicksburg. General Grant then returned to Memphis, ordered to Lake Providence, about sixty miles above us, McPherson's corps, the Seventeenth, and then came down again to give his personal supervision to the whole movement.

The Mississippi River was very high and rising, and we began that system of canals on which we expended so much hard work fruitlessly: first, the canal at Young's plantation, opposite Vicksburg; second, that at Lake Providence; and third, at the Yazoo Pass, leading in to the head-waters of the Yazoo River. Early in February the gunboats Indianola and Queen of the West ran the batteries of Vicksburg. The latter was afterward crippled in Red River, and was captured by the rebels; and the Indianola was butted and sunk about forty miles below Vicksburg. We heard the booming of the guns, but did not know of her loss till some days after. During the months of January and February, we were digging the canal and fighting off the water of the Mississippi, which continued to rise and threatened to drown us. We had no sure place of refuge except the narrow levee, and such steamboats as remained abreast of our camps. My two divisions furnished alternately a detail of five hundred men a day, to work on the canal. So high was the water in the beginning of March, that McClernand's corps was moved to higher ground, at Milliken's Bend, but I remained at Young's plantation, laid off a due proportion of the levee for each subdivision of my command, and assigned other parts to such steamboats as lay at the levee. My own headquarters were in Mrs. Grove's house, which had the water all around it, and could only be reached by a plank-walk from the levee, built on posts.

General Frederick Steele commanded the first division, and

General D. Stuart the second; this latter division had been reënforced by General Hugh Ewing's brigade, which had arrived from West Virginia.

At the time of its date I received the following note from General Grant:

MILLIKEN'S BEND, *March* 16, 1863

General SHERMAN.

DEAR SIR: I have just returned from a reconnoissance up Steele's Bayou, with the admiral (Porter), and five of his gunboats. With some labor in cutting tree-tops out of the way, it will be navigable for any class of steamers.

I want you to have your pioneer corps, or one regiment of good men for such work, detailed, and at the landing as soon as possible.

The party will want to take with them their rations, arms, and sufficient camp and garrison equipage for a few days. I will have a boat at any place you may designate, as early as the men can be there. The Eighth Missouri (being many of them boatmen) would be excellent men for this purpose.

As soon as you give directions for these men to be in readiness, come up and see me, and I will explain fully. The tug that takes this is instructed to wait for you. A full supply of axes will be required.

Very respectfully,

U. S. GRANT, *Major-General.*

This letter was instantly (8 A. M.) sent to Colonel Giles A. Smith, commanding the Eighth Missouri, with orders to prepare immediately. He returned it at 9.15, with an answer that the regiment was all ready. I went up to Milliken's Bend in the tug, and had a conference with the general, resulting in these orders:

HEADQUARTERS DEPARTMENT OF THE TENNESSEE, BEFORE VICKSBURG, *March* 16, 1863.

Major-General W. T. SHERMAN, *commanding Fifteenth Army Corps.*

GENERAL: You will proceed as early as practicable up

Steele's Bayou, and through Black Bayou to Deer Creek, and thence with the gunboats now there by any route they may take to get into the Yazoo River, for the purpose of determining the feasibility of getting an army through that route to the east bank of that river, and at a point from which they can act advantageously against Vicksburg.

Make such details from your army corps as may be required to clear out the channel of the various bayous through which transports would have to run, and to hold such points as in your judgment should be occupied.

I place at your disposal to-day the steamers Diligent and Silver Wave, the only two suitable for the present navigation of this route. Others will be supplied you as fast as required, and they can be got.

I have given directions (and you may repeat them) that the party going on board the steamer Diligent push on until they reach Black Bayou, only stopping sufficiently long at any point before reaching there to remove such obstructions as prevent their own progress. Captain Kossak, of the Engineers, will go with this party. The other boat-load will commence their work in Steele's Bayou, and make the navigation as free as possible all the way through.

There is but little work to be done in Steel's Bayou, except for about five miles about midway of the bayou. In this portion many overhanging trees will have to be removed, and should be dragged out of the channel.

Very respectfully,

U. S. GRANT, *Major-General.*

On returning to my camp at Young's Point, I started these two boats up the Yazoo and Steele's Bayou, with the Eighth Missouri and some pioneers, with axes, saws, and all the tools necessary. I gave orders for a part of Stuart's division to proceed in the large boats up the Mississippi River to a point at Gwin's plantation, where a bend of Steele's Bayou neared the main river; and the next day, with one or two staff-officers and orderlies, got a navy-tug, and hurried up to overtake Admiral Porter. About sixty miles up Steele's Bayou we came to the gunboat Price, Lieutenant [Selim E.] Woodworth, United States Navy, commanding, and then turned into Black Bayou, a narrow, crooked channel, obstructed by overhanging oaks, and filled with cypress and cotton-wood trees. The gunboats had forced their way through, pushing aside trees a foot in diameter. In about four miles we overtook the gunboat fleet just as it was emerging into Deer Creek. Along Deer Creek the alluvium was higher, and there was a large cotton-plantation belonging to a Mr. Hill, who was absent, and the Negroes were in charge of the place. Here I overtook Admiral Porter, and accompanied him a couple of miles up Deer Creek, which was much wider and more free of trees, with plantations on both sides at intervals. Admiral Porter thought he had passed the worst, and that he would be able to reach the Rolling Fork and Sunflower. He requested me to return and use all possible means to clear out Black Bayou. I returned to Hill's plantation, which was soon reached by Major Coleman, with a part of the Eighth Missouri; the bulk of the regiment and the pioneers had been distributed along the bayous, and set to work under the general supervision of Captain Kossak. The Diligent and Silver Wave then returned to Gwin's plantation and brought up Brigadier-General Giles A. Smith, with the Sixth Missouri, and part of the One Hundred and Sixteenth Illinois. Admiral Porter was then working up Deer Creek with his iron-clads, but he had left me a tug, which enabled me to reconnoitre the country, which was all under water except the narrow strip along Deer Creek. During the 19th I heard the heavy navy-guns booming more frequently than seemed consistent with mere guerrilla operations; and that night I got a message from Porter, written on tissue-paper, brought me through the swamp by a Negro, who had it concealed in a piece of tobacco.

The admiral stated that he had met a force of infantry and artillery which gave him great trouble by killing the men who had to expose themselves outside the iron armor to shove off the bows of the boats, which had so little headway that they would not steer. He begged me to come to his rescue as quickly as possible. Giles A. Smith had only about eight hundred men with him, but I ordered him to start up Deer Creek at once, crossing to the east side by an old bridge at Hill's plantation, which we had repaired for the purpose; to work his way up to the gunboat-fleet, and to report to the admiral that I would come up with every man I could raise as soon as possible. I was almost alone at Hill's, but took a canoe, paddled down Black Bayou to the gunboat Price, and there, luckily, found the Silver Wave with a load of men just arrived from Gwin's plantation. Taking some of the parties who were at work along the bayou into an empty coal-barge, we tugged it up by a navy-tug, followed by the Silver Wave, crashing through the trees, carrying away the pilot-house, smoke-stacks, and every thing above-deck; but the captain (McMillan, of Pittsburg) was a brave fellow, and realized the necessity. The night was absolutely black, and we could only make two and a half of the four miles. We then disembarked, and marched through the canebrake, carrying lighted candles in our hands, till we got into the open cotton-fields at Hill's plantation, where we lay down for a few hours' rest. These men were a part of Giles A. Smith's brigade, and part belonged to the brigade of T. Kilby Smith, the senior officer present being Lieutenant-Colonel Rice, Fifty-fourth Ohio, an excellent young officer. We had no horses.

On Sunday morning, March 21st, as soon as daylight appeared, we started, following the same route which Giles A. Smith had taken the day before; the battalion of the Thirteenth United States Regulars, Major Chase, in the lead. We could hear Porter's guns, and knew that moments were precious. Being on foot myself, no man could complain, and we generally went at the double-quick, with occasional rests. The road lay along Deer Creek, passing several plantations; and occasionally, at the bends, it crossed the swamp, where the water came above my hips. The smaller drummer-boys had to carry their drums on their heads, and most of the men slung their cartridge-boxes around their necks. The soldiers generally were glad to have their general and field officers afoot, but we gave them a fair specimen of marching, accomplishing about twenty-one miles by noon. Of course, our speed was accelerated by the sounds of the navy-guns, which became more and more distinct, though we could see nothing. At a plantation near some Indian mounds we met a detachment of the Eighth Missouri, that had been up to the fleet, and had been sent down as a picket to prevent any obstructions below. This picket reported that Admiral Porter had found Deer Creek badly obstructed, had turned back; that there was a rebel force beyond the fleet, with some six-pounders, and nothing between us and the fleet. So I sat down on the door-sill of a cabin to rest, but had not been seated ten minutes when, in the wood just ahead, not three hundred yards off, I heard quick and rapid firing of musketry. Jumping up, I ran up the road, and found Lieutenant-Colonel Rice, who said the head of his column had struck a small force of rebels with a working gang of Negroes, provided with axes, who on the first fire had broken and run back into the swamp. I ordered Rice to deploy his brigade, his left on the road, and extending as far into the swamp as the ground would permit, and then to sweep forward until he uncovered the gunboats. The movement was rapid and well executed, and we soon came to some large cotton-fields and could see our gunboats in Deer Creek, occasionally firing a heavy eight-inch gun across the cotton-field into the swamp behind. About that time a Major Kirby, of the Eighth Missouri, galloped down the road on a horse he had picked up the night before, and met me. He explained the situation of affairs, and offered me his horse. I got on *bareback,* and rode up the levee, the sailors coming out of their iron-clads and cheering most vociferously as I rode by, and as our men swept forward across the cotton-field in full view. I soon found Admiral Porter, who was on the deck of one of his iron-clads, with a shield made of the section of a smoke-stack, and I doubt if he was ever more glad to meet a friend than he was to see me. He explained that he had almost reached the Rolling Fork, when the woods became full of sharp-shooters, who, taking advantage of trees, stumps, and the levee, would shoot down every man that poked his nose outside the protection of their armor; so that he could not handle his clumsy boats in the narrow channel. The rebels had evidently dispatched a force from Haines's Bluff up the Sunflower to the Rolling Fork, had anticipated the movement of Admiral Porter's fleet, and had completely obstructed the channel of the upper part of Deer Creek by felling trees into it, so that further progress in that direction was simply impossible. It also happened that, at the instant of my arrival, a party of about four hundred rebels, armed and supplied with axes, had passed around the fleet and had got below it, intending in like manner to block up the channel by the felling of trees, so as to cut off retreat. This was the force we had struck so opportunely at the time before described. I inquired of Admiral Porter what he proposed to do, and he said he wanted to get out of that scrape as quickly as possible. He was actually working back when I met him, and, as we then had a sufficient force to cover his movement completely, he continued to back down Deer Creek. He informed me at one time things looked so critical that he had made up his mind to blow up the gunboats, and to escape with his men through the swamp to the Mississippi River. There being no longer any sharp-shooters to bother the sailors, they made good progress; still, it took three full days for the fleet to back out of Deer Creek into Black Bayou, at Hill's plantation, whence Admiral Porter proceeded to his post at the mouth of the Yazoo, leaving Captain [E. K] Owen in command of the fleet. I reported the facts to General Grant, who was sadly disappointed at the failure of the fleet to get through to the Yazoo above Haines's Bluff, and ordered us all to resume our camps at Young's Point. We accordingly steamed down, and regained our camps on the 27th.

On the 3d of April, a division of troops, commanded by Brigadier-General J. M. Tuttle, was assigned to my corps, and was designated the Third Division; and, on the 4th of April, Brigadier-General D. Stuart was relieved from the command of the Second Division, to which Major-General Frank P. Blair was appointed by an order from General Grant's headquarters. Stuart had been with me from the time we were at Benton Barracks, in command of the Fifty-fifth Illinois, then of a brigade, and finally of a division; but he had failed in securing a confirmation by the Senate to his nomination as brigadier-general, by reason of some old affair at Chicago, and, having resigned his commission as colonel, he was out of service. I esteemed him very highly, and was actually mortified that the service should thus be deprived of so excellent and gallant an officer. He afterward settled in New Orleans as a lawyer, and died about 1867 or 1868.

By this time it had become thoroughly demonstrated that we could not divert the main river Mississippi, or get practicable access to the east bank of the Yazoo, in the rear of Vicksburg, by any of the passes; and we were all in the habit of discussing the various chances of the future. General Grant's headquarters were at Milliken's Bend, in tents, and his army was strung along the river all the way from Young's Point up to Lake Providence, at least sixty miles. I had always contended that the best way to take Vicksburg was to resume the movement which had been so well begun the previous November, viz., for the main army to march by land down the country inland of the Mississippi River; while the gunboat-fleet and a minor land-force should threaten Vicksburg on its river-front.

I reasoned that, with the large force then subject to General Grant's orders—viz., four army corps—he could easily resume the movement from Memphis, by way of Oxford and Grenada, to Jackson, Mississippi, or down the ridge between the Yazoo and Big Black; but General Grant would not, for reasons other than military, take any course which looked like a step backward; and he himself concluded on the river movement below Vicksburg, so as to appear like connecting with General Banks, who at the same time was besieging Port Hudson from the direction of New Orleans.

Preliminary orders had already been given, looking to the digging of a canal, to connect the river at Duckport with Willow Bayou, back of Milliken's Bend, so as to form a channel for the conveyance of supplies, by way of Richmond, to New Carthage; and several steam dredge-boats had come from the upper rivers to assist in the work. One day early in April, I was up at General Grant's headquarters, and we talked over all these things with absolute freedom. Charles A. Dana, Assistant Secretary of War, was there, and [James H.] Wilson, Rawlins, Frank Blair, McPherson, etc. We all knew, what was notorious, that General McClernand was still intriguing against General Grant, in hopes to regain the command of the whole expedition, and that others were raising a clamor against General Grant in the newspapers at the North. Even Mr. Lincoln and General Halleck seemed to be shaken; but at no instant of time did we (his personal friends) slacken in our loyalty to him. One night, after such a discussion, and believing that General McClernand had no real plan of action shaped in his mind, I wrote my letter of April 8, 1863, to Colonel Rawlins, which letter is embraced in full at page 616 of Badeau's[1] book, and which I now reproduce here:

HEADQUARTERS FIFTEENTH ARMY CORPS,
CAMP NEAR VICKSBURG, *April 8, 1863.*

Colonel J. A. RAWLINS, *Assistant Adjutant-General to General* GRANT.

SIR: I would most respectfully suggest (for reasons which

[1] See Adam Badeau, *Military History of U. S. Grant* (New York: 1868–81), 3 volumes.

I will not name) that General Grant call on his corps commanders for their opinions, concise and positive, on the best general plan of a campaign. Unless this be done, there are men who will, in any result falling below the popular standard, claim that *their* advice was unheeded, and that fatal consequence resulted therefrom. My own opinions are—

First. That the Army of the Tennessee is now far in advance of the other grand armies of the United States.

Second. That a corps from Missouri should forthwith be moved from St. Louis to the vicinity of Little Rock, Arkansas; supplies collected there while the river is full, and land communication with Memphis opened *via* Des Arc on the White, and Madison on the St. Francis River.

Third. That as much of the Yazoo Pass, Goldwater, and Tallahatchie Rivers, as can be gained and fortified, be held, and the main army be transported thither by land and water; that the road back to Memphis be secured and reopened, and, as soon as the waters subside, Grenada be attacked, and the swamp-road across to Helena be patrolled by cavalry.

Fourth. That the line of the Yalabusha be the base from which to operate against the points where the Mississippi Central crosses Big Black, above Canton; and, lastly, where the Vicksburg & Jackson Railroad crosses the same river (Big Black). The capture of Vicksburg would result.

Fifth. That a minor force be left in this vicinity, not to exceed ten thousand men, with only enough steamboats to float and transport them to any desired point; this force to be held always near enough to act with the gunboats when the main army is known to be near Vicksburg—Haines's Bluff or Yazoo City.

Sixth. I do doubt the capacity of Willow Bayou (which I estimate to be fifty miles long and very tortuous) as a military channel, to supply an army large enough to operate against Jackson, Mississippi, or the Black River Bridge; and such a channel will be very vulnerable to a force coming from the west, which we must expect. Yet this canal will be most useful as the way to convey coals and supplies to a fleet that should navigate the lower reach of the Mississippi between Vicksburg and the Red River.

Seventh. The chief reason for operating *solely* by water was the season of the year and high water in the Tallahatchie and Yalabusha Rivers. The spring is now here, and soon these streams will be no serious obstacle, save in the ambuscades of the forest, and whatever works the enemy may have erected at or near Grenada. North Mississippi is too valuable for us to allow the enemy to hold it and make crops this year.

I make these suggestions, with the request that General Grant will read them and give them, as I know he will, a share of his thoughts. I would prefer that he should not answer this letter, but merely give it as much or as little weight as it deserves. Whatever plan of action he may adopt will receive from me the same zealous coöperation and energetic support as though conceived by myself. I do not believe General Banks will make any serious attack on Port Hudson this spring. I am, etc.,

W. T. SHERMAN, *Major-General.*

This is the letter which some critics have styled a "protest." We never had a council of war at any time during the Vicksburg campaign. We often met casually, regardless of rank or power, and talked and gossiped of things in general, as officers do and should. But my letter speaks for itself. It shows my opinions clearly at that stage of the game, and was meant partially to induce General Grant to call on General McClernand for a similar expression of opinion, but, so far as I know, he did not. He went on quietly to work out his own designs; and he has told me, since the war, that had we possessed in December, 1862, the experience of marching and maintaining armies without a regular base, which we afterward acquired, he would have gone on from Oxford as first contemplated, and would not have turned back because of the destruction of his depot at Holly Springs by Van Dorn. The distance from Oxford to the rear of Vicksburg is little greater than by the circuitous route we afterward followed, from Bruinsburg to Jackson and Vicksburg, during which we had neither depot nor train of supplies. I have never criticised General Grant's strategy on this or any other occasion, but I thought then that he had lost an opportunity, which cost him and us six months' extra-hard work, for we might have captured Vicksburg from the direction of Oxford in January, quite as easily as was afterward done in July, 1863.

General Grant's orders for the general movement past Vicksburg, by Richmond and Carthage, were dated April 20, 1863. McClernand was to lead off with his corps, McPherson next, and my corps (the Fifteenth) to bring up the rear. Preliminary thereto, on the night of April 16th, seven iron-clads led by Admiral Porter in person, in the Benton, with three transports, and ten barges in tow, ran the Vicksburg batteries by night. Anticipating a scene, I had four yawl-boats hauled across the swamp, to the reach of the river below Vicksburg, and manned them with soldiers, ready to pick up any of the disabled wrecks as they floated by. I was out in the stream when the fleet passed Vicksburg, and the scene was truly sublime. As soon as the rebel gunners detected the Benton, which was in the lead, they opened on her, and on the others in succession, with shot and shell; houses on the Vicksburg side and on the opposite shore were set on fire, which lighted up the whole river; and the roar of cannon, the bursting of shells, and finally the burning of the Henry Clay, drifting with the current, made up a picture of the terrible not often seen. Each gunboat returned the fire as she passed the town, while the transports hugged the opposite shore. When the Benton had got abreast of us, I pulled off to her, boarded, had a few words with Admiral Porter, and as she was drifting rapidly toward the lower batteries at Warrenton, I left, and pulled back toward the shore, meeting the gunboat Tuscumbia towing the transport Forest Queen into the bank out of the range of fire. The Forest Queen, Captain Conway, had been my flag-boat up the Arkansas, and for some time after, and I was very friendly with her officers. This was the only transport whose captain would not receive volunteers as a crew, but her own officers and *crew* stuck to their boat, and carried her safely below the Vicksburg batteries, and afterward rendered splendid service in ferrying troops across the river at Grand Gulf and Bruinsburg. In passing Vicksburg, she was damaged in the hull and had a steam-pipe cut away, but this was soon repaired. The Henry Clay was set on fire by bursting shells, and burned up; one of my yawls picked up her pilot floating on a piece of wreck, and the bulk of her crew escaped in their own yawl-boat to the shore above. The Silver Wave, Captain McMillan, the same that was with us up Steele's Bayou, passed safely, and she also rendered good service afterward.

Subsequently, on the night of April 26th, six other transports with numerous barges loaded with hay, corn, freight, and provisions, were drifted past Vicksburg; of these the Tigress was hit, and sunk just as she reached the river-bank below, on our side. I was there with my yawls, and saw Colonel Lagow, of General Grant's staff, who had passed the batteries in the Tigress, and I think he was satisfied never to attempt such a thing again. Thus General Grant's army had below Vicksburg an abundance of stores, and boats with which to cross the river. The road by which the troops marched was very bad, and it was not until the 1st of May that it was clear for my corps. While waiting my turn to march, I received a letter from General Grant, written at Carthage, saying that he proposed to cross over and attack Grand Gulf, about the end of April, and he thought I could put in my time usefully by making a "feint" on Haines's Bluff, but he did not like to order me to do it, because it might be reported at the North that I had again been "repulsed, etc." Thus we had to fight a senseless clamor at the North, as well as a determined foe and the obstacles of Nature. Of course, I answered him that I would make the "feint," regardless of public clamor at a distance, and I did make it most effectually; using all the old boats I could get about Milliken's Bend and the mouth of the Yazoo, but taking only ten small regiments, selected out of Blair's division, to make a show of force. We afterward learned that General Pemberton in Vicksburg had previously dispatched a large force to the assistance of General [John] Bowen, at Grand Gulf and Port Gibson, which force had proceeded as far as Hankinson's Ferry, when he discovered our ostentatious movement up the Yazoo, and recalled his men, and sent them up to Haines's Bluff to meet us. This detachment of rebel troops must have marched nearly sixty miles without rest, for afterward, on reaching Vicksburg, I heard that the men were perfectly exhausted, and lay along the road in groups, completely fagged out. This diversion, made with so much pomp and display, therefore completely fulfilled its purpose, by leaving General Grant to contend with a minor force, on landing at Bruinsburg, and afterward at Port Gibson and Grand Gulf.

In May the waters of the Mississippi had so far subsided that all our canals were useless, and the roads had become practicable. After McPherson's corps had passed Richmond, I took up the route of march, with Steele's and Tuttle's divisions. Blair's division remained at Milliken's Bend to protect our depots there, till relieved by troops from Memphis, and then he was ordered to follow us. Our route lay by Richmond and Roundabout Bayou; then, following Bayou Vidal we struck the Mississippi at Perkins's plantation. Thence the route followed Lake St. Joseph to a plantation called Hard Times, about five miles above Grand Gulf. The road was more or less occupied by wagons and detachments belonging to McPherson's corps; still we marched rapidly and reached Hard Times on the 6th of May. Along the Bayou or Lake St. Joseph were many very fine cotton-plantations, and I recall that of a Mr. Bowie, brother-in-law of the Hon. Reverdy Johnson, of Baltimore. The house was very handsome, with a fine, extensive grass-plot in front. We entered the yard, and, leaving our horses with the headquarters escort, walked to the house. On the front-porch I found a magnificent grand-piano, with several satin-covered arm-chairs, in one of which sat a Union soldier (one of McPherson's men), with his feet on the keys of the piano, and his musket and knapsack lying on the porch. I asked him what he was doing there, and he answered that he was "taking a rest"; this was manifest and I started him in a hurry to overtake his command. The house was tenantless, and had been completely ransacked; articles of dress and books were strewed about, and a handsome boudoir with mirror front had been cast down, striking a French bedstead, shivering the glass. The library was extensive, with a fine collection of books; and hanging on the wall were two full-length portraits of Reverdy Johnson and his wife, one of the most beautiful ladies of our country, with whom I had been acquainted in Washington at the time of General Taylor's administration. Behind the mansion was the usual double row of cabins called the "quarters." There I found an old Negro (a family servant) with several women, whom I sent to the house to put things in order; telling the old man that other troops would follow, and he must stand on the porch to tell any officers who came along that the property belonged to Mr. Bowie, who was the brother-in-law of our friend Mr. Reverdy Johnson, of Baltimore, asking them to see that no further harm was done. Soon after we left the house I saw some Negroes carrying away furniture which manifestly belonged to the house, and compelled them to carry it back; and after reaching camp that night, at Hard Times, I sent a wagon back to Bowie's plantation, to bring up to Dr. Hollingsworth's house the two portraits for safe keeping; but before the wagon had reached Bowie's the house was burned, whether by some of our men or by Negroes I have never learned.

At the river there was a good deal of scrambling to get across, because the means of ferriage were inadequate; but by the aid of the Forest Queen and several gunboats I got my command across during the 7th of May, and marched out to Hankinson's Ferry (eighteen miles), relieving General [Marcellus] Crocker's division of McPherson's corps. McClernand's corps and McPherson's were still ahead, and had fought the battle of Port Gibson, on the 11th. I overtook General Grant in person at Auburn, and he accompanied my corps all the way into Jackson, which we reached May 14th. McClernand's corps had been left in observation toward Edward's Ferry. McPherson had fought at Raymond, and taken the left-hand road toward Jackson, *via* Clinton, while my troops were ordered by General Grant in person to take the right-hand road leading through Mississippi Springs. We reached Jackson at the same time; McPherson fighting on the Clinton road, and my troops fighting just outside the town, on the Raymond road, where we captured three entire field-batteries, and about two hundred prisoners of war. The rebels, under General Joe Johnston, had retreated through the town northward on the Canton road. Generals Grant, McPherson, and I, met in the large hotel facing the State-House, where the former explained to us that he had intercepted dispatches from Pemberton to Johnston, which made it important for us to work smart to prevent a junction of their respective forces. McPherson was ordered to march back early the next day on the Clinton road to make junction with McClernand, and I was ordered to remain one day to break up railroads, to destroy the arsenal, a foundery, the cotton-factory of the Messrs. Green, etc., etc., and then to follow McPherson.

McPherson left Jackson early on the 15th, and General Grant during the same day. I kept my troops busy in tearing up railroad-tracks, etc., but early on the morning of the 16th received notice from General Grant that a battle was imminent near Edwards's Depot; that he wanted me to dispatch one of my divisions immediately, and to follow with the other as soon as I had completed the work of destruction. Steele's division started immediately, and later in the day I followed with the other division (Tuttle's). Just as I was leaving Jackson, a very fat man came to see me, to inquire if his hotel, a large, frame-building near the depot, were doomed to be burned. I told him we had no intention to burn it, or any

other house, except the machine-shops, and such buildings as
could easily be converted to hostile uses. He professed to be a
law-abiding Union man, and I remember to have said that this
fact was manifest from the sign of his hotel, which was the
"Confederate Hotel"; the sign "United States" being faintly
painted out, and "Confederate" painted over it! I remembered
that hotel, as it was the supper-station for the New Orleans
trains when I used to travel the road before the war. I had not
the least purpose, however, of burning it, but, just as we were
leaving the town, it burst out in flames and was burned to
the ground. I never found out exactly who set it on fire, but
was told that in one of our batteries were some officers and
men who had been made prisoners at Shiloh, with Prentiss's
division, and had been carried past Jackson in a railroad-train;
they had been permitted by the guard to go to this very hotel
for supper, and had nothing to pay but greenbacks, which
were refused, with insult, by this same law-abiding landlord.
These men, it was said, had quietly and stealthily applied the
fire underneath the hotel just as we were leaving the town.

About dark we met General Grant's staff-officer near Bolton Station, who turned us to the right, with orders to push
on to Vicksburg by what was known as the upper Jackson
Road, which crossed the Big Black at Bridgeport. During that
day (May 16th) the battle of Champion Hills had been
fought and won by McClernand's and McPherson's corps,
aided by one division of mine (Blair's), under the immediate
command of General Grant; and McPherson was then following the mass of Pemberton's army, disordered and retreating
toward Vicksburg by the Edwards's Ferry road. General
Blair's division had come up from the rear, was temporarily
attached to McClernand's corps, taking part with it in the
battle of Champion Hills, but on the 17th it was ordered by
General Grant across to Bridgeport, to join me there.

Just beyond Bolton there was a small hewn-log house,
standing back in a yard, in which was a well; at this some of
our soldiers were drawing water. I rode in to get a drink, and,
seeing a book on the ground, asked some soldier to hand it to
me. It was a volume of the Constitution of the United States,
and on the title-page was written the name of Jefferson Davis.
On inquiry of a Negro, I learned that the place belonged to
the then President of the Southern Confederation. His brother
Joe Davis's plantation was not far off; one of my staff-officers

went there, with a few soldiers, and took a pair of carriage-horses, without my knowledge at the time. He found Joe Davis at home, an old man, attended by a young and affectionate niece; but they were overwhelmed with grief to see their country overrun and swarming with Federal troops.

We pushed on, and reached the Big Black early, Blair's troops having preceded us by an hour or so. I found General Blair in person, and he reported that there was no bridge across the Big Black; that it was swimming-deep; and that there was a rebel force on the opposite side, intrenched. He had ordered a detachment of the Thirteenth United States Regulars, under Captain Charles Ewing, to strip some artillery-horses, mount the men, and swim the river above the ferry, to attack and drive away the party on the opposite bank. I did not approve of this risky attempt, but crept down close to the brink of the river-bank, behind a corn-crib belonging to a plantation-house near by, and saw the parapet on the opposite bank. Ordering a section of guns to be brought forward by hand behind this corn-crib, a few well-directed shells brought out of their holes the little party that was covering the crossing, viz., a lieutenant and ten men, who came down to the river-bank and surrendered. Blair's pontoon-train was brought up, consisting of India-rubber boats, one of which was inflated, used as a boat, and brought over the prisoners. A pontoon-bridge was at once begun, finished by night, and the troops began the passage. After dark, the whole scene was lit up with fires of pitch-pine. General Grant joined me there, and we sat on a log, looking at the passage of the troops by the light of those fires; the bridge swayed to and fro under the passing feet, and made a fine war-picture. At daybreak we moved on, ascending the ridge, and by 10 A. M. the head of my column, long drawn out, reached the Benton road, and gave us command of the peninsula between the Yazoo and Big Black. I dispatched Colonel Swan, of the Fourth Iowa Cavalry, to Haines's Bluff, to capture that battery from the rear, and he afterward reported that he found it abandoned, its garrison having hastily retreated into Vicksburg, leaving their guns partially disabled, a magazine full of ammunition, and a hospital full of wounded and sick men. Colonel Swan saw one of our gunboats lying about two miles below in the Yazoo, to which he signaled. She steamed up, and to its commander the cavalry turned over the battery at Haines's Bluff, and rejoined me in front of Vicksburg. Allowing a couple of hours for rest and to close up the column, I resumed the march straight on Vicksburg. About two miles before reaching the forts, the road forked; the left was the main Jackson road, and the right was the "graveyard" road, which entered Vicksburg near a large cemetery. General Grant in person directed me to take the right-hand road, but, as McPherson had not yet got up from the direction of the railroad-bridge at Big Black, I sent the Eighth Missouri on the main Jackson road, to push the rebel skirmishers into town, and to remain until relieved by McPherson's advance, which happened late that evening, May 18th. The battalion of the Thirteenth United States Regulars, commanded by Captain Washington, was at the head of the column on the right-hand road, and pushed the rebels close behind their parapets; one of my staff, Captain Pitzman, receiving a dangerous wound in the hip, which apparently disabled him for life. By night Blair's whole division had closed up against the defenses of Vicksburg, which were found to be strong and well manned; and, on General Steele's head of column arriving, I turned it still more to the right, with orders to work its way down the bluff, so as to make connection with our fleet in the Mississippi River. There was a good deal of desultory fighting that evening, and a man was killed by the side of General Grant and myself, as we sat by the road-side looking at Steele's division passing to the right. General Steele's men reached the road which led from Vicksburg up to Haines's Bluff, which road lay at the foot of the hills, and intercepted some prisoners and wagons which were coming down from Haines's Bluff.

All that night McPherson's troops were arriving by the main Jackson road, and McClernand's by another near the railroad, deploying forward as fast as they struck the rebel works. My corps (the Fifteenth) had the right of the line of investment; McPherson's (the Seventeenth) the centre; and McClernand's (the Thirteenth) the left, reaching from the river above to the railroad below. Our lines connected, and invested about three-quarters of the land-front of the fortifications of Vicksburg. On the supposition that the garrison of Vicksburg was demoralized by the defeats at Champion Hills and at the railroad crossing of the Big Black, General Grant ordered an assault at our respective fronts on the 19th. My troops reached the top of the parapet, but could not cross over. The rebel parapets were strongly manned, and the enemy fought hard and well. My loss was pretty heavy, falling chiefly on the Thirteenth Regulars, whose commanding officer, Captain Washington, was killed, and several other regiments were pretty badly cut up. We, however, held the ground up to the ditch till night, and then drew back only a short distance, and began to counter-trench. On the graveyard road, our parapet was within less than fifty yards of the rebel ditch.

On the 20th of May, General Grant called the three corps commanders together, viz., McClernand, McPherson, and Sherman. We compared notes, and agreed that the assault of the day before had failed, by reason of the natural strength of the position, and because we were forced by the nature of the ground to limit our attacks to the strongest parts of the enemy's line, viz., where the three principal roads entered the city. It was not a council of war, but a mere consultation, resulting in orders from General Grant for us to make all possible preparations for a renewed assault on the 22d, simultaneously, at 10 A. M. I reconnoitred my front thoroughly in person, from right to left, and concluded to make my real attack at the right flank of the bastion, where the graveyard road entered the enemy's intrenchments, and at another point in the curtain about a hundred yards to its right (our left); also to make a strong demonstration by Steele's division, about a mile to our right, toward the river. All our field-batteries were put in position, and were covered by good epaulements; the troops were brought forward, in easy support, concealed by the shape of the ground; and to the minute, viz., 10 A. M. of May 22d, the troops sprang to the assault. A small party, that might be called a forlorn hope, provided with plank to cross the ditch, advanced at a run, up to the very ditch; the lines of infantry sprang from cover, and advanced rapidly in line of battle. I took a position within two hundred yards of the rebel parapet, on the off slope of a spur of ground, where by advancing two or three steps I could see everything. The rebel line, concealed by the parapet, showed no sign of unusual activity, but as our troops came in fair view, the enemy rose behind their parapet and poured a furious fire upon our lines; and, for about two hours, we had a severe and bloody battle, but at every point we were repulsed. In the very midst of this, when shell and shot fell furious and fast, occurred that little episode which has been celebrated in song and story, of the boy Orion P. Howe, badly wounded, bearing me a message for cartridges, calibre 54, described in my letter to the Hon. E. M. Stanton, Secretary of War. This boy was afterward appointed a cadet to the United States Naval Academy, at Annapolis, but he could not graduate, and I do not now know what has become of him.

After our men had been fairly beaten back from off the parapet, and had got cover behind the spurs of ground close up to the rebel works, General Grant came to where I was, on foot, having left his horse some distance to the rear. I pointed out to him the rebel works, admitted that my assault had failed, and he said the result with McPherson and Mc-Clernand was about the same. While he was with me, an orderly or staff-officer came and handed him a piece of paper, which he read and handed to me. I think the writing was in pencil, on a loose piece of paper, and was in General McClernand's handwriting, to the effect that "his troops had captured the rebel parapet in his front," that "the flag of the Union waved over the stronghold of Vicksburg," and asking him (General Grant) to give renewed orders to McPherson and Sherman to press their attacks on their respective fronts, lest the enemy should concentrate on him (McClernand). General Grant said, "I don't believe a word of it"; but I reasoned with him, that this note was official, and must be credited, and I offered to renew the assault at once with new troops. He said he would instantly ride down the line to McClernand's front, and if I did not receive orders to the contrary, by 3 o'clock P. M., I might try it again. Mower's fresh brigade was brought up under cover, and some changes were made in Giles Smith's brigade; and, punctually at 3 P. M., hearing heavy firing down along the line to my left, I ordered the second assault. It was a repetition of the first, equally unsuccessful and bloody. It also transpired that the same thing had occurred with General McPherson, who lost in this second assault some most valuable officers and men, without adequate result; and that General McClernand, instead of having taken any single point of the rebel main parapet, had only taken one or two small outlying lunettes open to the rear, where his men were at the mercy of the rebels behind their main parapet, and most of them were actually thus captured. This affair caused great feeling with us, and severe criticism on General McClernand, which led finally to his removal from the command of the Thirteenth Corps, to which General Ord succeeded. The immediate cause, however, of General McClernand's removal was the publication of a sort of congratulatory order addressed to his troops, first published in St. Louis, in which he claimed that he had actually succeeded in making a lodgment in Vicksburg, but had lost it, owing to the fact that McPherson and Sherman did not fulfill their parts of the general plan of attack. This was simply untrue. The two several assaults made May 22d, on the lines of Vicksburg, had failed, by reason of the great strength of the position and the determined fighting of its garrison. I have since seen the position at Sevastopol, and without hesitation I declare that at Vicksburg to have been the more difficult of the two.

Thereafter our proceedings were all in the nature of a siege. General Grant drew more troops from Memphis, to prolong our general line to the left, so as completely to invest the place on its land-side, while the navy held the river both above and below. General Mower's brigade of Tuttle's division was also sent across the river to the peninsula, so that by May 31st Vicksburg was completely beleaguered. Good roads were constructed from our camps to the several landing-places on the Yazoo River, to which points out boats brought up ample supplies; so that we were in a splendid condition for a siege, while our enemy was shut up in a close fort, with a large civil population of men, women, and children to feed, in addition to his combatant force. If we could prevent sallies, or relief from the outside, the fate of the garrison of Vicksburg was merely a question of time.

I had my headquarters camp close up to the works, near the centre of my corps, and General Grant had his bivouac behind a ravine to my rear. We estimated Pemberton's whole force in Vicksburg at thirty thousand men, and it was well known that the rebel General Joseph E. Johnston was engaged in collecting another strong force near the Big Black, with the intention to attack our rear, and thus to afford Pemberton an opportunity to escape with his men. Even then the ability of General Johnston was recognized, and General Grant told me that he was about the only general on that side whom he feared. Each corps kept strong pickets well to the rear; but, as the rumors of Johnston's accumulating force reached us, General Grant concluded to take stronger measures. He had received from the North General [John] G. Parke's corps

(Ninth), which had been posted at Haines's Bluff; then, detailing one division from each of the three *corps d'armée* investing Vicksburg, he ordered me to go out, take a general command of all, and to counteract any movement on the part of General Johnston to relieve Vicksburg. I reconnoitred the whole country, from Haines's Bluff to the railroad bridge, and posted the troops thus: Parkes's two divisions from Haines's Bluff out to the Benton or ridge road; Tuttle's division, of my corps, joining on and extending to a plantation called Young's, overlooking Bear Creek valley, which empties into the Big Black above Messinger's Ferry; then McArthur's division, of McPherson's corps, took up the line, and reached to Osterhaus's division of McClernand's corps, which held a strong fortified position at the railroad-crossing of the Big Black River. I was of opinion that, if Johnston should cross the Big Black, he could by the favorable nature of the country be held in check till a concentration could be effected by us at the point threatened. From the best information we could gather, General Johnston had about thirty or forty thousand men. I took post near a plantation of one Trible, near Markham's, and frequently reconnoitred the whole line, and could see the enemy engaged in like manner, on the east side of Big Black; but he never attempted actually to cross over, except with some cavalry, just above Bear Creek, which was easily driven back. I was there from June 20th to the 4th of July. In a small log-house near Markham's was the family of Mr. Klein, whose wife was the daughter of Mrs. Day, of New Orleans, who in turn was the sister of Judge T. W. Bartley, my brother-in-law. I used frequently to drop in and take a meal with them, and Mrs. Klein was generally known as the general's cousin, which doubtless saved her and her family from molestation, too common on the part of our men.

One day, as I was riding the line near a farm known as Parson Fox's, I heard that the family of a Mr. Wilkinson, of New Orleans, was "refugeeing" at a house near by. I rode up, inquired, and found two young girls of that name, who said they were the children of General Wilkinson, of Louisiana, and that their brother had been at the Military School at Alexandria. Inquiring for their mother, I was told she was spending the day at Parson Fox's. As this house was on my route, I rode there, went through a large gate into the yard, followed by my staff and escort, and found quite a number of ladies sitting on the porch. I rode up and inquired if that were Parson Fox's. The parson, a fine-looking, venerable old man, rose, and said that he was Parson Fox. I then inquired for Mrs. Wilkinson, when an elderly lady answered that she was the person. I asked her if she were from Plaquemine Parish, Louisiana, and she said she was. I then inquired if she had a son who had been a cadet at Alexandria when General Sherman was superintendent, and she answered yes. I then announced myself, inquired after the boy, and she said he was inside of Vicksburg, an artillery lieutenant. I then asked about her husband, whom I had known, when she burst into tears, and cried out in agony, "You killed him at Bull Run, where he was fighting for his country!" I disclaimed killing anybody at Bull Run; but all the women present (nearly a dozen) burst into loud lamentations, which made it most uncomfortable for me, and I rode away. On the 3d of July, as I sat at my bivouac by the road-side near Trible's, I saw a poor, miserable horse, carrying a lady, and led by a little Negro boy, coming across a cotton-field toward me; as they approched I recognized poor Mrs. Wilkinson, and helped her to dismount. I inquired what had brought her to me in that style, and she answered that she *knew* Vicksburg was going to surrender, and she wanted to go right away to see her boy. I had a telegraph-wire to General Grant's headquarters, and had heard that there were symptoms of surrender, but as yet nothing definite. I tried to console and dissuade her, but she was resolved, and I could not help giving her a letter to General Grant, explaining to him who she was, and asking him to give her the earliest opportunity to see her son. The distance was fully twenty miles, but off she started, and I afterward learned that my letter had enabled her to see her son, who had escaped unharmed. Later in the day I got by telegraph General Grant's notice of the negotiations for surrender; and, by his directions, gave general orders to my troops to be ready at a moment's notice to cross the Big Black, and go for Joe Johnston.

The next day (July 4, 1863) Vicksburg surrendered, and orders were given for at once attacking General Johnston. The Thirteenth Corps (General Ord) was ordered to march rapidly, and cross the Big Black at the railroad-bridge; the Fifteenth by Messinger's, and the Ninth (General Parke) by Birdsong's Ferry—all to converge on Bolton. My corps crossed

the Big Black during the 5th and 6th of July, and marched
for Bolton, where we came in with General Ord's troops; but
the Ninth Corps was delayed in crossing at Birdsong's. Johnston had received timely notice of Pemberton's surrender,
and was in full retreat for Jackson. On the 8th all our troops
reached the neighborhood of Clinton, the weather fearfully
hot, and water scarce. Johnston had marched rapidly, and in
retreating had caused cattle, hogs, and sheep, to be driven
into the ponds of water, and there shot down; so that we had
to haul their dead and stinking carcasses out to use the water.
On the 10th of July we had driven the rebel army into Jackson, where it turned at bay behind the intrenchments, which
had been enlarged and strengthened since our former visit
in May. We closed our lines about Jackson; my corps (Fifteenth) held the centre, extending from the Clinton to the
Raymond road; Ord's (Thirteenth) on the right, reaching
Pearl River below the town; and Parkes's (Ninth) the left,
above the town.

On the 11th we pressed close in, and shelled the town from
every direction. One of Ord's brigades (Lauman's) got too
close, and was very roughly handled and driven back in disorder. General Ord accused the commander (General Lauman) of having disregarded his orders, and attributed to him
personally the disaster and heavy loss of men. He requested
his relief, which I granted, and General Lauman went to the
rear, and never regained his division. He died after the war,
in Iowa, much respected, as before that time he had been
universally esteemed a most gallant and excellent officer. The
weather was fearfully hot, but we continued to press the siege
day and night, using our artillery pretty freely; and on the
morning of July 17th the place was found evacauted. General
Steele's division was sent in pursuit as far as Brandon(fourteen miles), but General Johnston had carried his army safely
off, and pursuit in that hot weather would have been fatal to
my command.

Reporting the fact to General Grant, he ordered me to return, to send General Parke's corps to Haines's Bluff, General
Ord's back to Vicksburg, and he consented that I should en-
camp my whole corps near the Big Black, pretty much on the
same ground we had occupied before the movement, and
with the prospect of a period of rest for the remainder of the
summer. We reached our camps on the 27th of July.

Meantime, a division of troops, commanded by Brigadier-General W. Sooy Smith, had been added to my corps. General Smith applied for and received a sick-leave on the 20th of July; Brigadier-General Hugh Ewing was assigned to its command; and from that time it constituted the Fourth Division of the Fifteenth Army Corps.

Port Hudson had surrendered to General Banks on the 8th of July (a necessary consequence of the fall of Vicksburg), and thus terminated probably the most important enterprise of the civil war—the recovery of the complete control of the Mississippi River, from its source to its mouth—or, in the language of Mr. Lincoln, the Mississippi went "unvexed to the sea."

I put my four divisions into handsome, clean camps, looking to health and comfort alone, and had my headquarters in a beautiful grove near the house of that same Parson Fox where I had found the crowd of weeping rebel women waiting for the fate of their friends in Vicksburg.

The value of the capture of Vicksburg, however, was not measured by the list of prisoners, guns, and small-arms, but by the fact that its possession secured the navigation of the great central river of the continent, bisected fatally the Southern Confederacy, and set the armies which had been used in its conquest free for other purposes; and it so happened that the event coincided as to time with another great victory which crowned our arms far away, at Gettysburg, Pennsylvania. That was a defensive battle, whereas ours was offensive in the highest acceptation of the term, and the two, occurring at the same moment of time, should have ended the war; but the rebel leaders were mad, and seemed determined that their people should drink of the very lowest dregs of the cup of war, which they themselves had prepared.

The campaign of Vicksburg, in its conception and execution, belonged exclusively to General Grant, not only in the great whole, but in the thousands of its details. I still retain many of his letters and notes, all in his own handwriting, prescribing the routes of march for divisions and detachments, specifying even the amount of food and tools to be carried along. Many persons gave his adjutant-general, Rawlins, the credit for these things, but they were in error; for no commanding general of an army ever gave more of his personal attention to details, or wrote so many of his own orders, reports, and letters, as General Grant. His success at Vicksburg justly gave him great fame at home and abroad. The President conferred on him the rank of major-general in the regular army, the highest grade then existing by law; and General McPherson and I shared in his success by receiving similar commissions as brigadier-generals in the regular army.

But our success at Vicksburg produced other results not so favorable to our cause—a general relaxation of effort, and desire to escape the hard drudgery of camp: officers sought leaves of absence to visit their homes, and soldiers obtained furloughs and discharges on the most slender pretexts; even the General Government seemed to relax in its efforts to replenish our ranks with new men, or to enforce the draft, and the politicians were pressing their schemes to reorganize or patch up some form of civil government, as fast as the armies gained partial possession of the States.

In order to illustrate this peculiar phase of our civil war, I give at this place copies of certain letters which have not heretofore been published:

[PRIVATE]

WASHINGTON, *August* 29, 1863.

Major-General W. T. SHERMAN, *Vicksburg, Mississippi.*

MY DEAR GENERAL: The question of reconstruction in Louisiana, Mississippi, and Arkansas, will soon come up for decision of the Government, and not only the length of the war, but our ultimate and complete success, will depend upon its decision. It is a difficult matter, but I believe it can be successfully solved, if the President will consult opinions of cool and discreet men, who are capable of looking at it in all its bearings and effects. I think he is disposed to receive the advice of our generals who have been in these States, and know much more of their condition than gassy politicians in Congress. General Banks has written pretty fully on the subject. I wrote to General Grant, immediately after the fall of Vicksburg, for his views in regard to Mississippi, but he has not yet answered.

I wish you would consult with Grant, McPherson, and others of cool, good judgment and write me your views fully, as I may wish to use them with the President. You had better write me unofficially, and then your letter will not be put on file, and cannot hereafter be used against you. You have been in Washington enough to know how every thing a man writes or says is picked up by his enemies and misconstrued. With kind wishes for your further success,

I am yours truly,

H. W. HALLECK.

[PRIVATE AND CONFIDENTIAL.]

HEADQUARTERS, FIFTEENTH ARMY CORPS,
CAMP ON BIG BLACK, MISSISSIPPI, *September* 17, 1863.

H. W. HALLECK, *Commander-in-Chief, Washington, D. C.*

DEAR GENERAL: I have received your letter of August 29th, and with pleasure confide to you fully my thoughts on the important matters you suggest, with absolute confidence that you will use what is valuable, and reject the useless or superfluous.

That part of the continent of North America known as Louisiana, Mississippi, and Arkansas, is in my judgment the key to the whole interior. The valley of the Mississippi is America, and, although railroads have changed the economy of intercommunication, yet the water-channels still mark the lines of fertile land, and afford cheap carriage to the heavy products of it.

The inhabitants of the country on the Monongahela, the Illinois, the Minnesota, the Yellowstone, and Osage, are as directly concerned in the security of the Lower Mississippi as are those who dwell on its very banks in Louisiana; and now that the nation has recovered its possession, this generation of men will make a fearful mistake if they again commit its charge to a people liable to misuse their position, and assert, as was recently done, that, because they dwelt on the banks of his mighty stream, they had a right to control its navigation.

I would deem it very unwise at this time, or for years to come, to revive the State governments of Louisiana, etc., or to institute in this quarter any civil government in which the local people have much to say. They had a government so mild and paternal that they gradually forgot they had any at all, save what they themselves controlled; they asserted an absolute right to seize public moneys, forts, arms, and even to shut up the natural avenues of travel and commerce. They chose *war*—they ignored and denied all the obligations of the solemn contract of government and appealed to force.

We accepted the issue, and now they begin to realize that war is a two-edged sword, and it may be that many of the inhabitants cry for *peace*. I know them well, and the very impulses of their nature; and to deal with the inhabitants of that part of the South which borders on the great river, we must recognize the classes into which they have divided themselves:

First. The large planters, owning lands, slaves, and all kinds of personal property. These are, on the whole, the ruling class. They are educated, wealthy, and easily approached. In some districts they are bitter as gall, and have given up slaves, plantations, and all, serving in the armies of the Confederacy; whereas, in others, they are conservative. None dare admit a friendship for us, though they say freely that they were at the outset opposed to war and disunion. I *know* we can manage this class, but only by *action*. Argument is exhausted, and words have lost their usual meaning. Nothing but the logic of events touches their understanding; but, of late, this has worked a wonderful change. If our country were like Europe, crowded with people, I would say it would be easier to replace this class than to reconstruct it, subordinate to the policy of the nation; but, as this is not the case, it is better to allow the planters, with individual exceptions, gradually to recover their plantations, to hire any species of labor, and to adapt themselves to the new order of things. Still, their friendship and assistance to reconstruct order out of the present ruin cannot be depended on. They watch the operations of our armies, and hope still for a Southern Confederacy that will restore to them the slaves and privileges which they feel are otherwise lost forever. In my judgment, we have two more battles to win before we should even bother our minds with the idea of restoring civil order—viz., one near Meridian, in November, and one near Shreveport, in February and March next, when Red River is navigable by our gunboats. When these are done, then, and not until then, will the planters of Louisiana, Arkansas, and Mississippi, submit. Slavery is already gone, and, to cultivate the land, Negro or other labor must be hired. This, of itself, is a vast revolution, and time must be afforded to allow men to adjust their minds and habits to this new order of things. A civil government of the representative type would suit this class far less than a pure military rule, readily adapting itself to actual occurrences, and able to enforce its laws and orders promptly and emphatically.

Second. The smaller farmers, mechanics, merchants, and laborers. This class will probably number three-quarters of the whole; have, in fact, no real interest in the establishment of a Southern Confederacy, and have been led or driven into war on the false theory that they were to be benefited somehow—they knew not how. They are essentially tired of the war, and would slink back home if they could. These are the real *tiers état* of the South, and are hardly worthy a thought; for they swerve to and fro according to events which they do not comprehend or attempt to shape. When the time for reconstruction comes, they will want the old political system of caucuses, Legislatures, etc., to amuse them and make them believe they are real sovereigns; but in all things they will follow blindly the lead of the planters. The Southern politicians, who understand this class, use them as the French do their masses—seemingly consult their prejudices, while they make their orders and enforce them. We should do the same.

Third. The Union men of the South. I must confess I have little respect for this class. They allowed a clamorous set of demagogues to muzzle and drive them as a pack of curs. Afraid of shadows, they submit tamely to squads of dragoons, and permit them, without a murmur, to burn their cotton, take their horses, corn, and every thing; and, when we reach them, they are full of complaints if our men take a few fence-rails for fire, or corn to feed our horses. They give us no assistance or information, and are loudest in their complaints at the smallest excesses of our soldiers. Their sons, horses, arms, and every thing useful, are in the army against us, and they stay at home, claiming all the exemptions of peaceful citizens. I account them as nothing in this great game of war.

Fourth. The young bloods of the South: sons of planters, lawyers about towns, good billiard-players and sportsmen, men who never did work and never will. War suits them, and the rascals are brave, fine riders, bold to rashness, and dangerous subjects in every sense. They care not a sou for niggers, land, or any thing. They hate Yankees *per se,* and don't bother their brains about the past, present, or future. As long as they have good horses, plenty of forage, and an open country, they are happy. This is a larger class than most men suppose, and they are the most dangerous set of men that this war has turned loose upon the world. They are splendid riders, first-rate shots, and utterly reckless. Stewart, John Morgan, Forrest, and Jackson, are the types and leaders of this class. These men must all be killed or employed by us before we can hope for peace. They have no property or future, and therefore cannot be influenced by any thing, except personal considerations. I have two brigades of these fellows in my front, commanded by [George B.] Cosby, of the old army, and [John W.] Whitfield, of Texas. Stephen D. Lee is in command of the whole. I have frequent interviews with their officers, a good understanding with them, and am inclined to think, when the resources of their country are exhausted, we must employ them. They are the best cavalry in the world, but it will tax Mr. Chase's genius for finance to supply them with horses. At present horses cost them nothing; for they take where they find, and don't bother their brains as to who is to pay for them; the same may be said of the cornfields, which have, as they believe, been cultivated by a good-natured people for their special benefit. We propose to share with them the free use of these cornfields, planted by willing hands, that will never gather the crops.

Now that I have sketched the people who inhabit the district of country under consideration, I will proceed to discuss the future.

A civil government now, for any part of it, would be simply ridiculous. The people would not regard it, and even the military commanders of the antagonistic parties would treat it lightly. Governors would be simply petitioners for military assistance, to protect supposed friendly interests, and military commanders would refuse to disperse and weaken their armies for military reasons. Jealousies would arise between the two conflicting powers, and, instead of contributing to the end of the war, would actually defer it. Therefore, I contend that the interests of the United States, and of the real parties concerned, demand the continuance of the simple military rule, till after *all* the organized armies of the South are dispersed, conquered, and subjugated.

The people of all this region are represented in the Army of Virginia, at Charleston, Mobile, and Chattanooga. They have sons and relations in each of the rebel armies, and naturally are interested in their fate. Though we hold military possession of the key-points of their country, still they contend, and naturally, that should Lee succeed in Virginia, or Bragg at Chattanooga, a change will occur here also. We cannot for this reason attempt to reconstruct parts of the South as we conquer it, till all idea of the establishment of a Southern Confederacy is abandoned. We should avail ourselves of the present lull to secure the strategical points that will give us an advantage in the future military movements, and we should treat the idea of civil government as one in which we as a nation have a minor or subordinate interest. The opportunity is good to impress on the population the truth that they are more interested in civil government than we are; and that, to enjoy the protection of laws, they must not be passive observers of events, but must aid and sustain the constituted authorities in enforcing the laws; they must not only submit themselves, but should pay their share of taxes, and render personal services when called on.

It seems to me, in contemplating the history of the past two years, that all the people of our country, North, South, East, and West, have been undergoing a salutary political schooling, learning lessons which might have been acquired from the experience of other people; but we had all become so wise in our own conceit that we would only learn by actual experience of our own. The people even of small and unimportant localities, North as well as South, had reasoned themselves into the belief that their opinions were superior to the aggregated interest of the whole nation. Half our territorial nation rebelled, on a doctrine of secession that they themselves now scout; and a real numerical majority actually believed that a little State was endowed with such sovereignty that it could defeat the policy of the great whole. I think the present war has exploded that notion, and were this war to cease now, the experience gained, though dear, would be worth the expense.

Another great and important natural truth is still in contest, and can only be solved by war. Numerical majorities by vote have been our great arbiter. Heretofore all men have cheerfully submitted to it in questions left open, but numerical majorities are not necessarily physical majorities. The South, though numerically inferior, contend they can whip the Northern superiority of numbers, and therefore by natural law they contend that they are not bound to submit. This issue is the only real one, and in my judgment all else should be deferred to it. War alone can decide it, and it is the only question now left for us as a people to decide. Can we whip the South? If we can, our numerical majority has both the natural and constitutional right to govern them. If we cannot whip them, they contend for the natural right to select their own government, and they have the argument. Our armies must prevail over theirs; our officers, marshals, and courts, must penetrate into the innermost recesses of their land, before we have the natural right to demand their submission.

I would banish all minor questions, assert the broad doctrine that as a nation the United States has the right, and also the physical power, to penetrate to every part of our national domain, and that we will do it—that we will do it in our own time and in our own way; that it makes no difference whether it be in one year, or two, or ten, or twenty; that we will remove and destroy every obstacle, if need be, take every life, every acre of land, every particle of property, every thing that to us seems proper; that we will not cease till the end is attained; that all who do not aid us are enemies, and that we will not account to them for our acts. If the people of the South oppose, they do so at their peril; and if they stand by, mere lookers-on in this domestic tragedy, they have no right to immunity, protection, or share in the final results.

I even believe and contend further that, in the North, every member of the nation is bound by both natural and constitutional law to "maintain and defend the Government against all its enemies and opposers whomsoever." If they fail to do it they are derelict, and can be punished, or deprived of all advantages arising from the labors of those who do. If any man, North or South, withholds his share of taxes, or his physical assistance in this, the crisis of our history, he should be deprived of all voice in the future elections of this country, and might be banished, or reduced to the condition of a mere denizen of the land.

War is upon us, none can deny it. It is not the choice of the Government of the United States, but of a faction; the Government was forced to accept the issue, or to submit to a degradation fatal and disgraceful to all the inhabitants. In accepting war, *it* should be "pure and simple" as applied to the belligerents. I would keep it so, till all traces of the war are effaced; till those who appealed to it are sick and tired of it, and come to the emblem of our nation, and sue for peace. I would not coax them, or even meet them half-way, but make them so sick of war that generations would pass away before they would again appeal to it.

I know what I say when I repeat that the insurgents of the South sneer at all overtures looking to their interests. They scorn the alliance with the Copperheads; they tell me to my face that they respect Grant, McPherson, and our brave associates who fight manfully and well for a principle, but despise the Copperheads and sneaks at the North, who profess friendship for the South and opposition to the war, as mere covers for their knavery and poltroonery.

God knows that I deplore this fratricidal war as much as any man living, but it is upon us, a physical fact; and there is only one honorable issue from it. We must fight it out, army against army, and man against man; and I know, and you know, and civilians begin to realize the fact, that reconciliation and reconstruction will be easier through and by means of strong, well-equipped, and organized armies than through any species of conventions that can be framed. The issues are made, and all discussion is out of place and ridiculous. The section of thirty-pounder Parrott rifles now drilling before my tent is a more convincing argument than the largest Democratic meeting the State of New York can possibly assemble at Albany; and a simple order of the War Department to draft enough men to fill our skeleton regiments would be more convincing as to our national perpetuity than an humble pardon to Jeff. Davis and all his misled host.

The only government needed or deserved by the States of Louisiana, Arkansas, and Mississippi, now exists in Grant's army. This needs, simply, enough privates to fill its ranks; all else will follow in due season. This army has its well-defined code of laws and practice, and can adapt itself to the wants and necessities of a city, the country, the rivers, the sea, indeed to all parts of this land. It better subserves the interest and policy of the General Government, and the people here prefer it to any weak or servile combination that would at once, from force of habit, revive and perpetuate local prejudices and passions. The people of this country have forfeited all right to a voice in the councils of the nation. They know it and feel it, and in after-years they will be the better citizens from the dear-bought experience of the present crisis. Let them learn now, and learn it well, that good citizens must obey as well as command. Obedience to law, absolute —yea, even abject—is the lesson that this war, under Providence, will teach the free and enlightened American citizen. As a nation, we shall be the better for it.

I never have apprehended foreign interference in our family quarrel. Of course, governments founded on a different and it may be an antagonistic principle with ours naturally feel a pleasure at our complications, and, it may be, wish our downfall; but in the end England and France will join with us in jubilation at the triumph of constitutional government over faction. Even now the English manifest this. I do not profess to understand Napoleon's design in Mexico, and I do not see that his taking military possession of Mexico concerns us. We have as much territory now as we want. The Mexicans have failed in self-government, and it was a question as to what nation she should fall a prey. That is now solved, and I don't see that we are damaged. We have the finest part of the North American Continent, all we can people and can take care of; and, if we can suppress rebellion in our own land, and compose the strife generated by it, we shall have enough people, resources, and wealth, if well combined, to defy interference from any and every quarter.

I therefore hope the Government of the United States will continue, as heretofore, to collect, in well-organized armies, the physical strength of the nation; applying it, as heretofore, in asserting the national authority; and in persevering, without relaxation, to the end. This, whether near or far off, is not for us to say; but, fortunately, we have no choice. We must succeed—no other choice is left us except degradation. The South must be ruled by us, or she will rule us. We must conquer them, or ourselves be conquered. There is no middle course. They ask, and will have, nothing else, and talk of compromise is bosh; for we know they would even scorn the offer.

I wish the war could have been deferred for twenty years, till the superabundant population of the north could flow in and replace the losses sustained by war; but this could not be, and we are forced to take things as they are.

All therefore I can now venture to advise is to raise the draft to its maximum, fill the present regiments to as large a standard as possible, and push the war, pure and simple. Great attention should be paid to the discipline of our armies, for on them may be founded the future stability of the Government.

The cost of the war is, of course, to be considered, but finances will adjust themselves to the actual state of affairs; and, even if we would, we could not change the cost. Indeed, the larger the cost now, the less will it be in the end; for the end must be attained somehow, regardless of loss of life and treasure, and is merely a question of time.

Excuse so long a letter. With great respect, etc.,

W. T. SHERMAN, *Major-General.*

General Halleck, on receipt of this letter, telegraphed me that Mr. Lincoln had read it carefully, and had instructed him to obtain my consent to have it published. At the time, I preferred not to be drawn into any newpaper controversy, and so wrote to General Halleck.

Chapter 7

Chattanooga and Knoxville: "It Was a Magnificent Battle" July—December, 1863

AFTER THE FALL OF VICKSBURG, and its corollary, Port Hudson, the Mississippi River was wholly in the possession of the Union forces, and formed a perfect line of separation in the territories of our opponents. Thenceforth, they could not cross it save by stealth, and the military affairs on its west bank became unimportant. Grant's army had seemingly completed its share of the work of war, and lay, as it were, idle for a time. In person General Grant went to New Orleans to confer with General Banks, and his victorious army was somewhat dispersed. Parke's corps (Ninth) returned to Kentucky, and afterward formed part of the Army of the Ohio, under General Burnside; Ord's corps (Thirteenth) was sent down to Natchez, and gradually drifted to New Orleans and Texas; McPherson's (Seventeenth) remained in and near Vicksburg; Hurlbut's (Sixteenth) was at Memphis; and mine (Fifteenth) was encamped along the Big Black, about twenty miles east of Vicksburg. This corps was composed of four divisions: Steele's (the First) was posted at and near the railroad-bridge; Blair's (the Second), next in order, near Parson Fox's; the Third Division (Tuttle's) was on the ridge about the head of Bear Creek; and the Fourth (Ewing's) was at Messinger's Ford. My own headquarters were in tents in a fine grove of old oaks near Parson Fox's house, and the battalion of the Thirteenth Regulars was the headquarters guard.

All the camps were arranged for health, comfort, rest, and drill. It being midsummer, we did not expect any change till the autumn months, and accordingly made ourselves as comfortable as possible. There was a short railroad in operation from Vicksburg to the bridge across the Big Black, whence supplies in abundance were hauled to our respective camps. With a knowledge of this fact Mrs. Sherman came down from Ohio with Minnie, Lizzie, Willie, and Tom, to pay us a visit in our camp at Parson Fox's. Willie was then nine years old, was well advanced for his years, and took the most intense interest in the affairs of the army. He was a great favorite with the soldiers, and used to ride with me on horseback in the numerous drills and reviews of the time. He then had the promise of as long a life as any of my children, and displayed more interest in the war than any of them. He was called a "sergeant" in the regular battalion, learned the manual of arms, and regularly attended the parade and guard-mounting of the Thirteenth, back of my camp. We made frequent visits to Vicksburg, and always stopped with General McPherson, who had a large house, and boarded with a family (Mrs. Edwards's) in which were several interesting young ladies. General Grant occupied another house (Mrs. Lum's) in Vicksburg during that summer, and also had his family with him. The time passed very agreeably, diversified only by little events of not much significance, among which I will recount only one.

While we occupied the west bank of the Big Black, the east bank was watched by a rebel cavalry-division, commanded by General Armstrong. He had four brigades, commanded by Generals Whitfield, [Peter B.] Starke, Cosby, and Wirt Adams. Quite frequently they communicated with us by flags of truce on trivial matters, and we reciprocated, merely to observe them. One day a flag of truce, borne by a Captain B——, of Louisville, Kentucky, escorted by about twenty-five men, was reported at Messinger's Ferry, and I sent orders to let them come right into my tent. This brought them through the camps of the Fourth Division, and part of the Second; and as they drew up in front of my tent, I invited Captain B—— and another officer with him (a major from Mobile) to dismount, to enter my tent, and to make themselves at home. Their escort was sent to join mine, with orders to furnish them forage and every thing they wanted. B—— had brought a sealed letter for General Grant at Vicksburg, which was dispatched to him. In the evening we had a good supper, with wine and cigars, and, as we sat talking, B—— spoke of his father and mother, in Louisville, got leave to write them a long letter without its being read by any one, and then we talked about the war. He said: "What is the use of your persevering? It is simply impossible to subdue eight millions of people"; asserting that "the feeling in the South had become so embittered that a reconciliation was impossible." I answered that, "sitting as we then were, we appeared very comfortable, and surely there was no trouble in our becoming friends." "Yes," said he, "that is very true of us, but we are gentlemen of education, and can easily adapt ourselves to any condition of things; but this would not apply equally well to the common people, or to the common soldiers." I took him out to the camp-fires behind the tent, and there were the men of his escort and mine mingled together, drinking their coffee, and happy as soldiers always seem. I asked B—— what he thought of that, and he admitted that I had the best of the argument. Before I dismissed this flag of truce, his companion consulted me confidentially as to what disposition he ought to make of his family, then in Mobile, and I frankly gave him the best advice I could.

While we were thus lying idle in camp on the Big Black, the Army of the Cumberland, under General Rosecrans, was moving against Bragg at Chattanooga; and the Army of the Ohio, General Burnside, was marching toward East Tennessee. General Rosecrans was so confident of success that he somewhat scattered his command, seemingly to surround and capture Bragg in Chattanooga; but the latter, reënforced from Virginia, drew out of Chattanooga, concentrated his army at Lafayette, and at Chickamauga fell on Rosecrans, defeated him, and drove him into Chattanooga. The whole country seemed paralyzed by this unhappy event; and the authorities in Washington were thoroughly stampeded. From the East the Eleventh Corps ([Henry W.] Slocum), and the Twelfth Corps ([Oliver O.] Howard), were sent by rail to Nashville, and forward under command of General [Joseph E.] Hooker;

orders were also sent to General Grant, by Halleck, to send what reënforcements he could spare immediately toward Chattanooga.

Bragg had completely driven Rosecrans's army into Chattanooga; the latter was in actual danger of starvation, and the railroad to his rear seemed inadequate to his supply. The first intimation which I got of this disaster was on the 22d of September, by an order from General Grant to dispatch one of my divisions immediately into Vicksburg, to go toward Chattanooga, and I designated the First, General Osterhaus— Steele meantime having been appointed to the command of the Department of Arkansas, and had gone to Little Rock. General Osterhaus marched the same day, and on the 23d I was summoned to Vicksburg in person, where General Grant showed me the alarming dispatches from General Halleck, which had been sent from Memphis by General Hurlbut, and said, on further thought, that he would send me and my whole corps. But, inasmuch as one division of McPherson's corps (John E. Smith's) had already started, he instructed me to leave one of my divisions on the Big Black, and to get the other two ready to follow at once. I designated the Second, then commanded by Brigadier-General Giles A. Smith, and the Fourth, commanded by Brigadier-General [John A.] Corse.

On the 25th I returned to my camp on Big Black, gave all the necessary orders for these divisions to move, and for the Third (Tuttle's) to remain, and went into Vicksburg with my family. The last of my corps designed for this expedition started from camp on the 27th, reached Vicksburg the 28th, and were embarked on boats provided for them. General Halleck's dispatches dwelt upon the fact that General Rosecrans's routes of supply were overtaxed, and that we should move from Memphis eastward, repairing railroads as we progressed, as far as Athens, Alabama, whence I was to report to General Rosecrans, at Chattanooga, by letter.

I took passage for myself and family in the steamer Atlantic, Captain Henry McDougall. When the boat was ready to start, Willie was missing. Mrs. Sherman supposed him to have been with me, whereas I supposed he was with her. An officer of the Thirteenth went up to General McPherson's house for him, and soon returned, with Captain Clift leading him, carrying in his hands a small double-barreled shot-gun; and I joked him about carrying away captured property. In a short time we got off. As we all stood on the guards to look at our old camps at Young's Point, I remarked that Willie was not well, and he admitted that he was sick. His mother put him to bed, and consulted Dr. Roler, of the Fifty-fifth Illinois, who found symptoms of typhoid fever. The river was low; we made slow progress till above Helena; and, as we approached Memphis, Dr. Roler told me that Willie's life was in danger, and he was extremely anxious to reach Memphis for certain medicines and for consultation. We arrived at Memphis on the 2d of October, carried Willie up to the Gayoso Hotel, and got the most experienced physician there, who acted with Dr. Roler, but he sank rapidly, and died the evening of the 3d of October. The blow was a terrible one to us all, so sudden and so unexpected, that I could not help reproaching myself for having consented to his visit in that sickly region in the summer-time. Of all my children, he seemed the most precious. Born in San Francisco, I had watched with intense interest his development, and he seemed more than any of the children to take an interest in my special profession. Mrs. Sherman, Minnie, Lizzie, and Tom, were with him at the time, and we all, helpless and overwhelmed, saw him die. Being in the very midst of an important military enterprise, I had hardly time to pause and think of my personal loss. We procured a metallic casket, and had a military funeral, the battalion of the Thirteenth United States Regulars acting as escort from the Gayoso Hotel to the steamboat Grey Eagle, which conveyed him and my family up to Cairo, whence they proceeded to our home at Lancaster, Ohio, where he was buried. I here give my letter to Captain C. C. Smith, who commanded the battalion at the time, as exhibiting our intense feelings:

GAYOSO HOUSE, MEMPHIS, TENNESSEE, }
October 4, 1863—*Midnight.* }

Captain C. C. SMITH, *commanding Battalion Thirteenth United States Regulars.*

MY DEAR FRIEND: I cannot sleep to-night till I record an expression of the deep feelings of my heart to you, and to the officers and soldiers of the battalion, for their kind behavior to my poor child. I realize that you all feel for my family the attachment of kindred, and I assure you of full reciprocity.

Consistent with a sense of duty to my profession and office, I could not leave my post, and sent for the family to come to me in that fatal climate, and in that sickly period of the year, and behold the result! The child that bore my name, and in whose future I reposed with more confidence than I did in my own plan of life, now floats a mere corpse, seeking a grave in a distant land, with a weeping mother, brother, and sisters, clustered about him. For myself, I ask no sympathy. On, on I must go, to meet a soldier's fate, or live to see our country rise superior to all factions, till its flag is adored and respected by ourselves and by all the powers of the earth.

But Willie was, or thought he was, a sergeant in the Thirteenth. I have seen his eye brighten, his heart beat, as he beheld the battalion under arms, and asked me if they were not *real* soldiers. Child as he was, he had the enthusiasm, the pure love of truth, honor, and love of country, which should animate all soldiers.

God only knows why he should die thus young. He is dead, but will not be forgotten till those who knew him in life have followed him to that same mysterious end.

Please convey to the battalion my heart-felt thanks, and assure each and all that if in after-years they call on me or mine, and mention that they were of the Thirteenth Regulars when Willie was a sergeant, they will have a key to the affections of my family that will open all it has; that we will share with them our last blanket, our last crust! Your friend,

W. T. SHERMAN, *Major-General.*

Long afterward, in the spring of 1867, we had his body disinterred and brought to St. Louis, where he is now buried in a beautiful spot, in Calvary Cemetery, by the side of another child, "Charles," who was born at Lancaster, in the summer of 1864, died early, and was buried at Notre Dame, Indiana. His body was transferred at the same time to the same spot. Over Willie's grave is erected a beautiful marble monument, designed and executed by the officers and soldiers of that battalion which claimed him as a sergeant and comrade.

During the summer and fall of 1863 Major-General S. A. Hurlbut was in command at Memphis. He supplied me copies of all dispatches from Washington, and all the information he possessed of the events about Chattanooga. Two of these dispatches cover all essential points:

WASHINGTON CITY, *September 15, 1863—5 P. M.*
Major-General S. A. HURLBUT, *Memphis:*

All the troops that can possibly be spared in West Tennessee and on the Mississippi River should be sent without delay to assist General Rosecrans on the Tennessee River.

Urge Sherman to act with all possible promptness.

If you have boats, send them down to bring up his troops.

Information just received indicates that a part of Lee's army has been sent to reënforce Bragg.

H. W. HALLECK, *General-in-Chief.*

WASHINGTON, *September 19, 1863—4 P. M.*
Major-General S. A. HURLBUT, *Memphis, Tennessee:*

Give me definite information of the number of troops sent toward Decatur, and where they are. Also, what other troops are to follow, and when.

Has any thing been heard from the troops ordered from Vicksburg?

No efforts must be spared to support Rosecrans's right, and to guard the crossings of the Tennessee River.

H. W. HALLECK, *General-in-Chief.*

My special orders were to repair the Memphis & Charleston Railroad eastward as I progressed, as far as Athens, Alabama, to draw supplies by that route, so that, on reaching Athens, we should not be dependent on the roads back to Nashville, already overtaxed by the demand of Rosecrans's army.

On reaching Memphis, October 2d, I found that Osterhaus's division had already gone by rail as far as Corinth, and that John E. Smith's division was in the act of starting by cars. The Second Division, then commanded by Brigadier-General Giles A. Smith, reached Memphis at the same time with me; and the Fourth Division, commanded by Brigadier-General John M. Corse, arrived a day or two after. The railroad was in fair condition as far as Corinth, ninety-six miles, but the road was badly stocked with locomotives and cars, so that it took until the 9th to get off the Second Division, when I gave orders for the Fourth Division and wagon-trains to march by the common road.

On Sunday morning, October 11th, with a special train loaded with our orderlies and clerks, the horses of our staff, the battalion of the Thirteenth United States Regulars, and a few officers going forward to join their commands, among them Brigadier-General Hugh Ewing, I started for Corinth.

At Germantown, eight miles, we passed Corse's division (Fourth) on the march, and about noon the train ran by the depot at Colliersville, twenty-six miles out. I was in the rear car with my staff, dozing, but observed the train slacking speed and stopping about half a mile beyond the depot. I noticed some soldiers running to and fro, got out at the end of the car, and soon Colonel Anthony (Sixty-sixth Indiana), who commanded the post, rode up and said that his pickets had just been driven in, and there was an appearance of an attack by a large force of cavalry coming from the southeast. I ordered the men to get off the train, to form on the knoll near the railroad-cut, and soon observed a rebel officer riding toward us with a white flag. Colonel Anthony and Colonel Dayton (one of my aides) were sent to meet him, and to keep him in conversation as long as possible. They soon returned, saying it was the adjutant of the rebel general [James R.] Chalmers, who demanded the surrender of the place. I instructed them to return and give a negative answer, but to delay him as much as possible, so as to give us time for preparation. I saw Anthony, Dayton, and the rebel bearer of the flag, in conversation, and the latter turn his horse to ride back, when I ordered Colonel McCoy to run to the station, and get a message over the wires as quick as possible to Memphis and Germantown, to hurry forward Corse's division. I then ordered the train to back to the depot, and drew back the battalion of regulars to the small earth redoubt near it. The depot-building was of brick, and had been punctured with loop-holes. To its east, about two hundred yards, with a small square earthwork or fort, into which were put a part of the regulars along with the company of the Sixty-sixth Indiana already there. The rest of the men were distributed into the railroad-cut, and in some shallow rifle-trenches near the depot. We had hardly made these preparations when the enemy was seen forming in a long line on the ridge to the south, about four hundred yards off, and soon after two parties of cavalry passed the railroad on both sides of us, cutting the wires and tearing up some rails. Soon they opened on us with artillery (of which we had none), and their men were dismounting and preparing to assault. To the south of us was an extensive cornfield, with the corn still standing, and on the other side was the town of Colliersville. All the houses near, that could give shelter to the enemy, were ordered to be set on fire, and the men were instructed to keep well under cover and to reserve their fire for the assault, which seemed inevitable. A long line of rebel skirmishers came down through the cornfield, and two other parties approached us along the railroad on both sides.

In the fort was a small magazine containing some cartridges. Lieutenant James, a fine, gallant fellow, who was ordnance-officer on my staff, asked leave to arm the orderlies and clerks with some muskets which he had found in the depot, to which I consented; he marched them into the magazine, issued cartridges, and marched back to the depot to assist in its defense. Afterward he came to me, said a party of the enemy had got into the woods near the depot, and was annoying him, and he wanted to charge and drive it away. I advised him to be extremely cautious, as our enemy vastly outnumbered us, and had every advantage in position and artillery; but instructed him, if they got too near, he might make a sally. Soon after, I heard a rapid fire in that quarter, and Lieutenant James was brought in on a stretcher, with a ball through his breast, which I supposed to be fatal. The enemy closed down on us several times, and got possession of the rear of our train, from which they succeeded in getting five of our horses, among them my favorite mare Dolly; but our men were cool and practised shots (with great experience acquired at Vicksburg), and drove them back. With their artillery they knocked to pieces our locomotive and several of the cars, and set fire to the train; but we managed to get possession again, and extinguished the fire. Colonel [Joseph C.] Audenreid, aide-de-camp, was provoked to find that his valise of nice shirts had been used to kindle the fire. The fighting continued all round us for three or four hours, when we observed signs of drawing off, which I attributed to the rightful cause, the rapid approach of Corse's division, which arrived about dark, having marched the whole distance from Memphis, twenty-six miles, on the double-quick. The next day we repaired damages to the railroad and locomotive, and went on to Corinth.

At Corinth, on the 16th, I received the following important dispatches:

MEMPHIS, *October* 14, 1863—11 A.M.

Arrived this morning. Will be off in a few hours. My orders are only to go to Cairo, and report from there by telegraph. McPherson will be in Canton to-day. He will remain there until Sunday or Monday next, and reconnoitre as far eastward as possible with cavalry, in the mean time.

U. S. GRANT, *Major-General.*

WASHINGTON, *October* 14, 1863—1 P.M.
Major-General W. T. SHERMAN, *Corinth:*

Yours of the 10th is received. The important matter to be attended to is that of supplies. When Eastport can be reached by boats, the use of the railroad can be dispensed with; but until that time it must be guarded as far as used. The Kentucky Railroad can barely supply General Rosecrans. All these matters must be left to your judgment as circumstances may arise. Should the enemy be so strong as to prevent your going to Athens, or connecting with General Rosecrans, you will nevertheless have assisted him greatly by drawing away a part of the enemy's forces.

H. W. HALLECK, *Major-General.*

On the 18th, with my staff and a small escort, I rode forward to Burnsville, and on the 19th to Iuka, where, on the next day, I was most agreeably surprised to hear of the arrival at Eastport (only ten miles off) of two gunboats, under the command of Captain Phelps, which had been sent up the Tennessee River by Admiral Porter, to help us.

Satisfied that, to reach Athens and to communicate with General Rosecrans, we should have to take the route north of the Tennessee River, on the 24th I ordered the Fourth Division to cross at Eastport with the aid of the gunboats, and to move to Florence. About the same time, I received the general orders assigning General Grant to command the Military Division of the Mississippi, authorizing him, on reaching Chattanooga, to supersede General Rosecrans by General George H. Thomas, with other and complete authority.

General Frank P. Blair, who was then ahead with the two

divisions of Osterhaus and John E. Smith, was temporarily assigned to the command of the Fifteenth Corps. General Hurlbut remained at Memphis in command of the Sixteenth Corps, and General McPherson at Vicksburg with the Seventeenth These three corps made up the Army of the Tennessee.

I was still busy in pushing forward the repairs to the railroad-bridge at Bear Creek, and in patching up the many breaks between it and Tuscumbia, when on the 27th of October, as I sat on the porch of a house, I was approached by a dirty, black-haired individual with mixed dress and strange demeanor, who inquired for me, and, on being assured that I was in fact the man, he handed me a letter from General Blair at Tuscumbia, and another short one, which was a telegraph-message from General Grant at Chattanooga, addressed to me through General George Crook, commanding at Huntsville, Alabama, to this effect:

> Drop all work on Memphis & Charleston Railroad, cross the Tennessee, and hurry eastward with all possible dispatch toward Bridgeport, till you meet further orders from me.
>
> U. S. GRANT.

The bearer of this message was Corporal Pike, who described to me, in his peculiar way, that General Crook had sent him in a canoe; that he had paddled down the Tennessee River, over Muscle Shoals, was fired at all the way by guerrillas, but on reaching Tuscumbia he had providentially found it in possession of our troops. He had reported to General Blair, who sent him on to me at Iuka. This Pike proved to be a singular character; his manner attracted my notice at once, and I got him a horse, and had him travel with us eastward to about Elkton, whence I sent him back to General Crook at Huntsville; but told him, if I could ever do him a personal service, he might apply to me. The next spring when I was in Chattanooga, preparing for the Atlantic campaign, Corporal Pike made his appearance and asked a fulfillment of my promise. I inquired what he wanted, and he said he wanted to do something *bold*, something that would make him a hero. I explained to him, that we were getting ready to go for Joe Johnston at Dalton, that I expected to be in the neighborhood of Atlanta about the 4th of July, and wanted the bridge across the Savannah River at Augusta, Georgia, to be burnt about that time, to produce alarm and confusion behind the rebel army. I explained to Pike that the chances were three to one that he would be caught and hanged; but the greater the danger the greater seemed to be his desire to attempt it. I told him to select a companion, to disguise himself as an East Tennessee refugee, work his way over the mountains into North Carolina, and at the time appointed to float down the Savannah River and burn that bridge. In a few days he had made his preparations and took his departure. The bridge was not burnt, and I supposed that Pike had been caught and hanged.

When we reached Columbia, South Carolina, in February, 1865, just as we were leaving the town, in passing near the asylum, I heard my name called, and saw a very dirty fellow followed by a file of men running toward me, and as they got near I recognized Pike. He called to me to identify him as one of *my* men; he was then a prisoner under guard, and I instructed the guard to bring him that night to my camp some fifteen miles up the road, which was done. Pike gave me a graphic narrative of his adventures, which would have filled a volume; told me how he had made two attempts to burn the bridge, and failed; and said that at the time of our entering Columbia he was a prisoner in the hands of the rebels, under trial for his life, but in the confusion of their retreat he made his escape and got into our lines, where he was again made a prisoner by our troops because of his looks. Pike got some clothes, cleaned up, and I used him afterward to communicate with Wilmington, North Carolina. Some time after the war, he was appointed a lieutenant of the Regular Cavalry, and was killed in Oregon, by the accidental discharge of a pistol. Just before his death he wrote me, saying that he was tired of the monotony of garrison-life, and wanted to turn Indian, join the Cheyennes on the Plains, who were then giving us great trouble, and, after he had gained their confidence, he would betray them into our hands. Of course I wrote him that he must try and settle down and become a gentleman as well as an officer, apply himself to his duties, and forget the wild desires of his nature, which were well enough in time of war, but not suited to his new condition as an officer; but, poor fellow! he was killed by an accident, which probably saved him from a slower but harder fate.

At Iuka I issued all the orders to McPherson and Hurlbut necessary for the Department of the Tennessee during my absence, and, further, ordered the collection of a force out of the Sixteenth Corps, of about eight thousand men, to be commanded by General [Grenville] M. Dodge, with orders to follow as far east as Athens, Tennessee, there to await instructions. We instantly discontinued all attempts to repair the Charleston Railroad; and the remaining three divisions of the Fifteenth Corps marched to Eastport, crossed the Tennessee River by the aid of the gunboats, a ferry-boat, and a couple of transports which had come up, and hurried eastward.

In person I crossed on the 1st of November, and rode forward to Florence, where I overtook Ewing's division. The other divisions followed rapidly. On the road to Florence I was accompanied by my staff, some clerks, and mounted orderlies. Major Ezra Taylor was chief of artillery, and one of his sons was a clerk at headquarters. The latter seems to have dropped out of the column, and gone to a farm-house near the road. There was no organized force of the rebel army north of the Tennessee River, but the country was full of guerrillas. A party of these pounced down on the farm, caught young Taylor and another of the clerks, and after reaching Florence, Major Taylor heard of the capture of his son, and learned that when last seen he was stripped of his hat and coat, was tied to the tail-board of a wagon, and driven rapidly to the north of the road we had traveled. The major appealed to me to do something for his rescue. I had no cavalry to send in pursuit, but knowing that there was always an understanding between these guerrillas and their friends who staid at home, I sent for three or four of the principal men of Florence (among them a Mr. Foster, who had once been a Senator in Congress), explained to them the capture of young Taylor and his comrade, and demanded their immediate restoration. They, of course, remonstrated, denied all knowledge of the acts of these guerrillas, and claimed to be peaceful citizens of Alabama, residing at home. I insisted that these guerrillas were their own sons and neighbors; that they knew their haunts, and could reach them if they wanted, and they could effect the restoration to us of these men; and I said, moreover, they must do it within twenty-four hours, or I would take them, strip them of their hats and coats, and tie them to the tail-boards of our wagons till they were produced. They sent off messengers at once, and young Taylor and his comrade were brought back the next day.

Resuming our march eastward by the large road, we soon reached Elk River, which was wide and deep, and could only be crossed by a ferry, a process entirely too slow for the occasion; so I changed the route more by the north, to Elkton, Winchester, and Deckerd. At this point we came in communication with the Army of the Cumberland, and by telegraph with General Grant, who was at Chattanooga. He reiterated his orders for me and my command to hurry forward with all possible dispatch, and in person I reached Bridgeport during the night of November 13th, my troops following behind by several roads. At Bridgeport I found a garrison guarding the railroad-bridge and pontoon-bridge there, and staid with the quartermaster, Colonel William G. Le Duc (who was my school-mate at How's School in 1836). There I received a dispatch from General Grant, at Chattanooga, to come up in person, leaving my troops to follow as fast as possible. At that time there were two or three small steamboats on the river, engaged in carrying stores up as far as Kelly's Ferry. In one of these I took passage, and on reaching Kelly's Ferry found orderlies, with one of General Grant's private horses, waiting for me, on which I rode into Chattanooga, November 14th. Of course, I was heartily welcomed by Generals Grant, Thomas, and all, who realized the extraordinary efforts we had made to come to their relief.

The next morning we walked out to Fort Wood, a prominent salient of the defenses of the place, and from its parapet we had a magnificent view of the panorama. Lookout Mountain, with its rebel flags and batteries, stood out boldly, and an occasional shot fired toward Wauhatchee or Moccasin Point gave life to the scene. These shots could barely reach Chattanooga, and I was told that one or more shot had struck a hospital inside the lines. All along Missionary Ridge were the tents of the rebel beleaguering force; the lines of trench from Lookout up toward the Chickamauga were plainly visible; and rebel sentinels, in a continuous chain, were walking their posts in plain view, not a thousand yards off. "Why," said I, "General Grant, you are besieged"; and he said, "It is too true." Up to that moment I had no idea that things were so bad. The rebel lines actually extended from the river, below the town, to the river above, and the Army of the Cumberland was closely held to the town and its immediate defenses. General Grant pointed out to me a house on Missionary Ridge, where General Bragg's headquarters were known to be. He also explained the situation of affairs generally; that the mules and horses of Thomas's army were so starved that they could not haul his guns; that forage, corn, and provisions, were so scarce that the men in hunger stole the few grains of corn that were given to favorite horses; that the men of Thomas's army had been so demoralized by the battle of Chickamauga that he feared they could not be got out of their trenches to assume the offensive; that Bragg had detached Longstreet with a considerable force up into East Tennessee, to defeat and capture Burnside; that Burnside was in danger, etc.; and that he (Grant) was extremely anxious to attack Bragg in position, to defeat him, or at least to force him to recall Longstreet. The Army of the Cumberland had so long been in the trenches that he wanted my troops to hurry up, to take the offensive *first;* after which, he had no doubt the Cumberland army would fight well. Meantime the Eleventh and Twelfth Corps, under General Hooker, had been advanced from Bridgeport along the railroad to Wauhatchee, but could not as yet pass Lookout Mountain. A pontoon-bridge had been thrown across the Tennessee River at Brown's Ferry, by which supplies were hauled into Chattanooga from Kelly's and Wauhatchee.

Another bridge was in course of construction at Chattanooga, under the immediate direction of Quartermaster-General [Montgomery] Meigs, but at the time all wagons, etc., had to be ferried across by a flying-bridge. Men were busy and hard at work everywhere inside our lines, and boats for another pontoon-bridge were being rapidly constructed under Brigadier-General W. F. Smith, familiarly known as "Baldy Smith," and this bridge was destined to be used by my troops, at a point of the river about four miles above Chattanooga, just below the mouth of the Chickamauga River. General Grant explained to me that he had reconnoitred the rebel line from Lookout Mountain up to Chickamauga, and he believed that the northern portion of Missionary Ridge was not fortified at all; and he wanted me, as soon as my troops got up, to lay the new pontoon-bridge by night, cross over, and attack Bragg's right flank on that part of the ridge abutting on

Chickamauga Creek, near the tunnel; and he proposed that we should go at once to look at the ground. In company with Generals Thomas, W. F. Smith, Brannan, and others, we crossed by the flying-bridge, rode back of the hills some four miles, left our horses, and got on a hill overlooking the whole ground about the mouth of the Chickamauga River, and across to the Missionary Hills near the tunnel. Smith and I crept down behind a fringe of trees that lined the river-bank, to the very point selected for the new bridge, where we sat for some time, seeing the rebel pickets on the opposite bank, and almost hearing their words.

Having seen enough, we returned to Chattanooga; and in order to hurry up my command, on which so much depended, I started back to Kelly's in hopes to catch the steamboat that same evening; but on my arrival the boat had gone. I applied to the commanding officer, got a rough boat manned by four soldiers, and started down the river by night. I occasionally took a turn at the oars to relieve some tired man, and about midnight we reached Shell Mound, where General [Walter C.] Whitaker, of Kentucky, furnished us a new and good crew, with which we reached Bridgeport by daylight. I started Ewing's division in advance, with orders to turn aside toward Trenton, to make the enemy believe we were going to turn Bragg's left by pretty much the same road Rosecrans had followed; but with the other three divisions I followed the main road, *via* the Big Trestle at Whitesides, and reached General Hooker's headquarters, just above Wauhatchee, on the 20th; my troops strung all the way back to Bridgeport. It was on this occasion that the Fifteenth Corps gained its peculiar badge: as the men were trudging along the deeply-cut, muddy road, of a cold, drizzly day, one of our Western soldiers left his ranks and joined a party of the Twelfth Corps at their camp-fire. They got into conversation, the Twelfth Corps men asking what troops we were, etc., etc. In turn, our fellow (who had never seen a corps-badge, and noticed that every thing was marked with a star) asked if they were all brigadier-generals. Of course they were not, but the star was their corps-badge, and every wagon, tent, hat, etc., had its star. Then the Twelfth-Corps men inquired what corps he belonged to, and he answered, "The Fifteenth Corps." "What is your badge?" "Why," said he (and he was an Irishman), suiting the action to the word, "forty rounds in the cartridge-box, and twenty in the pocket!" At that time Blair commanded the corps; but Logan succeeded soon after, and, hearing the story, adopted the cartridge-box and forty rounds as the corps-badge.

The condition of the roads was such, and the bridge at Brown's so frail, that it was not until the 23d that we got three of my divisions behind the hills near the point indicated above Chattanooga for crossing the river. It was determined to begin the battle with these three divisions, aided by a division of Thomas's army, commanded by General Jeff. C. Davis, that was already near that point. All the details of the battle of Chattanooga, so far as I was a witness, are so fully given in my official report herewith, that I need add nothing to it. It was a magnificent battle in its conception, in its execution, and in its glorious results; hastened somewhat by the supposed danger of Burnside, at Knoxville, yet so completely successful, that nothing is left for cavil or fault-finding. The first day was lowering and overcast, favoring us greatly, because we wanted to be concealed from Bragg, whose position on the mountain-tops completely overlooked us and our movements. The second day was beautifully clear, and many a time, in the midst of its carnage and noise, I could not help stopping to look across that vast field of battle, to admire its sublimity.

The object of General Hooker's and my attacks on the extreme flanks of Bragg's position was, to disturb him to such an extent, that he would naturally detach from his centre as against us, so that Thomas's army could break through his centre. The whole plan succeeded admirably; but it was not until after dark that I learned the complete success at the centre, and received General Grant's orders to pursue on the north side of Chickamauga Creek.

HEADQUARTERS MILITARY DIVISION OF THE MISSISSIPPI, CHATTANOOGA, TENNESSEE, *November* 25, 1863.

Major-General SHERMAN.

GENERAL: No doubt you witnessed the handsome manner in which Thomas's troops carried Missionary Ridge this afternoon, and can feel a just pride, too, in the part taken by the forces under your command in taking first so much of the same range of hills, and then in attracting the attention of so many of the enemy as to make Thomas's part certain of success. The next thing now will be to relieve Burnside. I have heard from him to the evening of the 23d. At that time he had from ten to twelve days' supplies, and spoke hopefully of being able to hold out that length of time.

My plan is to move your forces out gradually until they reach the railroad between Cleveland and Dalton. Granger will move up the south side of the Tennessee with a column of twenty thousand men, taking no wagons, or but few, with him. His men will carry four days' rations, and the steamer Chattanooga, loaded with rations, will accompany the expedition.

I take it for granted that Bragg's entire force has left. If not, of course, the first thing is to dispose of him. If he has gone, the only thing necessary to do to-morrow will be to send out a reconnoissance to ascertain the whereabouts of the enemy. Yours truly,

U. S. GRANT, *Major-General.*

P.S.—On reflection, I think we will push Bragg with all our strength to-morrow, and try if we cannot cut off a good portion of his rear troops and trains. His men have manifested a strong disposition to desert for some time past, and we will now give them a chance. I will instruct Thomas accordingly. Move the advance force early, on the most easterly road taken by the enemy.   U. S. G.

This compelled me to reverse our column, so as to use the bridge across the Chickamauga at its mouth. The next day we struck the rebel rear at Chickamauga Station, and again near Graysville. There we came in contact with Hooker's and Palmer's troops, who had reached Ringgold. There I detached Howard to cross Taylor's Ridge, and strike the railroad which comes from the north by Cleveland to Dalton. Hooker's troops were roughly handled at Ringgold, and the pursuit was checked. Receiving a note from General Hooker, asking help, I rode forward to Ringgold to explain the movement of Howard; where I met General Grant, and learned that the rebels had again retreated toward Dalton. He gave orders to discontinue the pursuit, as he meant to turn his attention to General Burnside, supposed to be in great danger at Knoxville, about one hundred and thirty miles northeast. General

Grant returned and spent part of the night with me, at Graysville. We talked over matters generally, and he explained that
he had ordered General Gordon Granger, with the Fourth
Corps, to move forward rapidly to Burnside's help, and that
he must return to Chattanooga to push him. By reason of the
scarcity of food, especially of forage, he consented that, instead of going back, I might keep out in the country; for in
motion I could pick up some forage and food, especially on
the Hiawassee River, whereas none remained in Chattanooga.

Accordingly, on the 29th of November, my several columns
marched to Cleveland, and the next day we reached the Hiawassee at Charleston, where the Chattanooga & Knoxville
Railroad crosses it. The railroad-bridge was partially damaged by the enemy in retreating, but we found some abandoned stores. There and thereabouts I expected some rest for
my weary troops and horses; but, as I rode into town, I met
Colonel J. H. Wilson and C. A. Dana (Assistant Secretary of
War), who had ridden out from Chattanooga to find me, with
the following letter from General Grant, and copies of several dispatches from General Burnside, the last which had
been received from him by way of Cumberland Gap:

HEADQUARTERS MILITARY DIVISION OF THE MISSISSIPPI, }
   CHATTANOOGA, TENNESSEE, *November* 29, 1863. }

Major-General W. T. SHERMAN:

News are received from Knoxville to the morning of the
27th. At that time the place was still invested, but the attack on it was not vigorous. Longstreet evidently determined to starve the garrison out. Granger is on the way to
Burnside's relief, but I have lost all faith in his energy or
capacity to manage an expedition of the importance of this
one. I am inclined to think, therefore, I shall have to send
you. Push as rapidly as you can to the Hiawassee, and
determine for yourself what force to take with you from
that point. Granger has his corps with him, from which you
will select in conjunction with the force now with you. In
plain words, you will assume command of all the forces
now moving up the Tennessee, including the garrison at
Kingston, and from that force organize what you deem
proper to relieve Burnside. The balance send back to Chat-

tanooga. Granger has a boat loaded with provisions, which you can issue, and return the boat. I will have another loaded, to follow you. Use, of course, as sparingly as possible from the rations taken with you, and subsist off the country all you can.

It is expected that Foster is moving, by this time, from Cumberland Gap on Knoxville. I do not know what force he will have with him, but presume it will range from three thousand five hundred to five thousand. I leave this matter to you, knowing that you will do better acting upon your discretion than you could trammeled with instructions. I will only add, that the last advices from Burnside himself indicated his ability to hold out with rations only to about the 3d of December.

Very respectfully,

U. S. GRANGER, *Major-General commanding.*

This showed that, on the 27th of November, General Burnside was in Knoxville, closely besieged by the rebel General [James] Longstreet; that his provisions were short, and that, unless relieved by December 3d, he might have to surrender. General Grant further wrote that General Granger, instead of moving with great rapidity as ordered, seemed to move "slowly, and with reluctance"; and, although he (General Grant) hated to call on me and on my tired troops, there was no alternative. He wanted me to take command of every thing within reach, and to hurry forward to Knoxville.

All the details of our march to Knoxville are also given in my official report. By extraordinary efforts [Ely] Long's small brigade of cavalry reached Knoxville during the night of the 3d, purposely to let Burnside know that I was rapidly approaching with an adequate force to raise the siege.

With the head of my infantry column I reached Marysville, about fifteen miles short of Knoxville, on the 5th of December, when I received official notice from Burnside that Longstreet had raised the siege, and had started in retreat up the valley toward Virginia. Halting all the army, except Granger's two divisions, on the morning of the 6th, with General Granger and some of my staff I rode into Knoxville. Approaching from the south and west, we crossed the Holston on a pontoon-bridge, and in a large pen on the Knoxville side I saw a fine lot of cattle, which did not look much like starvation. I found General Burnside and staff domiciled in a large, fine mansion, looking very comfortable, and in a few words he described to me the leading events of the previous few days, and said he had already given orders looking to the pursuit of Longstreet. I offered to join in the pursuit, though in fact my men were worn out, and suffering in that cold season and climate. Indeed, on our way up I personally was almost frozen, and had to beg leave to sleep in the house of a family at Athens.

Burnside explained to me that, reënforced by Granger's two divisions of ten thousand men, he would be able to push Longstreet out of East Tennessee, and he hoped to capture much of his artillery and trains. Granger was present at our conversation, and most unreasonably, I thought, remonstrated against being left; complaining bitterly of what he thought was hard treatment to his men and himself. I know that this language and manner at that time produced on my mind a bad impression, and it was one of the causes which led me to relieve him as a corps commander in the campaign of the next spring. I asked General Burnside to reduce his wishes to writing, which he did in the letter of December 7th, embodied in my official report. General Burnside and I then walked along his lines and examined the salient, known as Fort Sanders, where, some days before, Longstreet had made his assault, and had sustained a bloody repulse.

Returning to Burnside's quarters, we all sat down to a good dinner, embracing roast-turkey. There was a regular dining-table, with clean table-cloth, dishes, knives, forks, spoons, etc., etc. I had seen nothing of this kind in my field experience, and could not help exclaiming that I thought "they were starving," etc.; but Burnside explained that Longstreet had at no time completely invested the place, and that he had kept open communication with the country on the south side of the river Holston, more especially with the French Broad settlements, from whose Union inhabitants he had received a good supply of beef, bacon, and corn-meal. Had I known of this, I should not have hurried my men so fast; but until I reached Knoxville I thought our troops there were actually in danger of starvation. Having supplied General Burnside all the help he wanted, we began our leisurely return to Chattanooga, which we reached on the 16th; when General Grant in person ordered me to restore to General Thomas the divisions of

Howard and Davis, which belonged to his army, and to conduct my own corps (the Fifteenth) to North Alabama for winter-quarters.

On the 19th of December I was at Bridgeport, and gave all the orders necessary for the distribution of the four divisions of the Fifteenth Corps along the railroad from Stevenson to Decatur, and the part of the Sixteenth Corps, commanded by General Dodge, along the railroad from Decatur to Nashville, to make the needed repairs, and to be in readiness for the campaign of the succeeding year; and on the 21st I went up to Nashville, to confer with General Grant and conclude the arrangements for the winer. At that time General Grant was under the impression that the next campaign would be up the valley of East Tennessee, in the direction of Virginia; and as it was likely to be the last and most important campaign of the war, it became necessary to set free as many of the old troops serving along the Mississippi River as possible. This was the real object and purpose of the Meridian campaign, and of Banks's expedition up Red River to Shreveport during that winter.

Chapter 8

Meridian Campaign:
"The Rebel Cavalry Were All
Around Us"
January—February, 1864

THE WINTER OF 1863-'64 opened very cold and severe; and
it was manifest after the battle of Chattanooga, November
25, 1863, and the raising of the siege of Knoxville, December
5th, that military operations in that quarter must in a measure cease, or be limited to Burnside's force beyond Knoxville.
On the 21st of December General Grant had removed his
heaquarters to Nashville, Tennessee, leaving General George
H. Thomas at Chattanooga, in command of the Department
of the Cumberland, and of the army round about that place;
and I was at Bridgeport, with orders to distribute my troops
along the railroad from Stevenson to Decatur, Alabama, and
from Decatur up toward Nashville.

General G. M. Dodge, who was in command of the detachment of the Sixteenth Corps, numbering about eight thousand
men, had not participated with us in the battle of Chattanooga,
but had remained at and near Pulaski, Tennessee, engaged in
repairing that railroad, as auxiliary to the main line which led
from Nashville to Stevenson, and Chattanooga. General John
A. Logan had succeeded to the command of the Fifteenth

Corps, by regular appointment of the President of the United States, and had relieved General Frank P. Blair, who had been temporarily in command of that corps during the Chattanooga and Knoxville movement.

At that time I was in command of the Department of the Tennessee, which embraced substantially the territory on the east bank of the Mississippi River, from Natchez up to the Ohio River, and thence along the Tennessee River as high as Decatur and Bellefonte, Alabama. General McPherson was at Vicksburg and General Hurlbut at Memphis, and from them I had the regular reports of affairs in that quarter of my command. The rebels still maintained a considerable force of infantry and cavalry in the State of Mississippi, threatening the river, whose navigation had become to us so delicate and important a matter. Satisfied that I could check this by one or two quick moves inland, and thereby set free a considerable body of men held as local garrisons, I went up to Nashville and represented the case to General Grant, who consented that I might go down the Mississippi River, where the bulk of my command lay, and strike a blow on the east of the river, while General Banks from New Orleans should in like manner strike another to the west; thus preventing any further molestation of the boats navigating the main river, and thereby widening the gap in the Southern Confederacy.

After having given all the necessary orders for the distribution, during the winter months, of that part of my command which was in Southern and Middle Tennessee, I went to Cincinnati and Lancaster, Ohio, to spend Christmas with my family; and on my return I took Minnie with me down to a convent at Reading, near Cincinnati, where I left her, and took the cars for Cairo, Illinois, which I reached January 3d, a very cold and bitter day. The ice was forming fast, and there was great danger that the Mississippi River would become closed to navigation. Admiral Porter, who was at Cairo, gave me a small gunboat (the Juliet), with which I went up to Paducah, to inspect that place, garrisoned by a small force, commanded by Colonel [Stephen] G. Hicks, Fortieth Illinois, who had been with me and was severely wounded at Shiloh. Returning to Cairo, we started down the Mississippi River, which was full of floating ice. With the utmost difficulty we made our way through it, for hours floating in the midst of immense cakes, that chafed and ground our boat so that at times we were in danger of sinking. But about the 10th of January we reached Memphis, where I found General Hurlbut, and explained to him my purpose to collect from his garrisons and those of McPherson about twenty thousand men, with which in February to march out from Vicksburg as far as Meridian, break up the Mobile & Ohio Railroad, and also the one leading from Vicksburg to Selma, Alabama. I instructed him to select two good divisions, and to be ready with them to go along. At Memphis I found Brigadier-General W. Sooy Smith, with a force of about twenty-five hundred cavalry, which he had by General Grant's orders brought across from Middle Tennessee, to assist in our general purpose, as well as to punish the rebel General Forrest, who had been most active in harassing our garrisons in West Tennessee and Mississippi.

After staying a couple of days at Memphis, we continued on in the gunboat Silver Cloud to Vicksburg, where I found General McPherson, and, giving him similar orders, instructed him to send out spies to ascertain and bring back timely information of the strength and location of the enemy. The winter continued so severe that the river at Vicksburg was full of floating ice, but in the Silver Cloud we breasted it manfully, and got back to Memphis by the 20th. A chief part of the enterprise was to destroy the rebel cavalry commanded by General Forrest, who were a constant threat to our railway communications in Middle Tennessee, and I committed this task to Brigadier-General W. Sooy Smith. General Hurlbut had in his command about seven thousand five hundred cavalry, scattered from Columbus, Kentucky, to Corinth, Mississippi, and we proposed to make up an aggregate cavalry force of about seven thousand "effective," out of these and the twenty-five hundred which General Smith had brought with him from Middle Tennessee. With this force General Smith was ordered to move from Memphis straight for Meridian, Mississippi, and to start by February 1st. I explained to him personally the nature of Forrest as a man, and of his peculiar force; told him that in his route he was sure to encounter Forrest, who always attacked with a vehemence for which he must be prepared, and that, after he had repelled the first attack, he must in turn assume the most determined offensive, overwhelm him and utterly destroy his whole force. I knew that Forrest could not have more than four thousand cavalry, and my own movement would give employment to every other man of the rebel army not immediately present with him, so that he (General Smith) might safely act on the hypothesis I have stated.

Having completed all these preparations in Memphis, being satisfied that the cavalry force would be ready to start by the 1st of February, and having seen General Hurlbut with his two divisions embark in steamers from Vicksburg, I also reëmbarked for the same destination on the 27th of January.

On the 1st of February we rendezvoused in Vicksburg, where I found a spy who had been sent out two weeks before, had been to Meridian, and brought back correct information of the state of facts in the interior of Mississippi. Lieutenant-General (Bishop) Polk was in chief command, with head-quarters at Meridian, and had two divisions of infantry, one of which (General Loring's) was posted at Canton, Mississippi, the other (General French's) at Brandon. He had also two divisions of cavalry—Armstrong's, composed of the three brigades of Ross, Stark, and Wirt Adams, which were scattered from the neighborhood of Yazoo City to Jackson and below; and Forrest's, which was united, toward Memphis, with headquarters at Como. General Polk seemed to have no suspicion of our intentions to disturb his serenity.

Accordingly, on the morning of February 3d, we started in two columns, each of two divisions, preceded by a light force of cavalry, commanded by Colonel E. F. Winslow. General McPherson commanded the right column, and General Hurlbut the left. The former crossed the Big Black at the railroad-bridge, and the latter seven miles above, at Messinger's. We were lightly equipped as to wagons, and marched without deployment straight for Meridian, distant one hundred and fifty miles. We struck the rebel cavalry beyond the Big Black, and pushed them pell-mell into and beyond Jackson during the 6th. The next day we reached Brandon, and on the 9th Morton, where we perceived signs of an infantry concentration, but the enemy did not give us battle, and retreated before us. The rebel cavalry were all around us, so we kept our columns compact and offered few or no chances for their dashes. As far as Morton we had occupied two roads, but there we were forced into one. Toward evening of the 12th, Hurlbut's column passed through Decatur, with orders to go into camp four miles beyond at a creek. McPherson's head of column was some four miles behind, and I personally detached one of Hurlbut's regiments to guard the cross-roads at Decatur till the head of McPherson's column should come in sight. Intending to spend the night in Decatur, I went to a double log-house, and arranged with the lady for some supper. We unsaddled our horses, tied them to the fence inside the yard, and, being tired, I lay down on a bed and fell asleep. Presently I heard shouts and hallooing, and then heard pistol-shots close to the house. My aide, Major Audenried, called me and said we were attacked by rebel cavalry, who were all around us. I jumped up and inquired where was the regiment of infantry I had myself posted at the cross-roads. He said a few moments before it had marched past the house, following the road by which General Hurlbut had gone, and I told him to run, over-take it, and bring it back. Meantime, I went out into the back-yard, saw wagons passing at a run down the road, and horse-men dashing about in a cloud of dust, firing their pistols, their shots reaching the house in which we were. Gathering the few orderlies and clerks that were about, I was preparing to get into a corn-crib at the back side of the lot, wherein to defend ourselves, when I saw Audenried coming back with the regiment, on a run, deploying forward as they came. This regiment soon cleared the place and drove the rebel cavalry back toward the south, whence they had come.

It transpired that the colonel of this infantry regiment, whose name I do not recall, had seen some officers of Mc-Pherson's staff (among them Inspector-General Strong) coming up the road at a gallop, raising a cloud of dust; supposing them to be the head of McPherson's column, and being anxious to get into camp before dark, he had called in his pickets and started down the road, leaving me perfectly exposed. Some straggling wagons, escorted by a New Jersey regiment, were passing at the time, and composed the rear of Hurlbut's train. The rebel cavalry, seeing the road clear of troops, and these wagons passing, struck them in flank, shot down the mules of three or four wagons, broke the column, and began a general skirmish. The escort defended their wagons as well as they could, and thus diverted their attention; otherwise I would surely have been captured. In a short time the head of McPherson's column came up, went into camp, and we spent the night in Decatur.

The next day we pushed on, and on the 14th entered Meridian, the enemy retreating before us toward Demopolis, Alabama. We at once set to work to destroy an arsenal, immense storehouses, and the railroad in every direction. We staid in Meridian five days, expecting every hour to hear of General Sooy Smith, but could get no tidings of him whatever. A large force of infantry was kept at work all the time in breaking up the Mobile & Ohio Railroad south and north; also the Jackson & Selma Railroad, east and west. I was determined to damage these roads so that they could not be used again for hostile purposes during the rest of the war. I never had the remotest idea of going to Mobile, but had purposely given out that idea to the people of the country, so as to deceive the enemy and to divert their attention. Many persons still insist that, because we did not go to Mobile on this occasion, I had failed.

The object of the Meridian expedition was to strike the roads inland, so to paralyze the rebel forces that we could take from the defense of the Mississippi River the equivalent of a corps of twenty thousand men, to be used in the next Georgia campaign; and this was actually done. At the same time, I wanted to destroy General Forrest, who, with an irregular force of cavalry, was constantly threatening Memphis and the river above, as well as our routes of supply in Middle Tennessee. In this we failed utterly, because General W. Sooy Smith did not fulfill his orders, which were clear and specific, as contained in my letter of instructions to him of January 27th, at Memphis, and my personal explanations to him at the same time. Instead of starting at the date ordered, February 1st, he did not leave Memphis till the 11th, waiting for some regiment that was ice-bound near Columbus, Kentucky; and then, when he did start, he allowed General Forrest to head him off and to defeat him with an inferior force, near West Point, below Okalona, on the Mobile & Ohio Railroad.

We waited at Meridian till the 20th to hear from General Smith, but hearing nothing whatever, and having utterly destroyed the railroads in and around that junction. I ordered General McPherson to move back slowly toward Canton. With [Edward F.] Winslow's cavalry, and Hurlbut's infantry, I turned north to Marion, and thence to a place called "Union," whence I dispatched the cavalry farther north to Philadelphia and Louisville, to feel as it were for General Smith, and then turned all the infantry columns toward Canton, Mississippi.

On the 26th we all reached Canton, but we had not heard a word of General Smith, nor was it until some time after (at Vicksburg) that I learned the whole truth of General Smith's movement and of his failure. Of course I did not and could not approve of his conduct, and I know that he yet chafes under the censure. I had set so much store on his part of the project that I was disappointed, and so reported officially to General Grant. General Smith never regained my confidence as a soldier, though I still regard him as a most accomplished gentleman and a skillful engineer. Since the close of the war he has appealed to me to relieve him of that censure, but I could not do it, because it would falsify history.

Having assembled all my troops in and about Canton, on the 27th of February I left them under the command of the senior major-general, Hurlbut, with orders to remain till about the 3d of March, and then to come into Vicksburg leisurely; and, escorted by Winslow's cavalry, I rode into Vicksburg on the last day of February. There I found letters from General Grant, at Nashville, and General Banks, at New Orleans, concerning his (General Banks's) projected movement up Red River. I was authorized by the former to contribute aid to General Banks for a limited time; but General Grant insisted on my returning in person to my own command about Huntsville, Alabama, as soon as possible, to prepare for the spring campaign.

About this time we were much embarrassed by a general order of the War Department, promising a thirty-days furlough to all soldiers who would "veteranize"—viz., reënlist for the rest of the war. This was a judicious and wise measure, because it doubtless secured the services of a very large portion of the men who had almost completed a three-years enlistment, and were therefore veteran soldiers in feeling and in habit. But to furlough so many of our men at that instant of time was like disbanding an army in the very midst of battle.

In order to come to a perfect understanding with General Banks, I took the steamer Diana and ran down to New Orleans to see him. Among the many letters which I found in Vicksburg on my return from Meridian was one from Captain [David] F. Boyd, of Louisiana, written from the jail in Natchez, telling me that he was a prisoner of war in our hands; had been captured in Louisiana by some of our scouts; and he bespoke my friendly assistance. Boyd was Professor of

Ancient Languages at the Louisiana Seminary of Learning during my administration in 1859-'60; was an accomplished scholar, of moderate views in politics, but, being a Virginian, was drawn, like all others of his kind, into the vortex of the rebellion by the events of 1861, which broke up colleges and every thing at the South. Natchez, at this time, was in my command, and was held by a strong division, commanded by Brigadier-General [John] W. Davidson. In the Diana we stopped at Natchez, and I made a hasty inspection of the place. I sent for Boyd, who was in good health, but quite dirty, and begged me to take him out of prison, and to effect his exchange. I receipted for him; took him along with me to New Orleans; offered him money, which he declined; allowed him to go free in the city; and obtained from General Banks a promise to effect his exchange, which was afterward done. Boyd is now my legitimate successor in Louisiana, viz., President of the Louisiana University, which is the present title of what had been the Seminary of Learning. After the war was over, Boyd went back to Alexandria, reorganized the old institution, which I visited in 1866; but the building was burnt down by an accident or by an incendiary about 1868, and the institution was then removed to Baton Rouge, where it now is, under its new title of the University of Louisiana.

We reached New Orleans on the 2d of March. I found General Banks, with his wife and daughter, living in a good house, and he explained to me fully the position and strength of his troops, and his plans of action for the approaching campaign. I dined with him, and, rough as I was—just out of the woods—attended, that night, a very pleasant party at the house of a lady, whose name I cannot recall, but who is now the wife of Captain Arnold, Fifth United States Artillery. At this party were also Mr. and Mrs. Frank Howe. I found New Orleans much changed since I had been familiar with in 1853 and in 1860-'61. It was full of officers and soldiers. Among the former were General [Thomas] W. Sherman, who had lost a leg at Port Hudson, and General P. Stone, whom I knew so well in California, and who is now in the Egyptian service as chief of staff. The bulk of General [Nathaniel P.] Banks's army was about Opelousas, under command of General [William B.] Franklin, ready to move on Alexandria. General Banks seemed to be all ready, but intended to delay his departure a few days to assist in the inauguration of a civil government for Louisiana, under Governor Hahn. In Lafayette Square I saw the arrangements of scaffoldng for the fireworks and benches for the audience. General Banks urged me to remain over the 4th of March, to participate in the ceremonies, which he explained would include the performance of the "Anvil Chorus" by all the bands of his army, and during the performance the church-bells were to be rung, and cannons were to be fired by electricity. I regarded all such ceremonies as out of place at a time when it seemed to me every hour and every minute were due to the war. General Banks's movement, however, contemplated my sending a force of ten thousand men in boats up Red River from Vicksburg, and that a junction should occur at Alexandria by March 17th. I therefore had no time to wait for the grand pageant of the 4th of March, but took my departure from New Orleans in the Diana the evening of March 3d.

On the next day, March 4th, I wrote to General Banks a letter, which was extremely minute in conveying to him how far I felt authorized to go under my orders from General Grant. At that time General Grant commanded the Military Division of the Mississippi, embracing my own Department of the Tennessee and that of General Steele in Arkansas, but not that of General Banks in Louisiana. General Banks was acting on his own powers, or under the instructions of General Halleck in Washington, and our assistance to him was designed as a loan of ten thousand men for a period of thirty days. The instructions of March 6th to General A. J. Smith, who commanded this detachment, were full and explicit on this point. The Diana reached Vicksburg on the 6th, where I found that the expeditionary army had come in from Canton. One division of five thousand men was made up out of Hurlbut's command, and placed under Brigadier-General T. Kilby Smith; and a similar division was made out of McPherson's and Hurlbut's troops, and placed under Brigadier-General Joseph A. Mower; the whole commanded by Brigadier-General A. J. Smith. General Hurlbut, with the rest of his command, returned to Memphis, and General McPherson remained at Vicksburg. General A. J. Smith's command was in due season embarked, and proceeded to Red River, which it ascended, convoyed by Admiral Porter's fleet. General Mower's division was landed near the outlet of the Atchafalaya, marched up by land and captured the fort below Alexandria known as Fort De Russy, and the whole fleet then proceeded up to Alexandria, reaching it on the day appointed, viz., March 17th, where it waited for the arrival of General Banks, who, however, did not come till some days after. These two divisions participated in the whole of General Banks's unfortunate Red River expedition, and were delayed so long up Red River, and subsequently on the Mississippi, that they did not share with their comrades the successes and glories of the Atlanta campaign, for which I had designed them; and, indeed, they did not join our army till just in time to assist General George H. Thomas to defeat General Hood before Nashville, on the 15th and 16th of December, 1864.

General Grant's letter of instructions, which was brought me by General [Daniel] Butterfield, who had followed me to New Orleans, enjoined on me, after concluding with General Banks the details for his Red River expedition, to make all necessary arrangements for furloughing the men entitled to that privilege, and to hurry back to the army at Huntsville, Alabama. I accordingly gave the necessary orders to General McPherson, at Vicksburg, and continued up the river toward Memphis. On our way we met Captain Badeau, of General Grant's staff, bearing the following letter, of March 4th, which I answered on the 10th, and sent the answer by General Butterfield, who had accompanied me up from New Orleans. Copies of both were also sent to General McPherson, at Vicksburg.

[PRIVATE.]

NASHVILLE, TENNESSEE, *March* 4, 1864.

DEAR SHERMAN: The bill reviving the grade of lieutenant-general in the army has become a law, and my name has been sent to the Senate for the place.

I now receive orders to report at Washington immediately, *in person,* which indicates either a confirmation or a likelihood of confirmation. I start in the morning to comply with the order, but I shall say very distinctly on my arrival there that I shall accept no appointment which will require me to make that city my headquarters. This, however, is not what I started out to write about.

While I have been eminently successful in this war, in at

least gaining the confidence of the public, no one feels more than I how much of this success is due to the energy, skill, and the harmonious putting forth of that energy and skill, of those whom it has been my good fortune to have occupying subordinate positions under me.

There are many officers to whom these remarks are applicable to a greater or less degree, proportionate to their ability as soldiers; but what I want is to express my thanks to you and McPherson, as *the men* to whom, above all others, I feel indebted for whatever I have had of success. How far your advice and suggestions have been of assistance, you know. How far your execution of whatever has been given you to do entitles you to the reward I am receiving, you cannot know as well as I do. I feel all the gratitude this letter would express, giving it the most flattering construction.

The word *you* I use in the plural, intending it for McPherson also. I should write to him, and will some day, but, starting in the morning, I do not know that I will find time just now.

Your friend,

U. S. GRANT, *Major-General.*

[PRIVATE AND CONFIDENTIAL.]

NEAR MEMPHIS, *March* 10, 1864.

General GRANT.

DEAR GENERAL: I have your more than kind and characteristic letter of the 4th, and will send a copy of it to General McPherson at once.

You do yourself injustice and us too much honor in assigning to us so large a share of the merits which have led to your high advancement. I know you approve the friendship I have ever professed to you, and will permit me to continue as heretofore to manifest it on all proper occasions.

You are now Washington's legitimate successor, and occupy a position of almost dangerous elevation; but if you can continue as heretofore to be yourself, simple, honest, and unpretending, you will enjoy through life the respect and love of friends, and the homage of millions of human beings who will award to you a large share for securing to them and their descendants a government of law and stability.

I repeat, you do General McPherson and myself too much honor. At Belmont you manifested your traits, neither of us being near; at Donelson also you illustrated your whole character. I was not near, and General McPherson in too subordinate a capacity to influence you.

Until you had won Donelson, I confess I was almost cowed by the terrible array of anarchical elements that presented themselves at every point; but that victory admitted the ray of light which I have followed ever since.

I believe you are as brave, patriotic, and just, as the great prototype Washington; as unselfish, kind-hearted, and honest, as a man should be; but the chief characteristic in your nature is the simple faith in success you have always manifested, which I can liken to nothing else than the faith a Christian has in his Saviour.

This faith gave you victory at Shiloh and Vicksburg. Also, when you have completed your best preparations, you go into battle without hesitation, as at Chattanooga—no doubts, no reserve; and I tell you that it was this that made us act with confidence. I knew wherever I was that you thought of me, and if I got in a tight place you would come—if alive.

My only points of doubt were as to your knowledge of grand strategy, and of books of science and history; but I confess your common-sense seems to have supplied all this.

Now as to the future. Do not stay in Washington. Halleck is better qualified than you are to stand the buffets of intrigue and policy. Come out West; take to yourself the whole Mississippi Valley; let us make it dead-sure, and I tell you the Atlantic slope and Pacific shores will follow its destiny as sure as the limbs of a tree live or die with the main trunk! We have done much; still much remains to be done. Time and time's influences are all with us; we could almost afford to sit still and let these influences work. Even in the seceded States your word *now* would go further than a President's proclamation, or an act of Congress.

For God's sake and for your country's sake, come out of Washington! I foretold to General Halleck, before he left Corinth, the inevitable result to him, and I now exhort you to come out West. Here lies the seat of the coming empire; and from the West, when our task is done, we will make short work of Charleston and Richmond, and the impoverished coast of the Atlantic.

Your sincere friend,

W. T. SHERMAN.

We reached Memphis on the 13th, where I remained some days, but on the 14th of March received from General Grant a disptach to hurry to Nashville in person by the 17th, if possible. Disposing of all matters then pending, I took a steamboat to Cairo, the cars thence to Louisville and Nashville, reaching that place on the 17th of March, 1864.

I found General Grant there. He had been to Washington and back, and was ordered to return East to command all the armies of the United States, and personally the Army of the Potomac. I was to succeed him in command of the Military Division of the Mississippi, embracing the Departments of the Ohio, Cumberland, Tennessee, and Arkansas. General Grant was of course very busy in winding up all matters of business, in transferring his command to me, and in preparing for what was manifest would be the great and closing campaign of our civil war. Mrs. Grant and some of their children were with him, and occupied a large house in Nashville, which was used as an office, dwelling, and every thing combined.

On the 18th of March I had issued orders assuming command of the Military Division of the Mississippi, and was seated in the office, when the general came in and said they were about to present him a sword, inviting me to come and see the ceremony. I went back into what was the dining-room of the house; on the table lay a rose-wood box, containing a sword, sash, spurs, etc., and round about the table were grouped Mrs. Grant, Nelly, and one or two of the boys. I was introduced to a large, corpulent gentleman, as the mayor, and another citizen, who had come down from Galena to make this presentation of a sword to their fellow-townsman. I think that Rawlins, Bowers, Badeau, and one or more of General Grant's personal staff, were present. The mayor rose and in the most dignified way read a finished speech to General Grant, who stood, as usual, very awkwardly; and the mayor closed his speech by handing him the resolutions of the City Council engrossed on parchment, with a broad ribbon and large seal attached. After the mayor had fulfilled his office so well, General Grant said: "Mr. Mayor, as I knew that this ceremony was to occur, and as I am not used to speaking, I have written something in reply." He then began to fumble in his pockets, first his breast-coat pocket, then his pants, vest, etc., and after considerable delay he pulled out a crumpled piece of common yellow cartridge-paper, which he handed to the mayor. His whole manner was awkward in the extreme, yet perfectly characteristic, and in strong contrast with the elegant parchment and speech of the mayor. When read, however, the substance of his answer was most excellent, short, concise, and, if it had been delivered by word of mouth, would have been all that the occasion required.

I could not help laughing at a scene so characteristic of the man who then stood prominent before the country, and to whom all had turned as the only one qualified to guide the nation in a war that had become painfully critical.

Chapter 9

Nashville to Kenesaw:
"I Slept on the Ground"
March—May, 1864

On the 18th day of March, 1864, at Nashville, Tennessee, I relieved Lieutenant-General Grant in command of the Military Division of the Mississippi, embracing the Departments of the Ohio, Cumberland, Tennessee, and Arkansas, commanded respectively by Major-Generals Schofield, Thomas, McPherson, and Steele. General Grant was in the act of starting East to assume command of all the armies of the United States, but more particularly to give direction in person to the Armies of the Potomac and James, operating against Richmond; and I accompanied him as far as Cincinnati on his way, to avail myself of the opportunity to discuss privately many little details incident to the contemplated changes, and of preparation for the great events then impending. Among these was the intended assignment to duty of many officers of note and influence, who had, by the force of events, drifted into inactivity and discontent. Among these stood prominent Generals McClellan, Burnside, and Fremont, in the East; and Generals Buell, McCook, Negley, and Crittenden, at the West. My understanding was that General Grant thought it wise and prudent to give all these officers appropriate commands, that would enable them to regain the influence they had lost; and, as a general reorganization of all the armies was then necessary, he directed me to keep in mind especially the claims of Generals Buell, McCook, and Crittenden, and endeavor to give them commands that would be as near their rank and dates of commission as possible; but I was to do nothing until I heard further from him on the subject, as he explained that he would have to consult the Secretary of War before making final orders. General Buell and his officers had been subjected to a long ordeal by a court of inquiry, touching their conduct of the campaign in Tennessee and Kentucky, that resulted in the battle of Perryville, or Chaplin's Hills, October 8, 1862, and they had been substantially acquitted; and, as it was manifest that we were to have some hard fighting, we were anxious to bring into harmony every man and every officer of skill in the profession of arms. Of these, Generals Buell and McClellan were prominent in rank, and also by reason of their fame acquired in Mexico, as well as in the earlier part of the civil war.

After my return to Nashville I addressed myself to the task of organization and preparation, which involved the general security of the vast region of the South which had been already conquered, more especially the several routes of supply and communication with the active armies at the front, and to organize a large army to move into Georgia, coincident with the advance of the Eastern armies against Richmond. I soon received from Colonel J. B. Fry—now of the Adjutant-General's Department, but then at Washington in charge of the Provost-Marshal-General's office—a letter asking me to do something for General Buell. I answered him frankly, telling him of my understanding with General Grant, and that I was still awaiting the expected order of the War Department, assigning General Buell to my command. Colonel Fry, as General Buell's special friend, replied that he was very anxious that I should make specific application for the services of General Buell by name, and inquired what I proposed to offer him. To this I answered that, after the agreement with General Grant that he would notify me from Washington, I could not with propriety press the matter, but if General Buell should be assigned to me specifically I was prepared to assign him to command all the troops on the Mississippi River from Cairo to Natchez, comprising about three divisions, or the equivalent of a *corps d'armée*. General Grant never afterward communicated to me on the subject at all; and I inferred that Mr. Stanton, who was notoriously vindictive in his prejudices, would not consent to the employment of these high officers. General Buell, toward the close of the war, published a bitter political letter, aimed at General Grant, reflecting on his general management of the war, and stated that both Generals [Edward R.] Canby and Sherman had offered him a subordinate command, which he had declined because he had once outranked us. This was not true as to me, or Canby either, I think, for both General Canby and I ranked him at West Point and in the old army, and he (General Buell) was only superior to us in the date of his commission as major-general, for a short period in 1862. This newspaper communication, though aimed at General Grant, reacted on himself, for it closed his military career. General Crittenden afterward obtained authority for service, and I offered him a division, but he declined it for the reason, as I understood it, that he had at one time commanded a corps.

I returned to Nashville from Cincinnati about the 25th of March, and started at once, in a special car attached to the regular train, to inspect my command at the front, going to Pulaski, Tennessee, where I found General G. M. Dodge; thence to Huntsville, Alabama, where I had left a part of my personal staff and the records of the department during the time we had been absent at Meridian; and there I found General McPherson, who had arrived from Vicksburg, and had assumed command of the Army of the Tennessee. General McPherson accompanied me, and we proceeded by the cars to Stevenson, Bridgeport, etc., to Chattanooga, where we spent a day or two with General George H. Thomas, and then continued on to Knoxville, where was General Schofield. He returned with us to Chattanooga, stopping by the way a few hours at Loudon, where were the headquarters of the Fourth Corps (Major-General Gordon Granger). General Granger, as usual, was full of complaints at the treatment of his corps since I had left him with General Burnside, at Knoxville, the preceding November; and he stated to me personally that he had a leave of absence in his pocket, of which he intended to take advantage very soon. About the end of March, therefore, the three army commanders and myself were together at Chattanooga. We had nothing like a council of war, but conversed freely and frankly on all matters of interest then in progress or impending. We all knew that, as soon as the spring was fairly open, we should have to move directly against our antagonist, General Jos. E. Johnston, then securely intrenched at Dalton, thirty miles distant; and the purpose of our conference at the time was to ascertain our own resources, and to distribute to each part of the army its appropriate share of work. We discussed every possible contingency likely to arise, and I simply instructed each army commander to make immediate preparations for a hard campaign, regulating the distribution of supplies that were coming up by rail from Nashville as equitably as possible. We also agreed on some subordinate changes in the organization of the three separate armies which were destined to take the field; among which was the consolidation of the Eleventh and Twelfth Corps (Howard and Slocum) into a single corps, to be commanded by General Jos. Hooker. General Howard was to be transferred to the Fourth Corps, *vice* Gordon Granger to avail himself of his leave of absence; and General Slocum was to be ordered down the Mississippi River, to command the District of Vicksburg. These changes required the consent of the President, and were all in due time approved.

The great question of the campaign was one of supplies. Nashville, our chief depot, was itself partially in a hostile country, and even the routes of supply from Louisville to Nashville by rail, and by way of the Cumberland River, had to be guarded. Chattanooga (our starting-point) was one hundred and thirty-six in front of Nashville, and every foot of the way, especially the many bridges, trestles, and culverts, had to be strongly guarded against the acts of a local hostile population and of the enemy's cavalry. Then, of course, as we advanced into Georgia, it was manifest that we should have to repair the railroad, use it, and guard it likewise. General Thomas's army was much the largest of the three, was best provided, and contained the best corps of engineers, railroad managers, and repair parties, as well as the best body of spies and provost-marshals. On him we were therefore compelled in a great measure to rely for these most useful branches of service. He had so long exercised absolute command and control over the railroads in his department, that the other armies were jealous, and these thought the Army of the Cumberland got the lion's share of the supplies and other advantages of the railroads. I found a good deal of feeling in the Army of the Tennessee on this score, and therefore took supreme control of the roads myself, placed all the army commanders on an equal footing, and gave to each the same control, so far as orders of transportation for men and stores were concerned. Thomas's spies brought him frequent and accurate reports of Jos. Johnston's army at Dalton, giving its strength anywhere between forty and fifty thousand men, and these were being reëforced by troops from Mississippi, and by the Georgia militia, under General G. W. Smith. General Johnston seemed to be acting purely on the defensive, so that we had time and leisure to take all our measures deliberately and fully. I fixed the date of May 1st, when all things should be in readiness for the grand forward movement, and then returned to Nashville; General Schofield going back to Knoxville, and McPherson to Huntsville, Thomas remaining at Chattanooga.

On the 2d of April, at Nashville, I wrote to General Grant, then at Washington, reporting to him the results of my visit to the several armies, and asked his consent to the several changes proposed, which was promptly given by telegraph. I then addressed myself specially to the troublesome question of transportation and supplies. I found the capacity of the railroads from Nashville forward to Decatur, and to Chattanooga, so small, especially in the number of locomotives and cars, that it was clear that they were barely able to supply the daily wants of the armies then dependent on them, with no power of accumulating a surplus in advance. The cars were daily loaded down with men returning from furlough, with cattle, horses, etc.; and, by reason of the previous desolation of the country between Chattanooga and Knoxville, General Thomas had authorized the issue of provisions to the suffering inhabitants.

We could not attempt an advance into Georgia without food, ammunition, etc.; and ordinary prudence dictated that we should have an accumulation at the front, in case of interruption to the railway by the act of the enemy, or by common accident. Accordingly, on the 6th of April, I issued a general order, limiting the use of the railroad-cars to transporting only the essential articles of food, ammunition, and supplies for the army proper, forbidding any further issues to citizens, and cutting off all civil traffic; requiring the commanders of posts within thirty miles of Nashville to haul out their own stores in wagons; requiring all troops destined for the front to march, and all beef-cattle to be driven on their own legs. This was a great help, but of course it naturally raised a howl. Some of the poor Union people of East Tennessee appealed to President Lincoln, whose kind heart responded promptly to their request. He telegraphed me to know if I could not modify or repeal my orders; but I answered him that a great campaign was impending, on which the fate of the nation hung; that our railroads had but a limited capacity, and could not provide for the necessities of the army and of the people too; that one or the other must quit, and we could not until the army of Jos. Johnston was conquered, etc., etc. Mr. Linocln seemed to acquiesce, and I advised the people to obtain and drive out cattle from Kentucky, and to haul out their supplies by the wagon-road from the same quarter, by way of Cumberland Gap. By these changes I nearly or quite doubled our daily accumulation of stores at the front, and yet even this was not found enough.

I accordingly called together in Nashville the master of transportation, Colonel Anderson, the chief quartermaster, General J[ames] L. Donaldson, and the chief commissary, General Amos Beckwith, for conference. I assumed the strength of the army to move from Chattanooga into Georgia at one hundred thousand men, and the number of animals to be fed, both for cavalry and draught, at thirty-five thousand; then, allowing for occasional wrecks of trains, which were very common, and for the interruption of the road itself by guerrillas and regular raids, we estimated it would require one hundred and thirty cars, of ten tons each, to reach Chattanooga daily, to be reasonably certain of an adequate supply. Even with this calculation, we could not afford to bring forward hay for the horses and mules, nor more than five pounds of oats or corn per day for each animal. I was willing to risk the question of forage in part, because I expected to find wheat and corn fields, and a good deal of grass, as we advanced into Georgia at that season of the year. The problem then was to deliver at Chattanooga and beyond one hundred and thirty car-loads daily, leaving the beef-cattle to be driven on the hoof, and all the troops in excess of the usual train-guards to march by the ordinary roads. Colonel Anderson promptly explained that he did not possess cars or locomotives enough to do this work. I then instructed and authorized him to hold on to all trains that arrived at Nashville from Louisville, and to allow none to go back until he had secured enough to fill the requirements of our problem. At the time he only had about sixty serviceable locomotives, and about six hundred cars of all kinds, and he represented that to provide for all contingencies he must have at least one hundred locomotives and one thousand cars. As soon as Mr. Guthrie, the President of the Louisville & Nashville Railroad, detected that we were holding on to all his locomotives and cars, he wrote me, earnestly remonstrating against it, saying that he would not be able with diminished stock to bring forward the necessary stores from Louisville to Nashville. I wrote to him, frankly telling him exactly how we were placed, appealed to his patriotism to stand by us, and advised him in like manner to hold on to all trains coming into Jeffersonville, Indiana. He and General Robert Allen, then quartermaster-general at Louisville, arranged a ferry-boat so as to transfer the trains over the Ohio River from Jeffersonville, and in a short time we had cars and locomotives from almost every road in the North; months afterward I was amused to see, away down in Georgia, cars marked "Pittsburg & Fort Wayne," "Delaware & Lackawanna," "Baltimore & Ohio," and indeed with the names of almost every railroad north of the Ohio River. How these railroad companies ever recovered their property, or settled their transportation accounts, I have never heard, but to this fact, as much as to any other single fact, I attribute the perfect success which afterward attended our campaigns; and I have always felt grateful to Mr. Guthrie, of Louisville, who had sense enough and patriotism enough to subordinate the interests of his railroad company to the cause of his country.

About this time, viz., the early part of April, I was much disturbed by a bold raid made by the rebel General Forrest up between the Mississippi and Tennessee Rivers. He reached the Ohio River at Paducah, but was handsomely repulsed by Colonel Hicks. He then swung down toward Memphis, assaulted and carried Fort Pillow, massacring a part of its garrison, composed wholly of Negro troops. At first I discredited the story of the massacre, because, in preparing for the Meridian campaign, I had ordered Fort Pillow to be evacuated, but it transpired afterward that General Hurlbut had retained a small garrison at Fort Pillow to encourage the enlistment of the blacks as soldiers, which was a favorite political policy at that day. The massacre at Fort Pillow occurred April 12, 1864, and has been the subject of congressional inquiry. No doubt Forrest's men acted like a set of barbarians, shooting down the helpless Negro garrison after the fort was in their possession; but I am told that Forrest personally disclaims any active participation in the assault, and that he stopped the firing as soon as he could. I also take it for granted that Forrest did not lead the assault in person, and consequently that he was to the rear, out of sight if not of hearing at the time, and I was told by hundreds of our men, who were at various times prisoners in Forrest's possession, that he was usually very kind to them. He had a desperate set of fellows under him, and at that very time there is no doubt the feeling of the Southern people was fearfully savage on this very point of our making soldiers out of their late slaves, and Forrest may have shared the feeling.

I also had another serious cause of disturbance about that time. I wanted badly the two divisions of troops which had been loaned to General Banks in the month of March previously, with the express understanding that their absence was to endure only one month, and that during April they were to come out of Red River, and be again within the sphere of my command. I accordingly instructed one of my inspector-generals, John M. Corse, to take a fleet steamboat at Nashville, proceed *via* Cairo, Memphis, and Vicksburg, to General Banks up the Red River, and to deliver the following letter of April 3d, as also others, of like tenor, to Generals A. J. Smith and Fred Steele, who were supposed to be with him:

HEADQUARTERS MILITARY DIVISION OF THE MISSISSIPPI,
NASHVILLE, TENNESSEE, *April* 3, 1864.

Major-General N. P. BANKS, *commanding Department of the Gulf, Red River.*

GENERAL: The thirty days for which I loaned you the command of General A. J. Smith will expire on the 10th instant. I send with this Brigadier-General J. M. Corse, to carry orders to General A. J. Smith, and to give directions for a new movement, which is preliminary to the general campaign. General Corse may see you and explain in full, but, lest he should not find you in person, I will simply state that Forrest, availing himself of the absence of our furloughed men and of the detachment with you, has pushed up between the Mississippi and Tennessee Rivers, even to the Ohio. He attacked Paducah, but got the worst of it, and he still lingers about the place. I hope that he will remain thereabouts till General A. J. Smith can reach his destined point, but this I can hardly expect; yet I want him to reach by the Yazoo a position near Grenada, thence to operate against Forrest, after which to march across to Decatur, Alabama. You will see that he has a big job, and therefore should start at once. From all that I can learn, my troops reached Alexandria, Louisiana, at the time agreed on, viz., March 17th, and I hear of them at Natchitoches, but cannot hear of your troops being above Opelousas.

Steele is also moving. I leave Steele's entire force to coöperate with you and the navy, but, as I before stated, I must have A. J. Smith's troops now as soon as possible.

I beg you will expedite their return to Vicksburg, if they have not already started, and I want them if possible to remain in the same boats they have used up Red River, as it will save the time otherwise consumed in transfer to other boats.

All is well in this quarter, and I hope by the time you turn against Mobile our forces will again act toward the same end, though from distant points. General Grant, now having lawful control, will doubtless see that all minor objects are disregarded, and that all the armies act on a common plan.

Hoping, when this reaches you, that you will be in possession of Shreveport, I am, with great respect, etc.,

W. T. SHERMAN, *Major-General commanding.*

Rumors were reaching us thick and fast of defeat and disaster in that quarter; and I feared then, what afterward actually happened, that neither General Banks nor Admiral Porter could or would spare those two divisions. On the 23rd of April, General Corse returned, bringing full answers to my letters, and I saw that we must go on without them. This was a serious loss to the Army of the Tennessee, which was also short by two other divisions that were on their veteran furlough, and were under orders to rendezvous at Cairo, before embarking for Clifton, on the Tennessee River.

Each division and brigade was provided a fair proportion

of wagons for a supply-train, and these were limited in their loads to carry food, ammunition, and clothing. Tents were forbidden to all save the sick and wounded, and one tent only was allowed to each headquarters for use as an office. These orders were not absolutely enforced, though in person I set the example, and did not have a tent, nor did any officer about me have one; but we had wall tent-flies, without poles, and no tent-furniture of any kind. We usually spread our flies over saplings, or on fence-rails or posts improvised on the spot. Most of the general officers, except Thomas, followed my example strictly; but he had a regular headquarters-camp. I frequently called his attention to the orders on this subject, rather jestingly than seriously. He would break out against his officers for having such luxuries, but, needing a tent himself, and being good-natured and slow to act, he never enforced my orders perfectly. In addition to his regular wagon-train, he had a big wagon which could be converted into an office, and this we used to call "Thomas's circus." Several times during the campaign I found quartermasters hid away in some comfortable nook to the rear, with tents and mess-fixtures which were the envy of the passing soldiers; and I frequently broke them up, and distributed the tents to the surgeons of brigades. Yet my orders actually reduced the transportation, so that I doubt if any army ever went forth to battle with fewer impedimenta, and where the regular and necessary supplies of food, ammunition, and clothing, were issued, as called for, so regularly and so well.

General Stoneman, having a division of about four thousand men and horses, was attached to Schofield's Army of the Ohio. General Garrard's division, of about four thousand five hundred men and horses, was attached to General Thomas's command; and he had another irregular division of cavalry, commanded by Brigadier-General E. McCook. There was also a small brigade of cavalry, belonging to the Army of the Cumberland, attached temporarily to the Army of the Tennessee, which was commanded by Brigadier-General Judson Kilpatrick. These cavalry commands changed constantly in strength and numbers, and were generally used on the extreme flanks, or for some special detached service, as will be hereinafter related. The Army of the Tennessee was still short by the two divisions detached with General Banks, up Red River, and two other divisions on furlough in Illinois, Indiana, and Ohio, but which were rendezvousing at Cairo, under Generals [Mortimer D.] Leggett and Crocker, to form a part of the Seventeenth Corps, which corps was to be commanded by Major-General Frank P. Blair, then a member of Congress, in Washington. On the 2d of April I notified him by letter that I wanted him to join and to command these two divisions, which ought to be ready by the 1st of May. General Blair, with these two divisions constituting the Seventeenth Army Corps, did not actually overtake us until we reached Acworth and Big Shanty, in Georgia, about the 9th of June, 1864.

In my letter of April 4th to General John A. Rawlins, chief of staff to General Grant at Washington, I described at length all the preparations that were in progress for the active campaign thus contemplated, and therein estimated Schofield at twelve thousand, Thomas at forty-five thousand, and Mc-Pherson at thirty thousand. At first I intended to open the campaign about May 1st, by moving Schofield on Dalton from Cleveland, Thomas on the same objective from Chattanooga, and McPherson on Rome and Kingston from Gunter's Landing. My intention was merely to threaten Dalton in front, and to direct McPherson to act vigorously against the railroad below Resaca, far to the rear of the enemy. But by reason of his being short of his estimated strength by the four divisions before referred to, and thus being reduced to about twenty-four thousand men, I did not feel justified in placing him so far away from the support of the main body of the army, and therefore subsequently changed the plan of campaign, so far as to bring that army up to Chattanooga, and to direct it thence through Ship's Gap against the railroad to Johnston's rear, at or near Resaca, distant from Dalton only eighteen miles, and in full communication with the other armies by roads behind Rocky-face Ridge, of about the same length.

On the 10th of April I received General Grant's letter of April 4th from Washington, which formed the basis of all the campaigns of the year 1864, and subsequently received another of April 19th, written from Culpeper, Virginia, both of which are now in my possession.

On the 28th of April I removed my headquarters to Chattanooga, and prepared for taking the field in person. General Grant had first indicated the 30th of April as the day for the simultaneous advance, but subsequently changed the day to May 5th. McPherson's troops were brought forward rapidly to Chattanooga, partly by rail and partly by marching. Thomas's troops were already in position (his advance being out as far as Ringgold—eighteen miles), and Schofield was marching down by Cleveland to Red Clay and Catoosa Springs. On the 4th of May, Thomas was in person at Ringgold, his left at Catoosa, and his right at Leet's Tan-yard. Schofield was at Red Clay, closing upon Thomas's left; and McPherson was moving rapidly into Chattanooga, and out toward Gordon's Mill.

On the 5th I rode out to Ringgold, and on the very day appointed by General Grant from his headquarters in Virginia the great campaign was begun. To give all the minute details will involve more than is contemplated, and I will endeavor only to trace the principal events, or rather to record such as weighed heaviest on my own mind at the time, and which now remain best fixed in my memory.

My general headquarters and official records remained back at Nashville, and I had near me only my personal staff and inspectors-general, with about half a dozen wagons, and a single company of Ohio sharp-shooters (commanded by Lieutenant [William] McCrory) as headquarters or camp guard. I also had a small company of irregular Alabama cavalry (commanded by Lieutenant Snelling), used mostly as orderlies and couriers. No wall-tents were allowed, only the flies. Our mess establishment was less in bulk than that of any of the brigade commanders; nor was this from an indifference to the ordinary comforts of life, but because I wanted to set the example, and gradually to convert all parts of that army into a mobile machine, willing and able to start at a minute's notice, and to subsist on the scantiest food. To reap absolute success might involve the necessity even of dropping all wagons, and to subsist on the chance food which the country was known to contain. I had obtained not only the United States census-tables of 1860, but a compilation made by the Controller of the State of Georgia for the purpose of taxation, containing in considerable detail the "population and statistics" of every county in Georgia. One of my aides (Captain Dayton) acted as assistant adjutant-general, with an order-book, letter-book, and writing-paper, that filled a small chest not much larger than an ordinary candle-box. The only reports and returns called for were the ordinary trimonthly returns of "effective strength." As these accumulated they were sent back to Nashville, and afterward were embraced in the archives of the Military Division of the Mississippi, changed in 1865 to the Military Division of the Missouri, and I suppose they were burned in the Chicago fire of 1870. Still, duplicates remain of all essential papers in the archives of the War Department.

The 6th of May was given to Schofield and McPherson to get into position, and on the 7th General Thomas moved in force against Tunnel Hill, driving off a mere picket-guard of the enemy, and I was agreeably surprised to find that no damage had been done to the tunnel or the railroad. From Tunnel Hill I could look into the gorge by which the railroad passed through a straight and well-defined range of mountains, presenting sharp palisade faces, and known as "Rocky Face." The gorge itself was called the "Buzzard Roost." We could plainly see the enemy in this gorge and behind it, and Mill Creek which formed the gorge, flowing toward Dalton, had been dammed up, making a sort of irregular lake, filling the road, thereby obstructing it, and the enemy's batteries crowned the cliffs on either side. The position was very strong, and I knew that such a general as was my antagonist (Jos. Johnston), who had been there six months, had fortified it to the maximum. Therefore I had no intention to attack the position seriously in front, but depended on McPherson to capture and hold the railroad to its rear, which would force Johnston to detach largely against him, or rather, as I expected, to evacuate his position at Dalton altogether. My orders to Generals Thomas and Schofield were merely to press strongly at all points in front, ready to rush in on the first appearance of "let go," and, if possible, to catch our enemy in the confusion of retreat.

All the movements of the 7th and 8th were made exactly as ordered, and the enemy seemed quiescent, acting purely on the defensive.

I had constant communication with all parts of the army, and on the 9th McPherson's head of column entered and passed through Snake Creek, perfectly undefended, and accomplished a complete surprise to the enemy. At its farther *débouché* he met a cavalry brigade, easily driven, which retreated hastily north toward Dalton, and doubtless carried to Johnston the first serious intimation that a heavy force of infantry and artillery was to his rear and within a few miles of his railroad. I got a short note from McPherson that day (written at 2 P. M., when he was within a mile and a half of the railroad, above and near Resaca), and we all felt jubilant. I renewed orders to Thomas and Schofield to be ready for the instant pursuit of what I expected to be a broken and disordered army, forced to retreat by roads to the east of Resaca, which were known to be very rough and impracticable.

That night I received further notice from McPherson that he had found Resaca too strong for a surprise; that in consequence he had fallen back three miles to the mouth of Snake-Creek Gap, and was there fortified. I wrote him the next day the following letters, copies of which are in my letter-book; but his to me were mere notes in pencil, not retained:

HEADQUARTERS MILITARY DIVISION OF THE MISSISSIPPI,
IN THE FIELD, TUNNEL HILL, GEORGIA,
May 11, 1864—*Morning.*

Major-General McPHERSON, *commanding Army of the Tennessee, Sugar Valley, Georgia.*

GENERAL: I received by courier (in the night) yours of 5 and 6:30 P. M. of yesterday.

You now have your twenty-three thousand men, and General Hooker is in close support, so that you can hold all of Jos. Johnston's army in check should he abandon Dalton. He cannot afford to abandon Dalton, for he has fixed it up on purpose to receive us, and he observes that we are close at hand, waiting for him to quit. He cannot afford a detachment strong enough to fight you, as his army will not admit of it.

Strengthen your position; fight any thing that comes; and threaten the safety of the railroad all the time. But, to tell the truth, I would rather the enemy would stay in Dalton two more days, when he may find in his rear a larger party than he expects in an open field. At all events, we can then choose our own ground, and he will be forced to move out of his works. I do not intend to put a column into Buzzard Roost-Gap at present.

See that you are in easy communication with me and with all headquarters. After to-day the supplies will be at Ringgold.

Yours,

W. T. SHERMAN, *Major-General commanding.*

HEADQUARTERS MILITARY DIVISION OF THE MISSISSIPPI,
    IN THE FIELD, TUNNEL HILL, GEORGIA,
        May 11, 1864—*Evening.*

General McPHERSON, Sugar Valley.

GENERAL: The indications are that Johnston is evacuating Dalton. In that event, Howard's corps and the cavalry will pursue; all the rest will follow your route. I will be down early in the morning.

Try to strike him if possible about the forks of the road.

Hooker must be with you now, and you may send General Garrard by Summerville to threaten Rome and that flank. I will cause all the lines to be felt at once.

        W. T. SHERMAN, *Major-General commanding.*

McPherson had startled Johnston in his fancied security, but had not done the full measure of his work. He had in hand twenty-three thousand of the best men of the army, and could have walked into Resaca (then held only by a small brigade), or he could have placed his whole force astride the railroad above Resaca, and there have easily withstood the attack of all of Johnston's army, with the knowledge that Thomas and Schofield were on his heels. Had he done so, I am certain that Johnston would not have ventured to attack him in position, but would have retreated eastward by Spring Place, and we should have captured half his army and all his artillery and wagons at the very beginning of the campaign.

Such an opportunity does not occur twice in a single life, but at the critical moment McPherson seems to have been a little timid. Still, he was perfectly justified by his orders, and fell back and assumed an unassailable defensive position in Sugar Valley, on the Resaca side of Snake-Creek Gap. As soon as informed of this, I determined to pass the whole army through Snake-Creek Gap, and to move on Resaca with the main army.

But during the 10th, the enemy showed no signs of evacuating Dalton, and I was waiting for the arrival of Garrard's and Stoneman's cavalry, known to be near at hand, so as to secure the full advantages of victory, of which I felt certain. Hooker's Twentieth Corps was at once moved down to within easy supporting distance of McPherson; and on the 11th, perceiving signs of evacuation of Dalton, I gave all the orders for the general movement, leaving the Fourth Corps (Howard) and Stoneman's cavalry in observation in front of Buzzard-Roost Gap, and directing all the rest of the army to march through Snake-Creek Gap, straight on Resaca. The roads were only such as the country afforded, mere rough wagon-ways, and these converged to the single narrow track through Snake-Creek Gap; but during the 12th and 13th the bulk of Thomas's and Schofield's armies were got through, and deployed against Resaca, McPherson on the right, Thomas in the centre, and Schofield on the left. Johnston, as I anticipated, had abandoned all his well-prepared defenses at Dalton, and was found inside of Resaca with the bulk of his army, holding his divisions well in hand, acting purely on the defensive, and fighting well at all points of conflict. A complete line of intrenchments was found covering the place, and this was strongly manned at all points. On the 14th we closed in, enveloping the town on its north and west, and during the 15th we had a day of continual battle and skirmish. At the same time I caused two pontoon-bridges to be laid across the Oostenaula River at Lay's Ferry, about three miles below the town, by which we could threaten Calhoun, a station on the railroad seven miles below Resaca. At the same time, May 14th, I dispatched General Garrard, with his cavalry division, down the Oostenaula by the Rome road, with orders to cross over, if possible, and to attack or threaten the railroad at any point below Calhoun and above Kingston.

During the 15th, without attempting to assault the fortified works, we pressed at all points, and the sound of cannon and musketry rose all day to the dignity of a battle. Toward evening McPherson moved his whole line of battle forward, till he had gained a ridge overlooking the town, from which his field-artillery could reach the railroad-bridge across the Oostenaula. The enemy made several attempts to drive him away, repeating the sallies several times, and extending them into the night; but in every instance he was repulsed with bloody loss.

Hooker's corps had also some heavy and handsome fighting that afternoon and night on the left, where the Dalton road entered the intrenchments, capturing a four-gun intrenched battery, with its men and guns; and generally all our men showed the finest fighting qualities.

Howard's corps had followed Johnston down from Dalton,

and was in line; Stoneman's division of cavalry had also got up, and was on the extreme left, beyond the Oostenaula.

On the night of May 15th Johnston got his army across the bridges, set them on fire, and we entered Resaca at daylight. Our loss up to that time was about six hundred dead and thirty-three hundred and seventy-five wounded—mostly light wounds that did not necessitate sending the men to the rear for treatment. That Johnston had deliberately designed in advance to give up such strong positions as Dalton and Resaca, for the purpose of drawing us farther south, is simply absurd. Had he remained in Dalton another hour, it would have been his total defeat, and he only evacuated Resaca because his safety demanded it. The movement by us through Snake-Creek Gap was a total surprise to him. My army about doubled his in size, but he had all the advantages of natural positions, of artificial forts and roads, and of concentrated action. We were compelled to grope our way through forests, across mountains, with a large army, necessarily more or less dispersed. Of course, I was disappointed not to have crippled his army more at that particular stage of the game; but, as it resulted, these rapid successes gave us the initiative, and the usual impulse of a conquering army.

Johnston having retreated in the night of May 15th, immediate pursuit was begun. A division of infantry (Jeff. C. Davis's) was at once dispatched down the valley toward Rome, to support Garrard's cavalry, and the whole army was ordered to pursue, McPherson by Lay's Ferry, on the right, Thomas directly by the railroad, and Schofield by the left, by the old road that crossed the Oostenaula above Echota or Newtown. We hastily repaired the railroad-bridge at Resaca, which had been partially burned, and built a temporary floating-bridge out of timber and materials found on the spot; so that Thomas got his advance corps over during the 16th, and marched as far as Calhoun, where he came into communication with McPherson's troops, which had crossed the Oostenaula at Lay's Ferry by our pontoon-bridges, previously laid. Inasmuch as the bridge at Resaca was overtaxed, Hooker's Twentieth Corps was also diverted to cross by the fords and ferries above Resaca, in the neighborhood of Echota.

On the 17th, toward evening, the head of Thomas's column, Newton's division, encountered the rear-guard of Johnston's army near Adairsville. I was near the head of column at the time, trying to get a view of the position of the enemy from an elevation in an open field. My party attracted the fire of a battery; a shell passed through the group of staff-officers and burst just beyond, which scattered us promptly. The next morning the enemy had disappeared, and our pursuit was continued to Kingston, which we reached during Sunday forenoon, the 19th.

From Resaca the railroad runs nearly due south, but at Kingston it makes junction with another railroad from Rome, and changes direction due east. At that time McPherson's head of column was about four miles to the west of Kingston, at a country place called "Woodlawn"; Schofield and Hooker were on the direct roads leading from Newtown to Cassville, diagonal to the route followed by Thomas. Thomas's head of column, which had followed the country roads alongside of the railroad, was about four miles east of Kingston, toward Cassville, when about noon I got a message from him that he had found the enemy, drawn up in line of battle, on some extensive, open ground, about half-way between Kingston and Cassville, and that appearances indicated a willingness and preparation for battle.

Hurriedly sending orders to McPherson to resume the march, to hasten forward by roads leading to the south of Kingston, so as to leave for Thomas's troops and trains the use of the main road, and to come up on his right, I rode forward rapidly, over some rough gravel hills, and above six miles from Kingston found General Thomas, with his troops deployed; but he reported that the enemy had fallen back in echelon of divisions, steadily and in superb order, into Cassville. I knew that the roads by which Generals Hooker and Schofield were approaching would lead them to a seminary near Cassville, and that it was all-important to secure the point of junction of these roads with the main road along which we were marching. Therefore I ordered General Thomas to push forward his deployed lines as rapidly as possible; and as night was approaching, I ordered two field-batteries to close up at a gallop on some woods which lay between us and the town of Cassville. We could not see the town by reason of these woods, but a high range of hills just back of the town was visible over the tree-tops. On these hills could be seen fresh-made parapets, and the movements of men, against whom I directed the artillery to fire at long range. The stout resistance made by the enemy along our whole front of a couple of miles indicated a purpose to fight at Cassville; and, as the night was closing in, General Thomas and I were together, along with our skirmish-lines near the seminary, on the edge of the town, where musket-bullets from the enemy were cutting the leaves of the trees pretty thickly about us. Either Thomas or I remarked that that was not the place for the two senior officers of a great army, and we personally went back to the battery, where we passed the night on the ground. During the night I had reports from McPherson, Hooker, and Schofield. The former was about five miles to my right rear, near the "nitre-caves"; Schofield was about six miles north, and Hooker between us, within two miles. All were ordered to close down on Cassville at daylight, and to attack the enemy wherever found. Skirmishing was kept up all night, but when day broke the next morning, May 20th, the enemy was gone, and our cavalry was sent in pursuit. These reported him beyond the Etowah River. We were then well in advance of our railroad-trains, on which we depended for supplies; so I determined to pause a few days to repair the railroad, which had been damaged but little, except at the bridge at Resaca, and then to go on.

Nearly all the people of the country seemed to have fled with Johnston's army; yet some few families remained, and from one of them I procured the copy of an order which Johnston had made at Adairsville, in which he recited that he had retreated as far as strategy required, and that his army must be prepared for battle at Cassville. The newspapers of the South, many of which we found, were also loud in denunciation of Johnston's falling back before us without a serious battle, simply resisting by his skirmish-lines and by his rear-guard. But his friends proclaimed that it was all *strategic*; that he was deliberately drawing us farther and farther into the meshes, farther and farther away from our base of supplies, and that in due season he would not only halt for battle, but assume the bold offensive. Of course it was to my interest to bring him to battle as soon as possible, when our numerical superiority was at the greatest; for he was picking up his detachments as he fell back, whereas I was compelled to make similar and stronger detachments to repair the railroads as we advanced, and to guard them. I found at Cassville many evidences of preparation for a grand battle, among them a long line of fresh intrenchments on the hill beyond the town, extending nearly three miles to the south, embracing the railroad-crossing. I was also convinced that the whole of Polk's corps had joined Johnston from Mississippi, and that he had in hand three full corps, viz., Hood's, Polk's, and Hardee's, numbering about sixty thousand men, and could not then imagine why he had declined battle, and did not learn the real reason till after the war was over, and then from General Johnston himself.

In the autumn of 1865, when in command of the Military Division of the Missouri, I went from St. Louis to Little Rock, Arkansas, and afterward to Memphis. Taking a steamer for Cairo, I found as fellow-passengers Generals Johnston and Frank Blair. We were, of course, on the most friendly terms, and on our way up we talked over our battles again, played cards, and questioned each other as to particular parts of our mutual conduct in the game of war. I told Johnston that I had seen his order of preparation, in the nature of an address to his army, announcing his purpose to retreat no more, but to accept battle at Cassville. He answered that such was his purpose; that he had left Hardee's corps in the open fields to check Thomas, and gain time for his formation on the ridge, just behind Cassville; and it was this corps which General Thomas had seen deployed, and whose handsome movement in retreat he had reported in such complimentary terms. Johnston described how he had placed [John B.] Hood's corps on the right, Polk's in the centre, and Hardee's on the left. He said he had ridden over the ground, given to each corps commander his position, and orders to throw up parapets during the night; that he was with Hardee on his extreme left as the night closed in, and as Hardee's troops fell back to the position assigned them for the intended battle of the next day; and that, after giving Hardee some general instructions, he and his staff rode back to Cassville. As he entered the town, or village, he met Generals Hood and Polk. Hood inquired of him if he had had any thing to eat, and he said no, that he was both hungry and tired, when Hood invited him to go and share a supper which had been prepared for him at a house close by. At the supper they discussed the chances of the impending battle, when Hood spoke of the ground assigned him as being enfiladed by our (Union) artillery, which

Johnston disputed, when General Polk chimed in with the remark that General Hood was right; that the cannon-shots fired by us at nightfall had enfiladed their general line of battle, and that for this reason he feared they could not hold their men. General Johnston was surprised at this, for he understood General Hood to be one of those who professed to criticise his strategy, contending that, instead of retreating, he should have risked a battle. General Johnston said he was provoked, accused them of having been in conference, with being beaten before battle, and added that he was unwilling to engage in a critical battle with an army so superior to his own in numbers, with two of his three corps commanders dissatisfied with the ground and positions assigned them. He then and there made up his mind to retreat still farther south, to put the Etowah River and the Allatoona range between us; and he at once gave orders to resume the retrograde movement.

This was my recollection of the substance of the conversation, of which I made no note at the time; but, at a meeting of the Society of the Army of the Cumberland some years after, at Cleveland, Ohio, about 1868, in a short after-dinner speech, I related this conversation, and it got into print. Subsequently, in the spring of 1870, when I was at New Orleans, *en route* for Texas, General Hood called to see me at the St. Charles Hotel, explained that he had seen my speech reprinted in the newspapers and gave me his version of the same event, describing the halt at Cassville, the general orders for battle on that ground, and the meeting at supper with Generals Johnston and Polk, when the chances of the battle to be fought the next day were freely and fully discussed; and he stated that he had argued against fighting the battle purely on the defensive, but had asked General Johnston to permit him with his own corps and part of Polk's to quit their lines, and to march rapidly to attack and overwhelm Schofield, who was known to be separated from Thomas by an interval of nearly five miles, claiming that he could have defeated Schofield, and got back to his position in time to meet General Thomas's attack in front. He also stated that he had then contended with Johnston for the "offensive-defensive" game, instead of the "pure defensive," as proposed by General Johnston; and he said that it was at this time that General Johnston had taken offense, and that it was for this reason he had ordered the retreat that night. As subsequent events estranged these two officers, it is very natural they should now differ on this point; but it was sufficient for us that the rebel army did retreat that night, leaving us masters of all the country above the Etowah River.

For the purposes of rest, to give time for the repair of the railroads, and to replenish supplies, we lay by some few days in that quarter—Schofield with Stoneman's cavalry holding the ground at Cassville Depot, Cartersville, and the Etowah Bridge; Thomas holding his ground near Cassville, and Mc-Pherson that near Kingston. The officer intrusted with the repair of the railroads was Colonel W. W. Wright, a railroad-engineer, who, with about two thousand men, was so industrious and skillful that the bridge at Resaca was rebuilt in three days, and cars loaded with stores came forward to Kingston on the 24th. The telegraph also brought us the news of the bloody and desperate battles of the Wilderness, in Virginia, and that General Grant was pushing his operations against Lee with terrific energy. I was therefore resolved to give my enemy no rest.

In early days (1844), when a lieutenant of the Third Artillery, I had been sent from Charleston, South Carolina, to Marietta, Georgia, to assist Inspector-General Churchill to take testimony concerning certain losses of horses and accoutrements by the Georgia Volunteers during the Florida War; and after completing the work at Marietta we transferred our party over to Bellefonte, Alabama. I had ridden the distance on horseback, and had noted well the topography of the country, especially that about Kenesaw, Allatoona, and the Etowah River. On that occasion I had stopped some days with a Colonel Tumlin, to see some remarkable Indian mounds on the Etowah River, usually called the "Hightower." I therefore knew that the Allatoona Pass was very strong, would be hard to force, and resolved not even to attempt it, but to turn the position, by moving from Kingston to Marietta *via* Dallas; accordingly I made orders on the 20th to get ready for the march to begin on the 23d. The Army of the Cumberland was ordered to march for Dallas, by Euharlee and Stilesboro'; Davis's division, then in Rome, by Van Wert; the Army of the Ohio to keep on the left of Thomas, by a place called Burnt Hickory; and the Army of the Tennessee to march for a position a little to the south, so as to be on the right of the general army, when grouped about Dallas.

The movement contemplated leaving our railroad, and to depend for twenty days on the contents of our wagons; and as the country was very obscure, mostly in a state of nature, densely wooded, and with few roads, our movements were necessarily slow. We crossed the Etowah by several bridges and fords, and took as many roads as possible, keeping up communication by cross-roads, or by couriers through the woods. I personally joined General Thomas, who had the centre, and was consequently the main column, or "column of direction." The several columns followed generally the valley of the Euharlee, a tributary coming into the Etowah from the south, and gradually crossed over a ridge of mount- tains, parts of which had once been worked over for gold, and were consequently full of paths and unused wagon-roads or tracks. A cavalry picket of the enemy at Burnt Hickory was captured, and had on his person an order from General Johnston, dated at Allatoona, which showed that he had detected my purpose of turning his position, and it accord- ingly became necessary to use great caution, lest some of the minor columns should fall into ambush, but, luckily the enemy was not much more familiar with that part of the country than we were. On the other side of the Allatoona range, the Pumpkin-Vine Creek, also a tributary of the Etowah, flowed north and west; Dallas, the point aimed at, was a small town on the other or east side of this creek, and was the point of concentration of a great many roads that led in every direction. Its possession would be a threat to Ma- rietta and Atlanta, but I could not then venture to attempt either, till I had regained the use of the railroad, at least as far down as its *débouché* from the Allatoona range of mountains. Therefore, the movement was chiefly designed to compel Johnston to give up Allatoona.

On the 25th all the columns were moving steadily on Dallas —McPherson and Davis away off to the right, near Van Wert; Thomas on the main road in the centre, with Hooker's Twentieth Corps ahead, toward Dallas; and Schofield to the left rear. For the convenience of march, Hooker had his three divisions on separate roads, all leading toward Dallas, when, in the afternoon, as he approached a bridge across Pumpkin-

Vine Creek, he found it held by a cavalry force, which was driven off, but the bridge was on fire. This fire was extinguished, and Hooker's leading division ([John W.] Geary's) followed the retreating cavalry on a road leading due east toward Marietta, instead of Dallas. This leading division, about four miles out from the bridge, struck a heavy infantry force, which was moving down from Allatoona toward Dallas, and a sharp battle ensued. I came up in person soon after, and as my map showed that we were near an important cross-road called "New Hope," from a Methodist meeting-house there of that name, I ordered General Hooker to secure it if possible that night. He asked for a short delay, till he could bring up his other two divisions, viz., of Butterfield and [Alpheus S.] Williams, but before these divisions had got up and were deployed, the enemy had also gained corresponding strength. The woods were so dense, and the resistance so spirited, that Hooker could not carry the position, though the battle was noisy, and prolonged far into the night. This point, "New Hope," was the accidental intersection of the road leading from Allatoona to Dallas with that from Van Wert to Marietta, was four miles northeast of Dallas, and from the bloody fighting there for the next week was called by the soldiers "Hell-Hole."

The night was pitch-dark, it rained hard, and the convergence of our columns toward Dallas produced much confusion. I am sure similar confusion existed in the army opposed to us, for we were all mixed up. I slept on the ground, without cover, alongside of a log, got little sleep, resolved at daylight to renew the battle, and to make a lodgment on the Dallas and Allatoona road if possible, but the morning revealed a strong line of intrenchments facing up, with a heavy force of infantry and guns. The battle was renewed, and without success. McPherson reached Dallas that morning, viz., the 26th, and deployed his troops to the southeast and east of the town, placing Davis's division of the Fourteenth Corps, which had joined him on the road from Rome, on his left; but this still left a gap of at least three miles between Davis and Hooker. Meantime, also, General Schofield was closing up on Thomas's left.

Satisfied that Johnston in person was at New Hope with all his army, and that it was so much nearer my "objective," the railroad, than Dallas, I concluded to draw McPherson from Dallas to Hooker's right, and gave orders accordingly; but McPherson also was confronted with a heavy force, and, as he began to withdraw according to his orders, on the morning of the 28th he was fiercely assailed on his right; a bloody battle ensued, in which he repulsed the attack, inflicting heavy loss on his assailants, and it was not until the 1st of June that he was enabled to withdraw from Dallas, and to effect a close junction with Hooker in front of New Hope. Meantime Thomas and Schofield were completing their deployments, gradually overlapping Johnston on his right, and thus extending our left nearer and nearer to the railroad, the nearest point of which was Acworth, about eight miles distant. All this time a continual battle was in progress by strong skirmish-lines, taking advantage of every species of cover, and both parties fortifying each night by rifle-trenches, with head-logs, many of which grew to be as formidable as first-class works of defense. Occasionally one party or the other would make a dash in the nature of a sally, but usually it sustained a repulse with great loss of life. I visited personally all parts of our lines nearly every day, was constantly within musket-range, and though the fire of musketry and cannon resounded day and night along the whole line, varying from six to ten miles, I rarely saw a dozen of the enemy at any one time; and these were always skirmishers dodging from tree to tree, or behind logs on the ground, or who occasionally showed their heads above the hastily-constructed but remarkably strong rifle-trenches. On the occasion of my visit to McPherson on the 30th of May, while standing with a group of officers, among whom were Generals McPherson, Logan, [William F.] Barry, and Colonel Taylor, my former chief of artillery, a Minié-ball passed through Logan's coat-sleeve, scratching the skin, and struck Colonel Taylor square in the breast; luckily he had in his pocket a famous memorandum-book, in which he kept a sort of diary, about which we used to joke him a good deal; its thickness and size saved his life, breaking the force of the ball, so that after traversing the book it only penetrated the breast to the ribs, but it knocked him down and disabled him for the rest of the campaign.

On the 1st of June General McPherson closed in upon the right, and, without attempting further to carry the enemy's strong position at New Hope Church, I held our general right in close contact with it, gradually, carefully, and steadily working by the left, until our strong infantry-lines had reached and secured possession of all the wagon-roads between New Hope, Allatoona, and Acworth, when I dispatched Generals Garrard's and Stoneman's divisions of cavalry into Allatoona, the first around by the west end of the pass, and the latter by the direct road. Both reached their destination without opposition, and orders were at once given to repair the railroad forward from Kingston to Allatoona, embracing the bridge across the Etowah River. Thus the real object of my move on Dallas was accomplished, and on the 4th of June I was preparing to draw off from New Hope Church, and to take position on the railroad in front of Allatoona, when, General Johnston himself having evacuated his position, we effected the change without further battle, and moved to the railroad, occupying it from Allatoona and Acworth forward to Big Shanty, in sight of the famous Kenesaw Mountain.

Thus, substantially in the month of May, we had steadily driven our antagonist from the strong positions of Dalton, Resaca, Cassville, Allatoona, and Dallas; had advanced our lines in strong, compact order from Chattanooga to Big Shanty, nearly a hundred miles of as difficult country as was ever fought over by civilized armies; and thus stood prepared to go on, anxious to fight, and confident of success as soon as the railroad communications were complete to bring forward the necessary supplies. It is now impossible to state accurately our loss of life and men in any one separate battle; for the fighting was continuous, almost daily, among trees and bushes, on ground where one could rarely see a hundred yards ahead.

Chapter 10

Battles About Kenesaw: "There Was No Alternative But to Attack" June, 1864

ON THE 1ST OF JUNE our three armies were well in hand, in the broken and densely-wooded country fronting the enemy intrenched at New Hope Church, about five miles north of Dallas. General Stoneman's division of cavalry had occupied Allatoona, on the railroad, and General Garrard's division was at the western end of the pass, about Stilesboro'. Colonel W. W. Wright, of the Engineers, was busily employed in repairing the railroad and rebuilding the bridge across the Etowah (or Hightower) River, which had been destroyed by the enemy on his retreat; and the armies were engaged in a general and constant skirmish along a front of about six miles— McPherson the right, Thomas the centre, and Schofield on the left. By gradually covering our front with parapet, and extending to the left, we approached the railroad toward Acworth and overlapped the enemy's right. By the 4th of June we had made such progress that Johnston evacuated his lines in the night, leaving us masters of the situation, when I deliberately shifted McPherson's army to the extreme left, at and in front of Acworth, with Thomas's about two miles on his right, and Schofield's on his right—all facing east. Heavy rains set in about the 1st of June, making the roads infamous; but our marches were short, as we needed time for the repair of the railroad, so as to bring supplies forward to Allatoona Station. On the 6th I rode back to Allatoona, seven miles, found it all that was expected, and gave orders for its fortification and preparation as a "secondary base." General Blair arrived at Acworth on the 8th with his two divisions of the Seventeenth Corps—the same which had been on veteran furlough—had come up from Cairo by way of Clifton, on the Tennessee River, and had followed our general route to Allatoona, where he had left a garrison of about fifteen hundred men. His effective strength, as reported, was nine thousand. These, with new regiments and furloughed men who had joined early in the month of May, equaled our losses from battle, sickness, and by detachments; so that the three armies still aggregated about one hundred thousand effective men.

On the 10th of June the whole combined army moved forward six miles, to "Big Shanty," a station on the railroad, whence we had a good view of the enemy's position, which embraced three prominent hills, known as Kenesaw, Pine Mountain, and Lost Mountain. On each of these hills the enemy had signal-stations and fresh lines of parapets. Heavy masses of infantry could be distinctly seen with the naked eye, and it was manifest that Johnston had chosen his ground well, and with deliberation had prepared for battle; but his line was at least ten miles in extent—too long, in my judgment, to be held successfully by his force, then estimated at sixty thousand. As his position, however, gave him a perfect view over our field, we had to proceed with due caution. McPherson had the left, following the railroad, which curved around the north base of Kenesaw; Thomas the centre, obliqued to the right, deploying below Kenesaw and facing Pine Hill; and Schofield, somewhat refused, was on the general right, looking south, toward Lost Mountain.

On the 11th the Etowah bridge was done; the railroad was repaired up to our very skirmish-line, close to the base of Kenesaw, and a loaded train of cars came to Big Shanty. The locomotive, detached, was run forward to a water-tank within the range of the enemy's guns on Kenesaw, whence the enemy opened fire on the locomotive; but the engineer was not afraid, went on to the tank, got water, and returned safely to his train, answering the guns with the screams of his engine, heightened by the cheers and shouts of our men.

The rains continued to pour, and made our developments slow and dilatory, for there were no roads, and these had to be improvised by each division for its own supply-train from the depot in Big Shanty to the camps. Meantime each army was deploying carefully before the enemy, intrenching every camp, ready as against a sally. The enemy's cavalry was also busy in our rear, compelling us to detach cavalry all the way back as far as Resaca, and to strengthen all the infantry posts as far as Nashville. Besides, there was great danger, always in my mind, that Forrest would collect a heavy cavalry command in Mississippi, cross the Tennessee River, and break up our railroad below Nashville. In anticipation of this very danger, I had sent General [Samuel B.] Sturgis to Memphis to take command of all the cavalry in that quarter, to go out toward Pontotoc, engage Forrest and defeat him; but on the 14th of June I learned that General Sturgis had himself been defeated on the 10th of June, and had been driven by Forrest back into Memphis in considerable confusion. I expected that this would soon be followed by a general raid on all our roads in Tennessee. General A. J. Smith, with the two divisions of the Sixteenth and Seventeenth Corps which had been with General Banks up Red River, had returned from that ill-fated expedition, and had been ordered to General Canby at New Orleans, who was making a diversion about Mobile; but, on hearing of General Sturgis's defeat, I ordered General Smith to go out from Memphis and renew the offensive, so as to keep Forrest off our roads. This he did finally, defeating Forrest at Tupelo, on the 13th, 14th, and 15th days of July; and he so stirred up matters in North Mississippi that Forrest could not leave for Tennessee. This, for a time, left me only the task of covering the roads against such minor detachments of cavalry as Johnston could spare from his immediate army, and I proposed to keep these too busy in their own defense to spare detachments.

By the 14th the rain slackened, and we occupied a continuous line of ten miles, intrenched, conforming to the irregular position of the enemy, when I reconnoitred, with a view to make a break in their line between Kenesaw and Pine Mountain. When abreast of Pine Mountain I noticed a rebel battery on its crest, with a continuous line of fresh rifle-trench about half-way down the hill. Our skirmishers were at the time engaged in the woods about the base of this hill between the lines, and I estimated the distance to the battery on the crest at about eight hundred yards. Near it, in plain view, stood a group of the enemy, evidently observing us with glasses. General Howard, commanding the Fourth Corps, was near by, and I called his attention to this group, and ordered him to compel it to keep behind its cover. He replied that his orders from General Thomas were to spare artillery-ammunition. This was right, according to the general policy, but I explained to him that we must keep up the *morale* of a bold offensive, that he must use his artillery, force the enemy to remain on the timid defensive, and ordered him to cause a battery close by to fire three volleys. I continued to ride down our line, and soon heard, in quick succession, the three volleys. The next division in order was Geary's, and I gave him similar orders. General Polk, in my opinon, was killed by the second volley fired from the first battery referred to.

In a conversation with General Johnston, after the war, he explained that on that day he had ridden in person from Marietta to Pine Mountain, held by [William B.] Bate's division, and was accompanied by Generals Hardee and Polk. When on Pine Mountain, reconnoitring, quite a group of soldiers, belonging to the battery close by, clustered about him. He noticed the preparations of our battery to fire, and cautioned these men to scatter. They did so, and he likewise hurried behind the parapet, from which he had an equally good view of our position; but General Polk, who was dignified and corpulent, walked back slowly, not wishing to appear too hurried or cautious in the presence of the men, and was struck across the breast by an unexploded shell, which killed him instantly. It has been asserted that I fired the gun which killed General Polk, and that I knew it was directed against that general. The fact is, at that distance we could not even tell that the group were officers at all; I was on horseback, a couple of hundred yards off, before my orders to fire were executed, had no idea that our shot had taken effect, and continued my ride down along the line to Schofield's extreme flank, returning late in the evening to my headquarters at Big Shanty, where I occupied an abandoned house. In a cotton-field back of that house was our signal-station, on the roof of an old gin-house. The signal-officer reported that by studying the enemy's signals he had learned the "key," and that he could read their signals. He explained to me that he had translated a signal about noon, from Pine Mountain to Marietta, "Send an ambulance for General Polk's body"; and later in the day another, "Why don't you send an ambulance for General Polk?" From this we inferred that General Polk had been killed, but how or where we knew not; and this inference was confirmed later in the same day by the report of some prisoners who had been captured.

On the 15th we advanced our general lines, intending to attack at any weak point discovered between Kenesaw and Pine Mountain; but Pine Mountain was found to be abandoned, and Johnston had contracted his front somewhat, on a direct line, connecting Kenesaw with Lost Mountain. Thomas and Schofield thereby gained about two miles of most difficult country, and McPherson's left lapped well around the north end of Kenesaw. We captured a good many prisoners, among them a whole infantry regiment, the Fourteenth Alabama, three hundred and twenty strong.

On the 16th the general movement was continued, when Lost Mountain was abandoned by the enemy. Our right naturally swung round, so as to threaten the railroad below Marietta, but Johnston had still further contracted and strengthened his lines, covering Marietta and all the roads below.

On the 17th and 18th the rain again fell in torrents, making army movements impossible, but we devoted the time to strengthening our positions, more especially the left and centre, with a view gradually to draw from the left to add to the right; and we had to hold our lines on the left extremely strong, to guard against a sally from Kenesaw against our depot at Big Shanty. Garrard's division of cavalry was kept busy on our left, McPherson had gradually extended to his right, enabling Thomas to do the same still farther; but the enemy's position was so very strong, and everywhere it was covered by intrenchments, that we found it as dangerous to assault as a permanent fort. We in like manner covered our lines of battle by similar works, and even our skirmishers learned to cover their bodies by the simplest and best forms of defensive works, such as rails or logs, piled in the form of a simple lunette, covered on the outside with earth thrown up at night.

The enemy and ourselves used the same form of rifle-trench, varied according to the nature of the ground, viz.: the trees and bushes were cut away for a hundred yards or more in front, serving as an abatis or entanglement; the parapets varied from four to six feet high, the dirt taken from a ditch outside and from a covered way inside, and this parapet was surmounted by a "head-log," composed of the trunk of a tree from twelve to twenty inches at the butt, lying along the interior crest of the parapet and resting in notches cut in other trunks which extended back, forming an inclined plane, in case the head-log should be knocked inward by a cannon-shot. The men of both armies became extremely skillful in the construction of these works, because each man realized their value and importance to himself, so that it required no orders for their construction. As soon as a regiment or brigade gained a position within easy distance for a sally, it would set to work with a will, and would construct such a parapet in a single night; but I endeavored to spare the soldiers this hard labor by authorizing each division commander to organize out of the freedmen who escaped to us a pioneer corps of two hundred men, who were fed out of the regular army supplies, and I promised them ten dollars a month, under an existing act of Congress. These pioneer detachments became very useful to us during the rest of the war, for they could work at night while our men slept; they in turn were not expected to fight, and could therefore sleep by day. Our enemies used their slaves for a similar purpose, but usually kept them out of the range of fire by employing them to fortify and strengthen the position to their rear *next* to be occupied in their general retrograde. During this campaign hundreds if not thousands of miles of similar intrenchments were built by both armies, and as a rule whichever party attacked one of them got the worst of it.

On the 19th of June the rebel army again fell back on its flanks, to such an extent that for a time I supposed it had retreated to the Chattahoochee River, fifteen miles distant; but as we pressed forward we were soon undeceived, for we found it still more concentrated, covering Marietta and the railroad. These successive contractions of the enemy's line encouraged us and discouraged him, but were doubtless justified by sound reasons. On the 20th Johnston's position was unusually strong. Kenesaw Mountain was his salient; his two flanks were refused and covered by parapets and by Noonday and Nose's Creeks. His left flank was his weak point, so long as he acted on the "defensive," whereas, had he designed to contract the extent of his line for the purpose of getting in reverse a force with which to strike "offensively" from his right, he would have done a wise act, and I was compelled to presume that such was his object. We were also so far from Nashville and Chattanooga that we were naturally sensitive for the safety of our railroad and depots, so that the left (McPherson) was held *very strong*.

About this time came reports that a large cavalry force of the enemy had passed around our left flank, evidently to strike this very railroad somewhere below Chattanooga. I therefore reënforced the cavalry stationed from Resaca to Cassville, and ordered forward from Huntsville, Alabama, the infantry division of General John E. Smith, to hold Kingston securely.

While we were thus engaged about Kenesaw, General Grant had his hands full with Lee, in Virginia. General Halleck was the chief of staff at Washington, and to him I communicated almost daily. I find from my letter-book that on the 21st of June I reported to him tersely and truly the condition of facts on that day: "This is the nineteenth day of rain, and the prospect of fair weather is as far off as ever. The roads are impassable; the fields and woods become quagmires after a few wagons have crossed over. Yet we are at work all the time. The left flank is across Noonday Creek, and the right is across Nose's Creek. The enemy still holds Kenesaw, a conical mountain, with Marietta behind it, and has his flanks retired, to cover that town and the railroad behind. I am all ready to attack the moment the weather and roads will permit troops and artillery to move with any thing like life."

The weather has a wonderful effect on troops: in action and on the march, rain is favorable; but in the woods, where all is blind and uncertain, it seems almost impossible for an army covering ten miles of front to act in concert during wet and stormy weather. Still I pressed operations with the utmost earnestness, aiming always to keep our fortified lines in absolute contact with the enemy, while with the surplus force we felt forward, from one flank or the other, for his line of communication and retreat. On the 22d of June I rode the whole line, and ordered General Thomas in person to advance his

extreme right corps (Hooker's); and instructed General Schofield, by letter, to keep his entire army, viz., the Twenty-third
Corps, as a strong right flank in close support of Hooker's
deployed line. During this day the sun came out, with some
promise of clear weather, and I had got back to my bivouac
about dark, when a signal-message was received, dated—

KULP HOUSE, 5:30 P. M.

General SHERMAN:

We have repulsed two heavy attacks, and feel confident,
our only apprehension being from our extreme right flank.
Three entire corps are in front of us.

Major-General HOOKER.

Hooker's corps (the Twentieth) belonged to Thomas's
army; Thomas's headquarters were two miles nearer to
Hooker than mine; and Hooker, being an old army officer,
knew that he should have reported this fact to Thomas and
not to me; I was, moreover, specially disturbed by the assertion in his report that he was uneasy about his *right flank*,
when Schofield had been specially ordered to protect that. I
first inquired of my adjutant, Dayton, if he were certain that
General Schofield had received his orders, and he answered
that the envelope in which he had sent them was receipted
by General Schofield himself. I knew, therefore, that General
Schofield must be near by, in close support of Hooker's right
flank. General Thomas had before this occasion complained
to me of General Hooker's disposition to "switch off," leaving wide gaps in his line, so as to be independent, and to
make *glory* on his own account. I therefore resolved not to
overlook his breach of discipline and propriety. The rebel
army was only composed of three corps; I had that very day
ridden six miles of their lines, found them everywhere
strongly occupied, and therefore Hooker could not have
encountered "three entire corps." Both McPherson and Schofield had also complained to me of this same tendency of
Hooker to widen the gap between his own corps and his
proper army (Thomas's), so as to come into closer contact
with one or other of the wings, asserting that he was the
senior by commission to both McPherson and Schofield, and
that in the event of battle he should assume command over
them, by virtue of his older commission.

They appealed to me to protect them. I had heard during that day some cannonading and heavy firing down toward the "Kulp House," which was about five miles southeast of where I was, but this was nothing unusual, for at the same moment there was firing along our lines full ten miles in extent. Early the next day (23d) I rode down to the "Kulp House," which was on a road leading from Powder Springs to Marietta, about three miles distant from the latter. On the way I passed through General Butterfield's division of Hooker's corps, which I learned had not been engaged at all in the battle of the day before; then I rode along Geary's and Ward's divisions, which occupied the field of battle, and the men were engaged in burying the dead. I found General Schofield's corps on the Powder Springs road, its head of column abreast of Hooker's right, therefore constituting "a strong right flank," and I met Generals Schofield and Hooker together. As rain was falling at the moment, we passed into a little church standing by the road-side, and I there showed General Schofield Hooker's signal-message of the day before. He was very angry, and pretty sharp words passed between them, Schofield saying that his head of column (Hascall's division) had been, at the time of the battle, actually in advance of Hooker's line; that the attack or sally of the enemy struck his troops before it did Hooker's; that General Hooker knew of it at the time; and he offered to go out and show me that the dead men of his advance division (Hascall's) were lying farther out than any of Hooker's. General Hooker pretended not to have known this fact. I then asked him why he had called on me for help, until he had used all of his own troops; asserting that I had just seen Butterfield's division, and had learned from his that he had not been engaged the day before at all; and I asserted that the enemy's sally must have been made by one corps (Hood's), in place of three, and that it had fallen on Geary's and Williams's divisions, which had repulsed the attack handsomely. As we rode away from that church General Hooker was by my side, and I told him that such a thing must not occur again; in other words, I reproved him more gently than the occasion demanded, and from that time he began to sulk. General Hooker had come from the East with great fame as a "fighter," and at Chattanooga he was glorified by his "battle above the clouds," which I fear turned his head. He seemed jealous of all the army commanders, because in years, former rank, and experience, he thought he was our superior.

On the 23d of June I telegraphed to General Halleck this summary, which I cannot again better state:

We continue to press forward on the principle of an advance against fortified positions. The whole country is one vast fort, and Johnston must have at least fifty miles of connected trenches, with abatis and finished batteries. We gain ground daily, fighting all the time. On the 21st General [David S.] Stanley gained a position near the south end of Kenesaw, from which the enemy attempted in vain to drive him; and the same day General T. J. Wood's division took a hill, which the enemy assaulted three times at night without success, leaving more than a hundred dead on the ground. Yesterday the extreme right (Hooker and Schofield) advanced on the Powder Springs road to within three miles of Marietta. The enemy made a strong effort to drive them away, but failed signally, leaving more than two hundred dead on the field. Our lines are now in close contact, and the fighting is incessant, with a good deal of artillery-fire. As fast as we gain one position the enemy has another all ready, but I think he will soon have to let go Kenesaw, which is the key to the whole country. The weather is now better, and the roads are drying up fast. Our losses are light, and, notwithstanding the repeated breaks of the road to our rear, supplies are ample.

During the 24th and 25th of June General Schofield extended his right as far as prudent, so as to compel the enemy to thin out his lines correspondingly, with the intention to make two strong assaults at points where success would give us the greatest advantage. I had consulted Generals Thomas, McPherson, and Schofield, and we all agreed that we could not with prudence stretch out any more, and therefore there was no alternative but to attack "fortified lines," a thing carefully avoided up to that time. I reasoned, if we could make a breach anywhere near the rebel centre, and thrust in a strong head of column, that with the one moiety of our army we could hold in check the corresponding wing of the enemy, and with the other sweep in flank and overwhelm the other half. The 27th of June was fixed as the day for the attempt, and in order to oversee the whole, and to be in close communcation with all parts of the army, I had a place cleared on the top of a hill to the rear of Thomas's centre, and had the telegraph-wires laid to it. The points of attack were chosen, and the troops were all prepared with as little demonstration as possible. About 9 A. M. of the day appointed, the troops moved to the assault, and all along our lines for ten miles a furious fire of artillery and musketry was kept up. At all points the enemy met us with determined courage and in great force. McPherson's attacking column fought up the face of the lesser Kenesaw, but could not reach the summit. About a mile to the right (just below the Dallas road) Thomas's assaulting column reached the parapet, where Brigadier-General [Charles G.] Harker was shot down mortally wounded, and Brigadier-General Daniel McCook (my old law-partner) was desperately wounded, from the effects of which he afterward died. By 11:30 the assault was in fact over, and had failed. We had not broken the rebel line at either point, but our assaulting columns held their ground within a few yards of the rebel trenches, and there covered themselves with parapet. McPherson lost about five hundred men and several valuable officers, and Thomas lost nearly two thousand men. This was the hardest fight of the campaign up to that date, and it is well described by Johnston in his "Narrative" (pages 342, 343) where he admits his loss in killed and wounded as—

	Men
Hood's corps (not reported)	—
Hardee's corps	286
Loring's (Polk's)	522
Total	808

This, no doubt, is a true and fair statement; but, as usual, Johnston overestimates our loss, putting it at six thousand, whereas our entire loss was about twenty-five hundred, killed and wounded.

While the battle was in progress at the centre, Schofield crosed Olley's Creek on the right, and gained a position threatening Johnston's line of retreat; and, to increase the effect, I ordered Stoneman's cavalry to proceed rapidly still farther to the right, to Sweetwater. Satisfied of the bloody cost of attacking intrenched lines, I at once thought of moving the whole army to the railroad at a point (Fulton) about ten miles below Marietta, or to the Chattahoochee River itself, a movement similar to the one afterward so successfully practised at Atlanta. All the orders were issued to bring forward supplies enough to fill our wagons, intending to strip the railroad back to Allatoona, and leave that place as our depot, to be covered as well as possible by Garrard's cavalry. General Thomas, as usual, shook his head, deeming it risky to leave the railroad; but something had to be done, and I had resolved on this move, as reported in my dispatch to General Halleck on July 1st:

General Schofield is now south of Olley's Creek, and on the head of Nickajack. I have been hurrying down provisions and forage, and to-morrow night propose to move McPherson from the left to the extreme right, back of General Thomas. This will bring my right within three miles of the Chattahoochee River, and about five miles from the railroad. By this movement I think I can force Johnston to move his whole army down from Kenesaw to defend his railroad and the Chattahoochee, when I will (by the left flank) reach the railroad below Marietta; but in this I must cut loose from the railroad with ten days' supplies in wagons. Johnston may come out of his intrenchments to attack Thomas, which is exactly what I want, for General Thomas is well intrenched on a line parallel with the enemy south of Kenesaw. I think that Allatoona and the line of the Etowah are strong enough for me to venture on this move. The movement is substantially down the Sandtown road straight for Atlanta.

McPherson drew out of his lines during the night of July 2d, leaving Garrard's cavalry, dismounted, occupying his trenches, and moved to the rear of the Army of the Cumberland, stretching down the Nickajack; but Johnston detected the movement, and promptly abandoned Marietta and Kenesaw. I expected as much, for, by the earliest dawn of the 3d of July, I was up at a large spy-glass mounted on a tripod, which Colonel Poe, United States Engineers, had at his bivouac close by our camp. I directed the glass on Kenesaw, and saw some of our pickets crawling up the hill cautiously;

soon they stood upon the very top, and I could plainly see their movements as they ran along the crest just abandoned by the enemy. In a minute I roused my staff, and started them off with orders in every direction for a pursuit by every possible road, hoping to catch Johnston in the confusion of retreat, especially at the crossing of the Chattahoochee River.

Chapter 11

Atlanta:
"The Men Were Skillful and Brave"
July, 1864

As BEFORE EXPLAINED, on the 3d of July, by moving McPherson's entire army from the extreme left, at the base of Kenesaw to the right, below Olley's Creek, and stretching it down the Nickajack toward Turner's Ferry of the Chattahoochee, we forced Johnston to choose between a direct assault on Thomas's intrenched position, or to permit us to make a lodgment on his railroad below Marietta, or even to cross the Chattahoochee. Of course, he chose to let go Kenesaw and Marietta, and fall back on an intrenched camp prepared by his orders in advance on the north and west bank of the Chattahoochee, covering the railroad-crossing and his several pontoon-bridges. I confess I had not learned beforehand of the existence of this strong place, in the nature of a *tête-du-pont*,[1] and had counted on striking him an effectual blow in the expected confusion of his crossing the Chattahoochee, a broad and deep river then to his rear. Ordering every part of the army to pursue vigorously on the morning of the 3d of July, I rode into Marietta, just quitted by the rebel rear-guard, and was terribly angry at the cautious pursuit by Garrard's cavalry, and even by the head of our infantry columns. But

---

[1] Ordinarily given as *tête-de-pont*—that is, a bridgehead.

Johnston had in advance cleared and multiplied his roads, whereas ours had to cross at right angles from the direction of Powder Springs toward Marietta, producing delay and confusion. By night Thomas's head of column ran up against a strong rear-guard intrenched at Smyrna camp-ground, six miles below Marietta, and there on the next day we celebrated our Fourth of July, by a noisy but not a desperate battle, designed chiefly to hold the enemy there till Generals McPherson and Schofield could get well into position below him, near the Chattahoochee crossings.

It was here that General [Edward F.] Noyes, late Governor of Ohio, lost his leg. I came very near being shot myself while reconnoitring in the second story of a house on our picket-line, which was struck several times by cannon-shot, and perfectly riddled with musket-balls.

During the night Johnston drew back all his army and trains inside the *tête-du-pont* at the Chattahoochee, which proved one of the strongest pieces of field-fortification I ever saw. We closed up against it, and were promptly met by a heavy and severe fire. Thomas was on the main road in immediate pursuit; next on his right was Schofield; and McPherson on the extreme right, reaching the Chattahoochee River below Turner's Ferry. Stoneman's cavalry was still farther to the right, along down the Chattahoochee River as far as opposite Sandtown; and on that day I ordered Garrard's division of cavalry up the river eighteen miles, to secure possession of the factories at Roswell, as well as to hold an important bridge and ford at that place.

About three miles out from the Chattahoochee the main road forked, the right branch following substantially the railroad, and the left one leading straight for Atlanta, *via* Paice's Ferry and Buckhead. We found the latter unoccupied and unguarded, and the Fourth Corps (Howard's) reached the river at Paice's Ferry. The right-hand road was perfectly covered by the *tête-du-pont* before described, where the resistance was very severe, and for some time deceived me, for I was pushing Thomas with orders to fiercely assault his enemy, supposing that he was merely opposing us to gain time to get his trains and troops across the Chattahoochee; but, on personally reconnoitring, I saw the abatis and the strong redoubts, which satisfied me of the preparations that had been made by Johnston in anticipation of this very event. While I was with General Jeff. C. Davis, a poor Negro came out of the abatis, blanched with fright, said he had been hidden under a log all day, with a perfect storm of shot, shells, and musket-balls, passing over him, till a short lull had enabled him to creep out and make himself known to our skirmishers, who in turn had sent him back to where we were. This Negro explained that he with about a thousand slaves had been at work a month or more on these very lines, which, as he explained, extended from the river about a mile above the railroad-bridge to Turner's Ferry below, being in extent from five to six miles.

Therefore, on the 5th of July we had driven our enemy to cover in the valley of the Chattahoochee, and we held possession of the river above for eighteen miles, as far as Roswell, and below ten miles to the mouth of the Sweetwater. Moreover, we held the high ground and could overlook his movements, instead of his looking down on us, as was the case at Kenesaw.

From a hill just back of Vining's Station I could see the houses in Atlanta, nine miles distant, and the whole intervening valley of the Chattahoochee; could observe the preparations for our reception on the other side, the camps of men and large trains of covered wagons; and supposed, as a matter of course, that Johnston had passed the river with the bulk of his army, and that he had only left on our side a corps to cover his bridges; but in fact he had only sent across his cavalry and trains. Between Howard's corps at Paice's Ferry and the rest of Thomas's army pressing up against this *tête-du-pont*, was a space concealed by dense woods, in crossing which I came near riding into a detachment of the enemy's cavalry; and later in the same day Colonel Frank Sherman, of Chicago, then on General Howard's staff, did actually ride straight into the enemy's camp, supposing that our lines were continuous. He was carried to Atlanta, and for some time the enemy supposed they were in possession of the commander-in-chief of the opposing army.

I knew that Johnston would not remain long on the west bank of the Chattahoochee, for I could easily practise on that ground to better advantage our former tactics of intrenching a moiety in his front, and with the rest of our army cross the river and threaten either his rear or the city of Atlanta itself, which city was of vital importance to the existence not only of his own army, but of the Confederacy itself.

In my dispatch of July 6th to General Halleck, at Washington, I state that—

Johnston (in his retreat from Kenesaw) has left two breaks in the railroad—one above Marietta and one near Vining's Station. The former is already repaired, and Johnston's army has heard the sound of our locomotives. The telegraph is finished to Vining's Station, and the field-wire has just reached my bivouac, and will be ready to convey this message as soon as it is written and translated into cipher.

I propose to study the crossings of the Chattahoochee, and, when all is ready, to move quickly. As a beginning, I will keep the troops and wagons well back from the river, and only display to the enemy our picket-line, with a few field-batteries along at random. I have already shifted Schofield to a point in our left rear, whence he can in a single move reach the Chattahoochee at a point above the railroad-bridge, where there is a ford. At present the waters are turbid and swollen from recent rains; but if the present hot weather lasts, the water will run down very fast. We have pontoons enough for four bridges, but, as our crossing will be resisted, we must manœuvre some. All the regular crossing-places are covered by forts, apparently of long construction; but we shall cross in due time, and, instead of attacking Atlanta direct, or any of its forts, I propose to make a circuit, destroying all its railroads. This is a delicate movement, and must be done with caution. Our army is in good condition and full of confidence; but the weather is intensely hot, and a good many men have fallen with sun-stroke. The country is high and healthy, and the sanitary condition of the army is good.

At this time Stoneman was very active on our extreme right, pretending to be searching the river below Turner's Ferry for a crossing, and was watched closely by the enemy's cavalry on the other side. McPherson, on the right, was equally demonstrative at and near Turner's Ferry. Thomas faced substantially the intrenched *tête-du-pont*, and had his left on the Chattahoochee River, at Paice's Ferry. Garrard's cavalry was up at Roswell, and McCook's small division of cavalry was intermediate, above Soap's Creek. Meantime, also, the railroad-construction party was hard at work, repairing the railroad up to our camp at Vining's Station.

Of course, I expected every possible resistance in crossing

the Chattahoochee River, and had made up my mind to feign on the right, but actually to cross over by the left. We had already secured a crossing-place at Roswell, but one nearer was advisable; General Schofield had examined the river well, found a place just below the mouth of Soap's Creek which he deemed advantageous, and was instructed to effect an early crossing there, and to intrench a good position on the other side, viz., the east bank. But, preliminary thereto, I had ordered General Rousseau, at Nashville, to collect, out of the scattered detachments of cavalry in Tennessee, a force of a couple of thousand men, to rendezvous at Decatur, Alabama, thence to make a rapid march for Opelika, to break up the railroad-links between Georgia and Alabama, and then to make junction with me about Atlanta; or, if forced, to go on to Pensacola, or even to swing across to some of our posts in Mississippi. General Rousseau asked leave to command this expedition himself, to which I consented, and on the 6th of July he reported that he was all ready at Decatur, and I gave him orders to start. He moved promptly on the 9th, crossed the Coosa below the "Ten Islands" and the Tallapoosa below "Horseshoe Bend," having passed through Talladega. He struck the railroad west of Opelika, tore it up for twenty miles, then turned north and came to Marietta on the 22d of July, whence he reported to me. This expedition was in the nature of a raid, and must have disturbed the enemy somewhat; but, as usual, the cavalry did not work hard, and their destruction of the railroad was soon repaired. Rousseau, when he reported to me in person before Atlanta, on the 23d of July, stated his entire loss to have been only twelve killed and thirty wounded. He brought in four hundred captured mules and three hundred horses, and also told me a good story. He said he was far down in Alabama, below Talladega, one hot, dusty day, when the blue clothing of his men was gray with dust; he had halted his column along a road, and he in person, with his staff, had gone to the house of a planter, who met him kindly on the front-porch. He asked for water, which was brought, and as the party sat on the porch in conversation he saw, in a stable-yard across the road, quite a number of good mules. He remarked to the planter, "My good sir, I fear I must take some of your mules." The planter remonstrated, saying he had already contributed liberally to the *good cause*; that it was only last week he had given to

General [Philip D.] Roddey ten mules. Rousseau replied, "Well, in this war you should be at least neutral—that is, you should be as liberal to us as to Roddey" (a rebel cavalry general). "Well, ain't you on our side?" "No," said Rousseau; "I am General Rousseau, and all these men you see are yanks." "Great God! is it possible? Are these Yanks? Who ever supposed they would come away down here in Alabama?" Of course, Rousseau took his ten mules.

Schofield effected his crossing at Soap's Creek very handsomely on the 9th, capturing the small guard that was watching the crossing. By night he was on the high ground beyond, strongly intrenched, with two good pontoon-bridges finished, and was prepared, if necessary, for an assault by the whole Confederate army. The same day [Theophilus T.] Garrard's cavalry also crossed over at Roswell, drove away the cavalry-pickets, and held its ground till relieved by [John] Newton's division of Howard's corps, which was sent up temporarily, till it in turn was relieved by Dodge's corps (Sixteenth) of the Army of the Tennessee, which was the advance of the whole of that army.

That night Johnston evacuated his trenches, crossed over the Chattahoochee, burned the railroad-bridge and his pontoon and trestle bridges, and left us in full possession of the north or west bank—besides which, we had already secured possession of the two good crossings at Roswell and Soap's Creek. I have always thought Johnston neglected his opportunity there, for he had lain comparatively idle while we got control of both banks of the river above him.

On the 13th I ordered McPherson, with the Fifteenth Corps, to move up to Roswell, to cross over, prepare good bridges, and to make a strong *tête-du-pont* on the farther side. Stoneman had been sent down to Campbellton, with orders to cross over and to threaten the railroad below Atlanta, if he could do so without too much risk; and General Blair, with the Seventeenth Corps, was to remain at Turner's Ferry, demonstrating as much as possible, thus keeping up the feint below while we were actually crossing above. Thomas was also ordered to prepare his bridges at Powers's and Paice's Ferries. By crossing the Chattahoochee above the railroad-bridge, we were better placed to cover our railroad and depots than below, though a movement across the river below the railroad, to the south of Atlanta, might have been more decisive. But we were already so far from home, and would be compelled to accept battle whenever offered, with the Chattahoochee to *our* rear, that it became imperative for me to take all prudential measures the case admitted of, and I therefore determined to pass the river above the railroad-bridge—McPherson on the left, Schofield in the centre, and Thomas on the right.

On the 13th I reported to General Halleck as follows:

All is well. I have now accumulated stores at Allatoona and Marietta, both fortified and garrisoned points. Have also three places at which to cross the Chattahoochee in our possession, and only await General Stoneman's return from a trip down the river, to cross the army in force and move on Atlanta.

Stoneman is now out two days, and had orders to be back on the fourth or fifth day at furthest.

From the 10th to the 15th we were all busy in strengthening the several points for the proposed passage of the Chattahoochee, in increasing the number and capacity of the bridges, rearranging the garrisons to our rear, and in bringing forward supplies. On the 15th General Stoneman got back to Powder Springs, and was ordered to replace General Blair at Turner's Ferry, and Blair, with the Seventeenth Corps, was ordered up to Roswell to join McPherson.

On the 17th we began the general movement against Atlanta, Thomas crossing the Chattahoochee at Powers's and Paice's, by pontoon-bridges; Schofield moving out toward Cross Keys, and McPherson toward Stone Mountain. We encountered but little opposition except by cavalry. On the 18th all the armies moved on a general right wheel. Thomas to Buckhead, forming line of battle facing Peach-Tree Creek; Schofield was on his left, and McPherson well over toward the railroad between Stone Mountain and Decatur, which he reached at 2 P. M. of that day, about four miles from Stone Mountain, and seven miles east of Decatur, and there he turned toward Atlanta, breaking up the railroad as he progressed, his advance-guard reaching Decatur about night, where he came into communication with Schofield's troops, which had also reached Decatur. About 10 A. M. of that day (July 18th), when the armies were all in motion, one of General Thomas's staff-officers brought me a citizen, one of

our spies, who had just come out of Atlanta, and had brought
a newspaper of the same day, or of the day before, containing
Johnston's order relinquishing the command of the Confederate forces in Atlanta, and Hood's order assuming the command. I immediately inquired of General Schofield, who was
his classmate at West Point, about Hood, as to his general
character, etc., and learned that he was bold even to rashness,
and courageous in the extreme; I inferred that the change of
commanders meant "fight." Notice of this important change
was at once sent to all parts of the army, and every division
commander was cautioned to be always prepared for battle in
any shape. This was just what we wanted, viz., to fight in open
ground, on any thing like equal terms, instead of being forced
to run up against prepared intrenchments; but, at the same
time, the enemy having Atlanta behind him, could choose the
time and place of attack, and could at pleasure mass a superior force on our weakest points. Therefore, we had to be
constantly ready for sallies.

On the 19th the three armies were converging toward Atlanta, meeting such feeble resistance that I really thought the
enemy intended to evacuate the place. McPherson was moving
astride of the railroad, near Decatur; Schofield along a road
leading toward Atlanta, by Colonel Howard's house and the
distillery; and Thomas was crossing "Peach-Tree" in line of
battle, building bridges for nearly every division as deployed.
There was quite a gap between Thomas and Schofield, which I
endeavored to close by drawing two of Howard's divisions
nearer Schofield. On the 20th I was with General Schofield
near the centre, and soon after noon heard heavy firing in
front of Thomas's right, which lasted an hour or so, and then
ceased. I soon learned that the enemy had made a furious
sally, the blow falling on Hooker's corps (the Twentieth), and
partially on Johnson's division of the Fourteenth, and Newton's of the Fourth. The troops had crossed Peach-Tree
Creek, were deployed, but at the time were resting for noon,
when, without notice, the enemy came pouring out of their
trenches down upon them, they became commingled, and
fought in many places hand to hand. General Thomas happened to be near the rear of Newton's division, and got
some field-batteries in a good position, on the north side of
Peach-Tree Creek, from which he directed a furious fire on
a mass of the enemy, which was passing around Newton's

left and exposed flank. After a couple of hours of hard and close conflict, the enemy retired slowly within his trenches, leaving his dead and many wounded on the field. Johnson's and Newton's losses were light, for they had partially covered their fronts with light parapet; but Hooker's whole corps fought in open ground, and lost about fifteen hundred men. He reported four hundred rebel dead left on the ground, and that the rebel wounded would number four thousand; but this was conjectural, for most of them got back within their own lines. We had, however, met successfully a bold sally, had repelled it handsomely, and were also put on our guard; and the event illustrated the future tactics of our enemy. This sally came from the Peach-Tree line, which General Johnston had carefully prepared in advance, from which to fight us *outside* of Atlanta. We then advanced our lines in compact order, close up to these finished intrenchments, overlapping them on our left. From various parts of our lines the houses inside of Atlanta were plainly visible, though between us were the strong parapets, with ditch, *fraise, chevaux-de-frise*,[2] and abatis, prepared long in advance by Colonel Jeremy F. Gilmer, formerly of the United States Engineers. McPherson had the Fifteenth Corps astride the Augusta Railroad, and the Seventeenth deployed on its left. Schofield was next on his right, then came Howard's, Hooker's, and [John M.] Palmer's corps, on the extreme right. Each corps was deployed with strong reserves, and their trains were parked to their rear. McPherson's trains were in Decatur, guarded by a brigade commanded by Colonel [John W.] Sprague of the Sixty-third Ohio. The Sixteenth Corps (Dodge's) was crowded out of position on the right of McPherson's line, by the contraction of the circle of investment; and, during the previous afternoon, the Seventeenth Corps (Blair's) had pushed its operations on the farther side of the Augusta Railroad, so as to secure possession of a hill, known as Leggett's Hill, because General Leggett's division had carried it by assault. Giles A. Smith's division was on Leggett's left, deployed with a weak left flank "in air," in military phraseology. It was in carrying this hill that Gen-

---

[2] *Fraise:* pointed spikes driven in a horizontal or inclined position into a rampart. *Chevaux-de-frise* (the plural form of *cheval-de-frise*): a defense consisting of spikes along a wall or of spikes driven into barrels and connected with barbed wire.

eral [Walter Q.] Gresham, a great favorite, was badly wounded; and there also Colonel Tom Reynolds, now of Madison, Wisconsin, was shot through the leg. When the surgeons were debating the propriety of amputating it in his hearing, he begged them to spare the leg, as it was very valuable, being an "imported leg." He was of Irish birth, and this well-timed piece of wit saved his leg, for the surgeons thought, if he could perpetrate a joke at such a time, they would trust to his vitality to save his limb.

During the night, I had full reports from all parts of our line, most of which was partially intrenched as against a sally, and finding that McPherson was stretching out too much on his left flank, I wrote him a note early in the morning not to extend so much by his left; for we had not troops enough to completely invest the place, and I intended to destroy utterly all parts of the Augusta Railroad to the east of Atlanta, then to withdraw from the left flank and add to the right. In that letter I ordered McPherson not to extend any farther to the left, but to employ General Dodge's corps (Sixteenth), then forced out of position, to destroy every rail and tie of the railroad, from Decatur up to his skirmish-line, and I wanted him (McPherson) to be ready, as soon as General Garrard returned from Covington (whither I had sent him), to move to the extreme right of Thomas, so as to reach if possible the railroad below Atlanta, viz., the Macon road. In the morning we found the strong line of parapet, "Peach-Tree line," to the front of Schofield and Thomas, abandoned, and our lines were advanced rapidly close up to Atlanta. For some moments I supposed the enemy intended to evacuate, and in person was on horseback at the head of Schofield's troops, who had advanced in front of the Howard House to some open ground, from which we could plainly see the whole rebel line of parapets, and I saw their men dragging up from the intervening valley, by the distillery, trees and saplings for abatis. Our skirmishers found the enemy down in this valley, and we could see the rebel main line strongly manned, with guns in position at intervals. Schofield was dressing forward his lines, and I could hear Thomas farther to the right engaged, when General McPherson and his staff rode up. We went back to the Howard House, a double frame-building with a porch, and sat on the steps, discussing the chances of battle, and of Hood's general character. McPherson had also been of the same class at West Point with Hood, Schofield, and [Philip H.] Sheridan. We agreed that we ought to be unusually cautious and prepared at all times for sallies and for hard fighting, because Hood, though not deemed much of a scholar, or of great mental capacity, was undoubtedly a brave, determined, and rash man; and the change of commanders at that particular crisis argued the displeasure of the Confederate Government with the cautious but prudent conduct of General Jos. Johnston.

McPherson was in excellent spirits, well pleased at the progress of events so far, and had come over purposely to see me about the order I had given him to use Dodge's corps to break up the railroad, saying that the night before he had gained a position on Leggett's Hill from which he could look over the rebel parapet, and see the high smoke-stack of a large foundry in Atlanta; that before receiving my order he had diverted Dodge's two divisions (then in motion) from the main road, along a diagonal one that led to his extreme left flank, then held by Giles A. Smith's division (Seventeenth Corps), for the purpose of strengthening that flank; and that he had sent some intrenching-tools there, to erect some batteries from which he intended to knock down that foundry, and otherwise to damage the buildings inside of Atlanta. He said he could put all his pioneers to work, and do with them in the time indicated all I had proposed to do with General Dodge's two divisions. Of course I assented at once, and we walked down the road a short distance, sat down by the foot of a tree where I had my map, and on it pointed out to him Thomas's position and his own. I then explained minutely that, after we had sufficiently broken up the Augusta road, I wanted to shift his whole army around by the rear to Thomas's extreme right, and hoped thus to reach the other railroad at East Point. While we sat there we could hear lively skirmishing going on near us (down about the distillery), and occasionally round-shot from twelve or twenty-four pound guns came through the trees in reply to those of Schofield, and we could hear similar sounds all along down the lines of Thomas to our right, and his own to the left; but presently the firing appeared a little more brisk (especially over about Giles A. Smith's division), and then we heard an occasional gun back toward Decatur. I asked him what it meant. We took my pocket-compass (which I always carried), and by noting the direction of the sound, we became satisfied that the firing was too far to our left rear to be explained by known facts, and he hastily called for his horse, his staff, and his orderlies.

McPherson was then in his prime (about thirty-four years old), over six feet high, and a very handsome man in every way, was universally liked, and had many noble qualities. He had on his boots outside his pantaloons, gauntlets on his hands, had on his major-general's uniform, and wore a sword-belt, but no sword. He hastily gathered his papers (save one, which I now possess) into a pocket-book, put it in his breast-pocket, and jumped on his horse, saying he would hurry down his line and send me back word what these sounds meant. His adjutant-general, Clark, Inspector-General Strong, and his aides, Captains Steele and Gile, were with him. Although the sound of musketry on our left grew in volume, I was not so much disturbed by it as by the sound of artillery back toward Decatur. I ordered Schofield at once to send a brigade back to Decatur (some five miles) and was walking up and down the porch of the Howard House, listening, when one of McPherson's staff, with his horse covered with sweat, dashed up to the porch, and reported that General McPherson was either "killed or a prisoner." He explained that when they had left me a few minutes before, they had ridden rapidly across to the railroad, the sounds of battle increasing as they neared the position occupied by General Giles A. Smith's division, and that McPherson had sent first one, then another of his staff to bring some of the reserve brigades of the Fifteenth Corps over to the exposed left flank; that he had reached the head of Dodge's corps (marching by the flank on the diagonal road as described), and had ordered it to hurry forward to the same point; that then, almost if not entirely alone, he had followed this road leading across the wooded valley behind the Seventeenth Corps, and had disappeared in these woods, doubtless with a sense of absolute security. The sound of musketry was there heard, and McPherson's horse came back, bleeding, wounded, and riderless. I ordered the staff-officer who brought this message to return at once, to find General Logan (the senior officer present with the Army of the Tennessee), to report the same facts to him, and to instruct him to drive back this supposed small force, which had evidently got around the Seventeenth Corps through the blind woods in rear of our left flank. I soon dispatched one of my own staff (McCoy, I think) to General Logan with similar orders, telling him to refuse his left flank, and to fight the battle (holding fast to Leggett's Hill) with the Army of the Tennessee; that I would personally look to Decatur and to the safety of his rear, and would reënforce him if he needed it. I dispatched orders to General Thomas on our right, telling him of this strong sally, and my inference that the lines in his front had evidently been weakened by reason thereof, and that he ought to take advantage of the opportunity to make a lodgment in Atlanta, if possible.

Meantime the sounds of the battle rose on our extreme left more and more furious, extending to the place where I stood, at the Howard House. Within an hour an ambulance came in (attended by Colonels Clark and Strong, and Captains Steele and Gile), bearing McPherson's body. I had it carried inside of the Howard House, and laid on a door wrenched from its hinges. Dr. Hewitt, of the army, was there, and I asked him to examine the wound. He opened the coat and shirt, saw where the ball had entered and where it came out, or rather lodged under the skin, and he reported that McPherson must have died in a few seconds after being hit; that the ball had ranged upward across his body, and passed near the heart. He was dressed just as he left me, with gauntlets and boots on, but his pocket-book was gone. On further inquiry I learned that his body must have been in possession of the enemy some minutes, during which time it was rifled of the pocket-book, and I was much concerned lest the letter I had written him that morning should have fallen into the hands of some one who could read and understand its meaning. Fortunately the spot in the woods where McPherson was shot was regained by our troops in a few minutes, and the pocket-book found in the haversack of a prisoner of war captured at the time, and it and its contents were secured by one of McPherson's staff.

While we were examining the body inside the house, the battle was progressing outside, and many shots struck the building, which I feared would take fire; so I ordered Captains Steele and Gile to carry the body to Marietta. They reached that place the same night, and, on application, I ordered his personal staff to go on and escort the body to his home, in Clyde, Ohio, where it was received with great honor, and it is now buried in a small cemetery, close by his mother's house, which cemetery is composed in part of the family orchard, in which he used to play when a boy.

The reports that came to me from all parts of the field revealed clearly what was the game of my antagonist, and the ground somewhat favored it. The railroad and wagon-road from Decatur to Atlanta lie along the summit, from which the waters flow, by short, steep valleys, into the "Peach-Tree" and Chattahoochee, to the west, and by other valleys, of gentler declivity, toward the east (Ocmulgee). The ridges and level ground were mostly cleared, and had been cultivated as corn or cotton fields; but where the valleys were broken, they were left in a state of nature—wooded, and full of undergrowth. McPherson's line of battle was across this railroad, along a general ridge, with a gentle but cleared valley to his front, between him and the defenses of Atlanta; and another valley, behind him, was clear of timber in part, but to his left rear the country was heavily wooded. Hood, during the night of July 21st, had withdrawn from his Peach-Tree line, had occupied the fortified line of Atlanta, facing north and east, with [Alexander P.] Stewart's—formerly Polk's—corps and part of Hardee's, and with G. W. Smith's division of militia. His own corps, and part of Hardee's, had marched out to the road leading from McDonough to Decatur, and had turned so as to strike the left and rear of McPherson's line "in air." At the same time he had sent Wheeler's division of cavalry against the trains parked in Decatur. Unluckily for us, I had sent away the whole of Garrard's division of cavalry during the night of the 20th, with orders to proceed to Covington, thirty miles east, to burn two important bridges across the Ulcofauhatchee and Yellow Rivers, to tear up the railroad, to damage it as much as possible from Stone Mountain eastward, and to be gone four days; so that McPherson had no cavalry in hand to guard that flank.

The enemy was therefore enabled, under cover of the forest, to approach quite near before he was discovered; indeed, his skirmish-line had worked through the timber and got into the field to the rear of Giles A. Smith's division of the Seventeenth Corps unseen, had captured Murray's battery of regular artillery, moving through these woods entirely unguarded, and had got possession of several of the hospital camps. The right of this rebel line struck Dodge's troops in motion; but, fortunately, this corps (Sixteenth) had only to halt, face to the left, and was in line of battle; and this corps not only held in check the enemy, but drove him back through the woods. About the same time this same force had struck General Giles A. Smith's left flank, doubled it back, captured four guns in position and the party engaged in building the very battery which was the special object of McPherson's visit to me, and almost enveloped the entire left flank. The men, however, were skillful and brave, and fought for a time with their backs to Atlanta. They gradually fell back, compressing their own line, and gaining strength by making junction with Leggett's division of the Seventeenth Corps, well and strongly posted on the hill. One or two brigades of the Fifteenth Corps, ordered by McPherson, came rapidly across the open field to the rear, from the direction of the railroad, filled up the gap from Blair's new left to the head of Dodge's column—now facing to the general left—thus forming a strong left flank, at right angles to the original line of battle. The enemy attacked, boldly and repeatedly, the whole of this flank, but met an equally fierce resistance; and on that ground a bloody battle raged from little after noon till into the night. A part of Hood's plan of action was to sally from Atlanta at the same moment; but this sally was not, for some reason, simultaneous, for the first attack on our extreme left flank had been checked and repulsed before the sally came from the direction of Atlanta. Meantime, Colonel Sprague, in Decatur, had got his teams harnessed up, and safely conducted his train to the rear of Schofield's position, holding in check [Joseph] Wheeler's cavalry till he had got off all his trains, with the exception of three or four wagons. I remained near the Howard House, receiving reports and sending orders, urging Generals Thomas and Schofield to take advantage of the absence from their front of so considerable a body as was evidently engaged on our left, and, if possible, to make a lodgment in Atlanta itself; but they reported that the lines to their front, at all accessible points, were strong, by nature and by art, and were fully manned. About 4 P. M. the expected sally came from Atlanta, directed mainly against Leggett's Hill and along the Decatur road. At Leggett's Hill they were met and bloodily repulsed. Along the railroad they were more successful. Sweeping over a small force with two guns, they reached our main line, broke through it, and got possession of [Francis] De Gress's battery of four twenty-pound Parrotts, killing every horse, and turning the guns against us. General Charles R. Wood's division of the Fifteenth Corps was on the extreme right of the Army of the Tennessee, between the railroad and the Howard House, where he connected with Schofield's troops. He reported to me in person that the line on his left had been swept back, and that his connection with General Logan, on Leggett's Hill, was broken. I ordered him to wheel his brigades to the left, to advance in echelon, and to catch the enemy in flank. General Schofield brought forward all his available batteries, to the number of twenty guns, to a position to the left front of the Howard House, whence we could overlook the field of action, and directed a heavy fire over the heads of General Wood's men against the enemy; and we saw Wood's troops advance and encounter the enemy, who had secured possession of the old line of parapet which had been held by our men. His right crossed this parapet, which he swept back, taking it in flank; and, at the same time, the division which had been driven back along the railroad was rallied by General Logan in person, and fought for their former ground. These combined forces drove the enemy into Atlanta, recovering the twenty-pound Parrott guns—but one of them was found "bursted" while in the possession of the enemy. The two six-pounders farther in advance were, however, lost, and had been hauled back by the enemy into Atlanta. Poor Captain de Gress came to me in tears, lamenting the loss of his favorite guns; when they were regained he had only a few men left, and not a single horse. He asked an order for a reëquipment, but I told him he must beg and borrow of others till he could restore his battery, now reduced to three guns. How he did so I do not know, but in a short time he did get horses, men, and finally another gun, of the same special pattern, and served them with splendid effect till the very close of the war. This battery had also been with me from Shiloh till that time.

The battle of July 22d is usually called the battle of Atlanta. It extended from the Howard House to General Giles A. Smith's position, about a mile beyond the Augusta Railroad, and then back toward Decatur, the whole extent of ground being fully seven miles. In part the ground was clear and in part densely wooded. I rode over the whole of it the next day, and it bore the marks of a bloody conflict. The enemy had retired during the night inside of Atlanta, and we remained masters of the situation outside. I purposely allowed the Army of the Tennessee to fight this battle almost unaided, save by demonstrations on the part of General Schofield and Thomas against the fortified lines to their immediate fronts, and by detaching, as described, one of Schofield's brigades to Decatur, because I knew that the attacking force could only be a part of Hood's army, and that, if any assistance were rendered by either of the other armies, the Army of the Tennessee would be jealous. Nobly did they do their work that day, and terrible was the slaughter done to our enemy, though at sad cost to ourselves.

On the 22nd of July General Rousseau reached Marietta, having returned from his raid on the Alabama road at Opelika, and on the next day General Garrard also returned from Covington, both having been measurably successful. The former was about twenty-five hundred strong, the latter about four thousand, and both reported that their horses were jaded and tired, needing shoes and rest. But, about this time, I was advised by General Grant (then investing Richmond) that the rebel Government had become aroused to the critical condition of things about Atlanta, and that I must look out for Hood being greatly reënforced. I therefore was resolved to push matters, and at once set about the original purpose of transferring the whole of the Army of the Tennessee to our right flank, leaving Schofield to stretch out so as to rest his left on the Augusta road, then torn up for thirty miles eastward; and, as auxiliary thereto, I ordered all the cavalry to be ready to pass around Atlanta on both flanks, to break up the Macon road at some point below, so as to cut off all supplies to the rebel army inside, and thus to force it to evacuate, or come out and fight us on equal terms.

But it first became necessary to settle the important question of who should succeed General McPherson? General Logan had taken command of the Army of the Tennessee by virtue of his seniority, and had done well; but I did not consider him equal to the command of three corps. Between him and General Blair there existed a natural rivalry. Both were men of great courage and talent, but were politicians by nature and experience, and it may be that for this reason they were mistrusted by regular officers like Generals Schofield, Thomas, and myself. It was all-important that there should exist a perfect understanding among the army commanders, and at a conference with General George H. Thomas at the headquarters of General Thomas J. Woods, commanding a division in the Fourth Corps, he (Thomas) remonstrated warmly against my recommending that General Logan should be regularly assigned to the command of the Army of the Tennessee by reason of his accidental seniority. We discussed fully the merits and qualities of every officer of high rank in the army, and finally settled on Major-General O. O. Howard as the best officer who was present and available for the purpose; on the 24th of July I telegraphed to General Halleck this preference, and it was promptly ratified by the President. General Howard's place in command of the Fourth Corps was filled by General Stanley, one of his division commanders, on the recommendation of General Thomas. All these promotions happened to fall upon West-Pointers, and doubtless Logan and Blair had some reason to believe that we intended to monopolize the higher honors of the war for the regular officers. I remember well my own thoughts and feelings at the time, and feel sure that I was not intentionally partial to any class. I wanted to succeed in taking Atlanta, and needed commanders who were purely and technically soldiers, men who would obey orders and execute them promptly and on time; for I knew that we would have to execute some most delicate manœuvres, requiring the utmost skill, nicety, and precision. I believed that General Howard would do all these faithfully and well, and I think the result has justified my choice. I regarded both Generals Logan and Blair as "volunteers," that looked to personal fame and glory as auxiliary and secondary to their political ambition, and not as professional soldiers.

As soon as it was known that General Howard had been chosen to command the Army of the Tennessee, General Hooker applied to General Thomas to be relieved of the command of the Twentieth Corps, and General Thomas forwarded his application to me approved and *heartily* recommended. I at once telegraphed to General Halleck, recommending General Slocum (then at Vicksburg) to be his successor, because Slocum had been displaced from the command of his corps at the time when the Eleventh and Twelfth were united and made the twentieth.

General Hooker was offended because he was not chosen to succeed McPherson; but his chances were not even considered; indeed, I had never been satisfied with him since his affair at the Kulp House, and had been more than once disposed to relieve him of his corps, because of his repeated attempts to interfere with Generals McPherson and Schofield. I am told that he says that Thomas and I were jealous of him; but this is hardly probable, for we on the spot did not rate his fighting qualities as high as he did, and I am, moreover, convinced that both he and General Butterfield went to the rear for personal reasons. We were then two hundred and fifty miles in advance of our base, dependent on a single line of railroad for our daily food. We had a bold, determined foe in our immediate front, strongly intrenched, with communication open to his rear for supplies and reënforcements, and every soldier realized that we had plenty of hard fighting ahead, and that all honors had to be fairly earned. General Hooker, moreover, when he got back to Cincinnati, reported (I was told) that we had run up against a rock at Atlanta, and that the country ought to be prepared to hear of disaster from that quarter.

Until General Slocum joined (in the latter part of August), the Twentieth Corps was commanded by General A. S. Williams, the senior division commander present. On the 25th of July the army, therefore, stood thus: the Army of the Tennessee (General O. O. Howard commanding) was on the left, pretty much on the same ground it had occupied during the battle of the 22d, all ready to move rapidly by the rear to the extreme right beyond Proctor's Creek; the Army of the Ohio (General Schofield) was next in order, with its left flank reaching the Augusta Railroad; next in order, conforming closely with the rebel intrenchments of Atlanta, was General Thomas's Army of the Cumberland, in the order of—the Fourth Corps (Stanley's); the Twentieth Corps (Williams's), and the Fourteenth Corps (Palmer's). Palmer's right division (Jefferson C. Davis's) was strongly refused along Proctor's Creek. This line was about five miles long, and was intrenched as against a sally about as strong as was our enemy. The cavalry was assembled in two strong divisions; that of [Daniel] McCook (including the brigade of Harrison which had been brought in from Opelika by General Rousseau) numbered about thirty-five hundred effective cavalry, and was posted to our right rear, at Turner's Ferry, where we had a good pontoon-bridge; and to our left rear, at and about

Decatur, were the two cavalry divisions of Stoneman, twenty-five hundred, and Garrard, four thousand, united for the time and occasion under the command of Major-General George Stoneman, a cavalry-officer of high repute. My plan of action was to move the Army of the Tennessee to the right rapidly and boldly against the railroad below Atlanta, and at the same time to send all the cavalry around by the right and left to make a lodgment on the Macon road about Jonesboro'.

All the orders were given, and the morning of the 27th was fixed for commencing the movement. On the 26th I received from General Stoneman a note asking permission (after having accomplished his orders to break up the railroad at Jonesboro') to go on to Macon to rescue our prisoners of war known to be held there, and then to push on to Andersonville, where was the great depot of Union prisoners, in which were penned at one time as many as twenty-three thousand of our men, badly fed and harshly treated. I wrote him an answer consenting substantially to his proposition, only modifying it by requiring him to send back General Garrard's division to its position on our left flank after he had broken up the railroad at Jonesboro'. Promptly, and on time, all got off, and General Dodge's corps (the Sixteenth, of the Army of the Tennessee) reached its position across Proctor's Creek the same evening, and early the next morning (the 28th) Blair's corps (the Seventeenth) deployed on his right, both corps covering their front with the usual parapet; the Fifteenth Corps (General Logan's) came up that morning on the right of Blair, strongly refused, and began to prepare the usual cover. As General Jeff. C. Davis's division was, as it were, left out of line, I ordered it on the evening before to march down toward Turner's Ferry, and then to take a road laid down on our maps which led from there toward East Point, ready to engage any enemy that might attack our general right flank, after the same manner as had been done to the left flank on the 22d.

Personally on the morning of the 28th I followed the movement, and rode to the extreme right, where we could hear some skirmishing and an occasional cannon-shot. As we approached the ground held by the Fifteenth Corps, a cannon-ball passed over my shoulder and killed the horse of an orderly behind; and seeing that this gun enfiladed the road by which we were riding, we turned out of it and rode down into a valley, where we left our horses and walked up to the hill held by Morgan L. Smith's division of the Fifteenth Corps. Near a house I met Generals Howard and Logan, who explained that there was an intrenched battery to their front, with the appearance of a strong infantry support. I then walked up to the ridge, where I found General Morgan L. Smith. His men were deployed and engaged in rolling logs and fence-rails, preparing a hasty cover. From this ridge we could overlook the open fields near a meeting-house known as "Ezra Church," close by the Poor-House. We could see the fresh earth of a parapet covering some guns (that fired an occasional shot), and there was also an appearance of activity beyond. General Smith was in the act of sending forward a regiment from his right flank to feel the position of the enemy, when I explained to him and to Generals Logan and Howard that they must look out for General Jeff. C. Davis's division, which was coming up from the direction of Turner's Ferry.

As the skirmish-fire warmed up along the front of Blair's corps, as well as along the Fifteenth Corps (Logan's), I became convinced that Hood designed to attack this right flank, to prevent, if possible, the extension of our line in that direction. I regained my horse, and rode rapidly back to see that Davis's division had been dispatched as ordered. I found General Davis in person, who was unwell, and had sent his division that morning early, under the command of his senior brigadier, [James D.] Morgan; but, as I attached great importance to the movement, he mounted his horse, and rode away to overtake and to hurry forward the movement, so as to come up on the left rear of the enemy, during the expected battle.

By this time the sound of cannon and musketry denoted a severe battle as in progress, which began seriously at 11½ A. M., and ended substantially by 4 P. M. It was a fierce attack by the enemy on our extreme right flank, well posted and partially covered. The most authentic account of the battle is given by General Logan, who commanded the Fifteenth Corps, in his official report to the Adjutant-General of the Army of the Tennessee, thus:

HEADQUARTERS FIFTEENTH ARMY CORPS,
BEFORE ATLANTA, GEORGIA, *July* 29, 1864.

Lieutenant-Colonel WILLIAM T. CLARK, *Assistant Adjutant-General, Army of the Tennessee, present.*

COLONEL: I have the honor to report that, in pursuance of orders, I moved my command into position on the right of the Seventeenth Corps, which was the extreme right of the army in the field, during the night of the 27th and morning of the 28th; and, while advancing in line of battle to a more favorable position, we were met by the rebel infantry of Hardee's and [Stephen D.] Lee's corps, who made a determined and desperate attack on us at 11½ A. M. of the 28th (yesterday).

My lines were only protected by logs and rails, hastily thrown up in front of them.

The first onset was received and checked, and the battle commenced and lasted until about three o'clock in the evening. During that time six successive charges were made, which were six times gallantly repulsed, each time with fearful loss to the enemy.

Later in the evening my lines were several times assaulted vigorously, but each time with like result.

The worst of the fighting occurred on Generals [William] Harrow's and Morgan L. Smith's fronts, which formed the centre and right of the corps.

The troops could not have displayed greater courage, nor greater determination not to give ground; had they shown less, they would have been driven from their position. . . .

JOHN A. LOGAN,
Major-General, commanding Fifteenth Army Corps.

General Howard, in transmitting this report, added:

I wish to express my high gratification with the conduct of the troops engaged. I never saw better conduct in battle. General Logan, though ill and much worn out, was indefatigable, and the success of the day is as much attributable to him as to any one man.

This was, of course, the first fight in which General Howard had commanded the Army of the Tennessee, and he evidently aimed to reconcile General Logan in his disappointment, and to gain the heart of his army, to which he was a stranger. He very properly left General Logan to fight his own corps, but exposed himself freely; and, after the firing had ceased, in the afternoon he walked the lines; the men, as reported to me, gathered about him in the most affectionate way, and he at once gained their respect and confidence. To this fact I at the time attached much importance, for it put me at ease as to the future conduct of that most important army.

At no instant of time did I feel the least uneasiness about the result on the 28th, but wanted to reap fuller results, hoping that Davis's division would come up at the instant of defeat, and catch the enemy in flank; but the woods were dense, the roads obscure, and as usual this division got on the wrong road, and did not come into position until about dark. In like manner, I thought that Hood had greatly weakened his main lines inside of Atlanta, and accordingly sent repeated orders to Schofield and Thomas to make an attempt to break in; but both reported that they found the parapets very strong and full manned.

Our men were unusually encouraged by this day's work, for they realized that we could compel Hood to come out from behind his fortified lines to attack us at a disadvantage. In conversation with me, the soldiers of the Fifteenth Corps, with whom I was on the most familiar terms, spoke of the affair of the 28th as the easiest thing in the world; that, in fact, it was a common slaughter of the enemy; they pointed out where the rebel lines had been, and how they themselves had fired deliberately, had shot down their antagonists, whose bodies still lay unburied, and marked plainly their lines of battle, which must have halted within easy musket-range of our men, who were partially protected by their improvised line of logs and fence-rails. All bore willing testimony to the courage and spirit of the foe, who, though repeatedly repulsed, came back with increased determination some six or more times.

The next morning the Fifteenth Corps wheeled forward to the left over the battle-field of the day before, and Davis's division still farther prolonged the line, which reached nearly to the ever-to-be-remembered "Sandtown road."

Then, by further thinning out Thomas's line, which was well intrenched, I drew another division of Palmer's corps (Ward's) around to the right, to further strengthen that flank. I was impatient to hear from the cavalry raid, then four days out, and was watching for its effect, ready to make a bold push for the possession of East Point. General Garrard's division returned to Decatur on the 31st, and reported that General Stoneman had posted him at Flat Rock, while he (Stoneman) went on. The month of July therefore closed with our infantry line strongly intrenched, but drawn out from the Augusta road on the left to the Sandtown road on the right, a distance of full ten measured miles.

The enemy, though evidently somewhat intimated by the results of their defeats on the 22d and 28th, still presented a bold front at all points, with fortified lines that defied a direct assault. Our railroad was done to the rear of our camps, Colonel W. W. Wright having reconstructed the bridge across the Chattahoochee in six days; and our garrisons and detachments to the rear had so effectually guarded the railroad that the trains from Nashville arrived daily, and our substantial wants were well supplied.

The month, though hot in the extreme, had been one of constant conflict, without intermission, and on four several occasions—viz., July 4th, 20th, 22d, and 28th—these affairs had amounted to real battles, with casualty lists by the thousands.

On the 24th of July I received a dispatch from Inspector-General James A. Hardie, then on duty at the War Department in Washington, to the effect that Generals Osterhaus and Alvin P. Hovey had been appointed major-generals. Both of these had begun the campaign with us in command of divisions, but had gone to the rear—the former by reason of sickness, and the latter dissatisfied with General Schofield and myself about the composition of his division of the Twenty-third Corps. Both were esteemed as first-class officers, who had gained special distinction in the Vicksburg campaign. But up to that time, when the newspapers announced daily promotions elsewhere, no prominent officers serving with me had been advanced a peg, and I felt hurt. I answered Hardie on the 25th, in a dispatch which has been made public, closing with this language: "If the rear be the post of honor, then we had better all change front on Washington." To my amazement, in a few days I received from President Lincoln himself an answer, in which he caught me fairly. I have not preserved a copy of that dispatch, and suppose it was burned up in the Chicago fire; but it was characteristic of Mr. Lincoln, and was dated the 26th or 27th day of July, contained unequivocal expressions of respect for those who were fighting hard and unselfishly, offering us a full share of the honors and rewards of the war, and saying that, in the cases of Hovey and Osterhaus, he was influenced mainly by the recommendations of Generals Grant and Sherman. On the 27th I replied direct, apologizing somewhat for my message to General Hardie, saying that I did not suppose such messages ever reached him personally, explaining that General Grant's and Sherman's recommendations for Hovey and Osterhaus had been made when the events of the Vicksburg campaign were fresh with us, and that my dispatch of the 25th to General Hardie had reflected chiefly the feelings of the officers then present with me before Atlanta. The result of all this, however, was good, for another dispatch from General Hardie, of the 28th, called on me to nominate eight colonels for promotion as brigadier-generals. I at once sent a circular note to the army-commanders to nominate two colonels from the Army of the Ohio and three from each of the others; and the result was, that on the 29th of July I telegraphed the names of—Colonel William Gross, Thirty-sixth Indiana; Colonel Charles C. Walcutt, Forty-sixth Ohio; Colonel James W. Riley, One Hundred and Fourth Ohio; Colonel L. P. Bradley, Fifty-first Illinois; Colonel J. W. Sprague, Sixty-third Ohio; Colonel Joseph A. Cooper, Sixth East Tennessee; Colonel John T. Croxton, Fourth Kentucky; Colonel William W. Belknap, Fifteenth Iowa. These were promptly appointed brigadier-generals, were already in command of brigades or divisions; and I doubt if eight promotions were ever made fairer, or were more honestly earned, during the whole war.

Chapter 12

Atlanta Captured:
"It Will Be a Used-up Community"
August—September, 1864

THE MONTH OF August opened hot and sultry, but our position before Atlanta was healthy, with ample supply of wood, water, and provisions. The troops had become habituated to the slow and steady progress of the siege; the skirmish-lines were held close up to the enemy, were covered by rifle-trenches or logs, and kept up a continuous clatter of musketry. The main lines were held farther back, adapted to the shape of the ground, with muskets loaded and stacked for instant use. The field-batteries were in select positions, covered by handsome parapets, and occasional shots from them gave life and animation to the scene. The men loitered about the trenches carelessly, or busied themselves in constructing ingenious huts out of the abundant timber, and seemed as snug, comfortable, and happy, as though they were at home. General Schofield was still on the extreme left, Thomas in the centre, and Howard on the right. Two divisions of the Fourteenth Corps ([Absolom] Baird's and Jeff. C. Davis's) were detached to the right rear, and held in reserve.

I thus awaited the effect of the cavalry movement against the railroad about Jonesboro', and had heard from General Garrard that Stoneman had gone on to Macon; during that

day (August 1st) Colonel [William G.] Brownlow, of a
Tennessee cavalry regiment, came in to Marietta from General McCook, and reported that McCook's whole division had
been overwhelmed, defeated, and captured at Newnan. Of
course, I was disturbed by this wild report, though I discredited it, but made all possible preparations to strengthen
our guards along the railroad to the rear, on the theory that
the force of cavalry which had defeated McCook would at
once be on the railroad about Marietta. At the same time
Garrard was ordered to occupy the trenches on our left,
while Schofield's whole army moved to the extreme right, and
extended the line toward East Point. Thomas was also ordered
still further to thin out his lines, so as to set free the other
division (Johnson's) of the Fourteenth Corps (Palmer's),
which was moved to the extreme right rear, and held in reserve
ready to make a bold push from that flank to secure a footing
on the Macon Railroad at or below East Point.

These changes were effected during the 2d and 3d days of
August, when General McCook came in and reported the
actual results of his cavalry expedition. He had crossed the
Chattahoochee River below Campbellton, by his pontoon-
bridge; had then marched rapidly across to the Macon Railroad at Lovejoy's Station, where he had reason to expect
General Stoneman; but, not hearing of him, he set to work,
tore up two miles of track, burned two trains of cars, and cut
away five miles of telegraph-wire. He also found the wagon-
train belonging to the rebel army in Atlanta, burned five
hundred wagons, killed eight hundred mules, and captured
seventy-two officers and three hundred and fifty men. Finding
his progress eastward, toward McDonough, barred by a superior force, he turned back to Newnan, where he found himself completely surrounded by infantry and cavalry. He had
to drop his prisoners and fight his way out, losing about six
hundred men in killed and captured, and then returned with
the remainder to his position at Turner's Ferry. This was bad
enough, but not so bad as had been reported by Colonel
Brownlow. Meantime, rumors came that General Stoneman
was down about Macon, on the east bank of the Ocmulgee.
On the 4th of August Colonel [Silas] Adams got to Marietta
with his small brigade of nine hundred men belonging to
Stoneman's cavalry, reporting, as usual, all the rest lost, and
this was partially confirmed by a report which came to me

all the way round by General Grant's headquarters before Richmond. A few days afterward Colonel [Horace] Capron also got in, with another small brigade perfectly demoralized, and confirmed the report that General Stoneman had covered the escape of these two small brigades, himself standing with a reserve of seven hundred men, with which he surrendered to a Colonel [Alfred] Iverson. Thus another of my cavalry divisions was badly damaged, and out of the fragments we hastily reorganized three small divisions under Brigadier-Generals Garrard, McCook, and [Judson] Kilpatrick.

Stoneman had not obeyed his orders to attack the railroad *first* before going to Macon and Andersonville, but had crossed the Ocmulgee River high up near Covington, and had gone down that river on the east bank. He reached Clinton, and sent out detachments which struck the railroad leading from Macon to Savannah at Griswold Station, where they found and destroyed seventeen locomotives and over a hundred cars; then went on and burned the bridge across the Oconee, and reunited the division before Macon. Stoneman shelled the town across the river, but could not cross over by the bridge, and returned to Clinton; where he found his retreat obstructed; as he supposed, by a superior force. There he became bewildered, and sacrificed himself for the safety of his command. He occupied the attention of his enemy by a small force of seven hundred men, giving Colonels Adams and Capron leave, with their brigades, to cut their way back to me at Atlanta. The former reached us entire, but the latter was struck and scattered at some place farther north, and came in by detachments. Stoneman surrendered, and remained a prisoner until he was exchanged some time after, late in September, at Rough and Ready.

I now became satisfied that cavalry could not, or would not, make a sufficient lodgment on the railroad below Atlanta, and that nothing would suffice but for us to reach it with the main army. Therefore the most urgent efforts to that end were made, and to Schofield, on the right, was committed the charge of this special object. He had his own corps (the Twenty-third), composed of eleven thousand and seventy-five infantry and eight hundred and eighty-five artillery, with McCook's broken division of cavalry, seventeen hundred and fifty-four men and horses. For this purpose I also placed the Fourteenth Corps (Palmer) under his orders. This corps numbered at the time seventeen thousand two hundred and eighty-eight infantry and eight hundred and twenty-six artillery; but General Palmer claimed to rank General Schofield in the date of his commission as major-general, and denied the latter's right to exercise command over him. General Palmer was a man of ability, but was not enterprising. His three divisions were compact and strong, well commanded, admirable on the defensive, but slow to move or to act on the offensive. His corps (the Fourteenth) had sustained, up to that time, fewer hard knocks than any other corps in the whole army, and I was anxious to give it a chance. I always expected to have a desperate fight to get possession of the Macon road, which was then the vital objective of the campaign. Its possession by us would, in my judgment, result in the capture of Atlanta, and give us the fruits of victory, although the destruction of Hood's army was the real object to be desired. Yet Atlanta was known as the "Gate-City of the South," was full of foundries, arsenals, and machine-shops, and I knew that its capture would be the death-knell of the Southern Confederacy.

On the 4th of August I ordered General Schofield to make a bold attack on the railroad, anywhere about East Point, and ordered General Palmer to report to him for duty. He at once denied General Schofield's right to command him; but, after examining the dates of their respective commissions, and hearing their arguments, I wrote to General Palmer.

August 4th—10:45 P. M.

From the statements made by yourself and General Schofield to-day, my decision is, that he ranks you as a major-general, being of the same date of present commission, by reason of his previous superior rank as *brigadier-general*. The movements of to-morrow are so important that the orders of the superior on that flank must be regarded as military orders, and not in the nature of coöperation. I did hope that there would be no necessity for my making this decision; but it is better for all parties interested that no question of rank should occur in actual battle. The Sandtown road, and the railroad, if possible, must be gained to-morrow, if it costs half your command. I regard the loss of time this afternoon as equal to the loss of two thousand men.

I also communicated the substance of this to General

Thomas, to whose army Palmer's corps belonged, who replied on the 5th:

> I regret to hear that Palmer has taken the course he has, and I know that he intends to offer his resignation as soon as he can properly do so. I recommend that his application be granted.

And on the 5th I again wrote to General Palmer, arguing the point with him, advising him, as a friend, not to resign at that crisis lest his motives might be misconstrued, and because it might damage his future career in civil life; but, at the same time, I felt it my duty to say to him that the operations on that flank, during the 4th and 5th, had not been satisfacory—not imputing to him, however, any want of energy or skill, but insisting that "the events did not keep pace with my desires." General Schofield had reported to me that night:

> I am compelled to acknowledge that I have totally failed to make any aggressive movement with the Fourteenth Corps. I have ordered General Johnson's division to replace General Hascall's this evening, and I propose to-morrow to take my own troops (Twenty-third Corps) to the right, and try to recover what has been lost by two days' delay. The force may likely be too small.

I sanctioned the movement, and ordered two of Palmer's divisions—Davis's and Baird's—to follow *en échelon*[1] in support of Schofield, and summoned General Palmer to meet me in person. He came on the 6th to my headquarters, and insisted on his resignation being accepted, for which formal act I referred him to General Thomas. He then rode to General Thomas's camp, where he made a written resignation of his office as commander of the Fourteenth Corps, and was granted the usual leave of absence to go to his home in Illinois, there to await further orders. General Thomas recommended that the resignation be accepted; that Johnson, the senior division commander of the corps, should be ordered back to Nash-

---

[1] *En echelon:* troops drawn up in parallel lines, usually with the units to the right or left of one another.

ville as chief of cavalry, and that Brigadier-General Jefferson
C. Davis, the next in order, should be promoted major-
general, and assigned to command the corps. These changes
had to be referred to the President, in Washington, and were,
in due time, approved and executed; and thenceforward I
had no reason to complain of the slowness or inactivity of
that splendid corps. It had been originally formed by General
George H. Thomas, had been commanded by him in person,
and had imbibed somewhat his personal character, viz., steadiness, good order, and deliberation—nothing hasty or rash,
but always safe, "slow, and sure."

On August 7th I telegraphed to General Halleck:

Have received to-day the dispatches of the Secretary of
War and of General Grant, which are very satisfactory. We
keep hammering away all the time, and there is no peace,
inside or outside of Atlanta. To-day General Schofield got
round the line which was assaulted yesterday by General
[James W.] Reilly's brigade, turned it and gained the ground
where the assault had been made, and got possession of all
our dead and wounded. He continued to press on that flank,
and brought on a noisy but not a bloody battle. He drove
the enemy behind his main breastworks, which cover the
railroad from Atlanta to East Point, and captured a good
many of the skirmishers, who are of his best troops—for the
militia hug the breastworks close. I do not deem it prudent
to extend any more to the right, but will push forward daily
by parallels, and make the inside of Atlanta too hot to be
endured. I have sent back to Chattanooga for two thirty-
pound Parrotts, with which we can pick out almost any house
in town. I am too impatient for a siege, and don't know but
this is as good a place to fight it out on, as farther inland.
One thing is certain, whether we get inside of Atlanta or not,
it will be a used-up community when we are done with it.

In Schofield's extension on the 5th, General Reilly's brigade had struck an outwork, which he promptly attacked, but,
as usual, got entangled in the trees and bushes which had been
felled, and lost about five hundred men, in killed and wounded;
but, as above reported, this outwork was found abandoned

the next day, and we could see from it that the rebels were extending their lines, parallel with the railroad, about as fast as we could add to our line of investment. On the 10th of August the Parrott thirty-pounders were received and placed in position; for a couple of days we kept up a sharp fire from all our batteries converging on Atlanta, and at every available point we advanced our infantry-lines, thereby shortening and strengthening the investment; but I was not willing to order a direct assault, unless some accident or positive neglect on the part of our antagonist should reveal an opening. However, it was manifest that no such opening was intended by Hood, who felt secure behind his strong defenses. He had repelled our cavalry attacks on his railroad, and had damaged us seriously thereby, so I expected that he would attempt the same game against our rear. Therefore I made extraordinary exertions to recompose our cavalry divisions, which were so essential, both for defense and offense. Kilpatrick was given that on our right rear, in support of Schofield's exposed flank; Garrard retained that on our general left; and McCook's division was held somewhat in reserve, about Marietta and the railroad. On the 10th, having occasion to telegraph to General Grant, then in Washington, I used this language:

Since July 28th Hood has not attempted to meet us outside his parapets. In order to possess and destroy effectually his communications, I may have to leave a corps at the railroad-bridge, well intrenched, and cut loose with the balance to make a circle of desolation around Atlanta. I do not propose to assault the works, which are too strong, nor to proceed by regular approaches. I have lost a good many regiments, and will lose more, by the expiration of service; and this is the only reason why I want reënforcements. We have killed, crippled, and captured more of the enemy than we have lost by his acts.

On the 12th of August I heard of the success of Admiral Farragut in entering Mobile Bay, which was regarded as a most valuable auxiliary to our operations at Atlanta; and learned that I had been commissioned a major-general in the regular army, which was unexpected, and not desired until successful in the capture of Atlanta. These did not change the fact that we were held in check by the stubborn defense of the place, and a conviction was forced on my mind that our enemy would hold fast, even though every house in the town should be battered down by our artillery. It was evident that we must decoy him out to fight us on something like equal terms, or else, with the whole army, raise the siege and attack his communications. Accordingly, on the 13th of August, I gave general orders for the Twentieth Corps to draw back to the railroad-bridge at the Chattahoochee, to protect our trains, hospitals, spare artillery, and the railroad-depot, while the rest of the army should move bodily to some point on the Macon Railroad below East Point.

Luckily, I learned just then that the enemy's cavalry, under General Wheeler, had made a wide circuit around our left flank, and had actually reached our railroad at Tilton Station, above Resaca, captured a drove of one thousand of our beef-cattle, and was strong enough to appear before Dalton, and demand of its commander, Colonel [William C.] Raum, the surrender of the place. General John E. Smith, who was at Kingston, collected together a couple of thousand men, and proceeded in cars to the relief of Dalton, when Wheeler retreated northward toward Cleveland. On the 16th another detachment of the enemy's cavalry appeared in force about Allatoona and the Etowah bridge, when I became fully convinced that Hood and had sent *all* of his cavalry to raid upon our railroads. For some days our communication with Nashville was interrupted by the destruction of the telegraph-lines, as well as railroad. I at once ordered strong reconnoissances forward from our flanks on the left by Garrard, and on the right by Kilpatrick. The former moved with so much caution that I was displeased; but Kilpatrick, on the contrary, displayed so much zeal and activity that I was attracted to him at once. He reached Fairburn Station, on the West Point road, and tore it up, returning safely to his position on our right flank. I summoned him to me, and was so pleased with his spirit and confidence, that I concluded to suspend the general movement of the main army, and to send him with his small division of cavalry to break up the Macon road about Jonesboro', in the hopes that it would force Hood to evacuate Atlanta, and that I should thereby not only secure possession of the city itself, but probably could catch Hood in the con-

fusion of retreat; and, further to increase the chances of success, I ordered General Thomas to detach two brigades of
Garrard's division of cavalry from the left to the right rear, to
act as a reserve in support of General Kilpatrick. Meantime,
also, the utmost activity was ordered along our whole front by
the infantry and artillery. Kilpatrick got off during the night of
the 18th, and returned to us on the 22d, having made the complete circuit of Atlanta. He reported that he had destroyed
three miles of the railroad about Jonesboro', which he reckoned would take ten days to repair; that he had encountered
a division of infantry and a brigade of cavalry ([Samuel]
Ross's); that he had captured a battery and destroyed three of
its guns, bringing one in as a trophy, and he also brought in
three battle-flags and seventy prisoners. On the 23d, however,
we saw trains coming into Atlanta from the south, when I became more than ever convinced that cavalry could not or
would not work hard enough to disable a railroad properly,
and therefore resolved at once to proceed to the execution of
my original plan. Meantime, the damage done to our own railroad and telegraph by Wheeler, about Resaca and Dalton, had
been repaired, and Wheeler himself was too far away to be of
any service to his own army, and where he could not do us
much harm, viz., up about the Hiawassee. On the 24th I rode
down to the Chattahoochee bridge, to see in person that it
could be properly defended by the single corps proposed to be
left there for that purpose, and found that the rebel works,
which had been built by Johnston to resist us, could be easily
utilized against themselves; and on returning to my camp, at
7:15 P. M. that same evening, I telegraphed to General Halleck as follows:

Heavy fires in Atlanta all day, caused by our artillery. I will
be all ready, and will commence the movement around Atlanta by the south, to-morrow night, and for some time you
will hear little of us. I will keep open a courier line back to
the Chattahoochee bridge, by way of Sandtown. The Twentieth Corps will hold the railroad-bridge, and I will move with
the balance of the army, provisioned for twenty days.

Meantime General Dodge (commanding the Sixteenth
Corps) had been wounded in the forehead, had gone to the

rear, and his two divisions were distributed to the Fifteenth and Seventeenth Corps. The real movement commenced on the 25th, at night. The Twentieth Corps drew back and took post at the railroad-bridge, and the Fourth Corps (Stanley) moved to his right rear, closing up with the Fourteenth Corps (Jeff. C. Davis) near Utoy Creek; at the same time Garrard's cavalry, leaving their horses out of sight, occupied the vacant trenches, so that the enemy did not detect the change at all. The next night (26th) the Fifteenth and Seventeenth Corps, composing the Army of the Tennessee (Howard), drew out of their trenches, made a wide circuit, and came up on the extreme right of the Fourth and Fourteenth Corps of the Army of the Cumberland (Thomas) along Utoy Creek, facing south. The enemy seemed to suspect something that night, using his artillery pretty freely; but I think he supposed we were going to retreat altogether. An artillery-shot, fired at random, killed one man and wounded another, and the next morning some of his infantry came out of Atlanta and found our camps abandoned. It was afterward related that there was great rejoicing in Atlanta "that the Yankees were gone"; the fact was telegraphed all over the South, and several trains of cars (with ladies) came up from Macon to assist in the celebration of their grand victory.

On the 28th (making a general left-wheel, pivoting on Schofield) both Thomas and Howard reached the West Point Railroad, extending from East Point to Red-Oak Station and Fairburn, where we spent the next day (29th) in breaking it up thoroughly. The track was heaved up in sections the length of a regiment, then separated rail by rail; bonfires were made of the ties and of fence-rails on which the rails were heated, carried to trees or telegraph-poles, wrapped around and left to cool. Such rails could not be used again; and, to be still more certain, we filled up many deep cuts with trees, brush, and earth, and commingled with them loaded shells, so arranged that they would explode on an attempt to haul out the bushes. The explosion of one such shell would have demoralized a gang of Negroes, and thus would have prevented even the attempt to clear the road.

Meantime Schofield, with the Twenty-third Corps, presented a bold front toward East Point, daring and inviting the enemy to sally out to attack him in position. His first movement was on the 30th, to Mount Gilead Church, then to Morrow's Mills, facing Rough and Ready. Thomas was on his right, within easy support, moving by cross-roads from Red Oak to the Fayetteville road, extending from Couch's to Renfrew's; and Howard was aiming for Jonesboro'.

I was with General Thomas that day, which was hot but otherwise very pleasant. We stopped for a short noon-rest near a little church (marked on our maps as Shoal-Creek Church), which stood back about a hundred yards from the road, in a grove of native oaks. The infantry column had halted in the road, stacked their arms, and the men were scattered about—some lying in the shade of the trees, and others were bringing corn-stalks from a large corn-field across the road to feed our horses, while still others had arms full of the roasting-ears, then in their prime. Hundreds of fires were soon started with the fence-rails, and the men were busy roasting the ears. Thomas and I were walking up and down the road which led to the church, discussing the chances of the movement, which he thought were extra-hazardous, and our path carried us by a fire at which a soldier was roasting his corn. The fire was built artistically; the man was stripping the ears of their husks, standing them in front of his fire, watching them carefully, and turning each ear little by little, so as to roast it nicely. He was down on his knees intent on his business, paying little heed to the stately and serious deliberations of his leaders. Thomas's mind was running on the fact that we had cut loose from our base of supplies, and that seventy thousand men were then dependent for their food on the chance supplies of the country (already impoverished by the requisitions of the enemy), and on the contents of our wagons. Between Thomas and his men there existed a most kindly relation, and he frequently talked with them in the most familiar way. Pausing awhile, and watching the operations of this man roasting his corn, he said, "What are you doing?" The man looked up smilingly: "Why, general, I am laying in a supply of provisions." "That is right, my man, but don't waste your provisions." As we resumed our walk, the man remarked, in a sort of musing way, but loud enough for me to hear: "There he goes, there goes the old man, economizing as usual." "Economizing" with corn, which cost only the labor of gathering and roasting!

As we walked, we could hear General Howard's guns at intervals, away off to our right front, but an ominous silence continued toward our left, where I was expecting at each moment to hear the sound of battle. That night we reached Renfrew's, and had reports from left to right (from General Schofield, about Morrow's Mills, to General Howard, within a couple of miles of Jonesboro'). The next morning (August 31st) all moved straight for the railroad. Schofield reached it near Rough and Ready, and Thomas at two points between there and Jonesboro'. Howard found an intrenched foe (Hardee's corps) covering Jonesboro', and his men began at once to dig their accustomed rifle-pits. Orders were sent to Generals Thomas and Schofield to turn straight for Jonesboro', tearing up the railroad-track as they advanced. About 3 P. M. the enemy sallied from Jonesboro' against the Fifteenth corps, but was easily repulsed, and driven back within his lines. All hands were kept busy tearing up the railroad, and it was not until toward evening of the 1st day of September that the Fourteenth Corps (Davis) closed down on the north front of Jonesboro', connecting on his right with Howard, and his left reaching the railroad, along which General Stanley was moving, followed by Schofield. General Davis formed his division in line about 4 P. M., swept forward over some old cotton-fields in full view, and went over the rebel parapet handsomely, capturing the whole of [Daniel C.] Govan's brigade, with two field-batteries of ten guns. Being on the spot, I checked Davis's movement, and ordered General Howard to send the two divisions of the Seventeenth Corps (Blair) round by his right rear, to get below Jonesboro', and to reach the railroad, so as to cut off retreat in that direction. I also dispatched orders after orders to hurry forward Stanley, so as to lap around Jonesboro' on the east, hoping thus to capture the whole of Hardee's corps. I sent first Captain Audenried (aide-de-camp), then Colonel Poe, of the Engineers, and lastly General Thomas himself (and that is the only time during the campaign I can recall seeing General Thomas urge his horse into a gallop). Night was approaching, and the country on the farther side of the railroad was densely wooded. General Stanley had come up on the left of Davis, and was deploying, though there could not have been on his front more than a skirmish-line. Had he moved straight on by the flank, or by a slight circuit to his left, he would have inclosed the whole ground occupied by Hardee's corps, and that corps could not have escaped us; but night came on, and Hardee did escape.

Meantime General Slocum had reached his corps (the

Twentieth), stationed at the Chattahoochee bridge, had relieved General A. S. Williams in command, and orders had
been sent back to him to feel forward occasionally toward
Atlanta, to observe the effect when we had reached the railroad. That night I was so restless and impatient that I could
not sleep, and about midnight there arose toward Atlanta
sounds of shells exploding, and other sound like that of
musketry. I walked to the house of a farmer close by my
bivouac, called him out to listen to the reverberations which
came from the direction of Atlanta (twenty miles to the north
of us), and inquired of him if he had resided there long. He
said he had, and that these sounds were just like those of a
battle. An interval of quiet then ensued, when again, about 4
A. M., arose other similar explosions, but I still remained in
doubt whether the enemy was engaged in blowing up his own
magazines, or whether General Slocum had not felt forward,
and become engaged in a real battle.

The next morning General Hardee was gone, and we all
pushed forward along the railroad south, in close pursuit, till
we ran up against his lines at a point just above Lovejoy's
Station. While bringing forward troops and feeling the new
position of our adversary, rumors came from the rear that the
enemy had evacuated Atlanta, and that General Slocum was
in the city. Later in the day I received a note in Slocum's own
handwriting, stating that he had heard during the night the
very sounds that I have referred to; that he had moved rapidly
up from the bridge about daylight, and had entered Atlanta
unopposed. His letter was dated inside the city, so there was
no doubt of the fact. General Thomas's bivouac was but a
short distance from mine, and, before giving notice to the
army in general orders, I sent one of my staff-officers to show
him the note. In a few minutes the officer returned, soon
followed by Thomas himself, who again examined the note,
so as to be perfectly certain that it was genuine. The news
seemed to him too good to be true. He snapped his fingers,
whistled, and almost danced, and, as the news spread to the
army, the shouts that arose from our men, the wild hallooing
and glorious laughter, were to us a full recompense for the
labor and toils and hardships through which we had passed
in the previous three months.

A courier-line was at once organized, messages were sent
back and forth from our camp at Lovejoy's to Atlanta, and to

our telegraph-station at the Chattahoochee bridge. Of course, the glad tidings flew on the wings of electricity to all parts of the North, where the people had patiently awaited news of their husbands, sons, and brothers, away down in "Dixie Land"; and congratulations came pouring back full of good-will and patriotism. This victory was most opportune; Mr. Lincoln himself told me afterward that even he had previously felt in doubt, for the summer was fast passing away; that General Grant seemed to be checkmated about Richmond and Petersburg, and my army seemed to have run up against an impassable barrier, when, suddenly and unexpectedly, came the news that "Atlanta was ours, and fairly won." On this text many a fine speech was made, but none more eloquent than that by Edward Everett, in Boston. A presidential election then agitated the North. Mr. Lincoln represented the national cause, and General McClellan had accepted the nomination of the Democratic party, whose platform was that the war was a failure, and that it was better to allow the South to go free to establish a separate government, whose corner-stone should be slavery. Success to our arms at that instant was therefore a political necessity; and it was all-important that something startling in our interest should occur before the election in November. The brilliant success at Atlanta filled that requirement, and made the election of Mr. Lincoln certain. Among the many letters of congratulation received, those of Mr. Lincoln and General Grant seem most important:

EXECUTIVE MANSION,
WASHINGTON, D. C., *September* 3, 1864.

The national thanks are rendered by the President to Major-General W. T. Sherman and the gallant officers and soldiers of his command before Atlanta, for the distinguished ability and perseverance displayed in the campaign in Georgia, which, under Divine favor, has resulted in the capture of Atlanta. The marches, battles, sieges, and other military operations, that have signalized the campaign, must render it famous in the annals of war, and have entitled those who have participated therein to the applause and thanks of the nation.

ABRAHAM LINCOLN,
President of the United States

CITY POINT, VIRGINIA, *September* 4, 1864—9 P.M.

Major-General SHERMAN:

I have just received your dispatch announcing the capture of Atlanta. In honor of your great victory, I have ordered a salute to be fired with *shotted* guns from every battery bearing upon the enemy. The salute will be fired within an hour, amid great rejoicing.

U. S. GRANT, *Lieutenant-General.*

These dispatches were communicated to the army in general orders, and we all felt duly encouraged and elated by the praise of those competent to bestow it.

The army still remained where the news of success had first found us, viz., Lovejoy's; but, after due reflection, I resolved not to attempt at that time a further pursuit of Hood's army, but slowly and deliberately to move back, occupy Atlanta, enjoy a short period of rest, and to think well over the next step required in the progress of events. Orders for this movement were made on the 5th September, and three days were given for each army to reach the place assigned it, viz.: the Army of the Cumberland in and about Atlanta; the Army of the Tennessee at East Point; and the Army of the Ohio at Decatur.

Personally I rode back to Jonesboro' on the 6th, and there inspected the rebel hospital, full of wounded officers and men left by Hardee in his retreat. The next night we stopped at Rough and Ready, and on the 8th of September we rode into Atlanta, then occupied by the Twentieth Corps (General Slocum). In the Court-House Square was encamped a brigade, embracing the Massachusetts Second and Thirty-third Regiments, which had two of the finest bands of the army, and their music was to us all a source of infinite pleasure during our sojourn in that city. I took up my headquarters in the house of Judge Lyons, which stood opposite one corner of the Court-House Square, and at once set about a measure already ordered, of which I had thought much and long, viz., to remove the entire civil population, and to deny to all civilians from the rear the expected profits of civil trade. Hundreds of sutlers and traders were waiting at Nashville and Chattanooga, greedy to reach Atlanta with their wares and goods, with which to drive a profitable trade with the inhabitants. I gave positive orders that none of these traders, except three (one for each separate army), should be permitted to come nearer than Chattanooga; and, moreover, I peremptorily required that all the citizens and families resident in Atlanta should go away, giving to each the option to go south or north, as their interests or feelings dictated. I was resolved to make Atlanta a pure military garrison or depot, with no civil population to influence military measures. I had seen Memphis, Vicksburg, Natchez, and New Orleans, all captured from the enemy, and each at once was garrisoned by a full division of troops, if not more; so that success was actually crippling our armies in the field by detachments to guard and protect the interests of a hostile population.

I gave notice of this purpose, as early as the 4th of September, to General Halleck, in a letter concluding with these words:

If the people raise a howl against my barbarity and cruelty, I will answer that war is war, and not popularity-seeking. If they want peace, they and their relatives must stop the war.

I knew, of course, that such a measure would be strongly criticised, but made up my mind to do it with the absolute certainty of its justness, and that time would sanction its wisdom. I knew that the people of the South would read in this measure two important conclusions: one, that we were in earnest; and the other, if they were sincere in their common and popular clamor "to die in the last ditch," that the opportunity would soon come.

Soon after our reaching Atlanta, General Hood had sent in by a flag of truce a proposition, offering a general exchange of prisoners, saying that he was authorized to make such an exchange by the Richmond authorities, out of the vast number of our men then held captive at Andersonville, the same whom General Stoneman had hoped to rescue at the time of his raid. Some of these prisoners had already escaped and got in, had described the pitiable condition of the remainder, and, although I felt a sympathy for their hardships and sufferings as deeply as any man could, yet as nearly all the prisoners who had been captured by us during the campaign had been sent, as fast as taken, to the usual depots North, they were then beyond my control. There were still about two thousand, mostly captured at Jonesboro', who had been sent back by cars, but had not passed Chattanooga. These I ordered back, and offered General Hood to exchange them for Stoneman, Buell, and such of my own army as would make up the equivalent; but I would not exchange for his prisoners *generally,* because I knew these would have to be sent to their own regiments, away from my army, whereas all we could give him could at once be put to duty in his immediate army. Quite an angry correspondence grew up between us, which was published at the time in the newspapers.

HEADQUARTERS ARMIES OF THE UNITED STATES,
CITY POINT, VIRGINIA, *September* 12, 1864.

Major-General W. T. SHERMAN, *commanding Military Division of the Mississippi.*

GENERAL: I send Lieutenant-Colonel Horace Porter, of my staff, with this. Colonel Porter will explain to you the exact condition of affairs here, better than I can do in the limits of a letter. Although I feel myself strong enough now for offensive operations, I am holding on quietly, to get advantage of recruits and convalescents, who are coming forward very rapidly. My lines are necessarily very long, extending from Deep Bottom, north of the James, across the peninsula formed by the Appomattox and the James, and south of the Appomattox to the Weldon road. This line is very strongly fortified, and can be held with comparatively few men; but, from its great length, necessarily takes many in the aggregate. I propose, when I do move, to extend my left so as to control what is known as the Southside, or Lynchburg & Petersburg road; then, if possible, to keep the Danville road cut. At the same time this move is made, I want to send a force of from six to ten thousand men against Wilmington. The way I propose to do this is to land the men north of Fort Fisher, and hold that point. At the same time a large naval fleet will be assembled there, and the iron-clads will run the batteries as they did at Mobile. This will give us the same control of the harbor of Wilmington that we now have of the harbor of Mobile. What you are to do with the forces at your command, I do not exactly see. The difficulties of supplying your army, except when they are constantly moving beyond where you are, I plainly see. If it had not been for Price's movement, Canby could have sent twelve thousand more men to Mobile. From your command on the Mississippi, an equal number could have been taken. With these forces, my idea would have been to divide them, sending one-half to Mobile, and the other half to Savannah. You could then move as proposed in your telegram, so as to threaten Macon and Augusta equally. Whichever one should be abandoned by the enemy, you could take and open up a new base of supplies. My object now in sending a staff-officer to you is not so much to suggest operations for you as to get your views, and to have plans matured by the time every thing can be got ready. It would probably be the 5th of October before any of the plans here indicated will be executed. If you have any promotions to recommend, send the names forward, and I will approve them.

In conclusion, it is hardly necessary for me to say that I feel you have accomplished the most gigantic undertaking given to any general in this war, and with a skill and ability that will be acknowledged in history as unsurpassed, if not unequaled. It gives me as much pleasure to record this in your favor as it would in favor of any living man, myself included.

Truly yours,   U. S. GRANT, *Lieutenant-General.*

HEADQUARTERS MILITARY DIVISION OF THE MISSISSIPPI, }
IN THE FIELD, ATLANTA, GEORGIA, *September* 20, 1864. }

Lieutenant-General U. S. GRANT, *Commander-in-Chief, City Point, Virginia.*

GENERAL: I have the honor to acknowledge, at the hands of Lieutenant-Colonel [Horace] Porter, of your staff, your letter of September 12th, and accept with thanks the honorable and kindly mention of the services of this army in the great cause in which we are all engaged.

I send by Colonel Porter all official reports which are completed, and will in a few days submit a list of names which are deemed worthy of promotion.

I think we owe it to the President to save him the invidious task of selection among the vast number of worthy applicants, and have ordered my army commanders to prepare their lists with great care, and to express their preferences, based upon claims of actual capacity and services rendered.

These I will consolidate, and submit in such a form that, if mistakes are made, they will at least be sanctioned by the best contemporaneous evidence of merit, for I know that vacancies do not exist equal in number to that of the officers who really deserve promotion.

As to the future, I am pleased to know that your army is being steadily reënforced by a good class of men, and I hope it will go on until you have a force that is numerically double that of your antagonist, so that with one part you can watch him, and with the other push out boldly from your left flank, occupy the Southside Railroad, compel him to attack you in position, or accept battle on your own terms.

We ought to ask our country for the largest possible armies that can be raised, as so important a thing as the self-existence of a great nation should not be left to the fickle chances of war.

Now that Mobile is shut out to the commerce of our enemy, it calls for no further effort on our part, unless the capture of the city can be followed by the occupation of the Alabama River and the railroad to Columbus, Georgia, when that place would be a magnificent auxiliary to my further progress into Georgia; but, until General Canby is much reënforced, and until he can more thoroughly subdue the scattered armies west of the Mississippi, I suppose that much cannot be attempted by him against the Alabama River and Columbus, Georgia.

The utter destruction of Wilmington, North Carolina, is of importance only in connection with the necessity of cutting off all foreign trade to our enemy, and if Admiral Farragut can get across the bar, and move quickly, I suppose he will succeed. From my knowledge of the mouth of Cape Fear River, I anticipate more difficulty in getting the heavy ships across the bar than in reaching the town of Wilmington; but, of course, the soundings of the channel are well known at Washington, as well as the draught of his iron-clads, so that it must be demonstrated to be feasible, or else it would not be attempted. If successful, I suppose that Fort Caswell will be occupied, and the fleet at once sent to the Savannah River. Then the reduction of that city is the next question. It once in our possession, and the river open to us, I would not hesitate to cross the State of Georgia with sixty thousand men, hauling same stores, and depending on the country for the balance. Where a million of people find subsistence, my army won't starve; but, as you know, in a country like Georgia, with few roads and innumerable streams, an inferior force can so delay an army and harass it, that it would not be a formidable object; but if the enemy knew that we had our boats in the

Savannah River I could rapidly move to Milledgeville, where there is abundance of corn and meat, and could so threaten Macon and Augusta that the enemy would doubtless give up Macon for Augusta; then I would move so as to interpose between Augusta and Savannah, and force him to give us Augusta, with the only powder-mills and factories remaining in the South, or let us have the use of the Savannah River. Either horn of the dilemma will be worth a battle. I would prefer his holding Augusta (as the probabilities are); for then, with the Savannah River in our possession, the taking of Augusta would be a mere matter of time. This campaign can be made in the winter.

But the more I study the game, the more am I convinced that it would be wrong for us to penetrate farther into Georgia without an objective beyond. It would not be productive of much good. I can start east and make a circuit south and back, doing vast damage to the State, but resulting in no permanent good; and by mere threatening to do so, I hold a rod over the Georgians, who are not over-loyal to the South. I will therefore give it as my opinion that your army and Canby's should be reënforced to the maximum; that, after you get Wilmington, you should strike for Savannah and its river; that General Canby should hold the Mississippi River, and send a force to take Columbus, Georgia, either by way of the Alabama or Appalachicola River; that I should keep Hood employed and put my army in fine order for a march on Augusta, Columbia, and Charleston; and start as soon as Wilmington is sealed to commerce, and the city of Savannah is in our possession.

I think it will be found that the movements of Price and Shelby, west of the Mississippi, are mere diversions. They cannot hope to enter Missouri except as raiders; and the truth is, that General Rosecrans should be ashamed to take my troops for such a purpose. If you will secure Wilmington and the city of Savannah from your centre, and let General Canby have command over the Mississippi River and country west of it, I will send a force to the Alabama and Appalachicola, provided you give me one hundred thousand of the drafted men to fill up my old regiments; and if you will fix a day to be in Savannah, I will insure our possession of Macon and a point on the river below Augusta. The possession of the Savannah River is more than fatal to the possibility of Southern independence. They may stand the fall of Richmond, but not of all Georgia.

I will have a long talk with Colonel Porter, and tell him every thing that may occur to me of interest to you.

In the mean time, know that I admire your dogged perseverance and pluck more than ever. If you can whip Lee and I can march to the Atlantic, I think Uncle Abe will give us a twenty days' leave of absence to see the young folks. Yours as ever,

W. T. SHERMAN, *Major-General.*

HEADQUARTERS MILITARY DIVISION OF THE MISSISSIPPI, ⎫
    IN THE FIELD, ATLANTA, GEORGIA, ⎬
        September 7, 1864. ⎭

General HOOD, *commanding Confederate Army.*

GENERAL: I have deemed it to the interest of the United States that the citizens now residing in Atlanta should remove, those who prefer it to go south, and the rest north. For the latter I can provide food and transportation to points of their election in Tennessee, Kentucky, or farther north. For the former I can provide transportation by cars as far as Rough and Ready, and also wagons; but, that their removal may be made with as little discomfort as possible, it will be necessary for you to help the families from Rough and Ready to the cars at Lovejoy's. If you consent, I will undertake to remove all the families in Atlanta who prefer to go south to Rough and Ready, with all their movable effects, viz.: clothing, trunks, reasonable furniture, bedding, etc., with their servants, white and black, with the proviso that no force shall be used toward the blacks, one way or the other. If they want to go with their masters or mistresses, they may do so; otherwise they will be sent away, unless they be men, when they may be employed by our quartermaster. Atlanta is no place for families or non-combatants, and I have no desire to send them north if you will assist in conveying them south. If this proposition meets your views, I will consent to a truce in the neighborhood of Rough and Ready, stipulating that any wagons, horses, animals, or persons sent there for the purposes herein stated, shall in no manner be harmed or molested; you in your turn agreeing that any cars, wagons, or carriages, persons or animals sent to the same point, shall not be interfered with. Each of us might send a guard of, say, one hundred men, to maintain order, and limit the truce to, say, two days after a certain time appointed.

I have authorized the mayor to choose two citizens to convey to you this letter, with such documents as the mayor may forward in explanation, and shall await your reply. I have the honor to be your obedient servant,

W. T. SHERMAN, *Major-General commanding.*

HEADQUARTERS ARMY OF TENNESSEE, }
OFFICE CHIEF OF STAFF, *September 9, 1864.* }

Major-General W. T. SHERMAN, *commanding United States Forces in Georgia.*

GENERAL: Your letter of yesterday's date, borne by James M. Ball and James R. Crew; citizens of Atlanta, is received. You say therein, "I deem it to be to the interest of the United States that the citizens now residing in Atlanta should remove," etc. I do not consider that I have any alternative in this matter. I therefore accept your proposition to declare a truce of two days, or such time as may be necessary to accomplish the purpose mentioned, and shall render all assistance in my power to expedite the transportation of citizens in this direction. I suggest that a staff-officer be appointed by you to superintend the removal from the city to Rough and Ready, while I appoint a like officer to control their removal farther south; that a guard of one hundred men be sent by either party as you propose, to maintain order at that place, and that the removal begin on Monday next.

And now, sir, permit me to say that the unprecedented measure you propose transcends, in studied and ingenious cruelty, all acts ever before brought to my attention in the dark history of war.

In the name of God and humanity, I protest, believing that you will find that you are expelling from their homes and firesides the wives and children of a brave people. I am, general, very respectfully, your obedient servant,

J. B. HOOD, *General.*

HEADQUARTERS MILITARY DIVISION OF THE MISSISSIPPI, }
IN THE FIELD, ATLANTA, GEORGIA, }
September 10, 1864. }

General J. B. HOOD, *commanding Army of Tennessee, Confederate Army.*

GENERAL: I have the honor to acknowledge the receipt of your letter of this date, at the hands of Messrs. Ball and Crew, consenting to the arrangements I had proposed to facilitate the removal south of the people of Atlanta, who prefer to go in that direction. I inclose you a copy of my orders, which will, I am satisfied, accomplish my purpose perfectly.

You style the measures proposed "unprecedented," and appeal to the dark history of war for a parallel, as an act of "studied and ingenious cruelty." It is not unprecedented; for General Johnston himself very wisely and properly removed the families all the way from Dalton down, and I see no reason why Atlanta should be excepted. Nor is it necessary to appeal to the dark history of war, when recent and modern examples are so handy. You yourself burned dwelling-houses along your parapet, and I have seen to-day fifty houses that you have rendered uninhabitable because they stood in the way of your forts and men. You defended Atlanta on a line so close to town that every cannon-shot and many musket-shots from our line of investment, that overshot their mark, went into the habitations of women and children. General Hardee did the same at Jonesboro', and General Johnston did the same, last summer, at Jackson, Mississippi. I have not accused you of heartless cruelty, but merely instance these cases of very recent occurrence, and could go on and enumerate hundreds of others, and challenge any fair man to judge which of us has the heart of pity for the families of a "brave people."

I say that it is kindness to these families of Atlanta to remove them now, at once, from scenes that women and children should not be exposed to, and the "brave people" should scorn to commit their wives and children to the rude barbarians who thus, as you say, violate the laws of war, as illustrated in the pages of its dark history.

In the name of common sense, I ask you not to appeal to a just God in such a sacrilegious manner. You who, in the midst of peace and prosperity, have plunged a nation into war—dark and cruel war—who dared and badgered us to battle, insulted our flag, seized our arsenals and forts that were left in the honorable custody of peaceful ordnance-sergeants, seized and made "prisoners of war" the very garrisons sent to protect your people against Negroes and Indians, long before any overt act was committed by the (to you) hated Lincoln Government; tried to force Kentucky and

Missouri into rebellion, spite of themselves; falsified the vote of Louisiana; turned loose your privateers to plunder unarmed ships; expelled Union families by the thousands, burned their houses, and declared, by an act of your Congress, the confiscation of all debts due Northern men for goods had and received! Talk thus to the marines, but not to me, who have seen these things, and who will this day make as much sacrifice for the peace and honor of the South as the best-born Southerner among you! If we must be enemies, let us be men, and fight it out as we propose to do, and not deal in such hypocritical appeals to God and humanity. God will judge us in due time, and he will pronounce whether it be more humane to fight with a town full of women and the families of a brave people at our back, or to remove them in time to places of safety among their own friends and people. I am, very respectfully, your obedient servant,

W. T. SHERMAN, *Major-General commanding.*

HEADQUARTERS ARMY OF TENNESSEE, }
September 12, 1864. }

Major-General W. T. SHERMAN, *commanding Military Division of the Mississippi.*

GENERAL: I have the honor to acknowledge the receipt of your letter of the 9th inst., with its inclosure in reference to the women, children, and others, whom you have thought proper to expel from their homes in the city of Atlanta. Had you seen proper to let the matter rest there, I would gladly have allowed your letter to close this correspondence, and, without your expressing it in words, would have been willing to believe that, while "the interests of the United States," in your opinion, compelled you to an act of barbarous cruelty, you regretted the necessity, and we would have dropped the subject; but you have chosen to indulge in statements which I feel compelled to notice, at least so far as to signify my dissent, and not allow silence in regard to them to be construed as acquiescence.

I see nothing in your communication which induces me to modify the language of condemnation with which I characterized your order. It but strengthens me in the opinion that it stands "preëminent in the dark history of war for studied and ingenious cruelty." Your original order was stripped of all pretenses; you announced the edict for the sole reason that it was "to the interest of the United States." This alone you offered to us and the civilized world as an all-sufficient reason for disregarding the laws of God and man. You say that "General Johnston himself very wisely and properly removed the families all the way from Dalton down." It is due to that gallant soldier and gentleman to say that no act of his distinguished career gives the least color to your unfounded aspersions upon his conduct. He depopulated no villages, nor towns, nor cities, either friendly or hostile. He offered and extended friendly aid to his unfortunate fellow-citizens who desired to flee from your fraternal embraces. You are equally unfortunate in your attempt to find a justification for this act of cruelty, either in the defense of Jonesboro', by General Hardee, or of Atlanta, by myself. General Hardee defended his position in front of Jonesboro' at the expense of injury to the houses; an ordinary, proper, and justifiable act of war. I defended Atlanta at the same risk and cost. If there was any fault in either case, it was your own, in not giving notice, especially in the case of Atlanta, of your purpose to shell the town, which is usual in war among civilized nations. No inhabitant was expelled from his home and fireside by the orders of General Hardee or myself, and therefore your recent order can find no support from the conduct of either of us. I feel no other emotion other than pain in reading that portion of your letter which attempts to justify your shelling Atlanta without notice under pretense that I defended Atlanta upon a line so close to town that every cannon-shot and many musket-balls from your line of investment, that overshot their mark, went into the habitations of women and children. I made no complaint of your firing into Atlanta in any way you thought proper. I make none now, but there are a hundred thousand witnesses that you fired into the habitations of women and children for weeks, firing far above and miles beyond my line of defense. I have too good an opinion, founded both upon observation and experience, of the skill of your artillerists, to credit the insinuation that they for several weeks unintentionally fired too high for my modest field-works, and slaughtered women and children by accident and want of skill.

The residue of your letter is rather discussion. It opens a wide field for the discussion of questions which I do not feel are committed to me. I am only a general of one of the armies of the Confederate States, charged with military operations in the field, under the direction of my superior officers, and I am not called upon to discuss with you the causes of the present war, or the political questions which led to or resulted from it. These grave and important questions have been committed to far abler hands than mine, and I shall only refer to them so far as to repel any unjust conclusion which might be drawn from my silence. You charge my country with "daring and badgering you to battle." The truth is, we sent commissioners to you, respectfully offering a peaceful separation, before the first gun was fired on either side. You say we insulted your flag. The truth is, we fired upon it, and those who fought under it, when you came to our doors upon the mission of subjugation. You say we seized upon your forts and arsenals, and made prisoners of the garrisons sent to protect us against Negroes and Indians. The truth is, we, by force of arms, drove out insolent intruders and took possession of our own forts and arsenals, to resist your claims to dominion over masters, slaves, and Indians, all of whom are to this day, with a unanimity unexampled in the history of the world, warring against your attempts to become their masters. You say that we tried to force Missouri and Kentucky into rebellion in spite of themselves. The truth is, my Government, from the beginning of this struggle to this hour, has again and again offered, before the whole world, to leave it to the unbiased will of these States, and all others, to determine for themselves whether they will cast their destiny with your Government or ours; and your Government has resisted this fundamental principle of free institutions with the bayonet, and labors daily, by force and fraud, to fasten its hateful tyranny upon the unfortunate freemen of these States. You say we falsified the vote of Louisiana. The truth is, Louisiana not only separated herself from your Government by nearly a unanimous vote of her people, but has vindicated the act upon every battlefield from Gettysburg to the Sabine, and has exhibited an heroic devotion to her decision which challenges the admiration and respect of every man capable of feeling sympathy for the oppressed or admiration for heroic valor. You say that we turned loose pirates to plunder your unarmed ships. The truth is, when you robbed us of our part of the navy, we built and bought a few vessels, hoisted the flag of our country, and swept the seas, in defiance of your navy, around the whole circumference of the globe. You say we have expelled Union families by thousands. The truth is, not a single family has been expelled from the Confederate States, that I am aware of; but, on the contrary, the moderation of our Government toward traitors has been a fruitful theme of denunciation by its enemies and well-meaning friends of our cause. You say my Government, by acts of Congress, has confiscated "all debts due Northern men for goods sold and delivered." The truth is, our Congress gave due and ample time to your merchants and traders to depart from our shores with their ships, goods, and effects, and only sequestrated the property of our enemies in retaliation for their acts—declaring us traitors, and confiscating our property wherever their power extended, either in their country or our own. Such are your accusations, and such are the facts known of all men to be true.

You order into exile the whole population of a city; drive men, women, and children from their homes at the point of the bayonet, under the plea that it is to the interest of your Government, and on the claim that it is an act of "kindness to these families of Atlanta." Butler only banished from New Orleans the registered enemies of his Government, and acknowledged that he did it as a punishment. You issue a sweeping edict, covering all the inhabitants of a city, and add insult to the injury heaped upon the defenseless by assuming that you have done them a kindness. This you follow by the assertion that you will "make as much sacrifice for the peace and honor of the South as the best-born Southerner." And, because I characterize what you call a kindness as being real cruelty, you presume to sit in judgment between me and my God; and you decide that my earnest prayer to the Almighty Father to save our women and children from what you call kindness, is a "sacrilegious, hypocritical appeal."

You came into our country with your army, avowedly for the purpose of subjugating free white men, women, and children, and not only intend to rule over them, but you make Negroes your allies, and desire to place over us an inferior race, which we have raised from barbarism to its present position, which is the highest ever attained by that race, in any country, in all time. I must, therefore, decline to accept your statements in reference to your kindness toward the people of Atlanta, and your willingness to sacrifice everything for the peace and honor of the South, and refuse to be governed by your decision in regard to matters between myself, my country, and my God.

You say, "Let us fight it out like men." To this my reply is—for myself, and I believe for all the true men, ay, and women and children, in my country—we will fight you to the death! Better die a thousand deaths than submit to live under you or your Government and your Negro allies!

Having answered the points forced upon me by your letter of the 9th of September, I close this correspondence with you; and, notwithstanding your comments upon my appeal to God in the cause of humanity, I again humbly and reverently invoke his almighty aid in defense of justice and right.

Respectfully, your obedient servant,

J. B. Hood, *General.*

ATLANTA, GEORGIA, *September* 11, 1864.

Major-General W. T. SHERMAN.

SIR: We the undersigned, Mayor and two of the Council for the city of Atlanta, for the time being the only legal organ of the people of the said city, to express their wants and wishes, ask leave most earnestly but respectfully to petition you to reconsider the order requiring them to leave Atlanta.

At first view, it struck us that the measure would involve extraordinary hardship and loss, but since we have seen the practical execution of it so far as it has progressed, and the individual condition of the people, and heard their statements as to the inconveniences, loss, and suffering attending it, we are satisfied that the amount of it will involve in the aggregate consequences appalling and heartrending.

Many poor women are in advanced state of pregnancy, others now having young children, and whose husbands for the greater part are either in the army, prisoners, or dead. Some say: "I have such a one sick at my house; who will wait on them when I am gone?" Others say: "What are we to do? We have no house to go to, and no means to buy, build, or rent any; no parents, relatives, or friends, to go to." Another says: "I will try and take this or that article of property, but such and such things I must leave behind, though I need them much." We reply to them: "General Sherman will carry your property to Rough and Ready, and General Hood will take it thence on." And they will reply to that: "But I want to leave the railroad at such a place, and cannot get conveyance from there on."

We only refer to a few facts, to try to illustrate in part how this measure will operate in practice. As you advanced, the people north of this fell back; and before your arrival here, a large portion of the people had retired south, so that the country south of this is already crowded, and without houses enough to accommodate the people, and we are informed that many are now staying in churches and other out-buildings.

This being so, how is it possible for the people still here (mostly women and children) to find any shelter? And how can they live through the winter in the woods—no shelter or subsistence, in the midst of strangers who know them not, and without the power to assist them much, if they were willing to do so?

This is but a feeble picture of the consequences of this measure. You know the woe, the horrors, and the suffering, cannot be described by words; imagination can only conceive of it, and we ask you to take these things into consideration.

We know your mind and time are constantly occupied with the duties of your command, which almost deters us from asking your attention to this matter, but thought it might be that you had not considered this subject in all of its awful consequences, and that on more reflection you, we hope, would not make this people an exception to all mankind, for we know of no such instance ever having occurred—surely never in the United States—and what has this *helpless* people done, that they should be driven from their homes, to wander strangers and outcasts, and exiles, and to subsist on charity?

We do not know as yet the number of people still here; of those who are here, we are satisfied a respectable number, if allowed to remain at home, could subsist for several months without assistance, and a respectable number for a much longer time, and who might not need assistance at any time.

In conclusion, we most earnestly and solemnly petition you to reconsider this order, or modify it, and suffer this unfortunate people to remain at home, and enjoy what little means they have.

Respectfully submitted:

> JAMES M. CALHOUN, *Mayor.*
> E. E. RAWSON, *Councilman.*
> S. C. WELLS, *Councilman.*

HEADQUARTERS MILITARY DIVISION OF THE MISSISSIPPI, IN THE FIELD, ATLANTA, GEORGIA, *September* 12, 1864.

JAMES M. CALHOUN, *Mayor*, E. E. RAWSON *and* S. C. WELLS, *representing City Council of Atlanta.*

GENTLEMEN: I have your letter of the 11th, in the nature of a petition to revoke my orders removing all the inhabitants from Atlanta. I have read it carefully, and give full credit to your statements of the distress that will be occasioned, and yet shall not revoke my orders, because they were not designed to meet the humanities of the case, but to prepare for the future struggles in which millions of good people outside of Atlanta have a deep interest. We must have peace, not only at Atlanta, but in all America. To secure this, we must stop the war that now desolates our once happy and favored country. To stop war, we must defeat the rebel armies which are arrayed against the laws and Constitution that all must respect and obey. To defeat those armies, we must prepare the way to reach them in their recesses, provided with the arms and instruments which enable us to accomplish our purpose. Now, I know the vindictive nature of our enemy, that we may have many years of military operations from this quarter; and, therefore, deem it wise and prudent to prepare in time. The use of Atlanta for warlike purposes is inconsistent with its character as a home for families. There will be no manufactures, commerce, or agriculture here, for the maintenance of families, and sooner or later want will compel the inhabitants to go. Why not go now, when all the arrangements are completed for the transfer, instead of the waiting till the plunging shot of contending armies will renew the scenes of the past month? Of course, I do not apprehend any such thing at this moment, but you do not suppose this army will be here until the war is over. I cannot discuss this subject with you fairly, because I cannot impart to you what we propose to do, but I assert that our military plans make it necessary for the inhabitants to go away, and I can only renew my offer of services to make their exodus in any direction as easy and comfortable as possible.

You cannot qualify war in harsher terms than I will. War is cruelty, and you cannot refine it; and those who brought war into our country deserve all the curses and maledictions a people can pour out. I know I had no hand in making this war, and I know I will make more sacrifices to-day than any of you to secure peace. But you cannot have peace and a division of our country. If the United States submits to a division now, it will not stop, but will go on until we reap the fate of Mexico, which is eternal war. The United States does and must assert its authority, wherever it once had power; for, if it relaxes one bit to pressure, it is gone, and I believe that such is the national feeling. This feeling assumes various shapes, but always comes back to that of Union. Once admit the Union, once more acknowledge the authority of the national Government, and, instead of devoting your houses and streets and roads to the dread uses of war, I and this army become at once your protectors and supporters, shielding you from danger, let it come from what quarter it may. I know that a few individuals cannot resist a torrent of error and passion, such as swept the South into rebellion, but you can point out, so that we may know those who desire a government, and those who insist on war and its desolation.

You might as well appeal against the thunder-storm as against these terrible hardships of war. They are inevitable, and the only way the people of Atlanta can hope once more to live in peace and quiet at home, is to stop the war, which can only be done by admitting that it began in error and is perpetuated in pride.

We don't want your Negroes, or your horses, or your

houses, or your lands, or any thing you have, but we do want and will have a just obedience to the laws of the United States. That we will have, and, if it involves the destruction of your improvements, we cannot help it.

You have heretofore read public sentiment in your newspapers, that live by falsehood and excitement; and the quicker you seek for truth in other quarters, the better. I repeat then that, by the original compact of Government, the United States had certain rights in Georgia, which have never been relinquished and never will be; that the South began war by seizing forts, arsenals, mints, custom-houses, etc., etc., long before Mr. Lincoln was installed, and before the South had one jot or tittle of provocation. I myself have seen in Missouri, Kentucky, Tennessee, and Mississippi, hundreds and thousands of women and children fleeing from your armies and desperadoes, hungry and with bleeding feet. In Memphis, Vicksburg, and Mississippi, we fed thousands upon thousands of the families of rebel soldiers left on our hands, and whom we could not see starve. Now that war comes home to you, you feel very different. You deprecate its horrors, but did not feel them when you sent car-loads of soldiers and ammunition, and moulded shells and shot, to carry war into Kentucky and Tennessee, to desolate the homes of hundreds and thousands of good people who only asked to live in peace at their old homes, and under the Government of their inheritance. But these comparisons are idle. I want peace, and believe it can only be reached through union and war, and I will ever conduct war with a view to perfect and early success.

But, my dear sirs, when peace does come, you may call on me for any thing. Then will I share with you the last cracker, and watch with you to shield your homes and families against danger from every quarter.

Now you must go, and take with you the old and feeble, feed and nurse them, and build for them, in more quiet places, proper habitations to shield them against the weather until the mad passions of men cool down, and allow the Union and peace once more to settle over your old homes at Atlanta.

Yours in haste,

W. T. SHERMAN, *Major-General commanding.*

HEADQUARTERS MILITARY DIVISION OF THE MISSISSIPPI, IN THE FIELD, ATLANTA, GEORGIA, *September* 14, 1864.

General J. B. HOOD, *commanding Army of the Tennessee, Confederate Army.*

GENERAL: Yours of September 12th is received, and has been carefully perused. I agree with you that this discussion by two soldiers is out of place, and profitless; but you must admit that you began the controversy by characterizing an official act of mine in unfair and improper terms. I reiterate my former answer, and to the only new matter contained in your rejoinder add: We have no "Negro allies" in this army; not a single Negro soldier left Chattanooga with this army, or is with it now. There are a few guarding Chattanooga, which General [James B.] Steedman sent at one time to drive Wheeler out of Dalton.

I was not bound by the laws of war to give notice of the shelling of Atlanta, a "fortified town, with magazines, arsenals, founderies, and public stores"; you were bound to take notice. See the books.

This is the conclusion of our correspondence, which I did not begin, and terminate with satisfaction.

I am, with respect, your obedient servant,
W. T. SHERMAN, *Major-General commanding.*

In order to effect the exchange of prisoners, to facilitate the exodus of the people of Atlanta, and to keep open communication with the South, we established a neutral camp, at and about the railroad-station next south of Atlanta, known as "Rough and Ready," to which point I dispatched Lieutenant-Colonel Willard Warner, of my staff, with a guard of one hundred men, and General Hood sent Colonel Clare, of his staff, with a similar guard; these officers and men harmonized perfectly, and parted good friends when their work was done. In the mean time I also had reconnoitred the entire rebel lines about Atlanta, which were well built, but were entirely too extensive to be held by a single corps or division of troops, so I instructed Colonel Poe, United States Engineers, on my staff, to lay off an inner and shorter line, susceptible of defense by a smaller garrison.

By the middle of September all these matters were in progress, the reports of the past campaign were written up and dispatched to Washington, and our thoughts began to turn toward the future. Admiral Farragut had boldly and successfully run the forts at the entrance to Mobile Bay, which resulted in the capture of Fort Morgan, so that General Canby was enabled to begin his regular operations against Mobile City, with a view to open the Alabama River to navigation. My first thoughts were to concert operations with him, either by way of Montgomery, Alabama, or by the Appalachicola; but so lone a line, to be used as a base for further operations eastward, was not advisable, and I concluded to await the initiative of the enemy, supposing that he would be forced to resort to some desperate campaign by the clamor raised at the South on account of the great loss to them of the city of Atlanta.

General Thomas occupied a house on Marietta Street, which had a veranda with high pillars. We were sitting there one evening, talking about things generally, when General Thomas asked leave to send his trains back to Chattanooga, for the convenience and economy of forage. I inquired of him if he supposed we would be allowed much rest at Atlanta, and he said he thought we would, or that at all events it would not be prudent for us to go much farther into Georgia because of our already long line of communication, viz., three hundred miles from Nashville. This was true; but there we were, and we could not afford to remain on the defensive, simply holding Atlanta and fighting for the saftey of its railroad. I insisted on his retaining all trains, and on keeping all his divisions ready to move at a moment's warning. All the army, officers and men, seemed to relax more or less, and sink into a condition of idleness. General Schofield was permitted to go to Knoxville, to look after matters in his Department of the Ohio; and Generals Blair and Logan went home to look after politics. Many of the regiments were entitled to, and claimed, their discharge, by reason of the expiration of their term of service; so that with victory and success came also many causes of disintegration.

The rebel General Wheeler was still in Middle Tennessee, threatening our railroads, and rumors came that Forrest was on his way from Mississippi to the same theatre, for the avowed purpose of breaking up our railroads and compelling us to fall back from our conquest. To prepare for this, or any other emergency, I ordered Newton's division of the Fourth Corps back to Chattanooga, and Corse's division of the Seventeenth Corps to Rome, and instructed General Rousseau at Nashville, Granger at Decatur, and Steadman at Chattanooga, to adopt the most active measures to protect and insure the safety of our roads.

Hood still remained about Lovejoy's Station, and, up to the 15th of September, had given no signs of his future plans; so that with this date I close the campaign of Atlanta.

Chapter 13

Pursuit of Hood:
"I Can Make Georgia Howl"
September—October, 1864

BY THE MIDDLE of September, matters and things had settled
down in Atlanta, so that we felt perfectly at home. The telegraph and railroads were repaired, and we had uninterrupted
communication to the rear. The trains arrived with regularity
and dispatch, and brought us ample supplies. General Wheeler
had been driven out of Middle Tennessee, escaping south
across the Tennessee River at Bainbridge; and things looked
as though we were to have a period of repose.

One day, two citizens, Messrs. Hill and Nelson, came into
our lines at Decatur, and were sent to my headquarters. They
represented themselves as former members of Congress, and
particular friends of my brother John Sherman; that Mr. Hill
had a son killed in the rebel army as it fell back before us
somewhere near Cassville, and they wanted to obtain the body,
having learned from a comrade where it was buried. I gave
them permission to go by rail to the rear, with a note to the
commanding officer, General John E. Smith, at Cartersville,
requiring him to furnish them an escort and an ambulance for
the purpose. I invited them to take dinner with our mess, and
we naturally ran into a general conversation about politics and
the devastation and ruin caused by the war. They had seen a

part of the country over which the army had passed, and could easily apply its measure of desolation to the remainder of the State, if necessity should compel us to go ahead.

Mr. Hill resided at Madison, on the main road to Augusta, and seemed to realize fully the danger; said that further resistance on the part of the South was madness, that he hoped Governor [Joseph E.] Brown, of Georgia, would so proclaim it, and withdraw his people from the rebellion, in pursuance of what was known as the policy of "separate State action." I told him, if he saw Governor Brown, to describe to him fully what he had seen, and to say that if he remained inert, I would be compelled to go ahead, devastating the State in its whole length and breadth; that there was no adequate force to stop us, etc.; but if he would issue his proclamation withdrawing his State troops from the armies of the Confederacy, I would spare the State, and in our passage across it confine the troops to the main roads, and would, moreover, pay for all the corn and food we needed. I also told Mr. Hill that he might, in my name, invite Governor Brown to visit Atlanta; that I would give him a safeguard, and that if he wanted to make a speech, I would guarantee him as full and respectable an audience as any he had ever spoken to. I believe that Mr. Hill, after reaching his home at Madison, went to Milledgeville, the capital of the State, and delivered the message to Governor Brown. I had also sent similar messages by Judge Wright of Rome, Georgia, and by Mr. King, of Marietta. On the 15th of September I telegraphed to General Halleck as follows:

My report is done, and will be forwarded as soon as I get in a few more of the subordinate reports. I am awaiting a courier from General Grant. All well; the troops are in good, healthy camps, and supplies are coming forward finely. Governor Brown has disbanded his militia, to gather the corn and sorghum of the State. I have reason to believe that he and [Alexander H.] Stephens want to visit me, and have sent them a hearty invitation. I will exchange two thousand prisoners with Hood, but no more.

Governor Brown's action at that time is fully explained by the following letter, since made public, which was then only known to us in part by hearsay:

EXECUTIVE DEPARTMENT,
MILLEDGEVILLE, GEORGIA, *September* 10, 1864.

General J. B. HOOD, *commanding Army of Tennessee.*

GENERAL: As the militia of the State were called out for the defense of Atlanta during the campaign against it, which has terminated by the fall of the city into the hands of the enemy, and as many of these left their homes without preparation (expecting to be gone but a few weeks), who have remained in service over three months (most of the time in the trenches), justice requires that they be permitted, while the enemy are preparing for the winter campaign, to return to their homes, and look for a time after important interests, and prepare themselves for such service as may be required when another campaign commences against other important points in the State. I therefore hereby withdraw said organization from your command. . . .

JOSEPH E. BROWN.

This militia had composed a division under command of Major-General Gustavus W. Smith, and were thus dispersed to their homes, to gather the corn and sorghum, then ripe and ready for the harvesters.

On the 17th I received by telegraph from President Lincoln this dispatch:

WASHINGTON, D. C., *September* 17, 1864—10 A. M.

Major-General SHERMAN:

I feel great interest in the subjects of your dispatch, mentioning corn and sorghum, and the contemplated visit to you.

A. LINCOLN, *President of the United States.*

I replied at once:

HEADQUARTERS MILITARY DIVISION OF THE MISSISSIPPI,
IN THE FIELD, ATLANTA, GEORGIA, *September* 17, 1864.

President LINCOLN, *Washington, D. C.:*

I will keep the department fully advised of all developments connected with the subject in which you feel interested.

Mr. Wright, former member of Congress from Rome, Georgia, and Mr. King, of Marietta, are now going between Governor Brown and myself. I have said to them that some of the people of Georgia are engaged in rebellion, begun in error and perpetuated in pride, but that Georgia can now save herself from the devastations of war preparing for her, only by withdrawing her quota out of the Confederate Army, and aiding me to expel Hood from the borders of the State; in which event, instead of desolating the land as we progress, I will keep our men to the high-roads and commons, and pay for the corn and meat we need and take.

I am fully conscious of the delicate nature of such assertions, but it would be a magnificent stroke of policy if we could, without surrendering principle or a foot of ground, arouse the latent enmity of Georgia against Davis.

The people do not hesitate to say that Mr. Stephens was and is a Union man at heart; and they say that Davis will not trust him or let him have a share in his Government.

W. T. Sherman, Major-General.

I have not the least doubt that Governor Brown, at that time, seriously entertained the proposition; but he hardly felt ready to act, and simply gave a furlough to the militia, and called a special session of the Legislature, to meet at Milledgeville, to take into consideration the critical condition of affairs in the State.

On the 20th of September Colonel Horace Porter arrived from General Grant, at City Point, bringing me the letter of September 12th, asking my general views as to what should next be done. He staid several days at Atlanta, and on his return carried back to Washington my full reports of the past campaign, and my letter of September 20th to General Grant in answer to his of the 12th.

About this time we detected signs of activity on the part of the enemy. On the 21st Hood shifted his army across from the Macon road, at Lovejoy's, to the West Point road, at Palmetto Station, and his cavalry appeared on the west side of the Chattahoochee, toward Powder Springs; thus, as it were, stepping aside, and opening wide the door for us to enter Central Georgia. I inferred, however, that his real purpose was to assume the offensive against our railroads, and on the 24th a heavy force of cavalry from Mississippi, under General Forrest, made its appearance at Athens, Alabama, and captured its garrison.

General Newton's division (of the Fourth Corps), and Corse's (of the Seventeenth), were sent back by rail, the former to Chattanooga, and the latter to Rome. On the 25th I telegraphed to General Halleck

Hood seems to be moving, as it were, to the Alabama line, leaving open the road to Macon, as also to Augusta; but his cavalry is busy on all our roads. A force, number estimated as high as eight thousand, are reported to have captured Athens, Alabama; and a regiment of three hundred and fifty men sent to its relief. I have sent Newton's division up to Chattanooga in cars, and will send another division to Rome. If I were sure that Savannah would soon be in our possession, I should be tempted to march for Milledgeville and Augusta; but I must first secure what I have. Jeff. Davis is at Macon.

W. T. SHERMAN, *Major-General.*

On the next day I telegraphed further that Jeff. Davis was with Hood at Palmetto Station. One of our spies was there at the time, who came in the next night, and reported to me the substance of his speech to the soldiers. It was a repetition of those he had made at Columbia, South Carolina, and Macon, Georgia, on his way out, which I had seen in the newspapers. Davis seemed to be perfectly upset by the fall of Atlanta, and to have lost all sense and reason. He denounced General Jos. Johnston and Governor Brown as little better than traitors; attributed to them personally the many misfortunes which had befallen their cause, and informed the soldiers that now the tables were to be turned; that General Forrest was already on our roads in Middle Tennessee; and that Hood's army would soon be there. He asserted that the Yankee army would have to retreat or starve, and that the retreat would prove more disastrous than was that of Napoleon from Moscow. He promised his Tennessee and Kentucky soldiers that their feet should soon tread their "native soil," etc., etc. He made no concealment of these vainglorious boasts, and thus gave us the full key to his future designs. To be forewarned was to be forearmed, and I think we took full advantage of the occasion.

On the 26th I received this dispatch:

CITY POINT, VIRGINIA, *September* 26, 1864—10 A. M.

Major-General SHERMAN, *Atlanta:*

It will be better to drive Forrest out of Middle Tennessee

as a first step, and do any thing else you may feel your force sufficient for. When a movement is made on any part of the sea-coast, I will advise you. If Hood goes to the Alabama line, will it not be impossible for him to subsist his army?

U. S. GRANT, Lieutenant-General.

Answer:

HEADQUARTERS MILITARY DIVISION OF THE MISSISSIPPI,
IN THE FIELD, ATLANTA, GEORGIA, *September* 26, 1864.

GENERAL: I have your dispatch of to-day. I have already sent one division (Newton's) to Chattanooga, and another (Corse's) to Rome.

Our armies are much reduced, and if I send back any more, I will not be able to threaten Georgia much. There are men enough to the rear to whip Forrest, but they are necessarily scattered to defend the roads.

Can you expedite the sending to Nashville of the recruits that are in Indiana and Ohio? They could occupy the forts.

Hood is now on the West Point road, twenty-four miles south of this, and draws his supplies by that road. Jefferson Davis is there to-day, and superhuman efforts will be made to break my road.

Forrest is now lieutenant-general, and commands all the enemy's cavalry.

W. T. SHERMAN, Major-General.

General Grant first thought I was in error in supposing that Jeff. Davis was at Macon and Palmetto, but on the 27th I received a printed copy of his speech made at Macon on the 22d, which was so significant that I ordered it to be telegraphed entire as far as Louisville, to be sent thence by mail to Washington, and on the same day received this distpach:

WASHINGTON, D. C., September 27, 1864—9 A. M.

Major-General SHERMAN, *Atlanta:*

You say Jeff. Davis is on a visit to General Hood. I judge that Brown and Stephens are the objects of his visit.

A. LINCOLN, President of the United States.

To which I replied:

HEADQUARTERS MILITARY DIVISION OF THE MISSISSIPPI,
IN THE FIELD, ATLANTA, GEORGIA, *September* 28, 1864.

President LINCOLN, *Washington, D. C.*:

I have positive knowledge that Mr. Davis made a speech at Macon, on the 22d, which I mailed to General Halleck yesterday. It was bitter against General Jos. Johnston and Governor Brown. The militia are on furlough. Brown is at Milledgeville, trying to get a Legislature to meet next month, but he is afraid to act unless in concert with other Governors. Judge Wright, of Rome, has been here, and Messrs. Hill and Nelson, former members of Congress, are here now, and will go to meet Wright at Rome, and then go back to Madison and Milledgeville.

Great efforts are being made to reënforce Hood's army, and to break up my railroads, and I should have at once a good reserve force at Nashville. It would have a bad effect, if I were forced to send back any considerable part of my army to guard roads, so as to weaken me to an extent that I could not act offensively if the occasion calls for it.

W. T. SHERMAN, *Major-General.*

All this time Hood and I were carrying on the foregoing correspondence relating to the exchange of prisoners, the removal of the people from Atlanta, and the relief of our prisoners of war at Andersonville. Notwithstanding the severity of their imprisonment, some of these men escaped from Andersonville, and got to me at Atlanta. They described their sad condition: more than twenty-five thousand prisoners confined in a stockade designed for only ten thousand; debarred the privilege of gathering wood out of which to make huts; deprived of sufficient healthy food, and the little stream that ran through their prison-pen poisoned and polluted by the offal from their cooking and butchering houses above. On the 22d of September I wrote to General Hood, describing the condition of our men at Andersonville, purposely refraining from casting odium on him or his associates for the treatment of these men, but asking his consent for me to procure from our generous friends at the North the articles of clothing and comfort which they wanted, viz., under-clothing, soap, combs, scissors, etc.—all needed to keep them in health—and to send these stores with a train, and an officer to issue them. General Hood, on the 24th, promptly consented, and I telegraphed to my friend Mr. James E. Yeatman, Vice-President of the Sanitary Commission at St. Louis, to send us all the under-clothing and soap he could spare, specifying twelve hundred fine-tooth combs, and four hundred pairs of shears to cut hair. These articles indicate the plague that most afflicted our prisoners at Andersonville.

Mr. Yeatman promptly responded to my request, expressed the articles, but they did not reach Andersonville in time, for the prisoners were soon after removed; these supplies did, however, finally overtake them at Jacksonville, Florida, just before the war closed.

On the 28th I received from General Grant two dispatches:

CITY POINT, VIRGINIA,
September 27, 1864—8.30 A. M.

Major-General SHERMAN:

It is evident, from the tone of the Richmond press and from other sources of information, that the enemy intend making a desperate effort to drive you from where you are. I have directed all new troops from the West, and from the East too, if necessary, in case none are ready in the West, to be sent to you. If General Burbridge is not too far on his way to Abingdon, I think he had better be recalled and his surplus troops sent into Tennessee.

U. S. GRANT, *Lieutenant-General.*

CITY POINT, VIRGINIA,
September 27, 1864—10.30 A. M.

Major-General SHERMAN:

I have directed all recruits and new troops from all the Western States to be sent to Nashville, to receive their further orders from you. I was mistaken about Jeff. Davis being in Richmond on Thursday last. He was then on his way to Macon.

U. S. GRANT, *Lieutenant-General.*

Forrest having already made his appearance in Middle Tennessee, and Hood evidently edging off in that direction, satisfied me that the general movement against our roads had begun. I therefore determined to send General Thomas back to Chattanooga, with another division (Morgan's, of the Fourteenth Corps), to meet the danger in Tennessee. General Thomas went up on the 29th, and Morgan's division followed the same day, also by rail. And I telegraphed to General Halleck:

I take it for granted that Forrest will cut our road, but think we can prevent him from making a serious lodgment. His cavalry will travel a hundred miles where ours will ten. I have sent two divisions up to Chattanooga and one to Rome, and General Thomas started to-day to drive Forrest out of Tennessee. Our roads should be watched from the rear, and I am glad that General Grant has ordered reserves to Nashville. I prefer for the future to make the movement on Milledgeville, Millen, and Savannah. Hood now rests twenty-four miles south, on the Chattahoochee, with his right on the West Point road. He is removing the iron of the Macon road. I can whip his infantry, but his cavalry is to be feared.

There was great difficulty in obtaining correct information about Hood's movements from Palmetto Station. I could not get spies to penetrate his camps, but on the 1st of October I was satisfied that the bulk of his infantry was at and across the Chattahoochee River, near Campbellton, and that his cavalry was on the west side, at Powder Springs. On that day I telegraphed to General Grant:

Hood is evidently across the Chattahoochee, below Sweetwater. If he tries to get on our road, this side of the Etowah, I shall attack him; but if he goes to the Selma & Talladega road, why will it not do to leave Tennessee to the forces which Thomas has, and the reserves soon to come to Nashville, and for me to destroy Atlanta and march across Georgia to Savannah or Charleston, breaking roads and doing irreparable damage? We cannot remain on the defensive.

The Selma & Talladega road herein referred to was an unfinished railroad from Selma, Alabama, through Talladega, to

Blue Mountain, a terminus sixty-five miles southwest of Rome and about fifteen miles southeast of Gadsden, where the rebel army could be supplied from the direction of Montgomery and Mobile, and from which point Hood could easily threaten Middle Tennessee. My first impression was, that Hood would make for that point; but by the 3d of October the indications were that he would strike our railroad nearer us, viz., about Kingston or Marietta.

Orders were at once made for the Twentieth Corps (Slocum's) to hold Atlanta and the bridges of the Chattahoochee, and the other corps were put in motion for Marietta.

The army had undergone many changes since the capture of Atlanta. General Schofield had gone to the rear, leaving General J[acob] D. Cox in command of the Army of the Ohio (Twenty-third Corps). General Thomas, also, had been dispatched to Chattanooga, with Newton's division of the Fourth Corps and Morgan's of the Fourteenth Corps, leaving General D. S. Stanley, the senior major-general of the two corps of his Army of the Cumberland, remaining and available for this movement, viz., the Fourth and Fourteenth, commanded by himself and Major-General Jeff. C. Davis; and after General Dodge was wounded, his corps (the Sixteenth) had been broken up, and its two divisions were added to the Fifteenth and Seventeenth Corps, constituting the Army of the Tennessee, commanded by Major-General O. O. Howard. Generals Logan and Blair had gone home to assist in the political canvass, leaving their corps, viz., the Fifteenth and Seventeenth, under the command of Major-Generals Osterhaus and T[homas] E. G. Ransom.

These five corps were very much reduced in strength, by detachments and by discharges, so that for the purpose of fighting Hood I had only about sixty thousand infantry and artillery, with two small divisions of cavalry (Kilpatrick's and Garrard's). General Elliott was the chief of cavalry to the Army of the Cumberland, and was the senior officer of that arm of service present for duty with me.

We had strong railroad guards at Marietta and Kenesaw, Allatoona, Etowah Bridge, Kingston, Rome, Resaca, Dalton, Ringgold, and Chattanooga. All the important bridges were likewise protected by good block-houses, admirably constructed, and capable of a strong defense against cavalry or infantry; and at nearly all the regular railroad-stations we had smaller detachments intrenched. I had little fear of the enemy's cavalry damaging our roads seriously, for they rarely made a break which could not be repaired in a few days; but it was absolutely necessary to keep General Hood's infantry off our main route of communication and supply. Forrest had with him in Middle Tennessee about eight thousand cavalry, and Hood's army was estimated at from thirty-five to forty thousand men, infantry and artillery, including Wheeler's cavalry, then about three thousand strong.

We crossed the Chattahoochee River during the 3d and 4th of October, rendezvoused at the old battle-field of Smyrna Camp, and the next day reached Marietta and Kenesaw. The telegraph-wires had been cut above Marietta, and learning that heavy masses of infantry, artillery, and cavalry, had been seen from Kenesaw (marching north), I inferred that Allatoona was their objective point; and on the 4th of October I signaled from Vining's Station to Kenesaw, and from Kenesaw to Allatoona, over the heads of the enemy, a message for General Corse, at Rome, to hurry back to the assistance of the garrison at Allatoona. Allatoona was held by a small brigade, commanded by Lieutenant-Colonel [John E.] Tourtellotte, my present aide-de-camp. He had two small redoubts on either side of the railroad, overlooking the village of Allatoona, and the warehouses, in which were stored over a million rations of bread.

Reaching Kenesaw Mountain about 8 A. M. of October 5th (a beautiful day), I had a superb view of the vast panorama to the north and west. To the southwest, about Dallas, could be seen the smoke of camp-fires, indicating the presence of a large force of the enemy, and the whole line of railroad from Big Shanty up to Allatoona (full fifteen miles) was marked by the fires of the burning railroad. We could plainly see the smoke of battle about Allatoona, and hear the faint reverberation of the cannon.

From Kenesaw I ordered the Twenty-third Corps (General Cox) to march due west on the Burnt Hickory road, and to burn houses or piles of brush as it progressed, to indicate the head of column, hoping to interpose this corps between Hood's main army at Dallas and the detachment then assailing Allatoona. The rest of the army was directed straight for Allatoona, northwest, distant eighteen miles. The signal-officer on Kenesaw reported that since daylight he had failed to obtain any answer to his call for Allatoona; but, while I was with him, he caught a faint glimpse of the tell-tale flag through an embrasure, and after much time he made out these letters—"C," "R," "S," "E," "H," "E," "R," and translated the message—"Corse is here." It was a source of great relief, for it gave me the first assurance that General Corse had received his orders, and that the place was adequately garrisoned.

I watched with painful suspense the indications of the battle raging there, and was dreadfully impatient at the slow progress of the relieving column, whose advance was marked by the smokes which were made according to orders, but about 2 P. M. I noticed with satisfaction that the smoke of battle about Allatoona grew less and less, and ceased altogether about 4 P. M. For a time I attributed this result to the effect of General Cox's march, but later in the afternoon the signal-flag announced the welcome tidings that the attack had been fairly repulsed, but that General Corse was wounded. The next day my aide, Colonel Dayton, received this characteristic dispatch:

ALLATOONA, GEORGIA, *October* 6, 1864—2 P. M.

Captain L. M. DAYTON, *Aide-de-Camp:*

I am short a cheek-bone and an ear, but am able to whip all h—l yet! My losses are very heavy. A force moving from Stilesboro' to Kingston gives me some anxiety. Tell me where Sherman is.

JOHN M. CORSE, *Brigadier-General.*

Inasmuch as the enemy had retreated southwest, and would probably next appear at Rome, I answered General Corse with orders to bet back to Rome with his troops as quickly as possible.

General Corse's report of this fight at Allatoona is very full and graphic. It is dated Rome, October 27, 1864; recites the fact that he received his orders by signal to go to the assistance of Allatoona on the 4th, when he telegraphed to Kingston for cars, and a train of thirty empty cars was started for him, but about ten of them got off the track and caused delay. By 7 P. M. he had at Rome a train of twenty cars, which he loaded up with Colonel [Richard] Rowett's brigade, and part of the

Twelfth Illinois Infantry; started at 8 P. M., reached Allatoona (distant thirty-five miles) at 1 A. M. of the 5th, and sent the train back for more men; but the road was in bad order, and no more men came in time. He found Colonel Tourtellotte's garrison composed of eight hundred and ninety men; his reënforcement was one thousand and fifty-four: total for the defense, nineteen hundred and forty-four. The outposts were already engaged, and as soon as daylight came he drew back the men from the village to the ridge on which the redoubts were built.

The enemy was composed of [Samuel] French's division of three brigades, variously reported from four to five thousand strong. This force gradually surrounded the place by 8 A. M., when General French sent in by flag of truce this note:

AROUND ALLATOONA, *October 5, 1864.*

Commanding Officer, United States Forces, Allatoona:

I have placed the forces under my command in such positions that you are surrounded, and to avoid a needless effusion of blood I call on you to surrender your forces at once, and unconditionally.

Five minutes will be allowed you to decide. Should you accede to this, you will be treated in the most honorable manner as prisoners of war.

I have the honor to be, very respectfully yours,

S. G. FRENCH,
Major-General commanding forces Confederate States.

General Corse answered immediately:

HEADQUARTERS FOURTH DIVISION, FIFTEENTH CORPS, ALLATOONA, GEORGIA, 8.30 A. M., *October 5, 1864.*

Major-General S. G. FRENCH, *Confederate States, etc.:*

Your communication demanding surrender of my command I acknowledge receipt of, and respectfully reply that we are prepared for the "needless effusion of blood" whenever it is agreeable to you.

I am, very respectfully, your obedient servant,

JOHN M. CORSE,
Brigadier-General commanding forces United States.

Of course the attack began at once, coming from front, flank, and rear. There were two small redoubts, with slight parapets and ditches, one on each side of the deep railroad-cut. These redoubts had been located by Colonel Poe, United States Engineers, at the time of our advance on Kenesaw, the previous June. Each redoubt overlooked the storehouses close by the railroad, and each could aid the other defensively by catching in flank the attacking force of the other. Our troops at first endeavored to hold some ground outside the redoubts, but were soon driven inside, when the enemy made repeated assaults, but were always driven back. About 11 A. M., Colonel Redfield, of the Thirty-ninth Iowa, was killed, and Colonel Rowett was wounded, but never ceased to fight and encourage his men. Colonel Tourtellotte was shot through the hips, but continued to command. General Corse was, at 1 P. M., shot across the face, the ball cutting his ear, which stunned him, but he continued to encourage his men and to give orders. The enemy (about 1.30 P. M.) made a last and desperate effort to carry one of the redoubts, but was badly cut to pieces by the artillery and infantry fire from the other, when he began to draw off, leaving his dead and wounded on the ground.

Before finally withdrawing, General French converged a heavy fire of his cannon on the block-house at Allatoona Creek, about two miles from the depot, set it on fire, and captured its garrison, consisting of four officers and eighty-five men. By 4 P. M. he was in full retreat south, on the Dallas road, and got by before the head of General Cox's column had reached it; still several ambulances and stragglers were picked up by this command on that road. General Corse reported two hundred and thirty-one rebel dead, four hundred and eleven prisoners, three regimental colors, and eight hundred muskets captured.

Among the prisoners was a Brigadier-General [William H.] Young, who thought that French's aggregate loss would reach two thousand. Colonel Tourtellotte says that, for days after General Corse had returned to Rome, his men found and buried at least a hundred more dead rebels, who had doubtless been wounded, and died in the woods near Allatoona. I know that when I reached Allatoona, on the 9th, I saw a good many dead men, which had been collected for burial.

Corse's entire loss, officially reported, was:

GARRISON	Killed	Wounded	Missing	Total
Officers	6	23	6	35
Men	136	330	206	672
Total	142	353	212	707

I esteemed this defense of Allatoona so handsome and important, that I made it the subject of a general order, viz., No. 86, of October 7, 1864:

> The general commanding avails himself of the opportunity, in the handsome defense made of Allatoona, to illustrate the most important principle in war, that fortified posts should be defended to the last, regardless of the relative numbers of the party attacking and attacked. . . . The thanks of this army are due and are hereby accorded to General Corse, Colonel Tourtellotte, Colonel Rowett, officers, and men, for their determined and gallant defense of Allatoona, and it is made an example to illustrate the importance of preparing in time, and meeting the danger, when present, boldly, manfully, and well.
>
> Commanders and garrisons of the posts along our railroad are hereby instructed that they must hold their posts to the last minute, sure that the time gained is valuable and necessary to their comrades at the front.
>
> By order of Major-General W. T. Sherman,
>
> L. M. DAYTON, *Aide-de-Camp.*

The rebels had struck our railroad a heavy blow, burning every tie, bending the rails for eight miles, from Big Shanty to above Acworth, so that the estimate for repairs called for thirty-five thousand new ties, and six miles of iron. Ten thousand men were distributed along the break to replace the ties, and to prepare the road-bed, while the regular repair-party, under Colonel W. W. Wright, came down from Chattanooga with iron, spikes, etc., and in about seven days the road was all right again. It was by such acts of extraordinary energy that we discouraged our adversaries, for the rebel soldiers felt that it was a waste of labor for them to march hurriedly, on wide circuits, day and night, to burn a bridge and tear up a mile or so of track, when they knew that we could lay it back so quickly. They supposed that we had men and money without limit, and that we always kept on hand, distributed along the road, duplicates of every bridge and culvert of any importance.

A good story is told of one who was on Kenesaw Mountain during our advance in the previous June or July. A group of rebels lay in the shade of a tree, one hot day, overlooking our camps about Big Shanty. One soldier remarked to his fellows:

"Well, the Yanks will have to git up and git now, for I heard General Johnston himself say that General Wheeler had blown up *the tunnel* near Dalton, and that the Yanks would have to retreat, because they could get no more rations."

"Oh, hell!" said a listener, "don't you know that old Sherman carries a *duplicate* tunnel along?"

After the war was over, General Johnston inquired of me who was our chief railroad-engineer. When I told him that it was Colonel W. W. Wright, a civilian, he was much surprised, said that our feats of bridge-building and repairs of roads had excited his admiration; and he instanced the occasion at Kenesaw in June, when an officer from Wheeler's cavalry had reported to him in person that he had come from General Wheeler, who had made a bad break in our road about Tilton Station, which he said would take at least a fortnight to repair; and, while they were talking, a train was seen coming down the road, which had passed that very break, and had reached me at Big Shanty as soon as the fleet horseman had reached him (General Johnston) at Marietta!

I doubt whether the history of war can furnish more examples of skill and bravery than attended the defense of the railroad from Nashville to Atlanta during the year 1864.

In person I reached Allatoona on the 9th of October, still in doubt as to Hood's immediate intentions. Our cavalry could do little against his infantry in the rough and wooded country about Dallas, which masked the enemy's movements; but General Corse, at Rome, with Spencer's First Alabama Cavalry and a mounted regiment of Illinois Infantry, could feel the country south of Rome about Cedartown and Villa Rica; and reported the enemy to be in force at both places. On the 9th I telegraphed to General Thomas, at Nashville, as follows:

I came up here to relieve our road. The Twentieth Corps remains at Atlanta. Hood reached the road and broke it up between Big Shanty and Acworth. He attacked Allatoona, but was repulsed. We have plenty of bread and meat, but forage is scarce. I want to destroy all the road below Chattanooga, including Atlanta, and to make for the sea-coast. We cannot defend this long line of road.

And on the same day I telegraphed to General Grant, at City Point:

It will be a physical impossibility to protect the roads, now that Hood, Forrest, Wheeler, and the whole batch of devils, are turned loose without home or habitation. I think Hood's movements indicate a diversion to the end of the Selma & Talladega road, at Blue Mountain, about sixty miles south-west of Rome, from which he will threaten Kingston, Bridge-port, and Decatur, Alabama. I propose that we break up the railroad from Chattanooga forward, and that we strike out with our wagons for Milledgeville, Millen, and Savannah. Until we can repopulate Georgia, it is useless for us to occupy it; but the utter destruction of its roads, houses, and people, will cripple their military resources. By attempting to hold the roads, we will lose a thousand men each month, and will gain no result. I can make this march, and make Georgia howl! We have on hand over eight thousand head of cattle and three million rations of bread, but no corn. We can find plenty of forage in the interior of the State.

Meantime the rebel General Forrest had made a bold cir-cuit in Middle Tennessee, avoiding all fortified points, and breaking up the railroad at several places; but, as usual, he did his work so hastily and carelessly that our engineers soon repaired the damage—then, retreating before General Rous-seau, he left the State of Tennessee, crossing the river near Florence, Alabama, and got off unharmed.

On the 10th of October the enemy appeared south of the Etowah River at Rome, when I ordered all the armies to march to Kingston, rode myself to Cartersville with the Twenty-third Corps (General Cox), and telegraphed from there to General Thomas at Nashville:

It looks to me as though Hood was bound for Tuscumbia. He is now crossing the Coosa River below Rome, looking west. Let me know if you can hold him with your forces now in Tennessee and the expected reenforcements, as, in that event, you know what I propose to do.

I will be at Kingston to-morrow. I think Rome is strong enough to resist any attack, and the rivers are all high. If he turns up by Summerville, I will get in behind him.

And on the same day to General Grant, at City Point:

Hood is now crossing the Coosa, twelve miles below Rome, bound west. If he passes over to the Mobile & Ohio Railroad, had I not better execute the plan of my letter sent you by Colonel Porter, and leave General Thomas, with the troops now in Tennessee, to defend the State? He will have an ample force when the reënforcements ordered reach Nashville.

I found General John E. Smith at Cartersville, and on the 11th rode on to Kingston, where I had telegraphic communications in all directions.

From General Corse, at Rome, I learned that Hood's army had disappeared, but in what direction he was still in doubt; and I was so strongly convinced of the wisdom of my proposition to change the whole tactics of the campaign, to leave Hood to General Thomas, and to march across Georgia for Savannah or Charleston, that I again telegraphed to General Grant:

We cannot now remain on the defensive. With twenty-five thousand infantry and the bold cavalry he has, Hood can constantly break my road. I would infinitely prefer to make a wreck of the road and of the country from Chattanooga to Atlanta, including the latter city; send back all my wounded and unserviceable men, and with my effective army move through Georgia, smashing things to the sea. Hood may turn into Tennessee and Kentucky, but I believe he will be forced to follow me. Instead of being on the defensive, I will be on the offensive. Instead of my guessing at what he means to do, he will have to guess at my plans. The difference in war would be fully twenty-five per cent. I can make Savannah, Charleston, or the mouth of the Chattahoochee (Appalachicola). Answer quick, as I know we will not have the telegraph long.

I received no answer to this at the time, and the next day went on to Rome, where the news came that Hood had made his appearance at Resaca, and had demanded the surrender of the place, which was commanded by Colonel [John B.] Weaver, reënforced by Brevet Brigadier-General [Green B.] Raum. General Hood had evidently marched with rapidity up the Chattooga Valley, by Summerville, Lafayette, Ship's Gap, and Snake-Creek Gap, and had with him his whole army, except a small force left behind to watch Rome. I ordered Resaca to be further reënforced by rail from Kingston, and ordered General Corse to make a bold reconnoissance down the Coosa Valley, which captured and brought into Rome some cavalry men and a couple of field-guns, with their horses and men. At first I thought of interposing my whole army in the Chattooga Valley, so as to prevent Hood's escape south; but I saw at a glance that he did not mean to fight, and in that event, after damaging the road all he could, he would be likely to retreat eastward by Spring Place, which I did not want him to do; and, hearing from General Raum that he still held Resaca safe, and that General Edward McCook had also got there with some cavalry reënforcements, I turned all the heads of columns for Resaca, viz., General Cox's, from Rome; General Stanley's, from McGuire's; and General Howard's, from Kingston. We all reached Resaca during that night, and the next morning (13th) learned that Hood's whole army had passed up the valley toward Dalton, burning the railroad and doing all the damage possible.

On the 12th he had demanded the surrender of Resaca in the following letter:

HEADQUARTERS ARMY OF TENNESSEE,
IN THE FIELD, *October* 12, 1864.

To the Officer commanding the United States Forces at Resaca, Georgia

SIR: I demand the immediate and unconditional surrender of the post and garrison under your command, and, should this be acceded to, all white officers and soldiers will be parolled in a few days. If the place is carried by assault, no prisoners will be taken.

Most respectfully, your obedient servant,

J. B. HOOD, *General.*

To this Colonel Weaver, then in command, replied:

> HEADQUARTERS SECOND BRIGADE, THIRD DIVISION, FIFTEENTH CORPS, RESACA, GEORGIA, *October* 12, 1864.

To General J. B. HOOD:

> Your communication of this date just received. In reply, I have to state that I am somewhat surprised at the concluding paragraph, to the effect that, if the place is carried by assault, no prisoners will be taken. In my opinion I can hold this post. If you want it, come and take it.
>
> I am, general, very respectfully, your most obedient servant,
>
> > CLARK R. WEAVER, *Commanding Officer.*

This brigade was very small, and as Hood's investment extended only from the Oostenaula, below the town, to the Connesauga above, he left open the approach from the south, which enabled General Raum and the cavalry of General Edward McCook to reënforce from Kingston. In fact, Hood, admonished by his losses at Allatoona, did not attempt an assault at all, but limited his attack to the above threat, and to some skirmishing, giving his attention chiefly to the destruction of the railroad, which he accomplished all the way up to Tunnel Hill, nearly twenty miles, capturing *en route* the regiment of black troops at Dalton (Johnson's Forty-fourth United States colored). On the 14th, I turned General Howard through Snake-Creek Gap, and sent General Stanley around by Tilton, with orders to cross the mountain to the west, so as to capture, if possible, the force left by the enemy in Snake-Creek Gap. We found this gap very badly obstructed by fallen timber, but got through that night, and the next day the main army was at Villanow. On the morning of the 16th, the leading division of General Howard's column, commanded by General Charles R. Woods, carried Ship's Gap, taking prisoners part of the Twenty-fourth South Carolina Regiment, which had been left there to hold us in check.

The best information there obtained located Hood's army at Lafayette, near which place I hoped to catch him and force him to battle; but, by the time we had got enough troops across the mountain at Ship's Gap, Hood had escaped down the valley of the Chattooga, and all we could do was to follow him as closely as possible. From Ship's Gap I dispatched couriers to Chattanooga, and received word back that General Schofield was there, endeavoring to coöperate with me, but Hood had broken up the telegraph, and thus had prevented quick communication. General Schofield did not reach me till the army had got down to Gaylesville, about the 21st of October.

It was at Ship's Gap that a courier brought me the cipher message from General Halleck which intimated that the authorities in Washington were willing I should undertake the march across Georgia to the sea. The translated dispatch named "Horse-i-bar Sound" as the point where the fleet would await my arrival. After much time I construed it to mean, "Ossabaw Sound," below Savannah, which was correct.

On the 16th I telegraphed to General Thomas, at Nashville:

Send me [George W.] Morgan's and Newton's old divisions. Reëstablish the road, and I will follow Hood wherever he may go. I think he will move to Blue Mountain. We can maintain our men and animals on the country.

General Thomas's reply was:

NASHVILLE, *October* 17, 1864—10.30 A. M.

Major-General SHERMAN:

Your dispatch from Ship's Gap, 5 P. M. of the 16th, just received. Schofield, whom I placed in command of the two divisions ([George D.] Wagner's and Morgan's), was to move up Lookout Valley this A. M., to intercept Hood, should he be marching for Bridgeport. I will order him to join you with the two divisions, and will reconstruct the road as soon as possible. Will also reorganize the guards for posts and block-houses. . . . Mower and Wilson have arrived, and are on their way to join you. I hope you will adopt Grant's idea of turning Wilson loose, rather than undertake the plan of a march with the whole force through Georgia to the sea, inasmuch as General Grant cannot coöperate with you as at first arranged.

GEORGE H. THOMAS, *Major-General.*

So it is clear that at that date neither General Grant nor General Thomas heartily favored my proposed plan of campaign. On the same day, I wrote to General Schofield at Chattanooga:

> Hood is not at Dear Head Cove. We occupy Ship's Gap and Lafayette. Hood is moving south *via* Summerville, Alpine, and Gadsden. If he enters Tennessee, it will be to the west of Huntsville, but I think he has given up all such idea. I want the road repaired to Atlanta; the sick and wounded men sent north of the Tennessee; my army recomposed; and I will then make the interior of Georgia feel the weight of war. It is folly for us to be moving our armies on the reports of scouts and citizens. We must maintain the offensive. Your first move on Trenton and Valley Head was right—the move to defend Caperton's Ferry is wrong. Notify General Thomas of these my views. We must follow Hood till he is beyond the reach of mischief, and then resume the offensive.

The correspondence between me and the authorities at Washington, as well as with the several army commanders, given at length in the report of the Committee on the Conduct of the War, is full on all these points.

After striking our road at Dalton, Hood was compelled to go on to Chattanooga and Bridgeport, or to pass around by Decatur and abandon altogether his attempt to make us let go our hold of Atlanta by attacking our communications. It was clear to me that he had no intention to meet us in open battle, and the lightness and celerity of his army convinced me that I could not possibly catch him on a stern-chase. We therefore quietly followed him down the Chattooga Valley to the neighborhood of Gadsden, but halted the main armies near the Coosa River, at the mouth of the Chattooga, drawing our supplies of corn and meat from the farms of that comparatively rich valley and of the neighborhood.

General Slocum, in Atlanta, had likewise sent out, under strong escort, large trains of wagons to the east, and brought back corn, bacon, and all kinds of provisions, so that Hood's efforts to cut off our supplies only reacted on his own people. So long as the railroads were in good order, our supplies came full and regular from the North; but when the enemy broke our railroads we were perfectly justified in stripping the inhabitants of all they had. I remember well the appeal of a very respectable farmer against our men driving away his fine flock of sheep. I explained to him that General Hood had broken our railroad; that we were a strong, hungry crowd, and needed plenty of food; that Uncle Sam was deeply interested in our continued health and would soon repair these roads, but meantime we must eat; we preferred Illinois beef, but mutton would have to answer. Poor fellow! I don't believe he was convinced of the wisdom or wit of my explanation. Very soon after reaching Lafayette we organized a line of supply from Chattanooga to Ringgold by rail, and thence by wagons to our camps about Gaylesville. Meantime, also, Hood had reached the neighborhood of Gadsden, and drew his supplies from the railroad at Blue Mountain.

On the 19th of October I telegraphed to General Halleck, at Washington:

Hood has retreated rapidly by all the roads leading south. Our advance columns are now at Alpine and Melville Post-Office. I shall pursue him as far as Gaylesville. The enemy will not venture toward Tennessee except around by Decatur. I propose to send the Fourth Corps back to General Thomas, and leave him, with that corps, the garrisons, and new troops, to defend the line of the Tennessee River; and with the rest I will push into the heart of Georgia and come out at Savannah, destroying all the railroads of the State. The break in our railroad at Big Shanty is almost repaired, and that about Dalton should be done in ten days. We find abundance of forage in the country.

On the same day I telegraphed to General L[angdon] C. Easton, chief-quartermaster, who had been absent on a visit to Missouri, but had got back to Chattanooga:

Go in person to superintend the repairs of the railroad, and make all orders in my name that will expedite its completion. I want it finished, to bring back from Atlanta to Chattanooga the sick and wounded men and surplus stores. On the 1st of November I want nothing in front of Chattanooga except what we can use as food and clothing and haul in our wagons. There is plenty of corn in the country, and we only want forage for the posts. I allow ten days for all this to be done, by which time I expect to be at or near Atlanta.

I telegraphed also to General Amos Beckwith, chief-commissary in Atlanta, who was acting as chief-quartermaster during the absence of General Easton:

> Hood will escape me. I want to prepare for my big raid. On the 1st of November I want nothing in Atlanta but what is necessary for war. Send all trash to the rear at once, and have on hand thirty days' food and but little forage. I propose to abandon Atlanta, and the railroad back to Chattanooga, to sally forth to ruin Georgia and bring up on the seashore. Make all dispositions accordingly. I will do down the Coosa until I am sure that Hood has gone to Blue Mountain.

On the 21st of October I reached Gaylesville, had my bivouac in an open field back of the village, and remained there till the 28th. During that time General Schofield arrived, with the two divisions of Generals Wagner (formerly Newton's) and Morgan, which were returned to their respective corps (the Fourth and Fourteenth), and General Schofield resumed his own command of the Army of the Ohio, then on the Coosa River, near Cedar Bluff. General Joseph A. Mower also arrived, and was assigned to command a division in the Seventeenth Corps; and General J. H. Wilson came, having been sent from Virginia by General Grant, for the purpose of commanding all my cavalry. I first intended to organize this cavalry into a corps of three small divisions, to be commanded by General Wilson; but the horses were well run down, and, at Wilson's instance, I concluded to retain only one division of four thousand five hundred men, with selected horses, under General Kilpatrick, and to send General Wilson back with all the rest to Nashville, to be reorganized and to act under General Thomas in the defense of Tennessee. Orders to this effect were made on the 24th of October.

General Grant, in designating General Wilson to command my cavalry, predicted that he would, by his personal activity, increase the effect of that arm "fifty per cent," and he advised that he should be sent south, to accomplish all that I had proposed to do with the main army; but I had not so much faith in cavalry as he had, and preferred to adhere to my original intention of going myself with a competent force.

About this time I learned that General Beauregard had

reached Hood's army at Gadsden; that, without assuming direct command of that army, he had authority from the Confederate Government to direct all its movements, and to call to his assistance the whole strength of the South. His orders, on assuming command, were full of alarm and desperation, dated—

HEADQUARTERS MILITARY DIVISION OF THE WEST,
October 17, 1864.

In assuming command, at this critical juncture, of the Military Division of the West, I appeal to my countrymen, of all classes and sections, for their generous support. In assigning me to this responsible position, the President of the Confederate States has extended to me the assurance of his earnest support. The Executives of your States meet me with similar expressions of their devotion to our cause. The noble army in the field, composed of brave men and gallant officers, are strangers to me, but I know they will do all that patriots can achieve. . . .

The army of Sherman still defiantly holds Atlanta. He can and must be driven from it. It is only for the good people of Georgia and surrounding States to speak the word, and the work is done. We have abundant provisions. There are men enough in the country, liable to and able for service, to accomplish the result. . . .

My countrymen, respond to this call as you have done in days that are past, and, with the blessing of a kind and overruling Providence, the enemy shall be driven from your soil. The security of your wives and daughters from the insults and outrages of a brutal foe shall be established soon, and be followed by a permanent and honorable peace. The claims of home and country, wife and children, uniting with the demands of honor and patriotism, summon us to the field. We cannot, dare not, will not fail to respond. Full of hope and confidence, I come to join you in your struggles, sharing your privations, and, with your brave and true men, to strike the blow that shall bring success to our arms, triumph to our cause, and peace to our country!

G. T. BEAUREGARD, *General.*

Notwithstanding this somewhat boastful order or appeal, General Beauregard did not actually accompany General

Hood on his disastrous march to Nashville, but took post at Corinth, Mississippi, to control the movement of his supplies and to watch me.

At Gaylesville the pursuit of Hood by the army under my immediate command may be said to have ceased. During this pursuit, the Fifteenth Corps was commanded by its senior major-general present, P. J. Osterhaus, in the absence of General John A. Logan; and the Seventeenth Corps was commanded by Brigadier-General T. E. G. Ransom, the senior officer present, in the absence of General Frank P. Blair.

General Ransom was a young, most gallant, and promising officer, son of the Colonel Ransom who was killed at Chapultepec, in the Mexican War. He had served with the Army of the Tennessee in 1862 and 1863, at Vicksburg, where he was severely wounded. He was not well at the time we started from Atlanta, but he insisted on going along with his command. His symptoms became more aggravated on the march, and when we were encamped near Gaylesville, I visited him in company with Surgeon John Moore, United States Army, who said that the case was one of typhoid fever, which would likely prove fatal. A few days after, viz., the 28th, he was being carried on a litter toward Rome; and as I rode from Gaylesville to Rome, I passed him by the way, stopped, and spoke with him, but did not then suppose he was so near his end. The next day, however, his escort reached Rome, bearing his dead body. The officer in charge reported that, shortly after I had passed, his symptoms became so much worse that they stopped at a farmhouse by the road-side, where he died that evening.

On the 26th of October I learned that Hood's whole army had made its appearance about Decatur, Alabama, and at once caused a strong reconnoissance to be made down the Coosa to near Gadsden, which revealed the truth that the enemy was gone, except a small force of cavalry, commanded by General Wheeler, which had been left to watch us. I then finally resolved on my future course, which was to leave Hood to be encountered by General Thomas, while I should carry into full effect the long-contemplated project of marching for the sea-coast, and thence to operate toward Richmond. But it was all-important to me and to our cause that General Thomas should have an ample force, equal to any and every emergency.

He then had at Nashville about eight or ten thousand new troops, and as many more civil employés of the Quartermaster's Department, which were not suited for the field, but would be most useful in manning the excellent forts that already covered Nashville. At Chattanooga, he had General Steedman's division, about five thousand men, besides garrisons for Chattanooga, Bridgeport, and Stevenson; at Murfreesboro' he also had General Rousseau's division, which was full five thousand strong, independent of the necessary garrisons for the railroad. At Decatur and Huntsville, Alabama, was the infantry division of General R. S. Granger, estimated at four thousand; and near Florence, Alabama, watching the crossings of the Tennessee, were General Edward Hatch's division of cavalry, four thousand; General [John T.] Croxton's brigade, twenty-five hundred; and Colonel Capron's brigade, twelve hundred; besides which, General J. H. Wilson had collected in Nashville about ten thousand dismounted cavalry, for which he was rapidly collecting the necessary horses for a remount. All these aggregated about forty-five thousand men. General A. J. Smith at that time was in Missouri, with the two divisions of the Sixteenth Corps which had been diverted to that quarter to assist General Rosecrans in driving the rebel General Price out of Missouri. This object had been accomplished, and these troops, numbering from eight to ten thousand, had been ordered to Nashville. To these I proposed at first to add only the Fourth Corps (General Stanley), fifteen thousand; and that corps was ordered from Gaylesville to march to Chattanooga, and thence report for orders to General Thomas; but subsequently, on the 30th of October, at Rome, Georgia, learning from General Thomas that the new troops promised by General Grant were coming forward very slowly, I concluded to further reënforce him by General Schofield's corps (Twenty-third), twelve thousand, which corps accordingly marched for Resaca, and there took the cars for Chattanooga. I then knew that General Thomas would have an ample force with which to encounter General Hood anywhere in the open field, besides garrisons to secure the railroad to his rear and as far forward as Chattanooga. And, moreover, I was more than convinced that he would have ample time for preparation; for, on that very day, General R. S. Granger had telegraphed me from Decatur, Alabama:

I omitted to mention another reason why Hood will go to

Tuscumbia before crossing the Tennessee River. He was evidently out of supplies. His men were all grumbling; the first thing the prisoners asked for was something to eat. Hood could not get any thing if he should cross this side of Rogersville.

I knew that the country about Decatur and Tuscumbia, Alabama, was bare of provisions, and inferred that General Hood would have to draw his supplies, not only of food, but of stores, clothing, and ammunition, from Mobile, Montgomery, and Selma, Alabama, by the railroad around by Meridian and Corinth, Mississippi, which we had most effectually disabled the previous winter.

General Hood did not make a serious attack on Decatur, but hung around it from October 26th to the 30th, when he drew off and marched for a point on the south side of the Tennessee River, opposite Florence, where he was compelled to remain nearly a month, to collect the necessary supplies for his contemplated invasion of Tennessee and Kentucky.

The Fourth Corps (Stanley) had already reached Chattanooga, and had been transported by rail to Pulaski, Tennessee; and General Thomas ordered General Schofield, with the Twenty-third Corps, to Columbia, Tennessee, a place intermediate between Hood (then on the Tennessee River, opposite Florence) and Forrest, opposite Johnsonville.

On the 31st of October General Croxton, of the cavalry, reported that the enemy had crossed the Tennessee River four miles above Florence, and that he had endeavored to stop him, but without success. Still, I was convinced that Hood's army was in no condition to march for Nashville, and that a good deal of further delay might reasonably be counted on. I also rested with much confidence on the fact that the Tennessee River below Muscle Shoals was strongly patrolled by gunboats, and that the reach of the river above Muscle Shoals, from Decatur as high up as our railroad at Bridgeport, was also guarded by gunboats, so that Hood, to cross over, would be compelled to select a point inaccessible to these gunboats. He actually did choose such a place, at the old railroad-piers, four miles above Florence, Alabama, which is below Muscle Shoals and above Colbert Shoals.

On the 31st of October Forrest made his appearance on the Tennessee River opposite Johnsonville (whence a new railroad led to Nashville), and with his cavalry and field-pieces actually crippled and captured two gunboats with five of our transports, a feat of arms which, I confess, excited my admiration.

There is no doubt that the month of October closed to us looking decidedly squally; but, somehow, I was sustained in the belief that in a very few days the tide would turn.

On the 1st of November I telegraphed very fully to General Grant, at City Point, who must have been disturbed by the wild rumors that filled the country, and on the 2d of November received (at Rome) this dispatch:

CITY POINT, *November* 1, 1864—6 P. M.

Major-General SHERMAN:

Do you not think it advisable, now that Hood has gone so far north, to entirely ruin him before starting on your proposed campaign? With Hood's army destroyed, you can go where you please with impunity. I believed and still believe, if you had started south while Hood was in the neighborhood of you, he would have been forced to go after you. Now that he is far away he might look upon the chase as useless, and he will go in one direction while you are pushing in the other. If you can see a chance of destroying Hood's army, attend to that first, and make your other move secondary.

U. S. GRANT, *Lieutenant-General.*

My answer is dated—

ROME, GEORGIA, *November* 2, 1864.

Lieutenant-General U. S. GRANT, *City Point, Virginia:*

Your dispatch is received. If I could hope to overhaul Hood, I would turn against him with my whole force; then he would retreat to the south-west, drawing me as a decoy away from Georgia, which is his chief object. If he ventures north of the Tennessee River, I may turn in that direction, and endeavor to get below him on his line of retreat; but thus far he has not gone above the Tennessee River. General Thomas will have a force strong enough to prevent his reaching any country in which we have an interest; and he has orders, if Hood turns to follow me, to push for Selma, Alabama. No single army can catch Hood, and I am convinced the best results will follow from our defeating Jeff. Davis's cherished plan of making me leave Georgia by manœuvring. Thus far I have confined my efforts to thwart this plan, and have reduced baggage so that I can pick up and start in any direction; but I regard the pursuit of Hood as useless. Still, if he attempts to invade Middle Tennessee, I will hold Decatur, and be prepared to move in that direction; but, unless I let go of Atlanta, my force will not be equal to his.

W. T. SHERMAN, Major-General.

By this date, under the intelligent and energetic action of Colonel W. W. Wright, and with the labor of fifteen hundred men, the railroad break of fifteen miles about Dalton was repaired so far as to admit of the passage of cars, and I transferred my headquarters to Kingston as more central; and from that place, on the same day (November 2d), again telegraphed to General Grant.

KINGSTON, GEORGIA, November 2, 1864.

Lieutenant-General U. S. GRANT, City Point, Virginia:

If I turn back, the whole effect of my campaign will be lost. By my movements I have thrown Beauregard (Hood) well to the west, and Thomas will have ample time and sufficient troops to hold him until the reënforcements from Missouri reach him. We have now ample supplies at Chattannooga and Atlanta, and can stand a month's interruption to our communications. I do not believe the Confederate army can reach our railroad-lines except by cavalry-raids, and Wilson will have cavalry enough to checkmate them. I am clearly of opinion that the best results will follow my contemplated movement through Georgia.

W. T. SHERMAN, Major-General.

That same day I received, in answer to the Rome dispatch, the following:

CITY POINT, VIRGINIA, November 2, 1864—11:30 A. M.

Major-General SHERMAN:

Your dispatch of 9 A. M. yesterday is just received. I dispatched you the same date, advising that Hood's army, now that it had worked so far north, ought to be looked upon now as the "object." With the force, however, that you have left with General Thomas, he must be able to take care of Hood and destroy him.

I do not see that you can withdraw from where you are to follow Hood, without giving up all we have gained in territory. I say, then, go on as you propose.

U. S. GRANT, *Lieutenant-General*

This was the first time that General Grant assented to the "march to the sea," and, although many of his warm friends and admirers insist that he was the author and projector of that march, and that I simply executed his plans, General Grant has never, in my opinion, thought so or said so. The truth is fully given in an original letter of President Lincoln, which I received at Savannah, Georgia, and have at this instant before me, every word of which is in his own familiar handwriting. It is dated—

WASHINGTON, *December* 26, 1864.

When you were about leaving Atlanta for the Atlantic coast, I was anxious, if not fearful; but, feeling that you were the better judge, and remembering "nothing risked, nothing gained," I did not interfere. Now, the undertaking being a success, the honor is all yours; for I believe none of us went further than to acquiesce; and, taking the work of General Thomas into account, as it should be taken, it is indeed a great success. Not only does it afford the obvious and immediate military advantages, but, in showing to the world that your army could be divided, putting the stronger part to an important new service, and yet leaving enough to vanquish the old opposing force of the whole, Hood's army, it brings those who sat in darkness to see a great light. But what next? I suppose it will be safer if I leave General Grant and yourself to decide.

A. LINCOLN.

Of course, this judgment, made after the event, was extremely flattering and was all I ever expected, a recognition of the truth and of its importance. I have often been asked, by well-meaning friends, when the thought of that march first entered my mind. I knew that an army which had penetrated Georgia as far as Atlanta could not turn back. It must go ahead, but when, how, and where, depended on many considerations. As soon as Hood had shifted across from

Lovejoy's to Palmetto, I saw the move in my "mind's eye"; and, after Jeff. Davis's speech at Palmetto, of September 26th, I was more positive in my conviction, but was in doubt as to the time and manner. When General Hood first struck our railroad above Marietta, we were not ready, and I was forced to watch his movements further, till he had "carromed" off to the west of Decatur. Then I was perfectly convinced, and had no longer a shadow of doubt. The only possible question was as to Thomas's strength and ability to meet Hood in the open field. I did not suppose that General Hood, though rash, would venture to attack fortified places like Allatoona, Resaca, Decatur, and Nashville; but he did so, and in so doing he played into our hands perfectly.

On the 2d of November I was at Kingston, Georgia, and my four corps—the Fifteenth, Seventeenth, Fourteenth, and Twentieth—with one division of cavalry, were strung from Rome to Atlanta. Our railroads and telegraph had been repaired, and I deliberately prepared for the march to Savannah, distant three hundred miles from Atlanta. All the sick and wounded men had been sent back by rail to Chattanooga; all our wagon-trains had been carefully overhauled and loaded, so as to be ready to start on an hour's notice, and there was no serious enemy in our front.

General Hood remained still at Florence, Alabama, occupying both banks of the Tennessee River, busy in collecting shoes and clothing for his men, and the necessary ammunition and stores with which to invade Tennessee, most of which had to come from Mobile, Selma, and Montgomery, Alabama, over railroads that were still broken. Beauregard was at Corinth, hastening forward these necessary preparations.

General Thomas was at Nashville, with Wilson's dismounted cavalry and a mass of new troops and quartermaster's employés amply sufficient to defend the place. The Fourth and Twenty-third Corps, under Generals Stanley and Schofield, were posted at Pulaski, Tennessee, and the cavalry of Hatch, Croxton, and Capron, were about Florence, watching Hood. Smith's (A. J.) two divisions of the Sixteenth Corps were still in Missouri, but were reported as ready to embark at Lexington for the Cumberland River and Nashville. Of course, General Thomas saw that on him would likely fall the real blow, and was naturally anxious. He still kept Granger's division at Decatur, Rousseau's at Murfreesboro', and Steedman's at Chattanooga, with strong railroad guards at all the essential points intermediate, confident that by means of this very railroad he could make his concentration sooner than Hood could possibly march up from Florence.

Meantime, General F. P. Blair had rejoined his corps (Seventeenth), and we were receiving at Kingston recruits and returned furlough-men, distributing them to their proper companies. Paymasters had come down to pay off our men before their departure to a new sphere of action, and commissioners were also on hand from the several States to take the vote of our men in the presidential election then agitating the country.

On the 6th of November, at Kingston, I wrote and telegraphed to General Grant, reviewing the whole situation, gave him my full plan of action, stated that I was ready to march as soon as the election was over, and appointed November 10th as the day for starting. On the 8th I received this dispatch.

CITY POINT, VIRGINIA, *November 7*, 1864—10.30 P. M.

Major-General SHERMAN:

Your dispatch of this evening received. I see no present reason for changing your plan. Should any arise, you will see it, or if I do I will inform you. I think every thing here is favorable now. Great good fortune attend you! I believe you will be eminently successful, and, at worst, can only make a march less fruitful of results than hoped for.

U. S. GRANT, *Lieutenant-General.*

Meantime trains of cars were whirling by, carrying to the rear an immense amount of stores which had accumulated at Atlanta, and at the other stations along the railroad; and General Steedman had come down to Kingston, to take charge of the final evacuation and withdrawal of the several garrisons below Chattanooga.

On the 10th of November the movement may be said to have fairly begun. All the troops designed for the campaign were ordered to march for Atlanta, and General Corse, before evacuating his post at Rome, was ordered to burn all the mills, factories, etc., etc., that could be useful to the enemy, should he undertake to pursue us, or resume military possession of the country. This was done on the night of the 10th, and next day Corse reached Kingston. On the 11th General Thomas and I interchanged full dispatches. He had heard of the arrival of General A. J. Smith's two divisions at Paducah, which would surely reach Nashville much sooner than General Hood could possibly do from Florence, so that he was perfectly satisfied with his share of the army.

On the 12th, with a full staff, I started from Kingston for Atlanta; and about noon of that day we reached Cartersville, and sat on the edge of a porch to rest, when the telegraph operator, Mr. Van Valkenburg, or Eddy, got the wire down from the poles to his lap, in which he held a small pocket instrument. Calling "Chattanooga," he received this message from General Thomas, dated—

NASHVILLE, *November* 12, 1864—8.30 A. M.

Major-General SHERMAN:

Your dispatch of twelve o'clock last night is received. I have no fears that Beauregard can do us any harm now, and, if he attempts to follow you, I will follow him as far as possible. If he does not follow you, I will then thoroughly organize my troops, and believe I shall have men enough to ruin him unless he gets out of the way very rapidly.

The country of Middle Alabama, I learn, is teeming with supplies this year, which will be greatly to our advantage. I have no additional news to report from the direction of Florence.

I am now convinced that the greater part of Beauregard's army is near Florence and Tuscumbia, and that you will have at least a clear road before you for several days, and that your success will fully equal your expectations.

GEORGE H. THOMAS, *Major-General.*

I answered simply: "Dispatch received—all right." About that instant of time, some of our men burnt a bridge, which severed the telegraph-wire, and all communication with the rear ceased thenceforth.

As we rode on toward Atlanta that night, I remember the railroad-trains going to the rear with a furious speed; the engineers and the few men about the trains waving us an affectionate adieu. It surely was a strange event—two hostile armies marching in opposite directions, each in the full belief that it was achieving a final and conclusive result in a great war; and I was strongly inspired with the feeling that the movement on our part was a direct attack upon the rebel army and the rebel capital at Richmond, though a full thousand miles of hostile country intervened, and that, for better or worse, it would end the war.

Chapter 14

March to the Sea:
"The Wild Adventure of a Crazy Fool"
November—December, 1864

ON THE 12TH OF November the railroad and telegraph communications with the rear were broken, and the army stood detached from all friends, dependent on its own resources and supplies. No time was to be lost; all the detachments were ordered to march rapidly for Atlanta, breaking up the railroad *en route,* and generally to so damage the country as to make it untenable to the enemy. By the 14th all the troops had arrived at or near Atlanta, and were, according to orders, grouped into two wings, the right and left, commanded respectively by Major-Generals O. O. Howard and H. W. Slocum, both comparatively young men, but educated and experienced officers, fully competent to their command.

The two general orders made for this march appear to me, even at this late day, so clear, emphatic, and well-digested, that no account of that historic event is perfect without them, and I give them entire, even at the seeming appearance of repetition; and, though they called for great sacrifice and labor on the part of the officers and men, I insist that these orders were obeyed as well as any similar orders ever were, by an army operating wholly in an enemy's country, and dispersed, as we necessarily were, during the subsequent period of nearly six months.

[Special Field Orders, No. 119.]

HEADQUARTERS MILITARY DIVISION OF THE MISSISSIPPI, }
IN THE FIELD, KINGSTON, GEORGIA, *November* 8, 1864. }

The general commanding deems it proper at this time to inform the officers and men of the Fourteenth, Fifteenth, Seventeenth, and Twentieth Corps, that he has organized them into an army for a special purpose, well known to the War Department and to General Grant. It is sufficient for you to know that it involves a departure from our present base, and a long and difficult march to a new one. All the chances of war have been considered and provided for, as far as human sagacity can. All he asks of you is to maintain that discipline, patience, and courage, which have characterized you in the past; and he hopes, through you, to strike a blow at our enemy that will have a material effect in producing what we all so much desire, his complete overthrow. Of all things, the most important is, that the men, during marches and in camp, keep their places and do not scatter about as stragglers or foragers, to be picked up by a hostile people in detail. It is also of utmost importance that our wagons should not be loaded with any thing but provisions and ammunition. All surplus servants, noncombatants, and refugees, should now go to the rear, and none should be encouraged to encumber us on the march. At some future time we will be able to provide for the poor whites and blacks who seek to escape the bondage under which they are now suffering. With these few simple cautions, he hopes to lead you to achievements equal in importance to those of the past.

By order of Major-General W. T. Sherman,

L. M. DAYTON, *Aide-de-Camp.*

[Special Field Orders, No. 120.]

HEADQUARTERS MILITARY DIVISION OF THE MISSISSIPPI, }
IN THE FIELD, KINGSTON, GEORGIA, *November* 9, 1864. }

1. For the purpose of military operations, this army is divided into two wings viz.:

The right wing, Major-General O. O. Howard commanding, composed of the Fifteenth and Seventeenth Corps; the left wing, Major-General H. W. Slocum commanding, composed of the Fourteenth and Twentieth Corps.

2. The habitual order of march will be, wherever practicable, by four roads, as nearly parallel as possible, and converging at points hereafter to be indicated in orders. The cavalry, Brigadier-General Kilpatrick commanding, will receive special orders from the commander-in-chief.

3. There will be no general train of supplies, but each corps will have its ammunition-train and provision-train distributed habitually as follows: Behind each regiment should follow one wagon and one ambulance; behind each brigade should follow a due proportion of ammunition-wagons, provision-wagons, and ambulances. In case of danger, each corps commander should change this order of march, by having his advance and rear brigades unencumbered by wheels. The separate columns will start habitually at 7 A. M., and make about fifteen miles per day, unless otherwise fixed in orders.

4. The army will forage liberally on the country during the march. To this end, each brigade commander will organize a good and sufficient foraging party, under the command of one or more discreet officers, who will gather, near the route traveled, corn or forage of any kind, meat of any kind, vegetables, corn-meal, or whatever is needed by the command, aiming at all times to keep in the wagons at least ten days' provisions for his command, and three days' forage. Soldiers must not enter the dwellings of the inhabitants, or commit any trespass; but, during a halt or camp, they may be permitted to gather turnips, potatoes, and other vegetables, and to drive in stock in sight of their camp. To regular foraging-parties must be instrusted the gathering of provisions and forage, at any distance from the road traveled.

5. To corps commanders alone is intrusted the power to destroy mills, houses, cotton-gins, etc.; and for them this general principle is laid down: In districts and neighborhoods where the army is unmolested, no destruction of such property should be permitted; but should guerrillas or

bushwackers molest our march, or should the inhabitants burn bridges, obstruct roads, or otherwise manifest local hostility, then army commanders should order and enforce a devastation more or less relentless, according to the measure of such hostility.

6. As for horses, mules, wagons, etc., belonging to the inhabitants, the cavalry and artillery may appropriate freely and without limit; discriminating, however, between the rich, who are usually hostile, and the poor and industrious, usually neutral or friendly. Foraging-parties may also take mules or horses, to replace the jaded animals of their trains, or to serve as pack-mules for the regiments or brigades. In all foraging, of whatever kind, the parties engaged will refrain from abusive or threatening language, and may, where the officer in command thinks proper, give written certificates of the facts, but no receipts; and they will endeavor to leave with each family a reasonable portion for their maintenance.

7. Negroes who are able-bodied and can be of service to the several columns may be taken along; but each army commander will bear in mind that the question of supplies is a very important one, and that his first duty is to see to those who bear arms.

8. The organization, at once, of a good pioneer battalion for each army corps, composed if possible of Negroes, should be attended to. This battalion should follow the advance-guard, repair roads and double them if possible, so that the columns will not be delayed after reaching bad places. Also, army commanders should practise the habit of giving the artillery and wagons the road, marching their troops on one side, and instruct their troops to assist wagons at steep hills or bad crossings of streams.

9. Captain O. M. Poe, chief-engineer, will assign to each wing of the army a pontoon-train, fully equipped and organized; and the commanders thereof will see to their being properly protected at all times.

By order of Major-General W. T. Sherman,

L. M. DAYTON, *Aide-de-Camp.*

The greatest possible attention had been given to the artillery and wagon trains. The number of guns had been reduced to sixty-five, or about one gun to each thousand men, and these were generally in batteries of four guns each.

Each gun, caisson, and forge, was drawn by four teams of horses. We had in all about twenty-five hundred wagons, with teams of six mules to each, and six hundred ambulances, with two horses to each. The loads were made comparatively light, about twenty-five hundred pounds net; each wagon carrying in addition the forage need by its own team. Each soldier carried on his person forty rounds of ammunition, and in the wagons were enough cartridges to make up about two hundred rounds per man, and in like manner two hundred rounds of assorted ammunition were carried for each gun.

The wagon-trains were divided equally between the four corps, so that each had about eight hundred wagons, and these usually on the march occupied five miles or more of road. Each corps commander managed his own train; and habitually the artillery and wagons had the road, while the men, with the exception of the advance and rear guards, pursued paths improvised by the side of the wagons, unless they were forced to use a bridge or causeway in common.

I reached Atlanta during the afternoon of the 14th, and found that all preparations had been made—Colonel Beckwith, chief commissary, reporting one million two hundred thousand rations in possession of the troops, which was about twenty days' supply, and he had on hand a good supply of beef-cattle to be driven along on the hoof. Of forage, the supply was limited, being of oats and corn enough for five days, but I knew that within that time we would reach a country well stocked with corn, which had been gathered and stored in cribs, seemingly for our use, by Governor Brown's militia.

Colonel Poe, United States Engineers, of my staff, had been busy in his special task of destruction. He had a large force at work, had leveled the great depot, round-house, and the machine-shops of the Georgia Railroad, and had applied fire to the wreck. One of these machine-shops had been used by the rebels as an arsenal, and in it were stored piles of shot and shell, some of which proved to be loaded, and that night was made hideous by the bursting of shells, whose fragments came uncomfortably near Judge Lyon's house, in which I was quartered. The fire also reached the block of stores near the depot, and the heart of the city was in flames all night, but the fire did not reach the parts of Atlanta where the court-house was, or the great mass of dwelling-houses.

The march from Atlanta began on the morning of November 15th, the right wing and cavalry following the railroad southeast toward Jonesboro', and General Slocum with the Twentieth Corps leading off to the east by Decatur and Stone Mountain, toward Madison. These were divergent lines, designed to threaten both Macon and Augusta at the same time, so as to prevent a concentration at our intended destination, or "objective," Milledgeville, the capital of Georgia, distant southeast about one hundred miles. The time allowed each column for reaching Milledgeville was seven days. I remained in Atlanta during the 15th with the Fourteenth Corps, and the rear-guard of the right wing, to complete the loading of the trains, and the destruction of the buildings of Atlanta which could be converted to hostile uses, and on the morning of the 16th started with my personal staff, a company of Alabama cavalry, commanded by Lieutenant Snelling, and an infantry company, commanded by Lieutenant McCrory, which guarded our small train of wagons.

My staff was then composed of Major L. M. Dayton, aide-de-camp and acting adjutant-general, Major J. C. McCoy, and Major J. C. Audenried, aides. Major Ward Nichols had joined some weeks before at Gaylesville, Alabama, and was attached as an acting aide-de-camp. Also Major Henry Hitchcock had joined at the same time as judge-advocate. Colonel Charles Ewing was inspector general, and Surgeon John Moore medical director. These constituted our mess. We had no tents, only the flies, with which we nightly made bivouacs with the assistance of the abundant pine-boughs, which made excellent shelter, as well as beds.

Colonel L. C. Easton was chief-quartermaster; Colonel Amos Beckwith, chief-commissary; Colonel O. M. Poe, chief-engineer; and Colonel T. G. Baylor, chief of ordnance. These invariably rode with us during the day, but they had a separate camp and mess at night.

General William F. Barry had been chief of artillery in the previous campaign, but at Kingston his face was so swollen with erysipelas that he was reluctantly compelled to leave us for the rear, and he could not, on recovering, rejoin us till we had reached Savannah.

About 7 A. M. of November 16th we rode out of Atlanta by the Decatur road, filled by the marching troops and wagons of the Fourteenth Corps; and reaching the hill, just outside of the old rebel works, we naturally paused to look back upon the scenes of our past battles. We stood upon the very ground whereon was fought the bloody battle of July 22d, and could see the copse of wood where McPherson fell. Behind us lay Atlanta, smouldering and in ruins, the black smoke rising high in air, and hanging like a pall over the ruined city. Away off in the distance, on the McDonough road, was the rear of Howard's column, the gun-barrels glistening in the sun, the white-topped wagons stretching away to the south; and right before us the Fourteenth Corps, marching steadily and rapidly, with a cheery look and swinging pace, that made light of the thousand miles that lay between us and Richmond. Some band, by accident, struck up the anthem of "John Brown's soul goes marching on"; the men caught up the strain, and never before or since have I heard the chorus of "Glory, glory, hallelujah!" done with more spirit, or in better harmony of time and place.

Then we turned our horses' heads to the east; Atlanta was soon lost behind the screen of trees, and became a thing of the past. Around it clings many a thought of desperate battle, of hope and fear, that now seem like the memory of a dream; and I have never seen the place since. The day was extremely beautiful, clear sunlight, with bracing air, and an unusual feeling of exhilaration seemed to pervade all minds—a feeling of something to come, vague and undefined, still full of venture and intense interest. Even the common soldiers caught the inspiration, and many a group called out to me as I worked my way past them, "Uncle Billy, I guess Grant is waiting for us at Richmond!" Indeed, the general sentiment was that we were marching for Richmond, and that there we should end the war, but how and when they seemed to care not; nor did they measure the distance, or count the cost in life, or bother their brains about the great rivers to be crossed, and the food required for man and beast, that had to be gathered by the way. There was a "devil-may-care" feeling pervading officers and men, that made me feel the full load of responsibility, for success would be accepted as a matter of course, whereas, should we fail, this "march" would be adjudged the wild adventure of a crazy fool. I had no purpose to march direct for Richmond by way of Augusta and Charlotte, but always designed to reach the sea-coast first at Savannah or Port Royal, South Carolina, and even kept in mind the alternative of Pensacola.

The first night out we camped by the road-side near

Lithonia. Stone Mountain, a mass of granite, was in plain view, cut out in clear outline against the blue sky; the whole horizon was lurid with the bonfires of rail-ties, and groups of men all night were carrying the heated rails to the nearest trees, and bending them around the trunks. Colonel Poe had provided tools for ripping up the rails and twisting them when hot; but the best and easiest way is the one I have described, of heating the middle of the iron-rails on bonfires made of the cross-ties, and then winding them around a telegraph-pole or the trunk of some convenient sapling. I attached much importance to this destruction of the railroad, gave it my own personal attention, and made reiterated orders to others on the subject.

The next day we passed through the handsome town of Covington, the soldiers closing up their ranks, the color-bearers unfurling their flags, and the bands striking up patriotic airs. The white people came out of their houses to behold the sight, spite of their deep hatred of the invaders, and the Negroes were simply frantic with joy. Whenever they heard my name, they clustered about my horse, shouted and prayed in their peculiar style, which had a natural eloquence that would have moved a stone. I have witnessed hundreds, if not thousands, of such scenes; and can now see a poor girl, in the very ecstasy of the Methodist "shout," hugging the banner of one of the regiments, and jumping up to the "feet of Jesus."

I remember, when riding around by a by-street in Covington, to avoid the crowd that followed the marching column, that some one brought me an invitation to dine with a sister of Sam. Anderson, who was a cadet at West Point with me; but the messenger reached me after we had passed the main part of the town. I asked to be excused, and rode on to a place designated for camp, at the crossing of the Ulcofauhachee River, about four miles to the east of the town. Here we made our bivouac, and I walked up to a plantation-house close by, where were assembled many Negroes, among them an old, gray-haired man, of as fine a head as I ever saw. I asked him if he understood about the war and its progress. He said he did; that he had been looking for the "angel of the Lord" ever since he was knee-high, and, though we professed to be fighting for the Union, he supposed that slavery was the cause, and that our success was to be his freedom. I asked him if all the Negro slaves comprehended this fact, and he said they surely did. I then explained to him that we wanted the slaves to remain where they were, and not to load us down with useless mouths, which would eat up the food needed for our fighting-men; that our success was their assured freedom; that we could receive a few of their young, hearty men as pioneers; but that, if they followed us in swarms of old and young, feeble and helpless, it would simply load us down and cripple us in our great task. I think Major Henry Hitchcock was with me on that occasion, and made a note of the conversation, and I believe that old man spread this message to the slaves, which was carried from mouth to mouth, to the very end of our journey, and that it in part saved us from the great danger we incurred of swelling our numbers so that famine would have attended our progress. It was at this very plantation that a soldier passed me with a ham on his musket, a jug of sorghum-molasses under his arm, and a big piece of honey in his-hand, from which he was eating, and, catching my eye, he remarked *sotto voce* and carelessly to a comrade, "Forage liberally on the country," quoting from my general orders. On this occasion, as on many others that fell under my personal observation, I reproved the man, explained that foraging must be limited to the regular parties properly detailed, and that all provisions thus obtained must be delivered to the regular commissaries, to be fairly distributed to the men who kept their ranks.

From Covington the Fourteenth Corps (Davis's), with which I was traveling, turned to the right for Milledgeville, *via* Shady Dale. General Slocum was ahead at Madison, with the Twentieth Corps, having torn up the railroad as far as that place, and thence had sent Geary's division on to the Oconee, to burn the bridges across that stream, when this corps turned south by Eatonton, for Milledgeville, the common "objective" for the first stage of the "march." We found abundance of corn, molasses, meal, bacon, and sweet-potatoes. We also took a good many cows and oxen, and a large number of mules. In all these the country was quite rich, never before having been visited by a hostile army; the recent crop had been excellent, had been just gathered and laid by for the winter. As a rule, we destroyed none, but kept our wagons full, and fed our teams bountifully.

The skill and success of the men in collecting forage was one of the features of this march. Each brigade commander had authority to detail a company of foragers, usually about fifty men, with one or two commissioned officers selected for their boldness and enterprise. This party would be dispatched before daylight with a knowledge of the intended day's march and camp; would proceed on foot five or six miles from the route traveled by their brigade, and then visit every plantation and farm within range. They would usually procure a wagon or family carriage, load it with bacon, corn-meal, turkeys, chickens, ducks, and every thing that could be used as food or forage, and would then regain the main road, usually in advance of their train. When this came up, they would deliver to the brigade commissary the supplies thus gathered by the way. Often would I pass these foraging-parties at the roadside, waiting for their wagons to come up, and was amused at their strange collections—mules, horses, even cattle, packed with old saddles and loaded with hams, bacon, bags of corn-meal, and poultry of every character and description. Although this foraging was attended with great danger and hard work, there seem to be a charm about it that attracted the soldiers, and it was a privilege to be detailed on such a party. Daily they returned mounted on all sorts of beasts, which were at once taken from them and appropriated to the general use; but the next day they would start out again on foot, only to repeat the experience of the day before. No doubt, many acts of pillage, robbery, and violence, were committed by these parties of foragers, usually called "bummers"; for I have since heard of jewelry taken from women, and the plunder of articles that never reached the commissary; but these acts were exceptional and incidental. I never heard of any cases of murder or rape;[1] and no army could have carried along sufficient food and forage for a march of three hundred miles; so that foraging in some shape was necessary. The country was sparsely settled, with no magistrates or civil authorities who could respond to requisitions, as is done in all the wars of Europe; so that this system of foraging was simply indispensable to our success.

[1] The Macon *Telegraph* for December 7, 1864 circulated the story of the widespread despoilation of Southern womanhood by Sherman's troops, but propaganda rather than truth was served by the *Telegraph's* report. Two cases of rape were known among Sherman's soldiers in 1864–65.

By it our men were well supplied with all the essentials of life and health, while the wagons retained enough in case of unexpected delay, and our animals were well fed. Indeed, when we reached Savannah, the trains were pronounced by experts to be the finest in flesh and appearance ever seen with any army.

Habitually each corps followed some main road, and the foragers, being kept out on the exposed flank, served all the military uses of flankers. The main columns gathered, by the roads traveled, much forage and food, chiefly meat, corn, and sweet-potatoes, and it was the duty of each division and brigade quartermaster to fill his wagons as fast as the contents were issued to the troops. The wagon-trains had the right to the road *always,* but each wagon was required to keep closed up, so as to leave no gaps in the column. If for any purpose any wagon or group of wagons dropped out of place, they had to wait for the rear. And this was always dreaded, for each brigade commander wanted his train up at camp as soon after reaching it with his men as possible.

I have seen much skill and industry displayed by these quartermasters on the march, in trying to load their wagons with corn and fodder by the way without losing their place in column. They would, while marching, shift the loads of wagons, so as to have six or ten of them empty. Then, riding well ahead, they would secure possession of certain stacks of fodder near the road, or cribs of corn, leave some men in charge, then open fences and a road back for a couple of miles, return to their trains, divert the empty wagons out of column, and conduct them rapidly to their forage, load up and regain their place in column without losing distance. On one occasion I remember to have seen ten or a dozen wagons thus loaded with corn from two or three full cribs, almost without halting. These cribs were built of logs, and roofed. The train-guard, by a lever, had raised the whole side of the crib a foot or two; the wagons drove close alongside, and the men in the cribs, lying on their backs, kicked out a wagon-load of corn in the time I have taken to describe it.

In a well-ordered and well-disciplined army, these things might be deemed irregular, but I am convinced that the ingenuity of these younger officers accomplished many things far better than I could have ordered, and the marches were thus made, and the distances were accomplished, in the most admirable way. Habitually we started from camp at the earliest break of dawn, and usually reached camp soon after noon. The marches varied from ten to fifteen miles a day, though sometimes on extreme flanks it was necessary to make as much as twenty, but the rate of travel was regulated by the wagons; and, considering the nature of the roads, fifteen miles per day was deemed the limit.

The pontoon-trains were in like manner distributed in about equal proportions to the four corps, giving each a section of about nine hundred feet. The pontoons were of the skeleton pattern, with cotton-canvas covers, each boat, with its proportion of balks and chesses, constituting a load for one wagon. By uniting two such sections together, we could make a bridge of eighteen hundred feet, enough for any river we had to traverse; but habitually the leading brigade would, out of the abundant timber, improvise a bridge before the pontoon-train could come up, unless in the cases of rivers of considerable magnitude, such as the Ocmulgee, Oconee, Ogeechee, Savannah, etc.

On the 20th of November I was still with the Fourteenth Corps, near Eatonton Factory, waiting to hear of the Twentieth Corps; and on the 21st we camped near the house of a man named Vann; the next day, about 4 P. M., General Davis had halted his head of column on a wooded ridge, overlooking an extensive slope of cultivated country, about ten miles short of Milledgeville, and was deploying his troops for camp when I got up. There was a high, raw wind blowing, and I asked him why he had chosen so cold and bleak a position. He explained that he had accomplished his full distance for the day, and had there an abundance of wood and water. He explained further that his advance-guard was a mile or so ahead; so I rode on, asking him to let his rear division, as it came up, move some distance ahead into the depression or valley beyond. Riding on some distance to the border of a plantation, I turned out of the main road into a cluster of wild-plum bushes, that broke the force of the cold November wind, dismounted, and instructed the staff to pick out the place for our camp.

The afternoon was unusually raw and cold. My orderly was at hand with his invariable saddle-bags, which contained a change of under-clothing, my maps, a flask of whiskey, and bunch of cigars. Taking a drink and lighting a cigar, I walked to a row of Negro-huts close by, entered one and found a soldier or two warming themselves by a wood-fire. I took their place by the fire, intending to wait there till our wagons had got up, and a camp made for the night. I was talking to the old Negro woman, when some one came and explained to me that, if I would come farther down the road, I could find a better place. So I started on foot, and found on the main road a good double-hewed-log house, in one room of which Colonel Poe, Dr. Moore, and others, had started a fire. I sent back orders to the "plum-bushes" to bring our horses and saddles up to this house, and an orderly to conduct our head-quarter wagons to the same place. In looking around the room, I saw a small box, like a candle-box, marked "Howell Cobb," and, on inquiring of a Negro, found that we were at the plantation of General Howell Cobb, of Georgia, one of the leading rebels of the South, then a general in the Southern army, and who had been Secretary of the United States Treasury in Mr. Buchanan's time. Of course, we confiscated his property, and found it rich in corn, beans, peanuts, and sorghum-molasses. Extensive fields were all round the house; I sent word back to General Davis to explain whose plantation it was, and instructed him to spare nothing. That night huge bonfires consumed the fence-rails, kept our soldiers warm, and the teamsters and men, as well as the slaves, carried off an immense quantity of corn and provisions of all sorts.

In due season the headquarter wagons came up, and we got supper. After supper I sat on a chair astride, with my back to a good fire, musing, and became conscious that an old Negro, with a tallow-candle in his hand, was scanning my face closely. I inquired, "What do you want, old man?" He answered, "Dey say you is Massa Sherman." I answered that such was the case, and inquired what he wanted. He only wanted to look at me, and kept muttering, "Dis nigger can't sleep dis night." I asked him why he trembled so, and he said that he wanted to be sure that we were in fact "Yankees," for on a former occasion some rebel cavalry had put on light-blue overcoats, personating Yankee troops, and many of the Negroes were deceived thereby, himself among the number— had shown them sympathy, and had in consequence been un-mercifully beaten therefor. This time he wanted to be certain before committing himself; so I told him to go out on the porch, from which he could see the whole horizon lit up with camp-fires, and he could then judge whether he had ever seen any thing like it before. The old man became convinced that the "Yankees" had come at last, about whom he had been dreaming all his life; and some of the staff-officers gave him a strong drink of whiskey, which set his tongue going. Lieutenant Snelling, who commanded my escort, was a Georgian, and recognized in this old Negro a favorite slave of his uncle, who resided about six miles off; but the old slave did not at first recognize his young master in our uniform. One of my staff-officers asked him what had become of his young master, George. He did not know, only that he had gone off to the war, and he supposed him killed, as a matter of course. His attention was then drawn to Snelling's face, when he fell on his knees and thanked God that he had found his young master alive and along with the Yankees. Snelling inquired all about his uncle and the family, asked my permission to go and pay his uncle a visit, which I granted, of course, and the next morning he described to me his visit. The uncle was not cordial, by any means, to find his nephew in the ranks of the host that was desolating the land, and Snelling came back, having exchanged his tired horse for a fresher one out of his uncle's stables, explaining that surely some of the "bummers" would have got the horse had he not.

The next morning, November 23d, we rode into Milledgeville, the capital of the State, whither the Twentieth Corps had preceded us; and during that day the left wing was all united, in and around Milledgeville. From the inhabitants we learned that some of Kilpatrick's cavalry had preceded us by a couple of days, and that all of the right wing was at and near Gordon, twelve miles off, viz., the place where the branch railroad came to Milledgeville from the Macon & Savannah road. The first stage of the journey was, therefore, complete, and absolutely successful.

General Howard soon reported by letter the operations of his right wing, which, on leaving Atlanta, had substantially followed the two roads toward Macon, by Jonesboro' and McDonough, and reached the Ocmulgee at Planters' Factory, which they crossed, by the aid of the pontoon-train, during the 18th and 19th of November. Thence, with the Seventeenth Corps (General Blair's) he (General Howard) had marched *via* Monticello toward Gordon, having dispatched Kilpatrick's cavalry, supported by the Fifteenth Corps (Osterhaus's), to feign on Macon. Kilpatrick met the enemy's cavalry about four miles out of Macon, and drove them rapidly back into the bridge-defenses held by infantry. Kilpatrick charged these, got inside the parapet, but could not hold it, and retired to his infantry supports, near Griswold Station. The Fifteenth Corps tore up the railroad-track eastward from Griswold, leaving Charles R. Wood's division behind as a rear-guard—one brigade of which was intrenched across the road, with some of Kilpatrick's cavalry on the flanks. On the 22d of November General G. W. Smith, with a division of troops, came out of Macon, attacked this brigade (Walcutt's) in position, and was handsomely repulsed and driven back into Macon. This brigade was in part armed with Spencer repeating-rifles, and its fire was so rapid that General Smith insists to this day that he encountered a whole division; but he is mistaken; he was beaten by one brigade ([Charles C.] Walcutt's), and made no further effort to molest our operations from that direction. General Walcutt was wounded in the leg, and had to ride the rest of the distance to Savannah in a carriage.

Therefore, by the 23d, I was in Milledgeville with the left wing, and was in full communication with the right wing at Gordon. The people of Milledgeville remained at home, except the Governor (Brown), the State officers, and Legislature, who had ignominiously fled, in the utmost disorder and confusion; standing not on the order of their going, but going at once—some by rail, some by carriages, and many on foot. Some of the citizens who remained behind described this flight of the "brave and patriotic" Governor Brown. He had occupied a public building known as the "Governor's Mansion," and had hastily stripped it of carpets, curtains, and furniture of all sorts, which were removed to a train of freight-cars, which carried away these things—even the cabbages and vegetables from his kitchen and cellar—leaving behind muskets, ammunition, and the public archives. On arrival at Milledgeville I occupied the same public mansion, and was soon overwhelmed with appeals for protection. General Slocum had previously arrived with the Twentieth Corps, had taken up his quarters at the Milledgeville Hotel, established a good provost-guard, and excellent order was maintained. The most frantic appeals had been made by the Governor and Legislature for help from every quarter, and the people of the State had been called out *en masse* to resist and destroy the invaders of their homes and firesides. Even the prisoners and convicts of the penitentiary were released on condition of serving as soldiers, and the cadets were taken from their military college for the same purpose. These constituted a small battalion, under General Harry Wayne, a former officer of the United States Army, and son of the then Justice Wayne of the Supreme Court. But these hastily retreated east across the Oconee River, leaving us a good bridge, which we promptly secured.

At Milledgeville we found newspapers from all the South, and learned the consternation which had filled the Southern mind at our temerity; many charging that we were actually fleeing for our lives and seeking safety at the hands of our fleet on the sea-coast. All demanded that we should be assailed, "front, flank, and rear"; that provisions should be destroyed in advance, so that we would starve; that bridges should be burned, roads obstructed, and no mercy shown us. Judging from the tone of the Southern press of that day, the outside world must have supposed us ruined and lost. I give a few of these appeals as samples, which to-day must sound strange to the parties who made them:

CORINTH, MISSISSIPPI, *November* 18, 1864.

To the People of Georgia:

Arise for the defense of your native soil! Rally around your patriotic Governor and gallant soldiers! Obstruct and destroy all the roads in Sherman's front, flank, and rear, and his army will soon starve in your midst. Be confident. Be resolute. Trust in an overruling Providence, and success will soon crown your efforts. I hasten to join you in the defense of your homes and firesides.

G. T. BEAUREGARD.

RICHMOND, *November* 18, 1864.

To the People of Georgia:

You have now the best opportunity ever yet presented to destroy the enemy. Put every thing at the disposal of our generals; remove all provisions from the path of the invader, and put all obstructions in his path.

Every citizen with his gun, and every Negro with his spade and axe, can do the work of a soldier. You can destroy the enemy by retarding his march.

Georgians, be firm! Act promptly, and fear not!

B. H. HILL, *Senator.*

I most cordially approve the above.

JAMES A. SEDDON, *Secretary of War.*

RICHMOND, *November* 19, 1864.

To the People of Georgia:

We have had a special conference with President Davis and the Secretary of War, and are able to assure you that they have done and are still doing all that can be done to meet the emergency that presses upon you. Let every man fly to arms! Remove your Negroes, horses, cattle, and provisions from Sherman's army, and burn what you cannot carry. Burn all bridges, and block up the roads in his route. Assail the invader in front, flank, and rear, by night and by day. Let him have no rest.

JULIAN HARTRIDGE,	MARK BLAUFORD,
J. H. REYNOLDS,	GENERAL N. LESTER,
JOHN T. SHOEMAKER,	JOSEPH M. SMITH,
	Members of Congress.

Of course, we were rather amused than alarmed at these threats, and made light of the feeble opposition offered to our progress. Some of the officers (in the spirit of mischief) gathered together in the vacant hall of Representatives, elected a Speaker, and constituted themselves the Legislature of the State of Georgia! A proposition was made to repeal the ordinance of secession, which was well debated, and resulted in its repeal by a fair vote! I was not present at these frolics, but heard of them at the time, and enjoyed the joke.

Meantime orders were made for the total destruction of the arsenal and its contents, and of such public buildings as could be easily converted to hostile uses. But little or no damage was done to private property, and General Slocum, with my approval, spared several mills, and many thousands of bales of cotton, taking what he knew to be worthless bonds, that the cotton should not be used for the Confederacy. Meantime the right wing continued its movement along the railroad toward Savannah, tearing up the track and destroying its iron. At the Oconee was met a feeble resistance from Harry Wayne's troops, but soon the pontoon-bridge was laid, and that wing crossed over. Kilpatrick's cavalry was brought into Milledgeville, and crossed the Oconee by the bridge near the town; and on the 23d I made the general orders for the next stage of the march as far as Millen. These were, substantially, for the right wing to follow the Savannah Railroad, by roads on its south; the left wing was to move to Sandersville, by Davisboro' and Louisville, while the cavalry was ordered by a circuit to the north, and to march rapidly for Millen, to rescue our prisoners of war confined there. The distance was about a hundred miles.

General Wheeler, with his division of rebel cavalry, had succeeded in getting ahead of us between Milledgeville and Augusta; and General W. J. Hardee had been dispatched by General Beauregard from Hood's army to oppose our progress directly in front. He had, however, brought with him no troops, but relied on his influence with the Georgians (of whose State he was a native) to arouse the people, and with them to annihilate Sherman's army!

On the 24th we renewed the march, and I accompanied the Twentieth Corps, which took the direct road to Sandersville, which we reached simultaneously with the Fourteenth Corps, on the 26th. A brigade of rebel cavalry was deployed before the town, and was driven in and through it by our skirmish-line. I myself saw the rebel cavalry apply fire to stacks of fodder standing in the fields at Sandersville, and gave orders to burn some unoccupied dwellings close by. On entering the town, I told certain citizens (who would be sure to spread the report) that, if the enemy attempted to carry out their threat to burn their food, corn, and fodder, in our route, I would most undoubtedly execute to the letter the general orders of devastation made at the outset of the campaign. With this exception, and one or two minor cases near Savannah, the people did not destroy food, for they saw clearly that it would be ruin to themselves.

At Sandersville I halted the left wing until I heard that the right wing was abreast of us on the railroad. During the evening a Negro was brought to me, who had that day been to the station (Tenille), about six miles south of the town. I inquired of him if there were any Yankees there, and he answered, "Yes." He described in his own way what he had seen. "First, there come along some cavalry-men, and they burned the depot; then come along some infantry-men, and they tore up the track, and burned it"; and just before he left they had "sot fire to the well!"

The next morning, viz., the 27th, I rode down to the station, and found General Corse's division (of the Fifteenth Corps) engaged in destroying the railroad, and saw the well which my Negro informant had seen "burnt." it was a square pit about twenty-five feet deep, boarded up, with wooden steps leading to the bottom, wherein was a fine copper pump, to lift the water to a tank above. The soldiers had broken up the pump, heaved in the steps and lining, and set fire to the mass of lumber in the bottom of the well, which corroborated the Negro's description.

From this point Blair's corps, the Seventeenth, took up the work of destroying the railroad, the Fifteenth Corps following another road leading eastward, farther to the south of the railroad. While the left wing was marching toward Louisville, north of the railroad, General Kilpatrick had, with his cavalry division, moved rapidly toward Waynesboro', on the branch railroad leading from Millen to Augusta. He found Wheeler's division of rebel cavalry there, and had considerable skirmishing with it; but, learning that our prisoners had been removed two days before from Millen, he returned to Louisville on the 29th, where he found the left wing. Here he remained a couple of days to rest his horses, and, receiving orders from me to engage Wheeler and give him all the fighting he wanted, he procured from General Slocum the assistance of the infantry division of General Baird, and moved back for Waynesboro' on the 2d of December, the remainder of the left wing continuing its march on toward Millen. Near Waynesboro' Wheeler was again encountered, and driven through the town and beyond Brier Creek, toward Augusta, thus keeping up the delusion that the main army was moving toward Augusta. General Kilpatrick's fighting and movements about Waynesboro' and Brier Creek were spirited, and produced a good effect by relieving the infantry column and the wagon-trains of all molestation during their march on Millen. Having thus covered that flank, he turned south and followed the movement of the Fourteenth Corps to Buckhead Church, north of Millen and near it.

On the 3d of December I entered Millen with the Seventeenth Corps (General Frank P. Blair), and there paused one day, to communicate with all parts of the army. General Howard was south of the Ogeechee River, with the Fifteenth Corps, opposite Scarboro'. General Slocum was at Buckhead Church, four miles north of Millen, with the Twentieth Corps. The Fourteenth (General Davis) was at Lumpkin's Station, on the Augusta road, about ten miles north of Millen, and the cavalry division was within easy support of this wing. Thus the whole army was in good position and in good condition. We had largely subsisted on the country; our wagons were full of forage and provisions; but, as we approached the seacoast, the country became more sandy and barren, and food became more scarce; still, with little or no loss, we had traveled two-thirds of our distance, and I concluded to push on for Savannah. At Millen I learned that General Bragg was in Augusta, and that General Wade Hampton had been ordered there from Richmond, to organize a large cavalry force with which to resist our progress.

General Hardee was ahead, between us and Savannah, with [Lafayette] McLaws's division, and other irregular troops, that could not, I felt assured, exceed ten thousand men. I caused the fine depot at Millen to be destroyed, and other damage done, and then resumed the march directly on Savannah, by the four main roads. The Seventeenth Corps (General Blair) followed substantially the railroad, and, along with it, on the 5th of December, I reached Ogeechee Church, about fifty miles from Savannah, and found there fresh earthworks, which had been thrown up by McLaws's division; but he must have seen that both his flanks were being turned, and prudently retreated to Savannah without a fight. All the columns then pursued leisurely their march toward Savannah, corn and forage becoming more and more scarce, but ricefields beginning to occur along the Savannah and Ogeechee Rivers, which proved a good substitute, both as food and forage. The weather was fine, the roads good, and every thing seemed to favor us. Never do I recall a more agreeable sensation than the sight of our camps by night, lit up by the fires of fragrant pine-knots. The trains were all in good order, and the men seemed to march their fifteen miles a day as though it were nothing. No enemy opposed us, and we could only occasionally hear the faint reverberation of a gun to our left rear, where we knew that General Kilpatrick was skirmishing with Wheeler's cavalry, which persistently followed him. But the infantry columns had met with no opposition whatsoever. McLaws's division was falling back before us, and we occasionally picked up a few of his men as prisoners, who insisted that we would meet with strong opposition at Savannah.

On the 8th, as I rode along, I found the column turned out of the main road, marching through the fields. Close by, in the corner of a fence, was a group of men standing around a handsome young officer, whose foot had been blown to pieces by a torpedo planted in the road. He was waiting for a surgeon to amputate his leg, and told me that he was riding along with the rest of his brigade-staff of the Seventeenth Corps, when a torpedo trodden on by his horse had exploded, killing the horse and literally blowing off all the flesh from one of his legs. I saw the terrible wound, and made full inquiry into the facts. There had been no resistance at that point, nothing to give warning of danger, and the rebels had planted eight-inch shells in the road, with friction-matches to explode them by being trodden on. This was not war, but murder, and it made me very angry. I immediately ordered a lot of rebel prisoners to be brought from the provost-guard, armed with picks and spades, and made them march in close order along the road, so as to explode their own torpedoes, or to discover and dig them up. They begged hard, but I reiterated the order, and could hardly help laughing at their stepping so gingerly along the road, where it was supposed sunken torpedoes might explode at each step, but they found no other torpedoes till near Fort McAllister. That night we reached Pooler's Station, eight miles from Savannah, and during the next two days, December 9th and 10th, the several corps reached the defenses of Savannah—the Fourteenth Corps on the left, touching the river; the Twentieth Corps next; then the Seventeenth; and the Fifteenth on the extreme right; thus completely investing the city. Wishing to reconnoitre the place in person, I rode forward by the Louisville road, into a dense wood of oak, pine, and cypress, left the horses, and walked down to the railroad-track, at a place where there was a side-track, and a cut about four feet deep. From that point the railroad was straight, leading into Savannah, and about eight hundred yards off were a rebel parapet and battery. I could see the cannoneers preparing to fire, and cautioned the officers near me to scatter, as we would likely attract a shot. Very soon I saw the white puff of smoke, and, watching close, caught sight of the ball as it rose in its flight, and, finding it coming pretty straight, I stepped a short distance to one side, but noticed a Negro very near me in the act of crossing the track at right angles. Some one called to him to look out; but, before the poor fellow understood his danger, the ball (a thirty-two-pound round shot) struck the ground, and rose in its first ricochet, caught the Negro under the right jaw, and literally carried away his head, scattering blood and brains about. A soldier close by spread an overcoat over the body, and we all concluded to get out of that railroad-cut. Meantime, General Mower's division of the Seventeenth Corps had crossed the canal to the right of the Louisville road, and had found the line of parapet continuous; so at Savannah we had again run up against the old familiar parapet, with its deep ditches, canals, and bayous, full of water; and it looked as though another siege was inevitable. I accordingly made a camp or bivouac near the Louisville road, about five miles from Savannah, and proceeded to invest the place closely, pushing forward reconnoissances at every available point.

As soon as it was demonstrated that Savannah was well fortified, with a good garrison, commanded by General William J. Hardee, a competent soldier, I saw that the first step was to open communication with our fleet, supposed to be waiting for us with supplies and clothing in Ossabaw Sound.

General Howard had, some nights previously, sent one of his best scouts, Captain [William] Duncan, with two men, in a canoe, to drift past Fort McAllister, and to convey to the fleet a knowledge of our approach. General Kilpatrick's cavalry had also been transferred to the south bank of the Ogeechee, with orders to open communication with the fleet. Leaving orders with General Slocum to press the siege, I instructed General Howard to send a division with all his engineers to King's Bridge, fourteen and a half miles south-west from Savannah, to rebuild it. On the evening of the 12th I rode over myself, and spent the night at Mr. King's house, where I found General Howard, with General Hazen's division of the Fifteenth Corps. His engineers were hard at work on the bridge, which they finished that night, and at sunrise Hazen's division passed over. I gave General Hazen, in person, his orders to march rapidly down the right bank of the Ogeechee, and without hesitation to assault and carry Fort McAllister by storm. I knew it to be strong in heavy artillery, as against an approach from the sea, but believed it open and weak to the rear. I explained to General Hazen, fully, that on his action depended the safety of the whole army, and the success of the campaign. Kilpatrick had already felt the fort, and had gone farther down the coast to Kilkenny Bluff, or St. Catharine's Sound, where, on the same day, he had communication with a vessel belonging to the blockading fleet; but, at the time, I was not aware of this fact, and trusted entirely to General Hazen and his division of infantry, the Second of the Fifteenth Corps, the same old division which I had commanded at Shiloh and Vicksburg, in which I felt a special pride and confidence.

Having seen General Hazen fairly off, accompanied by General Howard, I rode with my staff down the left bank of the Ogeechee, ten miles to the rice-plantation of a Mr. Cheeves, where General Howard had established a signal-station to overlook the lower river, and to watch for any vessel of the blockading squadron, which the Negroes reported to be expecting us, because they nightly sent up rockets, and daily dispatched a steamboat up the Ogeechee as near to Fort McAllister as it was safe.

On reaching the rice-mill at Cheeves's, I found a guard and a couple of twenty-pound Parrott guns, of De Gress's' battery, which fired an occasional shot toward Fort McAllister, plainly seen over the salt-marsh, about three miles distant. Fort McAllister had the rebel flag flying, and occasionally sent a heavy shot back across the marsh to where we were, but otherwise every thing about the place looked as peaceable and quiet as on the Sabbath.

The signal-officer had built a platform on the ridge-pole of the rice-mill. Leaving our horses behind the stacks of rice-straw, we all got on the roof of a shed attached to the mill, wherefrom I could communicate with the signal-officer above, and at the same time look out toward Ossabaw Sound, and across the Ogeechee River at Fort McAllister. About 2 P. M.

we observed signs of commotion in the fort, and noticed one or two guns fired inland, and some musket-skirmishing in the woods close by.

This betokened the approach of Hazen's division, which had been anxiously expected, and soon thereafter the signal-officer discovered about three miles above the fort a signal-flag, with which he conversed, and found it to belong to General Hazen, who was preparing to assault the fort, and wanted to know if I were there. On being assured of this fact, and that I expected the fort to be carried before night, I received by signal the assurance of General Hazen that he was making his preparations, and would soon attempt the assault. The sun was rapidly declining, and I was dreadfully impatient. At that very moment some one discovered a faint cloud of smoke, and an object gliding, as it were, along the horizon above the tops of the sedge toward the sea, which little by little grew till it was pronounced to be the smoke-stack of a steamer coming up the river. "It must be one of our squadron!" Soon the flag of the United States was plainly visible, and our attention was divided between this approaching steamer and the expected assault. When the sun was about an hour high, another signal-message came from General Hazen that he was all ready, and I replied to go ahead, as a friendly steamer was approaching from below. Soon we made out a group of officers on the deck of this vessel, signaling with a flag, "Who are you?" The answer went back promptly, "General Sherman." Then followed the question, "Is Fort McAllister taken?" "Not yet, but it will be in a minute!" Almost at that instant of time, we saw Hazen's troops come out of the dark fringe of woods that encompassed the fort, the lines dressed as on parade, with colors flying, and moving forward with a quick, steady pace. Fort McAllister was then all alive, its big guns belching forth dense clouds of smoke, which soon enveloped our assaulting lines. One color went down, but was up in a moment. On the lines advanced, faintly seen in the white, sulphurous smoke; there was a pause, a cessation of fire; the smoke cleared away, and the parapets were blue with our men, who fired their muskets in the air, and shouted so that we actually heard them, or felt that we did. Fort McAllister was taken, and the good news was instantly sent by the signal-officer to our navy friends on the approaching gunboat, for a point of timber had shut out Fort McAllister from their view, and they had not seen the action at all, but must have heard the cannonading.

During the progress of the assault, our little group on Cheeves's mill hardly breathed; but no sooner did we see our flags on the parapet than I exclaimed, in the language of the poor Negro at Cobb's plantation, "This nigger will have no sleep this night!"

I was resolved to communicate with our fleet that night, which happened to be a beautiful moonlight one. At the wharf belonging to Cheeves's mill was a small skiff, that had been used by our men in fishing or in gathering oysters. I was there in a minute, called for a volunteer crew, when several young officers, Nichols and Merritt among the number, said they were good oarsmen, and volunteered to pull the boat down to Fort McAllister. General Howard asked to accompany me; so we took seats in the stern of the boat, and our crew of officers pulled out with a will. The tide was setting in strong, and they had a hard pull, for, though the distance was but three miles in an air-line, the river was so crooked that the actual distance was fully six miles. On the way down we passed the wreck of a steamer which had been sunk some years before, during a naval attack on Fort McAllister.

Night had fairly set in when we discovered a soldier on the beach. I hailed him, and inquired if he knew where General Hazen was. He answered that the general was at the house of the overseer of the plantation (McAllister's), and that he could guide me to it. We accordingly landed, tied our boat to a driftlog, and followed our guide through bushes to a framehouse, standing in a grove of live-oaks, near a row of Negro quarters. General Hazen was there with his staff, in the act of getting supper; he invited us to join them, which we accepted promptly, for we were really very hungry. Of course, I congratulated Hazen most heartily on his brilliant success, and praised its execution very highly, as it deserved, and he explained to me more in detail the exact results. The fort was an inclosed work, and its land-front was in the nature of a bastion and curtains, with good parapet, ditch, *fraise*, and *chevaux-de-frise*, made out of the large branches of live-oaks. Luckily, the rebels had left the larger and unwieldy trunks on the ground, which served as a good cover for the skirmish-line, which crept behind these logs, and from them kept the artillerists from loading and firing their guns accurately.

The assault had been made by three parties in line, one from below, one from above the fort, and the third directly in rear, along the capital. All were simultaneous, and had to pass a good abatis and line of torpedoes, which actually killed more of the assailants than the heavy guns of the fort, which generally overshot the mark. Hazen's entire loss was reported, killed and wounded, ninety-two. Each party reached the parapet about the same time, and the garrison inside, of about two hundred and fifty men (about fifty of them killed or wounded), were in his power. The commanding officer, Major [Robert H.] Anderson, was at that moment a prisoner, and General Hazen invited him in to take supper with us, which he did.

Up to this time General Hazen did not know that a gunboat was in the river below the fort; for it was shut off from sight by a point of timber, and I was determined to board her that night, at whatever risk or cost, as I wanted some news of what was going on in the outer world. Accordingly, after supper, we all walked down to the fort, nearly a mile from the house where we had been, entered Fort McAllister, held by a regiment of Hazen's troops, and the sentinel cautioned us to be very careful, as the ground outside the fort was full of torpedoes. Indeed, while we were there, a torpedo exploded, tearing to pieces a poor fellow who was hunting for a dead comrade. Inside the fort lay the dead as they had fallen, and they could hardly be distinguished from their living comrades, sleeping soundly side by side in the pale moonlight. In the river, close by the fort, was a good yawl tied to a stake, but the tide was high, and it required some time to get it in to the bank; the commanding officer, whose name I cannot recall, manned the boat with a good crew of his men, and, with General Howard, I entered, and pulled down-stream, regardless of the warnings of all about the torpedoes.

The night was unusually bright, and we expected to find the gunboat within a mile or so; but, after pulling down the river fully three miles, and not seeing the gunboat, I began to think she had turned and gone back to the sound; but we kept on, following the bends of the river, and about six miles below McAllister we saw her light, and soon were hailed by the vessel at anchor. Pulling alongside, we announced ourselves, and were received with great warmth and enthusiasm on deck by half a dozen naval officers, among them Captain Williamson, United States Navy. She proved to be the Dandelion, a tender of the regular gunboat Flag, posted at the mouth of the Ogeechee. All sorts of questions were made and answered, and we learned that Captain Duncan had safely reached the squadron, had communicated the good news of our approach, and they had been expecting us for some days. They explained that Admiral [Louis M.] Dahlgren commanded the South-Atlantic Squadron, which was then engaged in blockading the coast from Charleston south, and was on his flag-ship, the Harvest Moon, lying in Wassaw Sound; that General J[ohn] G. Foster was in command of the Department of the South, with his headquarters at Hilton Head; and that several ships loaded with stores for the army were lying in Tybee Roads and in Port Royal Sound. From these officers I also learned that General Grant was still besieging Petersburg and Richmond, and that matters and things generally remained pretty much the same as when we had left Atlanta. All thoughts seemed to have been turned to us in Georgia, cut off from all communication with our friends; and the rebel papers had reported us to be harassed, defeated, starving, and fleeing for safety to the coast. I then asked for pen and paper, and wrote several hasty notes to General Foster, Admiral Dahlgren, General Grant, and the Secretary of War, giving in general terms the actual state of affairs, the fact of the capture of Fort McAllister, and of my desire that means should be taken to establish a line of supply from the vessels in port up the Ogeechee to the rear of the army. As a sample, I give one of these notes, addressed to the Secretary of War, intended for publication to relieve the anxiety of our friends at the North generally:

ON BOARD DANDELION, OSSABAW SOUND,
December 13, 1864—11.50 P. M.

To Hon. E. M. STANTON, *Secretary of War, Washington, D. C.:*

To-day, at 5 P. M., General Hazen's division of the Fifteenth Corps carried Fort McAllister by assault, capturing its entire garrison and stores. This opened to us Ossabaw Sound, and I pushed down to this gunboat to communicate with the fleet. Before opening communication we had completely destroyed all the railroads leading into Savannah, and invested the city. The left of the army is on the Savannah River three miles above the city, and the right on the Ogeechee, at King's Bridge. The army is in splendid order, and equal to any thing. The weather has been fine, and supplies were abundant. Our march was most agreeable, and we were not at all molested by guerrillas.

We reached Savannah three days ago, but, owing to Fort McAllister, could not communicate; but, now that we have McAllister, we can go ahead.

We have already captured two boats on the Savannah River, and prevented their gunboats from coming down.

I estimate the population of Savannah at twenty-five thousand, and the garrison at fifteen thousand. General Hardee commands.

We have not lost a wagon on the trip; but have gathered a large supply of Negroes, mules, horses, etc., and our teams are in far better condition than when we started.

My first duty will be to clear the army of surplus Negroes, mules, and horses. We have utterly destroyed over two hundred miles of rails, and consumed stores and provisions that were essential to Lee's and Hood's armies.

The quick work made with McAllister, the opening of communication with our fleet, and our consequent independence as to supplies, dissipate all their boasted threats to head us off and starve the army.

I regard Savannah as already *gained*.

Yours truly,

W. T. SHERMAN, *Major-General*.

By this time the night was well advanced, and the tide was running ebb-strong; so I asked Captain Williamson to tow us up as near Fort McAllister as he would venture for the torpedoes, of which the navy-officers had a wholesome dread. The Dandelion steamed up some three or four miles, till the lights of Fort McAllister could be seen, when she anchored, and we pulled to the fort in our own boat. General Howard and I then walked up to the McAllister House, where we found General Hazen and his officers asleep on the floor of one of the rooms. Lying down on the floor, I was soon fast asleep, but shortly became conscious that some one in the room was inquiring for me among the sleepers. Calling out, I was told that an officer of General Foster's staff had just arrived from a steamboat anchored below McAllister; that the general was extremely anxious to see me on important business, but that he was lame from an old Mexican-War wound, and could not possibly come to me. I was extremely weary from the incessant labor of the day and night before, but got up, and again walked down the sandy road to McAllister, where I found a boat awaiting us, which carried us some three miles down the river, to the steamer W. W. Coit (I think), on board of which we found General Foster. He had just come from Port Royal, expecting to find Admiral Dahlgren in Ossabaw Sound, and, hearing of the capture of Fort McAllister, he had come up to see me. He described fully the condition of affairs with his own command in South Carolina. He had made several serious efforts to effect a lodgment on the railroad which connects Savannah with Charleston near Pocotaligo, but had not succeeded in reaching the railroad itself, though he had a full division of troops, strongly intrenched, near Broad River, within cannon-range of the railroad. He explained, moreover, that there were at Port Royal abundant supplies of bread and provisions, as well as of clothing, designed for our use. We still had in our wagons and in camp abundance of meat, but we needed bread, sugar, and coffee, and it was all-important that a route of supply should at once be opened, for which purpose the aid and assistance of the navy were indispensable. We accordingly steamed down the Ogeechee River to Ossabaw Sound, in hopes to meet Admiral Dahlgren, but he was not there, and we continued on by the inland channel to Wassaw Sound, where we found the Harvest Moon, and Admiral Dahlgren. I was not personally acquainted with him at the time, but he was so extremely kind and courteous that I was at once attracted to him. There was nothing in his power, he said, which he would not do to assist us, to make our campaign absolutely successful. He undertook at once to find vessels of light draught to carry our supplies from Port Royal to Cheeves's Mill, or to King's Bridge above, whence they could be hauled by wagons to our several camps; he offered to return with me to Fort McAllister, to superintend the removal of the torpedoes, and to relieve me of all the details of this most difficult work. General Foster then concluded to go on to Port Royal, to send back to us six hundred thousand rations, and all the rifled guns of heavy calibre, and ammunition on hand, with which I thought we could reach the city of Savannah, from the positions already secured. Admiral Dahlgren then returned with me in the Harvest Moon to Fort McAllister. This consumed all of the 14th of December; and by the 15th I had again reached Cheeves's Mill, where my horse awaited me, and rode on to General Howard's headquarters at Anderson's plantation, on the plank-road, about eight miles back of Savannah. I reached this place about noon, and immediately sent orders to my own headquarters, on the Louisville road, to have them brought over to the plank-road, as a place more central and convenient; gave written notice to Generals Slocum and Howard of all the steps taken, and ordered them to get ready to receive the siege-guns, to put them in position to bombard Savannah, and to prepare for the general assault. The country back of Savannah is very low, and intersected with innumerable salt-water creeks, swamps, and rice-fields. Fortunately the weather was good and the roads were passable, but, should the winter rains set in, I knew that we would be much embarrassed. Therefore, heavy details of men were at once put to work to prepare a wharf and depot at King's Bridge, and the roads leading thereto were corduroyed in advance. The Ogeechee Canal was also cleared out for use; and boats, such as were common on the river plantations, were collected, in which to float stores from our proposed base on the Ogeechee to the points most convenient to the several camps.

Slocum's wing extended from the Savannah River to the canal, and Howard's wing from the canal to the extreme right, along down the Little Ogeechee. The enemy occupied not only the city itself, with its long line of outer works, but the many forts which had been built to guard the approaches from the sea—such as at Beaulieu, Rosedew, White Bluff, Bonaventura, Thunderbolt, Cansten's Bluff, Forts Tatnall, Boggs, etc., etc. I knew that General Hardee could not have a garrison strong enough for all these purposes, and I was therefore anxious to break his lines before he could receive reënforcements from Virginia or Augusta. General Slocum had already captured a couple of steamboats trying to pass down the Savannah River from Augusta, and had established some of his men on Argyle and Hutchinson Islands above the city, and wanted to transfer a whole corps to the South Carolina bank; but, as the enemy had iron-clad gunboats in the river, I did not deem it prudent, because the same result could be better accomplished from General Foster's position at Broad River.

Fort McAllister was captured as described, late in the evening of December 13th, and by the 16th many steamboats had passed up as high as King's Bridge; among them one which General Grant had dispatched with the mails for the army, which had accumulated since our departure from Atlanta, under charge of Colonel A. H. Markland. These mails were most welcome to all the officers and soldiers of the army, which had been cut off from friends and the world for two months, and this prompt receipt of letters from home had an excellent effect, making us feel that home was near. By this vessel also came Lieutenant Dunn, aide-de-camp, with the following letter of December 3d, from General Grant, and on the next day Colonel [Orville E.] Babcock, United States Engineers, arrived with the letter of December 6th, both of which are in General Grant's own handwriting, and are given entire:

HEADQUARTERS ARMIES OF THE UNITED STATES, }
CITY POINT, VIRGINIA, *December* 3, 1864. }

Major-General W. T. SHERMAN, *commanding Armies near Savannah, Georgia.*

GENERAL: The little information gleaned from the Southern press indicating no great obstacle to your progress, I have directed your mails (which had been previously collected in Baltimore by Colonel Markland, special agent of the Post-Office Department) to be sent as far as the blockading squadron off Savannah, to be forwarded to you as soon as heard from on the coast.

Not liking to rejoice before the victory is assured, I abstain from congratulating you and those under your command, until bottom has been struck. I have never had a fear, however, for the result.

Since you left Atlanta no very great progress has been made here. The enemy has been closely watched, though, and prevented from detaching against you. I think not one man has gone from here, except some twelve or fifteen hundred dismounted cavalry. Bragg has gone from Wilmington. I am trying to take advantage of his absence to get possession of that place. Owing to some preparations Admiral Porter and General Butler are making to blow up Fort Fisher (which, while hoping for the best, I do not believe a particle in), there is a delay in getting this expedition off. I hope they will be ready to start by the 7th, and that Bragg will not have started back by that time.

In this letter I do not intend to give you any thing like directions for future action, but will state a general idea I have, and will get your views after you have established yourself on the sea-coast. With your veteran army I hope to get control of the only two through routes from east to west possessed by the enemy before the fall of Atlanta. The condition will be filled by holding Savannah and Augusta, or by holding any other port to the east of Savannah and Branchville. If Wilmington falls, a force from there can coöperate with you.

Thomas has got back into the defenses of Nashville, with Hood close upon him. Decatur has been abandoned, and so have all the roads, except the main one leading to Chattanooga. Part of this falling back was undoubtedly necessary, and all of it may have been. It did not look so, however, to me. In my opinion, Thomas far outnumbers Hood in infantry. In cavalry Hood has the advantage in *morale* and numbers. I hope yet that Hood will be badly crippled, if not destroyed. The general news you will learn from the papers better than I can give it.

After all becomes quiet, and roads become so bad up here that there is likely to be a week or two when nothing can be done, I will run down the coast to see you. If you desire it, I will ask Mrs. Sherman to go with me.

Yours truly,   U. S. GRANT, *Lieutenant-General.*

HEADQUARTERS ARMIES OF THE UNITED STATES, ⎫
CITY POINT, VIRGINIA, *December* 6, 1864.   ⎭

Major-General W. T. SHERMAN, *commanding Military Division of the Mississippi.*

GENERAL: On reflection since sending my letter by the hands of Lieutenant Dunn, I have concluded that the most important operation toward closing out the rebellion will be to close out Lee and his army.

You have now destroyed the roads of the South so that it will probably take them three months without interruption to reëstablish a through line from east to west. In that time I think the job here will be effectually completed.

My idea now is that you establish a base on the sea-coast, fortify and leave in it all your artillery and cavalry, and enough infantry to protect them, and at the same time so threaten the interior that the militia of the South will have to be kept at home. With the balance of your command come here by water with all dispatch. Select yourself the officer to leave in command, but you I want in person. Unless you see objections to this plan which I cannot see, use every vessel going to you for purposes of transportation.

Hood has Thomas close in Nashville. I have said all I can to force him to attack, without giving the positive order until to-day. To-day, however, I could stand it no longer, and gave the order without any reserve. I think the battle will take place to-morrow. The result will probably be known in New York before Colonel Babcock (the bearer of this) will leave it. Colonel Babcock will give you full information of all operations now in progress. Very respectfully your obedient servant,

U. S. GRANT, *Lieutenant-General.*

The contents of these letters gave me great uneasiness, for I had set my heart on the capture of Savannah, which I believed to be practicable, and to be near; for me to embark for Virginia by sea was so complete a change from what I had supposed would be the course of events that I was very much concerned. I supposed, as a matter of course, that a fleet of vessels would soon pour in, ready to convey the army to Virginia, and as General Grant's orders contemplated my leaving the cavalry, trains, and artillery, behind, I judged Fort McAllister to be the best place for the purpose, and sent my chief-engineer, Colonel Poe, to that fort, to reconnoitre the ground, and to prepare it so as to make a fortified camp large enough to accommodate the vast herd of mules and horses that would thus be left behind. And as some time might be required to collect the necessary shipping, which I estimated at little less than a hundred steamers and sailing-vessels, I determined to push operations, in hopes to secure the city of Savannah before the necessary fleet could be available. All these ideas are given in my answer to General Grant's letters (dated December 16, 1864) herewith, which is a little more full than the one printed in the report of the Committee on the Conduct of the War, because in that copy I omitted the matter concerning General Thomas, which now need no longer be withheld:

HEADQUARTERS MILITARY DIVISION OF THE MISSISSIPPI, }
   IN THE FIELD, NEAR SAVANNAH, *December* 16, 1864. }

Lieutenant-General U. S. GRANT, *Commander-in-Chief, City Point, Virginia.*

GENERAL: I received, day before yesterday, at the hands of Lieutenant Dunn, your letter of December 3d, and last night, at the hands of Colonel Babcock, that of December 6th. I had previously made you a hasty scrawl from the tugboat Dandelion, in Ogeechee River, advising you that the army had reached the sea-coast, destroying all the railroads across the State of Georgia, investing closely the city of Savannah, and had made connection with the fleet.

Since writing that note, I have in person met and conferred with General Foster and Admiral Dahlgren, and made all the arrangements which were deemed essential for reducing the city of Savannah to our possession. But, since the receipt of yours of the 6th, I have initiated measures looking principally to coming to you with fifty or sixty thousand infantry, and incidently to capture Savannah, if time will allow.

At the time we carried Fort McAllister by assault so handsomely, with its twenty-two guns and entire garrison, I was hardly aware of its importance; but, since passing down the river with General Foster and up with Admiral Dahlgren. I realize how admirably adapted are Ossabaw Sound and Ogeechee River to supply an army operating against Savannah. Sea-going vessels can easily come to King's Bridge, a point on Ogeechee River, fourteen and a half miles due west of Savannah, from which point we have roads leading to all our camps. The country is low and sandy, and cut up with marshes, which in wet weather will be very bad, but we have been so favored with weather that they are all now comparatively good, and heavy details are constantly employed in double-corduroying the marshes, so that I have no fears even of bad weather. Fortunately, also by liberal and judicious foraging, we reached the sea-coast abundantly supplied with forage and provisions, needing nothing on arrival except bread. Of this we started from Atlanta, with from eight to twenty days' supply per corps, and some of the troops only had one day's issue of bread during the trip of thirty days; yet they did not want, for sweet-potatoes were very abundant, as well as corn-meal, and our soldiers took to them naturally. We started with about five thousand head of cattle, and arrived with over ten thousand, of course consuming mostly turkeys, chickens, sheep, hogs, and the cattle of the country. As to our mules and horses, we left Atlanta with about twenty-five hundred wagons, many of which were drawn by mules which had not recovered from the Chattanooga starvation, all of which were replaced, the poor mules shot, and our transportation is now in superb condition. I have no doubt the State of Georgia has lost, by our operations, fifteen thousand first-rate mules. As to horses, Kilpatrick collected all his remounts, and it looks to me, in riding along our columns, as though every officer had three or four led horses, and each regiment seems to be followed by at least fifty Negroes and foot-sore soldiers, riding on horses and mules. The custom was for each brigade to send out daily a foraging-party of about fifty men, on foot, who invariably returned mounted, with several wagons loaded with poultry, potatoes, etc., and as the army is composed of about forty brigades, you can estimate approximately the number of horses collected. Great numbers of these were shot by my order, because of the disorganizing effect on our infantry of having too many idlers mounted. General Easton is now engaged in collecting statistics on this subject, but I know the Government will never receive full accounts of our captures, although the result aimed at was fully attained, viz., to deprive our enemy of them. All these animals I will have sent to Port Royal, or collected behind Fort McAllister, to be used by General [Rufus] Saxton in his farming operations, or by the Quartermaster's Department, after they are systematically accounted for. While General Easton is collecting transportation for my troops to James River, I will throw to Port Royal Island all our means of transportation I can, and collect the rest near Fort McAllister, covered by the Ogeechee River and intrenchments to be erected, and for which Captain Poe, my chief-engineer, is now reconnoitring the ground, but in the mean time will act as I have begun, as though the city of Savannah were my objective: namely, the troops will continue to invest Savannah closely, making attacks and feints wherever we have fair ground to stand upon, and I will place some thirty-pound Parrotts, which I have got from General Foster, in position, near enough to reach the centre of the city, and then will demand its surrender. If General Hardee is alarmed, or fears starvation, he may surrender; otherwise I will bombard the city, but not risk the lives of our men by assaults across the narrow causeways, by which alone I can now reach it.

If I had time, Savannah, with all its dependent fortifications, would surely fall into our possession, for we hold all its avenues of supply.

The enemy has made two desperate efforts to get boats from above to the city, in both of which he has been foiled—General Slocum (whose left flank rests on the river) capturing and burning the first boat, and in the second instance driving back two gunboats and capturing the steamer Resolute, with seven naval officers and a crew of twenty-five seamen. General Slocum occupies Argyle Island and the upper end of Hutchinson Island, and has a brigade on the South Carolina shore opposite, and is very urgent to pass one of his corps over to that shore. But, in view of the change of plan made necessary by your order of the 6th, I will maintain things *in statu quo* till I have got all my transportation to the rear and out of the way, and until I have sea-transportation for the troops you require at James River, which I will accompany and command in person. Of course, I will leave Kilpatrick, with his cavalry (say five thousand three hundred), and, it may be, a division of the Fifteenth Corps; but, before determining on this, I must see General Foster, and may arrange to shift his force (now over above the Charleston Railroad, at the head of Broad River) to the Ogeechee, where, in coöperation with Kilpatrick's cavalry, he can better threaten the State of Georgia than from the direction of Port Royal. Besides, I would much prefer not to detach from my regular corps any of its veteran divisions, and would even prefer that other less valuable troops should be sent to reënforce Foster from some other quarter. My four corps, full of experience and full of ardor, coming to you *en masse,* equal to sixty thousand fighting-men, will be a reënforcement that Lee cannot disregard. Indeed, with my present command, I had expected, after reducing Savannah, instantly to march to Columbia, South Carolina; thence to Raleigh, and thence to report to you. But this would consume, it may be, six weeks' time after the fall of Savannah; whereas, by sea, I can probably reach you with my men and arms before the middle of January.

I myself am somewhat astonished at the attitude of things in Tennessee. I purposely delayed at Kingston until General Thomas assured me that he was all ready, and my last dispatch from him of the 12th of November was full of confidence, in which he promised me that he would ruin Hood if he dared to advance from Florence, urging me to go ahead, and give myself no concern about Hood's army in Tennessee.

Why he did not turn on him at Franklin, after checking and discomfiting him, surpasses my understanding. Indeed, I do not approve of his evacuating Decatur, but think he should have assumed the offensive against Hood from Pulaski, in the direction of Waynesburg. I know full well that General Thomas is slow in mind and in action; but he is judicious and brave, and the troops feel great confidence in him. I still hope he will outmanœuvre and destroy Hood.

As to matters in the Southeast, I think Hardee, in Savannah, has good artillerists, some five or six thousand good infantry, and, it may be, a mongrel mass of eight to ten thousand militia. In all our marching through Georgia, he has not forced us to use any thing but a skirmish-line, though at several points he had erected fortifications and tried to alarm us by bombastic threats. In Savannah he has taken refuge in a line constructed behind swamps and overflowed rice-fields, extending from a point on the Savannah River about three miles above the city, around by a branch of the Little Ogeechee, which stream is impassable from its salt-marshes and boggy swamps, crossed only by narrow causeways or common corduroy-roads.

There must be twenty-five thousand citizens, men, women, and children, in Savannah, that must also be fed, and how he is to feed them beyond a few days I cannot imagine. I know that his requisitions for corn on the interior countries were not filled, and we are in possession of the rice-fields and mills, which could alone be of service to him in this neighborhood. He can draw nothing from South Carolina, save from a small corner down in the southeast, and that by a disused wagon-road. I could easily get possession of this, but hardly deem it worth the risk of making a detachment, which would be in danger by its isolation from the main army. Our whole army is in fine condition as to health, and the weather is splendid. For that reason alone I feel a personal dislike to turning northward. I will keep Lieutenant Dunn here until I know the result of my demand for the surrender of Savannah, but, whether successful or not, shall not delay my execution of your order of the 6th, which will depend alone upon the time it will require to obtain transportation by sea.

I am, with respect, etc., your obedient servant,

W. T. SHERMAN, *Major-General United States Army.*

Having concluded all needful preparations, I rode from my headquarters, on the plank-road, over to General Slocum's headquarters, on the Macon road, and thence dispatched (by flag of truce) into Savannah, by the hands of Colonel Ewing, inspector-general, a demand for the surrender of the place. The following letters give the result. General Hardee refused to surrender, and I then resolved to make the attempt to break his line of defense at several places, trusting that some one would succeed.

HEADQUARTERS MILITARY DIVISION OF THE MISSISSIPPI, IN THE FIELD, SAVANNAH, GEORGIA, *December* 17, 1864.

General WILLIAM J. HARDEE, *commanding Confederate Forces in Savannah.*

GENERAL: You have doubtless observed, from your station at Rosedew that sea-going vessels now come through Ossabaw Sound and up the Ogeechee to the rear of my army, giving me abundant supplies of all kinds, and more especially heavy ordnance necessary for the reduction of Savannah. I have already received guns that can cast heavy and destructive shot as far as the heart of your city; also, I have for some days held and controlled every avenue by which the people and garrison of Savannah can be supplied, and I am therefore justified in demanding the surrender of the city of Savannah, and its dependent forts, and shall wait a reasonable time for your answer, before opening with heavy ordnance. Should you entertain the proposition, I am prepared to grant liberal terms to the inhabitants and garrison; but should I be forced to resort to assault, or the slower and surer process of starvation, I shall then feel justified in resorting to the harshest measures, and shall make little effort to restrain my army— burning to avenge the national wrong which they attach to Savannah and other large cities which have been so prominent in dragging our country into civil war. I inclose you a copy of General Hood's demand for the surrender of the town of Resaca, to be used by you for what it is worth.

I have the honor to be your obedient servant,

W. T. SHERMAN, *Major-General.*

HEADQUARTERS DEPARTMENT SOUTH CAROLINA, GEORGIA, AND FLORIDA, SAVANNAH, GEORGIA, *December* 17, 1864.

Major-General W. T. SHERMAN, *commanding Federal Forces near Savannah, Georgia.*

GENERAL: I have to acknowledge the receipt of a communication from you of this date, in which you demand "the surrender of Savannah and its dependent forts," on the ground that you "have received guns that can cast heavy and destructive shot into the heart of the city," and for the further reason that you "have, for some days, held and controlled every avenue by which the people and garrison can be supplied." You add that should you be "forced to resort to assault, or to the slower and surer process of starvation, you will then feel justified in resorting to the harshest measures, and will make little effort to restrain your army," etc., etc. The position of your forces (a half-mile beyond the outer line for the land-defense of Savannah) is, at the nearest point, at least four miles from the heart of the city. That and the interior line are both intact.

Your statement that you have, for some days, held and controlled every avenue by which the people and garrison can be supplied, is incorrect. I am in free and constant communication with my department.

Your demand for the surrender of Savannah and its dependent forts is refused.

With respect to the threats conveyed in the closing paragraphs of your letter (of what may be expected in case your demand is not complied with), I have to say that I have hitherto conducted the military operations intrusted to my direction in strict accordance with the rules of civilized warfare, and I should deeply regret the adoption of any course by you that may force me to deviate from them in future. I have the honor to be, very respectfully, your obedient servant,

W. J. HARDEE, *Lieutenant-General.*

HEADQUARTERS MILITARY DIVISION OF THE MISSISSIPPI,
IN THE FIELD, NEAR SAVANNAH, GEORGIA,
December 18, 1864—8 P. M.

Lieutenant-General U. S. GRANT, *City Point, Virginia.*

GENERAL: I wrote you at length (by Colonel Babcock) on the 16th instant. As I therein explained my purpose, yesterday I made a demand on General Hardee for the surrender of the city of Savannah, and to-day received his answer—refusing; copies of both letters are herewith inclosed. You will notice that I claim that my lines are within easy cannon-range of the heart of Savannah; but General Hardee asserts that we are four and a half miles distant. But I myself have been to the intersection of the Charleston and Georgia Central Railroads, and the three-mile post is but a few yards beyond, within the line of our pickets. The enemy has no pickets outside of his fortified line (which is a full quarter of a mile within the three-mile post), and I have the evidence of Mr. R. R. Cuyler, President of the Georgia Central Railroad (who was a prisoner in our hands), that the mile-posts are measured from the Exchange, which is but two squares back from the river. By to-morrow morning I will have six thirty-pound Parrotts in position, and General Hardee will learn whether I am right or not. From the left of our line, which is on the Savannah River, the spires can be plainly seen; but the country is so densely wooded with pine and live-oak, and lies so flat, that we can see nothing from any other portion of our lines. General Slocum feels confident that he can make a successful assault at one or two points in front of General Davis's (Fourteenth) corps. All of General Howard's troops (the right wing) lie behind the Little Ogeechee, and I doubt if it can be passed by troops in the face of an enemy. Still, we can make strong feints, and if I can get a sufficient number of boats, I shall make a coöperative demonstration up Vernon River or Wassaw Sound. I should like very much indeed to take Savannah before coming to you; but, as I wrote to you before, I will do nothing rash or hasty, and will embark for the James River as soon as General Easton (who is gone to Port Royal for that purpose) reports to me that he has an approximate number of vessels for the transportation of the contemplated force. I fear even this will cost more delay than you anticipate, for already the movement of our transports and the gunboats has required more time than I had expected. We have had dense fogs; there are more mud-banks in the Ogeechee than were reported, and there are no pilots whatever. Admiral Dahlgren promised to have the channel bouyed and staked, but it is not done yet. We find only six feet of water up to King's Bridge at low tide, about ten feet up to the rice-mill, and sixteen to Fort McAllister. All these points may be used by us, and we have a good, strong bridge across Ogeechee at King's by which our wagons can go to Fort McAllister, to which point I am sending all wagons not absolutely necessary for daily use, the Negroes, prisoners of war, sick, etc., *en route* for Port Royal. In relation to Savannah, you will remark that General Hardee refers to his still being in communication with his department. This language he thought would deceive me; but I am confirmed in the belief that the route to which he refers (the Union Plank-road on the South Carolina shore) is inadequate to feed his army and the people of Savannah, and General Foster assures me that he has his force on that very road, near the head of Broad River, so that cars no longer run between Charleston and Savannah. We hold this end of the Charleston Railroad, and have destroyed it from the three-mile post back to the bridge (about twelve miles). In anticipation of leaving this country, I am continuing the destruction of their railroads, and at this moment have two divisions and the cavalry at work breaking up the Gulf Railroad from the Ogeechee to the Altamaha; so that, even if I do not take Savannah, I will leave it in a bad way. But I still hope that events will give me time to take Savannah, even if I have to assault with some loss. I am satisfied that, unless we take it, the gunboats never will, for they can make no impression upon the batteries which guard every approach from the sea. I have a faint belief that, when Colonel Babcock reaches you,

you will delay operations long enough to enable me to succeed here. With Savannah in our possession, at some future time if not now, we can punish South Carolina as she deserves, and as thousands of the people in Georgia hoped we would do. I do sincerely believe that the whole United States, North and South, would rejoice to have this army turned loose on South Carolina, to devastate that State in the manner we have done in Georgia, and it would have a direct and immediate bearing on your campaign in Virginia.

I have the honor to be your obedient servant,

W. T. SHERMAN, *Major-General United States Army.*

As soon as the army had reached Savannah, and had opened communication with the fleet, I endeavored to ascertain what had transpired in Tennessee since our departure. We received our letters and files of newspapers, which contained full accounts of all the events there up to about the 1st of December. As before described, General Hood had three full corps of infantry—S. D. Lee's, A. P. Stewart's, and [Benjamin F.] Cheatham's, at Florence, Alabama—with Forrest's corps of cavalry, numbering in the aggregate about forty-five thousand men. General Thomas was in Nashville, Tennessee, quietly engaged in reorganizing his army out of the somewhat broken forces at his disposal. He had posted his only two regular corps, the Fourth and Twenty-third, under the general command of Major-General J. M. Schofield, at Pulaski, directly in front of Florence, with the three brigades of cavalry (Hatch, Croxton, and Capron), commanded by Major-General Wilson, watching closely for Hood's initiative.

This force aggregated about thirty thousand men, was therefore inferior to the enemy; and General Schofield was instructed, in case the enemy made a general advance, to fall back slowly toward Nashville, fighting, till he should be reenforced by General Thomas in person. Hood's movement was probably hurried by reason of my advance into Georgia; for on the 17th his infantry columns marched from Florence in the direction of Waynesboro', turning Schofield's position at Pulaski. The latter at once sent his trains to the rear, and on the 21st fell back to Columbia, Tennessee. General Hood followed up this movement, skirmished lightly with Schofield at Columbia, began the passage of Duck River, below the town, and Cheatman's corps reached the vicinity of Spring Hill, whither General Schofield had sent General Stanley, with two of his divisions, to cover the movement of his trains. During the night of November 29th General Schofield passed Spring Hill with his trains and army, and took post at Franklin, on the south side of Harpeth River. General Hood now attaches serious blame to General Cheatham for not attacking General Schofield in flank while in motion at Spring Hill, for he was bivouacked within eight hundred yards of the road at the time of the passage of our army. General Schofield reached Franklin on the morning of November 30th, and posted his army in front of the town, where some rifle-intrenchments had been constructed in advance. He had the two corps of Stanley and Cox (Fourth and Twenty-third), with Wilson's cavalry on his flanks, and sent his trains behind the Harpeth.

General Hood closed upon him the same day, and assaulted his position with vehemence, at one time breaking the line and wounding General Stanley seriously; but our men were veterans, cool and determined, and fought magnificently. The rebel officers led their men in person to the several persistent assaults, continuing the battle far into the night, when they drew off, beaten and discomfited.

Their loss was very severe, especially in general officers; among them Generals Cleburn and Adams, division commanders. Hood's loss on that day was afterward ascertained to be (Thomas's report): Buried on the field, seventeen hundred and fifty; left in hospital at Franklin, thirty-eight hundred; and seven hundred and two prisoners captured and held: aggregate, six thousand two hundred and fifty-two. General Schofield's loss, reported officially, was one hundred and eight-nine killed, one thousand and thirty-three wounded, and eleven hundred and four prisoners or missing: aggregate, twenty-three hundred and twenty-six. The next day General Schofield crossed the Harpeth without trouble, and fell back to the defenses of Nashville.

Meantime General Thomas had organized the employés of the Quartermaster's Department into a corps, commanded by the chief-quartermaster, General J[ames] L. Donaldson, and placed them in the fortifications of Nashville, under the general direction of Major-General Z[ealous] B. Tower, now of the United States Engineers. He had also received the two veteran divisions of the Sixteenth Corps, under General A. J.

Smith, long absent and long expected; and he had drawn from Chattanooga and Decatur (Alabama) the divisions of Steedman and of R. S. Granger. These, with General Schofield's army and about ten thousand good cavalry, under General J. H. Wilson, constituted a strong army, capable not only of defending Nashville, but of beating Hood in the open field. Yet Thomas remained inside of Nashville, seemingly passive, until General Hood had closed upon him and had intrenched his position.

General Thomas had furthermore held fast to the railroad leading from Nashville to Chattanooga, leaving strong guards at its principal points, as at Murfreesboro', Deckerd, Stevenson, Bridgeport, Whitesides, and Chattanooga. At Murfreesboro' the division of Rousseau was reënforced and strengthened up to about eight thousand men.

At that time the weather was cold and sleety, the ground was covered with ice and snow, and both parties for a time rested on the defensive. Thus matters stood at Nashville, while we were closing down on Savannah, in the early part of December, 1864; and the country, as well as General Grant, was alarmed at the seeming passive conduct of General Thomas; and General Grant at one time considered the situation so dangerous that he thought of going to Nashville in person, but General John A. Logan, happening to be at City Point, was sent out to supersede General Thomas; luckily for the latter, he acted in time, gained a magnificent victory, and thus escaped so terrible a fate.

On the 18th of December, at my camp by the side of the plank-road, eight miles back of Savannah, I received General Hardee's letter declining to surrender, when nothing remained but to assault. The ground was difficult, and, as all former assaults had proved so bloody, I concluded to make one more effort to completely surround Savannah on all sides, so as further to excite Hardee's fears, and, in case of success, to capture the whole of his army. We had already completely invested the place on the north, west, and south, but there remained to the enemy, on the east, the use of the old dike or plank-road leading into South Carolina, and I knew that Hardee would have a pontoon-bridge across the river. On examining my maps, I thought that the division of John P. Hatch, belonging to General Foster's command, might be moved from its then position at Broad River, by water, down to Bluffton, from which it could reach this plank-road, fortify and hold it—at some risk, of course, because Hardee could avail himself of his central position to fall on this detachment with his whole army. I did not want to make a mistake like "Ball's Bluff" at that period of the war; so, taking one or two of my personal staff, I rode back to King's Bridge, leaving with Generals Howard and Slocum orders to make all possible preparations, but not to attack, during my two or three days' absence; and there I took a boat for Wassaw Sound, whence Admiral Dahlgren conveyed me in his own boat (the Harvest Moon) to Hilton Head, where I represented the matter to General Foster, and he promptly agreed to give his personal attention to it. During the night of the 20th we started back, the wind blowing strong, Admiral Dahlgren ordered the pilot of the Harvest Moon to run into Tybee, and to work his way through to Wassaw Sound and the Ogeechee River by the Romney Marshes. We were caught by a low tide and stuck in the mud. After laboring some time, the admiral ordered out his barge; in it we pulled through this intricate and shallow channel, and toward evening of December 21st we discovered, coming toward us, a tug, called the Red Legs, belonging to the Quartermaster's Department, with a staff-officer on board, bearing letters from Colonel Dayton to myself and the admiral, reporting that the city of Savannah had been found evacuated on the morning of December 21st, and was then in our possession. General Hardee had crossed the Savannah River by a pontoon-bridge, carrying off his men and light artillery, blowing up his iron-clads and navy-yard, but leaving for us all the heavy guns, stores, cotton, railway-cars, steamboats, and an immense amount of public and private property. Admiral Dahlgren concluded to go toward a vessel (the Sonoma) of his blockading fleet, which lay at anchor near Beaulieu, and I transferred to the Red Legs, and hastened up the Ogeechee River to King's Bridge, whence I rode to my camp that same night. I there learned that, early on the morning of December 21st, the skirmishers had detected the absence of the enemy, and had occupied his lines simultaneously along their whole extent; but the left flank (Slocum), especially Geary's division of the Twentieth Corps, claimed to have been the first to reach the heart of the city.

Generals Slocum and Howard moved their headquarters at once into the city, leaving the bulk of their troops in camps outside. On the morning of December 22d I followed with my own headquarters, and rode down Bull Street to the custom-house, from the roof of which we had an extensive view over the city, the river, and the vast extent of marsh and rice-fields on the South Carolina side. The navy-yard, and the wreck of the iron-clad ram Savannah, were still smoldering, but all else looked quiet enough. Turning back, we rode to the Pulaski Hotel, which I had known in years long gone, and found it kept by a Vermont man with a lame leg, who used to be a clerk in the St. Louis Hotel, New Orleans, and I inquired about the capacity of his hotel for headquarters. He was very anxious to have us for boarders, but I soon explained to him that we had a full mess equipment along, and that we were not in the habit of paying board; that one wing of the building would suffice for our use, while I would allow him to keep an hotel for the accommodation of officers and gentlemen in the remainder. I then dispatched an officer to look around for a livery-stable that could accommodate our horses, and, while waiting there, an English gentleman, Mr. Charles Green, came and said that he had a fine house completely furnished, for which he had no use, and offered it as headquarters. He explained, moreover, that General Howard had informed him, the day before, that I would want his house for headquarters. At first I felt strongly disinclined to make use of any private dwelling, lest complaints should arise of damage and loss of furniture, and so expressed myself to Mr. Green; but, after riding about the city, and finding his house so spacious, so convenient, with large yard and stabling, I accepted his offer, and occupied that house during our stay in Savannah. He only reserved for himself the use of a couple of rooms above the dining-room, and we had all else, and a most excellent house it was in all respects.

I was disappointed that Hardee had escaped with his army, but on the whole we had reason to be content with the sub-stantial fruits of victory. The Savannah River was found to be badly obstructed by torpedoes, and by log piers stretched across the channel below the city, which piers were filled with the cobble stones that formerly paved the streets. Admiral Dahlgren was extremely active, visited me repeatedly in the city, while his fleet still watched Charleston, and all the ave-nues, for the blockade-runners that infested the coast, which were notoriously owned and managed by Englishmen, who used the island of New Providence (Nassau) as a sort of entrepot. One of these small blockade-runners came into Savannah after we were in full possession, and the master did not discover his mistake till he came ashore to visit the custom-house. Of course his vessel fell a prize to the navy. A heavy force was at once set to work to remove the torpedoes and obstructions in the main channel of the river, and, from that time forth, Savannah became the great depot of supply for the troops operating in that quarter.

Meantime, on the 15th and 16th of December, were fought, in front of Nashville, the great battles in which General Thomas so nobly fulfilled his promise to ruin Hood, the details of which are fully given in his own official reports, long since published. Rumors of these great victories reached us at Savannah by piecemeal, but his official report came on the 24th of December, with a letter from General Grant, giving in general terms the events up to the 18th, and I wrote at once through my chief of staff, General Webster, to General Thomas, complimenting him in the highest terms. His brilliant victory at Nashville was necessary to mine at Savannah to make a complete whole, and this fact was perfectly comprehended by Mr. Lincoln, who recognized it fully in his personal letter of December 26th, hereinbefore quoted at length, and which I also claimed at the time, in my Special Field Order No. 6, of January 8, 1865, here given:

[Special Field Order No. 6.]

HEADQUARTERS MILITARY DIVISION OF THE MISSISSIPPI, }
IN THE FIELD, SAVANNAH, GEORGIA, *January* 8, 1865. }

The general commanding announces to the troops composing the Military Division of the Mississippi that he has received from the President of the United States, and from Lieutenant-General Grant, letters conveying their high sense and appreciation of the campaign just closed, resulting in the capture of Savannah and the defeat of Hood's army in Tennessee.

In order that all may understand the importance of events, it is proper to revert to the situation of affairs in September last. We held Atlanta, a city of little value to us, but so important to the enemy that Mr. Davis, the head of the rebellious faction in the South, visited his army near

Palmetto, and commanded it to regain the place and also to ruin and destroy us, by a series of measures which he thought would be effectual. That army, by a rapid march, gained our railroad near Big Shanty, and afterward about Dalton. We pursued it, but it moved so rapidly that we could not overtake it, and General Hood led his army successfully far over toward Mississippi, in hope to decoy us out of Georgia. But we were not thus to be led away by him, and preferred to lead and control events ourselves. Generals Thomas and Schofield, commanding the departments to our rear, returned to their posts and prepared to decoy General Hood into their meshes, while we came on to complete the original journey. We quietly and deliberately destroyed Atlanta, and all the railroads which the enemy had used to carry on war against us, occupied his State capital, and then captured his commercial capital, which had been so strongly fortified from the sea as to defy approach from that quarter. Almost at the moment of our victorious entry into Savannah came the welcome and expected news that our comrades in Tennessee had also fulfilled nobly and well their part, had decoyed General Hood to Nashville and then turned on him, defeating his army thoroughly, capturing all his artillery, great numbers of prisoners, and were still pursuing the fragments down in Alabama. So complete a success in military operations, extending over half a continent, is an achievement that entitles it to a place in the military history of the world. The armies serving in Georgia and Tennessee, as well as the local garrisons of Decatur, Bridgeport, Chattanooga, and Murfreesboro', are alike entitled to the common honors, and each regiment may inscribe on its colors, at pleasure, the word "Savannah" or "Nashville." The general commanding embraces, in the same general success, the operations of the cavalry under Generals Stoneman, [Stephen G.] Burbridge, and [Alvan C.] Gillem, that penetrated into Southwest Virginia, and paralyzed the efforts of the enemy to disturb the peace and safety of East Tennessee. Instead of being put on the defensive, we have at all points assumed the bold offensive, and have completely thwarted the designs of the enemies of our country.

By order of Major-General W. T. Sherman,

L. M. Dayton, *Aide-de-Camp.*

Chapter 15

Savannah:
"The Beginning of Wisdom"
December, 1864—January, 1865

THE CITY OF Savannah was an old place, and usually accounted a handsome one. Its houses were of brick or frame, with large yards, ornamented with shrubbery and flowers; its streets perfectly regular, crossing each other at right angles; and at many of the intersections were small inclosures in the nature of parks. These streets and parks were lined with the handsomest shade-trees of which I have knowledge, viz., the willow-leaf live-oak, evergreens of exquisite beauty; and these certainly entitled Savannah to its reputation as a handsome town more than the houses, which, though comfortable, would hardly make a display on Fifth Avenue or the Boulevard Haussmann of Paris. The city was built on a plateau of sand about forty feet above the level of the sea, abutting against the river, leaving room along its margin for a street of stores and warehouses. The custom-house, court-house, post-office, etc., were on the plateau above. In rear of Savannah was a large park, with a fountain, and between it and the court-house was a handsome monument, erected to the memory of Count Pulaski, who fell in 1779 in the assault made on the city at the time it was held by the English during the Revolutionary War. Outside of Savannah there was very little to interest a stranger, except the cemetery of Bonaventura, and the ride along the Wilmington Channel by way of Thunderbolt, where might be seen some groves of the majestic live-oak trees, covered with gray and funereal moss, which were truly sublime in grandeur, but gloomy after a few days' camping under them.

Within an hour of taking up my quarters in Mr. Green's house, Mr. A. G. Browne, of Salem, Massachusetts, United States Treasury agent for the Department of the South, made his appearance to claim possession, in the name of the Treasury Department, of all captured cotton, rice, buildings, etc. Having use for these articles ourselves, and having fairly earned them, I did not feel inclined to surrender possession, and explained to him that the quartermaster and commissary could manage them more to my liking than he; but I agreed, after the proper inventories had been prepared, if there remained any thing for which we had no special use, I would turn it over to him. It was then known that in the warehouses were stored at least twenty-five thousand bales of cotton, and in the forts one hundred and fifty large, heavy sea-coast guns; although afterward, on a more careful count, there proved to be more than two hundred and fifty sea-coast or siege guns, and thirty-one thousand bales of cotton. At that interview Mr. Browne, who was a shrewd, clever Yankee, told me that a vessel was on the point of starting for Old Point Comfort, and, if she had good weather off Cape Hatteras, would reach Fortress Monroe by Christmas-day, and he suggested that I might make it the occasion of sending a welcome Christmas gift to the President, Mr. Lincoln, who peculiarly enjoyed such pleasantry. I accordingly sat down and wrote on a slip of paper, to be left at the telegraph-office at Fortress Monroe for transmission, the following:

SAVANNAH, GEORGIA, *December* 22, 1864.

To His Excellency President LINCOLN, *Washington, D. C.:*

I beg to present you as a Christmas-gift the city of Savannah, with one hundred and fifty heavy guns and plenty of ammunition, also about twenty-five thousand bales of cotton.

W. T. SHERMAN, *Major-General.*

This message actually reached him on Christmas-eve, was extensively published in the newspapers, and made many a household unusually happy on that festive day; and it was in the answer to this dispatch that Mr. Lincoln wrote me the letter of December 28th, already given, beginning with the words, "Many, many thanks," etc., which he sent at the hands of General John A. Logan, who happened to be in Washington, and was coming to Savannah, to rejoin his command.

On the 23d of December were made the following general orders for the disposition of the troops in and about Savannah:

[Special Field Order No. 139.]

HEADQUARTERS MILITARY DIVISION OF THE MISSISSIPPI, IN THE FIELD, SAVANNAH, GEORGIA, *December* 23, 1864.

Savannah, being now in our possession, the river partially cleared out, and measures having been taken to remove all obstructions, will at once be made a grand depot for future operations:

1. The chief-quartermaster, General Easton, will, after giving the necessary orders touching the transports in Ogeechee River and Ossabaw Sound, come in person to Savannah, and take possession of all public buildings, vacant storerooms, warehouses, etc., that may be now or hereafter needed for any department of the army. No rents will be paid by the Government of the United States during the war, and all buildings must be distributed according to the accustomed rules of the Quartermaster's Department, as though they were public property.

2. The chief commissary of subsistence, Colonel A. Beckwith, will transfer the grand depot of the army to the city of Savannah, secure possession of the needful buildings and offices, and give the necessary orders, to the end that the army may be supplied abundantly and well.

3. The chief-engineer, Captain Poe, will at once direct which of the enemy's forts are to be retained for our use, and which dismantled and destroyed. The chief ordnance-officer, Captain Baylor, will in like manner take possession of all property pertaining to his department captured from

the enemy, and cause the same to be collected and conveyed to points of security; all the heavy coast-guns will be dismounted and carried to Fort Pulaski.

4. The troops, for the present, will be grouped about the city of Savannah, looking to convenience of camps; General Slocum taking from the Savannah River around to the seven-mile post on the canal, and General Howard thence to the sea; General Kilpatrick will hold King's Bridge until Fort McAllister is dismantled, and the troops withdrawn from the south side of the Ogeechee, when he will take post about Anderson's plantation, on the plank-road, and picket all the roads leading from the north and west.

5. General Howard will keep a small guard at Forts Rosedale, Beaulieu, Wimberley, Thunderbolt, and Bonaventura, and he will cause that shore and Skidaway Island to be examined very closely, with a view to finding many and convenient points for the embarkation of troops and wagons on sea-going vessels.

By order of Major-General W. T. Sherman,

L. M. DAYTON, *Aide-de-Camp*.

[Special Field Order No. 143.]

HEADQUARTERS MILITARY DIVISION OF THE MISSISSIPPI,
IN THE FIELD, SAVANNAH, GEORGIA,
December 26, 1864.

The city of Savannah and surrounding country will be held as a military post, and adapted to future military uses, but, as it contains a population of some twenty thousand people, who must be provided for, and as other citizens may come, it is proper to lay down certain general principles, that all within its military jurisdiction may understand their relative duties and obligations.

1. During war, the military is superior to civil authority, and, where interests clash, the civil must give way; yet, where there is no conflict, every encouragement should be given to well-disposed and peaceful inhabitants to resume their usual pursuits. Families should be disturbed as little as possible in their residences, and tradesmen allowed the free use of their shops, tools, etc.; churches, schools, and

all places of amusement and recreation, should be encouraged, and streets and roads made perfectly safe to persons in their pursuits. Passes should not be exacted within the line of outer pickets, but if any person shall abuse these privileges by communicating with the enemy, or doing any act of hostility to the Government of the United States, he or she will be punished with the utmost rigor of the law. Commerce with the outer world will be resumed to an extent commensurate with the wants of the citizens, governed by the restrictions and rules of the Treasury Department.

2. The chief-quartermaster and commissary of the army may give suitable employment to the people, white and black, or transport them to such points as they may choose where employment can be had; and may extend temporary relief in the way of provisions and vacant houses to the worthy and needy, until such time as they can help themselves. They will select first the buildings for the necessary uses of the army; next, a sufficient number of stores, to be turned over to the Treasury agent for trade-stores. All vacant storehouses or dwellings, and all buildings belonging to absent rebels, will be construed and used as belonging to the United States, until such time as their titles can be settled by the courts of the United States.

3. The Mayor and City Council of Savannah will continue to exercise their functions, and will, in concert with the commanding officer of the post and the chief-quartermaster, see that the fire-companies are kept in organization, the streets cleaned and lighted, and keep up a good understanding between the citizens and soldiers. They will ascertain and report to the chief commissary of subsistence, as soon as possible, the names and number of worthy families that need assistance and support. The mayor will forthwith give public notice that the time has come when all must choose their course, viz., remain within our lines, and conduct themselves as good citizens, or depart in peace. He will ascertain the names of all who choose to leave Savannah, and report their names and residence to the chief-quartermaster, that measures may be taken to transport them beyond our lines.

4. Not more than two newspapers will be published in

Savannah; their editors and proprietors will be held to the strictest accountability, and will be punished severely, in person and property, for any libelous publication, mischievous matter, premature news, exaggerated statements, or any comments whatever upon the acts of the constituted authorities; they will be held accountable for such articles, even though copied from other papers.

By order of Major-General W. T. Sherman,

L. M. Dayton, *Aide-de-Camp.*

It was estimated that there were about twenty thousand inhabitants in Savannah, all of whom had participated more or less in the war, and had no special claims to our favor, but I regarded the war as rapidly drawing to a close, and it was becoming a political question as to what was to be done with the people of the South, both white and black, when the war was actually over. I concluded to give them the option to remain or to join their friends in Charleston or Augusta, and so announced in general orders. The mayor, Dr. Arnold, was completely "subjugated," and, after consulting with him, I authorized him to assemble his City Council to take charge generally of the interests of the people; but warned all who remained that they must be strictly subordinate to the military law, and to the interests of the General Government. About two hundred persons, mostly the families of men in the Confederate army, prepared to follow the fortunes of their husbands and fathers, and these were sent in a steamboat under a flag of truce, in charge of my aide Captain Audenried, to Charleston harbor, and there delivered to an officer of the Confederate army. But the great bulk of the inhabitants chose to remain in Savannah, generally behaved with propriety, and good social relations at once arose between them and the army. Shortly after our occupation of Savannah, a lady was announced at my headquarters by the orderly or sentinel at the front-door, who was ushered into the parlor, and proved to be the wife of General G. W. Smith, whom I had known about 1850, when Smith was on duty at West Point. She was a native of New London, Connecticut, and very handsome. She began her interview by presenting me a letter from her husband, who then commanded a division of the Georgia militia in the rebel army, which had just quitted Savannah, which letter began, "DEAR SHERMAN: The fortunes of war, etc., compel me to leave my wife in Savannah, and I beg for her your courteous protection," etc., etc. I inquired where she lived, and if anybody was troubling her. She said she was boarding with a lady whose husband had, in like manner with her own, gone off with Hardee's army; that a part of the house had been taken for the use of Major-General Ward, of Kentucky; that her landlady was approaching her confinement, and was nervous at the noise which the younger staff-officers made at night, etc. I explained to her that I could give but little personal attention to such matters, and referred her to General Slocum, whose troops occupied the city. I afterward visited her house, and saw, personally, that she had no reason to complain. Shortly afterward Mr. Hardee, a merchant of Savannah, came to me and presented a letter from his brother, the general, to the same effect, alleging that his brother was a civilian, had never taken up arms, and asked of me protection for his family, his cotton, etc. To him I gave the general assurance that no harm was designed to any of the people of Savannah who would remain quiet and peaceable, but that I could give him no guarantee as to his cotton, for over it I had no absolute control; and yet still later I received a note from the wife of General A. P. Stewart (who commanded a corps in Hood's army), asking me to come to see her. This I did, and found her to be a native of Cincinnati, Ohio, wanting protection, and who was naturally anxious about the fate of her husband, known to be with General Hood, in Tennessee, retreating before General Thomas. I remember that I was able to assure her that he had not been killed or captured, up to that date, and think that I advised her, instead of attempting to go in pursuit of her husband, to go to Cincinnati, to her uncle, Judge Storer, there await the issue of events.

Before I had reached Savannah, and during our stay there, the rebel officers and newspapers represented the conduct of the men of our army as simply infamous; that we respected neither age nor sex; that we burned every thing we came across—barns, stables, cotton-gins, and even dwelling-houses; that we ravished the women and killed the men, and perpetrated all manner of outrages on the inhabitants. Therefore it struck me as strange that Generals Hardee and Smith should commit their families to our custody, and even bespeak our personal care and attention. These officers knew well that these reports were exaggerated in the extreme, and yet tacitly assented to these false publications, to arouse the drooping energies of the people of the South.

As the division of Major-General John W. Geary, of the Twentieth Corps, was the first to enter Savannah, that officer was appointed to command the place, or to act as a sort of governor. He very soon established a good police, maintained admirable order, and I doubt if Savannah, either before or since, has had a better government than during our stay. The guard-mountings and parades, as well as the greater reviews, became the daily resorts of the ladies, to hear the music of our excellent bands; schools were opened, and the churches every Sunday were well filled with most devout and respectful congregations; stores were reopened, and markets for provisions, meat, wood, etc., were established, so that each family, regardless of race, color, or opinion, could procure all the necessaries and even luxuries of life, provided they had money. Of course, many families were actually destitute of this, and to these were issued stores from our own stock of supplies. I remember to have given to Dr. Arnold, the mayor, an order for the contents of a large warehouse of rice, which he confided to a committee of gentlemen, who went North (to Boston), and soon returned with one or more cargoes of flour, hams, sugar, coffee, etc., for gratuitous distribution, which relieved the most pressing wants until the revival of trade and business enabled the people to provide for themselves.

A lady, whom I had known in former years as Miss Josephine Goodwin, told me that, with a barrel of flour and some sugar which she had received gratuitously from the commissary, she had baked cakes and pies, in the sale of which she realized a profit of fifty-six dollars.

Meantime Colonel Poe had reconnoitred and laid off new lines of parapet, which would enable a comparatively small garrison to hold the place, and a heavy detail of soldiers was put to work thereon; Generals Easton and Beckwith had organized a complete depot of supplies; and, though vessels arrived almost daily with mails and provisions, we were hardly ready to initiate a new and hazardous campaign. I had not yet received from General Grant or General Halleck any

modification of the orders of December 6, 1864, to embark
my command for Virginia by sea; but on the 2d of January,
1865, General J[ohn] G. Barnard, United States Engineers, arrived direct from General Grant's headquarters, bearing the
following letter, in the general's own handwriting, which, with
my answer, is here given:

HEADQUARTERS ARMIES OF THE UNITED STATES, }
CITY POINT, VIRGINIA, *December* 27, 1864. }

Major-General W. T. SHERMAN, *commanding Military Division of the Mississippi.*

GENERAL: Before writing you definite instructions for
the next campaign, I wanted to receive your answer to my
letter written from Washington. Your confidence in being
able to march up and join this army pleases me, and I
believe it can be done. The effect of such a campaign will
be to disorganize the South, and prevent the organization
of new armies from their broken fragments. Hood is now
retreating, with his army broken and demoralized. His loss
in men has probably not been far from twenty thousand,
besides deserters. If time is given, the fragments may be
collected together and many of the deserters reassembled. If
we can, we should act to prevent this. Your spare army, as
it were, moving as proposed, will do it.

In addition to holding Savannah, it looks to me that an
intrenched camp ought to be held on the railroad between
Savannah and Charleston. Your movement toward Branchville will probably enable Foster to reach this with his own
force. This will give us a position in the South from which
we can threaten the interior without marching over long,
narrow causeways, easily defended, as we have heretofore
been compelled to do. Could not such a camp be established
about Pocotaligo or Coosawhatchie?

I have thought that, Hood being so completely wiped out
for present harm, I might bring A. J. Smith here, with fourteen to fifteen thousand men. With this increase I could
hold my lines, and move out with a greater force than Lee
has. It would compel Lee to retain all his present force in
the defenses of Richmond or abandon them entirely. This

latter contingency is probably the only danger to the easy success of your expedition. In the event you should meet Lee's army, you would be compelled to beat it or find the sea-coast. Of course, I shall not let Lee's army escape if I can help it, and will not let it go without following to the best of my ability.

Without waiting further directions, then, you may make your preparations to start on your northern expedition without delay. Break up the railroads in South and North Carolina, and join the armies operating against Richmond as soon as you can. I will leave out all suggestions about the route you should take, knowing that your information, gained daily in the course of events, will be better than any that can be obtained now.

It may not be possible for you to march to the rear of Petersburg; but, failing in this, you could strike either of the sea-coast ports in North Carolina held by us. From there you could take shipping. It would be decidedly preferable, however, if you could march the whole distance.

From the best information I have, you will find no difficulty in supplying your army until you cross the Roanoke. From there here is but a few days' march, and supplies could be collected south of the river to bring you through. I shall establish communication with you there, by steamboat and gunboat. By this means your wants can be partially supplied. I shall hope to hear from you soon, and to hear your plan, and about the time of starting.

Please instruct Foster to hold on to all the property in Savannah, and especially the cotton. Do not turn it over to citizens or Treasury agents, without orders of the War Department.

Very respectfully, your obedient servant,
U. S. GRANT, *Lieutenant-General.*

HEADQUARTERS MILITARY DIVISION OF THE MISSISSIPPI,
IN THE FIELD, SAVANNAH, GEORGIA,
January 2, 1865.

Lieutenant-General U. S. GRANT, *City Point.*

GENERAL: I have received, by the hands of General Barnard, your note of 26th and letter of 27th December.

I herewith inclose to you a copy of a *projet* which I have this morning, in strict confidence, discussed with my immediate commanders.

I shall need, however, larger supplies of stores, especially grain. I will inclose to you, with this, letters from General Easton, quartermaster, and Colonel Beckwith, commissary of subsistence, setting forth what will be required, and trust you will forward them to Washington with your sanction, so that the necessary steps may be taken at once to enable me to carry out this plan on time. . . .

W. H. SHERMAN, *Major-General.*

[Entirely confidential.]

PROJET FOR JANUARY

1. Right wing to move men and artillery by transports to head of Broad River and Beaufort; reëstablish Port Royal Ferry, and mass the wing at or in the neighborhood of Pocotaligo.

Left wing and cavalry to work slowly across the causeway toward Hardeeville, to open a road by which wagons can reach their corps about Broad River; also, by a rapid movement of the left, to secure Sister's Ferry, and Augusta road out to Robertsville.

In the mean time, all guns, shot, shell, cotton, etc., to be moved to a safe place, easy to guard, and provisions and wagons got ready for another *swath*, aiming to have our army in hand about the head of Broad River, say Pocotaligo, Robertsville, and Coosawhatchie, by the 15th January.

2. The whole army to move with loaded wagons by the roads leading in the direction of Columbia, which afford the best chance of forage and provisions. Howard to be at Pocotaligo by the 15th January, and Slocum to be at Robertsville, and Kilpatrick at or near Coosawhatchie about the same date. General Foster's troops to occupy Savannah, and gunboats to protect the rivers as soon as Howard gets Pocotaligo.

W. T. SHERMAN, *Major-General.*

Therefore, on the 2d of January, I was authorized to march with my entire army north by land, and concluded at once to secure a foothold or starting-point on the South Carolina side, selecting Pocotaligo and Hardeeville as the points of rendezvous for the two wings; but I still remained in doubt as to the wishes of the Administration, whether I should take Charleston *en route,* or confine my whole attention to the incidental advantages of breaking up the railways of South and North Carolina, and the greater object of uniting my army with that of General Grant before Richmond.

General Barnard remained with me several days, and was regarded then, as now, one of the first engineers of the age, perfectly competent to advise me on the strategy and objects of the new campaign. He expressed himself delighted with the high spirit of the army, the steps already taken, by which we had captured Savannah, and he personally inspected some of the forts, such as Thunderbolt and Causten's Bluff, by which the enemy had so long held at bay the whole of our navy, and had defeated the previous attempts made in April, 1862, by the army of General [Quincy A.] Gillmore, which had bombarded and captured Fort Pulaski, but had failed to reach the city of Savannah. I think General Barnard expected me to invite him to accompany us northward in his official capacity; but Colonel Poe, of my staff, had done so well, and was so perfectly competent, that I thought it unjust to supersede him by a senior in his own corps. I therefore said nothing of this to General Barnard, and soon after he returned to his post with General Grant, at City Point, bearing letters and full personal messages of our situation and wants.

We were very much in want of light-draught steamers for navigating the shallow waters of the coast, so that it took the Seventeenth Corps more than a week to transfer from Thunderbolt to Beaufort, South Carolina. Admiral Dahlgren had supplied the Harvest Moon and the Pontiac, and General Foster gave us a couple of hired steamers; I was really amused at the effect this short sea-voyage had on our men, most of whom had never before looked upon the ocean. Of course, they were fit subjects for sea-sickness, and afterward they begged me never again to send them to sea, saying they would rather march a thousand miles on the worst roads of the South than to spend a single night on the ocean. By the 10th General Howard had collected the bulk of the Seventeenth Corps (General Blair) on Beaufort Island, and began his march for Pocotaligo, twenty-five miles inland. They crossed the channel between the island and main-land during Saturday, the 14th of January, by a pontoon-bridge, and marched out to Garden's Corners, where there was some light skirmishing; the next day, Sunday, they continued on to Pocotaligo, finding the strong fort there abandoned, and accordingly made a lodgment on the railroad, having lost only two officers and eight men.

About the same time General Slocum crossed two divisions of the Twentieth Corps over the Savannah River, above the city, occupied Hardeeville by one division and Purysburg by another. Thus, by the middle of January, we had effected a lodgment in South Carolina, and were ready to resume the march northward; but we had not yet accumulated enough provisions and forage to fill the wagons, and other causes of delay occurred, of which I will make mention in due order.

On the last day of December, 1864, Captain [K. Randolph] Breese, United States Navy, flag-officer to Admiral Porter, reached Savannah, bringing the first news of General Butler's failure at Fort Fisher, and that the general had returned to James River with his land-forces, leaving Admiral Porter's fleet anchored off Cape Fear, in that tempestuous season. Captain Breese brought me a letter from the admiral, dated December 29th, asking me to send him from Savannah one of my old divisions, with which he said he would make short work of Fort Fisher; that he had already bombarded and silenced its guns, and that General Butler had failed because he was afraid to attack, or even give the order to attack, after (as Porter insisted) the guns of Fort Fisher had been actually silenced by the navy.

I answered him promptly on the 31st of December, that I proposed to march north *inland,* and that I would prefer to leave the rebel garrisons on the coast, instead of dislodging and piling them up in my front as we progressed. From the chances, as I then understood them, I supposed that Fort Fisher was garrisoned by a comparatively small force, while the whole division of General [Robert F.] Hoke remained about the city of Wilmington; and that, if Fort Fisher were captured, it would leave General Hoke free to join the larger force that would naturally be collected to oppose my progress northward. I accordingly answered Admiral Porter to this effect, declining to loan him the use of one of my divisions. It subsequently transpired, however, that; as soon as General Butler reached City Point, General Grant was unwilling to rest under a sense of failure, and accordingly dispatched back the same troops, reënforced and commanded by General A[lfred] H. Terry, who, on the 15th day of January, successfully assaulted and captured Fort Fisher, with its entire garrison. After the war was over, about the 20th of May, when I was giving my testimony before the Congressional Committee on the Conduct of the War, the chairman of the committee, Senator B[enjamin] F. Wade, of Ohio, told me that General Butler had been summoned before that committee during the previous January, and had just finished his demonstration to their entire satisfaction that Fort Fisher could not be carried by assault, when they heard the newsboy in the hall crying out an "extra." Calling him in, they inquired the news, and he answered, "Fort Fisher done took!" Of course, they all laughed, and none more heartily than General Butler himself.

On the 11th of January there arrived at Savannah a revenue-cutter, having on board Simeon Draper, Esq., of New York City, the Hon. E. M. Stanton, Secretary of War, Quartermaster-General Meigs, Adjutant-General Townsend, and a retinue of civilians, who had come down from the North to regulate the civil affairs of Savannah.

I was instructed by Mr. Stanton to transfer to Mr. Draper the custom-house, post-office, and such other public buildings as these civilians needed in the execution of their office, and to cause to be delivered into their custody the captured cotton.

Up to this time all the cotton had been carefully guarded, with orders to General Easton to ship it by the return-vessels to New York, for the adjudication of the nearest prize-court, accompanied with invoices and all evidence of title to ownership. Marks, numbers, and other figures, were carefully preserved on the bales, so that the court might know the history of each bale. But Mr. Stanton, who surely was an able lawyer, changed all this, and ordered the obliteration of all the marks; so that no man, friend or foe, could trace his identical cotton. I thought it strange at the ime, and think it more so now; for I am assured that claims, real and fictitious, have been *proved up* against this identical cotton of three times the quantity actually captured, and that reclamations on the Treasury have been *allowed* for more than the actual quantity captured, viz., thirty-one thousand bales.

Mr. Stanton staid in Savannah several days, and seemed very curious about matters and things in general. I walked with him through the city, especially the bivouacs of the several regiments that occupied the vacant squares, and he seemed particularly pleased at the ingenuity of the men in constructing their temporary huts. Four of the "dog-tents," or *tentes d'abri*, buttoned together, served for a roof, and the sides were made of clapboards, or rough boards brought from demolished houses or fences. I remember his marked admiration for the hut of a soldier who had made his door out of a handsome parlor mirror, the glass gone and its gilt frame serving for his door.

He talked to me a great deal about the Negroes, the former slaves, and I told him of many interesting incidents, illustrating their simple character and faith in our arms and progress. He inquired particularly about General Jeff. C. Davis, who, he said, was a Democrat, and hostile to the Negro. I assured him that General Davis was an excellent soldier, and I did not believe he had any hostility to the Negro; that in our army we had no Negro soldiers, and, as a rule, we preferred white soldiers, but that we employed a large force of them as servants, teamsters, and pioneers, who had rendered admirable service. He then showed me a newspaper account of General Davis taking up his pontoon-bridge across Ebenezer Creek, leaving sleeping Negro men, women, and children, on the other side, to be slaughtered by Wheeler's cavalry. I had heard such a rumor, and advised Mr. Stanton, before becoming prejudiced, to allow me to send for General Davis, which he did, and General Davis explained the matter to his entire satisfaction. The truth was, that, as we approached the seaboard, the freedmen in droves, old and young, followed the several columns to reach a place of safety. It so happened that General Davis's route into Savannah followed what was known as the "River-road," and he had to make constant use of his pontoon-train—the head of his column reaching some deep, impassable creek before the rear was fairly over another. He had occasionally to use the pontoons both day and night. On the occasion referred to, the bridge was taken up from Ebenezer Creek while some of the camp-followers remained asleep on the farther side, and these were pickd up by Wheeler's cavalry. Some of them, in their fright, were drowned in trying to swim over, and others may have been cruelly killed by Wheeler's men, but this was a mere supposition. At all events, the same thing might have resulted to General Howard, or to any other of the many most humane commanders who filled the army. General Jeff. C. Davis was strictly a soldier, and doubtless hated to have his wagons and columns encumbered by these poor Negroes, for whom we all felt sympathy, but a sympathy of a different sort from that of Mr. Stanton, which was not of pure humanity, but of *politics*. The Negro question was beginning to loom up among the political eventualities of the day, and many foresaw that not only would the slaves secure their freedom, but that they would also have votes. I did not dream of such a result then, but knew that slavery, as such, was dead forever, and did not suppose that the former slaves would be suddenly, without preparation, manufactured into voters, equal to all others, politically and socially. Mr. Stanton seemed desirous of coming into contact with the Negroes to confer with them, and he asked me to arrange an interview for him. I accordingly sent out and invited the most intelligent of the Negroes, mostly Baptist and Methodist preachers, to come to my rooms to meet the Secretary of War. Twenty responded, and were received in my room up-stairs in Mr. Green's house, where Mr. Stanton and Adjutant-General Townsend took down the conversation in the form of questions and answers. Each of the twenty gave his name and partial history, and then selected Garrison Frazier as their spokesman:

First Question. State what your understanding is in regard to the acts of Congress and President Lincoln's proclamation touching the colored people in the rebel States?

Answer. So far as I understand President Lincoln's proclamation to the rebel States, it is, that if they will lay down their arms and submit to the laws of the United States, before the 1st of January, 1863, all should be well; but if they did not, then all the slaves in the Southern States should be free, henceforth and forever. That is what I understood.

Second Question. State what you understand by slavery, and the freedom that was to be given by the President's proclamation?

Answer. Slavery is receiving by irresistible power the

work of another man, and not by his consent. The freedom, as I understand it, promised by the proclamation, is taking us from under the yoke of bondage and placing us where we can reap the fruit of our own labor, and take care of ourselves and assist the Government in maintaining our freedom.

. . . .

Fourth Question. State in what manner you would rather live—whether scattered among the whites, or in colonies by yourselves?

Answer. I would prefer to live by ourselves, for there is a prejudice against us in the South that will take years to get over; but I do not know that I can answer for my brethren.

(All but Mr. Lynch, a missionary from the North, agreed with Frazier, but he thought they ought to live together, along with the whites.)

. . . .

Eighth Question. If the rebel leaders were to arm the slaves, what would be its effect?

Answer. I think they would fight as long as they were before the "bayonet," and just as soon as they could get away they would desert, in my opinion.

. . . .

Tenth Question. Do you understand the mode of enlistment of colored persons in the rebel States by State agents, under the act of Congress; if yes, what is your understanding?

Answer. My understanding is, that colored persons enlisted by State agents are enlisted as substitutes, and give credit to the State and do not swell the army, because every black man enlisted by a State agent leaves a white man at home; and also that larger bounties are given, or promised, by the State agents than are given by the United States. The great object should be to push through this rebellion the shortest way; and there seems to be something wanting in the enlistment by State agents, for it don't strengthen the army, but takes one away for every colored man enlisted.

Eleventh Question. State what, in your opinion, is the best way to enlist colored men as soldiers?

Answer. I think; sir, that all compulsory operations

should be put a stop to. The ministers would talk to them, and the young men would enlist. It is my opinion that it would be far better for the State agents to stay at home and the enlistments be made for the United States under the direction of General Sherman.

Up to this time I was present, and, on Mr. Stanton's intimating that he wanted to ask some questions affecting me, I withdrew, and then he put the twelfth and last question:

Twelfth Question. State what is the feeling of the colored people toward General Sherman, and how far do they regard his sentiments and actions as friendly to their rights and interests, or otherwise?

Answer. We looked upon General Sherman, prior to his arrival, as a man, in the providence of God, specially set apart to accomplish this work, and we unanimously felt inexpressible gratitude to him, looking upon him as a man who should be honored for the faithful performance of his duty. Some of us called upon him immediately upon his arrival, and it is probable he did not meet the secretary with more courtesy than he did us. His conduct and deportment toward us characterized him as a friend and gentleman. We have confidence in General Sherman, and think what concerns us could not be in better hands. This is our opinion now, from the short acquaintance and intercourse we have had.

It certainly was a strange fact that the great War Secretary should have catechized Negroes concerning the character of a general who had commanded a hundred thousand men in battle, had captured cities, conducted sixty-five thousand men successfully across four hundred miles of hostile territory, and had just brought tens of thousands of freedmen to a place of security; but because I had not loaded down my army by other hundreds of thousands of poor Negroes, I was construed by others as hostile to the black race. I had received from General Halleck, at Washington, a letter warning me that there were certain influential parties near the President who were torturing him with suspicions of my fidelity to him and his Negro policy; but I shall always believe that Mr.

Lincoln, though a civilian, knew better, and appreciated my motives and character. Though this letter of General Halleck has always been treated by me as confidential, I now insert it here at length:

HEADQUARTERS OF THE ARMY,
WASHINGTON, D. C., *December* 30, 1864.

Major-General W. T. SHERMAN, *Savannah.*

MY DEAR GENERAL: I take the liberty of calling your attention, in this private and friendly way, to a matter which may possibly hereafter be of more importance to you than either of us may now anticipate.

While almost every one is praising your great march through Georgia, and the capture of Savannah, there is a certain class having now great influence with the President, and very probably anticipating still more on a change of cabinet, who are decidedly disposed to make a point against you. I mean in regard to "inevitable Sambo." They say that you have manifested an almost *criminal* dislike to the Negro, and that you are not willing to carry out the wishes of the Government in regard to him, but repulse him with contempt! They say you might have brought with you to Savannah more than fifty thousand, thus stripping Georgia of that number of laborers, and opening a road by which as many more could have escaped from their masters; but that, instead of this, you drove them from your ranks, prevented their following you by cutting the bridges in your rear, and thus caused the massacre of large numbers by Wheeler's cavalry.

To those who know you as I do, such accusation will pass as the idle winds, for we presume that you discouraged the Negroes from following you because you had not the means of supporting them, and feared they might seriously embarrass your march. But there are others, and among them some in high authority, who think or pretend to think otherwise, and they are decidedly disposed to make a point against you.

I do not write this to induce you to conciliate this class of men by doing any thing which you do not deem right and proper, and for the interest of the Government and the country; but simply to call your attention to certain things which are viewed here somewhat differently than from your stand-point. I will explain as briefly as possible:

Some here think that, in view of the scarcity of labor in the South, and the probability that a part, at least, of the able-bodied slaves will be called into the military service of the rebels, it is of the greatest importance to open outlets by which these slaves can escape into our lines, and they say that the route you have passed over should be made the route of escape, and Savannah the great place of refuge. These, I know, are the views of some of the leading men in the Administration, and they now express dissatisfaction that you did not carry them out in your great raid.

Now that you are in possession of Savannah, and there can be no further fears about supplies, would it not be possible for you to reopen these avenues of escape for the Negroes, without interfering with your military operations? Could not such escaped slaves find at least a partial supply of food in the rice-fields about Savannah, and cotton plantations on the coast?

I merely throw out these suggestions. I know that such a course would be approved by the Government, and I believe that a manifestation on your part of a desire to bring the slaves within our lines will do much to silence your opponents. You will appreciate my motives in writing this private letter.

Yours truly,
H. W. HALLECK.

There is no doubt that Mr. Stanton, when he reached Savannah, shared these thoughts, but luckily the Negroes themselves convinced him that he was in error, and that they understood their own interests far better than did the men in Washington, who tried to make political capital out of this Negro question. The idea that such men should have been permitted to hang around Mr. Lincoln, to torture his life by suspicions of the officers who were toiling with the single purpose to bring the war to a successful end, and thereby to liberate *all* slaves, is a fair illustration of the influences that poison a political capital.

My aim then was, to whip the rebels, to humble their pride, to follow them to their inmost recesses, and make them fear and dread us. "Fear of the Lord is the beginning of wisdom." I did not want them to cast in our teeth what General Hood had once done in Atlanta, that we had to call on *their* slaves to help us to subdue them. But, as regards kindness to the race, encouraging them to patience and forbearance, procuring them food and clothing, and providing them with land whereon to labor, I assert that no army ever did more for that race than the one I commanded in Savannah. When we reached Savannah, we were beset by ravenous State agents from Hilton Head, who enticed and carried away our servants, and the corps of pioneers which we had organized, and which had done such excellent service. On one occasion, my own aide-de-camp, Colonel Audenried, found at least a hundred poor Negroes shut up in a house and pen, waiting for the night, to be conveyed stealthily to Hilton Head. They appealed to him for protection, alleging that they had been told that they *must be* soldiers, that "Massa Lincoln" wanted them, etc. I never denied the slaves a full opportunity for voluntary enlistment, but I did prohibit force to be used, for I knew that the State agents were more influenced by the profit they derived from the large bounties then being paid than by any love of country or of the colored race. In the language of Mr. Frazier, the enlistment of every black man "did not strengthen the army, but took away one white man from the ranks."

During Mr. Stanton's stay in Savannah we discussed this Negro question very fully; he asked me to draft an order on the subject, in accordance with my own views, that would meet the pressing necessities of the case, and I did so. We went over this order, No. 15, of January 16, 1865, very carefully. The secretary made some verbal modifications, when it was approved by him in all its details, I published it, and it went into operation at once. It provided fully for the enlistment of colored troops, and gave the freedmen certain possessory rights to land, which afterward became matters of judicial inquiry and decision. Of course, the military authorities at that day, when war prevailed, had a perfect right to grant the possession of any vacant land to which they could extend military protection, but we did not undertake to give a fee-simple title; and all that was designed by these special field orders was to make temporary provisions for the freedmen and their families during the rest of the war, or until Congress should take action in the premises. All that I now propose to assert is, that Mr. Stanton, Secretary of War, saw these orders in the rough, and approved every paragraph thereof, before they were made public.

I saw a good deal of the secretary socially, during the time of his visit to Savannah. He kept his quarters on the revenue-cutter with Simeon Draper, Esq., which cutter lay at a wharf in the river, but he came very often to my quarters at Mr. Green's house. Though appearing robust and strong, he complained a good deal of internal pains, which he said threatened his life, and would compel him soon to quit public office. He professed to have come from Washington purposely for rest and recreation, and he spoke unreservedly of the bickerings and jealousies at the national capital; of the interminable quarrels of the State Governors about their quotas, and more particularly of the financial troubles that threatened the very existence of the Government itself. He said that the price of everything had so risen in comparison with the depreciated money, that there was danger of national bankruptcy, and he appealed to me, as a soldier and patriot, to hurry up matters so as to bring the war to a close.

He left for Port Royal about the 15th of January, and promised to go North without delay, so as to hurry back to me the supplies I had called for, as indispensable for the prosecution of the next stage of the campaign. I was quite impatient to get off myself, for a city-life had become dull and tame, and we were all anxious to get into the pine-woods again, free from the importunities of rebel women asking for protection, and of the civilians from the North who were coming to Savannah for cotton and all sorts of profit.

On the 18th of January General Slocum was ordered to turn over the city of Savannah to General J. G. Foster, commanding the Department of the South, who proposed to retain his own headquarters at Hilton Head, and to occupy Savannah by General [Cuvier] Grover's division of the Nineteenth Corps, just arrived from James River; and on the next day, viz., January 19th, I made the first general orders for the move.

These were substantially to group the right wing of the army at Pocotaligo, already held by the Seventeenth Corps, and the left wing and cavalry at or near Robertsville, in South Carolina. The army remained substantially the same as during the march from Atlanta, with the exception of a few changes in the commanders of brigades and divisions, the addition of some men who had joined from furlough, and the loss of others from the expiration of their term of service. My own personal staff remained the same, with the exception that General W. F. Barry had rejoined us at Savannah, perfectly recovered from his attack of erysipelas, and continued with us to the end of the war. Generals Easton and Beckwith remained at Savannah, in charge of their respective depots, with orders to follow and meet us by sea with supplies when we should reach the coast at Wilmington or New Bern, North Carolina.

Of course, I gave out with some ostentation, especially among the rebels, that we were going to Charleston or Augusta; but I had long before made up my mind to waste no time on either, further than to play off on their fears, thus to retain for their protection a force of the enemy which would otherwise concentrate in our front, and make the passage of some of the great rivers that crossed our route more difficult and bloody.

Having accomplished all that seemed necessary, on the 21st of January, with my entire headquarters, officers, clerks, orderlies, etc., with wagons and horses, I embarked in a steamer for Beaufort, South Carolina, touching at Hilton Head, to see General Foster. The weather was rainy and bad, but we reached Beaufort safely on the 23d, and found some of General Blair's troops there. The bulk of his corps (Seventeenth) was, however, up on the railroad about Pocotaligo, near the head of Broad River, to which their supplies were carried from Hilton Head by steamboats. General Hatch's division (of General Foster's command) was still at Coosawhatchie or Tullafinny, where the Charleston & Savannah Railroad crosses the river of that name. All the country between Beaufort and Pocotaligo was low alluvial land, cut up by an infinite number of salt-water sloughs and fresh-water creeks, easily susceptible of defense by a small force; and why the enemy had allowed us to make a lodgment at Pocotaligo so easily I did not understand, unless it resulted from fear or ignorance. It seemed to me then that the terrible energy they had displayed in the earlier stages of the war was beginning to yield to the slower but more certain industry and discipline of our Northern men. It was to me manifest that the soldiers and people of the South entertained an undue fear of our Western men, and, like children, they had invented such ghostlike stories of our prowess in Georgia, that they were scared by their own inventions. Still, this was a power, and I intended to utilize it. Somehow, our men had got the idea that South Carolina was the cause of all our troubles; her people were the first to fire on Fort Sumter, had been in a great hurry to precipitate the country into civil war; and therefore on them should fall the scourge of war in its worst form. Taunting messages had also come to us, when in Georgia, to the effect that, when we should reach South Carolina, we would find a people less passive, who would fight us to the bitter end, daring us to come over, etc.; so that I saw and felt that we would not be able longer to restrain our men as we had done in Georgia.

Personally I had many friends in Charleston, to whom I would gladly have extended protection and mercy, but they were beyond my personal reach, and I would not restrain the army lest its vigor and energy should be impaired; and I had every reason to expect bold and strong resistance at the many broad and deep rivers that lay across our path.

General Foster's Department of the South had been enlarged to embrace the coast of North Carolina, so that the few troops serving there, under the command of General Innis N. Palmer, at New Bern, became subject to my command. General A. H. Terry held Fort Fisher, and a rumor came that he had taken the city of Wilmington; but this was premature. He had about eight thousand men. General Schofield was also known to be *en route* from Nashville for North Carolina, with the entire Twenty-third Corps, so that I had every reason to be satisfied that I would receive additional strength as we progressed northward, and before I should need it.

General W. J. Hardee commanded the Confederate forces in Charleston, with the Salkiehatchie River as his line of defense. It was also know that General Beauregard had come from the direction of Tennessee, and had assumed the general command of all the troops designed to resist our progress.

The heavy winter rains had begun early in January, rendered the roads execrable, and the Savannah River became so swollen that it filled its many channels, overflowing the vast extent of rice-fields that lay on the east bank. This flood delayed our departure two weeks; for it swept away our pontoon-bridge at Savannah, and came near drowning John E. Smith's division of the Fifteenth Corps, with several heavy trains of wagons that were *en route* from Savannah to Pocotaligo by the old causeway.

General Slocum had already ferried two of his divisions across the river, when Sister's Ferry, about forty miles above Savannah, was selected for the passage of the rest of his wing and of Kilpatrick's cavalry. The troops were in motion for that point before I quitted Savannah, and Captain S. B. Luce, United States Navy, had reported to me with a gunboat (the Pontiac) and a couple of transports, which I requested him to use in protecting Sister's Ferry during the passage of Slocum's wing, and to facilitate the passage of the troops all he could. The utmost activity prevailed at all points, but it was manifest we could not get off much before the 1st day of February; so I determined to go in person to Pocotaligo, and there act as though we were bound for Charleston. On the 24th of January I started from Beaufort with a part of my staff, leaving the rest to follow at leisure, rode across the island to a pontoon-bridge that spanned the channel between it and the main-land, and thence rode by Garden's Corners to a plantation not far from Pocotaligo, occupied by General Blair. There we found a house, with a majestic avenue of live-oaks, whose limbs had been cut away by the troops for firewood, and desolation marked one of those splendid South Carolina estates where the proprietors formerly had dispensed a hospitality that distinguished the old *régime* of that proud State. I slept on the floor of the house, but the night was so bitter cold that I got up by the fire several times, and when it burned low I rekindled it with an old mantel-clock and the wreck of a bedstead which stood in a corner of the room— the only act of vandalism that I recall done by myself personally during the war.

The next morning I rode to Pocotaligo, and thence reconnoitred our entire line down to Coosawhatchie. Pocotaligo Fort was on low, alluvial ground, and near it began the sandy pine-land which connected with the firm ground extending inland, constituting the chief reason for its capture at the very first stage of the campaign. Hatch's division was ordered to that point from Coosawhatchie, and the whole of Howard's right wing was brought near by, ready to start by the 1st of February. I also reconnoitred the point of the Salkiehatchie River, where the Charleston Railroad crossed it, found the bridge protected by a rebel battery on the farther side, and could see a few men about it; but the stream itself was absolutely impassable, for the whole bottom was overflowed by its swollen waters to the breadth of a full mile. Nevertheless, a division (Mower's) of the Seventeenth Corps was kept active, seemingly with the intention to cross over in the direction of Charleston, and thus to keep up the delusion that that city was our immediate "objective." Meantime, I had reports from General Slocum of the terrible difficulties he had encountered about Sister's Ferry, where the Savannah River was reported nearly three miles wide, and it seemed for a time almost impossible for him to span it at all with his frail pontoons. About this time (January 25th), the weather cleared away bright and cold, and I inferred that the river would soon run down, and enable Slocum to pass the river before February 1st. One of the divisions of the Fifteenth Corps (Corse's) had also been cut off by the loss of the pontoon-bridge at Savannah, so that General Slocum had with him, not only his own two corps, but Corse's division and Kilpatrick's cavalry, without which it was not prudent for me to inaugurate the campaign. We therefore rested quietly about Pocotaligo, collecting stores and making final preparations, until the 1st of February, when I learned that the cavalry and two divisions of the Twentieth Corps were fairly across the river, and then gave the necessary orders for the march northward.

Chapter 16

In the Carolinas:
"They Abandoned Poor Columbia"
February—March, 1865

ON THE 1ST DAY of February, as before explained, the army designed for the active campaign from Savannah northward was composed of two wings, commanded respectively by Major-Generals Howard and Slocum, and was substantially the same that had marched from Atlanta to Savannah. The same general orders were in force, and this campaign may properly be classed as a continuance of the former.

The right wing, less Corse's division, Fifteenth Corps, was grouped at or near Pocotaligo, South Carolina, with its wagons filled with food, ammunition, and forage, all ready to start, and only waiting for the left wing, which was detained by the flood in the Savannah River.

The enemy occupied the cities of Charleston and Augusta, with garrisons capable of making a respectable if not successful defense, but utterly unable to meet our veteran columns in the open field. To resist or delay our progress north, General Wheeler had his division of cavalry (reduced to the size of a brigade by his hard and persistent fighting ever since the beginning of the Atlanta campaign), and General Wade Hampton had been dispatched from the Army of Virginia to his native State of South Carolina, with a great flourish of trumpets, and extraordinary powers to raise men, money, and horses, with which "to stay the progress of the invader," and "to punish us for our insolent attempt to invade the glorious State of South Carolina!" He was supposed at the time to have, at and near Columbia, two small divisions of cavalry commanded by himself and General Butler.

Of course, I had a species of contempt for these scattered and inconsiderable forces, knew that they could hardly delay us an hour; and the only serious question that occurred to me was, would General Lee sit down in Richmond (besieged by General Grant), and permit us, almost unopposed, to pass through the States of South and North Carolina, cutting off and consuming the very supplies on which he depended to feed his army in Virginia, or would he make an effort to escape from General Grant, and endeavor to catch us inland somewhere between Columbia and Raleigh? I knew full well at the time that the broken fragments of Hood's army (which had escaped from Tennessee) were being hurried rapidly across Georgia, by Augusta, to make junction in my front; estimating them at the maximum twenty-five thousand men, and Hardee's, Wheeler's, and Hampton's forces at fifteen thousand, made forty thousand; which, if handled with spirit and energy, would constitute a formidable force, and might make the passage of such rivers as the Santee and Cape Fear a difficult undertaking. Therefore, I took all possible precautions, and arranged with Admiral Dahlgren and General Foster to watch our progress inland by all the means possible, and to provide for us points of security along the coast; as, at Bull's Bay, Georgetown, and the mouth of Cape Fear River. Still, it was extremely desirable in *one* march to reach Goldsboro' in the State of North Carolina (distant four hundred and twenty-five miles), a point of great convenience for ulterior operations, by reason of the two railroads which meet there, coming from the sea-coast at Wilmington and New Bern. Before leaving Savannah I had sent to New Bern Colonel W. W. Wright, of the Engineers, with orders to look to these railroads, to collect rolling-stock, and to have the roads repaired out as far as possible in six weeks—the time estimated as necessary for us to march that distance.

The question of supplies remained still the one of vital importance, and I reasoned that we might safely rely on the country for a considerable quantity of forage and provisions, and that, if the worst came to the worst, we could live several months on the mules and horses of our trains. Nevertheless, time was equally material, and the moment I heard that General Slocum had finished his pontoon-bridge at Sister's Ferry, and that Kilpatrick's cavalry was over the river, I gave the general orders to march, and instructed all the columns to aim for the South Carolina Railroad to the west of Branchville, about Blackville and Midway.

The right wing moved up the Salkiehatchie, the Seventeenth Corps on the right, with orders on reaching Rivers's Bridge to cross over, and the Fifteenth Corps by Hickory Hill to Beaufort's Bridge. Kilpatrick was instructed to march by way of Barnwell; Corse's division and the Twentieth Corps to take such roads as would bring them into communication with the Fifteenth Corps about Beaufort's Bridge. All these columns started promptly on the 1st of February. We encountered Wheeler's cavalry, which had obstructed the road by felling trees, but our men picked these up and threw them aside, so that this obstruction hardly delayed us an hour. In person I accompanied the Fifteenth Corps (General Logan) by McPhersonville and Hickory Hill, and kept couriers going to and fro to General Slocum with instructions to hurry as much as possible, so as to make a junction of the whole army on the South Carolina Railroad about Blackville.

I spent the night of February 1st at Hickory Hill Post-Office, and that of the 2d at Duck Branch Post-Office, thirty-one miles out from Pocotaligo. On the 3d the Seventeenth Corps was opposite Rivers's Bridge, and the Fifteenth approached Beaufort's Bridge. The Salkiehatchie was still over its banks, and presented a most formidable obstacle. The enemy appeared in some force on the opposite bank, had cut away all the bridges which spanned the many deep channels of the swollen river, and the only available passage seemed to be along the narrow causeways which constituted the common roads. At Rivers's Bridge Generals Mower and Giles A. Smith lead their heads of column through this swamp, the water up to their shoulders, crossed over to the pine-land, turned upon the rebel brigade which defended the passage, and routed it in utter disorder. It was in this attack that General Wager Swayne lost his leg, and he had to be conveyed back to Pocotaligo. Still, the loss of life was very small, in proportion to the advantages gained, for the enemy at once abandoned the whole line of the Salkiehatchie, and the Fifteenth Corps passed over at Beaufort's Bridge, without opposition.

On the 5th of February I was at Beaufort's Bridge, by which time General A. S. Williams had got up with five brigades of the Twentieth Corps; I also heard of General Kilpatrick's being abreast of us, at Barnwell, and then gave orders for the march straight for the railroad at Midway. I still remained with the Fifteenth Corps, which, on the 6th of February, was five miles from Bamberg. As a matter of course, I expected severe resistance at this railroad, for its loss would sever all the communications of the enemy in Charleston with those in Augusta.

Early on the 7th, in the midst of a rain-storm, we reached the railroad, almost unopposed, striking it at several points. General Howard told me a good story concerning this, which will bear repeating: He was with the Seventeenth Corps, marching straight for Midway, and when about five miles distant he began to deploy the leading division, so as to be ready for battle. Sitting on his horse by the road-side, while the deployment was making, he saw a man coming down the road, riding as hard as he could, and as he approached he recognized him as one of his own "foragers," mounted on a white horse, with a rope bridle and a blanket for saddle. As he came near he called out, "Hurry up, general; we have got the railroad!" So, while we, the generals, were proceeding deliberately to prepare for a serious battle, a parcel of our foragers, in search of plunder, had got ahead and actually captured the South Carolina Railroad, a line of vital importance to the rebel Government.

As soon as we struck the railroad, details of men were set to work to tear up the rails, to burn the ties and twist the bars. This was a most important railroad, and I proposed to destroy it completely for fifty miles, partly to prevent a possibility of its restoration and partly to utilize the time necessary for General Slocum to get up.

The country thereabouts was very poor, but the inhabitants mostly remained at home. Indeed, they knew not where to go.

The enemy's cavalry had retreated before us, but his infantry was reported in some strength at Branchville, on the farther side of the Edisto; yet on the appearance of a mere squad of our men they burned their own bridges—the very thing I wanted, for we had no use for them, and they had.

We all remained strung along this railroad till the 9th of February—the Seventeenth Corps on the right, then the Fifteenth, Twentieth, and cavalry, at Blackville. General Slocum reached Blackville that day, with Geary's division of the Twentieth Corps, and reported the Fourteenth Corps (General Jeff. C. Davis's) to be following by way of Barnwell. On the 10th I rode up to Blackville, where I conferred with Generals Slocum and Kilpatrick, became satisfied that the whole army would be ready within a day, and accordingly made orders for the next movement north to Columbia, the right wing to strike Orangeburg *en route*. Kilpatrick was ordered to demonstrate strongly toward Aiken, to keep up the delusion that we might turn to Augusta; but he was notified that Columbia was the next objective, and that he should cover the left flank against Wheeler, who hung around it. I wanted to reach Columbia before any part of Hood's army could possibly get there. Some of them were reported as having reached Augusta, under the command of General Dick Taylor.

Having sufficiently damaged the railroad, and effected the junction of the entire army, the general march was resumed on the 11th, each corps crossing the South Edisto by separate bridges, with orders to pause on the road leading from Orangeburg to Augusta, till it was certain that the Seventeenth Corps had got possession of Orangeburg. This place was simply important as its occupation would sever the communications between Charleston and Columbia. All the heads of column reached this road, known as the Edgefield road, during the 12th, and the Seventeenth Corps turned to the right, against Orangeburg. When I reached the head of column opposite Orangeburg, I found Giles A. Smith's division halted, with a battery unlimbered, exchanging shots with a party on the opposite side of the Edisto. He reported that the bridge was gone, and that the river was deep and impassable. I then directed General Blair to send Mower's division below the town, some four or five miles, to effect a crossing there. He laid his pontoon-bridge, but the bottom on the other side was overflowed, and the men had to wade through it, in places as deep as their waists. I was with this division at the time, on foot, trying to pick my way across the overflowed bottom; but, as soon as the head of column reached the sand-hills, I knew that the enemy would not long remain in Orangeburg, and accordingly returned to my horse, on the west bank, and rode rapidly up to where I had left Giles A. Smith. I found him in possession of the broken bridge, abreast of the town, which he was repairing, and I was among the first to cross over and enter the town. By and before the time either Mower's or Giles A. Smith's skirmishers entered the place, several stores were on fire, and I am sure that some of the towns-people told me that a Jew merchant had set fire to his own cotton and store, and from this the fire had spread. This, however, was soon put out, and the Seventeenth Corps (General Blair) occupied the place during that night. I remember to have visited a large hospital, on the hill near the railroad depot, which was occupied by the orphan children who had been removed from the asylum in Charleston. We gave them protection, and, I think, some provisions. The railroad and depot were destroyed by order, and no doubt a good deal of cotton was burned, for we all regarded cotton as hostile property, a thing to be destroyed. General Blair was ordered to break up this railroad, forward to the point where it crossed the Santee, and then to turn for Columbia. On the morning of the 13th I again joined the Fifteenth Corps, which crossed the North Edisto by Snilling's Bridge, and moved straight for Columbia, around the head of Caw-Caw Swamp. Orders were sent to all the columns to turn for Columbia, where it was supposed the enemy had concentrated all the men they could from Charleston, Augusta, and even from Virginia. That night I was with the Fifteenth Corps, twenty-one miles from Columbia, where my aide, Colonel Audenried, picked up a rebel officer on the road, who, supposing him to be of the same service with himself, answered all his questions frankly, and revealed the truth that there was nothing in Columbia except Hampton's cavalry. The fact was, that General Hardee, in Charleston, took it for granted that we were after Charleston; the rebel troops in Augusta supposed they were "our objective"; so they abandoned poor Columbia to the care of Hampton's cavalry, which was confused by the rumors that poured in on it, so that both

Beauregard and Wade Hampton, who were in Columbia, seem to have lost their heads.

On the 14th the head of the Fifteenth Corps, Charles R. Woods's division, approached the Little Congaree, a broad, deep stream, tributary to the Main Congaree, six or eight miles below Columbia. On the opposite side of this stream was a newly-constructed fort, and on our side a wide extent of old cotton-fields, which had been overflowed, and was covered with a deep slime. General Woods had deployed his leading brigade, which was skirmishing forward, but he reported that the bridge was gone, and that a considerable force of the enemy was on the other side. I directed General Howard or Logan to send a brigade by a circuit to the left, to see if this stream could not be crossed higher up, but at the same time knew that General Slocum's route would bring him to Columbia behind this stream, and that his approach would uncover it. Therefore, there was no need of exposing much life. The brigade, however, found means to cross the Little Congaree, and thus uncovered the passage by the main road, so that General Woods's skirmishers at once passed over, and a party was set to work to repair the bridge, which occupied less than an hour, when I passed over with my whole staff. I found the new fort unfinished and unoccupied, but from its parapet could see over some old fields bounded to the north and west by hills skirted with timber. There was a plantation to our left, about half a mile; and on the edge of the timber was drawn up a force of rebel cavalry of about a regiment, which advanced, and charged upon some of our foragers, who were plundering the plantation; my aide, Colonel Audenried, who had ridden forward, came back somewhat hurt and bruised, for, observing this charge of cavalry, he had turned for us, and his horse fell with him in attempting to leap a ditch. General Woods's skirmish-line met this charge of cavalry, and drove it back into the woods and beyond. We remained on that ground during the night of the 15th, and I camped on the nearest dry ground behind the Little Congaree, where on the next morning were made the written orders for the government of the troops while occupying Columbia. These are dated February 16, 1865, in these words:

General Howard will cross the Saluda and Broad Rivers as

near their mouths as possible, occupy Columbia, destroy the public buildings, railroad property, manufacturing and machine shops; but will spare libraries, asylums, and private dwellings. He will then move to Winnsboro', destroying *en route* utterly that section of the railroad. He will also cause all bridges, trestles, water-tanks, and depots on the railroad back to the Wateree to be burned, switches broken, and such other destruction as he can find time to accomplish consistent with proper celerity.

These instructions were embraced in General Order No. 26, which prescribed the routes of march for the several columns as far as Fayetteville, North Carolina, and is conclusive that I then regarded Columbia as simply one point on our general route of march, and not as an important conquest.

During the 16th of February the Fifteenth Corps reached the point opposite Columbia, and pushed on for the Saluda Factory three miles above, crossed that stream, and the head of column reached Broad River just in time to find its bridge in flames, [Matthew C.] Butler's cavalry having just passed over into Columbia. The head of Slocum's column also reached the point opposite Columbia the same morning, but the bulk of his army was back at Lexington. I reached this place early in the morning of the 16th, met General Slocum there, and explained to him the purport of General Order No. 26, which contemplated the passage of his army across Broad River at Alston, fifteen miles above Columbia. Riding down to the river-bank, I saw the wreck of the large bridge which had been burned by the enemy, with its many stone piers still standing, but the superstructure gone. Across the Congaree River lay the city of Columbia, in plain, easy view. I could see the unfinished State-House, a handsome granite structure, and the ruins of the railroad depot, which were still smouldering. Occasionally a few citizens or cavalry could be seen running across the streets, and quite a number of Negroes were seemingly busy in carrying off bags of grain or meal, which were piled up near the burned depot.

Captain De Gress had a section of his twenty-pound Parrott guns unlimbered, firing into the town. I asked him what he was firing for; he said he could see some rebel cavalry occasionally at the intersections of the streets, and he had an idea that there was a large force of infantry concealed on the opposite bank, lying low, in case we should attempt to cross over directly into the town. I instructed him not to fire any more into the town, but consented to his bursting a few shells near the depot, to scare away the Negroes who were appropriating the bags of corn and meal which we wanted, also to fire three shots at the unoccupied State-House. I stood by and saw these fired, and then all firing ceased. Although this matter of firing into Columbia has been the subject of much abuse and investigation, I have yet to hear of any single person having been killed in Columbia by our cannon. On the other hand, the night before, when Woods's division was in camp in the open fields at Little Congaree, it was shelled all night by a rebel battery from the other side of the river. This provoked me much at the time, for it was wanton mischief, as Generals Beauregard and Hampton must have been convinced that they could not prevent our entrance into Columbia. I have always contended that I would have been justified in retaliating for this unnecessary act of war, but did not, though I always characterized it as it deserved.

The night of the 16th I camped near an old prison bivouac opposite Columbia, known to our prisoners of war as "Camp Sorghum," where remained the mud-hovels and holes in the ground which our prisoners had made to shelter themselves from the winter's cold and the summer's heat. The Fifteenth Corps was then ahead, reaching to Broad River, about four miles above Columbia; the Seventeenth Corps was behind, on the river-bank opposite Columbia; and the left wing and cavalry had turned north toward Alston.

The next morning, viz., February 17th, I rode to the head of General Howard's column, and found that during the night he had ferried Stone's brigade of Woods's division of the Fifteenth Corps across by rafts made of the pontoons, and that brigade was then deployed on the opposite bank to cover the construction of a pontoon-bridge nearly finished.

I sat with General Howard on a log, watching the men lay this bridge; and about 9 or 10 A. M. a messenger came from Colonel [George A.] Stone on the other side, saying that the Mayor of Columbia had come out of the city to surrender the place, and asking for orders. I simply remarked to General Howard that he had his orders, to let Colonel Stone go on into the city, and that we would follow as soon as the bridge was ready. By this same messenger I received a note in pencil from the Lady Superioress of a convent or school in Columbia, in which she claimed to have been a teacher in a convent in Brown County, Ohio, at the time my daughter Minnie was a pupil there, and therefore asking special protection. My recollection is, that I gave the note to my brother-in-law, Colonel Ewing, then inspector-general on my staff, with instructions to see this lady, and assure her that we contemplated no destruction of any private property in Columbia at all.

As soon as the bridge was done, I led my horse over it, followed by my whole staff. General Howard accompanied me with his, and General Logan was next in order, followed by General C. R. Woods, and the whole of the Fifteenth Corps. Ascending the hill, we soon emerged into a broad road leading into Columbia, between old fields of corn and cotton, and, entering the city, we found seemingly all its population, white and black, in the streets. A high and boisterous wind was prevailing from the north, and flakes of cotton were flying about in the air and lodging in the limbs of the trees, reminding us of a Northern snow-storm. Near the market-square we found Stone's brigade halted, with arms stacked, and a large detail of his men, along with some citizens, engaged with an old fire-engine, trying to put out the fire in a long pile of burning cotton-bales, which I was told had been fired by the rebel cavalry on withdrawing from the city that morning. I know that, to avoid this row of burning cotton-bales, I had to ride my horse on the sidewalk. In the market-square had collected an immense crowd of whites and blacks, among whom was the mayor of the city, Dr. [T. J.] Goodwin, quite a respectable old gentleman, who was extremely anxious to protect the interests of the citizens. He was on foot, and I on horseback, and it is probable I told him then not to be uneasy, that we did not intend to stay long, and had no purpose to injure the private citizens or private property. About this time I noticed several men trying to get through the crowd to speak with me, and called to some black people to make room for them; when they reached me, they explained that they were officers of our army, who had been prisoners, had escaped from the rebel prison and guard, and were of course overjoyed to find themselves safe with us. I told them that, as soon as things settled down, they should report to General Howard, who would provide for their safety, and enable them to travel with us. One of them handed me a paper, asking me to read it at my leisure; I put it in my breast-pocket and rode on. General Howard was still with me, and, riding down the street which led by the right to the Charleston depot, we found it and a large storehouse burned to the ground, but there were, on the platform and ground near by, piles of cotton bags filled with corn and corn-meal, partially burned.

A detachment of Stone's brigade was guarding this, and separating the good from the bad. We rode along the railroad-track, some three or four hundred yards, to a large foundry, when some man rode up and said the rebel cavalry were close by, and he warned us that we might get shot. We accordingly turned back to the market-square, and *en route* noticed that several of the men were evidently in liquor, when I called General Howard's attention to it. He left me and rode toward General Woods's head of column, which was defiling through the town. On reaching the market-square, I again met Dr. Goodwin, and inquired where he proposed to quarter me, and he said that he had selected the house of Blanton Duncan, Esq., a citizen of Louisville, Kentucky, then a resident there, who had the contract for manufacturing the Confederate money, and had fled with Hampton's cavalry. We all rode some six or eight squares back from the new State-House, and found a very good modern house, completely furnished, with stabling and a large yard, took it as our headquarters, and occupied it during our stay. I considered General Howard as in command of the place, and referred the many applicants for guards and protection to him. Before our headquarter-wagons had got up, I strolled through the streets of Columbia, found sentinels posted at the principal intersections, and generally good order prevailing, but did not again return to the main street, because it was filled with a crowd of citizens watching the soldiers marching by.

During the afternoon of that day, February 17th, the whole of the Fifteenth Corps passed through the town and out on the Camden and Winnsboro' roads. The Seventeenth Corps did not enter the city at all, but crossed directly over to the Winnsboro' road from the pontoon-bridge at Broad River, which was about four miles above the city.

After we had got, as it were, settled in Blanton Duncan's

house, say about 2 P. M., I overhauled my pocket according to custom, to read more carefully the various notes and memoranda received during the day, and found the paper which had been given me, as described, by one of our escaped prisoners. It proved to be the song of "Sherman's March to the Sea," which had been composed by Adjutant S[amuel] H. M. Byers, of the Fifth Iowa Infantry, when a prisoner in the asylum at Columbia, which had been beautifully writen off by a fellow-prisoner, and handed to me in person. This appeared to me so good that I at once sent for Byers, attached him to my staff, provided him with horse and equipment, and took him as far as Fayetteville, North Carolina, whence he was sent to Washington as bearer of dispatches. I insert the song here for convenient reference and preservation. Byers said that there was an excellent glee-club among the prisoners in Columbia, who used to sing it well, with an audience often of rebel ladies:

SHERMAN'S MARCH TO THE SEA.

Composed by Adjutant BYERS, *Fifth Iowa Infantry. Arranged and sung by the Prisoners in Columbia Prison.*

I.

Our camp-fires shone bright on the mountain
 That frowned on the river below,
As we stood by our guns in the morning,
 And eagerly watched for the foe;
When a rider came out of the darkness
 That hung over mountain and tree,
And shouted, "Boys, up and be ready!
 For Sherman will march to the sea!"

Chorus.

Then sang we a song of our chieftain,
 That echoed over river and lea;
And the stars of our banner shone brighter
 When Sherman marched down to the sea!

II.

Then cheer upon cheer for bold Sherman
 Went up from each valley and glen,
And the bugles reëchoed the music

That came from the lips of the men;
For we knew that the stars in our banner
  More bright in their splendor would be,
And that blessings from Northland would greet us,
  When Sherman marched down to the sea!
                    Then sang we a song, etc.

III.

Then forward, boys! forward to battle!
  We marched on our wearisome way,
We stormed the wild hills of Resaca—
  God bless those who fell on that day!
Then Kenesaw frowned in its glory,
  Frowned down on the flag of the free;
But the East and the West bore our standard,
  And Sherman marched on to the sea!
                    Then sang we a song, etc.

IV.

Still onward we pressed, till our banners
  Swept out from Atlanta's grim walls,
And the blood of the patriot dampened
  The soil where the traitor-flag falls;
But we paused not to weep for the fallen,
  Who slept by each river and tree,
Yet we twined them a wreath of the laurel,
  As Sherman marched down to the sea!
                    Then sang we a song, etc.

V.

Oh, proud was our army that morning,
  That stood where the pine darkly towers,
When Sherman said "Boys, you are weary,
  But to-day fair Savannah is ours!"
Then sang we the song of our chieftain,
  That echoed over river and lea,
And the stars in our banner shone brighter
  When Sherman camped down by the sea!

Toward evening of February 17th, the mayor, Dr. Goodwin, came to my quarters at Duncan's house, and remarked

that there was a lady in Columbia who professed to be a special friend of mine. On his giving her name, I could not recall it, but inquired as to her maiden or family name. He answered Poyas. It so happened that, when I was a lieutenant at Fort Moultrie, in 1842-'46, I used very often to visit a family of that name on the east branch of Cooper River, about forty miles from Fort Moultrie, and to hunt with the son, Mr. James Poyas, an elegant young fellow and a fine sportsman. His father, mother, and several sisters, composed the family, and were extremely hospitable. One of the ladies was very fond of painting in water-colors, which was one of my weaknesses, and on one occasion I had presented her with a volume treating of water-colors. Of course, I was glad to renew the acquaintance, and proposed to Dr. Goodwin that we should walk to her house and visit this lady, which we did. The house stood beyond the Charlotte depot, in a large lot, was of frame, with a high porch, which was reached by a set of steps outside. Entering this yard, I noticed ducks and chickens, and a general air of peace and comfort that was really pleasant to behold at that time of universal desolation; the lady in question met us at the head of the steps and invited us into a parlor which was perfectly neat and well furnished. After inquiring about her father, mother, sisters, and especially her brother James, my special friend, I could not help saying that I was pleased to notice that our men had not handled her house and premises as roughly as was their wont. "I owe it to you, general," she answered. "Not at all. I did not know you were here till a few minutes ago." She reiterated that she was indebted to me for the perfect safety of her house and property, and added, "You remember, when you were at our house on Cooper River in 1845, you gave me a book", and she handed me the book in question, on the fly-leaf of which was written: "To Miss —— Poyas, with the compliments of W. T. Sherman, First-lieutenant Third Artillery." She then explained that, as our army approached Columbia, there was a doubt in her mind whether the terrible Sherman who was devastating the land were W. T. Sherman or T. W. Sherman, both known to be generals in the Northern army; but, on the supposition that he was her old acquaintance, when Wade Hampton's cavalry drew out of the city, calling out that the Yankees were coming, she armed herself with this book, and awaited the crisis. Soon the shouts about the market-house announced that the Yankees had come; very soon men were seen running up and down the streets; a parcel of them poured over the fence, began to chase the chickens and ducks, and to enter her house. She observed one large man, with full beard, who exercised some authority, and to him she appealed in the name of "his general." "What do you know of Uncle Billy?" "Why," she said, "when he was a young man he used to be our friend in Charleston, and here is a book he gave me." The officer or soldier took the book, looked at the inscription, and, turning to his fellows, said: "Boys, that's so; that's Uncle Billy's writing, for I have seen it often before." He at once commanded the party to stop pillaging, and left a man in charge of the house, to protect her until the regular provost-guard should be established. I then asked her if the regular guard or sentinel had been as good to her. She assured me that he was a very nice young man; that he had been telling her all about his family in Iowa; and that at that very instant of time he was in another room minding her baby. Now, this lady had good sense and tact, and had thus turned aside a party who, in five minutes more, would have rifled her premises of all that was good to eat or wear. I made her a long social visit, and, before leaving Columbia, gave her a half-tierce of rice and about one hundred pounds of ham from our own mess-stores.

In like manner, that same evening I found in Mrs. Simons another acquaintance—the wife of the brother of Hon. James Simons, of Charleston, who had been Miss Wragg. When Columbia was on fire that night, and her house in danger, I had her family and effects carried to my own headquarters, gave them my own room and bed, and, on leaving Columbia the next day, supplied her with a half-barrel of hams and a half-tierce of rice. I mention these specific facts to show that, personally, I had no malice or desire to destroy that city or its inhabitants, as is generally believed at the South.

Having walked over much of the suburbs of Columbia in the afternoon, and being tired, I lay down on a bed in Blanton Duncan's house to rest. Soon after dark I became conscious that a bright light was shining on the walls; and, calling some one of my staff (Major Nichols, I think) to inquire the cause, he said there seemed to be a house on fire down about the market-house. The same high wind still prevailed, and, fearing the consequences, I bade him go in person to see if the provost-guard were doing its duty. He soon returned, and reported that the block of buildings directly opposite the burning cotton of that morning was on fire, and that it was spreading; but he had found General Woods on the ground, with plenty of men trying to put the fire out, or, at least, to prevent its extension. The fire continued to increase, and the whole heavens became lurid. I dispatched messenger after messenger to Generals Howard, Logan, and Woods, and received from them repeated assurances that all was being done that could be done, but that the high wind was spreading the flames beyond all control. These general officers were on the ground all night, and Hazen's division had been brought into the city to assist Woods's division, already there. About eleven o'clock at night I went down-town myself, Colonel Dayton with me; we walked to Mr. Simons's house, from which I could see the flames rising high in the air, and could hear the roaring of the fire. I advised the ladies to move to my headquarters, had our own headquarter-wagons hitched up, and their effects carried there, as a place of greater safety. The whole air was full of sparks and of flying masses of cotton, shingles, etc., some of which were carried four or five blocks, and started new fires. The men seemed generally under good control, and certainly labored hard to girdle the fire, to prevent its spreading; but, so long as the high wind prevailed, it was simply beyond human possibility. Fortunately, about 3 or 4 A. M., the wind moderated, and gradually the fire was got under control; but it had burned out the very heart of the city, embracing several churches, the old State-House, and the school or asylum of that very Sister of Charity who had appealed for my personal protection. Nickerson's Hotel, in which several of my staff were quartered, was burned down, but the houses occupied by myself, Generals Howard and Logan, were not burned at all. Many of the people thought that this fire was deliberately planned and executed. This is not true. It was accidental, and in my judgment began with the cotton which General Hampton's men had set fire to on leaving the city (whether by his orders or not is not material), which fire was partially subdued early in the day by our men; but, when night came, the high wind fanned it again into full blaze, carried it against the frame-houses, which caught like tinder, and soon spread beyond our control.

This whole subject has since been thoroughly and judicially investigated, in some cotton cases, by the mixed commission on American and British claims, under the Treaty of Washington, which commission failed to award a verdict in favor of the English claimants, and thereby settled the fact that the destruction of property in Columbia, during that night, did not result from the acts of the General Government of the United States—that is to say, from my army. In my official report of this conflagration, I distinctly charged it to General Wade Hampton, and confess I did so pointedly, to shake the faith of his people in him, for he was in my opinion a braggart, and professed to be the special champion of South Carolina.[1]

The morning sun of February 18th rose bright and clear over a ruined city. About half of it was in ashes and in smouldering heaps. Many of the people were houseless, and gathered in groups in the suburbs, or in the open parks and spaces, around their scanty piles of furniture. General Howard, in concert with the mayor, did all that was possible to provide other houses for them; and by my authority he turned over to the Sisters of Charity the Methodist College, and to the mayor five hundred beef-cattle, to help feed the people; I also gave the mayor (Dr. Goodwin) one hundred muskets, with which to arm a guard to maintain order after we should leave the neighborhood. During the 18th and 19th we remained in Columbia, General Howard's troops engaged in tearing up and destroying the railroad, back toward the Wateree, while a strong detail, under the immediate supervision of Colonel O. M. Poe, United States Engineers, destroyed the State Arsenal, which was found to be well supplied with shot, shell, and ammunition. These were hauled in wagons to the Saluda River, under the supervision of Colonel Baylor, chief of ordnance, and emptied into deep water, causing a very serious accident by the bursting of a percussion-shell, as it struck another on the margin of the water.

[1] Sherman's bald attempt to fix the blame on Wade Hampton for the destruction of Columbia drew a sharp retort from that South Carolinian: "History will brand him [Sherman] as a robber and incendiary and will deservedly 'damn him to everlasting fame.'" See Earl Schenck Miers, *The General Who Marched to Hell* (New York: 1951), 314–16.

The flame followed back a train of powder which had sifted out, reached the wagons, still partially loaded, and exploded them, killing sixteen men and destroying several wagons and teams of mules. We also destroyed several valuable founderies and the factory of Confederate money. The dies had been carried away, but about sixty hand-presses remained. There was also found an immense quantity of money, in various stages of manufacture, which our men spent and gambled with in the most lavish manner.

Having utterly ruined Columbia, the right wing began its march northward, toward Winnsboro', on the 20th, which we reached on the 21st, and found General Slocum, with the left wing, who had come by the way of Alston. Thence the right wing was turned eastward, toward Cheraw, and Fayetteville, North Carolina, to cross the Catawba River at Peay's Ferry. The cavalry was ordered to follow the railroad north as far as Chester, and then to turn east to Rocky Mount, the point indicated for the passage of the left wing. In person I reached Rocky Mount on the 22d, with the Twentieth Corps, which laid its pontoon-bridge and crossed over during the 23d. Kilpatrick arrived the next day, in the midst of heavy rain, and was instructed to cross the Catawba at once, by night, and to move up to Lancaster, to make believe we were bound for Charlotte, to which point I heard that Beauregard had directed all his detachments, including a corps of Hood's old army, which had been marching parallel with us, but had failed to make junction with the forces immediately opposing us. Of course, I had no purpose of going to Charlotte, for the right wing was already moving rapidly toward Fayetteville, North Carolina. The rain was so heavy and persistent that the Catawba River rose fast, and soon after I had crossed the pontoon-bridge at Rocky Mount it was carried away, leaving General Davis, with the Fourteenth Corps, on the west bank. The roads were infamous, so I halted the Twentieth Corps at Hanging Rock for some days, to allow time for the Fourteenth to get over.

General Davis had infinite difficulty in reconstructing his bridge, and was compelled to use the fifth chains of his wagons for anchor-chains, so that we were delayed nearly a week in that neighborhood. While in camp at Hanging Rock two prisoners were brought to me—one a chaplain, the other a boy, son of Richard Bacot, of Charleston, whom I had known as a cadet at West Point. They were just from Charleston, and had been sent away by General Hardee in advance, because he was, they said, evacuating Charleston. Rumors to the same effect had reached me through the Negroes, and it was, moreover, reported that Wilmington, North Carolina, was in possession of the Yankee troops; so that I had every reason to be satisfied that our march was fully reaping all the fruits we could possibly ask for. Charleston was, in fact, evacuated by General Hardee on the 18th of February, and was taken possession of by a brigade of General Foster's troops, commanded by General [Alexander] Schimmelpfennig, the same day. Hardee had availed himself of his only remaining railroad, by Florence to Cheraw; had sent there much of his ammunition and stores, and reached it with the effective part of the garrison in time to escape across the Pedee River before our arrival. Wilmington was captured by General Terry on the 22d of February; but of this important event we only knew by the vague rumors which reached us through rebel sources.

General Jeff. C. Davis got across the Catawba during the 27th, and the general march was resumed on Cheraw. Kilpatrick remained near Lancaster, skirmishing with Wheeler's and Hampton's cavalry, keeping up the delusion that we proposed to move on Charlotte and Salisbury, but with orders to watch the progress of the Fourteenth Corps, and to act in concert with it, on its left rear. On the 1st of March I was at Finlay's Bridge across Lynch's Creek, the roads so bad that we had to corduroy nearly every foot of the way; but I was in communication with all parts of the army; which had met no serious opposition from the enemy. On the 2d of March we entered the village of Chesterfield, skirmishing with Butler's cavalry, which gave ground rapidly. There I received a message from General Howard, who reported that he was already in Cheraw with the Seventeenth Corps, and that the Fifteenth was near at hand.

General Hardee had retreated eastward across the Pedee, burning the bridge. I therefore directed the left wing to march for Sneedsboro', about ten miles above Cheraw, to cross the Pedee there, while I in person proposed to cross over and join the right wing in Cheraw. Early in the morning of the 3d of March I rode out of Chesterfield along with the Twentieth

Corps, which filled the road, forded Thompson's Creek, and, at the top of the hill beyond, found a road branching off to the right, which corresponded with the one on my map leading to Cheraw. Seeing a Negro standing by the road-side, looking at the troops passing, I inquired of him what road that was. "Him lead to Cheraw, master!" "Is it a good road, and how far?" "A very good road, and eight or ten miles." "Any guerrillas?" "Oh! no, master, dey is gone two days ago; you could have played cards on der coat-tails, dey was in sich a hurry!" I was on my Lexington horse, who was very hand-some and restive, so I made signal to my staff to follow, as I proposed to go without escort. I turned my horse down the road, and the rest of the staff followed. General Barry took up the questions about the road, and asked the same Negro what he was doing there. He answered, "Dey say Massa Sherman will be along soon!" "Why," said General Barry, "that was General Sherman you were talking to." The poor Negro, almost in the attitude of prayer, exclaimed: "De great God! just look at his horse!" He ran up and trotted by my side for a mile or so, and gave me all the information he possessed, but he seemed to admire the horse more than the rider.

We reached Cheraw in a couple of hours in a drizzling rain, and, while waiting for our wagons to come up, I staid with General Blair in a large house, the property of a blockade-runner, whose family remained. General Howard occupied another house farther down-town. He had already ordered his pontoon-bridge to be laid across the Pedee, there a large, deep, navigable stream, and Mower's division was already across, skirmishing with the enemy about two miles out. Cheraw was found to be full of stores which had been sent up from Charleston prior to its evacuation, and which could not be removed. I was satisfied, from inquiries, that General Hardee had with him only the Charleston garrison, that the enemy had not divined our movements, and that consequently they were still scattered from Charlotte around to Florence, then behind us. Having thus secured the passage of the Pedee, I felt no uneasiness about the future, because there remained no further great impediment between us and Cape Fear River, which I felt assured was by that time in possession of our friends. The day was so wet that we all kept in-doors; and about noon General Blair invited us to take lunch with him. We passed down into the basement dining-room, where the regular family table was spread with an excellent meal; and during its progress I was asked to take some wine, which stood upon the table in venerable bottles. It was so very good that I inquired where it came from. General Blair simply asked, "Do you like it?" but I insisted upon knowing where he had got it; he only replied by asking if I liked it, and wanted some. He afterward sent to my bivouac a case containing a dozen bottles of the finest madeira I ever tasted; and I learned that he had captured, in Cheraw, the wine of some of the old aristocratic families of Charleston, who had sent it up to Cheraw for safety, and heard afterward that Blair had found about eight wagon-loads of this wine, which he distributed to the army generally, in very fair proportions.

After finishing our lunch, as we passed out of the dining-room, General Blair asked me if I did not want some saddle-blankets, or a rug for my tent, and, leading me into the hall to a space under the stairway, he pointed out a pile of carpets which had also been sent up from Charleston for safety. After our headquarter-wagons got up, and our bivouac was established in a field near by, I sent my orderly (Walter) over to General Blair, and he came back staggering under a load of carpets, out of which the officers and escort made excellent tent-rugs, saddle-cloths, and blankets. There was an immense amount of stores in Cheraw, which were used or destroyed; among them twenty-four guns, two thousand muskets, and thirty-six hundred barrels of gunpowder. By the carelessness of a soldier, an immense pile of this powder was exploded, which shook the town badly, and killed and maimed several of our men.

We remained in or near Cheraw till the 6th of March, by which time the army was mostly across the Pedee River, and was prepared to resume the march on Fayetteville. In a house where General Hardee had been, I found a late *New York Tribune*, of fully a month later date than any I had seen. It contained a mass of news of great interest to us, and one short paragraph which I thought extremely mischievous. I think it was an editorial, to the effect that at last the editor had the satisfaction to inform his readers that General Sherman would next be heard from about Goldsboro', because his supply-vessels from Savannah were known to be rendezvousing at Morehead City. Now, I knew that General Hardee had read that same paper, and that he would be perfectly able to draw his own inferences. Up to that moment I had endeavored so to feign to our left that we had completely misled our antagoists; but this was no longer possible, and I concluded that we must be ready for the concentration in our front of all the force subject to General Joseph Johnston's orders, for I was there also informed that he had been restored to the full command of the Confederate forces in South and North Carolina.

On the 6th of March I crossed the Pedee, and all the army marched for Fayetteville: the Seventeenth Corps kept well to the right, to make room; the Fifteenth Corps marched by a direct road; the Fourteenth Corps also followed a direct road from Sneedsboro', where it had crossed the Pedee; and the Twentieth Corps, which had come into Cheraw for the convenience of the pontoon-bridge, diverged to the left, so as to enter Fayetteville next after the Fourteenth Corps, which was appointed to lead into Fayetteville. Kilpatrick held his cavalry still farther to the left rear on the roads from Lancaster, by way of Wadesboro' and New Gilead, so as to cover our trains from Hampton's and Wheeler's cavalry, who had first retreated toward the north. I traveled with the Fifteenth Corps, and on the 8th of March reached Laurel Hill, North Carolina. Satisfied that our troops must be at Wilmington, I determined to send a message there; I called for my man, Corporal Pike, whom I had rescued as before described, at Columbia, who was then traveling with our escort, and instructed him in disguise to work his way to the Cape Fear River, secure a boat, and float down to Wilmington to convey a letter, and to report our approach. I also called on General Howard for another volunteer, and he brought me a very clever young sergeant, who is now a commissioned officer in the regular army. Each of these got off during the night by separate routes, bearing the following message, reduced to the same cipher we used in telegraphic messages:

HEADQUARTERS MILITARY DIVISION OF THE MISSISSIPPI,
IN THE FIELD, LAUREL HILL,
Wednesday, March 8, 1865.

Commanding Officer, Wilmington, North Carolina:

We are marching for Fayetteville, will be there Saturday, Sunday, and Monday, and will then march for Goldsboro'.

If possible, send a boat up Cape Fear River, and have word conveyed to General Schofield that I expect to meet him about Goldsboro'. We are all well and have done finely. The rains make our roads difficult, and may delay us about Fayetteville, in which case I would like to have some bread, sugar, and coffee. We have abundance of all else. I expect to reach Goldsboro' by the 20th instant.

W. T. SHERMAN, *Major-General.*

On the 9th I was with the Fifteenth Corps, and toward evening reached a little church called Bethel, in the woods, in which we took refuge in a terrible storm of rain, which poured all night, making the roads awful. All the men were at work corduroying the roads, using fence-rails and split saplings, and every foot of the way had thus to be corduroyed to enable the artillery and wagons to pass. On the 10th we made some little progress; on the 11th I reached Fayetteville, and found that General Hardee, followed by Wade Hampton's cavalry, had barely escaped across Cape Fear River, burning the bridge which I had hoped to save. On reaching Fayetteville I found General Slocum already in possession with the Fourteenth Corps, and all the rest of the army was near at hand. A day or two before, General Kilpatrick, to our left rear, had divided his force into two parts, occupying roads behind the Twentieth Corps, interposing between our infantry columns and Wade Hampton's cavalry. The latter, doubtless to make junction with General Hardee, in Fayetteville, broke across this line, captured the house in which General Kilpatrick and the brigade-commander, General [George E.] Spencer, were, and for a time held possession of the camp and artillery of the brigade. However, General Kilpatrick and most of his men escaped into a swamp with their arms, reorganized and returned, catching Hampton's men in turn, scattered and drove them away, recovering most of his camp and artillery; but Hampton got off with Kilpatrick's private horses and a couple hundred prisoners, of which he boasted much in passing through Fayetteville.

It was also reported that, in the morning after Hardee's army was all across the bridge at Cape Fear River, Hampton, with a small body-guard, had remained in town, ready to retreat and burn the bridge as soon as our forces made their appearance. He was getting breakfast at the hotel when the alarm was given, when he and his escort took saddle, but soon realized that the alarm came from a set of our foragers, who, as usual, were extremely bold and rash. On these he turned, scattered them, killing some and making others prisoners; among them General Howard's favorite scout, Captain Duncan. Hampton then crossed the bridge and burned it.

I took up my quarters at the old United States Arsenal, which was in fine order, and had been much enlarged by the Confederate authorities, who never dreamed that an invading army would reach it from the west; and I also found in Fayetteville the widow and daughter of my first captain (General Childs), of the Third Artillery, learned that her son Fred had been the ordnance-officer in charge of the arsenal, and had of course fled with Hardee's army.

During the 11th the whole army closed down upon Fayetteville, and immediate preparations were made to lay two pontoon-bridges, one near the burned bridge, and another about four miles lower down.

Sunday, March 12th, was a day of Sabbath stillness in Fayetteville. The people generally attended their churches, for they were a very pious people, descended in a large measure from the old Scotch Covenanters, and our men too were resting from the toils and labors of six weeks of as hard marching as ever fell to the lot of soldiers. Shortly after noon was heard in the distance the shrill whistle of a steamboat, which came nearer and nearer, and soon a shout, long and continuous, was raised down by the river, which spread farther and farther, and we all felt that it meant a messenger from home. The effect was electric, and no one can realize the feeling unless, like us, he has been for months cut off from all communication with friends, and compelled to listen to the croakings and prognostications of open enemies. But in a very few minutes came up through the town to the arsenal on the plateau behind a group of officers, among whom was a large, florid seafaring man, named Ainsworth, bearing a small mail-bag from General Terry, at Wilmington, having left at 2 P. M.

the day before. Our couriers had got through safe from Laurel Hill, and this was the prompt reply.

As in the case of our former march from Atlanta, intense anxiety had been felt for our safety, and General Terry had been prompt to open communciation. After a few minutes' conference with Captain Ainsworth about the capacity of his boat, and the state of facts along the river, I instructed him to be ready to start back at 6 P. M., and ordered Captain Byers to get ready to carry dispatches to Washington. I also authorized General Howard to send back by this opportunity some of the fugitives who had traveled with his army all the way from Columbia, among whom were Mrs. Feaster and her two beautiful daughters.

I immediately prepared letters for Secretary Stanton, Generals Halleck and Grant, and Generals Schofield, Foster, Easton, and Beckwith.

In quick succession I received other messages from General Terry, of older date, and therefore superseded by that brought by the tug Davidson, viz., by two naval officers, who had come up partly by canoes and partly by land; General Terry had also sent a cavalry regiment to search for us, under Colonel Kerwin, who had dispatched two officers and fifty men, who reached us at Fayetteville; so that, by March 12th, I was in full communication with General Terry and the outside world. Still, I was anxious to reach Goldsboro', there to make junction with General Schofield, so as to be ready for the next and last stage of the war. I then knew that my special antagonist, General Joseph Johnston, was back, with part of his old army; that he would not be misled by feints and false reports, and would somehow compel me to exercise more caution than I had hitherto done. I then over-estimated his force at thirty-seven thousand infantry, supposed to be made up of S. D. Lee's corps, four thousand; Cheatham's, five thousand; Hoke's, eight thousand; Hardee's, ten thousand; and other detachments, ten thousand; with Hampton's, Wheeler's, and Butler's cavalry, about eight thousand. Of these, only Hardee and the cavalry were immediately in our front, while the bulk of Johnston's army was supposed to be collecting at or near Raleigh. I was determined, however, to give him as little time for organization as possible, and accordingly crossed Cape Fear River, with all the army, during the 13th and 14th, leaving one division as a rear-guard, until the arsenal could be completely destroyed. This was deliberately and completely leveled on the 14th, when fire was applied to the wreck. Little other damage was done at Fayetteville.

On the 14th the tug Davidson again arrived from Wilmington, with General Dodge, quartermaster, on board, reporting that there was no clothing to be had at Wilmington; but he brought up some sugar and coffee, which were most welcome, and some oats. He was followed by a couple of gunboats, under command of Captain Young, United States Navy, who reached Fayetteville after I had left, and undertook to patrol the river as long as the stage of water would permit; and General Dodge also promised to use the captured steamboats for a like purpose. Meantime, also, I had sent orders to General Schofield, at New Bern, and to General Terry, at Wilmington, to move with their effective forces straight for Goldsboro', where I expected to meet them by the 20th of March.

On the 15th of March the whole army was across Cape Fear River, and at once began its march for Goldsboro'; the Seventeenth Corps still on the right, the Fifteenth next in order, then the Fourteenth and Twentieth on the extreme left; the cavalry acting in close concert with the left flank. With almost a certainty of being attacked on this flank, I had instructed General Slocum to send his corps-trains under strong escort by an interior road, holding four divisions ready for immediate battle. General Howard was in like manner ordered to keep his trains well to his right, and to have four divisions unencumbered, about six miles ahead of General Slocum, within easy support.

In the mean time, I had dispatched by land to Wilmington a train of refugees who had followed the army all the way from Columbia, South Carolina, under an escort of two hundred men, commanded by Major John A. Winson (One Hundred and Sixteenth Illinois Infantry), so that we were disencumbered, and prepared for instant battle on our left and exposed flank.

In person I accompanied General Slocum, and during the night of March 15th was thirteen miles out on the Raleigh road. This flank followed substantially a road along Cape Fear River north, encountered pretty stubborn resistance by

Hardee's infantry, artillery, and cavalry, and the ground favored our enemy; for the deep river, Cape Fear, was on his
right, and North River on his left, forcing us to attack him
square in front. I proposed to drive Hardee well beyond
Averysboro', and then to turn to the right by Bentonsville for
Goldsboro'. During the day it rained very hard, and I had
taken refuge in an old cooper-shop, where a prisoner of war
was brought to me (sent back from the skirmish-line by General Kilpatrick), who proved to be Colonel Albert Rhett,
former commander of Fort Sumter. He was a tall, slender,
and handsome young man, dressed in the most approved rebel
uniform, with high jackboots beautifully stitched, and was
dreadfully mortified to find himself a prisoner in our hands.
General Frank Blair happened to be with me at the moment,
and we were much amused at Rhett's outspoken disgust at
having been captured without a fight. He said he was a brigade commander, and that his brigade that day was Hardee's
rear-guard; that his command was composed mostly of the
recent garrisons of the batteries of Charleston Harbor, and
had little experience in woodcraft; that he was giving ground
to us as fast as Hardee's army to his rear moved back, and
during this operation he was with a single aide in the woods,
and was captured by two men of Kilpatrick's skirmish-line
that was following up his retrograde movement. These men
called on him to surrender, and ordered him, in language
more forcible than polite, to turn and ride back. He first supposed these men to be of Hampton's cavalry, and threatened
to report them to General Hampton for disrespectful language; but he was soon undeceived, and was conducted to
Kilpatrick, who sent him back to General Slocum's guard.

The rain was falling heavily, and, our wagons coming up,
we went into camp there, and had Rhett and General Blair
to take supper with us, and our conversation was full and quite
interesting. In due time, however, Rhett was passed over by
General Slocum to his provost-guard, with orders to be treated
with due respect, and was furnished with a horse to ride.

The next day (the 16th) the opposition continued stubborn,
and near Averysboro' Hardee had taken up a strong position,
before which General Slocum deployed Jackson's division (of
the Twentieth Corps), with part of Ward's. Kilpatrick was on
his right front. Coming up, I advised that a brigade should

make a wide circuit by the left, and, if possible, catch this line in flank. The movement was completely successful, the first line of the enemy was swept away, and we captured the larger part of Rhett's brigade, two hundred and seventeen men, including Captain Macbeth's battery of three guns, and buried one hundred and eight dead.

The deployed lines (Ward's and Jackson's) passed on, and found Hardee again intrenched; but the next morning he was gone, in full retreat toward Smithfield. In this action, called the battle of Averysboro', we lost twelve officers and sixty-five men killed, and four hundred and seventy-seven men wounded; a serious loss, because every wounded man had to be carried in an ambulance. The rebel wounded (sixty-eight) were carried to a house near by, all surgical operations necessary were performed by our surgeons, and then these wounded men were left in care of an officer and four men of the rebel prisoners, with a scanty supply of food, which was the best we could do for them. In person I visited this house while the surgeons were at work, with arms and legs lying around loose, in the yard and on the porch; and in a room on a bed lay a pale, handsome young fellow, whose left arm had just been cut off near the shoulder. Some one used my name, when he asked, in a feeble voice, if I were General Sherman. He then announced himself as Captain Macbeth, whose battery had just been captured; and said that he remembered me when I used to visit his father's house, in Charleston. I inquired about his family, and enabled him to write a note to his mother, which was sent her afterward from Goldsboro'. I have seen that same young gentleman since in St. Louis, where he was a clerk in an insurance-office.

While the battle of Averysboro' was in progress, and I was sitting on my horse, I was approached by a man on foot, without shoes or coat, and his head bandaged by a handkerchief. He announced himself as the Captain Duncan who had been captured by Wade Hampton in Fayetteville, but had escaped; and, on my inquiring how he happened to be in that plight, he explained that when he was a prisoner Wade Hampton's men had made him "get out of his coat, hat, and shoes," which they appropriated to themselves. He said Wade Hampton had seen them do it, and he had appealed to him personally for protection, as an officer, but Hampton answered him with a curse. I sent Duncan to General Kilpatrick, and heard afterward that Kilpatrick had applied to General Slocum for his prisoner, Colonel Rhett, whom he made march on foot the rest of the way to Goldsboro', in retaliation. There was a story afloat that Kilpatrick made him "get out" of those fine boots, but restored them because none of his own officers had feet delicate enough to wear them. Of course, I know nothing of this personally, and have never seen Rhett since that night by the cooper-shop; and suppose that he is the editor who recently fought a duel in New Orleans.

From Averysboro' the left wing turned east, toward Goldsboro', the Fourteenth Corps leading. I remained with this wing until the night of the 18th, when we were within twenty-seven miles of Goldsboro' and five from Bentonsville; and, supposing that all danger was over, I crossed over to join Howard's column, to the right, so as to be nearer to Generals Schofield and Terry, known to be approaching Goldsboro'. I overtook General Howard at Falling-Creek Church, and found his column well drawn out, by reason of the bad roads. I had heard some cannonading over about Slocum's head of column, and supposed it to indicate about the same measure of opposition by Hardee's troops and Hampton's cavalry before experienced; but during the day a messenger overtook me, and notified me that near Bentonsville General Slocum had run up against *Johnston's whole army.* I sent back orders for him to fight defensively to save time, and that I would come up with reënforcements from the direction of Cox's Bridge, by the road which we had reached near Falling-Creek Church. The country was very obscure, and the maps extremely defective.

By this movement I hoped General Slocum would hold Johnston's army facing west, while I would come on his rear from the east. The Fifteenth Corps, less one division (Hazen's), still well to the rear, was turned at once toward Bentonsville; Hazen's division was ordered to Slocum's flank, and orders were also sent for General Blair, with the Seventeenth Corps, to come to the same destination. Meantime the sound of cannon came from the direction of Bentonsville.

The night of the 19th caught us near Falling-Creek Church; but early the next morning the Fifteenth Corps, General C. R. Woods's division leading, closed down on Bentonsville, near which it was brought up by encountering a line of fresh parapet, crossing the road and extending north, toward Mill Creek. After deploying, I ordered General Howard to proceed with due caution, using skirmishers alone, till he had made junction with General Slocum, on his left. These deployments occupied all day, during which two divisions of the Seventeenth Corps also got up. At that time General Johnston's army occupied the form of a V, the angle reaching the road leading from Averysboro' to Goldsboro', and the flanks resting on Mill Creek, his lines embracing the village of Bentonsville.

General Slocum's wing faced one of these lines and General Howard's the other; and, in the uncertainty of General Johnston's strength, I did not feel disposed to invite a general battle, for we had been out from Savannah since the latter part of January, and our wagon-trains contained but little food. I had also received messages during the day from General Schofield, at Kinston, and General Terry, at Faison's Depot, approaching Goldsboro', both expecting to reach it by March 21st. During the 20th we simply held our ground and started our trains back to Kinston for provisions, which would be needed in the event of being forced to fight a general battle at Bentonsville. The next day (21st) it began to rain again, and we remained quiet till about noon, when General Mower, ever rash, broke through the rebel line on his extreme left flank, and was pushing straight for Bentonsville and the bridge across Mill Creek. I ordered him back to connect with his own corps; and, lest the enemy should concentrate on him, ordered the whole rebel line to be engaged with a strong skirmish-fire.

I think I made a mistake there, and should rapidly have followed Mower's lead with the whole of the right wing, which would have brought on a general battle, and it could not have resulted otherwise than successfully to us, by reason of our vastly superior numbers; but at the moment, for the reasons given, I preferred to make junction with Generals Terry and Schofield, before engaging Johnston's army, the strength of which was utterly unknown. The next day he was gone, and had retreated on Smithfield; and, the roads all being clear, our army moved to Goldsboro'. The heaviest fighting at Bentonsville was on the first day, viz., the 19th, when

Johnston's army struck the head of Slocum's columns, knocking back [William P.] Carlin's division; but, as soon as General Slocum had brought up the rest of the Fourteenth Corps into line, and afterward the Twentieth on its left, he received and repulsed all attacks, and held his ground as ordered, to await the coming back of the right wing. His loss, as reported, was nine officers and one hundred and forty-five men killed, eight hundred and sixteen wounded, and two hundred and twenty-six missing. He reported having buried of the rebel dead one hundred and sixty-seven, and captured three hundred and thirty-eight prisoners.

The loss of the right wing was two officers and thirty-five men killed, twelve officers and two hundred and eighty-nine men wounded, and seventy missing. General Howard reported that he had buried one hundred of the rebel dead, and had captured twelve hundred and eighty-seven prisoners.

Our total loss, therefore, at Bentonsville was:

	Officers	Men
Killed	11	180
Wounded	12	1,105
Missing	—	296
Total	23	1,581
Aggregate Loss		1,604

General Johnston, in his "Narrative" (p. 392), asserts that his entire force at Bentonsville, omitting Wheeler's and Butler's cavalry, only amounted to fourteen thousand one hundred infantry and artillery; and (p. 393) states his losses as follows:

DATE	Killed	Wounded	Missing
On the 19th	180	1,220	515
On the 20th	6	90	31
On the 21st	37	157	107
Total	223	1,467	653
Aggregate Loss		2,343	

Wide discrepancies exist in these figures: for instance, General Slocum accounts for three hundred and thirty-eight prisoners captured, and General Howard for twelve hundred and eighty-seven, making sixteen hundred and twenty-five in all, to Johnston's six hundred and fifty-three—a difference of eight hundred and seventy-two. I have always accorded to General Johnston due credit for boldness in his attack on our exposed flank at Bentonsville, but I think he understates his strength, and doubt whether at the time he had accurate returns from his miscellaneous army, collected from Hoke, Bragg, Hardee, Lee, etc. After the first attack on Carlin's division, I doubt if the fighting was as desperate as described by him, p. 385, *et seq.* I was close up with the Fifteenth Corps, on the 20th and 21st, considered the fighting as mere skirmishing, and know that my orders were to avoid a general battle, till we could be sure of Goldsboro', and of opening up a new base of supply. With the knowledge now possessed of his small force, of course I committed an error in not overwhelming Johnston's army on the 21st of March, 1865. But I was content then to let him go, and on the 22d of March rode to Cox's Bridge, where I met General Terry, with his two divisions of the Tenth Corps; and the next day we rode into Goldsboro', where I found General Schofield with the Twenty-third Corps, thus effecting a perfect junction of all the army at that point, as originally contemplated. During the 23d and 24th the whole army was assembled at Goldsboro'; General Terry's two divisions encamped at Faison's Depot to the south, and General Kilpatrick's cavalry at Mount Olive Station, near him, and there we all rested, while I directed my special attention to replenishing the army for the next and last stage of the campaign. Colonel W. W. Wright had been so indefatigable, that the New Bern Railroad was done, and a locomotive arrived in Goldsboro' on the 25th of March.

Thus was concluded one of the longest and most important marches ever made by an organized army in a civilized country. The distance from Savannah to Goldsboro' is four hundred and twenty-five miles, and the route traversed embraced five large navigable rivers, viz., the Edisto, Broad, Catawba, Pedee, and Cape Fear, at either of which a comparatively small force, well handled, should have made the passage most difficult, if not impossible. The country generally was in a state of nature, with innumerable swamps, with simply mud roads, nearly every mile of which had to be corduroyed. In our route we had captured Columbia, Cheraw, and Fayetteville, important cities and depots of supplies, had compelled the evacuation of Charleston City and Harbor, had utterly broken up all the railroads of South Carolina, and had consumed a vast amount of food and forage, essential to the enemy for the support of his own armies. We had in mid-winter accomplished the whole journey of four hundred and twenty-five miles in fifty days, averaging ten miles per day, allowing ten lay-days, and had reached Goldsboro' with the army in superb order, and the trains almost as fresh as when we had started from Atlanta.

It was manifest to me that we could resume our march, and come within the theatre of General Grant's field of operations in all April, and that there was no force in existence that could delay our progress, unless General Lee should succeed in eluding General Grant at Petersburg, make junction with General Johnston, and thus united meet me alone; and now that we had effected a junction with Generals Terry and Schofield, I had no fear even of that event. On reaching Goldsboro', I learned from General Schofield all the details of his operations about Wilmington and New Bern; also of the fight of the Twenty-third Corps about Kinston, with General Bragg. I also found Lieutenant Dunn, of General Grant's staff, awaiting me, with the general's letter of February 7th, covering instructions to Generals Schofield and Thomas; and his letter of March 16th, in answer to mine of the 12th, from Fayetteville.

Chapter 17

End of War:
"Peace to the Rio Grande"
April—May, 1865

As BEFORE DESCRIBED, the armies commanded respectively by
Generals J. M. Schofield, A. H. Terry, and myself, effected a
junction in and about Goldsboro', North Carolina, during the
22d and 23d of March, 1865, but it required a few days for
all the troops and trains of wagons to reach their respective
camps. In person I reached Goldsboro' on the 23d, and met
General Schofield, who described fully his operations in North
Carolina up to that date; and I also found Lieutenant Dunn,
aide-de-camp to General Grant, with a letter from him of
March 16th, giving a general description of the state of facts
about City Point. The next day I received another letter, more
full, dated the 22d, which I give herewith.

Nevertheless, I deemed it of great importance that I should
have a personal interview with the general, and determined
to go in person to City Point as soon as the repairs of the
railroad, then in progress under the personal direction of
Colonel W. W. Wright, would permit:

HEADQUARTERS ARMIES OF THE UNITED STATES,
CITY POINT, VIRGINIA, *March* 22, 1865.

Major-General W. T. SHERMAN, *commanding Military Division of the Mississippi.*

GENERAL: Although the Richmond papers do not communicate the fact, yet I saw enough in them to satisfy me that you occupied Goldsboro' on the 19th inst. I congratulate you and the army on what may be regarded as the successful termination of the third campaign since leaving the Tennessee River, less than one year ago.

Since Sheridan's very successful raid north of the James, the enemy are left dependent on the Southside and Danville roads for all their supplies. These I hope to cut next week. Sheridan is at "White House," shoeing up and resting his cavalry. I expect him to finish by Friday night and to start the following morning, *via* Long Bridge, Newmarket, Bermuda Hundred, and the extreme left of the army around Petersburg. He will make no halt with the armies operating here, but will be joined by a division of cavalry, five thousand five hundred strong, from the Army of the Potomac, and will proceed directly to the Southside and Danville roads. His instructions will be to strike the Southside road as near Petersburg as he can, and destroy it so that it cannot be repaired for three or four days, and push on to the Danville road, as near to the Appomattox as he can get. Then I want him to destroy the road toward Burkesville as far as he can; then push on to the Southside road, west of Burkesville, and destroy it effectually. From that point I shall probably leave it to his discretion either to return to this army, crossing the Danville road south of Burkesville, or go and join you, passing between Danville and Greensboro'. When this movement commences I shall move out by my left, with all the force I can, holding present intrenched lines. I shall start with no distinct view, further than holding Lee's forces from following Sheridan. But I shall be along myself, and will take advantage of any thing that turns up. If Lee detaches, I will attack; or if he comes out of his lines I will endeavor to repulse him, and follow it up to the best advantage.

It is most difficult to understand what the rebels intend to do; so far but few troops have been detached from Lee's army. Much machinery has been removed, and material has been sent to Lynchburg, showing a disposition to go there. Points, too, have been fortified on the Danville road.

Lee's army is much demoralized, and great numbers are deserting. Probably, from returned prisoners, and such conscripts as can be picked up, his numbers may be kept up. I estimate his force now at about sixty-five thousand men.

Wilson started on Monday, with twelve thousand cavalry, from Eastport. Stoneman started on the same day, from East Tennessee, toward Lynchburg. Thomas is moving the Fourth Corps to Bull's Gap. Canby is moving with a formidable force on Mobile and the interior of Alabama.

I ordered Gillmore, as soon as the fall of Charleston was known, to hold all important posts on the sea-coast, and to send to Wilmington all surplus forces. Thomas was also directed to forward to New Bern all troops belonging to the corps with you. I understand this will give you about five thousand men, besides those brought east by [Thomas F.] Meagher.

I have been telegraphing General Meigs to hasten up locomotives and cars for you. General [Daniel C.] McCallum, he informs me, is attending to it. I fear they are not going forward as fast as I would like.

Let me know if you want more troops, or any thing else.

Very respectfully, your obedient servant,

U. S. GRANT, *Lieutenant-General.*

The railroad was repaired to Goldsboro' by the evening of March 25th, when, leaving General Schofield in chief command, with a couple of staff-officers I started for City Point, Virginia, on a locomotive, in company with Colonel Wright, the constructing engineer. We reached New Bern that evening, which was passed in the company of General Palmer and his accomplished lady, and early the next morning we continued on to Morehead City, where General Easton had provided for us the small captured steamer Russia, Captain [William] Smith. We put to sea at once and steamed up the coast, reaching Fortress Monroe on the morning of the 27th, where I landed and telegraphed to my brother, Senator Sherman, at Washington, inviting him to come down and return with me to Goldsboro'. We proceeded on up James River to City

Point, which we reached the same afternoon. I found General Grant, with his family and staff, occupying a pretty group of huts on the bank of James River, overlooking the harbor, which was full of vessels of all classes, both war and merchant, with wharves and warehouses on an extensive scale. The general received me most heartily, and we talked over matters very fully. After I had been with him an hour or so, he remarked that the President, Mr. Lincoln, was then on board the steamer River Queen, lying at the wharf, and he proposed that we should call and see him. We walked down to the wharf, went on board, and found Mr. Lincoln alone, in the after-cabin. He remembered me perfectly, and at once engaged in a most interesting conversation. He was full of curiosity about the many incidents of our great march, which had reached him officially and through the newspapers, and seemed to enjoy very much the more ludicrous parts—about the "bummers," and their devices to collect food and forage when the outside world supposed us to be starving; but at the same time he expressed a good deal of anxiety lest some accident might happen to the army in North Carolina during my absence. I explained to him that that army was snug and comfortable, in good camps, at Goldsboro'; that it would require some days to collect forage and food for another march; and that General Schofield was fully competent to command it in my absence. Having made a good, long, social visit, we took our leave and returned to General Grant's quarters, where Mrs. Grant had provided tea. While at the table, Mrs. Grant inquired if we had seen *Mrs.* Lincoln. "No," said the general, "I did not ask for her"; and I added that I did not even know that she was on board. Mrs. Grant then exclaimed, "Well, you are a pretty pair!" and added that our neglect was unpardonable; when the general said we would call again the next day, and make amends for the unintended slight.

Early the next day, March 28th, all the principal officers of the army and navy called to see me, Generals [George G.] Meade, Ord, Ingalls, etc., and Admiral Porter. At this time the River Queen was at anchor out in the river, abreast of the wharf, and we again started to visit Mr. and *Mrs.* Lincoln. Admiral Porter accompanied us. We took a small tug at the wharf, which conveyed us on board, where we were again received most courteously by the President, who conducted us to the after-cabin. After the general compliments, General Grant inquired after *Mrs.* Lincoln, when the President went to her state-room, returned, and begged us to excuse her, as she was not well. We then again entered upon a general conversation, during which General Grant explained to the President that at that very instant of time General Sheridan was crossing James River from the north, by a pontoon-bridge below City Point; that he had a large, well-appointed force of cavalry, with which he proposed to strike the Southside and Danville Railroads, by which alone General Lee, in Richmond, supplied his army; and that, in his judgment, matters were drawing to a crisis, his only apprehension being that General Lee would not wait long enough. I also explained that my army at Goldsboro' was strong enough to fight Lee's army and Johnston's combined, provided that General Grant could come up within a day or so; that if Lee would only remain in Richmond another fortnight, I could march up to Burkesville, when Lee would have to starve inside of his lines, or come out from his intrenchments and fight us on equal terms.

Both General Grant and myself supposed that one or the other of us would have to fight one more bloody battle, and that it would be the *last*. Mr. Lincoln exclaimed, more than once, that there had been blood enough shed, and asked us if another battle could not be avoided. I remember well to have said that we could not control that event; that this necessarily rested with our enemy; and I inferred that both Jeff. Davis and General Lee would be forced to fight one more desperate and bloody battle. I rather supposed it would fall on me, somewhere near Raleigh; and General Grant added that, if Lee would only wait a few more days, he would have his army so disposed that if the enemy should abandon Richmond, and attempt to make junction with General Joseph Johnston in North Carolina, he (General Grant) would be on his heels. Mr. Lincoln more than once expressed uneasiness that I was not with my army at Goldsboro', when I again assured him that General Schofield was fully competent to command in my absence; that I was going to start back that very day, and that Admiral Porter had kindly provided for me the steamer Bat, which he said was much swifter than my own vessel, the Russia. During this interview I inquired of the

President if he was all ready for the end of the war. What was to be done with the rebel armies when defeated? And what should be done with the political leaders, such as Jeff. Davis, etc.? Should we allow them to escape, etc.? He said he was all ready; all he wanted of us was to defeat the opposing armies, and to get the men composing the Confederate armies back to their homes, at work on their farms and in their shops. As to Jeff. Davis, he was hardly at liberty to speak his mind fully, but intimated that he ought to clear out, "escape the country," only it would not do for him to say so openly. As usual, he illustrated his meaning by a story: "A man once had taken the total-abstinence pledge. When visiting a friend, he was invited to take a drink, but declined, on the score of his pledge; when his friend suggested lemonade, which was accepted. In preparing the lemonade, the friend pointed to the brandy-bottle, and said the lemonade would be more palatable if he were to pour in a little brandy; when his guest said, if he could do so 'unbeknown' to him, he would not object." From which illustration I inferred that Mr. Lincoln wanted Davis to escape, "unbeknown" to him.

I made no notes of this conversation at the time, but Admiral Porter, who was present, did, and in 1866 he furnished me an account thereof, which I insert below, but the admiral describes the first visit, of the 27th, whereas my memory puts Admiral Porter's presence on the following day. Still he may be right, and he may have been with us the day before, as I write this chiefly from memory. There were two distinct interviews; the first was late in the afternoon of March 27th, and the other about noon of the 28th, both in the after-cabin of the steamer River Queen; on both occasions Mr. Lincoln was full and frank in his conversation, assuring me that in his mind he was all ready for the civil reorganization of affairs at the South as soon as the war was over; and he distinctly authorized me to assure Governor [Zebulon] Vance and the people of North Carolina that, as soon as the rebel armies laid down their arms, and resumed their civil pursuits, they would at once be guaranteed all their rights as citizens of a common country; and that to avoid anarchy the State governments then in existence, with their civil functionaries, would be recognized by him as the government de facto till Congress could provide others.

I know, when I left him, that I was more than ever impressed by his kindly nature, his deep and earnest sympathy with the afflictions of the whole people, resulting from the war, and by the march of hostile armies through the South; and that his earnest desire seemed to be to end the war speedily, without more bloodshed or devastation, and to restore all the men of both sections to their homes. In the language of his second inaugural address, he seemed to have "charity for all, malice toward none," and, above all, an absolute faith in the courage, manliness, and integrity of the armies in the field. When at rest or listening, his legs and arms seemed to hang almost lifeless, and his face was care-worn and haggard; but, the moment he began to talk, his face lightened up, his tall form, as it were, unfolded, and he was the very impersonation of good-humor and fellowship. The last words I recall as addressed to me were that he would feel better when I was back at Goldsboro'. We parted at the gangway of the River Queen, about noon of March 28th, and I never saw him again. Of all the men I ever met, he seemed to possess more of the elements of greatness, combined with goodness, than any other.

As soon as possible, I arranged with General Grant for certain changes in the organization of my army; and the general also undertook to send to North Carolina some tug-boats and barges to carry stores from New Bern up as far as Kinston, whence they could be hauled in wagons to our camps, thus relieving our railroads to that extent. I undertook to be ready to march north by April 10th, and then embarked on the steamer Bat, Captain [John S.] Barnes, for North Carolina. We steamed down James River, and at Old Point Comfort took on board my brother, Senator Sherman, and Mr. Edwin Stanton, son of the Secretary of War, and proceeded at once to our destination. On our way down the river, Captain Barnes expressed himself extremely obliged to me for taking his vessel, as it had relieved him of a most painful dilemma. He explained that he had been detailed by Admiral Porter to escort the President's unarmed boat, the River Queen, in which capacity it became his special duty to look after Mrs. Lincoln. The day before my arrival at City Point, there had been a grand review of a part of the Army of the James, then commanded by General Ord. The President rode out from City Point with General Grant on horseback, accompanied by a numerous staff, including Captain Barnes and Mrs. Ord; but Mrs. Lincoln and Mrs. Grant had followed in a carriage.

The cavalcade reached the review-ground some five or six miles out from City Point, found the troops all ready, drawn up in line, and after the usual presentation of arms, the President and party, followed by Mrs. Ord and Captain Barnes on horseback, rode the lines, and returned to the reviewing stand, which meantime had been reached by Mrs. Lincoln and Mrs. Grant in their carriage, which had been delayed by the driver taking a wrong road. Mrs. Lincoln, seeing Mrs. Ord and Captain Barnes riding with the retinue, and supposing that Mrs. Ord had personated her, turned on Captain Barnes and gave him a fearful scolding; and even indulged in some pretty sharp upbraidings to Mrs. Ord.

This made Barnes's position very unpleasant, so that he felt much relieved when he was sent with me to North Carolina. The Bat was very fast, and on the morning of the 29th we were near Cape Hatteras; Captain Barnes, noticing a propeller coming out of Hatteras Inlet, made her turn back and pilot us in. We entered safely, steamed up Pamlico Sound into Neuse River, and the next morning, by reason of some derangement of machinery, we anchored about seven miles below New Bern, whence we went up in Captain Barnes's barge. As soon as we arrived at New Bern, I telegraphed up to General Schofield at Goldsboro' the fact of my return, and that I had arranged with General Grant for the changes made necessary in the reorganization of the army, and for the boats necessary to carry up the provisions and stores we needed, prior to the renewal of our march northward.

These changes amounted to constituting the left wing a distinct army, under the title of "the Army of Georgia," under command of General Slocum, with his two corps commanded by General Jeff. C. Davis and General Joseph A. Mower; the Tenth and Twenty-third Corps already constituted another army, "of the Ohio," under the command of Major-General Schofield, and his two corps were commanded by Generals J. D. Cox and A. H. Terry. These changes were necessary, because army commanders only could order courts-martial, grant discharges, and perform many other matters of discipline and administration which were indispensable;

but my chief purpose was to prepare the whole army for what seemed among the probabilities of the time—to fight both Lee's and Johnston's armies combined, in case their junction could be formed before General Grant could possibly follow Lee to North Carolina.

General George H. Thomas, who still remained at Nashville, was not pleased with these changes, for the two corps with General Slocum, viz., the Fourteenth and Twentieth, up to that time, had remained technically a part of his "Army of the Cumberland"; but he was so far away, that I had to act to the best advantage with the troops and general officers actually present. I had specially asked for General Mower to command the Twentieth Corps, because I regarded him as one of the boldest and best fighting generals in the whole army. His predecessor, General A. S. Williams, the senior division commander present, had commanded the corps well from Atlanta to Goldsboro', and it may have seemed unjust to replace him at that precise moment; but I was resolved to be prepared for a most desperate and, as then expected, a final battle, should it fall on me.

I returned to Goldsboro' from New Bern by rail the evening of March 30th, and at once addressed myself to the task of reorganization and replenishment of stores, so as to be ready to march by April 10th, the day agreed on with General Grant.

The railroads to our rear had also been repaired, so that stores were arriving very fast, both from Morehead City and Wilmington. The country was so level that a single locomotive could haul twenty-five and thirty cars to a train, instead of only ten, as was the case in Tennessee and Upper Georgia.

By the 5th of April such progress had been made, that I issued the following Special Field Orders, No. 48, prescribing the time and manner of the next march:

[Special Field Orders, No. 48.]

HEADQUARTERS MILITARY DIVISION OF THE
MISSISSIPPI, IN THE FIELD, GOLDSBORO',
NORTH CAROLINA, *April* 5, 1865.

Confidential to Army Commanders, Corps Commanders, and Chiefs of Staff Departments:

The next grand objective is to place this army (with its full equipment) north of Roanoke River, facing west, with a base for supplies at Norfolk, and at Winton or Murfrees-boro' on the Chowan, and in full communication with the Army of the Potomac, about Petersburg; and also to do the enemy as much harm as possible *en route:*

1. To accomplish this result the following general plan will be followed, or modified only by written orders from these headquarters, should events require a change:

(1.) On Monday, the 10th of April, all preparations are presumed to be complete, and the outlying detachments will be called in, or given directions to meet on the next march. All preparations will also be complete to place the railroad-stock back of Kinston on the one road, and below the Northeast Branch on the other.

(2.) On Tuesday, the 11th, the columns will draw out on their lines of march, say, about seven miles, and close up.

(3.) On Wednesday the march will begin in earnest, and will be kept up at the rate, say, of about twelve miles a day, or according to the amount of resistance. All the columns will dress to the left (which is the exposed flank), and commanders will study always to find roads by which they can, if necessary, perform a general left wheel, the wagons to be escorted to some place of security on the direct route of march. Foraging and other details may continue as heretofore, only more caution and prudence should be observed; and foragers should not go in advance of the *advance-guard,* but look more to our right rear for corn, bacon, and meal.

2. The left wing (Major-General Slocum commanding) will aim straight for the railroad-bridge near Smithfield; thence along up the Neuse River to the railroad-bridge over Neuse River, northeast of Raleigh (Powell's); thence to Warrenton, the general point of concentration.

The centre (Major-General Schofield commanding) will move to Whitley's Mill, ready to support the left until it is past Smithfield, when it will follow up (substantially) Little River to about Rolesville, ready at all times to move to the support of the left; after passing Tar River, to move to Warrenton.

The right wing (Major-General Howard commanding), preceded by the cavalry, will move rapidly on Pikeville and Nahunta, then swing across to Bulah to Folk's Bridge, ready to make junction with the other armies in case the enemy offers battle this side of Neuse River, about Smithfield; thence, in case of no serious opposition on the left, will work up toward Earpsboro', Andrews, B——, and Warrenton.

The cavalry (General Kilpatrick commanding), leaving its encumbrances with the right wing, will push as though straight for Weldon, until the enemy is across Tar River, and that bridge burned; then it will deflect toward Nashville and Warrenton, keeping up communication with general headquarters.

3. As soon as the army starts, the chief-quartermaster and commissary will prepare a resupply of stores at some point on Pamlico or Albemarle Sounds, ready to be conveyed to Kinston or Winton and Murfreesboro', according to developments. As soon as they have satisfactory information that the army is north of the Roanoke, they will forthwith establish a depot at Winton, with a sub-depot at Murfreesboro'. Major-General Schofield will hold, as heretofore, Wilmington (with the bridge across Northern Branch as an outpost), New Bern (and Kinston as its outpost), and will be prepared to hold Winton and Murfreesboro' as soon as the time arrives for that move. The navy has instructions from Admiral Porter to coöperate, and any commanding officer is authorized to call on the navy for assistance and coöperation, always in writing, setting forth the reasons, of which necessarily the naval commander must be the judge.

4. The general-in-chief will be with the centre habitually, but may in person shift to either flank where his presence may be needed, leaving a staff-officer to receive reports. He requires, absolutely, a report of each army or grand detachment each night, whether any thing material has occurred or not, for often the absence of an enemy is a very important fact in military prognostication.

By order of Major-General W. T. Sherman,

  L. M. Dayton, *Assistant Adjutant-General.*

But the whole problem became suddenly changed by the

news of the fall of Richmond and Petersburg, which reached us at Goldsboro', on the 6th of April. The Confederate Government, with Lee's army, had hastily abandoned Richmond, fled in great disorder toward Danville, and General Grant's whole army was in close pursuit. Of course, I inferred that General Lee would succeed in making junction with General Johnston, with at least a fraction of his army, somewhere to my front. I at once altered the foregoing orders, and prepared on the day appointed, viz., April 10th, to move straight on Raleigh, against the army of General Johnston, known to be at Smithfield, and supposed to have about thirty-five thousand men. Wade Hampton's cavalry was on his left front and Wheeler's on his right front, simply watching us and awaiting our initiative. Meantime the details of the great victories in Virginia came thick and fast, and on the 8th I received from General Grant this communication, in the form of a cipher-dispatch:

HEADQUARTERS ARMIES OF THE UNITED STATES, }
WILSON'S STATION, *April 5, 1865.*

Major-General SHERMAN, *Goldsboro', North Carolina:*

All indications now are that Lee will attempt to reach Danville with the remnant of his force. Sheridan, who was up with him last night, reports all that is left with him—horse, foot, and dragoons—at twenty thousand, much demoralized. We hope to reduce this number one-half. I will push on to Burkesville, and, if a stand is made at Danville, will, in a very few days, go there. If you can possibly do so, push on from where you are, and let us see if we cannot finish the job with Lee's and Johnston's armies. Whether it will be better for you to strike for Greensboro' or nearer to Danville, you will be better also to judge when you receive this. Rebel armies now are the only strategic points to strike at.

U. S. GRANT, *Lieutenant-General.*

I answered immediately that we would move on the 10th, prepared to follow Johnston wherever he might go. Promptly on Monday morning, April 10th, the army moved straight on Smithfield; the right wing making a circuit by the right, and the left wing, supported by the centre, moving on the two direct roads toward Raleigh, distant fifty miles. General Terry's and General Kilpatrick's troops moved from their positions on the south or west bank of the Neuse River in the same general direction, by Cox's Bridge. On the 11th we reached Smithfield, and found it abandoned by Johnston's army, which had retreated hastily on Raleigh, burning the bridges. To restore these consumed the remainder of the day, and during that night I received a message from General Grant, at Appomattox, that General Lee had surrendered to him his whole army, which I at once announced to the troops in orders:

[Special Field Orders, No. 54.]

HEADQUARTERS MILITARY DIVISION OF THE MISSISSIPPI, }
   IN THE FIELD, SMITHFIELD, NORTH CAROLINA, }
              April 12, 1865. }

The general commanding announces to the army that he has official notice from General Grant that General Lee surrendered to him his entire army, on the 9th inst., at Appomattox Court-House, Virginia.

Glory to God and our country, and all honor to our comrades in arms, toward whom we are marching!

A little more labor, a little more toil on our part, the great race is won, and our Government stands regenerated, after four long years of war.

            W. T. SHERMAN, *Major-General commanding.*

Of course, this created a perfect *furore* of rejoicing, and we all regarded the war as over, for I knew well that General Johnston had no army with which to oppose mine. So that the only questions that remained were, would he surrender at Raleigh? or would he allow his army to disperse into guerrilla-bands, to "die in the last ditch," and entail on his country an indefinite and prolonged military occupation, and of consequent desolation? I knew well that Johnston's army could not be caught; the country was too open; and, without wagons, the men could escape us, disperse, and assemble again at some place agreed on, and thus the war might be prolonged indefinitely.

I then remembered Mr. Lincoln's repeated expression that he wanted the rebel soldiers not only defeated, but "back at their homes, engaged in their civil pursuits." On the evening of the 12th I was with the head of Slocum's column, at Gulley's, and General Kilpatrick's cavalry was still ahead, fighting Wade Hampton's rear-guard, with orders to push it through Raleigh, while I would give a more southerly course to the infantry columns, so as, if possible, to prevent a retreat southward. On the 13th, early, I entered Raleigh, and ordered the several heads of column toward Ashville, in the direction of Salisbury or Charlotte. Before reaching Raleigh, a locomotive came down the road to meet me, passing through both Wade Hampton's and Kilpatrick's cavalry, bringing four gentlemen, with a letter from Governor Vance to me, asking protection for the citizens of Raleigh. These gentlemen were, of course, dreadfully excited at the dangers through which they had passed. Among them were ex-Senator Graham, Mr. Swain, president of Chapel Hill University, and a Surgeon Warren, of the Confederate army. They had come with a flag of truce, to which they were not entitled; still, in the interest of peace, I respected it, and permitted them to return to Raleigh with their locomotive, to assure the Governor and the people that the war was substantially over, and that I wanted the civil authorities to remain in the execution of their office till the pleasure of the President could be ascertained. On reaching Raleigh I found these same gentlemen, with Messrs. Badger, Bragg, Holden, and others, but Governor Vance had fled, and could not be prevailed on to return, because he feared an arrest and imprisonment. From the Raleigh newspapers of the 10th I learned that General Stoneman, with his division of cavalry, had come across the mountains from East Tennessee, had destroyed the railroad at Salisbury, and was then supposed to be approaching Greensboro'. I also learned that General Wilson's cavalry corps was "smashing things" down about Selma and Montgomery, Alabama, and was pushing for Columbus and Macon, Georgia; and I also had reason to expect that General Sheridan would come down from Appomattox to join us at Raleigh with his superb cavalry corps. I needed more cavalry to check Johnston's retreat, so that I could come up to him with my infantry, and therefore had good reason to delay. I ordered the railroad to be finished up to Raleigh, so that I could operate from it as a base, and then made—

[Special Field Orders, No. 55.]

HEADQUARTERS MILITARY DIVISION OF THE MISSISSIPPI, }
IN THE FIELD, RALEIGH, NORTH CAROLINA,
April 14, 1865. }

The next movement will be on Ashboro', to turn the position of the enemy at the "Company's Shops" in rear of Haw River Bridge, and at Greensboro', and to cut off his only available line of retreat by Salisbury and Charlotte:

1. General Kilpatrick will keep up a show of pursuit in the direction of Hillsboro' and Graham, but be ready to cross Haw River on General Howard's bridge, near Pittsboro', and thence will operate toward Greensboro', on the right front of the right wing.

2. The right wing, Major-General Howard commanding, will move out on the Chapel Hill road, and send a light division up in the direction of Chapel Hill University to act in connection with the cavalry; but the main columns and trains will move *via* Hackney's Cross-Roads, and Trader's Hill, Pittsboro', St. Lawrence, etc., to be followed by the cavalry and light division, as soon as the bridge is laid over Haw River.

3. The centre, Major-General Schofield commanding, move *via* Holly Springs, New Hill, Haywood, and Moffitt's Mills.

4. The left wing, Major-General Slocum commanding, will move rapidly by the Aven's Ferry road, Carthage, Caledonia, and Cox's Mills.

5. All the troops will draw well out on the roads designated during to-day and to-morrow, and on the following day will move with all possible rapidity for Ashboro'. No further destruction of railroads, mills, cotton, and produce, will be made without the specific orders of an army commander, and the inhabitants will be dealt with kindly, looking to an early reconciliation. The troops will be permitted, however, to gather forage and provisions as heretofore; only more care should be taken not to strip the poorer classes too closely.

By order of General W. T. Sherman,
L. M. DAYTON, *Assistant Adjutant-General.*

Thus matters stood, when on the morning of the 14th General Kilpatrick reported from Durham's Station, twenty-six miles up the railroad toward Hillsboro', that a flag of truce had come in from the enemy with a package from General Johnston addressed to me. Taking it for granted that this was preliminary to a surrender, I ordered the message to be sent me at Raleigh, and on the 14th received from General Johnston a letter dated April 13, 1865, in these words:

The results of the recent campaign in Virginia have changed the relative military condition of the belligerents. I am, therefore, induced to address you in this form the inquiry whether, to stop the further effusion of blood and devastation of property, you are willing to make a temporary suspension of active operations, and to communicate to Lieutenant-General Grant, commanding the armies of the United States, the request that he will take like action in regard to other armies, the object being to permit the civil authorities to enter into the needful arrangements to terminate the existing war.

To which I replied as follows:

HEADQUARTERS MILITARY DIVISION OF THE MISSISSIPPI,
IN THE FIELD, RALEIGH, NORTH CAROLINA,
April 14, 1865.

General J. E. JOHNSTON, *commanding Confederate Army.*

GENERAL: I have this moment received your communication of this date. I am fully empowered to arrange with you any terms for the suspension of further hostilities between the armies commanded by you and those commanded by myself, and will be willing to confer with you to that end. I will limit the advance of my main column, to-morrow, to Morrisville, and the cavalry to the university, and expect that you will also maintain the present position of your forces until each has notice of a failure to agree.

That a basis of action may be had, I undertake to abide by

the same terms and conditions as were made by Generals Grant and Lee at Appomattox Court-House, on the 9th intant, relative to our two armies; and, furthermore, to obtain from General Grant an order to suspend the movements of any troops from the direction of Virginia. General Stoneman is under my command, and my order will suspend any devastation or destruction contemplated by him. I will add that I really desire to save the people of North Carolina the damage they would sustain by the march of this army through the central or western parts of the State.

I am, with respect, your obedient servant,

W. T. SHERMAN, *Major-General.*

I sent my aide-de-camp, Colonel McCoy, up to Durham's Station with this letter, with instruction to receive the answer, to telegraph its contents back to me at Raleigh, and to arrange for an interview. On the 16th I received a reply from General Johnston, agreeing to meet me the next day at a point midway between our advance at Durham and his rear at Hillsboro'. I ordered a car and locomotive to be prepared to convey me up to Durham's at eight o'clock of the morning of April 17th. Just as we were entering the car, the telegraph-operator, whose office was up-stairs in the depot-building, ran down to me and said that he was at that instant of time receiving a most important dispatch in cipher from Morehead City, which I ought to see. I held the train for nearly half an hour, when he returned with the message translated and written out. It was from Mr. Stanton, announcing the assassination of Mr. Lincoln, the attempt on the life of Mr. Seward and son, and a suspicion that a like fate was designed for General Grant and all the principal officers of the Government. Dreading the effect of such a message at that critical instant of time, I asked the operator if any one besides himself had seen it; he answered no. I then bade him not to reveal the contents by word or look till I came back, which I proposed to do the same afternoon. The train then started, and, as we passed Morris's Station, General Logan, commanding the Fifteenth Corps, came into my car, and I told him I wanted to see him on my return, as I had something very important to communicate. He knew I was going to meet General Johnston, and volunteered to say that he hoped I would succeed in obtaining his surrender, as the whole army dreaded the long march to Charlotte (one hundred and seventy-five miles), already begun, but which had been interrupted by the receipt of General Johnston's letter of the 13th. We reached Durham's, twenty-six miles, about 10 A. M., where General Kilpatrick had a squadron of cavalry drawn up to receive me. We passed into the house in which he had his headquarters, and soon after mounted some led horses, which he had prepared for myself and staff. General Kilpatrick sent a man ahead with a white flag, followed by a small platoon, behind which we rode, and were followed by the rest of the escort. We rode up the Hillsboro' road for about five miles, when our flag-bearer discovered another coming to meet him. They met, and word was passed back to us that General Johnston was near at hand, when we rode forward and met General Johnston on horseback, riding side by side with General Wade Hampton. We shook hands, and introduced our respective attendants. I asked if there was a place convenient where we could be private, and General Johnston said he had passed a small farm-house a short distance back, when we rode back to it together side by side, our staff-officers and escorts following. We had never met before, though we had been in the regular army together for thirteen years; but it so happened that we had never before come together. He was some twelve or more years my senior; but we knew enough of each other to be well acquainted at once. We soon reached the house of a Mr. Bennett, dismounted, and left our horses with orderlies in the road. Our officers, on foot, passed into the yard, and General Johnston and I entered the small frame-house. We asked the farmer if we could have the use of his home for a few minutes, and he and his wife withdrew into a smaller log-house, which stood close by.

As soon as we were alone together I showed him the dispatch announcing Mr. Lincoln's assassination, and watched him closely. The perspiration came out in large drops on his forehead, and he did not attempt to conceal his distress. He denounced the act as a disgrace to the age, and hoped I did not charge it to the Confederate Government. I told him I could not believe that he or General Lee, or the officers of the Confederate army, could possibly be privy to acts of assassination; but I would not say as much for Jeff. Davis, George

Sanders, and men of that stripe. We talked about the effect of this act on the country at large and on the armies, and he realized that it made my situation extremely delicate. I explained to him that I had not yet revealed the news to my own personal staff or to the army, and that I dreaded the effect when made known in Raleigh. Mr. Lincoln was peculiarly endeared to the soldiers, and I feared that some foolish woman or man in Raleigh might say something or do something that would madden our men, and that a fate worse than that of Columbia would befall the place.

I then told Johnson that he must be convinced that he could not oppose my army, and that, since Lee had surrendered, he could do the same with honor and propriety. He plainly and repeatedly admitted this, and added that any further fighting would be "*murder*"; but he thought that, instead of surrendering piecemeal, we might arrange terms that would embrace *all* the Confederate armies. I asked him if he could control other armies than his own; he said, not then, but intimated that he could procure authority from Mr. Davis. I then told him that I had recently had an interview with General Grant and President Lincoln, and that I was possessed of their views; that with them and the people North there seemed to be no vindictive feeling against the Confederate armies, but there was against Davis and his political adherents; and that the terms that General Grant had given to General Lee's army were certainly most generous and liberal. All this he admitted, but always recurred to the idea of a universal surrender, embracing his own army, that of Dick Taylor in Louisiana and Texas, and of [Dabney H.] Maury, Forrest, and others, in Alabama and Georgia. General Johnston's account of our interview in his "Narrative" (page 402, *et seq.*) is quite accurate and correct, only I do not recall his naming the capitulation of Loeben, to which he refers. Our conversation was very general and extremely cordial, satisfying me that it could have but one result, and that which we all desired, viz., to end the war as quickly as possible; and, being anxious to return to Raleigh before the news of Mr. Lincoln's assassination could be divulged, on General Johnston's saying that he thought that, during the night, he could procure authority to act in the name of all the Confederate armies in existence, we agreed to meet again the next day at noon at the same place, and parted, he for Hillsboro' and I for Raleigh.

We rode back to Durham's Station in the order we had come, and then I showed the dispatch announcing Mr. Lincoln's death. I cautioned the officers to watch the soldiers closely, to prevent any violent retaliation by them, leaving that to the Government at Washington; and on our way back to Raleigh in the cars I showed the same dispatch to General Logan and to several of the officers of the Fifteenth Corps that were posted at Morrisville and Jones's Station, all of whom were deeply impressed by it; but all gave their opinion that this sad news should not change our general course of action.

As soon as I reached Raleigh I published the following orders to the army, announcing the assassination of the President, and I doubt if, in the whole land, there were more sincere mourners over his sad fate than were then in and about Raleigh. I watched the effect closely, and was gratified that there was no single act of retaliation; though I saw and felt that one single word by me would have laid the city in ashes, and turned its whole population houseless upon the country, if not worse:

[Special Field Orders, No. 56.]

HEADQUARTERS MILITARY DIVISION OF THE MISSISSIPPI,
IN THE FIELD, RALEIGH, NORTH CAROLINA,
April 17, 1865.

The general commanding announces, with pain and sorrow, that on the evening of the 14th instant, at the theatre in Washington city, his Excellency the President of the United States, Mr. Lincoln, was assassinated by one who uttered the State motto of Virginia. At the same time, the Secretary of State, Mr. Seward, while suffering from a broken arm, was also stabbed by another murderer in his own house, but still survives, and his son was wounded, supposed fatally. It is believed, by persons capable of judging, that other high officers were designed to share the same fate. Thus it seems that our enemy, despairing of meeting us in open, manly warefare, begins to resort to the assassin's tools.

Your general does not wish you to infer that this is universal, for he knows that the great mass of the Confederate army would scorn to sanction such acts, but he believes it the legitimate consequence of rebellion against rightful authority.

We have met every phase which this war has assumed, and must now be prepared for it in its last and worst shape, that of assassins and guerrillas; but woe unto the people who seek to expend their wild passions in such a manner, for there is but one dread result!

By order of Major-General W. T. Sherman,
    L. M. DAYTON, *Assistant Adjutant-General.*

During the evening of the 17th and morning of the 18th I saw nearly all the general officers of the army (Schofield, Slocum, Howard, Logan, Blair), and we talked over the matter of the conference at Bennett's house of the day before, and, without exception, all advised me to agree to some terms, for they all dreaded the long and harassing march in pursuit of a dissolving and fleeing army—a march that might carry us back again over the thousand miles that we had just accomplished. We all knew that if we could bring Johnston's army to bay, we could destroy it in an hour, but that was simply impossible in the country in which we found ourselves. We discussed all the probabilities, among which was, whether, if Johnston made a point of it, I should assent to the escape from the country of Jeff. Davis and his fugitive cabinet; and some one of my general officers, either Logan or Blair, insisted that, if asked for, we should even provide a vessel to carry them to Nassau from Charleston.

The next morning I again started in the cars to Durham's Station, accompanied by most of my personal staff, and by Generals Blair, Barry, Howard, etc., and, reaching General Kilpatrick's headquarters at Durham, we again mounted, and rode, with the same escort of the day before, to Bennett's house, reaching there punctually at noon. General Johnston had not yet arrived, but a courier shortly came, and reported him as on the way. It must have been nearly 2 P. M. when he arrived, as before, with General Wade Hampton. He had halted his escort out of sight, and we again entered Bennett's house, and I closed the door. General Johnston then assured me that he had authority over all the Confederate armies, so that they would obey his orders to surrender on the same terms with his own, but he argued that, to obtain so cheaply this desirable result, I ought to give his men and officers some assurance of their political rights after their surrender. I explained to him that Mr. Lincoln's proclamation of amnesty, of December 8, 1863, still in force, enabled every Confederate soldier and officer, below the rank of colonel, to obtain an absolute pardon, by simply laying down his arms, and taking the common oath of allegiance, and that General Grant, in accepting the surrender of General Lee's army, had extended the same principle to *all* the officers, General Lee included; such a pardon, I understood, would restore to them all their rights of citizenship. But he insisted that the officers and men of the Confederate army were unnecessarily alarmed about this matter, as a sort of bugbear. He then said that Mr. [John C.] Breckenridge was near at hand, and he thought that it would be well for him to be present. I objected, on the score that he was then in Davis's cabinet, and our negotiations should be confined strictly to belligerents. He then said Breckenridge was a major-general in the Confederate army, and might sink his character of Secretary of War. I consented, and he sent one of his staff-officers back, who soon returned with Breckenridge, and he entered the room. General Johnston and I then again went over the whole ground, and Breckenridge confirmed what he had said as to the uneasiness of the Southern officers and soldiers about their political rights in case of surrender. While we were in consultation, a messenger came with a parcel of papers, which General Johnston said were from Mr. [John H.] Reagan, Postmaster-General. He and Breckenridge looked over them, and, after some side conversation, he handed one of the papers to me. It was in Reagan's handwriting, and began with a long preamble and terms, so general and verbose, that I said they were inadmissible. Then recalling the conversation of Mr. Lincoln, at City Point, I sat down at the table, and wrote off the terms, which I thought concisely expressed his views and wishes, and explained that I was willing to submit these terms to the new President, Mr. Johnson, provided that both armies should remain *in statu quo* until the truce therein declared should expire. I had full faith that General Johnston would religiously respect the truce, which he did; and that I would be the gainer, for in the few days it would take to send the papers to Washington, and receive an answer, I could finish the rail-road up to Raleigh, and be the better prepared for a long chase.

Neither Mr. Breckenridge nor General Johnston wrote one word of that paper. I wrote it myself, and announced it as the best I could do, and they readily assented.

While copies of this paper were being made for signature, the officers of our staffs commingled in the yard at Bennett's house, and were all presented to Generals Johnston and Breckenridge. All without exception were rejoiced that the war was over, and that in a very few days we could turn our faces toward home. I remember telling Breckenridge that he had better get away, as the feeling of our people was utterly hostile to the political element of the South, and to him especially, because he was the Vice-President of the United States, who had as such announced Mr. Lincoln, of Illinois, duly and properly elected the President of the United States, and yet that he had afterward openly rebelled and taken up arms against the Government. He answered me that he surely would give us no more trouble, and intimated that he would speedily leave the country forever. I may have also advised him that Mr. Davis too should get abroad as soon as possible.

The papers were duly signed; we parted about dark, and my party returned to Raleigh. Early the next morning, April 19th, I dispatched by telegraph to Morehead City to prepare a fleet-steamer to carry a messenger to Washington, and sent Major Henry Hitchcock down by rail, bearing the following letters, and agreement with General Johnston, with instructions to be very careful to let nothing escape him to the greedy newspaper correspondents, but to submit his papers to General Halleck, General Grant, or the Secretary of War, and to bring me back with all expedition their orders and instructions.

On their face they recited that I had no authority to make final terms involving civil or political questions, but that I submitted them to the proper quarter in Washington for their action; and the letters fully explained that the military situation was such that the delay was an advantage to us. I cared little whether they were approved, modified, or disapproved *in toto;* only I wanted instructions. Many of my general officers, among whom, I am almost positive, were Generals Logan and Blair, urged me to accept the "terms," without reference at all to Washington, but I preferred the latter course:

HEADQUARTERS MILITARY DIVISION OF THE MISSISSIPPI, IN THE FIELD, RALEIGH, NORTH CAROLINA, *April* 18, 1865.

General H. W. HALLECK, *Chief of Staff, Washington, D. C.*

GENERAL: I received your dispatch describing the man Clark, detailed to assassinate me. He had better be in a hurry, or he will be too late.

The news of Mr. Lincoln's death produced a most intense effect on our troops. At first I feared it would lead to excesses; but now it has softened down, and can easily be guided. None evinced more feeling than General Johnston, who admitted that the act was calculated to stain his cause with a dark hue; and he contended that the loss was most serious to the South, who had begun to realize that Mr. Lincoln was the best friend they had.

I cannot believe that even Mr. Davis was privy to the diabolical plot, but think it the emanation of a set of young men of the South, who are very devils. I want to throw upon the South the care of this class of men, who will soon be as obnoxious to their industrial classes as to us.

Had I pushed Johnston's army to an extremity, it would have dispersed, and done infinite mischief. Johnston informed me that General Stoneman had been at Salisbury, and was now at Statesville. I have sent him orders to come to me.

General Johnston also informed me that General Wilson was at Columbus, Georgia, and he wanted me to arrest his progress. I leave that to you.

Indeed, if the President sanctions my agreement with Johnston, our interest is to cease all destruction.

Please give all orders necessary according to the views the Executive may take, and influence him, if possible, not to vary the terms at all, for I have considered every thing, and believe that, the Confederate armies once dispersed, we can adjust all else fairly and well.

      I am, yours, etc.,

        W. T. SHERMAN, *Major-General commanding.*

HEADQUARTERS MILITARY DIVISION OF THE MISSISSIPPI,
IN THE FIELD, RALEIGH, NORTH CAROLINA,
April 18, 1865.

Lieutenant-General U. S. GRANT, *or Major-General* HALLECK,
Washington, D. C.

GENERAL: I inclose herewith a copy of an agreement made this day between General Joseph E. Johnston and myself, which, if approved by the President of the United States, will produce peace from the Potomac to the Rio Grande. Mr. Breckenridge was present at our conference, in the capacity of major-general, and satisfied me of the ability of General Johnston to carry out to their full extent the terms of this agreement; and if you will get the President to simply indorse the copy, and commission me to carry out the terms, I will follow them to the conclusion.

You will observe that it is an absolute submission of the enemy to the lawful authority of the United States, and disperses his armies absolutely; and the point to which I attach most importance is, that the dispersion and disbandment of these armies is done in such a manner as to prevent their breaking up into guerrilla bands. On the other hand, we can retain just as much of an army as we please. I agreed to the mode and manner of the surrender of arms set forth, as it gives the States the means of repressing guerrillas, which we could not expect them to do if we stripped them of all arms.

Both Generals Johnston and Breckenridge admitted that slavery was dead, and I could not insist on embracing it in such a paper, because it can be made with the States in detail. I know that all the men of substance South sincerely want peace, and I do not believe they will resort to war again during this century. I have no doubt that they will in the future be perfectly subordinate to the laws of the United States. The moment my action in this matter is approved, I can spare five corps, and will ask for orders to leave General Schofield here with the Tenth Corps, and to march myself with the Fourteenth, Fifteenth, Seventeenth, Twentieth, and Twenty-third Corps *via* Burkesville and Gordonsville to Frederick or Hagerstown, Maryland, there to be paid and mustered out.

The question of finance is now the chief one, and every

soldier and officer not needed should be got home at work. I would like to be able to begin the march north by May 1st.

I urge, on the part of the President, speedy action, as it is important to get the Confederate armies to their homes as well as our own.

I am, with great respect, your obedient servant,

W. T. SHERMAN, *Major-General commanding.*

Memorandum, or Basis of Agreement, made this 18th *day of April,* A. D. 1865, *near Durham's Station, in the State of North Carolina, by and between General* JOSEPH E. JOHNSTON, *commanding the Confederate Army, and Major-General* WILLIAM T. SHERMAN, *commanding the Army of the United States in North Carolina, both present:*

1. The contending armies now in the field to maintain the *statu quo* until notice is given by the commanding general of any one to its opponent, and reasonable time—say, forty-eight hours—allowed.

2. The Confederate armies now in existence to be disbanded and conducted to their several State capitals, there to deposit their arms and public property in the State Arsenal; and each officer and man to execute and file an agreement to cease from acts of war, and to abide the action of the State and Federal authority. The number of arms and munitions of war to be reported to the Chief of Ordnance at Washington City, subject to the future action of the Congress of the United States, and, in the mean time, to be used solely to maintain peace and order within the borders of the States respectively.

3. The recognition, by the Executive of the United States, of the several State governments, on their officers and Legislatures taking the oaths prescribed by the Constitution of the United States, and, where conflicting State governments have resulted from the war, the legitimacy of all shall be submitted to the Supreme Court of the United States.

4. The reëstablishment of all the Federal Courts in the several States, with powers as defined by the Constitution of the United States and of the States respectively.

5. The people and inhabitants of all the States to be guaranteed, so far as the Executive can, their political rights and

franchises, as well as their rights of person and property, as defined by the Constitution of the United States and of the States respectively.

6. The Executive authority of the Government of the United States not to disturb any of the people by reason of the late war, so long as they live in peace and quiet, abstain from acts of armed hostility, and obey the laws in existence at the place of their residence.

7. In general terms—the war to cease; a general amnesty, so far as the Executive of the United States can command, on condition of the disbandment of the Confederate armies, the distribution of the arms, and the resumption of peaceful pursuits by the officers and men hitherto composing said armies.

Not being fully empowered by our respective principals to fulfill these terms, we individually and officially pledge ourselves to promptly obtain the necessary authority, and to carry out the above programme.

W. T. Sherman, *Major General,*
Commanding Army of the United States in North Carolina.
J. E. Johnston, *General,*
Commanding Confederate States Army in North Carolina.

Major Hitchcock got off on the morning of the 20th, and I reckoned that it would take him four or five days to go to Washington and back. During that time the repairs on all the railroads and telegraph-lines were pushed with energy, and we also got possession of the railroad and telegraph from Raleigh to Weldon, in the direction of Norfolk. Meantime the troops remained *statu quo,* our cavalry occupying Durham's Station and Chapel Hill. General Slocum's head of column was at Aven's Ferry on Cape Fear River, and General Howard's was strung along the railroad toward Hillsboro'; the rest of the army was in and about Raleigh.

On the 20th I reviewed the Tenth Corps, and was much pleased at the appearance of General [Charles J.] Paines's division of black troops, the first I had even seen as a part of an organized army; and on the 21st I reviewed the Twenty-third Corps, which had been with me to Atlanta, but had returned to Nashville, had formed an essential part of the army which fought at Franklin, and with which General Thomas had defeated General Hood in Tennessee. It had then been transferred rapidly by rail to Baltimore and Washington by General Grant's orders, and thence by sea to North Carolina. Nothing of interest happened at Raleigh till the evening of April 23d, when Major Hitchcock reported by telegraph his return to Morehead City, and that he would come up by rail during the night. He arrived at 6 A. M., April 24th, accompanied by General Grant and one or two officers of his staff, who had not telegraphed the fact of their being on the train, for prudential reasons. Of course, I was both surprised and pleased to see the general, soon learned that my terms with Johnston had been disapproved, was instructed by him to give the forty-eight hours' notice required by the terms of the truce, and afterward to proceed to attack or follow him. I immediately telegraphed to General Kilpatrick, at Durham's, to have a mounted courier ready to carry the following message, then on its way up by rail, to the rebel lines:

HEADQUARTERS MILITARY DIVISION OF THE MISSISSIPPI,
    IN THE FIELD, RALEIGH, NORTH CAROLINA,
        April 24, 1865—6 A. M.

General JOHNSTON, *commanding Confederate Army, Greensboro':*

You will take notice that the truce or suspension of hostilities agreed to between us will cease in forty-eight hours after this is received at your lines, under the first of the articles of agreement.

                W. T. SHERMAN, *Major-General.*

At the same time I wrote another short note to General Johnston, of the same date:

I have replies from Washington to my communications of April 18th. I am instructed to limit my operations to your immediate command, and not to atempt civil negotiations. I therefore demand the surrender of your army on the same terms as were given to General Lee at Appomattox, April 9th instant, purely and simply.

Of course, both these papers were shown to General Grant

at the time, before they were sent, and he approved of them.

At the same time orders were sent to all parts of the army to be ready to resume the pursuit of the enemy on the expiration of the forty-eight hours' truce, and messages were sent to General Gillmore (at Hilton Head) to the same effect, with instructions to get a similar message through to General Wilson, at Macon, by some means.

General Grant had brought with him, from Washington, written answers from the Secretary of War, and of himself, to my communications of the 18th, which I still possess, and here give the originals. They embrace the copy of a dispatch made by Mr. Stanton to General Grant, when he was pressing Lee at Appomattox, which dispatch, if sent me at the same time (as should have been done), would have saved a world of trouble. I did not understand that General Grant had come down to supersede me in command, nor did he intimate it, nor did I receive these communications as a serious reproof, but promptly acted on them, as is already shown; and in this connection I give my answer made to General Grant, at Raleigh, before I had received any answer from General Johnston to the demand for the surrender of his own army, as well as my answer to Mr. Stanton's letter, of the same date, both written on the supposition that I might have to start suddenly in pursuit of Johnston, and have no other chance to explain.

War Department, Washington City, *April* 21, 1865.

Lieutenant-General Grant.

General: The memorandum or basis agreed upon between General Sherman and General Johnston having been submitted to the President, they are disapproved. You will give notice of the disapproval to General Sherman, and direct him to resume hostilities at the earliest moment.

The instructions given to you by the late President, Abraham Lincoln, on the 3d of March, by my telegraph of that date, addressed to you, express substantially the views of President Andrew Johnson, and will be observed by General Sherman. A copy is herewith appended.

The President desires that you proceed immediately to

the headquarters of Major-General Sherman, and direct operations against the enemy.

Your truly,

EDWIN M. STANTON, *Secretary of War.*

The following telegram was received 2 P. M., City Point, March 4, 1865 (from Washington, 12 M., March 3, 1865):

[CIPHER.]

OFFICE UNITED STATES MILITARY TELEGRAPH, }
HEADQUARTERS ARMIES OF THE UNITED STATES. }

Lieutenant-General GRANT:

The President directs me to say to you that he wishes you to have no conference with General Lee, unless it be for the capitulation of Lee's army or on solely minor and purely military matters.

He instructs me to say that you are not to decide, discuss, or confer upon any political question; such questions the President holds in his own hands, and will submit them to no military conferences or conventions.

Meantime you are to press to the utmost your military advantages.

EDWIN M. STANTON, *Secretary of War.*

HEADQUARTERS ARMIES OF THE UNITED STATES, }
WASHINGTON, D. C., *April* 21, 1865. }

Major-General W. T. SHERMAN, *commanding Military Division of the Mississippi.*

GENERAL: The basis of agreement entered into between yourself and General J. E. Johnston, for the disbandment of the Southern army, and the extension of the authority of the General Government over all the territory belonging to it, sent for the approval of the President, is received.

I read it carefully myself before submitting it to the President and Secretary of War, and felt satisfied that it could not possibly be approved. My reason for these views I will give you at another time, in a more extended letter.

Your agreement touches upon question of such vital importance that, as soon as read, I addressed a note to the Secretary of War, notifying him of their receipt, and the importance of immediate action by the President; and suggested, in view of their importance, that the entire Cabinet be called together, that all might give an expression of their opinions upon the matter. The result was a disapproval by the President of the basis laid down; a disapproval of the negotiations altogether—except for the surrender of the army commanded by General Johnston, and directions to me to notify you of this decision. I cannot do so better than by sending you the inclosed copy of a dispatch (penned by the late President, though signed by the Secretary of War) in answer to me, on sending a letter received from General Lee, proposing to meet me for the purpose of submitting the question of peace to a convention of officers.

Please notify General Johnston, immediately on receipt of this, of the termination of the truce, and resume hostilities against his army at the earliest moment you can, acting in good faith.

Very respectfully your obedient servant,

U. S. GRANT, *Lieutenant-General.*

HEADQUARTERS MILITARY DIVISION OF THE MISSISSIPPI, IN THE FIELD, RALEIGH, NORTH CAROLINA, *April* 25, 1865.

Lieutenant-General U. S. GRANT, *present.*

GENERAL: I had the honor to receive your letter of April 21st, with inclosures, yesterday, and was well pleased that you came along, as you must have observed that I held the military control so as to adapt it to any phase the case might assume.

It is but just I should record the fact that I made my terms with General Johnston under the influence of the liberal terms you extended to the army of General Lee at Appomattox Court-House on the 9th, and the seeming policy of our Government, as evinced by the call of the Virginia Legislature and Governor back to Richmond, under yours and President Lincoln's very eyes.

It now appears this last act was done without any consultation with you or any knowledge of Mr. Lincoln, but rather in opposition to a previous policy well considered.

I have not the least desire to interfere in the civil policy of our Government, but would shun it as something not to my liking; but occasions do arise when a prompt seizure of results is forced on military commanders not in immediate communication with the proper authority. It is probable that the terms signed by General Johnston and myself were not clear enough on the point, well understood between us, that our negotiations did not apply to any parties outside the officers and men of the Confederate armies, which could easily have been remedied.

No surrender of any army not actually at the mercy of an antagonist was ever made without "terms," and these always define the military status of the surrendered. Thus you stipulated that the officers and men of Lee's army should not be molested at their homes so long as they obeyed the laws at the place of their residence.

I do not wish to discuss these points involved in our recognition of the State governments in actual existence, but will merely state my conclusions, to await the solution of the future.

Such action on our part in no manner recognizes for a moment the so-called Confederate Government, or makes us liable for its debts or acts.

The laws and acts done by the several States during the period of rebellion are void, because done without the oath prescribed by our Constitution of the United States, which is a "condition precedent."

We have a right to use any sort of machinery to produce military results; and it is the commonest thing for military commanders to use the civil governments *in actual existence* as a means to an end. I do believe we could and can use the present State governments lawfully, constitutionally, and as the very best possible means to produce the object desired, viz., entire and complete submission to the lawful authority of the United States.

As to punishment for past crimes, that is for the judiciary, and can in no manner of way be disturbed by our acts; and, so far as I can, I will use my influence that rebels shall suffer all the personal punishment prescribed by law, as also the civil liabilities arising from their past acts.

What we now want is the new form of law by which common men may regain the positions of industry, so long disturbed by the war.

I now apprehend that the rebel armies will disperse; and, instead of dealing with six or seven States, we will have to deal with numberless bands of desperadoes, headed by such men as [John] Mosby, Forrest, Red Jackson, and others, who know not and care not for danger and its consequences.

I am, with great respect, your obedient servant,

W. T. SHERMAN, *Major-General commanding.*

HEADQUARTERS MILITARY DIVISION OF THE MISSISSIPPI, IN THE FIELD, RALEIGH, NORTH CAROLINA, *April 25, 1865.*

Hon. E. M. STANTON, *Secretary of War, Washington.*

DEAR SIR: I have been furnished a copy of your letter of April 21st to General Grant, signifying your disapproval of the terms on which General Johnston proposed to disarm and disperse the insurgents, on condition of amnesty, etc. I admit my folly in embracing in a military convention any civil matters; but, unfortunately, such is the nature of our situation that they seem inextricably united, and I understood from you at Savannah that the financial state of the country demanded military success, and would warrant a little bending to policy.

When I had my conference with General Johnston I had the public examples before me of General Grant's terms to Lee's army, and General [Godfrey] Weitzel's invitation to the Virginia Legislature to assemble at Richmond.

I still believe the General Government of the United States has made a mistake; but that is none of my business—mine is a different task; and I had flattered myself that, by four years of patient, unremitting, and successful labor, I deserved no reminder such as is contained in the last paragraph of your letter to General Grant. You may assure the President that I heed his suggestion. I am truly, etc.,

W. T. SHERMAN, *Major-General commanding.*

On the same day, but later; I received an answer from

General Johnston, agreeing to meet me again at Bennett's house the next day, April 26th, at noon. He did not even know that General Grant was in Raleigh.

General Grant advised me to meet him, and to accept his surrender on the same terms as his with General Lee; and on the 26th I again went up to Durham's Station by rail, and rode out to Bennett's house, where we again met, and General Johnston, without hesitation, agreed to, and we executed, the following final terms:

Terms of a Military Convention, entered into this 26th day of April, 1865, at Bennett's House, near Durham's Station, North Carolina, between General JOSEPH E. JOHNSTON, *commanding the Confederate Army, and Major-General* W. T. SHERMAN, *commanding the United States Army in North Carolina:*

1. All acts of war on the part of the troops under General Johnston's command to cease from this date.

2. All arms and public property to be deposited at Greensboro', and delivered to an ordnance-officer of the United States Army.

3. Rolls of all the officers and men to be made in duplicate; one copy to be retained by the commander of the troops, and the other to be given to an officer to be designated by General Sherman. Each officer and man to give his individual obligation in writing not to take up arms against the Government of the United States, until properly released from this obligation.

4. The side-arms of officer, and their private horses and baggage, to be retained by them.

5. This being done, all the officers and men will be permitted to return to their homes, not to be disturbed by the United States authorities, so long as they observe their obligation and the laws in force where they may reside.

W. T. SHERMAN, *Major-General,*
Commanding United States Forces in North Carolina.

J. E. JOHNSTON, *General,*
Commanding Confederate States Forces in North Carolina.

Approved: U. S. GRANT, *Lieutenant-General.*

I returned to Raleigh the same evening, and, at my request, General Grant wrote on these terms his approval, and then I thought the matter was surely at an end. He took the original copy, on the 27th returned to New Bern, and thence went back to Washington.

I immediately made all the orders necessary to carry into effect the terms of this convention, devolving on General Schofield the details of granting the parols and making the muster-rolls of prisoners, inventories of property, etc., of General Johnston's army at and about Greensboro', North Carolina, and on General Wilson the same duties in Georgia; but, thus far, I had been compelled to communicate with the latter through rebel sources, and General Wilson was necessarily confused by the conflict of orders and information. I deemed it of the utmost importance to establish for him a more reliable base of information and supply, and accordingly resolved to go in person to Savannah for that purpose. But, before starting, I received a *New York Times,* of April 24th, containing the following extraordinary communications:

[First Bulletin.]

WAR DEPARTMENT, WASHINGTON, *April* 22, 1865.

Yesterday evening a bearer of dispatches arrived from General Sherman. An agreement for a suspension of hostilities, and a memorandum of what is called a basis for peace, had been entered into on the 18th inst. by General Sherman, with the rebel General Johnston. Brigadier-General Breckenridge was present at the conference.

A cabinet meeting was held at eight o'clock in the evening, at which the action of General Sherman was disapproved by the President, by the Secretary of War, by General Grant, and by every member of the cabinet. General Sherman was ordered to resume hostilities immediately, and was directed that the instructions given by the late President, in the following telegram, which was penned by Mr. Lincoln himself, at the Capitol, on the night of the 3d of March, were approved by President Andrew Johnson, and were reiterated to govern the action of military commanders.

On the night of the 3d of March, while President Lincoln and his cabinet were at the Capitol, a telegram from General Grant was brought to the Secretary of War, informing him that General Lee had requested an interview or conference, to make an arrangement for terms of peace. The letter of General Lee was published in a letter to Davis and to the rebel Congress. General Grant's telegram was submitted to Mr. Lincoln, who, after pondering a few minutes, took up his pen and wrote with his own hand the following reply, which he submitted to the Secretary of State and Secretary of War. It was then dated, addressed, and signed, by the Secretary of War, and telegraphed to General Grant:

WASHINGTON, *March* 3, 1865—12 P. M.

Lieutenant-General GRANT:

The President directs me to say to you that he wishes you to have no conference with General Lee, unless it be for the capitulation of General Lee's army, or on some minor or purely military matter. He instructs me to say that you are not to decide, discuss, or confer upon any political questions. Such questions the President holds in his own hands, and will submit them to no military conferences or conventions.

Meantime you are to press to the utmost your military advantages.

EDWIN M. STANTON, *Secretary of War.*

The orders of General Sherman to General Stoneman to withdraw from Salisbury and join him will probably open the way for Davis to escape to Mexico or Europe with his plunder, which is reported to be very large, including not only the plunder of the Richmond banks, but previous accumulations.

A dispatch received by this department from Richmond says: "It is stated here, by respectable parties, that the amount of specie taken south by Jeff. Davis and his partisans is very large, including not only the plunder of the Richmond banks, but previous accumulations. They hope, it is said, to make terms with General Sherman, or some other commander, by which they will be permitted, with their effects, including this gold plunder, to go to Mexico or Europe. Johnston's negotiations look to this end."

After the cabinet meeting last night, General Grant started for North Carolina, to direct operations against Johnston's army.

EDWIN M. STANTON, *Secretary of War*.

Here followed the terms, and Mr. Stanton's ten reasons for rejecting them.

The publication of this bulletin by authority was an outrage on me, for Mr. Stanton had failed to communicate to me in advance, as was his duty, the purpose of the Administration to limit our negotiations to purely military matters; but, on the contrary, at Savannah he had authorized me to control all matters, *civil* and military.

By this bulletin, he implied that I had previously been furnished with a copy of his dispatch of March 3d to General Grant, which was not so; and he gave warrant to the impression, which was sown broadcast, that I might be bribed by banker's gold to permit Davis to escape. Under the influence of this, I wrote General Grant the following letter of April 28th, which has been published in the Proceedings of the Committee on the Conduct of the War.

I regarded this bulletin of Mr. Stanton as a personal and official insult, which I afterward publicly resented.

HEADQUARTERS MILITARY DIVISION OF THE MISSISSIPPI, IN THE FIELD, RALEIGH, NORTH CAROLINA, *April* 28, 1865

Lieutenant-General U. S. GRANT, *General-in-Chief, Washington, D. C.*

GENERAL: Since you left me yesterday, I have seen the *New York Times* of the 24th, containing a budget of military news, authenticated by the signature of the Secretary of War, Hon. E. M. Stanton, which is grouped in such a way as to give the public very erroneous impressions. It embraces a copy of the basis of agreement between myself and General Johnston, of April 18th, with comments, which it will be time enough to discuss two or three years hence, after the Government has experimented a little more in the machinery by which power reaches the scattered people of the vast country known as the "South."

In the mean time, however, I did think that my rank (if not past services) entitled me at least to trust that the Secretary of War would keep secret what was communicated for the use of none but the cabinet, until further inquiry could be made, instead of giving publicity to it along with documents which I never saw, and drawing therefrom inferences wide of the truth. I never saw or had furnished me a copy of President Lincoln's dispatch to you of the 3d of March, nor did Mr. Stanton or any human being ever convey to me its substance, or any thing like it. On the contrary, I had seen General Weitzel's invitation to the Virginia Legislature, made in Mr. Lincoln's very presence, and failed to discover any other official hint of a plan of reconstruction, or any ideas calculated to allay the fears of the people of the South, after the destruction of their armies and civil authorities would leave them without any government whatever.

We should not drive a people into anarchy, and it is simply impossible for our military power to reach all the masses of their unhappy country.

I confess I did not desire to drive General Johnston's army into bands of armed men, going about without purpose, and capable only of infinite mischief. But you saw, on your arrival here, that I had my army so disposed that his escape was only possible in a disorganized shape; and as you did not choose to "direct military operations in this quarter," I inferred that you were satisfied with the military situation; at all events, the instant I learned what was proper enough, the disapproval of the President, I acted in such a manner as to compel the surrender of General Johnston's whole army on the same terms which you had prescribed to General Lee's army, when you had it surrounded and in your absolute power.

Mr. Stanton, in stating that my orders to General Stoneman were likely to result in the escape of "Mr. Davis to Mexico or Europe," is in deep error. General Stoneman was not at "Salisbury," but had gone back to "Statesville." Davis was between us, and therefore Stoneman was beyond him. By turning toward me he was approaching Davis, and, had he joined me as ordered, I would have had a mounted force greatly needed for Davis's capture, and for other purposes. Even now I don't know that Mr. Stanton wants Davis caught, and as my official papers, deemed sacred, are hastily published to the world, it will be imprudent for me to state what has been done in that regard.

As the editor of the *Times* has (it may be) logically and fairly drawn from this singular document the conclusion that I am insubordinate, I can only deny the intention.

I have never in my life questioned or disobeyed an order, though many and many a time have I risked my life, health, and reputation, in obeying orders, or even hints to execute plans and purposes, not to my liking. It is not fair to withhold from me the plans and policy of Government (if any there be), and expect me to guess at them; for facts and events appear quite different from different stand-points. For four years I have been in camp dealing with soldiers, and I can assure you that the conclusion at which the cabinet arrived with such singular unanimity differs from mine. I conferred freely with the best officers in this army as to the points involved in this controversy, and, strange to say, they were singularly unanimous in the other conclusion. They will learn with pain and amazement that I am deemed insubordinate, and wanting in common-sense; that I, who for four years have labored day and night, winter and summer, who have brought an army of seventy thousand men in magnificent condition across a country hitherto deemed impassable, and placed it just where it was wanted, on the day appointed, have brought discredit on our Government! I do not wish to boast of this, but I do say that it entitled me to the courtesy of being consulted, before publishing to the world a proposition rightfully submitted to higher authority for adjudication, and then accompanied by statements which invited the dogs of the press to be let loose upon me. It is true that non-combatants, men who sleep in comfort and security while we watch on the distant lines, are better able to judge than we poor soldiers, who rarely see a newspaper, hardly hear from our families, or stop long enough to draw our pay. I envy not the task of "reconstruction," and am delighted that the Secretary of War has relieved me of it.

As you did not undertake to assume the management of the affairs of this army, I infer that, on personal inspection, your mind arrived at a different conclusion from that of the Secretary of War. I will therefore go on to execute your orders to the conclusion, and, when done, will with intense satisfaction leave to the civil authorities the execution of the task of which they seem so jealous. But, as an honest man and soldier, I invite them to go back to Nashville and follow my path, for they will see some things and hear some things that may disturb their philosophy.

With sincere respect,

W. T. SHERMAN, *Major-General commanding.*

P.S.—As Mr. Stanton's most singular paper has been published, I demand that this also be made public, though I am in no manner responsible to the press, but to the law, and my proper superiors.

W. T. S., *Major-General.*

On the 28th I summoned all the army and corps commanders together at my quarters in the Governor's mansion at Raleigh, where every thing was explained to them, and all orders for the future were completed. Generals Schofield, Terry, and Kilpatrick, were to remain on duty in the Department of North Carolina, already commanded by General Schofield, and the right and left wings were ordered to march under their respective commanding generals North by easy stages to Richmond, Virginia, there to await my return from the South.

On the 29th of April, with a part of my personal staff, I proceeded by rail to Wilmington, North Carolina, where I found Generals [John R.] Hawley and [Edward E.] Potter, and the little steamer Russia, Captain Smith, awaiting me. After a short pause in Wilmington, we embarked, and proceeded down the coast to Port Royal and the Savannah River, which we reached on the 1st of May. There Captain Hosea, who had just come from General Wilson at Macon, met us, bearing letters for me and General Grant, in which General Wilson gave a brief summary of his operations up to date. He had marched from Eastport, Mississippi, "five hundred miles in thirty days, took six thousand three hundred prisoners, twenty-three colors, and one hundred and fifty-six guns, defeating Forrest, scattering the militia, and destroying every railroad, iron establishment, and factory, in North Alabama and Georgia."

He spoke in the highest terms of his cavalry, as "cavalry," claiming that it could not be *excelled*, and he regarded his corps as a model for modern cavalry in organization, armament, and discipline. Its strength was given at thirteen thousand five hundred men and horses on reaching Macon. Of course I was extremely gratified at his just confidence, and saw that all he wanted for efficient action was a sure base of supply, so that he need no longer depend for clothing, ammunition, food, and forage, on the country, which, now that war had ceased, it was our solemn duty to protect, instead of plunder. I accordingly ordered the captured steamer Jeff. Davis to be loaded with stores, to proceed at once up the Savannah River to Augusta, with a small detachment of troops to occupy the arsenal, and to open communication with General Wilson at Macon; and on the next day, May 2d, this steamer was followed by another with a full cargo of clothing, sugar, coffee, and bread, sent from Hilton Head by the department commander, General Gillmore, with a stronger guard commanded by General [Edward L.] Molineux. Leaving to General Gillmore, who was present, and in whose department General Wilson was, to keep up the supplies at Augusta, and to facilitate as far as possible General Wilson's operations inland, I began my return on the 2d of May. We went into Charleston Harbor, passing the ruins of old Forts Moultrie and Sumter without landing. We reached the city of Charleston, which was held by part of the division of General John P. Hatch, the same that we had left at Pocotaligo. We walked the old familiar streets—Broad, King, Meeting, etc.—but desolation and ruin were everywhere. The heart of the city had been burned during the bombardment, and the rebel garrison at the time of its final evacuation had fired the railroad-depots, which fire had spread, and was only subdued by our troops after they had reached the city.

I inquired for many of my old friends, but they were dead or gone, and of them all I only saw a part of the family of Mrs. Pettigru. I doubt whether any city was ever more terribly punished than Charleston, but, as her people had for years been agitating for war and discord, and had finally inaugurated the civil war by an attack on the small and devoted garrison of Major Anderson, sent there by the General

Government to defend them, the judgment of the world will be, that Charleston deserved the fate that befell her. Resuming our voyage, we passed into Cape Fear River by its mouth at Fort Caswell and Smithville, and out by the new channel at Fort Fisher, and reached Morehead City on the 4th of May. We found there the revenue-cutter Wayanda, on board of which were the Chief-Justice, Mr. Chase, and his daughter Nettie, now Mrs. Hoyt. The Chief-Justice at that moment was absent on a visit to New Bern, but came back the next day. Meantime, by means of the telegraph, I was again in correspondence with General Schofield at Raleigh. He had made great progress in parolling the officers and men of Johnston's army at Greensboro', but was embarrassed by the utter confusion and anarchy that had resulted from a want of understanding on many minor points, and on the political questions that had to be met at the instant. In order to facilitate the return to their homes of the Confederate officers and men, he had been forced to make with General Johnston the following supplemental terms, which were of course ratified and approved:

MILITARY CONVENTION OF APRIL 26, 1865.

SUPPLEMENTAL TERMS.

1. The field transportation to be loaned to the troops for their march to their homes, and for subsequent use in their industrial pursuits. Artillery-horses may be used in field-transportation, if necessary.

2. Each brigade or separate body to retain a number of arms equal to *one-seventh* of its effective strength, which, when the troops reach the capitals of their States, will be disposed of as the general commanding the department may direct.

3. Private horses, and other private property of both officers and men, to be retained by them.

4. The commanding general of the Military Division of West Mississippi, Major-General Canby, will be requested to give transportation by water, from Mobile or New Orleans, to the troops from Arkansas and Texas.

5. The obligations of officers and soldiers to be signed by their immediate commanders.

6. Naval forces within the limits of General Johnston's command to be included in the terms of this convention.

J. M. SCHOFIELD, *Major-General,*
Commanding United States Forces in North Carolina.
J. E. JOHNSTON, *General,*
Commanding Confederate States Forces in North Carolina.

The total number of prisoners of war parolled by General Schofield, at Greensboro', North Carolina, as afterward officially reported, amounted to	36,817
And the total number who surrendered in Georgia and Florida, as reported by General J. H. Wilson, was	52,453
Aggregate surrendered under the capitulation of General J. E. Johnston.............	89,270

On the morning of the 5th I also received from General Schofield this dispatch:

RALEIGH, NORTH CAROLINA, *May* 5, 1865.

To Major-General W. T. SHERMAN, *Morehead City:*

When General Grant was here, as you doubtless recollect, he said the lines (for trade and intercourse) had been extended to embrace this and other States south. The order, it seems, has been modified so as to include only Virginia and Tennessee. I think it would be an act of wisdom to open this State to trade at once.

I hope the Government will make known its policy as to the organs of State government without delay. Affairs must necessarily be in a very unsettled state until that is done. The people are now in a mood to accept almost any thing which promises a definite settlement. "What is to be done with the freedmen?" is the question of all, and it is the all-important question. It requires prompt and wise action to prevent the Negroes from becoming a huge elephant on our hands. If I am to govern this State, it is important for me to know it at once. If another is to be sent here, it cannot be done too soon, for he probably will undo the most that I shall have done. I shall be glad to hear from you fully, when you have time to write. I will send your message to General Wilson at once.

J. M. SCHOFIELD, *Major-General.*

I was utterly without instructions from any source on the points of General Schofield's inquiry, and under the existing state of facts could not even advise him, for by this time I was in possession of the second bulletin of Mr. Stanton, published in all the Northern papers, with comments that assumed that I was a common traitor and a public enemy; and high officials had even instructed my own subordinates to disobey my lawful orders. General Halleck, who had so long been in Washington as the chief of staff, had been sent on the 21st of April to Richmond, to command the armies of the Potomac and James, in place of General Grant, who had transferred his headquarters to the national capital, and he (General Halleck) was therefore in supreme command in Virginia, while my command over North Carolina had never been revoked or modified.

[Second Bulletin.]

To Major-General DIX:

The department has received the following dispatch from Major-General Halleck, commanding the Military Division of the James. Generals Canby and Thomas were instructed some days ago that Sherman's arrangements with Johnston were disapproved by the President, and they were ordered to disregard it and push the enemy in every direction.

E. M. STANTON, *Secretary of War.*

RICHMOND, VIRGINIA, *April* 26—9:30 P. M.

Hon. E. M. STANTON, *Secretary of War:*

Generals Meade, Sheridan, and Wright, are acting under orders to pay no regard to any truce or orders of General Sherman respecting hostilities, on the ground that Sherman's agreement could bind his command only, and no other.

They are directed to push forward, regardless of orders from any one except from General Grant, and cut off Johnston's retreat.

Beauregard has telegraphed to Danville that a new arrangement has been made with Sherman, and that the advance of the Sixth Corps was to be suspended until further orders.

I have telegraphed back to obey no orders of Sherman, but to push forward as rapidly as possible.

The bankers here have information to-day that Jeff. Davis's specie is moving south from Goldsboro', in wagons, as fast as possible.

I suggest that orders be telegraphed, through General Thomas, that Wilson obey no orders from Sherman, and notifying him and Canby, and all commanders on the Mississippi, to take measures to intercept the rebel chiefs and their plunder.

The specie taken with them is estimated here at from six to thirteen million dollars.

H. W. HALLECK, *Major-General commanding.*

Subsequently, before the Committee on the Conduct of the War, in Washington, on the 22d of May, I testified fully on this whole matter, and will abide the judgment of the country on the patriotism and wisdom of my public conduct in this connection. General Halleck's measures to capture General Johnston's army, actually surrendered to me at the time, at Greensboro', on the 26th of April, simply excited my contempt for a judgment such as he was supposed to possess. The assertion that Jeff. Davis's specie-train, of six to thirteen million dollars, was reported to be moving south from Goldsboro' in wagons as fast as possible, found plenty of willing ears, though my army of eighty thousand men had been at Goldsboro' from March 22d to the date of his dispatch, April 26th; and such a train would have been composed of from fifteen to thirty-two six-mule teams to have hauled this specie, even if it all were in gold. I suppose the exact amount of treasure which Davis had with him is now known to a cent; some of it was paid to his escort, when it disbanded at and near Washington, Georgia, and at the time of his capture he had a small parcel of gold and silver coin, not to exceed ten thousand dollars, which is now retained in the United States Treasury-vault at Washington, and shown to the curious.

The thirteen millions of treasure, with which Jeff. Davis was to corrupt our armies and buy his escape, dwindled down to the contents of a hand-valise!

To say that I was merely angry at the tone and substance of these published bulletins of the War Department, would hardly express the state of my feelings. I was outraged beyond measure, and was resolved to resent the insult, cost what it might. I went to the Wayanda and showed them to Mr. Chase, with whom I had a long and frank conversation, during which he explained to me the confusion caused in Washington by the assassination of Mr. Lincoln, the sudden accession to power of Mr. Johnson, who was then supposed to be bitter and vindictive in his feelings toward the South, and the wild pressure of every class of politicians to enforce on the new President their pet schemes. He showed me a letter of his own, which was in print, dated Baltimore, April 11th, and another of April 12th, addressed to the President, urging him to recognize the freedmen as equal in all respects to the whites. He was the first man, of any authority or station, who ever informed me that the Government of the United States would insist on extending to the former slaves of the South the elective franchise, and he gave as a reason the fact that the slaves, grateful for their freedom, for which they were indebted to the armies and Government of the North, would, by their votes, offset the disaffected and rebel element of the white population of the South. At that time quite a storm was prevailing at sea, outside, and our two vessels lay snug at the wharf at Morehead City. I saw a good deal of Mr. Chase, and several notes passed between us, of which I have the originals yet. Always claiming that the South had herself freed all her slaves by rebellion, and that Mr. Lincoln's proclamation of freedom (of September 22, 1862) was binding on all officers of the General Government, I doubted the wisdom of at once clothing them with the elective franchise, without some previous preparation and qualification; and then realized the national loss in the death at that critical moment of Mr. Lincoln, who had long pondered over the difficult questions involved, who, at all events, would have been honest and frank, and would not have withheld from his army commanders at least a hint that would have been to them a guide. It was plain to me, therefore, that the manner of his assassination had stampeded the civil authorities in Washington, had unnerved them, and that they were then undecided as to the measures indispensably necessary to prevent anarchy at the South.

On the 7th of May the storm subsided, and we put to sea, Mr. Chase to the south, on his proposed tour as far as New Orleans, and I for James River. I reached Fortress Monroe on the 8th, and thence telegraphed my arrival to General Grant, asking for orders. I found at Fortress Monroe a dispatch from General Halleck, professing great friendship, and inviting me to accept his hospitality at Richmond. I answered by a cipher-dispatch that I had seen his dispatch to Mr. Stanton, of April 26th, embraced in the second bulletin, which I regarded as insulting, declined his hospitality, and added that I preferred we should not meet as I passed through Richmond. I thence proceeded to City Point in the Russia, and on to Manchester, opposite Richmond, *via* Petersburg, by rail. I found that both wings of the army had arrived from Raleigh, and were in camp in and around Manchester, whence I again telegraphed General Grant, on the 9th of May, for orders, and also reported my arrival to General Halleck by letter. I found that General Halleck had ordered General Davis's corps (the Fourteenth) for review by himself. This I forbade. All the army knew of the insult that had been made me by the Secretary of War and General Halleck, and watched me closely to see if I would tamely submit. During the 9th I made a full and complete report of all these events, from the last report made at Goldsboro' up to date, and the next day received orders to continue the march to Alexandria, near Washington.

On the morning of the 11th we crossed the pontoon-bridge at Richmond, marched through that city, and out on the Hanover Court-House road, General Slocum's left wing leading. The right wing (General Logan) followed the next day, viz., the 12th. Meantime, General O. O. Howard had been summoned to Washington to take charge of the new Bureau of Refugees, Freedmen, and Abandoned Lands, and, from that time till the army was finally disbanded, General John A. Logan was in command of the right wing, and of the Army of the Tennessee. The left wing marched through Hanover Court-House, and thence took roads well to the left by Chilesburg; the Fourteenth Corps by New Market and Culpeper, Manassas, etc.; the Twentieth Corps by Spotsylvania Court-House and Chancellorsville. The right wing followed the more direct road by Fredericksburg. On my way north I endeavored to see as much of the battle-fields of the Army of the Potomac as I could, and therefore shifted from one column to the other, visiting *en route* Hanover Court-House, Spotsylvania, Fredericksburg, Dumfries, etc., reaching Alexandria during the afternoon of May 19th, and pitched my camp by the roadside, about half-way between Alexandria and the Long Bridge. During the same and next day the whole army reached Alexandria, and camped round about it; General Meade's Army of the Potomac had possession of the camps above, opposite Washington and Georgetown.

The next day (by invitation) I went over to Washington and met many friends—among them General Grant and President Johnson. The latter occupied rooms in the house on the corner of Fifteenth and H Streets, belonging to Mr. Hooper. He was extremely cordial to me, and knowing that I was chafing under the censures of the War Department, especially of the two war bulletins of Mr. Stanton, he volunteered to say that he knew of neither of them till seen in the newspapers, and that Mr. Stanton had shown neither to him nor to any of his associates in the cabinet till they were published. Nearly all the members of the cabinet made similar asurances to me afterward, and, as Mr. Stanton made no friendly advances, and offered no word of explanation or apology, I declined General Grant's friendly offices for a reconciliation, but, on the contrary, resolved to resent what I considered an insult, as publicly as it was made. My brother, Senator Sherman, who was Mr. Stanton's neighbor, always insisted that Mr. Stanton had been frightened by the intended assassination of himself, and had become embittered thereby. At all events, I found strong military guards around his house, as well as all the houses occupied by the cabinet and by the principal officers of Government; and a sense of insecurity pervaded Washington, for which no reason existed.

On the 19th I received a copy of War Department Special Order No. 239, Adjutant-General's office, of May 18th, ordering a grand review, by the President and cabinet, of all the armies then near Washington; General Meade's to occur on Tuesday, May 23d, mine on Wednesday, the 24th; and on the 20th I made the necessary orders for my part. Meantime I had also arranged (with General Grant's approval) to remove, after the review, my armies from the south side of the Potomac to the north; both for convenience and because our men had found that the grounds assigned them had been used so long for camps that they were foul and unfit.

By invitation I was on the reviewing-stand, and witnessed the review of the Army of the Potomac (on the 23d), commanded by General Meade in person. The day was beautiful, and the pageant was superb. Washington was full of strangers, who filled the streets in holiday-dress, and every house was decorated with flags. The army marched by divisions in close column around the Capitol, down Pennsylvania Avenue, past the President and cabinet, who occupied a large stand prepared for the occasion, directly in front of the White House.

I had telegraphed to Lancaster for Mrs. Sherman, who arrived that day, accompanied by her father, the Hon. Thomas Ewing, and my son Tom, then eight years old.

During the afternoon and night of the 23d, the Fifteenth, Seventeenth, and Twentieth Corps, crossed Long Bridge, bivouacked in the streets about the Capital, and the Fourteenth Corps closed up to the bridge. The morning of the 24th was extremely beautiful, and the ground was in splendid order for our review. The streets were filled with people to see the pageant, armed with bouquets of flowers for their favorite regiments or heroes, and every thing was propitious. Punctually at 9 A. M. the signal-gun was fired, when in person, attended by General Howard and all my staff, I rode slowly down Pennsylvania Avenue, the crowds of men, women, and children, densely lining the sidewalks, and almost obstructing the way. We were followed close by General Logan and the head of the Fifteenth Corps. When I reached the Treasury-building, and looked back, the sight was simply magnificent. The column was compact, and the glittering muskets looked like a solid mass of steel, moving with the regularity of a pendulum. We passed the Treasury-building, in front of which and of the White House was an immense throng of people, for whom extensive stands had been prepared on both sides of the avenue. As I neared the brick-house opposite the lower corner of Lafayette Square, some one asked me to notice Mr. Seward, who, still feeble and bandaged for his wounds, had been removed there that he might behold the troops. I moved in that direction and took off my hat to Mr. Seward, who sat at an upper window. He recognized the salute, returned it, and then we rode on steadily past the President, saluting with our swords. All on his stand arose and acknowledged the salute. Then, turning into the gate of the presidential grounds, we left our horses with orderlies, and went upon the stand, where I found Mrs. Sherman, with her father and son. Passing them, I shook hands with the President, General Grant, and each member of the cabinet. As I approached Mr. Stanton, he offered me his hand, but I declined it publicly, and the fact was universally noticed. I then took my post on the left of the President, and for six hours and a half stood, while the army passed in the order of the Fifteenth, Seventeenth, Twentieth, and Fourteenth Corps. It was, in my judgment, the most magnificent army in existence—sixty-five thousand men, in splendid *physique,* who had just completed a march of nearly two thousand miles in a hostile country, in good drill, and who realized that they were being closely scrutinized by thousands of their fellow-countrymen and by foreigners. Division after division passed, each commander of an army corps or division coming on the stand during the passage of his command, to be presented to the President, cabinet, and spectators. The steadiness and firmness of the tread, the careful dress on the guides, the uniform intervals between the companies, all eyes directly to the front, and the tattered and bullet-riven flags, festooned with flowers, all attracted universal notice. Many good people, up to that time, had looked upon our Western army as a sort of mob; but the world then saw, and recognized the fact, that it was an army in the proper sense, well organized, well commanded and disciplined; and there was no wonder that it had swept throuhg the South like a tornado. For six hours and a half that strong tread of the Army of the West resounded along Pennsylvania Avenue; not a soul of that vast crowd of spectators left his place; and, when the rear of the column had passed by, thousands of the spectators still lingered to express their sense of confidence in the strength of a Government which could claim such an army.

Some little scenes enlivened the day, and called for the laughter and cheers of the crowd. Each division was followed by six ambulances, as a representative of its baggage-train. Some of the division commanders had added, by way of variety, goats, milch-cows, and pack-mules, whose loads consisted of game-cocks, poultry, hams, etc., and some of them had the families of freed slaves along, with the women leading their children. Each division was preceded by its corps of black pioneers, armed with picks and spades. These marched abreast in double ranks, keeping perfect dress and step, and added much to the interest of the occasion. On the whole, the grand review was a splendid success, and was a fitting conclusion to the campaign and the war.

I will now conclude by a copy of my general orders taking leave of the army, which ended my connection with the war, though I afterward visited and took a more formal leave of the officers and men on July 4, 1865, at Louisville, Kentucky:

[Special Field Orders, No. 76.]

HEADQUARTERS MILITARY DIVISION OF THE MISSISSIPPI,
IN THE FIELD, WASHINGTON, D. C., *May* 30, 1865.

The general commanding announces to the Armies of the Tennessee and Georgia that the time has come for us to part. Our work is done, and armed enemies no longer defy us. Some of you will go to your homes, and others will be retained in military service till further orders.

And now that we are all about to separate, to mingle with the civil world, it becomes a pleasing duty to recall to mind the situation of national affairs when, but little more than a year ago, we were gathered about the cliffs of Lookout Mountain, and all the future was wrapped in doubt and uncertainty.

Three armies had come together from distant fields, with separate histories, yet bound by one common cause—the union of our country, and the perpetuation of the Government of our inheritance. There is no need to recall to your memories Tunnel Hill, with Rocky-Face Mountain and Buzzard-Roost Gap, and the ugly forts of Dalton behind.

We were in earnest, and paused not for danger and difficulty, but dashed through Snake-Creek Gap and fell on Resaca; then on to the Etowah, to Dallas, Kenesaw; and the heats of summer found us on the banks of the Chattahoochee, far from home, and dependent on a single road for supplies. Again we were not to be held back by any obstacle, and crossed over and fought four hard battles for the possession of the citadel of Atlanta. That was the crisis of our history. A doubt still clouded our future, but we solved the problem, destroyed Atlanta, struck boldly across the State of Georgia, severed all the main arteries of life to our enemy, and Christmas found us at Savannah.

Waiting there only long enough to fill our wagons, we again began a march which, for peril, labor, and results, will compare with any ever made by an organized army. The floods of the Savannah, the swamps of the Combahee and Edisto, the "high hills" and rocks of the Santee, the flat quagmires of the Pedee and Cape Fear Rivers, were all passed in mid-winter, with its floods and rains, in the face of an accumulating enemy; and, after the battles of Averysboro' and Bentonsville, we once more came out of the wilderness, to meet our friends at Goldsboro'. Even then we paused only long enough to get new clothing, to reload our wagons, again pushed on to Raleigh and beyond, until we met our enemy suing for peace, instead of war, and offering to submit to the injured laws of his and our country. As long as that enemy was defiant, nor mountains nor rivers, nor swamps, nor hunger, nor cold, had checked us; but when he, who had fought us hard and persistently, offered submission, your general thought it wrong to pursue him farther, and negotiations followed, which resulted, as you all know, in his surrender.

How far the operations of this army contributed to the final overthrow of the Confederacy and the peace which now dawns upon us, must be judged by others, not by us; but that you have done all that men could do has been admitted by those in authority, and we have a right to join in the universal joy that fills our land because the war is *over*, and our Government stands vindicated before the world by the joint action of the volunteer armies and navy of the United States.

To such as remain in the service, your general need only remind you that success in the past was due to hard work and discipline, and that the same work and discipline are equally important in the future. To such as go home, he will only say that our favored country is so grand, so extensive, so diversified in climate, soil, and productions, that every man may find a home and occupation suited to his taste; none should yield to the natural impatience sure to result from our past life of excitement and adventure. You will be invited to seek new adventures abroad; do not yield to the temptation, for it will lead only to death and disappointment.

Your general now bids you farewell, with the full belief that, as in war you have been good soldiers, so in peace you will make good citizens; and if, unfortunately, new war should arise in our country, "Sherman's army" will be the first to buckle on its old armor, and come forth to defend and maintain the Government of our inheritance.

By order of Major-General W. T. Sherman,

L. M. DAYTON, *Assistant Adjutant-General.*

List of the Average Number of Miles marched by the Different Army Corps of the United States Forces under Command of Major-General W. T. SHERMAN, *United States Army, during his Campaigns in 1863—'64—'65.*

ROUTE	NUMBER OF MILES						
	Fourth Corps.	Fourteenth Corps.	Fifteenth Corps.	Sixteenth Corps.	Sixteenth Corps (Left Wing).	Seventeenth Corps.	Twentieth Corps.
From Vicksburg to Meridian, and back	......	......	......	330	......	335	......
From Memphis to Chattanooga	......	......	330	......	......	......	......
From Chattanooga to Knoxville, and back	110	......	230	......	......	......	......
From Chattanooga to Huntsville (Point Rock), Langston, etc., and back	......	......	240	......	......	......	......
From Clifton to Rome	......	......	......	......	......	261	......
From Chattanooga to Atlanta (average distance traversed in manoeuvring)	......	178	178	......	178	89	178
Pursuit of Hood, and back to Atlanta	......	270	270	......	......	270	270
From Atlanta to Savannah	......	283	285	......	......	290	287
From Savannah to Goldsboro'	......	425	423	......	......	478	420
From Goldsboro' to Washington, D. C.	......	430	333	......	......	353	370
Total distance in miles	110	1,586	2,289	330	178	2,076	1,525

Compiled from campaign maps at headquarters Military Division of the Mississippi, St. Louis, Missouri.

WILLIAM KOSSACK, *Captain,*
Additional Aide-de-Camp on Engineer Duty.